S

MORTON PUBLIC LIBRARY DISTRICT

W9-BZB-069

07/19/2003

MORTON PUBLIC LIBRARY DISTRICT

A13001 251205

808.88 OXF
The Oxford dictionary of
modern quotations

The Oxford Dictionary of

Modern Quotations

35.00

The Oxford Dictionary of
Modern Quotations

SECOND EDITION

edited by **Elizabeth Knowles**

OXFORD
UNIVERSITY PRESS

OXFORD
UNIVERSITY PRESS

Great Clarendon Street, Oxford OX2 6DP

Oxford University Press is a department of the University of Oxford.
It furthers the University's objective of excellence in research, scholarship,
and education by publishing worldwide in

Oxford New York

Auckland Bangkok Buenos Aires Cape Town Chennai
Dar es Salaam Delhi Hong Kong Istanbul Karachi Kolkata
Kuala Lumpur Madrid Melbourne Mexico City Mumbai Nairobi
São Paulo Shanghai Singapore Taipei Tokyo Toronto

with an associated company in Berlin

Oxford is a registered trade mark of Oxford University Press
in the UK and in certain other countries

Published in the United States
by Oxford University Press Inc., New York

© Oxford University Press 2002

The moral rights of the author have been asserted

Database right Oxford University Press (maker)

First Edition published 1991
Second Edition first published 2002

All rights reserved. No part of this publication may be reproduced,
stored in a retrieval system, or transmitted, in any form or by any means,
without the prior permission in writing of Oxford University Press,
or as expressly permitted by law, or under terms agreed with the appropriate
reprographics rights organization. Enquiries concerning reproduction
outside the scope of the above should be sent to the Rights Department,
Oxford University Press, at the address above

You must not circulate this book in any other binding or cover
and you must impose this same condition on any acquirer

British Library Cataloguing in Publication Data
Data available

Library of Congress Cataloging in Publication Data
Data available

ISBN 0-19-866275-0

10 9 8 7 6 5 4 3 2 1

Designed by Jane Stevenson
Typeset in Photina and Argo
by Interactive Sciences Ltd
Printed in Great Britain
on acid-free paper by
T. J. International Ltd, Padstow, Cornwall

Contents

Introduction vii

How to Use the Dictionary xi

Dictionary

SPECIAL CATEGORIES

Advertising slogans 3
Cartoons 56
Catchphrases 58
Epitaphs 109
Film lines 115
Film titles 118
Last words 190
Misquotations 226
Newspaper headlines and leaders 240
Official advice 245
Opening lines 247
Political sayings and slogans 261
Taglines for films 314
Telegrams 316

Keyword Index 353

Thematic Index 477

Administration, Age, America, Art, Britain, Business, Computing, Drinks, Education, Environment, Europe, Family, Fashion, Film, Fitness, Food, Future, Health, Law, Literature, Love, Marriage, Men and Women, Music, Past, Photography, Politics, Popular Culture, Present, Press, Quotations, Religion, Royalty, Science, Sex, Society, Sport, Technology, Television, Transport, Travel, War, Youth

Project Team

Editor	Elizabeth Knowles
Associate Editor	Susan Ratcliffe
Library Research	Ralph Bates Marie Diaz
Reading Programme	Verity Mason Helen Rappaport Richard Ramage
Data Capture	Muriel Summersgill
Proof-reading	Kim Allen Penny Trumble

Introduction

The second edition of the *Oxford Dictionary of Modern Quotations* charts the history of our modern times through quotations, from remembered sayings of past years to the voices of today. All quotations are from the twentieth or twenty-first century, and the book concentrates on authors who were alive in or after 1914 (taking the First World War as the cultural watershed of the modern period.) It is intended that the *Dictionary* will both record the key moments of the past which still have resonance for us, and reflect the interests and concerns of today.

Past and present often seem to intermingle. We may think of 'asylum-seekers' as a phenomenon of today, but Bertolt Brecht writes in the 1930s of those who 'went, as often changing countries as changing shoes'. Rebecca West, speaking of Yugoslavia in the same decade, concludes that if she were to ask one of the peasants there 'In your lifetime, have you known peace?' and were magically able to pursue her question back through the generations, 'I would never hear the word "Yes", if I carried my questioning of the dead back for a thousand years.' At a memorial service in New York after the terrorist attacks of September 2001, Tony Blair chose to quote from Thornton Wilder's novel *The Bridge of San Luis Rey* (1927), 'Even memory is not necessary for love. There is a land of the living and a land of the dead and the bridge is love.'

Some quotations recall landmark events. Norman Mailer describes the days of the Cuban Missile Crisis in 1962 as the time when 'the world stood like a playing card on edge'. The loss of the Hindenburg airship in 1937 is still remembered in the words of the horrified young radio announcer who witnessed it, 'It's bursting into flames . . . Oh, the humanity!' Jacqueline Kennedy Onassis gives voice to the feelings of a generation about the Kennedy assassination when she tells an interviewer, 'There'll be great Presidents again . . . but there'll never be another Camelot.'

Some people attempt deliberately to sum up their own times. Bob Dylan says of the 1960s that 'It was like a flying saucer landed. That's what the sixties were like. Everybody heard about it, but only a few really saw it.' 'The drummer and percussionist Nick Mason, on the other hand, looks more sceptically at one particular aspect of the decade: 'the record companies seemed to sign anything with long hair; if it was a sheepdog, so what.' Phil Collins explains why he 'thought punk was a good idea—like someone shaking an apple tree until all the bad ones fell off and you'd just got the good ones left.' Alice Cooper contrasts two approaches: 'The hippies wanted peace and love. We wanted Ferraris, blondes and switchblades.'

It is of course possible to misjudge one's era (as the American politician George McGovern comments wryly, 'Sometimes when they say you're ahead of your time, it's just a polite way of saying you have a real bad sense of timing'). An interviewer at Yale in 1946, hearing that the young Bernard Knox had fought with the International Brigade in the Spanish Civil War, judges, 'You were a premature anti-Fascist.' The unnamed academic was presumably moved by the same spirit as Joseph Starnes of the House Un-American Committee (HUAC) hearings, when in 1938 he asked the theatre director Hallie Flanagan 'this Marlowe. Is he a Communist?' (Nine years later HUAC had formulated its famous question, 'Are you now, or have you ever been, a member of the Communist Party?') Social anxieties are also highlighted by **Newspaper headlines**, from 'Sawdust Caesars' (Mods and Rockers, 1964), and 'The filth and the fury' (Sex Pistols, 1976), to the notorious 'Named shamed' of 2000. Maeve Binchy offers a corrective to assumptions of a golden past: 'It's not perfect, but to me on balance Right Now is better than the Good Old Days.'

Similar voices find echoes through the decades. Emmeline Pankhurst's recommendation of the broken window pane as a political argument is in line with Florynce Kennedy's succinct recipe for political activism, 'When you want to get to the suites, start in the streets.' Barbara Castle takes the same approach: 'If there is no fire in women's bellies it will all become a very dainty process. Organize yourselves and speak out.'

Sometimes the note is unforgiving. 'That man has offered me unsolicited advice for six years, all of it bad,' says Calvin Coolidge in 1928, when asked to support the presidential nomination of his eventual successor Herbert Hoover. In 1953 Dwight Eisenhower sounds a note of revulsion when explaining why he will not enter a battle of words with Senator McCarthy: 'I just will not—I *refuse*—to get into the gutter with that guy.' The lawyer Joseph Welch, defending the US Army in 1954 against allegations of harbouring subversive activities, is similarly outraged in his direct challenge, 'Have you no sense of decency, sir? At long last, have you no sense of decency?' (The televised confrontation was in fact deeply damaging to McCarthy.)

Political circumstances may change. Devolution has been a key issue in recent British politics, and the first session of the new Scottish Parliament is opened resoundingly by Winifred Ewing, 'The Scottish Parliament which adjourned on 25 March in the year 1707 is hereby reconvened', an event of which Sean Connery reflects, 'We have waited nearly 300 years.' Muriel Gray has her own take on these matters, explaining why she prefers devolution to full independence, 'Of course I want political autonomy but not cultural autonomy. You just have to watch the Scottish Baftas to want to kill yourself.'

A number of those quoted consider their own professional lives. 'I opened the door for a lot of people, and they just ran through', says Bo Diddley. Janis Joplin summarizes her popularity, 'Onstage I make love to twenty-five thousand people, then I go home alone.' John Mills reflects, 'I have worked with more submarines than leading ladies.' The American businessman Robert B. Shapiro, whose first view of corporate life was that 'It was the best game I'd ever seen', comes to the conclusion that 'this is not a game. This is one of the realest things you get to do in life.' For the Australian novelist Peter Carey, 'My fictional project has always been the invention or discovery of my own country.' Kate Adie describes trying to 'dig in' while with troops in the Gulf War: 'I dug the smallest trench you ever saw. The colonel told me it was pathetic and then offered an incentive: no trench, no lunch.' Julie Burchill tells us that it was answering an advertisement in *New Musical Express* for a 'hip young gunslinger' that started her on her career in journalism.

Walt Disney, seeing rushes for one of his last films, comments ruefully, 'I don't know, fellows, I guess I'm getting too old for animation.' The Canadian supermodel Linda Evangelista is uncompromising: I don't get out of bed for less than $10,000 a day.' The Australian runner Cathy Freeman thinks that, 'Running's like breathing. It's just something that comes really naturally.' After the death of Katherine Graham, owner of the *Washington Post* at the time of Watergate, the *Post*'s former Editor Ben Bradlee comments, 'Maybe not all of you are familiar with what it takes to make a great newspaper. It takes a great owner. Period.' Tom Brokaw, on the other hand, points up some of the difficulties of journalism, after the American networks had twice made premature calls of a win in Florida on the night of the presidential election of 2001: 'We don't just have egg on our face. We have omelette all over our suits.'

Domestic life evokes a range of comment. P. J. O'Rourke notes feelingly that, 'Anybody can have one kid. But going from one kid to two is like going from owning a dog to running a zoo.' Vikram Seth has his own view of babies: 'A pity that the blubbering blobs Come unequipped with volume knobs.' Food and drink are of constant interest, although Colin Powell, appointed US Secretary of State, opts for the simple approach: 'To save a lot of cable traffic now, I have no food preferences, no drink preferences; a cheeseburger will be fine.' (Gordon Gecko in the 1987 film *Wall Street* goes somewhat further: 'Lunch is for wimps.')

Progress ('What have the Romans ever done for us?' to quote from *Monty Python's Life of Brian* at **Film lines**) is often a matter of debate. Delia Smith selects a traditional object as exemplifying the best principles: 'A hen's egg is, simply, a work of art, a masterpiece of design, construction, and brilliant packaging.' The World Wide Web is variously described as 'fantasyland . . . There is no way that anyone can find anything on the Web without having to adopt the thought patterns of a weirdo' (Germaine Greer), or 'a tremendous grassroots revolution' (Tim Berners-Lee). Comfort in this area is offered by a cartoon caption, 'On the Internet, nobody knows you're a dog' (Peter Steiner in the *New Yorker*: see **Cartoons**).

Surreal comedy is still with us. Monty Python's Spanish Inquisition, appearing when nobody expects it, can now be paired with Eddie Izzard's vision of how an Anglican Inquisition might have interrogated its victims: '"Cake or death?" "Cake, please."' John Cleese remarks on his personal regrets about the popularity of his 'Ministry of Silly Walks' sketch: 'I was saddled with the bloody thing. It's probably why I've had to have a hip replacement.'

It is frequently said that modern quotations are generally cynical soundbites, but while there are plenty of these, others are genuinely inspirational. The Czech-born Israeli historian Yehuda Bauer formulates three additional commandments 'which we ought to adopt and commit ourselves to: thou shalt not be a perpetrator; thou shalt not be a victim; and thou shalt never, but never, be a bystander.' The actor Michael J. Fox speaks of having to cope with Parkinson's disease, 'It's all about losing your brain without losing your mind', and Tony Benn pays a moving tribute to the memory of his wife Caroline, 'She taught us how to live and she taught us how to die—and you can't ask more than that.'

Nelson Mandela, looking back at his life, reflects, 'One of the things I learnt when I was negotiating was that until I changed myself I could not change others.' The Canadian wheelchair athlete Ron Hansen says simply, 'You have to be the best with what you have.' Ian McEwan notes the association of the three-word message 'I love you' with victims of the terrorist actions in America in September 2001: 'I love you . . . That is what they were all saying down their phones, from the hijacked planes and the burning towers.'

A number of special category sections have been incorporated into the main author sequence, from **Advertising slogans** ('The future's bright, the future's Orange') to **Telegrams** by way of captions from **Official advice** ('Duck and cover', 'Just say no') and **Taglines** for films ('In space no one can hear you scream'). A full list of these sections can be found on p. v. There is also a selective thematic index, to guide readers to quotations on such topics as **Environment** ('We have met the enemy, and he is us'), **Television** ('the rudest voice wins'), and **War** ('the first war of the twenty-first century').

Each author entry has a direction to any quotations *about* that author elsewhere in the *Dictionary*. For example, at the entry for Al Gore, who by his own account 'used to be the next President of the United States', there is a direction to the quotation in which his cousin Gore Vidal explains why he will be voting instead for Ralph Nader: 'In the long run, Gore is thicker than Nader.'

As with other central titles in our Oxford Quotations family, we have had the good fortune to be able to build on the foundation of earlier collections: the first edition of the *Oxford Dictionary of Modern Quotations* (1991) and the *Oxford Dictionary of Twentieth Century Quotations* (1998).

We have once more drawn on our bank of new quotations, fed by our regular reading programme, and further enhanced through suggestions, questions, and comments received from the general public, as from colleagues in the Dictionary and Reference Departments. Peter Hennessy and Peter Kemp were kind enough to read and comment on an earlier version of this text, and of the many people who have contributed to our resources and replied to questions, thanks are especially due to Leslie Anne Connell, Jean Harker, Emma Lenz, Erin McKean, Bruce Moore, Jesse Sheidlower, Bill Trumble, and Georgie Wilkinson. Susie Dent, Alysoun Owen, and Helen Cox have given unfailing support, and Susan Ratcliffe's work as Associate Editor has once more been of inestimable value.

It has as always been of absorbing interest to see the history of modern times reflected through quotations. We hope that our readers will again share in the pleasure felt by the editorial staff in compiling the book.

ELIZABETH KNOWLES

Oxford 2001

How to Use the Dictionary

The sequence of entries is by alphabetical order of author, usually by surname but with occasional exceptions such as members of royal families (e.g. **Diana, Princess of Wales** and **Elizabeth II**), and Popes (**John Paul II**), or authors known by a pseudonym ('**Saki**'). In general authors' names are given in the form by which they are best known, so we have **Harold Macmillan** (not Lord Stockton), **Iris Murdoch** (not Jean Iris Murdoch), and **H. G. Wells** (not Herbert George Wells).

Anonymous quotations are included under that heading, or in one of the special category sections (see below).

Author names are followed by dates of birth and death (where known) and brief descriptions; cross-references are then given to quotations about that author elsewhere in the text (*on Capote: see* **Vidal** 328:9). Cross-references are also made to other entries in which the author appears, e.g. '*see also* **Epitaphs** 109:2' and '*see also* **Lennon and McCartney**'. Within each author entry, quotations are separated by literary form (novels, plays, poems: see further below) and within each group arranged by alphabetical order of title, 'a' and 'the' being ignored. Foreign-language text is given if it is felt that the quotation is familiar in the language of origin ('*Vorsprung durch Technik*').

Quotations from diaries, letters, and speeches are given in chronological order and usually follow the literary or published works quoted, with the form for which the author is best known taking precedence. Thus in the case of political figures, speeches appear first, just as poetry quotations come second for an author regarded primarily as a novelist.

Quotations from secondary sources such as biographies and other writers' works come at the end of the entry. Quotations to which a date in the author's lifetime can be assigned are arranged in chronological order, in sequence with diary entries, letters, and speeches. Other quotations from secondary sources and attributed quotations without an identifiable date are arranged in alphabetical order of quotation text.

Within the alphabetical sequence there are a number of special category entries, such as **Advertising slogans**, **Catchphrases**, **Film lines**, **Misquotations**, and **Newspaper headlines and leaders**. Quotations in these sections are arranged alphabetically according to the first word of the quotation (ignoring 'a' and 'the').

Contextual information regarded as essential to a full appreciation of the quotation precedes the text in an italicized note; information seen as providing useful amplification follows in an italicized note. Each quotation is accompanied by a bibliographical note of the source from which the quotation is taken; titles and dates of publication are given, but full finding references are not. Titles of published volumes (*Autumn Journal* by Louis MacNeice and *Oscar and Lucinda* by Peter Carey) appear in italics; titles of short stories and poems not published as volumes in their own right, and individual song titles, are given in roman type inside inverted commas ('Big Yellow Taxi' by Joni Mitchell and 'The Shadow of the Shark' by G. K. Chesterton).

Cross-references to specific quotations are used to direct the reader to another related item. In each case a reference is given to an author's name or to the title of the special category entry, followed by the page number and then the unique quotation number on that page ('see **Reagan** 271:14'and 'see **Film lines** 115:11'). In some cases, a quotation dating from before 1900 constitutes a direct source; when this happens, the source quotation is given directly below the quotation to which it relates. Authors who have their own entries are typographically distinguished by the use of bold ('of Robert **Menzies**', 'by Mae **West**') in context or source notes.

Indexes

Keyword Index

The most significant words from each quotation appear in the keyword index, allowing individual quotations to be traced. Both the keywords and the entries following each keyword, including those in foreign languages, are in strict alphabetical order. Singular and plural nouns (with their possessive forms) are grouped separately. References to are the author's name (often in abbreviated form, as AUNG for Aung San Suu Kyi) followed by the page number and the number of the unique quotation on the page. Thus AUNG 19:7 means quotation number 7 on page 19, in the entry for Aung San Suu Kyi.

Thematic Index

In addition, a selection of quotations on designated subjects can be traced through the thematic index. Each subject heading is followed by a line from each of the quotations on the theme. References are to the author's name, with page and quotation number, as in the keyword index.

Diane Abbott 1953–

British Labour politician

1 Being an MP is the sort of job all working-class parents want for their children—clean, indoors and no heavy lifting.

in *Independent* 18 January 1994

George Abbott 1887–1995

American director, producer, and dramatist

2 If you want to be adored by your peers and have standing ovations wherever you go—live to be over ninety.

in *The Times* 2 February 1995; obituary

Dannie Abse 1923–

Welsh-born doctor and poet

3 I know the colour rose, and it is lovely,
But not when it ripens in a tumour;
And healing greens, leaves and grass, so springlike
In limbs that fester are not springlike.

'Pathology of Colours' (1968)

Bella Abzug 1920–

American politician

4 Richard Nixon impeached himself. He gave us Gerald Ford as his revenge.

in *Rolling Stone*; Linda Botts *Loose Talk* (1980)

Goodman Ace 1899–1982

American humorist

5 TV—a clever contraction derived from the words Terrible Vaudeville . . . we call it a medium because nothing's well done.

letter, to Groucho Marx, in *The Groucho Letters* (1967)

Chinua Achebe 1930–

Nigerian novelist

6 The world is like a Mask dancing. If you want to see it well you do not stand in one place.

Arrow of God (1988)

7 In such a regime, I say, you died a good death if your life had inspired someone to come forward and shoot your murderer in the chest—without asking to be paid.

A Man of the People (1966)

Dean Acheson 1893–1971

American statesman, Secretary of State 1949–53

8 Great Britain has lost an empire and has not yet found a role.

speech at the Military Academy, West Point, 5 December 1962

9 A memorandum is written not to inform the reader but to protect the writer.

in *Wall Street Journal* 8 September 1977

Giuseppe Adami 1878–1946 and **Renato Simoni** 1875–1952

Italian librettists

10 *Nessun dorma.*

None shall sleep.

Turandot (1926 opera, music by Puccini) closing lines (after Gozzi's drama, 1762)

Douglas Adams 1952–2001

English science fiction writer

11 Don't panic.

The Hitch Hiker's Guide to the Galaxy (1979) preface

12 The Answer to the Great Question Of . . . Life, the Universe and Everything . . . [is] Forty-two.

The Hitch Hiker's Guide to the Galaxy (1979)

Franklin P. Adams 1881–1960

American journalist and humorist

13 Years ago we discovered the exact point, the dead centre of middle age. It occurs when you are too young to take up golf and too old to rush up to the net.

Nods and Becks (1944)

14 Elections are won by men and women chiefly because most people vote against somebody rather than for somebody.

Nods and Becks (1944); see **Fields** 113:14

Gerry Adams 1948–

Northern Irish politician; President of Sinn Féin

1 We want him to be the last British Prime Minister with jurisdiction in Ireland.

of Tony ***Blair***

in *Irish Times* 18 October 1997

2 Peace cannot be built on exclusion. That has been the price of the past 30 years.

in *Daily Telegraph* 11 April 1998

Phillip Adams 1939–

Australian film director and producer

3 Adams' first law of television: the weight of the backside is greater than the force of the intellect.

in 1970; attributed, Stephen Murray-Smith (ed.) *The Dictionary of Australian Quotations* (1984)

4 Fame often comes to those who are thinking about something else, whereas celebrity comes to those who think about nothing else. Celebrity is . . . a forgery of fame: it has the form but lacks the content.

in 1982; attributed, Stephen Murray-Smith (ed.) *The Dictionary of Australian Quotations* (1984)

Harold Adamson 1906–80

American songwriter

5 Comin' in on a wing and a pray'r.

derived from the contemporary comment of a war pilot, speaking from a disabled plane to ground control

title of song (1943)

Kate Adie 1945–

British journalist

6 I was expected to dig a trench in this hard, stony ground. I dug the smallest trench you ever saw. The colonel told me it was pathetic and then offered an incentive: no trench, no lunch.

recalling the Gulf War

in *Observer* 11 February 2001

Alfred Adler 1870–1937

Austrian psychologist and psychiatrist

7 The truth is often a terrible weapon of aggression. It is possible to lie, and even to murder, for the truth.

The Problems of Neurosis (1929)

Polly Adler 1900–62

American writer

8 A house is not a home.

title of book (1954)

Theodor Adorno 1903–69

German philosopher, sociologist, and musicologist

9 It is barbarous to write a poem after Auschwitz.

I. Buruma *Wages of Guilt* (1994)

■ Advertising slogans

see box opposite

see also **Taglines for films**

Herbert Agar 1897–1980

American poet and writer

10 The truth which makes men free is for the most part the truth which men prefer not to hear.

A Time for Greatness (1942); see below

And ye shall know the truth, and the truth shall make you free.

Bible St John

James Agate 1877–1947

British drama critic and novelist

11 A professional is a man who can do his job when he doesn't feel like it. An amateur is a man who can't do his job when he does feel like it.

diary, 19 July 1945

12 Shaw's plays are the price we pay for Shaw's prefaces.

diary, 10 March 1933

Advertising slogans

1 Access—your flexible friend.
Access credit card, 1981 onwards

2 An ace caff with quite a nice museum attached.
the Victoria and Albert Museum, February 1989

3 All human life is there.
the *News of the World*; used by Maurice Smelt in the late 1950s; see below

Cats and monkeys—monkeys and cats—all human life is there!
Henry James *The Madonna of the Future* (1879)

4 American Express? . . . That'll do nicely, sir.
American Express credit card, 1970s

5 And all because the lady loves Milk Tray.
Cadbury's Milk Tray chocolates, 1968 onwards

6 Australians wouldn't give a XXXX for anything else.
Castlemaine lager, 1986 onwards

7 Beanz meanz Heinz.
Heinz baked beans, c.1967; coined by Maurice Drake

8 Bovril . . . Prevents that sinking feeling.
Bovril, 1920; coined by H. H. Harris (1920)

9 . . . But I know a man who can.
Automobile Association, 1980s

10 Can you tell Stork from butter?
Stork margarine, from c.1956

11 Cool as a mountain stream.
Consulate menthol cigarettes, early 1960s onwards

12 A diamond is forever.
De Beers Consolidated Mines, 1940s onwards; coined by Frances Gerety; see **Loos** 202:12

13 Does she . . . or doesn't she?
Clairol hair colouring, 1950s

14 Don't be vague, ask for Haig.
Haig whisky, c.1936

15 Don't forget the fruit gums, Mum.
Rowntree's fruit gums, 1958–61; coined by Roger Musgrave

16 Drinka Pinta Milka Day.
National Dairy Council, 1958; coined by Bertrand Whitehead

17 Even your closest friends won't tell you.
Listerine mouthwash, US, in *Woman's Home Companion* November 1923

18 Full of Eastern promise.
Fry's Turkish Delight, 1950s onwards

19 The future's bright, the future's Orange.
slogan for Orange telecom company, mid 1990s

20 Go to work on an egg.
British Egg Marketing Board, from 1957; perhaps written by Fay **Weldon** or Mary Gowing

21 Guinness is good for you.
reply universally given to researchers asking people why they drank Guinness
adopted by Oswald Greene, c.1929; see **Advertising slogans** 4:13

22 Happiness is a cigar called Hamlet.
Hamlet cigars; see **Ephron** 108:6, **Lennon** 196:1, **Schulz** 291:11

23 Have a break, have a Kit-Kat.
Rowntree's Kit-Kat, from c.1955

24 Heineken refreshes the parts other beers cannot reach.
Heineken lager, 1975 onwards; coined by Terry Lovelock

25 Horlicks guards against night starvation.
Horlicks malted milk drink, 1930s

26 If you want to get ahead, get a hat.
the Hat Council, 1965

27 I liked it so much, I bought the company!
Remington Shavers, 1980; spoken by the company's new owner Victor Kiam (1926–2001)

28 I'm only here for the beer.
Double Diamond beer, 1971 onwards; coined by Ros Levenstein

29 It beats as it sweeps as it cleans.
Hoover vacuum cleaners, devised in 1919 by Gerald Page-Wood

▶

▸ Advertising slogans continued

1 It's finger lickin' good.
Kentucky fried chicken, from 1958

2 It's good to listen.
British Telecom, from 1997; see **Advertising slogans** 4:3

3 It's good to talk.
British Telecom, from 1994; see **Advertising slogans** 4:2

4 It's tingling fresh. It's fresh as ice.
Gibbs toothpaste; the first advertising slogan heard on British television, 22 September 1955

5 I was a seven-stone weakling.
Charles Atlas body-building, originally in US

6 Keep that schoolgirl complexion.
Palmolive soap, from 1917; coined by Charles S. Pearce

7 Kills all known germs.
Domestos bleach, 1959

8 Let the train take the strain.
British Rail, 1970 onwards

9 Let your fingers do the walking.
Bell system Telephone Directory Yellow Pages, 1960s

10 A Mars a day helps you work, rest and play.
Mars bar, *c.*1960 onwards; coined by Norman Gaff (d. 1988)

11 Maybe, just maybe.
British national lottery, from 1998

12 The mint with the hole.
Life-Savers, US, 1920; and Rowntree's Polo mints, UK, from 1947

13 My Goodness, My Guinness.
Guinness stout, 1935; coined by Dicky Richards; see **Advertising slogans** 3:21

14 Never knowingly undersold.
motto of the John Lewis Partnership, from *c.*1920; coined by John Spedan Lewis (1885–1963)

15 Nice one, Cyril.
taken up by supporters of Cyril Knowles, Tottenham Hotspur footballer; the Spurs team later made a record featuring the line
Wonderloaf, 1972

16 No manager ever got fired for buying IBM.
IBM

17 Oxo gives a meal man-appeal.
Oxo beef extract, *c.* 1960

18 Persil washes whiter—and it shows.
Persil washing powder, 1970s

19 Put a tiger in your tank.
Esso petrol, 1964

20 Say it with flowers.
Society of American Florists, 1917, coined by Patrick O'Keefe (1872–1934)

21 Sch . . . you know who.
Schweppes mineral drinks, 1960s

22 Someone, somewhere, wants a letter from you.
British Post Office, 1960s

23 Stop me and buy one.
Wall's ice cream, from spring 1922; coined by Cecil Rodd

24 Tell Sid.
privatization of British Gas, 1986

25 Things go better with Coke.
Coca-Cola, 1963

26 Top people take *The Times*.
The Times newspaper, from January 1959

27 *Vorsprung durch Technik.*
Progress through technology.
Audi cars, from 1986

28 We are the Ovaltineys,
Little [*or* Happy] girls and boys.
'We are the Ovaltineys' (song from *c.*1935); Ovaltine drink

29 We're number two. We try harder.
Avis car rentals

30 We won't make a drama out of a crisis.
Commercial Union insurance

31 Where's the beef?
Wendy's Hamburgers, from January 1984; coined by Cliff Freeman; see **Mondale** 229:1

32 You're never alone with a Strand.
Strand cigarettes, 1960; coined by John May

Spiro T. Agnew 1918–96

American Republican politician

1 I didn't say I wouldn't go into ghetto areas. I've been in many of them and to some extent I would have to say this: If you've seen one city slum you've seen them all.

in *Detroit Free Press* 19 October 1968; see below

See one promontory (said Socrates of old), one mountain, one sea, one river, and see all.

Robert Burton (1577–1640) *The Anatomy of Melancholy* (1621–51)

2 In the United States today, we have more than our share of the nattering nabobs of negativism.

speech in San Diego, 11 September 1970

Bertie Ahern 1951–

Irish Fianna Fáil statesman, Taoiseach since 1997

3 It is a day we should treasure. Today is about the promise of a bright future, a day when we hope a line will be drawn under the bloody past.

in *Guardian* 11 April 1998

4 This is the first time since 1918 in an act of self-determination that everyone on this island, on the one issue, has had the opportunity to pass their verdict.

opening the Fianna Fáil referendum campaign on the Good Friday agreement

in *Irish Times* 9 May 1998

Caroline Aherne 1963–

British comic actress and writer

5 To be blessed with a mind that can write often means you'll be cursed with a mind that will torture you.

in *Sunday Times* 15 April 2001

Jonathan Aitken 1942–

British Conservative politician

6 If it falls to me to start a fight to cut out the cancer of bent and twisted journalism in our country with the simple sword of truth and the trusty shield of British fair play, so be it.

statement, London, 10 April 1995

Anna Akhmatova 1889–1966

Russian poet

7 It was a time when only the dead smiled,
happy in their peace.

Requiem (1935–40)

8 Stars of death stood over us,
and innocent Russia squirmed
under the bloody boots,
under the wheels of black Marias.

Requiem (1935–40)

9 They took you away at dawn,
I walked after you as though you were being borne out,
the children were crying in the dark room,
the candle swam by the ikon-stand.
The cold of the ikon on your lips.
Death sweat on your brow . . . Do not forget!
I will howl by the Kremlin towers
like the wives of the Streltsy.

on the arrest of her friend N. N. Punin during the Stalinist purges

Requiem (1935–40)

Zoë Akins 1886–1958

American poet and dramatist

10 The Greeks had a word for it.

title of play (1930)

Alain (Émile-Auguste Chartier) 1868–1951

French poet and philosopher

11 *Rien n'est plus dangereux qu'une idée, quand on n'a qu'une idée.*

Nothing is more dangerous than an idea, when you have only one idea.

Propos sur la religion (1938) no. 74

Edward Albee 1928–

American dramatist

12 Who's afraid of Virginia Woolf?

title of play (1962); see **Churchill** 65:12

Madeleine Albright 1937–

American diplomat, Secretary of State 1997–2001

1 Hallelujah . . . Never again will your fates be tossed around like poker chips on a bargaining table.
accepting the admission papers for Hungary, Poland, and the Czech Republic to become members of Nato
in *Daily Telegraph* 13 March 1999

2 Busy times.
in a week which saw the overthrow of Slobodan Milosevic and the breakdown of the Middle East peace process
in *Newsweek* 16 October 2000

Brian Aldiss 1925–

English science fiction writer

3 Keep violence in the mind
Where it belongs.
Barefoot in the Head (1969) 'Charteris'

Buzz Aldrin 1930–

American astronaut; second man on the moon

4 Beautiful! Beautiful! Magnificent desolation.
of the lunar landscape
on the first moon walk, 20 July 1969

Nelson Algren 1909–

American novelist

5 A walk on the wild side.
title of novel (1956)

6 Never play cards with a man called Doc. Never eat at a place called Mom's. Never sleep with a woman whose troubles are worse than your own.
in *Newsweek* 2 July 1956

Muhammad Ali (Cassius Clay) 1942–

American boxer

7 I'm the greatest.
catch-phrase used from 1962, in *Louisville Times* 16 November 1962

8 Float like a butterfly, sting like a bee.
summary of his boxing strategy
G. Sullivan *Cassius Clay Story* (1964); probably originated by Drew 'Bundini' Brown

9 I ain't got no quarrel with the Viet Cong.
refusing to be drafted to fight in Vietnam
at a press conference in Miami, Florida, February 1966

Fred Allen 1894–1956

American humorist

10 California is a fine place to live—if you happen to be an orange.
in *American Magazine* December 1945

11 Committee—a group of men who individually can do nothing but as a group decide that nothing can be done.
attributed

Woody Allen 1935–

American film director, writer, and actor
on Allen: see **Farrow** 111:10*; see also* **Film titles** 118:15

12 That [sex] was the most fun I ever had without laughing.
Annie Hall (1977 film, with Marshall Brickman)

13 Don't knock masturbation. It's sex with someone I love.
Annie Hall (1977 film, with Marshall Brickman)

14 Is sex dirty? Only if it's done right.
Everything You Always Wanted to Know about Sex (1972 film)

15 My brain? It's my second favourite organ.
Sleeper (1973 film, with Marshall Brickman)

16 It's not that I'm afraid to die. I just don't want to be there when it happens.
Death (1975)

17 More than any other time in history, mankind faces a crossroads. One path leads to despair and utter hopelessness. The other, to total extinction. Let us pray we have the wisdom to choose correctly.
Side Effects (1980) 'My Speech to the Graduates'

1 A fast word about oral contraception. I asked a girl to go to bed with me and she said 'no'.
at a nightclub in Chicago, March 1964, recorded on *Woody Allen Volume Two*

2 Not only is there no God, but try getting a plumber on weekends.
in *New Yorker* 27 December 1969 'My Philosophy'

3 If only God would give me some clear sign! Like making a large deposit in my name at a Swiss bank.
'Selections from the Allen Notebooks' in *New Yorker* 5 November 1973

4 On bisexuality: It immediately doubles your chances for a date on Saturday night.
in *New York Times* 1 December 1975

5 I don't want to achieve immortality through my work . . . I want to achieve it through not dying.
Eric Lax *Woody Allen and his Comedy* (1975)

6 I recently turned sixty. Practically a third of my life is over.
in *Observer* 10 March 1996

Svetlana Alliluyeva 1925–

daughter of Joseph **Stalin**

7 He is gone, but his shadow still stands over all of us. It still dictates to us and we, very often, obey.
of her father, Joseph ***Stalin***
Twenty Letters to a Friend (1967)

Robert Altman 1922–

American film director

8 What's a cult? It just means not enough people to make a minority.
in *Guardian* 11 April 1981

Lord Altrincham

see **John Grigg**

Luis Walter Alvarez 1911–88

American physicist

9 There is no democracy in physics. We can't say that some second-rate guy has as much right to opinion as Fermi.
D. S. Greenberg *The Politics of Pure Science* (1969)

Leo Amery 1873–1955

British Conservative politician

10 Speak for England.
to Arthur Greenwood in the House of Commons, 2 September 1939: see **Boothby** 40:9

11 I will quote certain other words. I do it with great reluctance, because I am speaking of those who are old friends and associates of mine, but they are words which, I think, are applicable to the present situation. This is what Cromwell said to the Long Parliament when he thought it was no longer fit to conduct the affairs of the nation: 'You have sat too long here for any good you have been doing. Depart, I say, and let us have done with you. In the name of God, go.'
speech, House of Commons, 7 May 1940; see below

You have sat too long here for any good you have been doing. Depart, I say, and let us have done with you. In the name of God, go!
Oliver Cromwell (1599–1658) addressing the Rump Parliament, 20 April 1653, oral tradition

Barbara Amiel

British journalist, wife of Conrad **Black**

12 You're considered to have a rare kind of social disease if you espouse neo-conservative ideas in Canada.
in *Toronto Star* 15 November 1980; attributed

Hardy Amies 1909–

English couturier

13 She is only 5ft 4in, and to make someone that height look regal is difficult. Fortunately she holds herself very well.
of the Queen
interview in *Sunday Telegraph* 9 February 1997

14 A man should look as if he bought his clothes with intelligence, put them on with care, then forgot about them.
in *Mail on Sunday* 27 May 2001

Kingsley Amis 1922–95

English novelist and poet

1 His mouth had been used as a latrine by some small creature of the night, and then as its mausoleum.

Lucky Jim (1953)

2 Alun's life was coming to consist more and more exclusively of being told at dictation speed what he knew.

The Old Devils (1986)

3 Outside every fat man there was an even fatter man trying to close in.

One Fat Englishman (1963); see **Orwell** 249:9

4 Should poets bicycle-pump the human heart
Or squash it flat?
Man's love is of man's life a thing apart;
Girls aren't like that.

'A Bookshop Idyll' (1956); see below

Man's love is of man's life a thing apart,
'Tis woman's whole existence.

Lord Byron (1788–1824) *Don Juan* (1819–24)

5 The delusion that there are thousands of young people about who are capable of benefiting from university training, but have somehow failed to find their way there, is . . . a necessary component of the expansionist case . . . More will mean worse.

in *Encounter* July 1960

6 If you can't annoy somebody with what you write, I think there's little point in writing.

in *Radio Times* 1 May 1971

7 No pleasure is worth giving up for the sake of two more years in a geriatric home in Weston-super-Mare.

in *The Times* 21 June 1994; attributed

Martin Amis 1949–

English novelist

8 Weapons are like money; no one knows the meaning of *enough*.

Einstein's Monsters (1987)

9 Consciousness *isn't* intolerable. It is beautiful: the eternal creation and dissolution of mental forms.

Time's Arrow (1991)

Maxwell Anderson 1888–1959

American dramatist

10 But it's a long, long while
From May to December;
And the days grow short
When you reach September.

'September Song' (1938 song)

Maxwell Anderson 1888–1959 and Lawrence Stallings 1894–1968

American dramatists

11 What price glory?

title of play (1924)

Robert Anderson 1917–

American dramatist

12 Tea and sympathy.

title of play (1957)

Ursula Andress 1936–

Swiss actress

13 This bikini made me a success.

on the swimsuit she wore emerging from the sea in the 1962 film Dr No

in *Newsweek* 22 January 2001

Maya Angelou 1928–

American novelist and poet

14 Children's talent to endure stems from their ignorance of alternatives.

I Know Why The Caged Bird Sings (1969) ch.17

15 Lift up your eyes
Upon this day breaking for you.
Give birth again
To the dream.

Here, on the pulse of this new day,
You may have the grace to look up and out
And into your sister's eyes,
And into your brother's face,

Your country,
And say simply
Very simply
With hope
Good morning.
'On the Pulse of Morning' (1993)

1 You may shoot me with your words,
You may cut me with your eyes,
You may kill me with your hatefulness,
But still, like air, I'll rise.
'Still I Rise' (1978)

2 The sadness of the women's movement is that they don't allow the necessity of love. See, I don't personally trust any revolution where love is not allowed.
in *California Living* 14 May 1975

3 In all my work what I try to say is that as human beings we are more alike than we are unalike.
interview in *New York Times* 20 January 1993

Paul Anka 1941–

Canadian singer and composer

4 I've lived a life that's full, I've travelled each and ev'ry highway
And more, much more than this. I did it my way.
'My Way' (1969 song)

Kofi Annan 1938–

Ghanaian diplomat, Secretary General of the United Nations since 1997

5 You can do a lot with diplomacy, but of course you can do a lot more with diplomacy backed up by fairness and force.
of the agreement reached with Iraq over weapons inspections, February 1998
in *Mail on Sunday* 1 March 1998

6 The peace we seek in Iraq, as everywhere, is one that reflects the lessons of our terrible century: that peace is not true or lasting if it is bought at any cost; that only peace with justice can honour the victims of war and violence; and that, without democracy, tolerance and human rights for all, no peace is truly safe.
speech to the Council on Foreign Relations, New York, January 1999

Noel Annan 1916–2000

English historian and writer

7 The cardinal virtue was no longer to love one's country. It was to feel compassion for one's fellow men and women.
of his own generation
Our Age (1990)

Anne, Princess Royal 1950–

British princess; daughter of **Elizabeth II**

8 I don't work that way . . . The very idea that all children want to be cuddled by a complete stranger, I find completely amazing.
on her work for Save the Children
in *Daily Telegraph* 17 January 1998

Anonymous

see also **Advertising slogans, Newspaper headlines, Official advice, Political sayings and slogans, Sayings and slogans, Taglines for films**

9 An abomination unto the Lord, but a very present help in time of trouble.
definition of a lie
an amalgamation of the *Bible* Proverbs 12.22 and Psalms 46.1, often attributed to Adlai **Stevenson**

10 All human beings are born free and equal in dignity and rights.
Universal Declaration of Human Rights (1948) article 1

11 Anyone here been raped and speaks English?
shouted by a British TV reporter in a crowd of Belgian civilians waiting to be airlifted out of the Belgian Congo, c.1960
Edward Behr *Anyone Here been Raped and Speaks English?* (1981)

12 *Arbeit macht frei.*
Work liberates.
words inscribed on the gates of Dachau concentration camp, 1933, and subsequently on those of Auschwitz

13 The best defence against the atom bomb is not to be there when it goes off.
contributor to *British Army Journal*, in *Observer* 20 February 1949

1 Bigamy is having one husband too many. Monogamy is the same.
Erica Jong *Fear of Flying* (1973) epigraph

2 A bigger bang for a buck.
description of Charles E. **Wilson**'s defence policy, in *Newsweek* 22 March 1954

3 Can't act. Slightly bald. Also dances.
studio official's comment on Fred Astaire
Bob Thomas *Astaire* (1985)

4 A community in which power, wealth and opportunity are in the hands of the many not the few, where the rights we enjoy reflect the duties we owe . . . in which the enterprise of the market and the rigour of competition are joined with the forces of partnership and cooperation.
new Clause Four of the Labour Party constitution, passed at a special conference 29 April 1995; see **Anonymous** 12:9

5 Do not stand at my grave and weep:
I am not there. I do not sleep.
I am a thousand winds that blow.
I am the diamond glints on snow.
I am the sunlight on ripened grain
I am the gentle autumn's rain.
When you awaken in the morning's
hush,
I am the swift uplifting rush
Of quiet birds in circled flight.
I am the soft stars that shine at night.
Do not stand at my grave and cry;
I am not there, I did not die.
quoted in letter left by British soldier Stephen Cummins when killed by the IRA, March 1989
origin uncertain; attributed to various authors

6 Expletive deleted.
frequent editorial amendment of transcripts of Richard ***Nixon*** *during the Watergate inquiry*
Submission of Recorded Presidential Conversations . . . by President Richard M. Nixon 30 April 1974

7 Exterminate . . . the treacherous English, walk over General French's contemptible little army.
annexe to British Expeditionary Force Routine Orders, 24 September 1914 (allegedly quoting Kaiser ***Wilhelm II*** *but probably fabricated by the British)*
A. Ponsonby *Falsehood in Wartime* (1928)

8 Faster than a speeding bullet! . . . Look! Up in the sky! It's a bird! It's a plane! It's Superman! Yes, it's Superman! . . . who—disguised as Clark Kent, mild-mannered reporter for a great metropolitan newspaper—fights a never ending battle for truth, justice and the American way!
Superman (US radio show, 1940 onwards) preamble

9 The first and only thing they have to do is to decide how a resigned commission behaves.
unidentified British official in Brussels of the European Commission
in *Daily Telegraph* 18 March 1999

10 For ours is the harbour, the bridge and
the Bradman for ever and ever.
Australian parody of the Lord's Prayer, 1930s

11 God is not dead but alive and working on a much less ambitious project.
graffito quoted in *Guardian* 26 November 1975; see **Anonymous** 11:6

12 Hark the herald angels sing
Mrs Simpson's pinched our king.
children's rhyme at the time of the Abdication in 1936, quoted in letter from Clement Attlee, 26 December 1938; see below

Hark! the herald-angels sing
Glory to the new born king.
alteration, in George Whitefield's *Hymns for Social Worship* (1753), of Charles Wesley's 'Hymn for Christmas' (1739)

13 Hear ye! Hear ye! All persons are commanded to keep silent, on pain of imprisonment, while the House of Representatives is exhibiting to the Senate of the United States articles of impeachment against William Jefferson Clinton, President of the United States.
formal announcement read by the serjeant-at-arms
in *Guardian* 8 January 1999

14 Here we go, here we go, here we go.
song sung especially by football supporters, 1980s

15 Hip young gunslinger.
New Musical Express *advertisement for a journalist in 1976, answered by Julie* ***Burchill***
Julie Burchill *I Knew I Was Right* (1998)

16 The idea that the PM gets integrated advice is nonsense. You could not see a more *unjoined* system. To say they have imported the White House to No.

10—Washington to Downing Street—is absolutely right.

a senior Whitehall figure on the Blair administration, January 2000

Peter Hennessy *The Prime Minister: the Office and its Holders since 1945* (2000)

1 If I should die and leave you here awhile,
Be not like others, sore undone, who keep
Long vigils by the silent dust, and weep.
For my sake—turn again to life and smile,
Nerving thy heart and trembling hand to do
Something to comfort other hearts than thine.
Complete those dear unfinished tasks of mine
And I, perchance, may therein comfort you.

read at the funeral of **Diana**, Princess of Wales; variously attributed (origins discussed in Nigel Rees 'Quote . . . Unquote' Newsletter October 1997)

2 If you really want to make a million . . . the quickest way is to start your own religion.

previously attributed to L. Ron Hubbard 1911–86 in B. Corydon and L. Ron Hubbard Jr. *L. Ron Hubbard* (1987), but attribution subsequently rejected by L. Ron Hubbard Jr., who also dissociated himself from this book

3 The iron lady.

name given to Margaret ***Thatcher****, then Leader of the Opposition, by the Soviet defence ministry newspaper* Red Star, *which accused her of trying to revive the cold war*

in *Sunday Times* 25 January 1976

4 It became necessary to destroy the town to save it.

statement issued by US Army, referring to Ben Tre in Vietnam; in *New York Times* 8 February 1968

5 It is becoming difficult to find anyone in the Commission who has even the slightest sense of responsibility.

report on the European Commission; in *Guardian* 17 March 1999

6 Jacques Brel is alive and well and living in Paris.

title of musical entertainment (1968–72) which triggered numerous imitations; see **Anonymous** 10:11

7 *Jedem das Seine.*

To each his own.

often quoted as 'Everyone gets what he deserves'

inscription on the gate of Buchenwald concentration camp, *c.* 1937; see **Bold** 40:1

8 *Je suis Marxiste—tendance Groucho.*

I am a Marxist—of the Groucho tendency.

slogan found at Nanterre in Paris, 1968

9 Kilroy was here.

graffito popularized by American servicemen in the Second World War

10 Liberty is always unfinished business.

title of 36th Annual Report of the American Civil Liberties Union, 1 July 1955–30 June 1956

11 Life is a sexually transmitted disease.

graffito found on the London Underground; D. J. Enright (ed.) *Faber Book of Fevers and Frets* (1989)

12 Lloyd George knew my father,
My father knew Lloyd George.

sung to the tune of 'Onward, Christian Soldiers'; possibly by Tommy Rhys Roberts (1910–75)

13 Mademoiselle from Armenteers,
Hasn't been kissed for forty years,
Hinky, dinky, parley-voo.

song of the First World War, variously attributed to Edward Rowland and to Harry Carlton

14 The noise, my dear! And the people!

of the retreat from Dunkirk, May 1940

A. Rhodes *Sword of Bone* (1942)

15 Nostalgia isn't what it used to be.

graffito, taken as title of book by Simone Signoret, 1978

16 Not so much a programme, more a way of life!

title of satirical BBC television series, 1964

17 Once again we stop the mighty roar of London's traffic.

In Town Tonight (BBC radio series, 1933–60) preamble

18 Prudence is the other woman in Gordon's life.

of Gordon ***Brown***

unidentified aide, quoted in BBC News online (Budget Briefing), 20 March 1998

1 Psychological flaws.

on which, according to an unnamed source, Gordon **Brown** *needed to 'get a grip'*

in *Observer* 18 January 1998; attributed to Alastair **Campbell** by Bernard **Ingham** in minutes of the Parliamentary Select Committee on Public Administration, 2 June 1998, but denied by Campbell in evidence to the Committee, 23 June 1998

2 Science finds, industry applies, man conforms.

subtitle of guidebook to 1933 Chicago World's Fair

3 The singer not the song.

from a West Indian calypso; title of a novel (1959) by Audrey Erskine Lindop

4 Some television programmes are so much chewing gum for the eyes.

John Mason Brown quoting a friend of his young son, interview, 28 July 1955

J. B. Simpson *Best Quotes* (1957)

5 There shall be a Scottish parliament.

first clause of the Scotland Act, 1998; see **Dewar** 91:2

6 [This film] is so cryptic as to be almost meaningless. If there is a meaning, it is doubtless objectionable.

banning Jean **Cocteau***'s film* The Seashell and the Clergyman *(1929)*

The British Board of Film Censors, in J. C. Robertson *Hidden Cinema* (1989)

7 This is a rotten argument, but it should be good enough for their lordships on a hot summer afternoon.

annotation to a ministerial brief, said to have been read out inadvertently in the House of Lords

Lord Home *The Way the Wind Blows* (1976)

8 Though I yield to no one in my admiration for Mr Coolidge, I do wish he did not look as if he had been weaned on a pickle.

anonymous remark, in Alice Roosevelt Longworth *Crowded Hours* (1933)

9 To secure for the workers by hand or by brain the full fruits of their industry and the most equitable distribution thereof that may be possible upon the basis of the common ownership of the means of production, distribution, and exchange.

Clause Four of the Labour Party's Constitution of 1918 (revised 1929); the commitment to common ownership of services was largely removed in 1995; see **Anonymous** 10:4

10 We do not need a loose cannon like her.

an unidentified junior minister commenting on the intervention into the campaign against landmines by **Diana***, Princess of Wales*

in *Times* 15 January 1997

11 We trained hard . . . but it seemed that every time we were beginning to form up into teams we would be reorganized. I was to learn later in life that we tend to meet any new situation by reorganizing; and a wonderful method it can be for creating the illusion of progress while producing confusion, inefficiency, and demoralization.

modern saying, frequently (and wrongly) attributed to Petronius Arbiter

12 We value excellence as well as fairness, independence as dearly as mateship.

draft preamble to the Australian constitution, made public 23 March 1999

13 When cult is added to power
even the chairman makes mistakes.
Xiaoping suffered criticism (in the
 Cultural Revolution)
and the people raised him up.
Now he represents bureaucracy
and official corruption.
The country does not want him,
the people do not want him.

poem put up in the Forbidden City in 1989, shortly before the tanks moved into Tiananmen Square

quoted in obituary of **Deng** Xiaoping, in *Guardian* 20 February 1997

14 Winston is back.

Board of Admiralty signal to the Fleet on Winston **Churchill***'s reappointment as First Sea Lord, 3 September 1939*

Martin Gilbert *Winston S. Churchill* (1976)

15 You should make a point of trying every experience once, excepting incest and folk-dancing.

Arnold Bax (1883–1953), quoting 'a sympathetic Scot' in *Farewell My Youth* (1943)

16 You were a premature anti-Fascist.

interviewer for Yale Classics Department in 1946, on hearing that the young Bernard Knox had fought with the International Brigade in the Spanish Civil War

Bernard Knox 'Premature Anti-Fascist' (Bill Susman Lecture Series, New York, 1998)

Jean Anouilh 1910–87

French dramatist

1 The spring is wound up tight. It will uncoil of itself. That is what is so convenient in tragedy. The least little turn of the wrist will do the job. Anything will set it going.

Antigone (1944, tr. L. Galantiere, 1957)

2 Tragedy is clean, it is restful, it is flawless.

Antigone (1944, tr. L. Galantiere, 1957)

3 There will always be a lost dog somewhere that will prevent me from being happy.

La Sauvage (1938)

Guillaume Apollinaire 1880–1918

French poet

4 *Les souvenirs sont cors de chasse*
Dont meurt le bruit parmi le vent.

Memories are hunting horns
Whose sound dies on the wind.

'Cors de Chasse' (1912)

5 When man wanted to make a machine that would walk he created the wheel, which does not resemble a leg.

Les Mamelles de Tirésias (1918)

Yasser Arafat 1929–

Palestinian statesman, Palestinian President since 1996

6 Palestine is the cement that holds the Arab world together, or it is the explosive that blows it apart.

in *Time* 11 November 1974

Louis Aragon 1897–1982

French poet, essayist, and novelist

7 *Ô mois des floraisons mois des métamorphoses*
Mai qui fut sans nuage et Juin poignardé
Je n'oublierai jamais les lilas ni les roses
Ni ceux que le printemps dans ses plis a gardé.

O month of flowerings, month of metamorphoses,
May without cloud and June that was stabbed,
I shall never forget the lilac and the roses
Nor those whom spring has kept in its folds.

'Les lilas et les roses' (1940)

Diane Arbus 1923–71

American photographer

8 Most people go through life dreading they'll have a traumatic experience. Freaks are born with their trauma. They've already passed it. They're aristocrats.

Diane Arbus (1972)

9 A photograph is a secret about a secret. The more it tells you the less you know.

Patricia Bosworth *Diane Arbus: a Biography* (1985)

Mary Archer 1944–

British scientist, wife of Jeffrey Archer
on Archer: see **Caulfield** 57:11

10 I think we explored the further reaches of 'for better or for worse' more than some other married couples.

on her marriage during the 1980s

at Jeffrey Archer's trial for perjury, London, 29 June 2001

Elizabeth Arden 1876–1966

Canadian-born American businesswoman

11 Nothing that costs only a dollar is worth having.

attributed; in *Fortune* October 1973

Robert Ardrey 1908–80

American dramatist and evolutionist

12 Not in innocence, and not in Asia, was mankind born.

African Genesis (1961)

Hannah Arendt 1906–75

American political philosopher

1 It was as though in those last minutes he [Eichmann] was summing up the lessons that this long course in human wickedness had taught us—the lesson of the fearsome, word-and-thought-defying *banality of evil.*

Eichmann in Jerusalem (1963)

2 The most radical revolutionary will become a conservative on the day after the revolution.

in *New Yorker* 12 September 1970

3 Under conditions of tyranny it is far easier to act than to think.

W. H. Auden *A Certain World* (1970)

Louis Armstrong 1901–71

American singer and jazz musician
see also **Misquotations** 226:10

4 All music is folk music, I ain't never heard no horse sing a song.

in *New York Times* 7 July 1971

Neil Armstrong 1930–

American astronaut; first man on the moon

5 Houston, Tranquillity Base here. The Eagle has landed.

radio message as the lunar module touched down

in *The Times* 21 July 1969

6 That's one small step for a man, one giant leap for mankind.

landing on the moon

in *New York Times* 21 July 1969; interference in transmission obliterated 'a'

Robert Armstrong 1927–

British civil servant, Head of the Civil Service, 1981–7

7 It contains a misleading impression, not a lie. It was being economical with the truth.

referring to a letter during the 'Spycatcher' trial, Supreme Court, New South Wales; the expression 'over-economical with the truth' had been applied to Harold ***Wilson*** *by the Earl of Dalkeith in the House of Commons, 4 July 1968*

in *Daily Telegraph* 19 November 1986; see below; see also **Clark** 69:12

Falsehood and delusion are allowed in no case whatsoever: But, as in the exercise of all the virtues, there is an economy of truth.

Edmund Burke (1729–97) *Two letters on Proposals for Peace* (1796)

Roseanne Arnold 1953–

American comedian

8 If I were Her what would really piss me off the worst is that they cannot even get My gender right for Christsakes.

Roseanne (1990)

L. A. Artsimovich 1909–73

Russian scientist

9 The joke definition according to which 'Science is the best way of satisfying the curiosity of individuals at government expense' is more or less correct.

in *Novy Mir* January 1967

Isaac Asimov 1920–92

Russian-born biochemist and science fiction writer

10 The three fundamental Rules of Robotics . . . One, a robot may not injure a human being, or, through inaction, allow a human being to come to harm . . . Two . . . a robot must obey the orders given it by human beings except where such orders would conflict with the First Law . . . three, a robot must protect its own existence as long as such protection does not conflict with the First or Second Laws.

I, Robot (1950) 'Runaround'

11 Science fiction writers foresee the inevitable, and although problems and catastrophes may be inevitable, solutions are not.

'How Easy to See the Future' in *Natural History* April 1975

12 When, however, the lay public rallies around an idea that is denounced by distinguished but elderly scientists and supports that idea with great fervour and emotion—the distinguished but elderly scientists are then, after all, probably right.

corollary to Arthur C. ***Clarke****'s law; see* **Clarke** 70:3

Arthur C. Clarke 'Asimov's Corollary' in K. Frazier (ed.) *Paranormal Borderlands of Science* (1981)

1 The first law of dietetics seems to be: if it tastes good, it's bad for you.

attributed

Herbert Henry Asquith 1852–1928

British Liberal statesman; Prime Minister, 1908–16; husband of Margot **Asquith**

2 We had better wait and see.

referring, in 1910, to the rumour that the House of Lords was to be flooded with new Liberal peers to ensure the passage of the Finance Bill

Roy Jenkins *Asquith* (1964)

3 Happily there seems to be no reason why we should be anything more than spectators.

of the approaching war

letter to Venetia Stanley, 24 July 1914

4 It is fitting that we should have buried the Unknown Prime Minister [Bonar Law] by the side of the Unknown Soldier.

R. Blake *The Unknown Prime Minister* (1955)

5 [The War Office kept three sets of figures:] one to mislead the public, another to mislead the Cabinet, and the third to mislead itself.

A. Horne *Price of Glory* (1962)

Margot Asquith 1864–1945

British political hostess; wife of Herbert **Asquith**

6 Kitchener is a great poster.

More Memories (1933)

7 The *t* is silent, as in *Harlow*.

to Jean Harlow, who had mispronounced her name

T. S. Matthews *Great Tom* (1973)

Nancy Astor 1879–1964

American-born British Conservative politician
on Astor: see **Churchill** 69:2

8 One reason why I don't drink is because I wish to know when I am having a good time.

in *Christian Herald* June 1960

9 I married beneath me, all women do.

in *Dictionary of National Biography* (1917–)

Brooks Atkinson 1894–1984

American journalist and critic

10 After each war there is a little less democracy to save.

Once Around the Sun (1951) 7 January

11 In every age 'the good old days' were a myth. No one ever thought they were good at the time. For every age has consisted of crises that seemed intolerable to the people who lived through them.

Once Around the Sun (1951) 8 February

Jacques Attali 1943–

French economist and writer

12 Machines are the new proletariat. The working class is being given its walking papers.

Millenium: Winners and Losers in the Coming World Order (1991)

David Attenborough 1926–

English naturalist and broadcaster

13 I'm not over-fond of animals. I am merely astounded by them.

in *Independent* 14 January 1995

Clement Attlee 1883–1967

British Labour statesman; Prime Minister, 1945–51
on Attlee: see **Churchill** 68:4, 69:5, **de Gaulle** 88:9

14 I must remind the Right Honourable

Gentleman that a monologue is not a decision.

*to Winston **Churchill**, who had complained that a matter had been raised several times in Cabinet, c.1945*

Francis Williams *A Prime Minister Remembers* (1961)

1 The voice we heard was that of Mr Churchill but the mind was that of Lord Beaverbrook.

*on **Churchill**'s accusing the Labour Party of planning to set up a Gestapo*

speech on radio, 5 June 1945

2 A period of silence on your part would be welcome.

letter to Harold Laski, 20 August 1945

3 Few thought he was even a starter
There were many who thought
themselves smarter
But he ended PM
CH and OM
An earl and a knight of the garter.

describing himself

letter to Tom Attlee, 8 April 1956

4 [Russian Communism is] the illegitimate child of Karl Marx and Catherine the Great.

speech at Aarhus University, 11 April 1956

5 Democracy means government by discussion, but it is only effective if you can stop people talking.

speech at Oxford, 14 June 1957

6 Often the 'experts' make the worst possible Ministers in their own fields. In this country we prefer rule by amateurs.

speech at Oxford, 14 June 1957

7 If the King asks you to form a Government you say 'Yes' or 'No', not 'I'll let you know later!'

Kenneth Harris *Attlee* (1982)

Margaret Atwood 1939–

Canadian novelist

8 His father was self-made, but his mother was constructed by others, and such edifices are notoriously fragile.

Alias Grace (1996)

9 He's coming to hate the gratitude of women. It's like being fawned on by rabbits, or like being covered with syrup: you can't get it off . . . Their gratitude isn't real; what they really mean by it is that he should be grateful to them.

Alias Grace (1996)

10 The threshold of a new house is a lonely place.

The Handmaid's Tale (1985)

W. H. Auden 1907–73

English poet

11 Sob, heavy world,
Sob as you spin
Mantled in mist, remote from the happy.

The Age of Anxiety (1947) pt. 4 'The Dirge'

12 Blessed Cecilia, appear in visions
To all musicians, appear and inspire:
Translated Daughter, come down and
startle
Composing mortals with immortal fire.

Anthem for St Cecilia's Day (1941) pt. 1; set to music by Benjamin Britten, to whom it was dedicated, as *Hymn to St Cecilia* op. 27 (1942)

13 I'll love you, dear, I'll love you
Till China and Africa meet
And the river jumps over the mountain
And the salmon sing in the street,

I'll love you till the ocean
Is folded and hung up to dry
And the seven stars go squawking
Like geese about the sky.

'As I Walked Out One Evening' (1940)

14 The glacier knocks in the cupboard,
The desert sighs in the bed,
And the crack in the tea-cup opens
A lane to the land of the dead.

'As I Walked Out One Evening' (1940)

15 The desires of the heart are as crooked as
corkscrews
Not to be born is the best for man.

'Death's Echo' (1937); see below

Not to be born is, past all prizing, best.

Sophocles (c.496–406 BC) *Oedipus Coloneus* (translation by R. C. Jebb); see **Yeats** 347:9

16 Happy the hare at morning, for she
cannot read
The Hunter's waking thoughts.

Dog beneath the Skin (with Christopher **Isherwood**, 1935)

1 To save your world you asked this man
to die:
Would this man, could he see you now,
ask why?
'Epitaph for the Unknown Soldier' (1955)

2 When he laughed, respectable senators
burst with laughter,
And when he cried the little children died
in the streets.
'Epitaph on a Tyrant' (1940); see below

As long as he lived, he was the guiding-star of a whole brave nation, and when he died the little children cried in the streets.
of William of Orange; John Lothrop Motley (1814–77) *The Rise of the Dutch Republic* (1856)

3 Stop all the clocks, cut off the telephone,
Prevent the dog from barking with a
juicy bone,
Silence the pianos and with muffled drum
Bring out the coffin, let the mourners
come.
'Funeral Blues' (1936)

4 He was my North, my South, my East
and West,
My working week and my Sunday rest,
My noon, my midnight, my talk, my
song;
I thought that love would last for ever: I
was wrong.
'Funeral Blues' (1936)

5 To us he is no more a person
now but a whole climate of opinion.
'In Memory of Sigmund Freud' (1940)

6 You were silly like us; your gift survived
it all:
The parish of rich women, physical
decay,
Yourself. Mad Ireland hurt you into
poetry.
'In Memory of W. B. Yeats' (1940)

7 For poetry makes nothing happen: it
survives
In the valley of its saying where
executives
Would never want to tamper.
'In Memory of W. B. Yeats' (1940)

8 Earth, receive an honoured guest:
William Yeats is laid to rest.
Let the Irish vessel lie
Emptied of its poetry.
'In Memory of W. B. Yeats' (1940)

9 In the nightmare of the dark
All the dogs of Europe bark,
And the living nations wait,
Each sequestered in its hate;

Intellectual disgrace
Stares from every human face,
And the seas of pity lie
Locked and frozen in each eye.
'In Memory of W. B. Yeats' (1940)

10 Time that with this strange excuse
Pardoned Kipling and his views,
And will pardon Paul Claudel,
Pardons him for writing well.
'In Memory of W. B. Yeats' (1940)

11 Look, stranger, at this island now.
title of poem (1936)

12 Lay your sleeping head, my love,
Human on my faithless arm.
'Lullaby' (1940)

13 About suffering they were never wrong,
The Old Masters: how well they
understood
Its human position; how it takes place
While someone else is eating or opening
a window or just walking dully along.
'Musée des Beaux Arts' (1940)

14 Even the dreadful martyrdom must run
its course
Anyhow in a corner, some untidy spot
Where the dogs go on with their doggy
life and the torturer's horse
Scratches its innocent behind on a tree.
'Musée des Beaux Arts' (1940)

15 To the man-in-the-street, who, I'm sorry
to say,
Is a keen observer of life,
The word 'Intellectual' suggests straight
away
A man who's untrue to his wife.
New Year Letter (1941)

16 This is the Night Mail crossing the
Border,
Bringing the cheque and the postal order,
Letters for the rich, letters for the poor,
The shop at the corner, the girl next
door.
'Night Mail' (1936)

17 Private faces in public places

Are wiser and nicer
Than public faces in private places.
Orators (1932) dedication

1 Out on the lawn I lie in bed,
Vega conspicuous overhead.
'Out on the lawn I lie in bed' (1936)

2 Some thirty inches from my nose
The frontier of my Person goes,
And all the untilled air between
Is private *pagus* or demesne.
Stranger, unless with bedroom eyes
I beckon you to fraternize,
Beware of rudely crossing it:
I have no gun, but I can spit.
'Prologue: the Birth of Architecture' (1966)

3 Once we had a country and we thought it fair,
Look in the atlas and you'll find it there:
We cannot go there now, my dear, we cannot go there now.
'Refugee Blues' (1940)

4 I and the public know
What all schoolchildren learn,
Those to whom evil is done
Do evil in return.
'September 1, 1939' (1940)

5 But who can live for long
In an euphoric dream;
Out of the mirror they stare,
Imperialism's face
And the international wrong.
'September 1, 1939' (1940)

6 All I have is a voice
To undo the folded lie,
The romantic lie in the brain
Of the sensual man-in-the-street
And the lie of Authority
Whose buildings grope the sky:
There is no such thing as the State
And no one exists alone;
Hunger allows no choice
To the citizen or the police;
We must love one another or die.
'September 1, 1939' (1940)

7 A shilling life will give you all the facts.
title of poem (1936)

8 Each year brings new problems of Form and Content,
new foes to tug with: at Twenty I tried to
vex my elders, past Sixty it's the young whom
I hope to bother.
'Shorts I' (1969)

9 A poet's hope: to be,
like some valley cheese,
local, but prized elsewhere.
'Shorts II' (1976)

10 Sir, no man's enemy.
title of poem (1930)

11 Harrow the house of the dead; look shining at
New styles of architecture, a change of heart.
'Sir, No Man's Enemy' (1930)

12 To-morrow for the young the poets exploding like bombs,
The walks by the lake, the weeks of perfect communion;
To-morrow the bicycle races
Through the suburbs on summer evenings: but to-day the struggle.
'Spain 1937' (1937)

13 History to the defeated
May say Alas but cannot help or pardon.
'Spain 1937' (1937)

14 To ask the hard question is simple.
title of poem (1933)

15 Was he free? Was he happy? The question is absurd:
Had anything been wrong, we should certainly have heard.
'The Unknown Citizen' (1940)

16 Of course, Behaviourism 'works'. So does torture. Give me a no-nonsense, down-to-earth behaviourist, a few drugs, and simple electrical appliances, and in six months I will have him reciting the Athanasian Creed in public.
A Certain World (1970) 'Behaviourism'

17 It is a sad fact about our culture that a poet can earn much more money writing or talking about his art than he can by practising it.
The Dyer's Hand (1963) foreword

18 Man is a history-making creature who can neither repeat his past nor leave it behind.
The Dyer's Hand (1963) 'D. H. Lawrence'

19 When I find myself in the company of scientists, I feel like a shabby curate who has strayed by mistake into a drawing room full of dukes.

The Dyer's Hand (1963) 'The Poet and the City'

1 Some books are undeservedly forgotten; none are undeservedly remembered.

The Dyer's Hand (1963) 'Reading'

2 Art is born of humiliation.

Stephen Spender *World Within World* (1951)

3 LSD? Nothing much happened, but I did get the distinct impression that some birds were trying to communicate with me.

George Plimpton (ed.) *The Writer's Chapbook* (1989)

4 My face looks like a wedding-cake left out in the rain.

Humphrey Carpenter *W. H. Auden* (1981)

5 Nothing I wrote in the thirties saved one Jew from Auschwitz.

attributed

Stan Augarten

6 Computers are composed of nothing more than logic gates stretched out to the horizon in a vast numerical irrigation system.

State of the Art: A Photographic History of the Integrated Circuit (1983)

Aung San Suu Kyi 1945–

Burmese political leader

7 It's very different from living in academia in Oxford. We called someone vicious in the *Times Literary Supplement*. We didn't know what vicious was.

on returning to Burma (Myanmar)

in *Observer* 25 September 1988

8 In societies where men are truly confident of their own worth, women are not merely tolerated but valued.

videotape speech at NGO Forum on Women, China, early September 1995

Revd W. Awdry 1911–97

English writer of children's books

see also **Epitaphs** 109:8

9 You've a lot to learn about trucks, little Thomas. They are silly things and must be kept in their place. After pushing them about here for a few weeks you'll know almost as much about them as Edward. Then you'll be a Really Useful Engine.

Thomas the Tank Engine (1946)

10 Railways and the Church have their critics, but both are the best ways of getting a man to his ultimate destination.

in *Daily Telegraph* 22 March 1997; obituary

Alan Ayckbourn 1939–

English dramatist

11 My mother used to say, Delia, if S-E-X ever rears its ugly head, close your eyes before you see the rest of it.

Bedroom Farce (1978)

12 This place, you tell them you're interested in the arts, you get messages of sympathy.

Chorus of Disapproval (1986)

A. J. Ayer 1910–89

English philosopher

13 No moral system can rest solely on authority.

Humanist Outlook (1968) introduction

14 It seems that I have spent my entire time trying to make life more rational and that it was all wasted effort.

in *Observer* 17 August 1986

15 Even logical positivists are capable of love.

Kenneth Tynan *Profiles* (1989)

16 If I had been someone not very clever, I would have done an easier job like publishing. That's the easiest job I can think of.

attributed

17 Why should you mind being wrong if someone can show you that you are?

attributed

Pam Ayres 1947–

English writer of humorous verse

1 Medicinal discovery,
It moves in mighty leaps,
It leapt straight past the common cold
And gave it us for keeps.

'Oh no, I got a cold' (1976)

Isaac Babel 1894–1940

Russian short-story writer

2 Now a man talks frankly only with his wife, at night, with the blanket over his head.

remark c.1937; Solomon Volkov *St Petersburg* (1996)

3 They didn't let me finish.

to his wife, on the day of his arrest by the NKVD, 16 May 1939

Lauren Bacall 1924–

American actress
see also **Film lines** 117:1

4 I think your whole life shows in your face and you should be proud of that.

in *Daily Telegraph* 2 March 1988

5 A man's illness is his private territory and, no matter how much he loves you and how close you are, you stay an outsider. You are healthy.

By Myself (1978)

Francis Bacon 1909–92

Irish painter

6 What I see is a marvellous painting. But how are you going to make it? And, of course, as I don't know how to make it, I rely then on chance and accident making it for me.

David Sylvester (ed.) *Interviews with Francis Bacon* (ed. 3, 1987)

Lord Baden-Powell 1857–1941

English soldier; founder of the Boy Scouts, 1908

7 The scouts' motto is founded on my initials, it is: BE PREPARED.

Scouting for Boys (1908)

David Bailey 1938–

English photographer
see also **Sayings and slogans** 290:1

8 It takes a lot of imagination to be a good photographer. You need less imagination to be a painter, because you can invent things. But in photography everything is so ordinary; it takes a lot of looking before you learn to see the ordinary.

interview in *The Face* December 1984

9 I never cared for fashion much. Amusing little seams and witty little pleats. It was the girls I liked.

in *Independent* 5 November 1990

10 I hate manly men. Four men in a car talking about football is my idea of hell.

in *Observer* 2 May 1999

Ewen Bain

see **Cartoons** 56:7

Beryl Bainbridge 1933–

English novelist

11 Some people like being burdened. It gives them an interest.

An Awfully Big Adventure (1989)

12 Women are programmed to love completely, and men are programmed to spread it around.

interview in *Daily Telegraph* 10 September 1996

Bruce Bairnsfather

see **Cartoons** 56:12

Joan Bakewell 1933–

English broadcaster and writer
on Bakewell: see **Muir** 234:10

1 I'm afraid I'm addicted to fat and love British beef. BSE holds no terror for me because . . . I am as likely to get it as win the National Lottery.

on her main difficulty in following a healthy diet

in *Independent* 30 August 1997 'Quote Unquote'

James Baldwin 1924–87

American novelist and essayist

2 Children have never been very good at listening to their elders, but they have never failed to imitate them. They must, they have no other models.

Nobody Knows My Name (1961) 'Fifth Avenue, Uptown: a letter from Harlem'

3 Anyone who has ever struggled with poverty knows how extremely expensive it is to be poor.

Nobody Knows My Name (1961) 'Fifth Avenue, Uptown: a letter from Harlem'

4 At the root of the American Negro problem is the necessity of the American white man to find a way of living with the Negro in order to be able to live with himself.

in *Harper's Magazine* October 1953 'Stranger in a Village'

5 Money, it turned out, was exactly like sex, you thought of nothing else if you didn't have it and thought of other things if you did.

in *Esquire* May 1961 'Black Boy looks at the White Boy'

6 It comes as a great shock around the age of 5, 6 or 7 to discover that the flag to which you have pledged allegiance, along with everybody else, has not pledged allegiance to you. It comes as a great shock to see Gary Cooper killing off the Indians and, although you are rooting for Gary Cooper, that the Indians are you.

speaking for the proposition that 'The American Dream is at the expense of the American Negro'

speech at the Cambridge Union, England, 17 February 1965

7 If they take you in the morning, they will be coming for us that night.

in *New York Review of Books* 7 January 1971 'Open Letter to my Sister, Angela Davis'

Stanley Baldwin 1867–1947

British Conservative statesman; Prime Minister, 1923–4, 1924–9, 1935–7
on Baldwin: see **Churchill** 68:1, **Curzon** 83:7; *see also* **Kipling** 184:9, **Misquotations** 226:12

8 They [parliament] are a lot of hard-faced men who look as if they had done very well out of the war.

J. M. Keynes *Economic Consequences of the Peace* (1919)

9 A platitude is simply a truth repeated until people get tired of hearing it.

speech, House of Commons, 29 May 1924

10 The bomber will always get through. The only defence is in offence, which means that you have to kill more women and children more quickly than the enemy if you want to save yourselves.

speech, House of Commons, 10 November 1932

11 Since the day of the air, the old frontiers are gone. When you think of the defence of England you no longer think of the chalk cliffs of Dover; you think of the Rhine. That is where our frontier lies.

speech, House of Commons, 30 July 1934

12 This House today is a theatre which is being watched by the whole world. Let us conduct ourselves with that dignity which His Majesty is showing in this hour of his trial.

speech, House of Commons, 10 December 1936

13 Do not run up your nose dead against the Pope or the NUM!

Lord Butler *The Art of Memory* (1982); see **Macmillan** 211:4

Arthur James Balfour
1848–1930

British Conservative statesman; Prime Minister, 1902–5

1 His Majesty's Government view with favour the establishment in Palestine of a national home for the Jewish people, and will use their best endeavours to facilitate the achievement of this object, it being clearly understood that nothing shall be done which may prejudice the civil and religious rights of existing non-Jewish communities in Palestine, or the rights and political status enjoyed by Jews in any other country.

known as the 'Balfour Declaration'; see **Weizmann** 332:14

letter to Lord Rothschild 2 November 1917

2 I make it a rule never to stare at people when they are in obvious distress.

on being asked what he thought of the behaviour of the German delegation at the signing of the Treaty of Versailles

Max Egremont *Balfour* (1980)

J. G. Ballard 1930–

British writer

3 A car crash harnesses elements of eroticism, aggression, desire, speed, drama, kinaesthetic factors, the stylizing of motion, consumer goods, status—all these in one event. I myself see the car crash as a tremendous sexual event really: a liberation of human and machine libido (if there is such a thing).

interview in *Penthouse* September 1970

4 Some refer to it as a cultural Chernobyl. I think of it as a cultural Stalingrad.

of Euro Disney

in *Daily Telegraph* 2 July 1994; see **Mnouchkine** 228:11

Whitney Balliett 1926–

American writer

5 A critic is a bundle of biases held loosely together by a sense of taste.

Dinosaurs in the Morning (1962) introductory note

6 The sound of surprise.

title of book on jazz (1959)

Pierre Balmain 1914–82

French couturier

7 The trick of wearing mink is to look as though you were wearing a cloth coat. The trick of wearing a cloth coat is to look as though you are wearing mink.

in *Observer* 25 December 1955

E. Digby Baltzell 1915–1996

American educationist and sociologist

8 There is a crisis in American leadership in the middle of the twentieth century that is partly due, I think, to the declining authority of an establishment which is now based on an increasingly castelike White-Anglo Saxon-Protestant (WASP) upper class.

The Protestant Establishment (1964)

Tallulah Bankhead 1903–68

American actress

9 Cocaine habit-forming? Of course not. I ought to know. I've been using it for years.

Tallulah (1952)

10 There is less in this than meets the eye.

describing a revival of Maeterlinck's play Aglavaine and Selysette

Alexander Woollcott *Shouts and Murmurs* (1922)

11 I'm as pure as the driven slush.

in *Saturday Evening Post* 12 April 1947

12 I read Shakespeare and the Bible and I can shoot dice. That's what I call a liberal education.

attributed

13 They used to shoot her through gauze. You should shoot me through linoleum.

on Shirley Temple

attributed

Imamu Amiri Baraka 1934–

American poet and dramatist

1 God has been replaced, as he has all over the West, with respectability and air conditioning.
Midstream (1963)

2 A man is either free or he is not. There cannot be any apprenticeship for freedom.
in *Kulchur* Spring 1962 'Tokenism'

Daniel Barenboim 1942–

Argentine-born Israeli pianist and conductor

3 There are some times in life when you have to do what's right. Yes, I'd go through it all again.
of his relationship with his wife Jacqueline du Pré, who died from multiple sclerosis in 1987
in *Sunday Times* 21 January 2001

Pat Barker 1943–

English novelist

4 Another person's life, observed from outside, always has a shape and definition that one's own life lacks.
The Ghost Road (1995)

5 The Somme is like the Holocaust. It revealed things about mankind that we cannot come to terms with and cannot forget. It can never become the past.
on winning the Booker Prize 1995
in *Athens News* 9 November 1995

Ronnie Barker 1929–

English comedian

6 The marvellous thing about a joke with a double meaning is that it can only mean one thing.
Sauce (1977)

Frederick R. Barnard

7 One picture is worth ten thousand words.
in *Printers' Ink* 10 March 1927

Clive Barnes 1927–

British journalist and critic

8 This is the kind of show to give pornography a dirty name.
of Oh, Calcutta!
in *New York Times* 18 June 1969

Julian Barnes 1946–

English novelist

9 The land of embarrassment and breakfast.
of Britain
Flaubert's Parrot (1984) ch. 7

10 Do not imagine that Art is something which is designed to give gentle uplift and self-confidence. Art is not a *brassière*. At least, not in the English sense. But do not forget that *brassière* is the French for life-jacket.
Flaubert's Parrot (1984)

11 Books say: she did this because. Life says: she did this. Books are where things are explained to you; life is where things aren't.
Flaubert's Parrot (1984)

12 Does history repeat itself, the first time as tragedy, the second time as farce? No, that's too grand, too considered a process. History just burps, and we taste again that raw-onion sandwich it swallowed centuries ago.
A History of the World in 10½ Chapters (1989); see below

Hegel says somewhere that all great events and personalities in world history reappear in one fashion or another. He forgot to add: the first time as tragedy, the second as farce.
Karl Marx (1818–83) *The Eighteenth Brumaire of Louis Bonaparte* (1852)

13 If you want to get to know someone better, you shouldn't take them out for a candlelit dinner, you should watch them at work. When they're full of concentration, only not concentrating on you.
Love, Etc. (2000)

14 Love is just a system for getting someone to call you darling after sex.
Talking It Over (1991)

J. M. Barrie 1860–1937

Scottish writer and dramatist
on Barrie: see **Guedalla** 142:1, **Hope** 159:7

1 His lordship may compel us to be equal upstairs, but there will never be equality in the servants' hall.
The Admirable Crichton (performed 1902)

2 To die will be an awfully big adventure.
Peter Pan (1928); see **Last words** 191:8

3 Do you believe in fairies? Say quick that you believe! If you believe, clap your hands!
Peter Pan (1928)

4 There are few more impressive sights in the world than a Scotsman on the make.
What Every Woman Knows (performed 1908)

5 Someone said that God gave us memory so that we might have roses in December.
Rectorial Address at St Andrew's, 3 May 1922

6 Courage is the thing. All goes if courage goes!
Rectorial Address at St Andrews, 3 May 1922; see **Lewis** 198:14

John Barrymore 1882–1942

American actor

7 My only regret in the theatre is that I could never sit out front and watch me.
Eddie Cantor *The Way I See It* (1959)

Karl Barth 1886–1968

Swiss Protestant theologian

8 Men have never been good, they are not good and they never will be good.
Christian Community (1948)

9 He will not be like an ant which has foreseen everything in advance, but like a child in a forest, or on Christmas Eve: one who is always rightly astonished by events, by the encounters and experiences which overtake him.
of the justified man
Church Dogmatics (1936)

Roland Barthes 1915–80

French writer and critic

10 I think that cars today are almost the exact equivalent of the great Gothic cathedrals: I mean the supreme creation of an era, conceived with passion by unknown artists, and consumed in image if not in usage by a whole population which appropriates them as a purely magical object.
Mythologies (1957) 'La nouvelle Citroën'

Vernon Bartlett 1894–1983

British journalist and writer

11 I, and many others who had interviews with him, were at first impressed by his sincerity, and later realized that he was sincere only in his belief that he was destined to rule the world.
of Adolf ***Hitler***
I Know What I Liked (1974)

Bernard Baruch 1870–1965

American financier and presidential adviser

12 We are today in the midst of a cold war.
'cold war' was suggested to him by H. B. ***Swope****, former editor of the* New York World
speech to South Carolina Legislature 16 April 1947

13 To me old age is always fifteen years older than I am.
in *Newsweek* 29 August 1955

14 Vote for the man who promises least; he'll be the least disappointing.
M. Berger *New York* (1960)

15 A political leader must keep looking over his shoulder all the time to see if the boys are still there. If they aren't still there, he's no longer a political leader.
in *New York Times* 21 June 1965

Jacques Barzun 1907–

American historian and educationist

16 If it were possible to talk to the unborn,

one could never explain to them how it feels to be alive, for life is washed in the speechless real.

The House of Intellect (1959)

H. M. Bateman

see **Cartoons** 56:6

Jean Baudrillard 1929–

French sociologist and cultural critic

1 The microwave, the waste disposal, the orgasmic elasticity of the carpets, this soft resort-style civilization irresistibly evokes the end of the world.

America (1986)

Yehuda Bauer 1926–

Czech-born Israeli historian

2 I come from a people who gave the ten commandments to the world. Time has come to strengthen them by three additional ones, which we ought to adopt and commit ourselves to: thou shalt not be a perpetrator; thou shalt not be a victim; and thou shalt never, but never, be a bystander.

speech to the German Bundestag, 1998, quoted in his own speech to the Stockholm International Forum on the Holocaust, 26 July 2000

L. Frank Baum

see **Harburg** 146:1

John Bayley 1925–

English academic

3 It is rather like falling from stair to stair in a series of bumps.

on his wife Iris ***Murdoch****'s progressive loss of memory from Alzheimer's disease*

in an interview, *Daily Telegraph* 8 February 1997

Lord Beatty 1871–1936

British Admiral of the Fleet, 1916–19

4 There's something wrong with our bloody ships today.

at the Battle of Jutland, 1916

Winston Churchill *The World Crisis 1916–1918* (1927)

Lord Beaverbrook 1879–1964

Canadian-born British newspaper proprietor and Conservative politician

on Beaverbrook: see **Attlee** 16:1, **Kipling** 184:9

5 Our cock won't fight.

of ***Edward VIII****, during the abdication crisis of 1936*

F. Donaldson *Edward VIII* (1974)

6 Now who is responsible for this work of development on which so much depends? To whom must the praise be given? To the boys in the back rooms. They do not sit in the limelight. But they are the men who do the work.

in *Listener* 27 March 1941

7 I ran the paper [*Daily Express*] purely for propaganda, and with no other purpose.

evidence to Royal Commission on the Press, 18 March 1948, in A. J. P. Taylor *Beaverbrook* (1972)

8 Who's in charge of the clattering train?

habitual question about an organization

A. Chisholm and M. Davie *Beaverbrook* (1992)

Samuel Beckett 1906–89

Irish dramatist, novelist, and poet

9 We could have saved sixpence. We have saved fivepence. (*Pause*) But at what cost?

All That Fall (1957)

10 CLOV: Do you believe in the life to come?
HAMM: Mine was always that.

Endgame (1958)

11 Where I am, I don't know, I'll never know, in the silence you don't know, you must go on, I can't go on, I'll go on.

The Unnamable (1959)

1 Nothing to be done.
Waiting for Godot (1955)

2 There's a man all over for you, blaming on his boots the faults of his feet.
Waiting for Godot (1955)

3 One of the thieves was saved. (*Pause*) It's a reasonable percentage.
Waiting for Godot (1955)

4 ESTRAGON: Charming spot. Inspiring prospects. Let's go.
VLADIMIR: We can't.
ESTRAGON: Why not?
VLADIMIR: We're waiting for Godot.
Waiting for Godot (1955)

5 Nothing happens, nobody comes, nobody goes, it's awful!
Waiting for Godot (1955)

6 He can't think without his hat.
Waiting for Godot (1955)

7 VLADIMIR: That passed the time.
ESTRAGON: It would have passed in any case.
VLADIMIR: Yes, but not so rapidly.
Waiting for Godot (1955)

8 Habit is a great deadener.
Waiting for Godot (1955)

9 Ever tried. Ever failed. No matter. Try again. Fail again. Fail better.
Worstward Ho (1983)

10 I couldn't have done it otherwise, gone on I mean. I could not have gone on through the awful wretched mess of life without having left a stain upon the silence.
Deirdre Bair *Samuel Beckett* (1978)

11 Even death is unreliable: instead of zero it may be some ghastly hallucination, such as the square root of minus one.
attributed

12 I am what her savage loving has made me.
of his mother
James Knowlson *Damned to Fame* (1996)

13 INTERVIEWER: You are English, Mr Beckett?
BECKETT: *Au contraire.*
attributed

David Beckham 1975–

English footballer

14 We have enjoyed the last couple of days.
following England's defeat of Germany in the qualifying stages of the World Cup
in *Daily Telegraph* 4 September 2001

Harry Bedford and Terry Sullivan

British songwriters

15 I'm a bit of a ruin that Cromwell knocked about a bit.
'It's a Bit of a Ruin that Cromwell Knocked about a Bit' (1920 song, written for Marie Lloyd)

Thomas Beecham 1879–1961

English conductor

16 Good music is that which penetrates the ear with facility and quits the memory with difficulty.
speech, c.1950, in *New York Times* 9 March 1961

17 The English may not like music, but they absolutely love the noise it makes.
in *New York Herald Tribune* 9 March 1961

18 Too much counterpoint; what is worse, Protestant counterpoint.
of J. S. Bach
in *Guardian* 8 March 1971

19 Two skeletons copulating on a corrugated tin roof.
describing the harpsichord
H. Atkins and A. Newman *Beecham Stories* (1978)

Max Beerbohm 1872–1956

English critic, essayist, and caricaturist

20 She was one of the people who say 'I don't know anything about music really, but I know what I like.'
Zuleika Dobson (1911)

21 Vulgarity has its uses. Vulgarity often cuts ice which refinement scrapes at vainly.
letter, 21 May 1921

Brendan Behan 1923–64

Irish dramatist

1 PAT: He was an Anglo-Irishman.
MEG: In the blessed name of God what's that?
PAT: A Protestant with a horse.
The Hostage (1958)

2 When I came back to Dublin, I was courtmartialled in my absence and sentenced to death in my absence, so I said they could shoot me in my absence.
The Hostage (1958)

on being asked 'What was the message of your play' after a performance of The Hostage:

3 Message? Message? What the hell do you think I am, a bloody postman?
Dominic Behan *My Brother Brendan* (1965); see **Goldwyn** 137:10

4 There's no such thing as bad publicity except your own obituary.
Dominic Behan *My Brother Brendan* (1965)

Clive Bell 1881–1964

English art critic

5 Art and Religion are, then, two roads by which men escape from circumstance to ecstasy.
Art (1914)

6 I will try to account for the degree of my aesthetic emotion. That, I conceive, is the function of the critic.
Art (1914)

7 Only reason can convince us of those three fundamental truths without a recognition of which there can be no effective liberty: that what we believe is not necessarily true; that what we like is not necessarily good; and that all questions are open.
Civilization (1928)

George Bell 1883–1958

Anglican clergyman, Bishop of Chichester

8 The policy is obliteration, openly acknowledged. This is not a justifiable act of war.
of the saturation bombing of Berlin
speech, House of Lords, 9 February 1944

Gertrude Bell 1868–1926

English traveller, archaeologist, and government servant

9 I feel at times like the Creator about the middle of the week. He must have wondered what it was going to be like, as I do.
creating Iraq, at the Cairo Conference 1921; attributed

Hilaire Belloc 1870–1953

British poet, essayist, historian, novelist, and Liberal politician

10 Believing Truth is staring at the sun.
title of poem (1938)

11 And always keep a-hold of Nurse
For fear of finding something worse.
Cautionary Tales (1907) 'Jim'

12 Sir! you have disappointed us!
We had intended you to be
The next Prime Minister but three:
The stocks were sold; the Press was squared;
The Middle Class was quite prepared.
But as it is! . . . My language fails!
Go out and govern New South Wales!
Cautionary Tales (1907) 'Lord Lundy'

13 Matilda told such Dreadful Lies,
It made one Gasp and Stretch one's Eyes.
Cautionary Tales (1907) 'Matilda'

14 For every time She shouted 'Fire!'
They only answered 'Little Liar!'
Cautionary Tales (1907) 'Matilda'

15 I said to Heart, 'How goes it ?' Heart replied:
'Right as a Ribstone Pippin!' But it lied.
'The False Heart' (1910)

16 I'm tired of Love: I'm still more tired of Rhyme.
But Money gives me pleasure all the time.
'Fatigued' (1923)

17 Remote and ineffectual Don
That dared attack my Chesterton.
'Lines to a Don' (1910)

18 Lord Finchley tried to mend the Electric Light

Himself. It struck him dead: And serve him right!
It is the business of the wealthy man
To give employment to the artisan.
More Peers (1911) 'Lord Finchley'

1 Like many of the Upper Class
He liked the Sound of Broken Glass.
New Cautionary Tales (1930) 'About John'; see **Waugh** 331:6

2 The accursed power which stands on Privilege
(And goes with Women, and Champagne, and Bridge)
Broke—and Democracy resumed her reign:
(Which goes with Bridge, and Women and Champagne).
'On a Great Election' (1923)

3 I am a sundial, and I make a botch
Of what is done much better by a watch.
'On a Sundial' (1938)

4 When I am dead, I hope it may be said:
'His sins were scarlet, but his books were read.'
'On His Books' (1923)

5 Pale Ebenezer thought it wrong to fight,
But Roaring Bill (who killed him) thought it right.
'The Pacifist' (1938)

6 Do you remember an Inn,
Miranda?
Do you remember an Inn? . . .
And the fleas that tease in the High Pyrenees
And the wine that tasted of the tar?
'Tarantella' (1923)

7 Be content to remember that those who can make omelettes properly can do nothing else.
A Conversation with a Cat (1931)

Saul Bellow 1915–

American novelist
see also **Opening lines** 247:3

8 New York makes one think of the collapse of civilization, about Sodom and Gomorrah, the end of the world. The end wouldn't come as a surprise here. Many people already bank on it.
Mr Sammler's Planet (1970)

9 Nobody likes being written about in their lifetime, it's as though the FBI and the CIA were suddenly to splash your files in the paper.
on his forthcoming biography
in *Guardian* 10 September 1997

Robert Benchley 1889–1945

American humorist
see also **Film lines** 116:10, **Telegrams** 316:8

10 The surest way to make a monkey of a man is to quote him.
My Ten Years in a Quandary (1936)

11 In America there are two classes of travel—first class, and with children.
Pluck and Luck (1925)

12 It took me fifteen years to discover that I had no talent for writing, but I couldn't give it up because by that time I was too famous.
Nathaniel Benchley *Robert Benchley* (1955)

13 One square foot less and it would be adulterous.
of the cramped office he shared with Dorothy ***Parker***
in *New Yorker* 5 January 1946

Julien Benda 1867–1956

French philosopher and novelist

14 *La trahison des clercs.*
The treachery of the intellectuals.
title of book (1927)

Stephen Vincent Benét 1898–1943

American poet and novelist

15 I have fallen in love with American names,
The sharp, gaunt names that never get fat.
'American Names' (1927)

16 Bury my heart at Wounded Knee.
'American Names' (1927)

William Rose Benét

1886–1950

American poet

1 Blake saw a treefull of angels at Peckham Rye,
And his hands could lay hold on the tiger's terrible heart.
Blake knew how deep is Hell, and Heaven how high,
And could build the universe from one tiny part.

'Mad Blake' (1918)

Tony Benn 1925–

British Labour politician, who in 1963 disclaimed his hereditary peerage

2 Not a reluctant peer but a persistent commoner.

at a Press Conference, 23 November 1960

3 Some of the jam we thought was for tomorrow, we've already eaten.

attributed, 1969; see below

The rule is, jam to-morrow and jam yesterday—but never jam today.

Lewis Carroll (1832–98) *Through the Looking-Glass* (1872)

4 I did not enter the Labour Party forty-seven years ago to have our manifesto written by Dr Mori, Dr Gallup and Mr Harris.

in *Guardian* 13 June 1988

5 A faith is something you die for; a doctrine is something you kill for: there is all the difference in the world.

in *Observer* 16 April 1989

questions habitually asked by Tony Benn on meeting somebody in power:

6 What power have you got? Where did you get it from? In whose interests do you exercise it? To whom are you accountable? How do we get rid of you?

'The Independent Mind', lecture at Nottingham, 18 June 1993

7 If you file your waste-paper basket for 50 years, you have a public library.

in *Daily Telegraph* 5 March 1994

8 A quotation is what a speaker wants to say—unlike a soundbite which is all that an interviewer allows you to say.

letter to Antony Jay, August 1996

9 We should put the spin-doctors in spin clinics, where they can meet other spin patients and be treated by spin consultants. The rest of us can get on with the proper democratic process.

in *Independent* 25 October 1997

10 When I think of Cool Britannia, I think of old people dying of hypothermia.

at the Labour Party Conference

in *Daily Star* 30 September 1998

11 She taught us how to live and she taught us how to die—and you can't ask more than that.

oration at memorial service for his wife Caroline, 6 March 2001

in *Daily Telegraph* 7 March 2001

Alan Bennett 1934–

English actor and dramatist

12 I go to the theatre to be entertained, I want to be taken out of myself, I don't want to see lust and rape and incest and sodomy and so on, I can get all that at home.

Beyond the Fringe (1963) 'Man of Principles'

13 Outside Shakespeare the word treason to me means nothing. Only, you pissed in our soup and we drank it.

Coral Browne to Guy Burgess

An Englishman Abroad (1989)

14 I have never understood this liking for war. It panders to instincts already catered for within the scope of any respectable domestic establishment.

Forty Years On (1969)

15 Memories are not shackles, Franklin, they are garlands.

Forty Years On (1969)

16 Sapper, Buchan, Dornford Yates, practitioners in that school of Snobbery with Violence that runs like a thread of good-class tweed through twentieth-century literature.

Forty Years On (1969)

1 To be Prince of Wales is not a position. It is a predicament.
The Madness of King George (1995 film); in the 1992 play *The Madness of George III* the line was 'To be heir to the throne . . . '

2 Brought up in the provinces in the forties and fifties one learned early the valuable lesson that life is generally something that happens elsewhere.
introduction to *Talking Heads* (1988)

Arnold Bennett 1867–1931

English novelist

3 A cause may be inconvenient, but it's magnificent. It's like champagne or high heels, and one must be prepared to suffer for it.
The Title (1918)

4 Literature's always a good card to play for Honours. It makes people think that Cabinet ministers are educated.
The Title (1918)

A. C. Benson 1862–1925

English writer

5 Land of Hope and Glory, Mother of the Free,
How shall we extol thee who are born of thee?
Wider still and wider shall thy bounds be set;
God who made thee mighty, make thee mightier yet.
'Land of Hope and Glory' written to be sung as the Finale to Elgar's *Coronation Ode* (1902)

Stella Benson 1892–1933

English novelist

6 Call no man foe, but never love a stranger.
This is the End (1917)

Edmund Clerihew Bentley 1875–1956

English writer

7 The Art of Biography
Is different from Geography.
Geography is about Maps,
But Biography is about Chaps.
Biography for Beginners (1905) introduction

8 George the Third
Ought never to have occurred.
One can only wonder
At so grotesque a blunder.
'George the Third' (1929)

9 Sir Christopher Wren
Said, 'I am going to dine with some men.
If anybody calls
Say I am designing St Paul's.'
'Sir Christopher Wren' (1905)

Eric Bentley 1916–

10 Ours is the age of substitutes: instead of language, we have jargon; instead of principles, slogans; and, instead of genuine ideas, Bright Ideas.
in *New Republic* 29 December 1952

Lloyd Bentsen 1921–

American Democratic politician

*responding to Dan **Quayle**'s claim to have 'as much experience in the Congress as Jack **Kennedy** had when he sought the presidency':*

11 Senator, I served with Jack Kennedy. I knew Jack Kennedy. Jack Kennedy was a friend of mine. Senator, you're no Jack Kennedy.
in the vice-presidential debate, 5 October 1988

Ingmar Bergman 1918–

Swedish film director

12 After years of playing with images of life and death, life has made me shy.
message sent when his daughter Linn Ullman collected the Palme of Palmes for him at the Cannes Film Festival
in *Observer* 18 May 1997

Irving Berlin 1888–1989

American songwriter

13 Anything you can do, I can do better,
I can do anything better than you.
'Anything You Can Do' (1946 song)

1 Heaven—I'm in Heaven—And my heart beats so that I can hardly speak;
And I seem to find the happiness I seek
When we're out together dancing cheek-to-cheek.
'Cheek-to-Cheek' (1935 song)

2 God bless America,
Land that I love,
Stand beside her and guide her
Thru the night with a light from above.
From the mountains to the prairies,
To the oceans white with foam,
God bless America,
My home sweet home.
'God Bless America' (1939 song)

3 There may be trouble ahead,
But while there's moonlight and music and love and romance,
Let's face the music and dance.
'Let's Face the Music and Dance' (1936 song)

4 A pretty girl is like a melody
That haunts you night and day.
'A Pretty Girl is like a Melody' (1919 song)

5 The song is ended (but the melody lingers on).
title of song (1927)

6 There's no business like show business.
title of song (1946)

7 I'm puttin' on my top hat,
Tyin' up my white tie,
Brushin' off my tails.
'Top Hat, White Tie and Tails' (1935 song)

8 I'm dreaming of a white Christmas,
Just like the ones I used to know.
'White Christmas' (1942 song)

9 Listen, kid, take my advice, never hate a song that has sold half a million copies.
to Cole ***Porter****, of the song 'Rosalie'*
Philip Furia *Poets of Tin Pan Alley* (1990)

Isaiah Berlin 1909–97

British philosopher

10 There exists a great chasm between those, on one side, who relate everything to a single central vision . . . and, on the other side, those who pursue many ends, often unrelated and even contradictory . . . The first kind of intellectual and artistic personality belongs to the hedgehogs, the second to the foxes.
The Hedgehog and the Fox (1953); see below

The fox knows many things—the hedgehog one *big* one.
Archilochus (7th century BC) fragment

11 Liberty is liberty, not equality or fairness or justice or human happiness or a quiet conscience.
Two Concepts of Liberty (1958)

12 Few new truths have ever won their way against the resistance of established ideas save by being overstated.
Vico and Herder (1976)

13 Rousseau was the first militant lowbrow.
in *Observer* 9 November 1952

J. D. Bernal 1901–71

Irish-born physicist

14 Men will not be content to manufacture life: they will want to improve on it.
The World, the Flesh and the Devil (1929)

Cassie Bernall

see **Last words** 191:10

Georges Bernanos 1888–1948

French novelist and essayist

15 The wish for prayer is a prayer in itself.
Journal d'un curé de campagne (1936)

Eric Berne 1910–70

American psychiatrist

16 Games people play: the psychology of human relationships.
title of book (1964)

Lord Berners 1883–1950

English composer, artist, and writer

17 He's always backing into the limelight.
of T. E. ***Lawrence***
oral tradition

Tim Berners-Lee 1955–

English computer scientist

1 The Web is a tremendous grassroots revolution. All these people coming from very different directions achieved a change. There's a tremendous message of hope for humanity in that.
in *Independent* 17 May 1999

Carl Bernstein 1944–

American journalist

2 This convention, they got the show business right. They got their message out. They got their candidate to look exactly like they wanted him to look. Great achievement.
of the 2000 Republican convention which nominated George W. ***Bush*** *as presidential candidate*
on *Larry King Live* (CNN) 4 August 2000

Carl Bernstein 1944– and Bob Woodward 1943–

American journalists

3 All the President's men.
title of book (1974) on the Watergate scandal

Yogi Berra 1925–

American baseball player

4 It ain't over till it's over.
comment on National League pennant race, 1973, quoted in many versions

5 The future ain't what it used to be.
attributed

6 If people don't want to come out to the ball park, nobody's going to stop 'em.
of baseball games
attributed

7 It was déjà vu all over again.
attributed

Daniel Berrigan 1921–

American priest and peace campaigner

8 This is a war run to show the world, and particularly the Third World, where exactly it stands in relation to our technology.
of the Vietnam War
attributed, 1973

Chuck Berry 1931–

American rock and roll singer

9 Roll over, Beethoven, and tell Tchaikovsky the news.
'Roll Over, Beethoven' (1956 song)

John Berryman 1914–72

American poet

10 People will take balls,
Balls will be lost always, little boy,
And no one buys a ball back.
'The Ball Poem' (1948)

11 We must travel in the direction of our fear.
'A Point of Age' (1942)

12 Life, friends, is boring. We must not say so . . .
And moreover my mother taught me as a boy
(repeatingly) 'Ever to confess you're bored
means you have no

Inner Resources.'
77 Dream Songs (1964) no. 14

13 I seldom go to films. They are too exciting,
said the Honourable Possum.
77 Dream Songs (1964) no. 53

Pierre Berton 1920–

Canadian writer

14 Somebody who knows how to make love in a canoe.
definition of a Canadian
in *Toronto Star, Canadian Magazine* 22 December 1973

Theobald von Bethmann Hollweg 1856–1921

Chancellor of Germany, 1909–17

1 Just for a word 'neutrality'—a word which in wartime has so often been disregarded—just for a scrap of paper, Great Britain is going to make war on a kindred nation who desires nothing better than to be friends with her.

summary of a report by Sir Edward Goschen to Sir Edward Grey in *British Documents on Origins of the War 1898–1914* (1926)

John Betjeman 1906–84

English poet

on Betjeman: see **Ewart** 110:6

2 He sipped at a weak hock and seltzer
As he gazed at the London skies
Through the Nottingham lace of the
curtains
Or was it his bees-winged eyes?

'The Arrest of Oscar Wilde at the Cadogan Hotel' (1937)

3 And girls in slacks remember Dad,
And oafish louts remember Mum,
And sleepless children's hearts are glad,
And Christmas-morning bells say
'Come!'

'Christmas' (1954)

4 And is it true? And is it true,
This most tremendous tale of all,
Seen in a stained-glass window's hue,
A Baby in an ox's stall?

'Christmas' (1954)

5 Oh! Chintzy, Chintzy cheeriness,
Half dead and half alive!

'Death in Leamington' (1931)

6 Spirits of well-shot woodcock, partridge,
snipe
Flutter and bear him up the Norfolk sky.

'Death of King George V' (1937)

7 Old men who never cheated, never
doubted,
Communicated monthly, sit and stare
At the new suburb stretched beyond the
run-way
Where a young man lands hatless from
the air.

'Death of King George V' (1937)

8 Phone for the fish-knives, Norman
As Cook is a little unnerved;
You kiddies have crumpled the serviettes
And I must have things daintily served.

'How to get on in Society' (1954)

9 It's awf'lly bad luck on Diana,
Her ponies have swallowed their bits;
She fished down their throats with a
spanner
And frightened them all into fits.

'Hunter Trials' (1954)

10 The Church's Restoration
In eighteen-eighty-three
Has left for contemplation
Not what there used to be.

'Hymn' (1931)

11 Think of what our Nation stands for,
Books from Boots' and country lanes,
Free speech, free passes, class distinction,
Democracy and proper drains.

'In Westminster Abbey' (1940)

12 Gaily into Ruislip Gardens
Runs the red electric train,
With a thousand Ta's and Pardon's
Daintily alights Elaine;
Hurries down the concrete station
With a frown of concentration,
Out into the outskirt's edges
Where a few surviving hedges
Keep alive our lost Elysium—rural
Middlesex again.

'Middlesex' (1954)

13 Come, friendly bombs, and fall on
Slough!
It isn't fit for humans now,
There isn't grass to graze a cow.
Swarm over, Death!

'Slough' (1937)

14 Miss J. Hunter Dunn, Miss J. Hunter
Dunn,
Furnish'd and burnish'd by Aldershot
sun.

'A Subaltern's Love-Song' (1945)

15 Love-thirty, love-forty, oh! weakness of
joy,
The speed of a swallow, the grace of a
boy,
With carefullest carelessness, gaily you
won,

I am weak from your loveliness, Joan Hunter Dunn.
'A Subaltern's Love-Song' (1945)

1 Ghastly good taste, or a depressing story of the rise and fall of English architecture.
title of book (1933)

Bruno Bettelheim 1903–90

Austrian-born American psychologist

2 The most extreme agony is to feel that one has been utterly forsaken.
Surviving and other essays (1979)

Aneurin Bevan 1897–1960

British Labour politician
on Bevan: see **Bevin** 35:6, **Churchill** 67:13

3 This island is made mainly of coal and surrounded by fish. Only an organizing genius could produce a shortage of coal and fish at the same time.
speech at Blackpool, 24 May 1945

4 No amount of cajolery, and no attempts at ethical or social seduction, can eradicate from my heart a deep burning hatred for the Tory Party . . . So far as I am concerned they are lower than vermin.
speech at Manchester, 4 July 1948

5 He is still fighting Blenheim all over again. His only answer to a difficult situation is send a gun-boat.
of Winston ***Churchill***
speech at Labour Party Conference, 2 October 1951

6 We know what happens to people who stay in the middle of the road. They get run down.
in *Observer* 6 December 1953

7 Damn it all, you can't have the crown of thorns *and* the thirty pieces of silver.
on his position in the Labour Party, c.1956
Michael Foot *Aneurin Bevan* vol. 2 (1973)

8 I am not going to spend any time whatsoever in attacking the Foreign Secretary . . . If we complain about the tune, there is no reason to attack the monkey when the organ grinder is present.
on the Suez crisis
speech, House of Commons, 16 May 1957

9 If you carry this resolution you will send Britain's Foreign Secretary naked into the conference chamber.
on a motion proposing unilateral nuclear disarmament by the UK
speech at Labour Party Conference, 3 October 1957

10 I know that the right kind of leader for the Labour Party is a desiccated calculating machine who must not in any way permit himself to be swayed by indignation. If he sees suffering, privation or injustice he must not allow it to move him, for that would be evidence of the lack of proper education or of absence of self-control. He must speak in calm and objective accents and talk about a dying child in the same way as he would about the pieces inside an internal combustion engine.
generally taken as referring to Hugh ***Gaitskell****, although Bevan specifically denied it*
Michael Foot *Aneurin Bevan* (1973) vol. 2

11 This so-called affluent society is an ugly society still. It is a vulgar society. It is a meretricious society. It is a society in which priorities have gone all wrong.
speech in Blackpool, 29 November 1959; see **Galbraith** 130:4

12 I read the newspapers avidly. It is my one form of continuous fiction.
in *The Times* 29 March 1960

13 I stuffed their mouths with gold.
on his handling of the consultants during the establishment of the National Health Service
B. Abel-Smith *The Hospitals 1800–1948* (1964)

William Henry Beveridge 1879–1963

British economist

14 Ignorance is an evil weed, which dictators may cultivate among their dupes, but which no democracy can afford among its citizens.
Full Employment in a Free Society (1944)

1 Want is one only of five giants on the road of reconstruction . . . the others are Disease, Ignorance, Squalor and Idleness.

Social Insurance and Allied Services (1942)

Ernest Bevin 1881–1951

British Labour politician and trade unionist
on Bevin: see **Foot** 121:3

2 I hope you will carry no resolution of an emergency character telling a man with a conscience like Lansbury what he ought to do . . . It is placing the Executive in an absolutely wrong position to be taking your conscience round from body to body to be told what you ought to do with it.

often quoted as 'hawking his conscience round the Chancelleries of Europe'

Labour Party Conference Report (1935)

3 My [foreign] policy is to be able to take a ticket at Victoria Station and go anywhere I damn well please.

in *Spectator* 20 April 1951

4 I didn't ought never to have done it. It was you, Willie, what put me up to it.

to Lord Strang, after officially recognizing Communist China

C. Parrott *Serpent and Nightingale* (1977)

5 If you open that Pandora's Box, you never know what Trojan 'orses will jump out.

on the Council of Europe

Roderick Barclay *Ernest Bevin and the Foreign Office* (1975)

on the observation that Aneurin ***Bevan*** *was sometimes his own worst enemy:*

6 Not while I'm alive 'e ain't!

also attributed to Bevin of Herbert ***Morrison***

Roderick Barclay *Ernest Bevin and Foreign Office* (1975)

Benazir Bhutto 1953–

Pakistani stateswoman; Prime Minister 1988–90 and 1993–96

7 Every dictator uses religion as a prop to keep himself in power.

interview on *60 Minutes*, CBS-TV, 8 August 1986

Steve Biko 1946–77

South African anti-apartheid campaigner

8 The liberal must understand that the days of the Noble Savage are gone; that the blacks do not need a go-between in this struggle for their own emancipation. No true liberal should feel any resentment at the growth of black consciousness. Rather, all true liberals should realize that the place for their fight for justice is within their white society. The liberals must realize that they themselves are oppressed if they are true liberals and therefore they must fight for their own freedom and not that of the nebulous 'they' with whom they can hardly claim identification. The liberal must apply himself with absolute dedication to the idea of educating his white brothers.

'Black Souls in White Skins?' (written 1970), in *Steve Biko—I Write What I Like* (1978)

9 The most potent weapon in the hands of the oppressor is the mind of the oppressed.

statement as witness, 3 May 1976

Maeve Binchy 1940–

Irish writer

10 People don't come in my size until they're old . . . I used to think people were born with big bones and large frames, but apparently these grow when you're about sixty-eight.

Circle of Friends (1990)

11 It's not perfect, but to me on balance Right Now is a lot better than the Good Old Days.

in *Irish Times* 15 November 1997

Laurence Binyon 1869–1943

English poet

12 They shall grow not old, as we that are left grow old.
Age shall not weary them, nor the years condemn.
At the going down of the sun and in the morning

We will remember them.

regularly recited as part of the ritual for Remembrance Day parades; see **Epitaphs** 110:4

'For the Fallen' (1914)

Nigel Birch 1906–81

British Conservative politician

1 My God! They've shot our fox!

on hearing of the resignation of Hugh ***Dalton****, Labour Chancellor of the Exchequer, after the leak of Budget secrets*

comment, 13 November 1947

John Bird 1936–

English actor and satirist

2 That was the week that was.

title of satirical BBC television series, 1962–3

Harrison Birtwistle 1934–

English composer

3 You can't stop. Composing's not voluntary, you know. There's no choice, you're not free. You're landed with an idea and you have responsibility to that idea.

in *Observer* 14 April 1996

Elizabeth Bishop 1911–79

American poet

4 The state with the prettiest name,
the state that floats in brackish water,
held together by mangrove roots.

'Florida' (1946)

5 Topography displays no favourites;
North's as near as West.
More delicate than the historians' are the
map-makers' colours.

'The Map' (1946)

6 Lullaby.
Let nations rage,
let nations fall.
The shadow of the crib makes an
enormous cage
upon the wall.

'Songs for a Coloured Singer' (1946)

7 If she speaks of a chair you can practically sit on it.

of Marianne ***Moore***

notebook, *c.*1934/5; D. Kalstone *Becoming a Poet* (1989)

8 I am sorry for people who can't write letters. But I suspect also that you and I . . . love to write them because it's kind of like working without really doing it.

letter to Kit and Ilse Barker, 5 September 1953

Björk 1965–

Icelandic pop star

9 Icelandic peoples were the ones who memorized sagas . . . We were the first rappers of Europe.

attributed, January 1996

Conrad Black 1944–

Canadian-born British businessman and newspaper proprietor, husband of Barbara **Amiel**

10 Whenever businessmen have tried to defend themselves, they have tended to bellow ultra-right clichés like wounded dinosaurs.

Peter C. Newman *The Establishment Man* (1982)

11 We can't spend ourselves rich; we can't drink ourselves sober; and we will pay an unbearable price if we don't remember that the power to tax is the power to destroy.

in *Report on Business Magazine* January 1987

12 I take this step with regret, but without rancour.

renouncing his Canadian citizenship to take up a peerage

in *Daily Telegraph* 19 May 2001

James Black 1924–

British analytical pharmacologist; winner of the Nobel prize for medicine

13 In the culture I grew up in you did your work and you did not put your arm around it to stop other people from looking—you took the earliest possible opportunity to make knowledge available.

on modern scientific research

in *Daily Telegraph* 11 December 1995

Otis Blackwell 1931– and **Jack Hammer**

American songwriter

1 Goodness gracious great balls of fire.

'Great Balls of Fire' (1957 song)

Tony Blair 1953–

British Labour statesman; Prime Minister since 1997

on Blair: see **Adams** 2:1, **Hague** 142:13, **Thatcher** 318:1

2 Labour is the party of law and order in Britain today. Tough on crime and tough on the causes of crime.

as Shadow Home Secretary

speech at the Labour Party Conference, 30 September 1993

3 Those who seriously believe we cannot improve on words written for the world of 1918 when we are now in 1995 are not learning from our history but living it.

on the proposed revision of Clause IV

in *Independent* 11 January 1995; see **Anonymous** 10:4, 12:9

4 Ask me my three main priorities for Government, and I tell you: education, education and education.

speech at the Labour Party Conference, 1 October 1996

5 We are not the masters. The people are the masters. We are the servants of the people . . . What the electorate gives, the electorate can take away.

addressing Labour MPs on the first day of the new Parliament, 7 May 1997

in *Guardian* 8 May 1997; see **Misquotations** 227:3

6 She was the People's Princess, and that is how she will stay . . . in our hearts and in our memories forever.

on hearing of the death of ***Diana****, Princess of Wales*

in *Times* 1 September 1997

7 I am from the Disraeli school of Prime Ministers in their relations with the Monarch.

at the Queen's golden wedding celebration, 20 November 1997; see **Elizabeth II** 106:6

in *Daily Telegraph* 21 November 1997

8 My project will be complete when the Labour Party learns to love Peter Mandelson.

P. Routledge *Mandy* (1999)

9 We need two or three eye-catching initiatives . . . I should be personally associated with as much of this as possible.

leaked memorandum, 29 April 2000; in *Times* 18 July 2000

10 This is not a battle betweeen the United States and terrorism, but between the free and democratic world and terrorism. We therefore here in Britain stand shoulder to shoulder with our American friends in this hour of tragedy and we, like them, will not rest until this evil is driven from our world.

in Downing Street, London, 11 September 2001

Eubie Blake 1883–1983

American ragtime pianist

at the age of ninety-seven, Blake was asked at what age the sex drive goes:

11 You'll have to ask somebody older than me.

attributed

12 If I'd known I was gonna live this long, I'd have taken better care of myself.

on reaching the age of 100

in *Observer* 13 February 1983

Lesley Blanch 1907–

British writer

13 She was an Amazon. Her whole life was spent riding at breakneck speed towards the wilder shores of love.

The Wilder Shores of Love (1954)

Danny Blanchflower 1926–93

English footballer

1 The great fallacy is that the game is first and last about winning. It is nothing of the kind. The game is about glory, it is about doing things in style and with a flourish, about going out and beating the lot, not waiting for them to die of boredom.

attributed, 1972

Arthur Bliss 1891–1975

English composer

2 What is called the serenity of age is only perhaps a euphemism for the fading power to feel the sudden shock of joy or sorrow.

As I Remember (1970)

Karen Blixen

see Isak **Dinesen**

Judy Blume 1938–

American writer

3 Are you there God? It's me, Margaret.
I just told my mother I want a bra.
Please help me grow God. You know where.
I want to be like everyone else.

Are You There God? It's Me, Margaret (1970)

Edmund Blunden 1896–1974

English poet

4 I am for the woods against the world,
But are the woods for me?

'The Kiss' (1931)

5 I have been young, and now am not too old;
And I have seen the righteous forsaken,
His health, his honour and his quality taken.
This is not what we were formerly told.

'Report on Experience' (1929)

David Blunkett 1947–

British Labour politician, Minister for Education, 1992–7; Home Secretary from 1997

6 Let me say this very slowly indeed. Watch my lips: no selection by examination or interview under a Labour government.

in *Daily Telegraph* (electronic edition) 5 October 1995

7 I was parodying George Bush . . . Watch my lips was a joke. If I were doing it again I would say 'no more selection'.

in *Sunday Telegraph* 12 March 2000; see **Bush** 49:7

8 I don't use or recognize the term 'bog standard' but what I do recognize is the critical importance of honesty about what some children, in some schools, have had to put up with over the years.

at Labour spring conference, 17 February 2001; see **Campbell** 51:14

Alfred Blunt 1879–1957

English Protestant cleric, Bishop of Bradford

9 The benefit of the King's Coronation depends, under God, upon two elements: First, on the faith, prayer, and self-dedication of the King himself, and on that it would be improper for me to say anything except to commend him, and ask you to commend him, to God's grace, which he will so abundantly need . . . if he is to do his duty faithfully. We hope that he is aware of his need. Some of us wish that he gave more positive signs of his awareness.

referring to ***Edward VIII****'s relationship with Mrs Simpson, which until then had not been publicly mentioned; see* **Anonymous** 10:12

speech to Bradford Diocesan Conference, 1 December 1936

Robert Bly 1926–

American writer

10 Every modern male has, lying at the bottom of his psyche, a large, primitive being covered with hair down to his feet. Making contact with this Wild Man is the

step the Eighties male or the Nineties male has yet to take.
Iron John (1990)

Ronald Blythe 1922–

English writer

1 An industrial worker would sooner have a £5 note but a countryman must have praise.
Akenfield (1969)

2 With full-span lives having become the norm, people may need to learn how to be aged as they once had to learn how to be adult.
The View in Winter (1979)

David Boaz 1953–

American lawyer

3 Alcohol didn't cause the high crime rates of the '20s and '30s, Prohibition did. Drugs don't cause today's alarming crime rates, but drug prohibition does.
quoted by Judge James C. Paine, addressing the Federal Bar Association in Miami, 1991
'The Legalization of Drugs' 27 April 1988

Ivan F. Boesky 1937–

American businessman

4 Greed is all right . . . Greed is healthy. You can be greedy and still feel good about yourself.
commencement address, Berkeley, California, 18 May 1986; see **Film lines** 115:11

Louise Bogan 1897–1970

American poet

5 Women have no wilderness in them,
They are provident instead,
Content in the tight hot cell of their hearts
To eat dusty bread.
'Women' (1923)

Dirk Bogarde 1921–99

British actor and writer

6 I realised I was looking at Dante's Inferno.
of Belsen during the liberation
in *Daily Telegraph* 10 May 1999; obituary

7 You haven't cracked me yet!
to the interviewer Russell Harty
in *Daily Telegraph* 10 May 1999; obituary

Humphrey Bogart

see **Film lines** 115:12, 115:17, 117:5

John B. Bogart 1848–1921

American journalist

8 When a dog bites a man, that is not news, because it happens so often. But if a man bites a dog, that is news.
F. M. O'Brien *Story of the* [New York] *Sun* (1918); often attributed to Charles A. Dana

Niels Bohr 1885–1962

Danish physicist

9 Of course not, but I am told it works even if you don't believe in it.
when asked whether he really believed a horseshoe hanging over his door would bring him luck, c.1930
A. Pais *Inward Bound* (1986)

10 Anybody who is not shocked by this subject has failed to understand it.
of quantum mechanics
attributed; *Nature* 23 August 1990

Eavan Boland 1944–

Irish poet

11 Imagine how they stood there, what they stood with
that their possessions may become our power.
Cardboard. Iron. Their hardships parcelled in them.
'The Emigrant Irish' (1987)

12 I think of what great art removes:

Hazard and death, the future and the
past.

'From the painting *Back from Market* by Chardin' (1967)

Alan Bold 1943-

Scottish poet

1 This happened near the core
Of a world's culture. This
Occurred among higher things.
This was a philosophical conclusion.
Everybody gets what he deserves.

The bare drab rubble of the place.
The dull damp stone. The rain.
The emptiness. The human lack.

'June 1967 at Buchenwald' (1969); see **Anonymous** 11:7

2 Scotland, land of the omnipotent No.

'A Memory of Death' (1969)

3 Our job is to try
To change things.
After Hiroshima
You ask a poet to sing.

'Recitative' (1965)

Robert Bolt 1924–95

English dramatist

4 Morality's *not* practical. Morality's a gesture. A complicated gesture learned from books.

A Man for All Seasons (1960)

5 It profits a man nothing to give his soul for the whole world . . . But for Wales—!

A Man for All Seasons (1960); see below

For what shall it profit a man, if he shall gain the whole world, and lose his own soul?

Bible St Mark

Violet Bonham Carter

see **Telegrams** 316:4

Dietrich Bonhoeffer 1906–45

German Lutheran theologian and pastor

6 It is the nature, and the advantage, of strong people that they can bring out the crucial questions and form a clear opinion about them. The weak always have to decide between alternatives that are not their own.

Widerstand und Ergebung (1951)

Bono 1960-

Irish rock star

7 That will make some sense out of the nonsense of the millennium.

urging cancellation of Third World debt as a way of marking the millennium

in *Independent* 14 June 1999

Christopher Booker 1937- and **Richard North** 1946-

British writers

8 Castle of lies: why Britain must get out of Europe.

title of book (1996)

Connie Booth

see John **Cleese** and Connie Booth

Robert Boothby 1900–86

British Conservative politician

9 *You* speak for Britain!

to Arthur Greenwood, acting Leader of the Labour Party, after Neville ***Chamberlain*** *had failed to announce an ultimatum to Germany; perhaps taking up an appeal already voiced by Leo* ***Amery***

Harold Nicolson diary, 2 September 1939; see **Amery** 7:10

Betty Boothroyd 1929-

Labour politician; Speaker of the House of Commons, 1992–2000

10 My desire to get here was like miners' coal dust, it was under my fingers and I couldn't scrub it out.

of Parliament

Glenys Kinnock and Fiona Millar (eds.) *By Faith and Daring* (1993)

11 The level of cynicism about Parliament and the accompanying alienation of many of the young from the democratic process is troubling. Let's make a start by

remembering that the function of Parliament is to hold the executive to account.

in her valedictory statement as Speaker
in the House of Commons, 26 July 2000

1 Time's up!

concluding her valedictory statement
in the House of Commons, 26 July 2000

James H. Boren 1925–

American bureaucrat

2 Guidelines for bureaucrats: (1) When in charge, ponder. (2) When in trouble, delegate. (3) When in doubt, mumble.
in *New York Times* 8 November 1970

Jorge Luis Borges 1899–1986

Argentinian writer

3 I come from a vertiginous country where the lottery forms a principal part of reality.
Fictions (1956) 'The Babylon Lottery'

4 The original is unfaithful to the translation.

of Henley's translation of Vathek
Sobre el 'Vathek' de William Beckford; in *Obras Completas* (1974)

5 The Falklands thing was a fight between two bald men over a comb.

application of a proverbial phrase
in *Time* 14 February 1983

Horatio Bottomley 1860–1933

British newspaper proprietor and financier

6 What poor education I have received has been gained in the University of Life.
speech at the Oxford Union, 2 December 1920

reply to a prison visitor who asked if he were sewing:

7 No, reaping.
S. T. Felstead *Horatio Bottomley* (1936)

Louis Bousquet

French songwriter

8 *Nous en rêvons la nuit, nous y pensons le jour,*
Ce n'est que Madelon, mais pour nous, c'est l'amour.

We dream of her by night, we think of her by day,
It's only Madelon, but for us, it's love.
'Quand Madelon' (1914), French soldiers' song of the First World War

Elizabeth Bowen 1899–1973

Anglo-Irish novelist

9 It is about five o'clock in an evening that the first hour of spring strikes—autumn arrives in the early morning, but spring at the close of a winter day.
The Death of the Heart (1938)

10 The heart may think it knows better: the senses know that absence blots people out. We have really no absent friends.
The Death of the Heart (1938)

11 I suppose art is the only thing that can go on mattering once it has stopped hurting.
Heat of the Day (1949)

12 There is no end to the violations committed by children on children, quietly talking alone.
The House in Paris (1935)

13 Jealousy is no more than feeling alone against smiling enemies.
The House in Paris (1935)

14 A high altar on the move.

of Edith ***Sitwell***
V. Glendinning *Edith Sitwell* (1981)

David Bowie 1947–

English rock musician

15 We can be heroes
Just for one day.
'Heroes' (1977 song)

16 Ground control to Major Tom.
'Space Oddity' (1969 song)

17 What the music says may be serious, but as a medium it should not be questioned, analysed, or taken so seriously. I think it should be tarted up, made into a prostitute, a parody of itself.
in *Rolling Stone* 1 April 1971

1 We have created a child who will be so exposed to the media that he will be lost to his parents by the time he is 12.
in *Melody Maker* 22 January 1972

2 The 1970s for me started the 21st century—it was the beginning of a true pluralism in social attitudes.
An Earthling at 50 ITV programme; in *Sunday Times* 12 January 1997

Boy George 1961–

English pop singer and songwriter

3 She's a gay man trapped in a woman's body.
of ***Madonna***
Take It Like a Man (1995)

4 Sex has never been an obsession with me. It's just like eating a bag of crisps. Quite nice, but nothing marvellous. Sex is not simply black and white. There's a lot of grey.
in *Sun* 21 October 1982

Charles Boyer

see **Misquotations** 226:2

Benjamin C. Bradlee 1921–

American journalist, former Editor of the Washington Post

5 Maybe not all of you are familiar with what it takes to make a great newspaper. It takes a great owner. Period.
at the funeral of Katherine Graham, owner of the Washington Post *during his Editorship*
in *Daily Telegraph* 24 July 2001

Omar Bradley 1893–1981

American general

6 The way to win an atomic war is to make certain it never starts.
speech on Armistice Day, 1948

7 We have grasped the mystery of the atom and rejected the Sermon on the Mount.
speech on Armistice Day, 1948

8 The world has achieved brilliance without wisdom, power without conscience. Ours is a world of nuclear giants and ethical infants.
speech on Armistice Day, 1948

9 Red China is not the powerful nation seeking to dominate the world. Frankly, in the opinion of the Joint Chiefs of Staff, this strategy would involve us in the wrong war, at the wrong place, at the wrong time, and with the wrong enemy.
US Congress Senate Committee on Armed Services (1951)

Don Bradman 1908–2001

Australian cricketer
on Bradman: see **Anonymous** 10:10

10 When you play Test cricket you don't give Englishmen an inch. Play it tough, all the way.
telling Keith Miller to 'bowl faster'
Jack Fingleton *Batting from Memory* (1981)

11 Every ball is for me the first ball.
attributed; Colin Jarman (ed.) *Guinness Dictionary of Sports Quotations* (1990)

Marlon Brando

see **Film lines** 115:14*; see also* **Glass**

Richard Branson 1950–

English businessman

12 We spend most of our lives working. So why do so few people have a good time doing it? Virgin is the possibility of good times.
interview in *New York Times* 28 February 1993

Georges Braque 1882–1963

French painter

13 Art is meant to disturb, science reassures.
Le Jour et la nuit: Cahiers 1917–52

14 Truth exists; only lies are invented.
Le Jour et la nuit: Cahiers 1917–52

John W. Bratton

see James B. **Kennedy** and John W. Bratton

Werner von Braun 1912–77

German-born American rocket engineer

1 Don't tell me that man doesn't belong out there. Man belongs wherever he wants to go—and he'll do plenty well when he gets there.

on space

in *Time* 17 February 1958

2 Basic research is what I am doing when I don't know what I am doing.

R. L. Weber *A Random Walk in Science* (1973)

Bertolt Brecht 1898–1956

German dramatist

3 Terrible is the temptation to be good.

The Caucasian Chalk Circle (1948)

4 ANDREA: Unhappy the land that has no heroes! . . .
GALILEO: No. Unhappy the land that needs heroes.

The Life of Galileo (1939)

5 The aim of science is not to open the door to infinite wisdom, but to set a limit to infinite error.

The Life of Galileo (1939)

6 They have gone too long without a war here. Where is morality to come from in such a case, I ask? Peace is nothing but slovenliness, only war creates order.

Mother Courage (1939)

7 The finest plans are always ruined by the littleness of those who ought to carry them out, for the Emperors can actually do nothing.

Mother Courage (1939)

8 Don't tell me peace has broken out, when I've just bought fresh supplies.

Mother Courage (1939)

9 The resistible rise of Arturo Ui.

title of play (1941)

10 Oh, the shark has pretty teeth, dear,
And he shows them pearly white.
Just a jack-knife has Macheath, dear
And he keeps it out of sight.

The Threepenny Opera (1928)

11 Food comes first, then morals.

The Threepenny Opera (1928)

12 What is robbing a bank compared with founding a bank?

The Threepenny Opera (1928)

13 Who built Thebes of the seven gates?
In the books you will find the names of
kings.
Did the kings haul up the lumps of rock?
. . .
Where, the evening that the wall of
China was finished
Did the masons go?

'Questions From A Worker Who Reads' (1935)

14 Would it not be easier
In that case for the government
To dissolve the people
And elect another?

on the uprising against the Soviet occupying forces in East Germany in 1953

'The Solution' (1953)

15 Truly, I'm living in a time of darkness.

'To Those Born Later' (1939)

16 Yes, we went, as often changing
countries as changing shoes
Through the wars of the classes,
despairing
Each time we found an abuse, and no
sense of outrage.

'To Those Born Later' (1939)

Sydney Brenner 1927–

British scientist

17 A modern computer hovers between the obsolescent and the nonexistent.

attributed in *Science* 5 January 1990

Aristide Briand 1862–1932

French statesman

18 The high contracting powers solemnly declare . . . that they condemn recourse to war and renounce it . . . as an instrument of their national policy towards each other . . . The settlement or the solution of all disputes or conflicts of

whatever nature or of whatever origin they may be which may arise . . . shall never be sought by either side except by pacific means.

draft, 20 June 1927, later incorporated into the Kellogg Pact, 1928

Edward Bridges 1892–1969

British civil servant, Cabinet Secretary and Head of the Civil Service

1 I confidently expect that we shall continue to be grouped with mothers-in-law and Wigan Pier as one of the recognized objects of ridicule.

of civil servants

Portrait of a Profession (1950)

Vera Brittain 1893–1970

English writer

2 Politics are usually the executive expression of human immaturity.

Rebel Passion (1964)

Russell Brockbank

see **Cartoons** 56:2

Joseph Brodsky 1940–96

Russian-born American poet

3 As a form of moral insurance, at least, literature is much more dependable than a system of beliefs or a philosophical doctrine.

'Uncommon Visage', Nobel lecture 1987, in *On Grief and Reason* (1996)

4 There is no other antidote to the vulgarity of the human heart than doubt and good taste, which one finds fused in works of great literature.

'Letter to a President [Václav Havel]' (1993), in *On Grief and Reason* (1996)

Tom Brokaw 1940–

American journalist

5 We don't just have egg on our face. We have omelette all over our suits.

on the networks' premature calls of a win in Florida in the presidential election, first to Al ***Gore*** *and then to George W.* ***Bush***

in *Atlanta Constitution-Journal* 9 November 2000 (online edition)

Jacob Bronowski 1908–74

Polish-born mathematician and humanist

6 The world can only be grasped by action, not by contemplation . . . The hand is the cutting edge of the mind.

The Ascent of Man (1973)

7 The essence of science: ask an impertinent question, and you are on the way to a pertinent answer.

The Ascent of Man (1973)

8 The wish to hurt, the momentary intoxication with pain, is the loophole through which the pervert climbs into the minds of ordinary men.

The Face of Violence (1954)

9 Therapy has become what I think of as the tenth American muse.

attributed

Rupert Brooke 1887–1915

English poet

see also **Opening lines** 247:4

10 Blow out, you bugles, over the rich Dead!
There's none of these so lonely and poor of old,
But, dying, has made us rarer gifts than gold.
These laid the world away; poured out the red
Sweet wine of youth.

'The Dead' (1914)

11 Unkempt about those hedges blows
An English unofficial rose.

'The Old Vicarage, Grantchester' (1915)

12 For Cambridge people rarely smile,
Being urban, squat, and packed with guile.

'The Old Vicarage, Grantchester' (1915)

13 Stands the Church clock at ten to three?
And is there honey still for tea?

'The Old Vicarage, Grantchester' (1915)

14 Now, God be thanked Who has matched us with His hour,

And caught our youth, and wakened us
from sleeping,
With hand made sure, clear eye, and
sharpened power,
To turn, as swimmers into cleanness
leaping.
'Peace' (1914)

Anita Brookner 1928–

British novelist and art historian

1 Good women always think it is their fault when someone else is being offensive. Bad women never take the blame for anything.
Hotel du Lac (1984)

2 They were reasonable people, and no one was to be hurt, not even with words.
Hotel du Lac (1984)

3 Dr Weiss, at forty, knew that her life had been ruined by literature.
A Start in Life (1981)

Gwendolyn Brooks 1917–2000

American poet

4 Exhaust the little moment. Soon it dies.
And be it gash or gold it will not come
Again in this identical disguise.
'Exhaust the little moment' (1949)

5 Abortions will not let you forget.
You remember the children you got that
you did not get . . .
'The Mother' (1945)

6 The time
cracks into furious flower. Lifts its face
all unashamed. And sways in wicked
grace.
'The Second Sermon on the Warpland' (1968)

J. Brooks

7 A four-legged friend, a four-legged friend,
He'll never let you down.
sung by Roy Rogers about his horse Trigger
'A Four Legged Friend' (1952)

Heywood Broun 1888–1939

American journalist

8 Everybody favours free speech in the slack moments when no axes are being ground.
in *New York World* 23 October 1926

9 Just as every conviction begins as a whim so does every emancipator serve his apprenticeship as a crank. A fanatic is a great leader who is just entering the room.
in *New York World* 6 February 1928

Christy Brown 1932–81

Irish writer

10 Painting became everything to me . . . Through it I made articulate all that I saw and felt, all that went on inside the mind that was housed within my useless body like a prisoner in a cell.
My Left Foot (1954)

Gordon Brown 1951–

British Labour politician

11 Ideas which stress the growing importance of international cooperation and new theories of economic sovereignty across a wide range of areas—macroeconomics, the environment, the growth of post neo-classical endogenous growth theory and the symbiotic relationships between growth and investment in people and infrastructure.
New Labour Economics speech, September 1994, 'winner' of the ironic Plain English No Nonsense Award for 1994

12 It is about time we had an end to the old Britain, where all that matters is the privileges you were born with, rather than the potential you actually have.
speech, 25 May 2000

13 She is my mentor and my tormentor.
*on Barbara **Castle***
in *Guardian* 6 October 2000

H. Rap Brown 1943–

American Black Power leader

1 I say violence is necessary. It is as American as cherry pie.

speech, 27 July 1967

Lew Brown 1893–1958

American songwriter

see also **De Sylva** 90:8

2 Life is just a bowl of cherries.

title of song (1931)

Cecil Browne 1932–

American businessman

3 But not so odd
As those who choose
A Jewish God,
But spurn the Jews.

reply to verse by William Norman Ewer; see **Ewer** 110:9

Frederick 'Boy' Browning 1896–1965

British soldier

4 I think we might be going a bridge too far.

expressing reservations about the Arnhem 'Market Garden' operation

on 10 September 1944; R. E. Urquhart *Arnhem* (1958)

Lenny Bruce 1925–66

American comedian

5 The liberals can understand everything but people who don't understand them.

John Cohen (ed.) *The Essential Lenny Bruce* (1967)

6 People should be taught what is, not what should be. All my humour is based on destruction and despair. If the whole world were tranquil, without disease and violence, I'd be standing in the breadline.

The Essential Lenny Bruce (1967)

7 I'll die young, but it's like kissing God.

on his drug addiction

attributed

Gro Harlem Brundtland 1939–

Norwegian stateswoman; Prime Minister 1981, 1986–89, and 1990–96

8 I do not know of any environmental group in any country that does not view its government as an adversary.

in *Time* 25 September 1989

Frank Bruno 1961–

English boxer

9 Boxing's just show business with blood.

in *Guardian* 20 November 1991

10 Know what I mean, Harry?

supposed to have been said in interview with sports commentator Harry Carpenter, possibly apocryphal

Anita Bryant 1940–

American singer

11 If homosexuality were the normal way, God would have made Adam and Bruce.

in *New York Times* 5 June 1977

Bill Bryson 1951–

American travel writer

12 I had always thought that once you grew up you could do anything you wanted—stay up all night or eat ice-cream straight out of the container.

The Lost Continent (1989)

13 What an odd thing tourism is. You fly off to a strange land, eagerly abandoning all the comforts of home, and then expend vast quantities of time and money in a largely futile attempt to recapture the comforts that you wouldn't have lost if you hadn't left home in the first place.

Neither Here Nor There (1991)

Zbigniew Brzezinski 1928–

US Secretary of State and National Security Advisor

14 Russia can be an empire or a democracy,

but it cannot be both.
in *Foreign Affairs* March/April 1994 'The Premature Partnership'

Martin Buber 1878–1965

Austrian-born religious philosopher and Zionist

1 Through the Thou a person becomes I.
Ich und Du (1923)

John Buchan 1875–1940

Scottish novelist; Governor-General of Canada, 1935–40
on Buchan: see **Bennett** 29:16

2 It's a great life if you don't weaken.
Mr Standfast (1919)

3 An atheist is a man who has no invisible means of support.
H. E. Fosdick *On Being a Real Person* (1943)

Pat Buchanan 1938–

American politician and presidential candidate

4 My guess is I probably got some votes down there that really did not belong to me and I do not feel well about that.
on the surprising number of votes cast for the ultra-right wing Buchanan in Palm Beach, Florida
in *Guardian* 10 November 2000

Frank Buchman 1878–1961

American evangelist; founder of the Moral Re-Armament movement

5 There is enough in the world for everyone's need, but not enough for everyone's greed.
Remaking the World (1947)

6 I thank heaven for a man like Adolf Hitler, who built a front line of defence against the anti-Christ of Communism.
in *New York World-Telegram* 26 August 1936

Art Buchwald 1925–

American humorist

7 War is too serious a business to be left to computers.
in *International Herald Tribune* 14/15 June 1980

Gene Buck 1885–1957 and **Herman Ruby** 1891–1959

American songwriters

8 That Shakespearian rag,—
Most intelligent, very elegant.
'That Shakespearian Rag' (1912 song); see **Eliot** 105:2

Edward Bullard 1907–80

English geophysicist

9 Rutherford was a disaster. He started the 'something for nothing' tradition . . . the notion that research can always be done on the cheap . . . The war taught us differently. If you want quick and effective results you must put the money in.
P. Grosvenor and J. McMillan *The British Genius* (1973); see **Rutherford** 283:13

Arthur Buller 1874–1944

British botanist and mycologist

10 There was a young lady named Bright,
Whose speed was far faster than light;
She set out one day
In a relative way
And returned on the previous night.
'Relativity' in *Punch* 19 December 1923

Basil Bunting 1900–85

English poet

11 Praise the green earth. Chance has
appointed her
home, workshop, larder, middenpit.
Her lousy skin scabbed here and there by
cities provides us with name and nation.
'Attis: or, Something Missing' (1931)

12 Dance tiptoe, bull,
black against may.
'Briggflatts' (1965)

Luis Buñuel 1900–83

Spanish film director
see also **Film titles** 118:5

1 Thanks to God, I am still an atheist.
in *Le Monde* 16 December 1959

Julie Burchill 1960–

English journalist and writer
see also **Anonymous** 10:15

2 Now, at last, this sad, glittering century has an image worthy of it: a wandering, wondering girl, a silly Sloane turned secular saint, coming home in her coffin to RAF Northolt like the good soldier she was.
in *Guardian* 2 September 1997

Lord Burford 1939–

British aristocrat

3 This bill, drafted in Brussels, is treason.
urging rejection of the bill to abolish the right of hereditary peers to sit in the House of Lords
interruption to debate in the House of Lords, 26 October 1999

Anthony Burgess 1917–93

English novelist and critic
see also **Opening lines** 247:10

4 A clockwork orange.
title of novel (1962)

5 He said it was artificial respiration, but now I find I am to have his child.
Inside Mr Enderby (1963)

6 The US presidency is a Tudor monarchy plus telephones.
George Plimpton (ed.) *Writers at Work* (4th Series, 1977)

Johnny Burke 1908–64

American songwriter

7 Every time it rains, it rains
Pennies from heaven.
Don't you know each cloud contains
Pennies from heaven?
'Pennies from Heaven' (1936 song); see **Thatcher** 316:11

8 Like Webster's Dictionary, we're Morocco bound.
'The Road to Morocco' (1942 song)

Thomas E. Burnett Jnr *d.* 2001

American businessman

9 I love you, honey. I know we're all going to die—but there's three of us who are going to do something about it.
final phone call to his wife from the hijacked Flight 93, which crashed south of Pittsburgh
in *Independent* 13 September 2001

Burnum Burnum 1936–97

Australian political activist

10 We wish no harm to England's native people. We are here to bring you good manners, refinement and an opportunity to make a *Koompartoo*, a fresh start.
in 1988, the year of Australia's bicentenary, on planting an Aboriginal flag on the white cliffs of Dover and 'claiming' England for the Aboriginal people
on 26 January 1988; in obituary, *Independent* 20 August 1997

William S. Burroughs 1914–97

American novelist
see also **Last words** 191:1

11 Kerouac opened a million coffee bars and sold a million pairs of Levis to both sexes. Woodstock rises from his pages.
The Adding Machine (1985) 'Remembering Jack Kerouac'

12 Junk is the ideal product . . . the ultimate merchandise. No sales talk necessary. The client will crawl through a sewer and beg to buy.
The Naked Lunch (1959) introduction

13 The face of 'evil' is always the face of total need.
The Naked Lunch (1959)

Benjamin Hapgood Burt
1880–1950

American songwriter

1 'You can tell a man who "boozes" by the company he chooses'
And the pig got up and slowly walked away.
'The Pig Got Up and Slowly Walked Away' (1933 song)

2 When you're all dressed up and no place to go.
title of song (1913)

Nat Burton

British songwriter

3 There'll be bluebirds over the white cliffs of Dover,
Tomorrow, just you wait and see.
'The White Cliffs of Dover' (1941 song)

Barbara Bush 1925–

wife of George Bush; First Lady, 1989–93

4 Somewhere out in this audience may even be someone who will one day follow in my footsteps, and preside over the White House as the President's spouse. I wish him well!
remarks at Wellesley College Commencement, 1 June 1990

George Bush 1924–

American Republican statesman; 41st President of the US, 1989–93; husband of Barbara **Bush** and father of George W. **Bush**
on Bush: see **Richards** 274:5

5 Oh, the vision thing.
responding to the suggestion that he turn his attention from short-term campaign objectives and look to the longer term
in *Time* 26 January 1987

6 What's wrong with being a boring kind of guy?
during the campaign for the Republican nomination; in *Daily Telegraph* 28 April 1988

7 Read my lips: no new taxes.
campaign pledge on taxation
in *New York Times* 19 August 1988; see **Blunkett** 38:7

8 I'm President of the United States, and I'm not going to eat any more broccoli!
in *New York Times* 23 March 1990

9 And now, we can see a new world coming into view. A world in which there is the very real prospect of a new world order.
speech, in *New York Times* 7 March 1991

George W. Bush 1946–

American Republican statesman; 43rd President of the US from 2001; son of George **Bush**
see also **Castro** 57:9, **Gore** 138:1

10 New Hampshire has long been known as the bump in the road for front runners—and this year is no exception.
after being defeated in the New Hampshire primary
in *Sunday Times* 6 February 2000

11 We will make no distinction between terrorists who committed these acts and those who harbour them.
after the terrorist attacks of 11 September
televised address, 12 September 2001

12 It is time for us to win the first war of the 21st century.
of the 'war on terrorism'
at a White House press conference, 16 September 2001

13 Today we feel what Franklin Roosevelt called the warm courage of national unity. This unity against terror is now extending across the world.
address in Washington National Cathedral, 14 September 2001, at the day of mourning for those killed in the terrorist attacks of 11 September
in *Times* 15 September 2001; see **Roosevelt** 277:17

Laura Bush 1946–

wife of George W. **Bush**; First Lady since 2001

14 The president of the United States of America is more than a man, or a

woman as I hope the case will sometime be. The president is the most visible symbol of our country, of its heart and its values and its leadership in the world.

at the Republican Convention, 1 August 2000

Nicholas Murray Butler 1862–1947

President of Columbia University, 1901–45

1 An expert is one who knows more and more about less and less.

Commencement address at Columbia University; attributed

R. A. ('Rab') Butler 1902–82

British Conservative politician

2 REPORTER: Mr Butler, would you say that this [Anthony Eden] is the best Prime Minister we have?

R. A. BUTLER: Yes.

interview at London Airport, 8 January 1956

3 Politics is the Art of the Possible. That is what these pages show I have tried to achieve—not more—and that is what I have called my book.

The Art of the Possible (1971); see below; see **Galbraith** 130:11

Politics is the art of the possible.

Bismarck (1815–98) conversation with Meyer von Waldeck, 11 August 1867

A. S. Byatt 1936–

English novelist

4 What literature can and should do is change the people who teach the people who don't read the books.

interview in *Newsweek* 5 June 1995

James Branch Cabell 1879–1958

American novelist and essayist

5 The optimist proclaims that we live in the best of all possible worlds; and the pessimist fears this is true.

The Silver Stallion (1926); see below

In this best of possible worlds . . . all is for the best.

Voltaire (1694–1778) *Candide* (1759)

Irving Caesar 1895–

American songwriter

6 Picture you upon my knee,
Just tea for two and two for tea.

'Tea for Two' (1925 song)

John Cage 1912–92

American composer, pianist, and writer

7 I have nothing to say
and I am saying it and that is poetry.

'Lecture on nothing' (1961)

James Cagney

see **Film lines** 115:1, **Misquotations** 227:6

James M. Cain 1892–1977

American novelist

8 The postman always rings twice.

title of novel (1934)

Michael Caine 1933–

English film actor

9 Not many people know that.

title of book (1984)

Joseph Cairns 1920–

British industrialist and politician

10 The betrayal of Ulster, the cynical and entirely undemocratic banishment of its properly elected Parliament and a relegation to the status of a fuzzy wuzzy colony is, I hope, a last betrayal contemplated by Downing Street because it is the last that Ulster will countenance.

speech on retiring as Lord Mayor of Belfast, 31 May 1972

Charles Calhoun 1897–1972

American songwriter

1 Shake, rattle and roll.

title of song (1954)

James Callaghan 1912–

British Labour statesman; Prime Minister 1976–9

see also **Misquotations** 226:3

2 Leaking is what you do; briefing is what *I* do.

when giving evidence to the Franks Committee on Official Secrecy in 1971

Franks Report (1972); oral evidence

3 You cannot now, if you ever could, spend your way out of a recession.

speech at Labour Party Conference, 28 September 1976

4 You never reach the promised land. You can march towards it.

in a television interview, 20 July 1978

5 I had known it was going to be a 'winter of discontent'.

television interview, 8 February 1979; in *Daily Telegraph* 9 February 1979; see below; see **Newspaper headlines** 241:4

Now is the winter of our discontent
Made glorious summer by this sun of
York.

William Shakespeare (1564–1616) *Richard III* (1591)

6 It's the first time in recorded history that turkeys have been known to vote for an early Christmas.

in the debate resulting in the fall of the Labour government, when the pact between Labour and the Liberals had collapsed, and the Scottish and Welsh Nationalists had also withdrawn their support

in the House of Commons, 28 March 1979

7 There are times, perhaps once every thirty years, when there is a sea-change in politics. It then does not matter what you say or what you do. There is a shift in what the public wants and what it approves of. I suspect there is now such a sea-change—and it is for Mrs Thatcher.

during the election campaign of 1979

Bernard Donoughue *Prime Minister* (1987)

of the popularity of Margaret ***Thatcher:***

8 The further you got from Britain, the more admired you found she was.

in *Spectator* 1 December 1990

Italo Calvino 1923–85

Italian novelist and short-story writer

9 Everything has already begun before, the first line of the first page of every novel refers to something that has already happened outside the book.

If on a Winter's Night a Traveller (1979)

Helder Camara 1909–99

Brazilian priest

10 When I give food to the poor they call me a saint. When I ask why the poor have no food they call me a communist.

attributed

Alastair Campbell 1957–

British journalist, Press Secretary to the Prime Minister from 1997

see also **Anonymous** 12:1

11 Labour spin doctors aren't supposed to like Tory MPs. But Alan Clark was an exceptional man.

in *Mirror* 8 September 1999

12 I have no intention of getting into a war of words with the WI.

after Tony ***Blair*** *was heckled at the Women's Institute's annual conference for making what was regarded as a party political speech*

in *Guardian* 8 June 2000

13 There are parts of this that he can't explain. There are things he cannot explain to himself. He has been slightly detached.

on Peter ***Mandelson****'s claim that his resignation had been rushed through before he could justify himself*

press briefing, 28 January 2001

14 The day of the bog-standard comprehensive is over.

press briefing, 12 February 2001; see **Blunkett** 38:8

Mrs Patrick Campbell
1865–1940

English actress
on Campbell: see **Woollcott** 345:10

1 I'm out of a job. London wants flappers, and I can't flap.
of the theatre of 1927
Margot Peters *Mrs Pat* (1984)

2 The deep, deep peace of the double-bed after the hurly-burly of the chaise-longue.
on her recent marriage
Alexander Woollcott *While Rome Burns* (1934) 'The First Mrs Tanqueray'

3 It doesn't matter what you do in the bedroom as long as you don't do it in the street and frighten the horses.
Daphne Fielding *The Duchess of Jermyn Street* (1964)

Roy Campbell 1901–57

South African poet

4 You praise the firm restraint with which
they write—
I'm with you there, of course:
They use the snaffle and the curb all
right,
But where's the bloody horse?
'On Some South African Novelists' (1930)

5 South Africa, renowned both far and
wide
For politics and little else beside.
The Wayzgoose (1928)

Albert Camus 1913–60

French novelist, dramatist, and essayist
see also **Opening lines** 247:2

6 You know what charm is: a way of getting the answer yes without having asked any clear question.
The Fall (1957)

7 We are all special cases. We all want to appeal against something! Everyone insists on his innocence, at all costs, even if it means accusing the rest of the human race and heaven.
The Fall (1957)

8 I'll tell you a big secret, *mon cher*. Don't wait for the last judgement. It takes place every day.
The Fall (1957)

9 Poor people's memory is less nourished than that of the rich; it has fewer landmarks in space because they seldom leave the place where they live, and fewer reference points in time . . . Of course, there is the memory of the heart that they say is the surest kind, but the heart wears out with sorrow and labour, it forgets sooner under the weight of fatigue.
The First Man (1994)

10 The struggle itself towards the heights is enough to fill a human heart. One must imagine that Sisyphus is happy.
The Myth of Sisyphus (1942)

11 Politics and the fate of mankind are formed by men without ideals and without greatness. Those who have greatness within them do not go in for politics.
Notebooks 1935–42 (1963)

12 An intellectual is someone whose mind watches itself.
Notebooks 1935–42 (1963)

13 What is a rebel? A man who says no.
The Rebel (1953)

14 All modern revolutions have ended in a reinforcement of the State.
The Rebel (1953)

15 Every revolutionary ends as an oppressor or a heretic.
The Rebel (1951)

16 When the imagination sleeps, words are emptied of their meaning.
Resistance, Rebellion and Death (1961) 'Reflections on the Guillotine'

17 What I know most surely about morality and the duty of man I owe to sport.
often quoted as '. . . I owe to football'
Herbert R. Lottman *Albert Camus* (1979)

18 Without work, all life goes rotten, but when work is soulless, life stifles and dies.
attributed; E. F. Schumacher *Good Work* (1979)

Dennis Canavan 1942–

Scottish labour politician

1 Members of Parliament are representatives of the people, we are not party puppets sent down to Westminster to vote simply the way the whips instruct us to.

in *Scotsman* 12 November 1998

Elias Canetti 1905–94

Bulgarian-born writer and novelist

2 The fear of burglars is not only the fear of being robbed, but also the fear of a sudden and unexpected clutch out of the darkness.

Crowds and Power (1960)

3 All the things one has forgotten scream for help in dreams.

Die Provinz der Menschen (1973)

Moya Cannon 1956–

Irish poet

4 Our windy, untidy loft
where old people had flung up old junk
they'd thought might come in handy
ploughs, ladles, bears, lions, a clatter of
heroes.

'The Stars' (1997)

Eric Cantona 1966–

French footballer

5 When seagulls follow a trawler, it is because they think sardines will be thrown into the sea.

to the media at the end of a press conference, 31 March 1995

Robert Capa 1913–54

Hungarian-born American photojournalist

6 If your pictures aren't good enough, you aren't close enough.

Russell Miller *Magnum: Fifty years at the Front Line of History* (1997)

Al Capone 1899–1947

Italian-born American gangster

7 Once in the racket you're always in it.

in *Philadelphia Public Ledger* 18 May 1929

8 Don't you get the idea I'm one of these goddam radicals. Don't get the idea I'm knocking the American system.

interview, c.1929, with Claud Cockburn; Claud Cockburn *In Time of Trouble* (1956)

Truman Capote 1924–84

American writer and novelist
on Capote: see **Vidal** 328:9

9 Other voices, other rooms.

title of novel (1948)

Al Capp 1907–79

American cartoonist

10 A product of the untalented, sold by the unprincipled to the utterly bewildered.

on abstract art

in *National Observer* 1 July 1963

Neville Cardus 1889–1975

English critic and writer

11 If everything else in this nation of ours were lost but cricket—her Constitution and the laws of England of Lord Halsbury—it would be possible to reconstruct from the theory and practice of cricket all the eternal Englishness which has gone to the establishment of that Constitution and the laws aforesaid.

Cricket (1930)

George Carey 1935–

British Anglican clergyman, Archbishop of Canterbury from 1991

12 I see it as an elderly lady, who mutters away to herself in a corner, ignored most of the time.

on the Church of England

in *Readers Digest* (British ed.) March 1991

Peter Carey 1943–

Australian writer

1 She understood, as women often do more easily than men, that the declared meaning of a spoken sentence is only its overcoat, and the real meaning lies underneath its scarves and buttons.

Oscar and Lucinda (1989)

2 My fictional project has always been the invention or discovery of my own country.

interview in *Boldtype* (online journal) March 1999

Stokely Carmichael 1941–98

American Black Power leader

3 The only position for women in SNCC is prone.

response to a question about the position of women

at a Student Nonviolent Coordinating Committee conference, November 1964

Stokely Carmichael 1941–98 and **Charles Vernon Hamilton** 1929–

American Black Power leaders

4 The adoption of the concept of Black Power is one of the most legitimate and healthy developments in American politics and race relations in our time. . . . It is a call for black people in this country to unite, to recognize their heritage, to build a sense of community. It is a call for black people to begin to define their own goals, to lead their own organizations and to support those organizations. It is a call to reject the racist institutions and values of this society.

Black Power (1967)

Dale Carnegie 1888–1955

American writer and lecturer

5 How to win friends and influence people.

title of book (1936)

Lord Carrington 1919–

British Conservative politician

6 Q: If Mrs Thatcher were run over by a bus . . . ?
LORD CARRINGTON: It wouldn't dare.

during the Falklands War

Russell Lewis *Margaret Thatcher* (1984)

Edward Carson 1854–1935

Northern Irish lawyer and politician

7 From the day I first entered parliament up to the present, devotion to the union has been the guiding star of my political life.

in *Dictionary of National Biography* (1917–)

Rachel Carson 1907–64

American zoologist

8 Over increasingly large areas of the United States, spring now comes unheralded by the return of the birds, and the early mornings are strangely silent where once they were filled with the beauty of bird song.

The Silent Spring (1962)

Angela Carter 1940–92

English novelist

9 Clothes are our weapons, our challenges, our visible insults.

Nothing Sacred (1982) 'Notes for a Theory of Sixties Style'

10 Comedy is tragedy that happens to *other* people.

Wise Children (1991)

Howard Carter 1874–1939

English archaeologist

11 Yes, wonderful things.

when asked what he could see on first looking into the tomb of Tutankhamun, 26 November 1922; his notebook records the words as 'Yes, it is wonderful'

H. V. F. Winstone *Howard Carter and the discovery of the tomb of Tutankhamun* (1993)

Jimmy Carter 1924–

American Democratic statesman, 39th President of the US, 1977–81

1 I'm Jimmy Carter, and I'm going to be your next president.

to the son of a campaign supporter, November 1975

I'll Never Lie to You (1976); see **Gore** 138:2

2 I've looked on a lot of women with lust. I've committed adultery in my heart many times. This is something that God recognizes I will do—and I have done it—and God forgives me for it.

in *Playboy* November 1976

Sydney Carter 1915–

English folk-song writer

3 It's God they ought to crucify
Instead of you and me,
I said to the carpenter
A-hanging on the tree.

'Friday Morning' (1967)

4 Dance then wherever you may be,
I am the Lord of the Dance, said he,
And I'll lead you all, wherever you may be
And I'll lead you all in the dance, said he.

'Lord of the Dance' (1967)

5 One more step along the world I go.

'One More Step'

Henri Cartier-Bresson 1908–

French photographer and artist

6 To me, photography is the simultaneous recognition, in a fraction of a second, of the significance of an event as well as of a precise organisation of forms which give that event its proper expression.

The Decisive Moment (1952)

Barbara Cartland 1901–2000

English writer

7 After forty a woman has to choose between losing her figure or her face. My advice is to keep your face, and stay sitting down.

Libby Purves 'Luncheon à la Cartland'; in *The Times* 6 October 1993; similar remarks have been attributed since *c.*1980

■ **Cartoons**

see box overleaf

Pablo Casals 1876–1973

Spanish cellist, conductor, and composer

8 It is like a beautiful woman who has not grown older, but younger with time, more slender, more supple, more graceful.

of the cello

in *Time* 29 April 1957

9 The man who works and is not bored is never old.

J. Lloyd Webber (ed.) *Song of the Birds* (1985)

Roger Casement 1864–1916

Irish nationalist; executed for treason in 1916

10 Self-government is our right, a thing born in us at birth, a thing no more to be doled out to us, or withheld from us, by another people than the right to life itself—than the right to feel the sun, or smell the flowers, or to love our kind.

statement at the conclusion of his trial, the Old Bailey, London, 29 June 1916

11 Where all your rights become only an accumulated wrong; where men must beg with bated breath for leave to subsist in their own land, to think their own thoughts, to sing their own songs, to garner the fruits of their own labours . . . then surely it is a braver, a saner and truer thing, to be a rebel in act and deed against such circumstances as these than tamely to accept it as the natural lot of men.

statement at the conclusion of his trial, the Old Bailey, London, 29 June 1916

Cartoons

1 All right, have it your own way—you heard a seal bark!

showing a man and his wife in bed, with a seal looking over the headboard

caption in *New Yorker* 30 January 1932, by James **Thurber**

2 Fog in Channel—Continent isolated.

newspaper placard in cartoon, *Round the Bend with Brockbank* (1948) by the British cartoonist Russell Brockbank (1913–); the phrase 'Continent isolated' was quoted as already current by John Gunther *Inside Europe* (1938)

3 I feel like a fugitive from th' law of averages.

showing Willie and Joe, American GIs, under fire

caption in *Up Front* (1945), by Bill Mauldin (1921–)

4 It's a naive domestic Burgundy without any breeding, but I think you'll be amused by its presumption.

caption in *New Yorker* 27 March 1937, by James **Thurber**

5 MOTHER: It's broccoli, dear.
CHILD: I say it's spinach, and I say the hell with it.

caption in *New Yorker* 8 December 1928, by E. B. **White**

6 The man who . . .

illustrating social gaffes resulting from snobbery

opening words of the caption for a series of cartoons (first appearing in 1912) by H. M. Bateman (1887–1970)

7 No son—they're not the same—devolution takes longer.

father to his son, who is reading a book on evolution

caption in *Scots Independent* January 1978, by Ewen Bain (1925–89)

8 On the Internet, nobody knows you're a dog.

a large dog at a desk, paw on keyboard, enlightening a smaller friend

caption in *New Yorker*, July 1993, by the American cartoonist Peter Steiner

9 The price of petrol has been raised by a penny. Official.

a torpedoed sailor with oil-stained face lying on a raft; the message was intended to be a warning against wasting petrol, but it was taken by some as suggesting that lives were being put at risk for profit

caption in *Daily Mirror* 3 March 1942; cartoon by Philip Zec (1909–83) and caption by 'Cassandra' (William Connor, 1909–67).

10 We have met the enemy and he is us.

the cartoon-strip character, Pogo the opossum, looking at litter under a tree; used as an Earth Day poster in 1971

Pogo cartoon, 1970, by the American cartoonist Walt Kelly (1913–73); the comment is a modification of the message in which Commodore Perry (1785–1819) reported his victory over the British in the battle of Lake Erie, 1813, 'We have met the enemy, and they are ours'

11 Well, if I called the wrong number, why did you answer the phone?

in *New Yorker* 5 June 1937, by James **Thurber**

12 Well, if you knows of a better 'ole, go to it.

Old Bill and a friend in a shellhole under fire

caption in *Fragments from France* (1915), by the British cartoonist Bruce Bairnsfather (1888–1959)

13 You mean I'm supposed to stand on that?

a reluctant elephant (symbol of the Republican Party) is propelled towards a small platform resting on an unstable tower of buckets beneath a tar-barrel; the label on the barrel introduced the term 'McCarthyism'

caption in *Washington Post* 29 March 1950; by the American cartoonist 'Herblock' (Herbert Lawrence Block, 1910–2001)

Johnny Cash 1932–

American singer and songwriter

1 Many a good man I saw fall
And even now, every time I dream
I hear the men and the monkeys in the jungle scream.

Drive on, it don't mean nothin'
My children love me, but they don't understand
And I got a woman who knows her man.
'Drive On' (1993)

2 It was a real slow walk in a real sad rain.
'Drive On' (1993)

A. M. Cassandre 1901–68

French illustrator

3 A good poster is a visual telegram.
attributed

Hugh Casson 1910–

English architect

4 We have now to plan no longer for soft little animals pottering about on their own two legs, but for hard steel canisters hurtling about with these same little animals inside them.
C. Williams-Ellis *Around the World in 90 Years* (1978)

Barbara Castle 1910–

British Labour politician
on Castle: see **Brown** 45:13

5 I will fight for what I believe in until I drop dead. And that's what keeps you alive.
in *Guardian* 14 January 1998

6 Women have to do more to help themselves. If there is no fire in women's bellies it will all become a very dainty process. Organize yourselves and speak out.
on the 25th anniversary of the Sex Discrimination Act
in *Independent on Sunday* 21 January 2001

Ted Castle 1907–79

British journalist

7 In place of strife.
title of Government White Paper, 17 January 1969, suggested by Castle to his wife, Barbara Castle, then Secretary of State for Employment
Barbara Castle diary, 15 January 1969

Fidel Castro 1927–

Cuban statesman, Prime Minister 1959–76 and President since 1976
on Castro: see **Ceauşescu** 61:4

8 Capitalism is using its money; we socialists throw it away.
in *Observer* 8 November 1964

9 Hopefully he is not as stupid as he seems, nor as Mafia-like as his predecessors were.
on George W. ***Bush***
in *Newsweek* 5 February 2001

■ Catchphrases

see box overleaf

see also **Grenfell** 140:11, **Laurel** 189:14

Willa Cather 1873–1947

American novelist

10 Oh, the Germans classify, but the French arrange!
Death Comes For the Archbishop (1927)

Mr Justice Caulfield 1914–

British lawyer

11 Remember Mary Archer in the witness box. Your vision of her will probably never disappear. Has she elegance? Has she fragrance? Would she have—without the strain of this trial—a radiance?
summing up of court case between Jeffrey Archer and the Star, *July 1987*
in *The Times* 24 July 1987

Catchphrases

1 CECIL: After you, Claude.
CLAUDE: No, after you, Cecil.
ITMA (BBC radio programme, 1939–49), written by Ted Kavanagh (1892–1958)

2 And now for something completely different.
Monty Python's Flying Circus (BBC TV programme, 1969–74)

3 Anyone for tennis?
said to be typical of drawing-room comedies, much associated with Humphrey Bogart (1899–1957); perhaps from George Bernard Shaw 'Anybody on for a game of tennis?' *Misalliance* (1914)

4 Are yer courtin'?
Have a Go! (BBC radio quiz programme, 1946–67), used by Wilfred Pickles (1904–78)

5 Are you sitting comfortably? Then I'll begin.
sometimes 'Then we'll begin'
Listen with Mother (BBC radio programme for children, 1950–82), used by Julia Lang (1921–)

6 The butler did it!
a solution for detective stories
Nigel Rees, in *Sayings of the Century* (1984), quotes a correspondent who recalls hearing it at a cinema *c.*1916 but the origin of the phrase has not been traced

7 Can I do you now, sir?
spoken by 'Mrs Mopp'
ITMA (BBC radio programme, 1939–49), written by Ted Kavanagh (1892–1958)

8 Can you hear me, mother?
used by Sandy Powell (1900–82)

9 The day war broke out.
customary preamble to radio monologues in the role of a Home Guard, used by Robb Wilton (1881–1957)
from *c.*1940

10 Didn't she [*or* he *or* they] do well?
used by Bruce Forsyth (1928–) in 'The Generation Game' on BBC Television, 1973 onwards

11 Don't forget the diver.
spoken by 'The Diver'; based on 'a memory of the pier at New Brighton where Tommy Handley used to go as a child . . . A man in a bathing suit . . . whined "Don't forget the diver, sir."'
ITMA (BBC radio programme, 1939–49), written by Ted Kavanagh (1892–1958)

12 Don't have nightmares. Do sleep well.
habitual closing words for BBC1's *Crimewatch* (1984–), spoken by Nick Ross

13 Eat my shorts!
The Simpsons (American TV series, 1990–), created by Matt Groening

14 Ee, it was agony, Ivy.
Ray's a Laugh (BBC radio programme, 1949–61), written by Ted Ray (1906–77)

15 Evening, all.
opening words spoken by Jack Warner as Sergeant Dixon in *Dixon of Dock Green* (BBC television series, 1956–76), written by Ted Willis (1918–)

16 Everybody wants to get inta the act!
used by Jimmy Durante (1893–1980)

17 An everyday story of country folk.
introduction to *The Archers* (BBC radio serial, 1950 onwards), written by Geoffrey Webb and Edward J. Mason

18 Exterminate! Exterminate!
the Daleks in *Dr Who* (BBC television series, from 1963) written by Terry Nation

19 A good idea—son.
Educating Archie, 1950–3 BBC radio comedy series, written by Eric Sykes (1923–) and Max Bygraves (1922–)

20 Good morning, sir—was there something?
used by Sam Costa in radio comedy series *Much-Binding-in-the-Marsh*, written by Richard Murdoch (1907–90) and Kenneth Horne (1900–69), started 2 January 1947

21 Goodnight, children . . . everywhere.
closing words normally spoken by 'Uncle Mac' in the 1930s and 1940s
on *Children's Hour* (BBC Radio programme); written by Derek McCulloch (1892–1978)

22 Have you read any good books lately?
used by Richard Murdoch in radio comedy series *Much-Binding-in-the-Marsh*, written by Richard Murdoch (1907–90) and Kenneth Horne (1900–69), started 2 January 1947

▶

▸ Catchphrases continued

1 Hello, good evening, and welcome.
used by David **Frost** (1939–) in 'The Frost Programme' on BBC Television, 1966 onwards

2 Here come de judge.
from the song-title 'Here comes the judge' (1968); written by Dewey 'Pigmeat' Markham, Dick Alen, Bob Astor, and Sarah Harvey

3 Here's one I made earlier.
culmination to directions for making a model out of empty yoghurt pots, coat-hangers, and similar domestic items
children's BBC television programme *Blue Peter*, 1963 onwards

4 I didn't get where I am today without . . . .
used by the manager C. J. in BBC television series *The Fall and Rise of Reginald Perrin*, 1976–80); based on David Nobbs *The Death of Reginald Perrin* (1975)

5 I don't like this game, let's play another game—let's play doctor and nurses.
phrase first used by Bluebottle in 'The Phantom Head-Shaver' in *The Goon Show* (BBC radio series) 15 October 1954, written by Spike **Milligan**; the catch-phrase was often 'I do not like this game'

6 I don't mind if I do.
spoken by 'Colonel Chinstrap'
ITMA (BBC radio programme, 1939–49), written by Ted Kavanagh (1892–1958)

7 I go—I come back.
spoken by 'Ali Oop'
ITMA (BBC radio programme, 1939–49), written by Ted Kavanagh (1892–1958)

8 I have a cunning plan.
Baldrick's habitual over-optimistic promise in *Blackadder II* (1987 television series), written by Richard Curtis and Ben Elton (1959–)

9 I'm Bart Simpson: who the hell are you?
The Simpsons (American TV series, 1990–), created by Matt Groening

10 I'm in charge.
used by Bruce Forsyth (1928–) in 'Sunday Night at the London Palladium' on ITV, 1958 onwards

11 I'm worried about Jim.
frequent line in *Mrs Dale's Diary*, BBC radio series 1948–69

12 It all depends what you mean by . . .
habitually used by C. E. M. **Joad** when replying to questions on 'The Brains Trust' (formerly 'Any Questions'), BBC radio (1941–8)

13 It's being so cheerful as keeps me going.
spoken by 'Mona Lott'
ITMA (BBC radio programme, 1939–49), written by Ted Kavanagh (1892–1958)

14 I've arrived and to prove it I'm here!
Educating Archie, 1950–3 BBC radio comedy series, written by Eric Sykes (1923–) and Max Bygraves (1922–)

15 I've started so I'll finish.
said when a contestant's time runs out while a question is being put
Magnus Magnusson (1929–) *Mastermind*, BBC television (1972–97)

16 Just like that!
used by Tommy Cooper (1921–84)

17 Keep on truckin'.
used by Robert Crumb (1943–) in cartoons from *c.*1972

18 Left hand down a bit!
The Navy Lark (BBC radio series, 1959–77), written by Laurie Wyman

19 Let's be careful out there.
Hill Street Blues (television series, 1981 onwards), written by Steven Bochco and Michael Kozoll

20 Mind my bike!
used by Jack Warner (1895–1981) in the BBC radio series *Garrison Theatre*, 1939 onwards

21 Nice to see you—to see you, nice.
used by Bruce Forsyth (1928–) in 'The Generation Game' on BBC Television, 1973 onwards

22 Oh, calamity!
used by Robertson Hare (1891–1979)

23 Ohhh, I don't *believe* it!
Victor Meldrew in *One Foot in the Grave* (BBC television series, 1989–), written by David Renwick

▶

▸ Catchphrases continued

1 Pass the sick bag, Alice.
used by John Junor (1919–97); in *Sunday Express* and elsewhere

2 Seriously, though, he's doing a grand job!
used by David **Frost** (1939–) in 'That Was The Week That Was', on BBC Television, 1962-3

3 Shome mishtake, shurely?
in *Private Eye* magazine, 1980s

4 So farewell then . . .
frequent opening of poems by 'E. J. Thribb' in Private Eye *magazine, usually as an obituary*
1970s onwards

5 Take me to your leader.
from science-fiction stories

6 The truth is out there.
The X Files (American television series, 1993–), created by Chris Carter

7 Very interesting . . . but stupid.
Rowan and Martin's Laugh-In (American television series, 1967–73), written by Dan Rowan (1922–87) and Dick Martin (1923–)

8 The weekend starts here.
Ready, Steady, Go, British television series, c.1963

9 We have ways of making you talk.
perhaps originating in the line 'We have ways of making men talk' in *Lives of a Bengal Lancer* (1935 film), written by Waldemar Young et al.

10 What's up, Doc?
Bugs Bunny cartoons, written by Tex Avery (1907–80), from c.1940

11 Who loves ya, baby?
used by Telly Savalas (1926–94) in American TV series *Kojak* (1973-8)

12 You are the weakest link . . . goodbye.
used by Anne Robinson on the television game-show *The Weakest Link* (2000–)

13 You bet your sweet bippy.
Rowan and Martin's Laugh-In (American television series, 1967–73), written by Dan Rowan (1922–87) and Dick Martin (1923–)

14 You might very well think that. I couldn't possibly comment.
the Chief Whip's habitual response to questioning
House of Cards (televised 1990); written by Michael Dobbs (1948–)

15 You're going to like this . . . not a lot . . . but you'll like it!
used by Paul Daniels (1938–) in his conjuring act, especially on television from 1981 onwards

16 You rotten swines. I told you I'd be deaded.
phrase first used by Bluebottle in 'Hastings Flyer' in *The Goon Show* (BBC radio series) 3 January 1956, written by Spike **Milligan**

17 Your starter for ten.
phrase often used by Bamber Gascoigne (1935–) in *University Challenge* (ITV quiz series, 1962–87)

18 You silly twisted boy.
phrase first used in 'The Dreaded Batter Pudding Hurler' in *The Goon Show* (BBC radio series) 12 October 1954, written by Spike **Milligan**

Charles Causley 1917–

English poet and schoolmaster

19 Draw the blanket of ocean
Over the frozen face.
He lies, his eyes quarried by glittering fish,
Staring through the green freezing sea-glass
At the Northern Lights.
'Convoy' (1957)

20 Watch where he comes walking
Out of the Christmas flame,
Dancing, double-talking:

Herod is his name.
'Innocents' Song' (1961)

21 Timothy Winters comes to school
With eyes as wide as a football-pool,
Ears like bombs and teeth like splinters:
A blitz of a boy is Timothy Winters.
'Timothy Winters' (1957)

Constantine Cavafy
1863–1933

Greek poet

1 What are we waiting for, gathered in the market-place?
The barbarians are to arrive today.
'Waiting for the Barbarians' (1904)

2 And now, what will become of us without the barbarians?
Those people were a kind of solution.
'Waiting for the Barbarians' (1904)

Edith Cavell 1865–1915

English nurse

3 Patriotism is not enough. I must have no hatred or bitterness towards anyone.
on the eve of her execution by the Germans for assisting in the escape of British soldiers from occupied Belgium
in *The Times* 23 October 1915

Nicolae Ceauşescu 1918–89

Romanian Communist statesman, first President of the Socialist Republic of Romania 1974–89
on Ceauşescu: see **O'Donoghue** 244:11

4 Fidel Castro is right. You do not quieten your enemy by talking with him like a priest, but by burning him.
at a Communist Party meeting 17 December 1989
in *Guardian* 11 January 1990

Paul Celan 1920–70

German poet

5 A man lives in the house he plays with his vipers he writes
he writes when it grows dark to Deutschland your golden hair Margareta
Your ashen hair Shulamith we shovel a grave in the air there you won't lie too cramped.
'Deathfugue' (written 1944)

6 He shouts play death more sweetly this Death is a master from Deutschland
he shouts scrape your strings darker you'll rise then as smoke to the sky
you'll have a grave then in the clouds there you won't lie too cramped.
'Deathfugue' (written 1944)

7 *Der Tod ist ein Meister aus Deutschland.*
Death is a master from Germany.
'Deathfugue' (written 1944)

8 There's nothing in the world for which a poet will give up writing, not even when he is a Jew and the language of his poems is German.
letter to relatives, 2 August 1948

Neville Chamberlain
1869–1940

British Conservative statesman; Prime Minister, 1937–40
on Chamberlain: see **Jenkins** 169:10

9 How horrible, fantastic, incredible it is that we should be digging trenches and trying on gas-masks here because of a quarrel in a far away country between people of whom we know nothing.
on Germany's annexation of the Sudetenland
radio broadcast, 27 September 1938

10 This is the second time in our history that there has come back from Germany to Downing Street peace with honour. I believe it is peace for our time.
speech from 10 Downing Street, 30 September 1938; see below

Lord Salisbury and myself have brought you back peace—but a peace I hope with honour.
Benjamin Disraeli (1804–81) speech on returning from the Congress of Berlin, 16 July 1878

11 This morning, the British Ambassador in Berlin handed the German government a final Note stating that, unless we heard from them by eleven o'clock that they were prepared at once to withdraw their troops from Poland, a state of war would exist between us. I have to tell you now that no such undertaking has been received, and that consequently this country is at war with Germany.
radio broadcast, 3 September 1939

12 Whatever may be the reason—whether it was that Hitler thought he might get away with what he had got without fighting for it, or whether it was that after all the preparations were not sufficiently complete—however, one thing is certain—he missed the bus.

speech at Central Hall, Westminster, 4 April 1940

Raymond Chandler 1888–1959

American writer of detective fiction

1 It was a blonde. A blonde to make a bishop kick a hole in a stained glass window.

Farewell, My Lovely (1940)

2 Crime isn't a disease, it's a symptom. Cops are like a doctor that gives you aspirin for a brain tumour.

The Long Good-Bye (1953)

3 Down these mean streets a man must go who is not himself mean, who is neither tarnished nor afraid.

in *Atlantic Monthly* December 1944 'The Simple Art of Murder'

4 If my books had been any worse, I should not have been invited to Hollywood, and if they had been any better, I should not have come.

letter to Charles W. Morton, 12 December 1945

5 Would you convey my compliments to the purist who reads your proofs and tell him or her that I write in a sort of broken-down patois which is something like the way a Swiss waiter talks, and that when I split an infinitive, God damn it, I split it so it will stay split.

letter to Edward Weeks, 18 January 1947

6 When in doubt have a man come through the door with a gun in his hand.

attributed

Coco Chanel 1883–1971

French couturière

7 Clothes by a man who doesn't know women, never had one, and dreams of being one!

of Dior's New Look

in *Vanity Fair* June 1994

8 You ask if they were happy. This is not a characteristic of a European. To be contented—that's for the cows.

A. Madsen *Coco Chanel* (1990)

9 Youth is something very new: twenty years ago no one mentioned it.

Marcel Haedrich *Coco Chanel, Her Life, Her Secrets* (1971)

Henry ('Chips') Channon 1897–1958

American-born British Conservative politician and diarist

10 I like my 'abroad' to be Catholic and sensual.

diary, 18 January 1924

11 What is more dull than a discreet diary? One might just as well have a discreet soul.

diary, 26 July 1935

12 I gather it has now been decided not to embrace the Russian bear, but to hold out a hand and accept its paw gingerly. No more. The worst of both worlds.

diary, 16 May 1939

Charlie Chaplin 1889–1977

English film actor and director

13 All I need to make a comedy is a park, a policeman and a pretty girl.

My Autobiography (1964)

14 Words are cheap. The biggest thing you can say is 'elephant'.

on the universality of silent films

B. Norman *The Movie Greats* (1981)

Arthur Chapman 1873–1935

American poet

15 Out where the handclasp's a little
stronger,
Out where the smile dwells a little longer,
That's where the West begins.

Out Where the West Begins (1916)

John Jay Chapman 1862–1933

American essayist and poet

1 The present in New York is so powerful that the past is lost.

Emerson and Other Essays (rev. ed. 1909), preface

Charles, Prince of Wales 1948–

Heir apparent to the British throne; former husband of **Diana**, Princess of Wales

when asked if he was 'in love':

2 Yes . . . whatever that may mean.

after the announcement of his engagement

interview, 24 February 1981; see **Duffy** 95:7

3 A monstrous carbuncle on the face of a much-loved and elegant friend.

on the proposed extension to the National Gallery

speech in London, 30 May 1984

4 I just come and talk to the plants, really—very important to talk to them, they respond I find.

television interview, 21 September 1986

Lord Charteris 1913–99

British courtier, Private Secretary to the Queen, 1972–7

5 The Duchess of York is a vulgarian. She is vulgar, vulgar, vulgar, and that is that.

in *Spectator* 5 January 1995

Bruce Chatwin 1940–89

English writer and traveller

6 Finding in 'primitive' languages a dearth of words for moral ideas, many people assumed these ideas did not exist. But the concepts of 'good' or 'beautiful', so essential to Western thought, are meaningless unless they are rooted to things.

In Patagonia (1977)

7 If you walk hard enough, you probably don't need any other God.

In Patagonia (1977)

G. K. Chesterton 1874–1936

English essayist, novelist, and poet

on Chesterton: see **Belloc** 27:17, **Epitaphs** 109:16*; see also* **Telegrams** 316:1

8 Talk about the pews and steeples
And the Cash that goes therewith!
But the souls of Christian peoples . . .
Chuck it, Smith!

satirizing F. E. ***Smith****'s response to the Welsh Disestablishment Bill*

'Antichrist' (1915)

9 I tell you naught for your comfort,
Yea, naught for your desire,
Save that the sky grows darker yet
And the sea rises higher.

The Ballad of the White Horse (1911)

10 For the great Gaels of Ireland
Are the men that God made mad,
For all their wars are merry,
And all their songs are sad.

The Ballad of the White Horse (1911)

11 The strangest whim has seized me . . . .
After all
I think I will not hang myself today.

'Ballade of Suicide' (1915)

12 When fishes flew and forests walked
And figs grew upon thorn,
Some moment when the moon was blood
Then surely I was born.

With monstrous head and sickening cry
And ears like errant wings,
The devil's walking parody
On all four-footed things.

'The Donkey' (1900)

13 Fools! For I also had my hour;
One far fierce hour and sweet:
There was a shout about my ears,
And palms before my feet.

'The Donkey' (1900)

14 They died to save their country and they only saved the world.

'English Graves' (1922)

15 From all that terror teaches,
From lies of tongue and pen,
From all the easy speeches
That comfort cruel men,
From sale and profanation
Of honour and the sword,

From sleep and from damnation,
Deliver us, good Lord!
'A Hymn' (1915)

1 Strong gongs groaning as the guns boom far,
Don John of Austria is going to the war.
'Lepanto' (1915)

2 Before the Roman came to Rye or out to Severn strode,
The rolling English drunkard made the rolling English road.
A reeling road, a rolling road, that rambles round the shire,
And after him the parson ran, the sexton and the squire;
A merry road, a mazy road, and such as we did tread
The night we went to Birmingham by way of Beachy Head.
'The Rolling English Road' (1914)

3 For there is good news yet to hear and fine things to be seen,
Before we go to Paradise by way of Kensal Green.
'The Rolling English Road' (1914)

4 Smile at us, pay us, pass us; but do not quite forget.
For we are the people of England, that never have spoken yet.
'The Secret People' (1915)

5 Tea, although an Oriental,
Is a gentleman at least;
Cocoa is a cad and coward,
Cocoa is a vulgar beast.
'Song of Right and Wrong' (1914)

6 And Noah he often said to his wife when he sat down to dine,
'I don't care where the water goes if it doesn't get into the wine.'
'Wine and Water' (1914)

7 After the first silence the small man said to the other: 'Where does a wise man hide a pebble?'
And the tall man answered in a low voice: 'On the beach.'
The small man nodded, and after a short silence said: 'Where does a wise man hide a leaf?'
And the other answered: 'In the forest.'
The Innocence of Father Brown (1911)

8 One sees great things from the valley; only small things from the peak.
The Innocence of Father Brown (1911)

9 Thieves respect property. They merely wish the property to become their property that they may more perfectly respect it.
The Man who was Thursday (1908)

10 The men who really believe in themselves are all in lunatic asylums.
Orthodoxy (1908)

11 Tradition means giving votes to the most obscure of all classes, our ancestors. It is the democracy of the dead.
Orthodoxy (1908)

12 All conservatism is based upon the idea that if you leave things alone you leave them as they are. But you do not. If you leave a thing alone you leave it to a torrent of change.
Orthodoxy (1908)

13 It isn't that they can't see the solution. It is that they can't see the problem.
The Scandal of Father Brown (1935)

14 They say travel broadens the mind; but you must have the mind.
'The Shadow of the Shark' (1921)

15 The Christian ideal has not been tried and found wanting. It has been found difficult; and left untried.
What's Wrong with the World (1910) pt. 1 'The Unfinished Temple'

16 The prime truth of woman, the universal mother . . . that if a thing is worth doing, it is worth doing badly.
What's Wrong with the World (1910) pt. 4 'Folly and Female Education'

17 Journalism largely consists in saying 'Lord Jones Dead' to people who never knew that Lord Jones was alive.
The Wisdom of Father Brown (1914)

18 When men stop believing in God they don't believe in nothing; they believe in anything.
widely attributed, although not traced in his works; first recorded as 'The first effect of not believing in God is to believe in anything' in Emile Cammaerts *Chesterton: The Laughing Prophet* (1937)

Maurice Chevalier 1888–1972

French singer and actor

1 Considering the alternative, it's not too bad at all.

on being asked what he felt about the advancing years, on his seventy-second birthday

Michael Freedland *Maurice Chevalier* (1981)

Joseph Benedict 'Ben' Chifley 1885–1951

Australian Labor statesman, Prime Minister 1945–9

2 We have a great objective—the light on the hill—which we aim to reach by working for the betterment of mankind not only here but anywhere we may give a helping hand.

speech to the Annual Conference of the New South Wales branch of the Australian Labor Party, 12 June 1949

Erskine Childers 1870–1922

Anglo-Irish writer and Irish nationalist

see also **Last words** 190:2

3 The riddle of the sands.

title of novel (1903)

Lawton Chiles 1930–

American politician

4 You are misunderstood, maligned, viewed by the press as a Pulitzer Prize ready to be won.

on the problems of investigative journalism for politicians

in *St Petersburg (Florida) Times* 6 March 1991

Jaques Chirac 1932–

French statesman, Prime Minister 1974–6 and 1986–8, President since 1995

5 For its part, France wants you to take part in this great undertaking.

on European Monetary Union

speech to both British Houses of Parliament, 15 May 1996

Noam Chomsky 1928–

American linguistics scholar

6 Colourless green ideas sleep furiously.

illustrating that grammatical structure is independent of meaning

Syntactic Structures (1957)

7 The Internet is an élite organization; most of the population of the world has never even made a phone call.

on the limitations of the World Wide Web

in *Observer* 18 February 1996

Jean Chrétien 1934–

Canadian Liberal statesman, Prime Minister since 1993

8 Leadership means making people feel good.

in *Toronto Star* 7 June 1984

9 The art of politics is learning to walk with your back to the wall, your elbows high, and a smile on your face. It's a survival game played under the glare of lights.

Straight from the Heart (1985)

Agatha Christie 1890–1976

English writer of detective fiction

on Christie: see **Thomas** 318:19

10 He [Hercule Poirot] tapped his forehead. 'These little grey cells. It is "up to them".'

The Mysterious Affair at Styles (1920)

11 I'm a sausage machine, a perfect sausage machine.

G. C. Ramsey *Agatha Christie* (1972)

Frank E. Churchill 1901–1942

12 Who's afraid of the big bad wolf?

title of song (1933; probably written in collaboration with Ann Ronell)

Winston Churchill 1874–1965

British Conservative statesman; Prime Minister, 1940–5, 1951–5

on Churchill: see **Anonymous** 12:14, **Attlee** 15:14, 16:1, **Bevan** 34:5, **Murrow** 236:2; *see also* **Misquotations** 227:1

1 It cannot in the opinion of His Majesty's Government be classified as slavery in the extreme acceptance of the word without some risk of terminological inexactitude.

speech in the House of Commons, 22 February 1906

2 Business carried on as usual during alterations on the map of Europe.

on the self-adopted 'motto' of the British people

speech at Guildhall, 9 November 1914

3 The whole map of Europe has been changed . . . but as the deluge subsides and the waters fall short we see the dreary steeples of Fermanagh and Tyrone emerging once again.

speech in the House of Commons, 16 February 1922

4 Anyone can rat, but it takes a certain amount of ingenuity to re-rat.

on rejoining the Conservatives twenty years after leaving them for the Liberals, c.1924

Kay Halle *Irrepressible Churchill* (1966)

5 I remember, when I was a child, being taken to the celebrated Barnum's circus, which contained an exhibition of freaks and monstrosities, but the exhibit on the programme which I most desired to see was the one described as 'The Boneless Wonder'. My parents judged that that spectacle would be too revolting and demoralizing for my youthful eyes, and I have waited 50 years to see the boneless wonder sitting on the Treasury Bench.

of Ramsay ***MacDonald***

speech in the House of Commons, 28 January 1931

6 Dictators ride to and fro upon tigers which they dare not dismount. And the tigers are getting hungry.

letter, 11 November 1937

7 I cannot forecast to you the action of Russia. It is a riddle wrapped in a mystery inside an enigma.

radio broadcast, 1 October 1939

8 I have nothing to offer but blood, toil, tears and sweat.

speech in the House of Commons, 13 May 1940

9 What is our policy? . . . to wage war against a monstrous tyranny, never surpassed in the dark, lamentable catalogue of human crime.

speech in the House of Commons, 13 May 1940

10 What is our aim? . . . Victory, victory at all costs, victory in spite of all terror; victory, however long and hard the road may be; for without victory, there is no survival.

speech in the House of Commons, 13 May 1940

11 We shall not flag or fail. We shall go on to the end. We shall fight in France, we shall fight on the seas and oceans, we shall fight with growing confidence and growing strength in the air, we shall defend our island, whatever the cost may be. We shall fight on the beaches, we shall fight on the landing grounds, we shall fight in the fields and in the streets, we shall fight in the hills; we shall never surrender.

speech in the House of Commons, 4 June 1940

12 What General Weygand called the 'Battle of France' is over. I expect that the Battle of Britain is about to begin. Upon this battle depends the survival of Christian civilization. Upon it depends our own British life and the long continuity of our institutions and our Empire. The whole fury and might of the enemy must very soon be turned on us. Hitler knows that he will have to break us in this island or lose the war. If we can stand up to him all Europe may be free and the life of the world may move forward into broad, sunlit uplands; but if we fail then the whole world, including the United States, and all that we have known and cared for, will sink into the abyss of a new dark age made more sinister, and perhaps more prolonged, by the lights of a perverted science. Let us therefore brace ourselves to our duty, and so bear ourselves that, if the British Empire and its Commonwealth lasts for a thousand years, men will still say, 'This was their finest hour.'

speech in the House of Commons, 18 June 1940

1 Never in the field of human conflict was so much owed by so many to so few.

on the Battle of Britain

speech in the House of Commons, 20 August 1940

2 As far as I can see you have used every cliché except 'God is Love' and 'Please adjust your dress before leaving'.

on a long-winded report from Anthony ***Eden***

in *Life* 9 December 1940; when this story was repeated in the *Daily Mirror*, Churchill denied that it was true

3 Give us the tools and we will finish the job.

addressing President ***Roosevelt***

radio broadcast, 9 February 1941

4 The British nation is unique in this respect. They are the only people who like to be told how bad things are, who like to be told the worst.

speech in the House of Commons, 10 June 1941

5 The people of London with one voice would say to Hitler: 'You have committed every crime under the sun . . . We will have no truce or parley with you, or the grisly gang who work your wicked will. You do your worst—and we will do our best.'

speech at County Hall, London, 14 July 1941

6 It becomes still more difficult to reconcile Japanese action with prudence or even with sanity. What kind of a people do they think we are?

speech to US Congress, 26 December 1941

7 When I warned them [the French Government] that Britain would fight on alone whatever they did, their generals told their Prime Minister and his divided Cabinet, 'In three weeks England will have her neck wrung like a chicken.' Some chicken! Some neck!

speech to Canadian Parliament, 30 December 1941

8 We mean to hold our own. I have not become the King's First Minister in order to preside over the liquidation of the British Empire.

speech in London, 10 November 1942

9 Now this is not the end. It is not even the beginning of the end. But it is, perhaps, the end of the beginning.

on the Battle of Egypt

speech at the Mansion House, London, 10 November 1942

10 National compulsory insurance for all classes for all purposes from the cradle to the grave.

radio broadcast, 21 March 1943

11 There is no finer investment for any community than putting milk into babies.

radio broadcast, 21 March 1943

12 The empires of the future are the empires of the mind.

speech at Harvard, 6 September 1943

13 Unless the right hon. Gentleman changes his policy and methods and moves without the slightest delay, he will be as great a curse to this country in time of peace, as he was a squalid nuisance in time of war.

of Aneurin ***Bevan***

speech in the House of Commons, 6 December 1945

14 From Stettin in the Baltic to Trieste in the Adriatic an iron curtain has descended across the Continent.

'iron curtain' previously had been applied by others to the Soviet Union or her sphere of influence, e.g. Ethel Snowden Through Bolshevik Russia *(1920), Dr* ***Goebbels*** Das Reich *(25 February 1945), and by Churchill himself in a cable to President* ***Truman*** *(4 June 1945)*

speech at Westminster College, Fulton, Missouri, 5 March 1946

15 Democracy is the worst form of Government except all those other forms that have been tried from time to time.

speech in the House of Commons, 11 November 1947

16 This is the sort of English up with which I will not put.

Ernest Gowers *Plain Words* (1948) 'Troubles with Prepositions'

1 No, not dead. But the candle in that great turnip has gone out.

in reply to the comment 'One never hears of ***Baldwin*** *nowadays—he might as well be dead'*

Harold Nicolson diary, 17 August 1950

2 Naval tradition? Monstrous. Nothing but rum, sodomy, prayers, and the lash.

often quoted as 'rum, sodomy, and the lash', as in Peter Gretton Former Naval Person *(1968)*

Harold Nicolson diary, 17 August 1950

3 To jaw-jaw is always better than to war-war.

speech at White House, 26 June 1954

4 A modest man who has a good deal to be modest about.

of Clement ***Attlee***

in *Chicago Sunday Tribune Magazine of Books* 27 June 1954

5 I am prepared to meet my Maker. Whether my Maker is prepared for the great ordeal of meeting me is another matter.

at a news conference in Washington, 1954, in *New York Times* 25 January 1965

6 It was the nation and the race dwelling all round the globe that had the lion's heart. I had the luck to be called upon to give the roar. I also hope that I sometimes suggested to the lion the right place to use his claws.

speech at Westminster Hall, 30 November 1954

7 I have taken more out of alcohol than alcohol has taken out of me.

Quentin Reynolds *By Quentin Reynolds* (1964)

8 In defeat unbeatable: in victory unbearable.

of Lord ***Montgomery***

E. Marsh *Ambrosia and Small Beer* (1964)

9 I wrote my name at the top of the page. I wrote down the number of the question '1'. After much reflection I put a bracket round it thus '(1)'. But thereafter I could not think of anything connected with it that was either relevant or true. . . . It was from these slender indications of scholarship that Mr Welldon drew the conclusion that I was worthy to pass into Harrow. It is very much to his credit.

My Early Life (1930)

10 By being so long in the lowest form [at Harrow] I gained an immense advantage over the cleverer boys. They all went on to learn Latin and Greek . . . . But I was taught English. . . . Thus I got into my bones the essential structure of the ordinary British sentence—which is a noble thing. . . . Naturally I am biased in favour of boys learning English. I would make them all learn English: and then I would let the clever ones learn Latin as an honour, and Greek as a treat.

My Early Life (1930)

11 It is a good thing for an uneducated man to read books of quotations.

My Early Life (1930)

12 In war: resolution. In defeat: defiance. In victory: magnanimity. In peace: goodwill.

The Second World War (1948) vol. 1 epigraph

13 I felt as if I were walking with destiny, and that all my past life had been but a preparation for this hour and this trial.

The Second World War (1948) vol. 1

14 The loyalties which centre upon number one are enormous. If he trips he must be sustained. If he makes mistakes they must be covered. If he sleeps he must not be wantonly disturbed. If he is no good he must be pole-axed. But this last extreme process cannot be carried out every day; and certainly not in the days just after he has been chosen.

The Second World War (1949) vol. 2

15 If Hitler invaded hell I would make at least a favourable reference to the devil in the House of Commons.

The Second World War (1950) vol. 3

16 It may almost be said, 'Before Alamein we never had a victory. After Alamein we never had a defeat.'

The Second World War (1951) vol. 4

17 Jellicoe was the only man on either side who could lose the war in an afternoon.

The World Crisis (1927)

18 The ability to foretell what is going to happen tomorrow, next week, next month, and next year. And to have the

ability afterwards to explain why it didn't happen.
describing the qualifications desirable in a politician
B. Adler *Churchill Wit* (1965)

1 I am fond of pigs. Dogs look up to us. Cats look down on us. Pigs treat us as equals.
attributed, in M. Gilbert *Never Despair* (1988)

2 NANCY ASTOR: If I were your wife I would put poison in your coffee!
CHURCHILL: And if I were your husband I would drink it.
Consuelo Vanderbilt Balsan *Glitter and Gold* (1952)

3 A remarkable example of modern art. It certainly combines force with candour.
on the notorious 80th birthday portrait by Graham Sutherland, later destroyed by Lady Churchill
Martin Gilbert *Churchill: A Life* (1991)

4 The Prime Minister has nothing to hide from the President of the United States.
on stepping from his bath in the presence of a startled President ***Roosevelt***
recalled by Roosevelt's son in *Churchill* (BBC television series presented by Martin Gilbert, 1992)

5 A sheep in sheep's clothing.
of Clement ***Attlee***
Lord Home *The Way the Wind Blows* (1976)

6 BESSIE BRADDOCK: Winston, you're drunk.
CHURCHILL: Bessie, you're ugly. But tomorrow I shall be sober.
J. L. Lane (ed.) *Sayings of Churchill* (1992)

Count Galeazzo Ciano 1903–44

Italian fascist politician; son-in-law of Mussolini

7 Victory has a hundred fathers, but no-one wants to recognise defeat as his own.
often quoted as '. . . but defeat is an orphan'
diary, 9 September 1942

E. M. Cioran 1911–95

Romanian-born French philosopher

8 Without the possibility of suicide, I would have killed myself long ago.
in *Independent* 2 December 1989

9 I do nothing, granted. But I see the hours pass—which is better than trying to fill them.
in *Guardian* 11 May 1993

Eric Clapton 1945–

English guitarist, singer, and songwriter

10 Rock is like a battery that must always go back to blues to get recharged.
attributed; M. Palmer *Small Talk, Big Names* (1993)

Alan Clark 1928–99

British Conservative politician, son of Kenneth **Clark**
on Clark: see **Campbell** 51:11

11 There are no true friends in politics. We are all sharks circling, and waiting, for traces of blood to appear in the water.
diary, 30 November 1990

12 Our old friend economical . . . with the *actualité*.
under cross-examination at the Old Bailey during the Matrix Churchill case
in *Independent* 10 November 1992; see **Armstrong** 14:7

13 Safe is spelled D-U-L-L. Politics has got to be a fun activity, otherwise people turn their back on it.
on being selected as parliamentary candidate for Kensington and Chelsea, 24 January 1997
in *Daily Telegraph* 25 January 1997

Joe Clark 1939–

Canadian Conservative statesman, Prime Minister 1979–80

14 I'm not the greatest. I'm the best available.
of his election as Conservative leader
in *Maclean's* 21 February 1977

Kenneth Clark 1903–83

English art historian, father of Alan **Clark**

1 It's a curious fact that the all-male religions have produced no religious imagery—in most cases have positively forbidden it. The great religious art of the world is deeply involved with the female principle.

Civilisation (1969)

Arthur C. Clarke 1917–

English science fiction writer

2 Any sufficiently advanced technology is indistinguishable from magic.

The Lost Worlds of 2001 (1972)

3 If an elderly but distinguished scientist says that something is possible he is almost certainly right, but if he says that it is impossible he is very probably wrong.

in *New Yorker* 9 August 1969; see **Asimov** 14:12

4 How inappropriate to call this planet Earth when it is clearly Ocean.

in *Nature* 8 March 1990

5 The only genuine consciousness-expanding drug.

of science fiction

letter claiming coinage in *New Scientist* 2 April 1994

6 The intelligent minority of this world will mark 1 January 2001 as the real beginning of the 21st century and the Third Millennium.

in *Newsweek* 8 January 2001

Kenneth Clarke 1940–

British Conservative politician, Chancellor of the Exchequer 1993–7

7 Tell your kids to get their scooters off my lawn.

allegedly said to the Party Chairman, Brian Mawhinney, of young Central Office personnel; see **Wilson** 341:9

television report, 5 December 1996; in *Guardian* 7 December 1996

8 I do not wear a bleeper. I can't speak in soundbites. I refuse to repeat slogans. . . . I hate focus groups. I absolutely hate image consultants.

in *New Statesman* 12 February 1999

9 Blithering economic nonsense.

of Michael Portillo's position on the euro, as outlined in his Conference speech

in *Daily Telegraph* 4 October 2000

Philip 'Tubby' Clayton 1885–1972

Australian-born British clergyman, founder of Toc H

10 CHAIRMAN: What is service?
CANDIDATE: The rent we pay for our room on earth.

admission ceremony of Toc H, a society founded after the First World War to provide Christian fellowship and social service

Tresham Lever *Clayton of Toc H* (1971)

Eldridge Cleaver 1935–98

American political activist

11 You're either part of the solution or you're part of the problem.

speech in San Francisco, 1968, in R. Scheer *Eldridge Cleaver, Post Prison Writings and Speeches* (1969)

John Cleese 1939–

English comedy writer and actor

12 The audience roared with laughter and my heart sank. I was saddled with the bloody thing. It's probably why I've had to have a hip replacement.

on the Ministry of Silly Walks sketch for Monty Python

in *Mail on Sunday* 11 March 2001

John Cleese 1939– and **Connie Booth**

British comedy writer and actor; British comedy actress

see also **Monty Python's Flying Circus**

13 They're Germans. Don't mention the war.

Fawlty Towers 'The Germans' (BBC TV programme, 1975)

Georges Clemenceau
1841–1929

French statesman; Prime Minister of France, 1906–9, 1917–20

1 My home policy: I wage war; my foreign policy: I wage war. All the time I wage war.

speech to French Chamber of Deputies, 8 March 1918

2 What do you expect when I'm between two men of whom one [Lloyd George] thinks he is Napoleon and the other [Woodrow Wilson] thinks he is Jesus Christ?

to André Tardieu, on being asked why he always gave in to ***Lloyd George*** *at the Paris Peace Conference, 1918*

letter from Harold Nicolson to his wife, Vita Sackville-West, 20 May 1919

3 It is easier to make war than to make peace.

speech at Verdun, 20 July 1919

4 Oh, to be seventy again!

on seeing a pretty girl on his eightieth birthday

James Agate diary, 19 April 1938

5 War is too serious a matter to entrust to military men.

attributed to Clemenceau, e.g. in Hampden Jackson *Clemenceau and the Third Republic* (1946), but also to Briand and Talleyrand; see **Buchwald** 47:7, **de Gaulle** 88:9

Harlan Cleveland 1918–

American government official

6 The revolution of rising expectations.

phrase coined, 1950; Arthur Schlesinger *A Thousand Days* (1965)

Hillary Rodham Clinton
1947–

American lawyer, wife of Bill **Clinton**, First Lady 1993–2001

7 I am not standing by my man, like Tammy Wynette. I am sitting here because I love him, I respect him, and I honour what he's been through and what we've been through together.

interview on *60 Minutes*, CBS-TV, 27 January 1992; see **Wynette** 346:4

8 I could have stayed home and baked cookies and had teas. But what I decided was to fulfil my profession, which I entered before my husband was in public life.

comment on questions raised by rival Democratic contender Edmund G. Brown Jr.; in *Albany Times-Union* 17 March 1992

9 The great story here . . . is this vast right-wing conspiracy that has been conspiring against my husband since the day he announced for president.

interview on *Today* (NBC television), 27 January 1998

10 A hard dog to keep on the porch.

on her husband

in *Guardian* 2 August 1999

11 Today we voted as Democrats and Republicans. Tomorrow we begin again as New Yorkers.

acceptance speech on winning her seat as Senator for New York

on BBC *Today* (BBC Radio 4) 8 November 2000

William Jefferson ('Bill') Clinton 1946–

American Democratic statesman; 42nd President of the US 1993–2001; husband of Hillary Rodham **Clinton**
see also **Political sayings and slogans** 261:19

12 I experimented with marijuana a time or two. And I didn't like it, and I didn't inhale.

in *Washington Post* 30 March 1992

13 The comeback kid!

description of himself after coming second in the New Hampshire primary in the 1992 presidential election (since 1952, no presidential candidate had won the election without first winning in New Hampshire)

Michael Barone and Grant Ujifusa *The Almanac of American Politics 1994*

14 I did not have sexual relations with that woman.

in a television interview, Daily Telegraph (electronic edition) 27 January 1998

1 Peace is no longer a dream. It is a reality.
of the Northern Ireland referendum on the Good Friday agreement
in *Sunday Times* 24 May 1998

2 I did have a relationship with Ms Lewinsky that was not appropriate. In fact, it was wrong.
broadcast to the American people, 18 August 1998
in *Times* 19 August 1998

3 It depends on what the meaning of 'is' is.
videotaped evidence to the grand jury; tapes broadcast 21 September 1998
in *Guardian* 22 September 1998

4 Today we are learning the language in which God created life.
on the deciphering of 90% of the human genome
in *Independent* 27 June 2000

5 The American people have spoken—but it's going to take a little while to determine exactly what they said.
on the US presidential election
in *Mail on Sunday* 12 November 2000

6 I tried to walk a fine line between acting lawfully and testifying falsely but I now recognize that I did not fully accomplish that goal.
in *Daily Telegraph* 20 January 2001

Brian Clough 1935–

English football player and manager

7 If I'm ever feeling a bit uppity, whenever I get on my high horse, I go and take another look at my dear Mam's mangle that has pride of place in the dining-room.
Clough: The Autobiography (1994)

Kurt Cobain 1967–94

American rock singer, guitarist, and songwriter, husband of Courtney **Love**
see also **Young** 349:12

8 I'd rather be dead than cool.
'Stay Away' (1991 song)

Claud Cockburn 1904–81

British writer and journalist

9 Small earthquake in Chile. Not many dead.
winning entry for a dullest headline competition at The Times
In Time of Trouble (1956)

Jean Cocteau 1889–1963

French dramatist and film director
on Cocteau: see **Anonymous** 12:6

10 Life is a horizontal fall.
Opium (1930)

11 Being tactful in audacity is knowing how far one can go too far.
Le Rappel à l'ordre (1926)

12 The worst tragedy for a poet is to be admired through being misunderstood.
Le Rappel à l'ordre (1926)

13 If it has to choose who is to be crucified, the crowd will always save Barabbas.
Le Rappel à l'ordre (1926)

J. M. Coetzee 1940–

South African novelist

14 The essence of servanthood is the servant's intimacy with the master's dirt.
In the Heart of the Country (1977)

15 When we dream that we are dreaming, the moment of awakening is at hand.
In the Heart of the Country (1977)

George M. Cohan 1878–1942

American actor-manager and dramatist

16 Over there, over there,
Send the word, send the word over there
That the Yanks are coming, the Yanks are coming,
The drums rum-tumming everywhere.
So prepare, say a prayer,
Send the word, send the word to beware.
We'll be over, we're coming over
And we won't come back till it's over, over there.
'Over There' (1917 song)

Leonard Cohen 1934–

Canadian singer and writer

1 I don't consider myself a pessimist. I think of a pessimist as someone who is waiting for it to rain. And I feel soaked to the skin.

in *Observer* 2 May 1993

David Coleman 1926–

British sports commentator

2 He just can't believe what isn't happening to him.

attributed, 1980

3 That's the fastest time ever run—but it's not as fast as the world record.

Barry Fantoni (ed.) *Private Eye's Colemanballs 3* (1986)

Ornette Coleman 1930–

American jazz musician

4 Jazz is the only music in which the same note can be played night after night but differently each time.

W. H. Mellers *Music in a New Found Land* (1964)

Colette 1873–1954

French novelist

5 The world of the emotions that are so lightly called physical.

Le Blé en herbe (1923)

6 Her childhood, then her adolescence, had taught her patience, hope, silence and the easy manipulation of the weapons and virtues of all prisoners.

Chéri (1920)

7 Let's buy a pack of cards, good wine, bridge scores, knitting needles, all the paraphernalia needed to fill an enormous void, everything needed to hide that horror—the old woman.

Chéri (1920)

R. G. Collingwood 1889–1943

English philosopher and archaeologist

8 Perfect freedom is reserved for the man who lives by his own work and in that work does what he wants to do.

Speculum Mentis (1924)

Charles Collins

English songwriter

9 My old man said, 'Follow the van,
Don't dilly-dally on the way!'

'Don't Dilly-Dally on the Way' (1919 song, with Fred Leigh); popularized by Marie Lloyd

Michael Collins 1890–1922

Irish nationalist leader and politician

10 Think—what I have got for Ireland? Something which she has wanted these past seven hundred years. Will anyone be satisfied at the bargain? Will anyone? I tell you this—early this morning I signed my death warrant.

on signing the treaty establishing the Irish Free State; he was shot from ambush in the following year

letter, 6 December 1921

on arriving at Dublin Castle for the handover by British forces on 16 January 1922, and being told that he was seven minutes late:

11 We've been waiting seven hundred years, you can have the seven minutes.

Tim Pat Coogan *Michael Collins* (1990); attributed

Phil Collins 1951–

British rock musician

12 I thought punk was a good idea—like someone shaking an apple tree until all the bad ones fell off and you'd just got the good ones left.

D. Bowler and D. Dray *Genesis: a biography* (1992)

John Robert Colombo 1936–

Canadian writer

13 Canada could have enjoyed:
English government,

French culture,
and American know-how.

Instead it ended up with:
English know-how,
French government,
and American culture.

'O Canada' (1965)

Betty Comden 1919– and Adolph Green 1915–

American songwriters

1 The party's over, it's time to call it a day.

'The Party's Over' (1956 song); see **Crosland** 81:11

Henry Steele Commager 1902–

American historian

2 It was observed half a century ago that what is a stone wall to a layman, to a corporate lawyer is a triumphant arch. Much the same might be said of civil rights and freedoms. To the layman the Bill of Rights seems to be a stone wall against the misuse of power. But in the hands of a congressional committee, or often enough of a judge, it turns out to be so full of exceptions and qualifications that it might be a whole series of arches.

'The Right to Dissent' in *Current History* October 1955; see below

A law, Hinnissey, that might look like a wall to you or me wud look like a triumphal arch to th'expeeryenced eye iv a lawyer.

Peter Finley Dunne (1867–1936) 'Mr Dooley on the Power of the Press' in *American Magazine* 1906

Denis Compton 1918–97

British cricketer

3 I couldn't bat for the length of time required to score 500. I'd get bored and fall over.

to Brian Lara, who had recently scored 501 not out, a world record in first-class cricket

in *Daily Telegraph* 27 June 1994

Ivy Compton-Burnett 1884–1969

English novelist

4 Time has too much credit . . . It is not a great healer. It is an indifferent and perfunctory one. Sometimes it does not heal at all. And sometimes when it seems to, no healing has been necessary.

Darkness and Day (1951)

5 Well, of course, people are only human . . . But it really does not seem much for them to be.

A Family and a Fortune (1939)

6 People don't resent having nothing nearly as much as too little.

A Family and a Fortune (1939)

7 There are different kinds of wrong. The people sinned against are not always the best.

The Mighty and their Fall (1961)

8 A leopard does not change his spots, or change his feeling that spots are rather a credit.

More Women than Men (1933)

9 We must use words as they are used or stand aside from life.

Mother and Son (1955)

10 There is more difference within the sexes than between them.

Mother and Son (1955)

Gerry Conlon 1954–

first member of the Guildford Four to be released from prison

11 The life sentence goes on. It's like a runaway train that you can't just get off.

of life after his conviction was quashed by the Court of Appeal

in *Irish Post* 13 September 1997

Sean Connery 1930–

Scottish actor

12 It is Scotland's rightful heritage that its people should create a modern

Parliament . . . This entire issue is above and beyond any political party.
of Scottish devolution, in the Referendum campaign
speech in Edinburgh, 7 September 1997

1 We have waited nearly 300 years. My hope is that it will evolve with dignity and integrity and it will truly reflect the new voice of Scotland. My position on Scotland has never changed in 30-odd years. Scotland should be nothing less than an equal of other nations of the world.
in *Daily Telegraph* 27 April 1999

Billy Connolly 1942–

Scottish comedian

2 Marriage is a wonderful invention; but, then again, so is a bicycle repair kit.
Duncan Campbell *Billy Connolly* (1976)

3 I don't want a Stormont. I don't want a wee pretendy government in Edinburgh.
on the prospective Scottish Parliament; often quoted as 'a wee pretendy Parliament'
interview on *Breakfast with Frost* (BBC TV), 9 February 1997

4 When I read 'Be real, don't get caught acting,' I thought, 'How the hell do you do that?'
John Miller *Judi Dench: With a Crack in Her Voice* (1998)

Cyril Connolly 1903–74

English writer

5 As repressed sadists are supposed to become policemen or butchers, so those with an irrational fear of life become publishers.
Enemies of Promise (1938)

6 Whom the gods wish to destroy they first call promising.
Enemies of Promise (1938)

7 There is no more sombre enemy of good art than the pram in the hall.
Enemies of Promise (1938)

8 I have called this style the Mandarin style, since it is beloved by literary pundits, by those who would make the written word as unlike as possible to the spoken one. It is the style of those writers whose tendency is to make their language convey more than they mean or more than they feel, it is the style of most artists and all humbugs.
Enemies of Promise (1938)

9 Imprisoned in every fat man a thin one is wildly signalling to be let out.
The Unquiet Grave (1944); see **Amis** 8:3, **Orwell** 249:9

10 Our memories are card-indexes consulted, and then put back in disorder by authorities whom we do not control.
during the Blitz
The Unquiet Grave (1944)

11 M is for Marx
And Movement of Masses
And Massing of Arses.
And Clashing of Classes.
'Where Engels Fears to Tread' (1945)

12 It is closing time in the gardens of the West and from now on an artist will be judged only by the resonance of his solitude or the quality of his despair.
in *Horizon* December 1949—January 1950

13 It is the one war in which everyone changes sides.
on the generation gap
Tom Driberg, speech in House of Commons, 30 October 1959

James Connolly 1868–1916

Irish nationalist and labour leader; executed after the Easter Rising, 1916

14 The worker is the slave of capitalist society, the female worker is the slave of that slave.
The Re-conquest of Ireland (1915)

Jimmy Connors 1952–

American tennis player

15 New Yorkers love it when you spill your guts out there. Spill your guts at Wimbledon and they make you stop and clean it up.
at Flushing Meadow
in *Guardian* 24 December 1984 'Sports Quotes of the Year'

Joseph Conrad 1857–1924

Polish-born British novelist

1 The horror! The horror!
Heart of Darkness (1902)

2 The terrorist and the policeman both come from the same basket.
The Secret Agent (1907)

3 Reality, as usual, beats fiction out of sight.
commenting on 'this wartime atmosphere'
letter 11 August 1915

Shirley Conran 1932–

English writer

4 Life is too short to stuff a mushroom.
Superwoman (1975)

5 Conran's Law of Housework—it expands to fill the time available plus half an hour.
Superwoman 2 (1977); see **Parkinson** 254:5

A. J. Cook 1885–1931

English labour leader; Secretary of the Miners' Federation of Great Britain, 1924–31

6 Not a penny off the pay, not a second on the day.
often quoted with 'minute' substituted for 'second'
speech at York, 3 April 1926

Robin Cook 1946–

British Labour politician, Foreign Secretary 1997–2001

7 Our foreign policy must have an ethical dimension and must support the demands of other people for the democratic rights on which we insist for ourselves.
mission statement by the new Foreign Secretary, 12 May 1997
in *Times* 13 May 1997

Calvin Coolidge 1872–1933

American Republican statesman, 30th President of the US, 1923–9
on Coolidge: see **Anonymous** 12:8, **Parker** 253:17

8 There is no right to strike against the public safety by anybody, anywhere, any time.
telegram to Samuel Gompers, 14 September 1919

9 The chief business of the American people is business.
speech in Washington, 17 January 1925

10 I do not choose to run for President in nineteen twenty-eight.
statement issued at Rapid City, South Dakota, 2 August 1927

11 That man has offered me unsolicited advice for six years, all of it bad.
in 1928, when asked to support the Presidential nomination of his eventual successor ***Herbert Hoover***
Donald R. McCoy *Calvin Coolidge: the Quiet President* (1967)

when asked by Mrs Coolidge what a sermon had been about:

12 'Sins,' he said. 'Well, what did he say about sin?' 'He was against it.'
John H. McKee *Coolidge: Wit and Wisdom* (1933); perhaps apocryphal

13 They hired the money, didn't they?
on war debts incurred by England and others
J. H. McKee *Coolidge: Wit and Wisdom* (1933)

14 Nothing in the world can take the place of persistence. Talent will not; nothing is more common than unsuccessful men with talent. Genius will not; unrewarded genius is almost a proverb. Education will not; the world is full of educated derelicts. Persistence and determination are omnipotent. The slogan 'press on' has solved and always will solve the problems of the human race.
attributed in the programme of a memorial service for Coolidge in 1933

15 When a great many people are unable to find work, unemployment results.
attributed

Alice Cooper 1948–

American rock singer

1 The hippies wanted peace and love. We wanted Ferraris, blondes and switchblades.

in *Independent* 5 May 2001

Duff Cooper 1890–1954

British Conservative politician and writer

2 Your two stout lovers frowning at one another across the hearth rug, while your small, but perfectly formed one kept the party in a roar.

letter to Lady Diana Manners, later his wife, October 1914

Artemis Cooper *Durable Fire* (1983)

Wendy Cope 1945–

English poet

3 Bloody men are like bloody buses—
You wait for about a year
And as soon as one approaches your stop
Two or three others appear.

'Bloody Men' (1992)

4 Making cocoa for Kingsley Amis.

title of poem (1986)

5 I used to think all poets were Byronic—
Mad, bad and dangerous to know.
And then I met a few. Yes it's ironic—
I used to think all poets were Byronic.
They're mostly wicked as a ginless tonic
And wild as pension plans.

'Triolet' (1986); see below

Mad, bad, and dangerous to know.

Lady Caroline Lamb (1785–1828) writing of Byron in her journal after their first meeting at a ball in March 1812; Elizabeth Jenkins *Lady Caroline Lamb* (1932)

Aaron Copland 1900–90

American composer, pianist, and conductor

6 The whole problem can be stated quite simply by asking, 'Is there a meaning to music?' My answer to that would be, 'Yes.' And 'Can you state in so many words what the meaning is?' My answer to that would be, 'No.'

What to Listen for in Music (1939)

Francis Ford Coppola 1939–

American film director, writer, and producer

7 Your work parallels your life, but in the sense of a glass full of water where people look at it and say, 'Oh, the water's the same shape as the glass!'

in *Guardian* 15 October 1988

Ralph Cornes

8 Computers are anti-Faraday machines. He said he couldn't understand anything until he could count it, while computers count everything and understand nothing.

in *Guardian* 28 March 1991

Bernard Cornfeld 1927–

American businessman

9 Do you sincerely want to be rich?

stock question to salesmen

C. Raw et al. *Do You Sincerely Want to be Rich?* (1971)

Frances Cornford 1886–1960

English poet; wife of Francis M. **Cornford**

10 How long ago Hector took off his plume,
Not wanting that his little son should cry,
Then kissed his sad Andromache goodbye—
And now we three in Euston waiting-room.

'Parting in Wartime' (1948)

11 O fat white woman whom nobody loves,
Why do you walk through the fields in gloves,
When the grass is soft as the breast of doves
And shivering-sweet to the touch?
O why do you walk through the fields in gloves,
Missing so much and so much?

'To a Fat Lady seen from the Train' (1910)

Francis M. Cornford 1874–1943

English classical scholar; husband of Frances **Cornford**

1 Every public action, which is not customary, either is wrong, or, if it is right, is a dangerous precedent. It follows that nothing should ever be done for the first time.

Microcosmographia Academica (1908)

2 That branch of the art of lying which consists in very nearly deceiving your friends without quite deceiving your enemies.

on propaganda

Microcosmographia Academica (1922 ed.)

Baron Pierre de Coubertin 1863–1937

French sportsman and educationist, founder of the modern Olympics

3 The important thing in life is not the victory but the contest; the essential thing is not to have won but to have fought well.

speech in London, 24 July 1908

Émile Coué 1857–1926

French psychologist

4 Every day, in every way, I am getting better and better.

to be said 15 to 20 times, morning and evening

De la suggestion et de ses applications (1915)

Douglas Coupland 1961–

Canadian author

5 Generation X: tales for an accelerated culture.

title of book (1991)

Jacques Cousteau 1910–97

French underwater explorer

see also **Epitaphs** 109:2

6 The sea is the universal sewer.

testimony before the House Committee on Science and Astronautics, 28 January 1971

7 Mankind has probably done more damage to the earth in the 20th century than in all of previous human history.

'Consumer Society is the Enemy' in *New Perspectives Quarterly* Summer 1996

Noël Coward 1899–1973

English dramatist, actor, and composer

8 Dance, dance, dance, little lady!
Leave tomorrow behind.

'Dance, Little Lady' (1928 song)

9 Don't let's be beastly to the Germans
When our Victory is ultimately won.

'Don't Let's Be Beastly to the Germans' (1943 song)

10 I believe that since my life began
The most I've had is just
A talent to amuse.

'If Love Were All' (1929 song)

11 I'll see you again,
Whenever spring breaks through again.

'I'll See You Again' (1929 song)

12 London Pride has been handed down to us.
London Pride is a flower that's free.
London Pride means our own dear town to us,
And our pride it for ever will be.

'London Pride' (1941 song)

13 Mad about the boy,
It's pretty funny but I'm mad about the boy.
He has a gay appeal
That makes me feel
There may be something sad about the boy.

'Mad about the Boy' (1932 song)

14 Mad dogs and Englishmen
Go out in the midday sun.
The Japanese don't care to,
The Chinese wouldn't dare to,

The Hindus and Argentines sleep firmly
from twelve to one,
But Englishmen detest a siesta.
'Mad Dogs and Englishmen' (1931 song)

1 Don't put your daughter on the stage,
Mrs Worthington,
Don't put your daughter on the stage.
'Mrs Worthington' (1935 song)

2 Poor little rich girl
You're a bewitched girl,
Better beware!
'Poor Little Rich Girl' (1925 song)

3 Someday I'll find you,
Moonlight behind you,
True to the dream I am dreaming.
'Someday I'll Find You' (1930 song)

4 The Stately Homes of England,
How beautiful they stand,
To prove the upper classes
Have still the upper hand.
'The Stately Homes of England' (1938 song); see below

The stately homes of England,
How beautiful they stand!
Amidst their tall ancestral trees,
O'er all the pleasant land.
Felicia Hemans (1793–1835) 'The Homes of England' (1849)

5 There are bad times just around the
corner,
There are dark clouds travelling through
the sky
And it's no good whining
About a silver lining
For we know from experience that they
won't roll by.
'There are Bad Times Just Around the Corner' (1953 song)

6 Very flat, Norfolk.
Private Lives (1930)

7 Extraordinary how potent cheap music is.
Private Lives (1930)

8 Certain women should be struck regularly, like gongs.
Private Lives (1930)

9 Dear 338171 (May I call you 338?).
letter to T. E. Lawrence, 25 August 1930

10 Just say the lines and don't trip over the furniture.
advice on acting
D. Richards *The Wit of Noël Coward* (1968)

11 Television is for appearing on, not looking at.
D. Richards *The Wit of Noël Coward* (1968)

refusing to allow his biographer to out him as gay, despite the example of the theatre critic T. C. Worsley:

12 You forget that the great British public would not care if Cuthbert Worsley had slept with mice.
in *Independent on Sunday Magazine* 12 November 1995

Lord Cranborne 1946–

British Conservative peer, former Leader in the Lords

13 [I was sacked for] running in like an ill-trained spaniel.
of his independent negotiation with the government on Lords reform, and subsequent dismissal by William Hague
in *Daily Telegraph* 3 December 1998

14 There was this odd mixture of misery and the limpet—the miserable limpet if you like—which was a great inhibition to his premiership.
of John ***Major***
on *The Major Years* pt 3, BBC1, 25 October 1999

15 One of the reasons he would be good is that he is idle. There is a lot to be said for idle leaders.
on Kenneth ***Clarke*** *as candidate for the Conservative leadership*
in *Sunday Times* 24 June 2001

Hart Crane 1899–1932

American poet

16 Stars scribble on our eyes the frosty
sagas,
The gleaming cantos of unvanquished
space.
'Cape Hatteras' (1930)

17 Cowslip and shad-blow, flaked like
tethered foam
Around bared teeth of stallions, bloomed
that spring

When first I read thy lines, rife as the loam
Of prairies, yet like breakers cliffward leaping!
. . . My hand
in yours,
Walt Whitman—
so—

'Cape Hatteras' (1930)

1 We have seen
The moon in lonely alleys make
A grail of laughter of an empty ash can.

'Chaplinesque' (1926)

2 So the 20th Century—so
whizzed the Limited—roared by and left
three men, still hungry on the tracks, ploddingly
watching the tail lights wizen and converge, slipping
gimleted and neatly out of sight.

'The River' (1930)

3 O Sleepless as the river under thee,
Vaulting the sea, the prairies' dreaming sod,
Unto us lowliest sometime sweep, descend
And of the curveship lend a myth to God.

'To Brooklyn Bridge' (1930)

4 You who desired so much—in vain to ask—
Yet fed your hunger like an endless task,
Dared dignify the labor, bless the quest—
Achieved that stillness ultimately best,

Being, of all, least sought for: Emily, hear!

'To Emily Dickinson' (1927)

Robert Crawford 1959–

Scottish poet

5 In Scotland we live between and across languages.

Identifying Poets (1993)

Edith Cresson 1934–

French politician and European Commissioner

6 *Je ne regrette rien.*
I have no regrets.

on the inquiry into fraud at the European Commission

in an interview, 16 March 1999; '*Non, je ne regrette rien*' was the title of a song (1960) by Michel Vaucaire, sung by Edith Piaf

7 Perhaps I have been a little careless.

after the appearance of the report into fraud at the European Commission

in an interview, 16 March 1999

Ivor Crewe 1945–

British political scientist

8 The British public has always displayed a healthy cynicism of MPs. They have taken it for granted that MPs are self-serving impostors and hypocrites who put party before country and self before party.

addressing the Nolan inquiry into standards in public life

in *Guardian* 18 January 1995

Francis Crick 1916–

English biophysicist

on Crick: see **Wolpert** 344:5

9 Almost all aspects of life are engineered at the molecular level, and without understanding molecules we can only have a very sketchy understanding of life itself.

What Mad Pursuit (1988)

Francis Crick 1916– and James D. Watson 1928–

English biophysicist; American biologist

10 It has not escaped our notice that the specific pairing we have postulated immediately suggests a possible copying mechanism for the genetic material.

proposing the double helix as the structure of DNA, and hence the chemical mechanism of heredity

in *Nature* 25 April 1953

Quentin Crisp 1908–99

English writer

1 There was no need to do any housework at all. After the first four years the dirt doesn't get any worse.

The Naked Civil Servant (1968)

2 An autobiography is an obituary in serial form with the last instalment missing.

The Naked Civil Servant (1968)

Julian Critchley 1930–2000

British Conservative politician and journalist

3 The only safe pleasure for a parliamentarian is a bag of boiled sweets.

in *Listener* 10 June 1982

4 She cannot see an institution without hitting it with her handbag.

of Margaret ***Thatcher***

in *The Times* 21 June 1982

Richmal Crompton 1890–1969

English author of books for children

5 I'll thcream and thcream and thcream till I'm thick. I can.

Violet Elizabeth's habitual threat

Still—William (1925)

David Cronenberg 1943–

Canadian film director

see also **Taglines for films** 314:1

6 Canadians are very reluctant to confront the creature from the Black Lagoon—which is our collective unconscious, really. But that creature wants to come out.

in *Maclean's* 14 February 1983; attributed

7 Everybody's a mad scientist, and life is their lab. We're all trying to experiment to find a way to live, to solve problems, to fend off madness and chaos.

Chris Rodley (ed.) *Cronenberg on Cronenberg* (1992), ch. 1

8 I don't have a moral plan. I'm a Canadian.

attributed

Bing Crosby 1903–77

American singer and film actor

on Crosby: see also **Epitaphs** 109:12

9 Where the blue of the night
Meets the gold of the day,
Someone waits for me.

'Where the Blue of the Night' (1931 song); with Roy Turk and Fred Ahlert

Anthony Crosland 1918–77

British Labour politician; Foreign Secretary 1976–7

10 If it's the last thing I do, I'm going to destroy every fucking grammar school in England. And Wales, and Northern Ireland.

c.1965, while Secretary of State for Education and Science

Susan Crosland *Tony Crosland* (1982)

11 The party's over.

cutting back central government's support for rates, as Minister of the Environment in the 1970s

Anthony Sampson *The Changing Anatomy of Britain* (1982); see **Comden** 74:1

Amanda Cross 1926–

American crime writer

12 In former days, everyone found the assumption of innocence so easy; today we find fatally easy the assumption of guilt.

Poetic Justice (1970)

Douglas Cross

American songwriter

13 I left my heart in San Francisco
High on a hill it calls to me.
To be where little cable cars climb half-way to the stars,
The morning fog may chill the air—
I don't care!

'I Left My Heart in San Francisco' (1954 song)

Richard Crossman 1907–74

British Labour politician
on Crossman: see **Dalton** 83:12

1 While there is death there is hope.
on the death of Hugh ***Gaitskell*** *in 1963*
Tam Dalyell *Dick Crossman* (1989)

2 The Civil Service is profoundly deferential—'Yes, Minister! No, Minister! If you wish it, Minister!'
diary, 22 October 1964

Aleister Crowley 1875–1947

English diabolist

3 Do what thou wilt shall be the whole of the Law.
Book of the Law (1909); see below

Do what you like.
François Rabelais (c.1494–c.1553) *Gargantua* (1534)

e. e. cummings 1894–1962

American poet

4 anyone lived in a pretty how town
(with up so floating many bells down)
spring summer autumn winter
he sang his didn't he danced his did.
50 Poems (1949) no. 29

5 'next to of course god america i
love you land of the pilgrims' and so forth oh
say can you see by the dawn's early my
country 'tis of centuries come and go
and are no more what of it we should worry.
is 5 (1926)

6 a politician is an arse upon
which everyone has sat except a man.
1 x 1 (1944) no. 10

7 plato told

him: he couldn't
believe it (jesus

told him; he
wouldn't believe
it).
1 x 1 (1944) no. 13

8 pity this busy monster, manunkind,
not. Progress is a comfortable disease.
1 x 1 (1944) no. 14

9 We doctors know
a hopeless case if—listen: there's a hell
of a good universe next door; let's go.
1 x 1 (1944) no. 14

10 when man determined to destroy
himself he picked the was
of shall and finding only why
smashed it into because.
1 x 1 (1944) no. 26

11 i like my body when it is with your
body. It is so quite new a thing.
Muscles better and nerves more.
'Sonnets–Actualities' no. 8 (1925)

12 the Cambridge ladies who live in furnished souls
are unbeautiful and have comfortable minds.
'Sonnets–Realities' no. 1 (1923)

William Thomas Cummings 1903–45

American priest

13 There are no atheists in the foxholes.
C. P. Romulo *I Saw the Fall of the Philippines* (1943)

Peter Cunnah

see **Petrie**

J. V. Cunningham 1911–

American poet

14 And all's coherent.
Search in this gloss
No text inherent:
The text was loss.

The gain is gloss.
'To the Reader' (1947)

Mario Cuomo 1932–

American Democratic politician

15 You campaign in poetry. You govern in prose.
in *New Republic*, Washington, DC, 8 April 1985

Don Cupitt 1934–

British theologian

1 Christmas is the Disneyfication of Christianity.

in *Independent* 19 December 1996

John Curtin 1885–1945

Australian Labor statesman, Prime Minister 1941–5

2 Australia looks to America, free of any pangs as to our traditional links or kinship with the United Kingdom.

of the threat from Japan, and British reluctance to recall Australian troops from the Middle East

in *Herald* (Melbourne) 27 December 1941

3 Poor Bob. It's very sad; he would rather make a point than make a friend.

of Robert ***Menzies***

Howard Beale *This Inch of Time* (1977); attributed

Tony Curtis 1925–

American actor

4 It's like kissing Hitler.

when asked what it was like to kiss Marilyn ***Monroe***

A. Hunter *Tony Curtis* (1985)

Michael Curtiz 1888–1962

Hungarian-born American film director

5 Bring on the empty horses!

while directing The Charge of the Light Brigade *(1936 film)*

David Niven *Bring on the Empty Horses* (1975)

Lord Curzon 1859–1925

British Conservative politician; Viceroy of India 1898–1905

6 When a group of Cabinet Ministers begins to meet separately and to discuss independent action, the death-tick is audible in the rafters.

in November 1922, shortly before the fall of ***Lloyd George****'s Coalition Government*

David Gilmour *Curzon* (1994)

7 Not even a public figure. A man of no experience. And of the utmost insignificance.

of Stanley ***Baldwin****, appointed Prime Minister in 1923 in succession to Bonar Law*

Harold Nicolson *Curzon: the Last Phase* (1934)

8 Dear me, I never knew that the lower classes had such white skins.

supposedly said by Curzon when watching troops bathing during the First World War

K. Rose *Superior Person* (1969)

9 Gentlemen do not take soup at luncheon.

E. L. Woodward *Short Journey* (1942)

Dalai Lama 1935–

Spiritual head of Tibetan Buddhism

10 Frankly speaking it is difficult to trust the Chinese. Once bitten by a snake you feel suspicious even when you see a piece of rope.

attributed, 1981

Richard J. Daley 1902–76

American Democratic politician and Mayor of Chicago

11 The policeman isn't there to create disorder; the policeman is there to preserve disorder.

to the press, on the riots during the Democratic Convention in 1968

Milton N. Rakove *Don't Make No Waves: Don't Back No Losers* (1975)

Hugh Dalton 1887–1962

British Labour politician

on Dalton: see **Birch** 36:1

12 He is loyal to his own career but only incidentally to anything or anyone else.

of Richard ***Crossman***

diary, 17 September 1941

Tam Dalyell 1932–

Scottish-born Labour politician

13 Under the new Bill, shall I still be able to vote on many matters in relation to West Bromwich but not West Lothian, as I was under the last Bill, and will my right hon.

Friend [James Callaghan, MP for Cardiff] be able to vote on many matters in relation to Carlisle but not Cardiff?
formulation of the 'West Lothian question', identifying the constitutional anomaly that would arise if devolved assemblies were established for Scotland and for Wales but not for England
in the House of Commons, 3 November 1977

1 The West-Lothian-West-Bromwich problem pinpoints a basic design fault in the steering of the devolutionary coach which will cause it to crash into the side of the road.
in the House of Commons, 14 November 1977

2 I make no apology for returning yet again to the subject of the sinking of the *Belgrano*.
on the question of whether the Argentine cruiser Belgrano *had been a legitimate target in the Falklands War*
in the House of Commons, 13 May 1983

Joe Darion 1917–2001

American songwriter

3 Dream the impossible dream.
'The Quest' (1965 song)

Bill Darnell

Canadian environmentalist

4 Make it a *green* peace.
at a meeting of the Don't Make a Wave Committee, which preceded the formation of Greenpeace
in Vancouver, 1970; Robert Hunter *The Greenpeace Chronicle* (1979); see **Hunter** 163:5

Clarence Darrow 1857–1938

American lawyer

5 I do not consider it an insult, but rather a compliment to be called an agnostic. I do not pretend to know where many ignorant men are sure—that is all that agnosticism means.
speech at trial of John Thomas Scopes for teaching Darwin's theory of evolution in school, 15 July 1925

6 I would like to see a time when man loves his fellow man and forgets his colour or his creed. We will never be civilized until that time comes. I know the Negro race has a long road to go. I believe that the life of the Negro race has been a life of tragedy, of injustice, of oppression. The law has made him equal, but man has not.
speech in Detroit, 19 May 1926

7 When I was a boy I was told that anybody could become President. I'm beginning to believe it.
Irving Stone *Clarence Darrow for the Defence* (1941)

Francis Darwin 1848–1925

English botanist; son of Charles Darwin

8 In science the credit goes to the man who convinces the world, not to the man to whom the idea first occurs.
in *Eugenics Review* April 1914

Ian Davidson 1950–

Scottish Labour politician

9 Anyone in the Labour Party hierarchy who believes that new Labour is popular in Scotland should get out more.
after Labour was beaten into third place in the Ayr by-election for the Scottish Parliament
in *Scotsman* 18 March 2000

Robertson Davies 1913–95

Canadian novelist

10 I see Canada as a country torn between a very northern, rather extraordinary, mystical spirit which it fears and its desire to present itself to the world as a Scotch banker.
The Enthusiasms of Robertson Davies (1990)

11 It's an excellent life of somebody else. But I've really lived inside myself, and she can't get in there.
on a biography of himself
interview in *The Times* 4 April 1995

Ron Davies 1946–

British Labour politician

1 It was a moment of madness for which I have subsequently paid a very, very heavy price.

of the episode on Clapham Common leading to his resignation as Welsh Secretary

interview with BBC Wales and HTV, 30 October 1998

W. H. Davies 1871–1940

Welsh poet

2 A rainbow and a cuckoo's song
May never come together again;
May never come
This side the tomb.

'A Great Time' (1914)

3 It was the Rainbow gave thee birth,
And left thee all her lovely hues.

'Kingfisher' (1910)

4 What is this life if, full of care,
We have no time to stand and stare.

'Leisure' (1911)

5 Come, lovely Morning, rich in frost
On iron, wood and glass . . .

Come, rich and lovely Winter's Eve,
That seldom handles gold;
And spread your silver sunsets out,
In glittering fold on fold.

'Silver Hours' (1932)

Bette Davis

see **Film lines** 115:4, 115:7, 117:12

Philip J. Davis 1923– and Reuben Hersh 1927–

American mathematicians

6 One began to hear it said that World War I was the chemists' war, World War II was the physicists' war, World War III (may it never come) will be the mathematicians' war.

The Mathematical Experience (1981)

Sammy Davis Jnr. 1925–90

American entertainer

7 Being a star has made it possible for me to get insulted in places where the average Negro could never *hope* to go and get insulted.

Yes I Can (1965)

Richard Dawkins 1941–

English biologist

8 [Natural selection] has no vision, no foresight, no sight at all. If it can be said to play the role of watchmaker in nature, it is the *blind* watchmaker.

The Blind Watchmaker (1986); see below

Suppose I had found a *watch* upon the ground, and it should be enquired how the watch happened to be in that place . . . the inference, we think, is inevitable; that the watch must have had a maker.

William Paley (1743–1805) *Natural Theology* (1802)

9 However many ways there may be of being alive, it is certain that there are vastly more ways of being dead.

The Blind Watchmaker (1986)

10 The essence of life is statistical improbability on a colossal scale.

The Blind Watchmaker (1986); see **Fisher** 114:11

11 The selfish gene.

title of book (1976)

12 They are in you and in me; they created us, body and mind; and their preservation is the ultimate rationale for our existence . . . they go by the name of genes, and we are their survival machines.

The Selfish Gene (1976)

Christopher Dawson 1889–1970

English historian of ideas and social culture

13 As soon as men decide that all means are permitted to fight an evil, then their good

becomes indistinguishable from the evil that they set out to destroy.
The Judgement of the Nations (1942)

Lord Dawson of Penn
1864–1945

English doctor; physician to King George V
on Dawson: see **Moynihan** 233:11

1 The King's life is moving peacefully towards its close.
bulletin, 20 January 1936; K. Rose *King George V* (1983)

Robin Day 1923–2000

British broadcaster
on Day: see **Howerd** 160:13

2 Television . . . thrives on unreason, and unreason thrives on television . . . [Television] strikes at the emotions rather than the intellect.
Grand Inquisitor (1989)

3 I was never a journalist. I was always an institution.
in *Independent* 29 January 2000

Moshe Dayan 1915–81

Israeli statesman and general

4 War is the most exciting and dramatic thing in life. In fighting to the death you feel terribly relaxed when you manage to come through.
in *Observer* 13 February 1972

Cecil Day-Lewis 1904–72

Anglo-Irish poet and critic

5 Do not expect again a phoenix hour,
The triple-towered sky, the dove complaining,
Sudden the rain of gold and heart's first ease
Traced under trees by the eldritch light of sundown.
'From Feathers to Iron' (1935)

6 Tempt me no more; for I
Have known the lightning's hour,
The poet's inward pride,
The certainty of power.
The Magnetic Mountain (1933)

7 You that love England, who have an ear for her music,
The slow movement of clouds in benediction,
Clear arias of light thrilling over her uplands,
Over the chords of summer sustained peacefully.
The Magnetic Mountain (1933)

8 Tell them in England, if they ask
What brought us to these wars,
To this plateau beneath the night's
Grave manifold of stars—

It was not fraud or foolishness,
Glory, revenge, or pay:
We came because our open eyes
Could see no other way.
'The Volunteer' (1938)

9 It is the logic of our times,
No subject for immortal verse—
That we who lived by honest dreams
Defend the bad against the worse.
'Where are the War Poets?' (1943)

10 Every good poem, in fact, is a bridge built from the known, familiar side of life over into the unknown. Science too, is always making expeditions into the unknown. But this does not mean that science can supersede poetry. For poetry enlightens us in a different way from science; it speaks directly to our feelings or imagination. The findings of poetry are no more and no less true than science.
Poetry for You (1944)

John Dean 1938–

American lawyer and White House counsel during the Watergate affair

11 We have a cancer within, close to the Presidency, that is growing.
from the [Nixon] Presidential Transcripts, 21 March 1973

Millvina Dean 1911–

English youngest survivor of the Titanic disaster

1 I can't bear iced drinks . . . the iceberg, you know. Perhaps some champagne, though.

while visiting the house in Kansas City, Missouri, in which her family would have lived if her father had not drowned

in *Times* 20 August 1997

Simone de Beauvoir 1908–86

French novelist and feminist

2 It is not in giving life but in risking life that man is raised above the animal; that is why superiority has been accorded in humanity not to the sex that brings forth but to that which kills.

The Second Sex (1949)

3 One is not born a woman: one becomes one.

The Second Sex (1949)

4 Few tasks are more like the torture of Sisyphus than housework, with its endless repetition . . . The housewife wears herself out marking time: she makes nothing, simply perpetuates the present.

The Second Sex (1949)

Louis de Bernières 1954–

British novelist and short-story writer

5 The human heart likes a little disorder in its geometry.

Captain Corelli's Mandolin (1994) ch. 26

6 The trouble with fulfilling your ambitions is you think you will be transformed into some sort of archangel and you're not. You still have to wash your socks.

in *Independent* 14 February 1999

Edward de Bono 1933–

British writer and physician

7 Some people are aware of another sort of thinking which . . . leads to those simple ideas that are obvious only after they have been thought of . . . the term 'lateral thinking' has been coined to describe this other sort of thinking; 'vertical thinking' is used to denote the conventional logical process.

The Use of Lateral Thinking (1967)

8 Unhappiness is best defined as the difference between our talents and our expectations.

in *Observer* 12 June 1977

Guy Debord 1931–94

French philosopher

9 Villages, unlike towns, have always been ruled by conformism, isolation, petty surveillance, boredom and repetitive malicious gossip about the same families. Which is a precise enough description of the global spectacle's present vulgarity.

on the concept of the 'global village'; see **McLuhan** 210:6

Comments on the Society of the Spectacle (1988)

Régis Debray 1940–

French Marxist theorist

10 Propaganda can be defined as the art of managing one's legend.

Charles de Gaulle: Futurist of the Nation (1994)

11 International life is right-wing, like nature. The social contract is left-wing, like humanity.

Charles de Gaulle (1994)

Eugene Victor Debs 1855–1926

Founder of the Socialist party of America

12 When great changes occur in history, when great principles are involved, as a rule the majority are wrong. The minority are right.

speech at his trial for sedition in Cleveland, Ohio, 11 September 1918

13 While there is a lower class, I am in it; while there is a criminal element, I am of it; while there is a soul in prison, I am not free.

speech at his trial for sedition, in Cleveland, Ohio, 14 September 1918

John de Chastelain 1937–

British-born Canadian soldier and diplomat

1 The pike in the thatch is not quite the same as the surface-to-air missile in the thatch.

on decommissioning in Northern Ireland

interview in *Daily Telegraph* 11 June 1999

W. F. Deedes 1913–

British journalist and former Conservative politician

2 The man who said nobody ever lost money by underrating public taste has been proved wrong.

of the Millennium Dome

in *Mail on Sunday* 4 June 2000; see **Mencken** 221:10

Edgar Degas 1834–1917

French artist

3 Art is vice. You don't marry it legitimately, you rape it.

P. Lafond *Degas* (1918)

Charles de Gaulle 1890–1970

French general; President of France, 1959–69

see also **Opening lines** 248:2

4 France has lost a battle. But France has not lost the war!

proclamation, 18 June 1940

5 Faced by the bewilderment of my countrymen, by the disintegration of a government in thrall to the enemy, by the fact that the institutions of my country are incapable, at the moment, of functioning, I General de Gaulle, a French soldier and military leader, realize that I now speak for France.

speech in London, 19 June 1940

6 Since they whose duty it was to wield the sword of France have let it fall shattered to the ground, I have taken up the broken blade.

speech, 13 July 1940

7 *Je vous ai compris.*

I have understood you.

speech at Algiers, 4 June 1958

8 Yes, it is Europe, from the Atlantic to the Urals, it is Europe, it is the whole of Europe, that will decide the fate of the world.

speech to the people of Strasbourg, 23 November 1959

9 Politics are too serious a matter to be left to the politicians.

replying to ***Attlee****'s remark that 'De Gaulle is a very good soldier and a very bad politician'*

Clement Attlee *A Prime Minister Remembers* (1961); see **Clemenceau** 71:5

10 *Europe des patries.*

A Europe of nations.

widely associated with De Gaulle, c.1962, and taken as encapsulating his views, although perhaps not coined by him

J. Lacouture *De Gaulle: the Ruler* (1991)

11 How can you govern a country which has 246 varieties of cheese?

E. Mignon *Les Mots du Général* (1962)

12 Treaties, you see, are like girls and roses: they last while they last.

speech at Elysée Palace, 2 July 1963

13 *Vive Le Québec Libre.*

Long Live Free Quebec.

speech in Montreal, 24 July 1967

14 The sword is the axis of the world and its power is absolute.

Vers l'armée de métier (1934)

15 And now she is like everyone else.

on the death of his daughter, who had been born with Down's syndrome

attributed

16 One does not put Voltaire in the Bastille.

when asked to arrest ***Sartre****, in the 1960s*

in *Encounter* June 1975

17 The EEC is a horse and carriage: Germany is the horse and France is the coachman.

attributed; Bernard Connolly *The Rotten Heart of Europe* (1995)

J. de Knight 1919– and M. Freedman 1893–1962

18 (We're gonna) rock around the clock.

title of song (1953)

Walter de la Mare 1873–1956

English poet and novelist

1 Oh, no man knows
Through what wild centuries
Roves back the rose.
'All That's Past' (1912)

2 He is crazed with the spell of far Arabia,
They have stolen his wits away.
'Arabia' (1912)

3 Beauty vanishes; beauty passes;
However rare—rare it be.
'Epitaph' (1912)

4 Look thy last on all things lovely,
Every hour.
'Fare Well' (1918)

5 'Is there anybody there?' said the
Traveller,
Knocking on the moonlit door.
'The Listeners' (1912)

6 'Tell them I came, and no one answered,
That I kept my word,' he said.
'The Listeners' (1912)

7 Softly along the road of evening,
In a twilight dim with rose,
Wrinkled with age, and drenched with
dew,
Old Nod, the shepherd, goes.
'Nod' (1912)

8 Slowly, silently, now the moon
Walks the night in her silver shoon.
'Silver' (1913)

9 Behind the blinds I sit and watch
The people passing—passing by;
And not a single one can see
My tiny watching eye.
'The Window' (1913)

Shelagh Delaney 1939–

English dramatist

10 Women never have young minds. They are born three thousand years old.
A Taste of Honey (1959)

Frederick Delius 1862–1934

English composer, of German and Scandinavian descent

11 It is only that which cannot be expressed otherwise that is worth expressing in music.
in *Sackbut* September 1920 'At the Crossroads'

Jerry Della Femina 1936–

American advertising executive

12 Advertising is the most fun you can have with your clothes on.
From Those Wonderful Folks Who Gave You Pearl Harbor (1971)

Agnes de Mille 1908–

American dancer and choreographer

13 The truest expression of a people is in its dances and its music. Bodies never lie.
in *New York Times Magazine* 11 May 1975

Jack Dempsey 1895–1983

American boxer

14 Honey, I just forgot to duck.
to his wife, on losing the World Heavyweight title, 23 September 1926; after a failed attempt on his life in 1981, Ronald ***Reagan*** *quipped 'I forgot to duck'*
J. and B. P. Dempsey *Dempsey* (1977)

Catherine Deneuve 1943–

French actress

15 The paparazzi are nothing but dogs of war.
after the death in a car crash of ***Diana****, Princess of Wales*
in *Daily Telegraph* 3 September 1997

Deng Xiaoping 1904–97

Chinese Communist statesman, from 1977 paramount leader of China

on Deng: see **Anonymous** 12:13

1 It doesn't matter if a cat is black or white, as long as it catches mice.

in the early 1960s; in *Daily Telegraph* 20 February 1997, obituary

2 I should love to be around in 1997 to see with my own eyes Hong Kong's return to China.

in 1984; in *Daily Telegraph* 20 February 1997, obituary

Lord Denning 1899–1999

British judge

3 The Treaty [of Rome] is like an incoming tide. It flows into the estuaries and up the rivers. It cannot be held back.

in 1975; Anthony Sampson *The Essential Anatomy of Britain* (1992)

4 The keystone of the rule of law in England has been the independence of judges. It is the only respect in which we make any real separation of powers.

The Family Story (1981)

5 Properly exercised the new powers of the executive lead to the welfare state; but abused they lead to the totalitarian state.

Anthony Sampson *The Changing Anatomy of Britain* (1982)

6 We shouldn't have all these campaigns to get the Birmingham Six released if they'd been hanged. They'd have been forgotten and the whole community would be satisfied.

in *Spectator* 18 August 1990

Jacques Derrida 1930–

French philosopher and critic

7 *Il n'y a pas de hors-texte.*

There is nothing outside of the text.

Of Grammatology (1967)

Buddy De Sylva 1895–1950 and Lew Brown 1893–1958

American and Russian-born American songwriters

8 The moon belongs to everyone,
The best things in life are free,
The stars belong to everyone,
They gleam there for you and me.

'The Best Things in Life are Free' (1927 song)

Eamonn de Valera 1882–1975

American-born Irish statesman, Taoiseach 1937–48, 1951–4, and 1957–9, and President of the Republic of Ireland 1959–73

on de Valera: see **Lloyd George** 201:12

9 Whenever I wanted to know what the Irish people wanted, I had only to examine my own heart and it told me straight off what the Irish people wanted.

speech in Dáil Éireann, 6 January 1922

10 Further sacrifice of life would now be in vain . . . Military victory must be allowed to rest for the moment with those who have destroyed the Republic.

message to the Republican armed forces, 24 May 1923

11 That Ireland which we dreamed of would be the home of a people who valued material wealth only as a basis of right living, of a people who were satisfied with frugal comfort and devoted their leisure to the things of the spirit; a land whose countryside would be bright with cosy homesteads, whose fields and villages would be joyous with sounds of industry, the romping of sturdy children, the contests of athletic youths, the laughter of comely maidens; whose firesides would be the forums of the wisdom of serene old age.

St Patrick's Day broadcast, 17 March 1943

Peter De Vries 1910–93

American novelist

12 Gluttony is an emotional escape, a sign something is eating us.

Comfort Me With Apples (1956)

1 The value of marriage is not that adults produce children but that children produce adults.
The Tunnel of Love (1954)

Donald Dewar 1937–2000

Scottish Labour politician; First Minister for Scotland 1999–2000

2 'There shall be a Scottish parliament.' Through long years, those words were first a hope, then a belief, then a promise. Now they are a reality.
at the official opening of the Scottish Parliament
speech, 1 July 1999; see **Anonymous** 12:5

3 We look forward to the time when this moment will be seen as a turning point: the day when democracy was renewed in Scotland, when we revitalised our place in this our United Kingdom.
at the official opening of the Scottish Parliament
speech, 1 July 1999

Lord Dewar 1864–1930

British industrialist

4 [There are] only two classes of pedestrians in these days of reckless motor traffic—the quick, and the dead.
George Robey *Looking Back on Life* (1933)

Thomas E. Dewey 1902–71

American politician and presidential candidate
see also **Newspaper headlines** 240:4

5 That's why it's time for a change!
phrase used extensively in campaigns of 1944, 1948, and 1952
campaign speech in San Francisco, 21 September 1944

Sergei Diaghilev 1872–1929

Russian ballet impresario

6 *Étonne-moi.*
Astonish me.
to Jean ***Cocteau***
W. Fowlie (ed.) *Journals of Jean Cocteau* (1956)

7 Tchaikovsky thought of committing suicide for fear of being discovered as a homosexual, but today, if you are a composer and *not* homosexual, you might as well put a bullet through your head.
Vernon Duke *Listen Here!* (1963)

John Diamond 1953–2001

British journalist

8 In the face of such overwhelming statistical possibilities, hypochondria has always seemed to me to be the only rational position to take on life.
C: Because Cowards Get Cancer Too (1998)

Diana, Princess of Wales 1961–97

former wife of **Charles**, Prince of Wales
on Diana: see **Blair** 37:6, **Dowd** 94:6, **Duffy** 95:7, **Elizabeth II** 106:4, **John** 170:13, **Motion** 233:7, **Spencer** 303:11

9 If men had to have babies, they would only ever have one each.
in *Observer* 29 July 1984

10 I'd like to be a queen in people's hearts but I don't see myself being Queen of this country.
interview on *Panorama*, BBC1 TV, 20 November 1995

11 There were three of us in this marriage, so it was a bit crowded.
interview on *Panorama*, BBC1 TV, 20 November 1995

12 She won't go quietly, that's the problem. I'll fight to the end.
interview on *Panorama*, BBC1 TV, 20 November 1995

13 The press is ferocious. It forgives nothing, it only hunts for mistakes . . . In my position anyone sane would have left a long time ago.
contrasting British and foreign press reporting
in *Le Monde* 27 August 1997

Paul Dickson 1939–

American writer

1 Rowe's Rule: the odds are five to six that the light at the end of the tunnel is the headlight of an oncoming train.

in *Washingtonian* November 1978

Clarissa Dickson Wright

British barrister and cook

2 The feminist movement seems to have beaten the manners out of men, but I didn't see them put up a lot of resistance.

in *Mail on Sunday* 24 September 2000

Bo Diddley 1928–

American rock musician

3 I opened the door for a lot of people, and they just ran through and left me holding the knob.

in 1971; M. Wrenn *Bitch, Bitch, Bitch* (1988)

Joan Didion 1934–

American writer

4 Was there ever in anyone's life span a point free in time, devoid of memory, a night when choice was any more than the sum of all the choices gone before?

Run River (1963)

Howard Dietz 1896–1983

American songwriter

5 *Ars gratia artis.*

Art for art's sake.

motto of Metro-Goldwyn-Mayer film studios, apparently intended to say 'Art is beholden to the artists'

Bosley Crowthier *The Lion's Share* (1957); see below

L'art pour l'art.

Art for art's sake.

Benjamin Constant (1767–1834) *Journal intime* 11 February 1804

Joe DiMaggio 1914–99

American baseball player

6 A ball player's got to be kept hungry to become a big leaguer. That's why no boy from a rich family ever made the big leagues.

in *New York Times* 30 April 1961

Ernest Dimnet

French priest, writer, and lecturer

7 Architecture, of all the arts, is the one which acts the most slowly, but the most surely, on the soul.

What We Live By (1932)

Isak Dinesen (Karen Blixen) 1885–1962

Danish novelist and short-story writer

8 A herd of elephant . . . pacing along as if they had an appointment at the end of the world.

Out of Africa (1937)

9 What is man, when you come to think upon him, but a minutely set, ingenious machine for turning, with infinite artfulness, the red wine of Shiraz into urine?

Seven Gothic Tales (1934) 'The Dreamers'

Paul Dirac 1902–84

British theoretical physicist, of Swiss descent

10 I think it is a general rule that the originator of a new idea is not the most suitable person to develop it, because his fears of something going wrong are really too strong.

The Development of Quantum Theory (1971)

11 It is more important to have beauty in one's equations than to have them fit experiment . . . It seems that if one is working from the point of view of getting beauty in one's equations, and if one has a really sound insight, one is on a sure line of progress. If there is not complete agreement between the results of one's work and experiment, one should not allow oneself to be too discouraged, because the discrepancy may well be due to minor features that are not properly taken into account and that will get cleared up with further developments of the theory.

in *Scientific American* May 1963

1 It is nice, but in one of the chapters the author made a mistake. He describes the sun as rising twice on the same day.

on the novel Crime and Punishment

G. Gamow *Thirty Years that Shook Physics* (1966)

Walt Disney 1901–66

American animator and film producer

2 I don't know, fellows, I guess I'm getting too old for animation.

on seeing rushes from The Jungle Book (1967 *film*)

Richard Schickel *The Disney Version* (1986)

3 Fancy being remembered around the world for the invention of a mouse!

during his last illness

Leonard Mosley *Disney's World* (1985)

Frank Dobson 1940–

British Labour politician

4 I trudge the streets rather than trade the soundbite. I . . . would not know a focus group if I met one. I am unspun.

in *Sunday Times* 27 February 2000

5 The ego has landed.

of Ken ***Livingstone****'s independent candidacy for Mayor of London*

in *Times* 7 March 2000; see **Armstrong** 14:5

Ken Dodd 1931–

British comedian

6 Freud's theory was that when a joke opens a window and all those bats and bogeymen fly out, you get a marvellous feeling of relief and elation. The trouble with Freud is that he never had to play the old Glasgow Empire on a Saturday night after Rangers and Celtic had both lost.

in *Guardian* 30 April 1991; quoted in many forms since the mid-1960s

Robert ('Bob') Dole 1923–

American Republican politician

announcing his decision to relinquish his Senate seat and step down as majority leader:

7 I will seek the presidency with nothing to fall back on but the judgement of the people and with nowhere to go but the White House or home.

on Capitol Hill, 15 May 1996; in *Daily Telegraph* 16 May 1996

8 It's a lot more fun winning. It hurts to lose.

conceding the US presidential election, 6 November 1996

in *Daily Telegraph* 7 November 1996

J. P. Donleavy 1926–

Irish-American novelist

9 When you don't have any money, the problem is food. When you have money, it's sex. When you have both, it's health.

The Ginger Man (1955)

Mark Doty 1953–

American poet

10 and I swear sometimes
when I put my head to his chest
I can hear the virus humming

like a refrigerator.

'Atlantis' (1996)

Keith Douglas 1920–44

English poet

11 And all my endeavours are unlucky
explorers
come back, abandoning the expedition.

'On Return from Egypt, 1943–4' (1946)

12 Remember me when I am dead
And simplify me when I'm dead.

'Simplify me when I'm Dead' (1941)

13 For here the lover and killer are mingled

who had one body and one heart.
And death, who had the soldier singled
has done the lover mortal hurt.
'Vergissmeinnicht, 1943'

Norman Douglas 1868–1952

Scottish-born novelist and essayist

1 To find a friend one must close one eye. To keep him—two.
Almanac (1941)

2 You can tell the ideals of a nation by its advertisements.
South Wind (1917)

O. Douglas (Anna Buchan) 1877–1948

Scottish writer, sister of John **Buchan**

3 It is wonderful how much news there is when people write every other day; if they wait for a month, there is nothing that seems worth telling.
Penny Plain (1920)

4 I know heaps of quotations, so I can always make quite a fair show of knowledge.
The Setons (1917)

William O. Douglas 1898–1980

American lawyer

5 Free speech is not to be regulated like diseased cattle and impure butter. The audience . . . that hissed yesterday may applaud today, even for the same performance.
dissenting opinion in *Kingsley Books, Inc. v. Brown* 1957

Maureen Dowd 1952–

American journalist

6 The Princess of Wales was the queen of surfaces, ruling over a kingdom where fame was the highest value and glamour the most cherished attribute.
in *New York Times* 3 September 1997

7 These are not grounds for impeachment. These are grounds for divorce.
on the Lewinsky affair.
in *Guardian* 14 September 1998

Arthur Conan Doyle 1859–1930

Scottish-born writer of detective fiction
see also **Misquotations** 226:6

8 Matilda Briggs . . . was a ship which is associated with the giant rat of Sumatra, a story for which the world is not yet prepared.
The Case-Book of Sherlock Homes (1927)

9 Good old Watson! You are the one fixed point in a changing age.
His Last Bow (1917)

10 The charlatan is always the pioneer. From the astrologer came the astronomer, from the alchemist the chemist, from the mesmerist the experimental psychologist. The quack of yesterday is the professor of tomorrow.
Tales of Terror and Mystery (1922) 'The Leather Funnel'

Roddy Doyle 1958–

Irish novelist

11 They'd been in the folk mass choir when they were in school but that, they knew now, hadn't really been singing. Jimmy said that real music was sex . . . They were starting to agree with him. And there wasn't much sex in Morning Has Broken or The Lord Is My Shepherd.
The Commitments (1987)

12 I said one Hail Mary and four Our Fathers, because I preferred the Our Fathers to the Hail Mary and it was longer and better.
Paddy Clarke Ha Ha Ha (1993)

Margaret Drabble 1939–

English novelist

13 England's not a bad country . . . It's just a mean, cold, ugly, divided, tired, clapped-out, post-imperial, post-

industrial slag-heap covered in
polystyrene hamburger cartons.
A Natural Curiosity (1989)

1 Affluence was, quite simply, a question of texture . . . The threadbare carpets of infancy, the coconut matting, the ill-laid linoleum, the utility furniture . . . had all spoken of a life too near the bones of subsistence, too little padded, too severely worn.
The Needle's Eye (1972)

2 Perhaps the rare and simple pleasure of being seen for what one is compensates for the misery of being it.
A Summer Bird-Cage (1963)

John Drinkwater 1882–1937

English poet and dramatist

3 Deep is the silence, deep
On moon-washed apples of wonder.
'Moonlit Apples' (1917)

Alexander Dubček 1921–92

Czechoslovak statesman; First Secretary of the Czechoslovak Communist Party, 1968–9

4 In the service of the people we followed such a policy that socialism would not lose its human face.
describing the Prague Spring, 1968
in *Rudé Právo* 19 July 1968

W. E. B. Du Bois 1868–1963

American social reformer and political activist

5 The problem of the twentieth century is the problem of the colour line—the relation of the darker to the lighter races of men in Asia and Africa, in America and the islands of the sea.
The Souls of Black Folk (1905)

6 One thing alone I charge you. As you live, believe in life! Always human beings will live and progress to greater, broader and fuller life. The only possible death is to lose belief in this truth simply because the great end comes slowly, because time is long.
last message, written 26 June, 1957, and read at his funeral, 1963

Carol Ann Duffy 1965–

English poet

7 Whatever 'in love' means,
true love is talented.
Someone vividly gifted in love has gone.
on the death of ***Diana****, Princess of Wales*
'September, 1997' (1997); see **Charles** 63:2

John Foster Dulles 1888–1959

American international lawyer and politician

8 The ability to get to the verge without getting into the war is the necessary art . . . We walked to the brink and we looked it in the face.
in *Life* 16 January 1956; see **Stevenson** 308:11

Daphne Du Maurier

see **Opening lines** 247:11

Isadora Duncan

see **Last words** 190:3

Ronald Duncan 1914–82

English dramatist

9 Where in this wide world can man find
nobility without pride,
Friendship without envy, or beauty
without vanity?
'In Praise of the Horse' (1962)

Ian Dunlop 1940–

British art historian

10 The shock of the new.
title of book about modern art (1972)

Helen Dunmore 1952–

British novelist and poet

11 That killed head straining through the
windscreen
with its frill of bubbles in the eye-sockets

is not trying to tell you something—
it is telling you something.
'Poem on the Obliteration of 100,000 Iraqi Soldiers' (1994)

Douglas Dunn 1942–

Scottish poet

1 In a country like this
Our ghosts outnumber us . . .
'At Falkland Palace' (1988)

2 My poems should be Clyde-built, crude and sure,
With images of those dole-deployed
To honour the indomitable Reds,
Clydesiders of slant steel and angled cranes;
A poetry of nuts and bolts, born, bred,
Embattled by the Clyde, tight and impure.
'Clydesiders' (1974)

3 Look to the living, love them, and hold on.
in 'Disenchantments' (1993)

4 They ruined us. They conquered continents.
We filled their uniforms. We cruised the seas.
We worked their mines and made their histories.
You work, we rule, they said. We worked; they ruled.
They fooled the tenements. All men were fooled.
'Empires' (1979)

5 I am light with meditation, religiose
And mystic with a day of solitude.
'Reading Pascan in the Lowlands' (1985)

Sean Dunne 1956–97

Irish poet

6 The country wears their going like a scar,
Today their relatives save to support and
Send others in planes for the new diaspora.
'Letter from Ireland' (1991)

Paul Durcan 1944–

Irish poet

7 Some of us made it
To the forest edge, but many of us did not
Make it, although their unborn children did—
Such as you whom the camp commandant branded
Sid Vicious of the Sex Pistols. Jesus, break his fall:
There—but for the clutch of luck—go we all.
'The Death by Heroin of Sid Vicious' (1980)

Ray Durem 1915–63

American poet

8 Some of my best friends are white boys.
when I meet 'em
I treat 'em
just the same as if they was people.
'Broadminded' (written 1951)

Leo Durocher 1906–91

American baseball coach

9 Nice guys. Finish last.
casual remark at a practice ground, July 1946
Nice Guys Finish Last (as the remark generally is quoted, 1975)

Lawrence Durrell 1912–90

English novelist, poet, and travel writer

10 I love to feel events overlapping each other, crawling over one another like wet crabs in a basket.
Balthazar (1958)

11 No history much? Perhaps. Only this ominous
Dark beauty flowering under veils,
Trapped in the spectrum of a dying style:
A village like an instinct left to rust,
Composed around the echo of a pistol-shot.
'Sarajevo' (1951)

12 Our cathedrals are like abandoned computers now, but they used to be prayer factories once.
in *Listener* 20 April 1978

Friedrich Dürrenmatt 1921–

Swiss writer

1 What was once thought can never be unthought.

The Physicists (1962)

Ian Dury 1942–2000

British rock singer and songwriter

2 Sex and drugs and rock and roll.

title of song (1977)

Robert Duvall

see **Film lines** 116:4

Andrea Dworkin 1946–

American feminist and writer

3 Seduction is often difficult to distinguish from rape. In seduction, the rapist bothers to buy a bottle of wine.

in 1976; *Letters from a War Zone* (1988)

Bob Dylan 1941–

American singer and songwriter

4 How many roads must a man walk down
Before you can call him a man? . . .
The answer, my friend, is blowin' in the wind,
The answer is blowin' in the wind.

'Blowin' in the Wind' (1962 song)

5 They're selling postcards of the hanging.

'Desolation Row' (1965)

6 And someone says, You're in the wrong place, my friend
You better leave.'

'Desolation Row' (1965)

7 Don't think twice, it's all right.

title of song (1963)

8 I saw ten thousand talkers whose tongues were all broken,
I saw guns and sharp swords, in the hands of young children . . .
And it's a hard rain's a gonna fall.

'A Hard Rain's A Gonna Fall' (1963 song)

9 Money doesn't talk, it swears.

'It's Alright, Ma (I'm Only Bleeding)' (1965 song)

10 She takes just like a woman, yes, she does
She makes love just like a woman, yes, she does
And she aches just like a woman
But she breaks like a little girl.

'Just Like a Woman' (1966 song)

11 How does it feel
To be on your own
With no direction home
Like a complete unknown
Like a rolling stone?

'Like a Rolling Stone' (1965 song)

12 She knows there's no success like failure
And that failure's no success at all.

'Love Minus Zero / No Limit' (1965 song)

13 Hey! Mr Tambourine Man, play a song for me.
I'm not sleepy and there is no place I'm going to.

'Mr Tambourine Man' (1965 song)

14 Ah, but I was so much older then,
I'm younger than that now.

'My Back Pages' (1964 song)

15 Señor, señor, do you know where we're headin'?
Lincoln County Road or Armageddon?

'Señor (Tale of Yankee Power)' (1978 song)

16 All that foreign oil controlling American soil.

'Slow Train' (1979 song)

17 Come mothers and fathers,
Throughout the land
And don't criticize
What you can't understand.
Your sons and your daughters
Are beyond your command
Your old road is
Rapidly agin'
Please get out of the new one
If you can't lend your hand
For the times they are a-changin'!

'The Times They Are A-Changing' (1964 song)

18 But I can't think for you
You'll have to decide,
Whether Judas Iscariot

Had God on his side.
'With God on our Side' (1963 song)

1 It was like a flying saucer landed. That's what the sixties were like. Everybody heard about it, but only a few really saw it.
James Miller *Almost Grown: the Rise of Rock* (1999)

Greg Dyke 1947–

British journalist and television executive, BBC Director-General

2 I set about attacking what became known in the BBC as the three Cs—consultants, cars and croissants.
in *Sunday Times* 29 April 2001

Esther Dyson

American businesswoman 1951–

description of herself:

3 The court jester of the information industry. I try to have the ears of kings but I have the people's interests at heart.
online interview (*SmartBooks.com*) publicizing her book *Release 2.0* (1997)

4 Crime is crime, but that doesn't mean you can have a law making everyone keep their curtains up to help the police.
on the British government's Regulation of Investigatory Powers bill
in *Times* 6 July 2000

5 It is cute to have the British pound, it is quaint. But Britain has more hope if it joins them and fights for what it wants.
on why Britain should join the euro
in *Times* 6 July 2000

Clint Eastwood

see **Film lines** 115:10

Abba Eban 1915–

Israeli diplomat

6 History teaches us that men and nations behave wisely once they have exhausted all other alternatives.
speech in London, 16 December 1970

Arthur Eddington 1882–1944

British astrophysicist

7 I shall use the phrase 'time's arrow' to express this one-way property of time which has no analogue in space.
The Nature of the Physical World (1928)

8 If an army of monkeys were strumming on typewriters they *might* write all the books in the British Museum.
The Nature of the Physical World (1928); see **Wilensky** 338:16

9 If someone points out to you that your pet theory of the universe is in disagreement with Maxwell's equations—then so much the worse for Maxwell's equations. If it is found to be contradicted by observation—well, these experimentalists do bungle things sometimes. But if your theory is found to be against the second law of thermodynamics I can give you no hope; there is nothing for it but to collapse in deepest humiliation.
The Nature of the Physical World (1928)

10 I am standing on the threshold about to enter a room. It is a complicated business. In the first place I must shove against an atmosphere pressing with a force of fourteen pounds on every square inch of my body. I must make sure of landing on a plank travelling at twenty miles a second round the sun— a fraction of a second too early or too late, the plank would be miles away. I must do this whilst hanging from a round planet, head outward into space, and with a wind of aether blowing at no one knows how many miles a second through every interstice of my body.
The Nature of the Physical World (1928)

11 I ask you to look both ways. For the road to a knowledge of the stars leads through the atom; and important knowledge of the atom has been reached through the stars.
Stars and Atoms (1928)

12 Science is an edged tool, with which men play like children, and cut their own fingers.
attributed; R. L. Weber *More Random Walks in Science* (1982)

Anthony Eden 1897–1977

British Conservative statesman; Prime Minister, 1955–7; husband of Clarissa **Eden**
on Eden: see **Butler** 50:2, **Churchill** 67:2, **Muggeridge** 234:6

1 We are in an armed conflict; that is the phrase I have used. There has been no declaration of war.

on the Suez crisis

speech in the House of Commons, 1 November 1956

Clarissa Eden 1920–

wife of Anthony **Eden**

2 For the past few weeks I have really felt as if the Suez Canal was flowing through my drawing room.

speech at Gateshead, 20 November 1956

Marriott Edgar 1880–1951

British comic writer

3 There's a famous seaside place called
Blackpool,
That's noted for fresh air and fun,
And Mr and Mrs Ramsbottom
Went there with young Albert, their
son.

'The Lion and Albert' (1932)

Edward VIII (Duke of Windsor) 1894–1972

King of the United Kingdom, 1936; husband of the Duchess of **Windsor**
on Edward: see **Anonymous** 10:12, **Beaverbrook** 25:5, **Blunt** 38:9, **George V** 133:4, **Mary** 218:12; *see also* **Misquotations** 227:2

4 At long last I am able to say a few words of my own . . . you must believe me when I tell you that I have found it impossible to carry the heavy burden of responsibility and to discharge my duties as King as I would wish to do without the help and support of the woman I love.

following his abdication

radio broadcast, 11 December 1936

5 The thing that impresses me most about America is the way parents obey their children.

in *Look* 5 March 1957

Barbara Ehrenreich 1941–

American sociologist and writer

6 Exercise is the yuppie version of bulimia.

The Worst Years of Our Lives (1991) 'Food Worship'

Paul Ralph Ehrlich 1932–

American biologist

7 The first rule of intelligent tinkering is to save all the parts.

in *Saturday Review* 5 June 1971

John Ehrlichman 1925–99

American government official in the **Nixon** administration

8 I think we ought to let him hang there. Let him twist slowly, slowly in the wind.

Nixon had withdrawn his support for Patrick Gray, nominated as director of the FBI, although Gray himself had not been informed

in *Washington Post* 27 July 1973

Max Ehrmann 1872–1945

American poet

9 Go placidly amid the noise and the haste,
and remember what peace there may
be in silence.

often wrongly dated to 1692, the date of foundation of a church in Baltimore whose vicar circulated the poem in 1956

'Desiderata' (1948)

Adolf Eichmann 1906–62

German Nazi administrator

10 Today, 15 years after 8 May 1945, I know . . . that a life of obedience, led by orders, instructions, decrees and directives, is a very comfortable one in which one's creative thinking is diminished.

memoirs, in *Independent* 13 August 1999

Albert Einstein 1879–1955

German-born theoretical physicist; originator of the theory of relativity

on Einstein: see **Picasso** 258:7, **Squire** 305:5

1 Science without religion is lame, religion without science is blind.

Science, Philosophy and Religion (1941)

2 $E = mc^2$.

the usual form of Einstein's original statement: 'If a body releases the energy L in the form of radiation, its mass is decreased by L/V^2'

in *Annalen der Physik* 18 (1905)

3 God is subtle but he is not malicious.

remark made during a week at Princeton beginning 9 May 1921, later carved above the fireplace of the Common Room of Fine Hall (the Mathematical Institute), Princeton University

4 I am convinced that *He* [God] does not play dice.

letter to Max Born, 4 December 1926

5 I am an absolute pacifist . . . It is an instinctive feeling. It is a feeling that possesses me, because the murder of men is disgusting.

interview with Paul Hutchinson, in *Christian Century* 28 August 1929

6 If my theory of relativity is proven correct, Germany will claim me as a German and France will declare that I am a citizen of the world. Should my theory prove untrue, France will say that I am a German and Germany will declare that I am a Jew.

address at the Sorbonne, Paris, possibly early December 1929, in *New York Times* 16 February 1930

7 I never think of the future. It comes soon enough.

in an interview, given on the *Belgenland*, December 1930

8 I am not only a pacifist but a militant pacifist. I am willing to fight for peace. Nothing will end war unless the people themselves refuse to go to war.

interview with G. S. Viereck, January 1931

9 As a human being, one has been endowed with just enough intelligence to be able to see clearly how utterly inadequate that intelligence is when confronted with what exists.

letter to Queen Elisabeth of Belgium, 19 September 1932

10 The eternal mystery of the world is its comprehensibility . . . The fact that it is comprehensible is a miracle.

usually quoted as 'The most incomprehensible fact about the universe is that it is comprehensible'

in *Franklin Institute Journal* March 1936 'Physics and Reality'

11 Some recent work by E. Fermi and L. Szilard, which has been communicated to me in manuscript, leads me to expect that the element uranium may be turned into a new and important source of energy in the immediate future. Certain aspects of the situation which has arisen seem to call for watchfulness and, if necessary, quick action on the part of the Administration.

warning of the possible development of an atomic bomb, and leading to the setting up of the Manhattan Project

letter to Franklin **Roosevelt**, 2 August 1939, drafted by Leo Szilard and signed by Einstein

12 The unleashed power of the atom has changed everything save our modes of thinking and we thus drift toward unparalleled catastrophe.

telegram to prominent Americans, 24 May 1946

13 If *A* is a success in life, then *A* equals *x* plus *y* plus *z*. Work is *x*; *y* is play; and *z* is keeping your mouth shut.

in *Observer* 15 January 1950

14 Common sense is nothing more than a deposit of prejudices laid down in the mind before you reach eighteen.

Lincoln Barnett *The Universe and Dr Einstein* (1950 ed.)

15 The grand aim of all science [is] to cover the greatest number of empirical facts by logical deduction from the smallest possible number of hypotheses or axioms.

Lincoln Barnett *The Universe and Dr Einstein* (1950 ed.)

16 If I would be a young man again and had to decide how to make my living, I would not try to become a scientist or scholar or teacher. I would rather choose to be a plumber or a peddler in the hope to find that modest degree of independence still available under present circumstances.

in *Reporter* 18 November 1954

1 The distinction between past, present and future is only an illusion, however persistent.

letter to Michelangelo Besso, 21 March 1955

2 One must divide one's time between politics and equations. But our equations are much more important to me.

C. P. Snow 'Einstein'; M. Goldsmith et al. (eds.) *Einstein* (1980)

3 Nationalism is an infantile sickness. It is the measles of the human race.

Helen Dukas and Banesh Hoffman *Albert Einstein, the Human Side* (1979)

4 When I was young, I found out that the big toe always ends up making a hole in a sock. So I stopped wearing socks.

to Philippe Halsman; A. P. French *Einstein: A Centenary Volume* (1979)

Loren Eiseley 1907–77

American anthropologist, educator, and author

5 A man who has once looked with the archaeological eye will never see quite normally. He will be wounded by what other men call trifles. It is possible to refine the sense of time until an old show in the grass or a pile of nineteenth century beer bottles in an abandoned mining town tolls in one's head like a hall clock.

The Night Country (1971)

6 Every man contains within himself a ghost continent—a place circled as warily as Antarctica was circled two hundred years ago by Captain James Cook.

The Unexpected Universe (1969)

Dwight D. Eisenhower
1890–1969

American general and Republican statesman, 34th President of the US, 1953–61

on Eisenhower: see **Joplin** 173:2, **Political sayings and slogans** 261:15

7 Every gun that is made, every warship launched, every rocket fired signifies, in the final sense, a theft from those who hunger and are not fed, those who are cold and are not clothed. This world in arms is not spending money alone. It is spending the sweat of its labourers, the genius of its scientists, the hopes of its children.

speech in Washington, 16 April 1953

8 I just will not—I *refuse*—to get into the gutter with that guy.

explaining why he did not try to restrain Senator ***McCarthy***

in 1953; in *American National Biography* (online edition) 'Joseph McCarthy'

9 You have broader considerations that might follow what you might call the 'falling domino' principle. You have a row of dominoes set up. You knock over the first one, and what will happen to the last one is that it will go over very quickly.

speech at press conference, 7 April 1954

10 I think that people want peace so much that one of these days governments had better get out of the way and let them have it.

broadcast discussion, 31 August 1959

11 No easy problems ever come to the President of the United States. If they are easy to solve, somebody else has solved them.

in *Parade Magazine* 8 April 1962

12 In preparing for battle I have always found that plans are useless, but planning is indispensable.

Richard Nixon *Six Crises* (1962); attributed

Alfred Eisenstaedt 1898–1995

German-born American photographer and photojournalist

1 It's more important to click with people than to click the shutter.

in *Life* 24 August 1995 (electronic edition), obituary

T. S. Eliot 1888–1965

Anglo-American poet, critic, and dramatist

on Eliot: see **Elizabeth** 106:12, **Leavis** 194:4, **Lewis** 198:12

2 Because I do not hope to turn again
Because I do not hope
Because I do not hope to turn.

Ash-Wednesday (1930) pt. 1

3 Teach us to care and not to care
Teach us to sit still.

Ash-Wednesday (1930) pt. 1

4 Lady, three white leopards sat under a juniper-tree
In the cool of the day.

Ash-Wednesday (1930) pt. 2

5 What is hell?
Hell is oneself,
Hell is alone, the other figures in it
Merely projections.

The Cocktail Party (1950)

6 Success is relative:
It is what we can make of the mess we have made of things.

The Family Reunion (1939)

7 Round and round the circle
Completing the charm
So the knot be unknotted
The cross be uncrossed
The crooked be made straight
And the curse be ended.

The Family Reunion (1939)

8 Time present and time past
Are both perhaps present in time future,
And time future contained in time past.

Four Quartets 'Burnt Norton' (1936) pt. 1

9 Footfalls echo in the memory
Down the passage which we did not take
Towards the door we never opened
Into the rose-garden.

Four Quartets 'Burnt Norton' (1936) pt. 1

10 Human kind
Cannot bear very much reality.

Four Quartets 'Burnt Norton' (1936) pt. 1.

11 At the still point of the turning world.

Four Quartets 'Burnt Norton' (1936) pt. 2

12 Words strain,
Crack and sometimes break, under the burden,
Under the tension, slip, slide, perish,
Decay with imprecision, will not stay in place,
Will not stay still.

Four Quartets 'Burnt Norton' (1936) pt. 5

13 In my beginning is my end.

Four Quartets 'East Coker' (1940) pt. 1; see below

In my end is my beginning.

Mary, Queen of Scots (1542–87) motto embroidered with an emblem of her mother, Mary of Guise

14 That was a way of putting it—not very satisfactory:
A periphrastic study in a worn-out poetical fashion,
Leaving one still with the intolerable wrestle
With words and meanings.

Four Quartets 'East Coker' (1940) pt. 2

15 The houses are all gone under the sea.
The dancers are all gone under the hill.

Four Quartets 'East Coker' (1940) pt. 2

16 O dark dark dark. They all go into the dark,
The vacant interstellar spaces, the vacant into the vacant.

Four Quartets 'East Coker' (1940) pt. 3

17 The wounded surgeon plies the steel
That questions the distempered part;
Beneath the bleeding hands we feel
The sharp compassion of the healer's art
Resolving the enigma of the fever chart.

Four Quartets 'East Coker' (1940) pt. 4

18 Trying to learn to use words, and every attempt
Is a wholly new start, and a different kind of failure.

Four Quartets 'East Coker' (1940) pt. 5

19 I do not know much about gods; but I think that the river

Is a strong brown god.
Four Quartets 'The Dry Salvages' (1941) pt. 1

1 We had the experience but missed the meaning.
Four Quartets 'The Dry Salvages' (1941) pt. 2

2 And what the dead had no speech for, when living,
They can tell you, being dead: the communication
Of the dead is tongued with fire beyond the language of the living.
Four Quartets 'Little Gidding' (1942) pt. 1

3 Ash on an old man's sleeve
Is all the ash the burnt roses leave.
Four Quartets 'Little Gidding' (1942) pt. 2

4 The death of hope and despair,
This is the death of air.
Four Quartets 'Little Gidding' (1942) pt. 2

5 Since our concern was speech, and speech impelled us
To purify the dialect of the tribe.
Four Quartets 'Little Gidding' (1942) pt. 2

6 And the end of all our exploring
Will be to arrive where we started
And know the place for the first time.
Four Quartets 'Little Gidding' (1942) pt. 5

7 What we call the beginning is often the end
And to make an end is to make a beginning.
The end is where we start from.
Four Quartets 'Little Gidding' (1942) pt. 5

8 A people without history
Is not redeemed from time, for history is a pattern
Of timeless moments. So, while the light fails
On a winter's afternoon, in a secluded chapel
History is now and England.
Four Quartets 'Little Gidding' (1942) pt. 5

9 And all shall be well and
All manner of thing shall be well
When the tongues of flame are in-folded
Into the crowned knot of fire
And the fire and the rose are one.
Four Quartets 'Little Gidding' (1942) pt. 5; see below

Sin is behovely, but all shall be well and all shall be well and all manner of thing shall be well.
Julian of Norwich (1343–after 1416) *Revelations of Divine Love*

10 Here I am, an old man in a dry month
Being read to by a boy, waiting for rain.
'Gerontion' (1920)

11 After such knowledge, what forgiveness?
'Gerontion' (1920)

12 Tenants of the house,
Thoughts of a dry brain in a dry season.
'Gerontion' (1920)

13 We are the hollow men
We are the stuffed men
Leaning together
Headpiece filled with straw. Alas!
'The Hollow Men' (1925)

14 Here we go round the prickly pear
Prickly pear prickly pear.
'The Hollow Men' (1925)

15 Between the idea
And the reality
Between the motion
And the act
Falls the Shadow.
'The Hollow Men' (1925)

16 This is the way the world ends
Not with a bang but a whimper.
'The Hollow Men' (1925)

17 A cold coming we had of it,
Just the worst time of the year
For a journey, and such a long journey:
The ways deep and the weather sharp,
The very dead of winter.
'Journey of the Magi' (1927); see below

It was no summer progress. A cold coming they had of it, at this time of the year; just, the worst time of the year, to take a journey, and specially a long journey, in. The ways deep, the weather sharp, the days short, the sun farthest off *in solstitio brumali*, the very dead of Winter.
Lancelot Andrewes (1555–1626) *Of the Nativity* (1622)

18 There was a Birth, certainly,
We had evidence and no doubt. I had seen birth and death
But had thought they were different.
'Journey of the Magi' (1927)

1 With an alien people clutching their gods.
'Journey of the Magi' (1927)

2 Let us go then, you and I,
When the evening is spread out against the sky
Like a patient etherized upon a table.
'Love Song of J. Alfred Prufrock' (1917); see **Lewis** 198:12

3 In the room the women come and go
Talking of Michelangelo.
'Love Song of J. Alfred Prufrock' (1917)

4 The yellow fog that rubs its back upon the window-panes.
'Love Song of J. Alfred Prufrock' (1917)

5 I have measured out my life with coffee spoons.
'Love Song of J. Alfred Prufrock' (1917)

6 I should have been a pair of ragged claws
Scuttling across the floors of silent seas.
'Love Song of J. Alfred Prufrock' (1917)

7 No! I am not Prince Hamlet, nor was meant to be;
Am an attendant lord, one that will do
To swell a progress, start a scene or two,
Advise the prince.
'Love Song of J. Alfred Prufrock' (1917)

8 I grow old . . . I grow old . . .
I shall wear the bottoms of my trousers rolled.

Shall I part my hair behind? Do I dare to eat a peach?
I shall wear white flannel trousers, and walk upon the beach.
I have heard the mermaids singing, each to each.

I do not think that they will sing to me.
'Love Song of J. Alfred Prufrock' (1917); see below

Teach me to hear mermaids singing.
John Donne (1572–1631) *Songs and Sonnets* 'Song: Go and catch a falling star'

9 Yet we have gone on living,
Living and partly living.
Murder in the Cathedral (1935)

10 The last temptation is the greatest treason:
To do the right deed for the wrong reason.
Murder in the Cathedral (1935)

11 Clear the air! clean the sky! wash the wind!
Murder in the Cathedral (1935)

12 He always has an alibi, and one or two to spare:
At whatever time the deed took place—
MACAVITY WASN'T THERE!
Old Possum's Book of Practical Cats (1939) 'Macavity: the Mystery Cat'

13 Where is the Life we have lost in living?
Where is the wisdom we have lost in knowledge?
Where is the knowledge we have lost in information?
The Rock (1934)

14 . . . Here were decent godless people:
Their only monument the asphalt road
And a thousand lost golf balls.
The Rock (1934)

15 Birth, and copulation, and death.
That's all the facts when you come to brass tacks.
Sweeney Agonistes (1932) 'Fragment of an Agon'

16 Any man has to, needs to, wants to
Once in a lifetime, do a girl in.
Sweeney Agonistes (1932) 'Fragment of an Agon'

17 I gotta use words when I talk to you.
Sweeney Agonistes (1932) 'Fragment of an Agon'

18 The nightingales are singing near
The Convent of the Sacred Heart,

And sang within the bloody wood
When Agamemnon cried aloud
And let their liquid siftings fall
To stain the stiff dishonoured shroud.
'Sweeney among the Nightingales' (1919)

19 April is the cruellest month, breeding
Lilacs out of the dead land.
The Waste Land (1922) pt. 1

20 I read, much of the night, and go south in the winter.
The Waste Land (1922) pt. 1

21 I will show you fear in a handful of dust.
The Waste Land (1922) pt. 1

22 And still she cried, and still the world pursues,
'Jug Jug' to dirty ears.
The Waste Land (1922) pt. 2; see below

O 'tis the ravished nightingale.
Jug, jug, jug, jug, tereu, she cries.
John Lyly (c.1554–1606) *Campaspe* (1584)

1 I think we are in rats' alley
Where the dead men lost their bones.
The Waste Land (1922) pt. 2

2 O O O O that Shakespeherian Rag—
It's so elegant
So intelligent.
The Waste Land (1922) pt. 2; see **Buck** 47:8

3 Hurry up please it's time.
The Waste Land (1922) pt. 2

4 But at my back from time to time I hear
The sound of horns and motors, which shall bring
Sweeney to Mrs Porter in the spring.
O the moon shone bright on Mrs Porter
And on her daughter
They wash their feet in soda water.
The Waste Land (1922) pt. 3; see below

But at my back I always hear
Time's wingèd chariot hurrying near.
Andrew Marvell (1621–78) 'To His Coy Mistress' (1681)

5 At the violet hour, when the eyes and back
Turn upward from the desk, when the human engine waits
Like a taxi throbbing waiting.
The Waste Land (1922) pt. 3

6 I Tiresias, old man with wrinkled dugs.
The Waste Land (1922) pt. 3

7 When lovely woman stoops to folly and
Paces about her room again, alone,
She smoothes her hair with automatic hand,
And puts a record on the gramophone.
The Waste Land (1922) pt. 3; see below

When lovely woman stoops to folly
And finds too late that men betray.
Oliver Goldsmith (1728–74) *The Vicar of Wakefield* (1766)

8 Webster was much possessed by death
And saw the skull beneath the skin.
'Whispers of Immortality' (1919)

9 Culture may even be described simply as that which makes life worth living.
Notes Towards a Definition of Culture (1948)

10 The only way of expressing emotion in the form of art is by finding an 'objective correlative'; in other words, a set of objects, a situation, a chain of events which shall be the formula of that *particular* emotion; such that when the external facts, which must terminate in sensory experience, are given, the emotion is immediately evoked.
The Sacred Wood (1920) 'Hamlet and his Problems'

11 Immature poets imitate; mature poets steal.
The Sacred Wood (1920) 'Philip Massinger'

12 Someone said: 'The dead writers are remote from us because we *know* so much more than they did.' Precisely, and they are that which we know.
The Sacred Wood (1920) 'Tradition and Individual Talent'

13 Poetry is not a turning loose of emotion, but an escape from emotion; it is not the expression of personality but an escape from personality.
The Sacred Wood (1920) 'Tradition and Individual Talent'

14 In the seventeenth century a dissociation of sensibility set in, from which we have never recovered; and this dissociation, as is natural, was due to the influence of the two most powerful poets of the century, Milton and Dryden.
Selected Essays (1932) 'The Metaphysical Poets' (1921)

15 [*The Waste Land*] was only the relief of a personal and wholly insignificant grouse against life; it is just a piece of rhythmical grumbling.
The Waste Land (ed. Valerie Eliot, 1971) epigraph

Queen Elisabeth of Belgium
1876–1965

German-born consort of King Albert of the Belgians

16 Between them [Germany] and me there is now a bloody curtain which has descended forever.
on Germany's invasion of Belgium in 1914
attributed

Elizabeth II 1926–

Queen of the United Kingdom from 1952; wife of Prince **Philip**
on Elizabeth II: see **Grigg** 141:3, **Philip** 257:11

1 I declare before you all that my whole life, whether it be long or short, shall be devoted to your service and the service of our great Imperial family to which we all belong.
broadcast speech, as Princess Elizabeth, to the Commonwealth from Cape Town, 21 April 1947

2 I think everybody really will concede that on this, of all days, I should begin my speech with the words 'My husband and I'.
speech at Guildhall, London, on her 25th wedding anniversary
in *The Times* 21 November 1972

3 In the words of one of my more sympathetic correspondents, it has turned out to be an 'annus horribilis'.
speech at Guildhall, London, 24 November 1992

4 I for one believe that there are lessons to be drawn from her life and from the extraordinary and moving reaction to her death.
broadcast from Buckingham Palace on the evening before the funeral of ***Diana****, Princess of Wales, 5 September 1997*
in *The Times* 6 September 1997

5 I sometimes sense the world is changing almost too fast for its inhabitants, at least for us older ones.
on her tour of Pakistan, 8 October 1997
in *Times* 9 October 1997

6 Please don't be too effusive.
adjuration to the Prime Minister, at their weekly meeting on the speech he was to make to celebrate her golden wedding
in *Daily Telegraph* 21 November 1997; see **Blair** 37:7

7 Think what we would have missed if we had never . . . used a mobile phone or surfed the Net—or, to be honest, listened to other people talking about surfing the Net.
reflecting on developments in the past 50 years
in *Daily Telegraph* 21 November 1997

Elizabeth, the Queen Mother 1900–2002

Queen Consort of **George VI**
see also **Telegrams** 316:7

8 I'm glad we've been bombed. It makes me feel I can look the East End in the face.
to a London policeman, 13 September 1940
J. Wheeler-Bennett *King George VI* (1958)

9 The Princesses would never leave without me and I couldn't leave without the King, and the King will never leave.
on the suggestion that the royal family be evacuated during the Blitz
Penelope Mortimer *Queen Elizabeth* (1986)

10 How small and selfish is sorrow. But it bangs one about until one is senseless.
letter to Edith Sitwell, shortly after the death of ***George VI***
Victoria Glendinning *Edith Sitwell* (1983)

after an operation to remove a fishbone stuck in her throat:

11 After all these years of fishing, the fish are having their revenge.
in November 1982, attributed; Christopher Dobson (ed.) *Queen Elizabeth the Queen Mother: Chronicle of a Remarkable Life* (2000)

12 We had this rather lugubrious man in a suit, and he read a poem . . . I think it was called The Desert. And first the girls got the giggles and then I did and then even the King.
of an evening at Windsor during the war, at which T. S. ***Eliot*** *read from 'The Waste Land' to the King and Queen and the Princesses*
private conversation, reported in *Spectator* 30 June 1990

Elizabeth, Countess von Arnim 1866–1941

Australian-born British writer

13 Guests can be, and often are, delightful, but they should never be allowed to get the upper hand.
All the Dogs in My Life (1936)

Alf Ellerton

14 Belgium put the kibosh on the Kaiser.
title of song (1914)

Duke Ellington 1899–1974

American jazz pianist, composer, and band-leader

see also **Mills** 224:13

1 Playing 'Bop' is like scrabble with all the vowels missing.
in *Look* 10 August 1954

Alice Thomas Ellis 1932–

English novelist

2 Claudia's the sort of person who goes through life holding on to the sides.
The Other Side of the Fire (1983)

3 Our only hope rests on the off-chance that God does exist.
Unexplained Laughter (1985)

Havelock Ellis 1859–1939

English sexologist

4 What we call 'progress' is the exchange of one nuisance for another nuisance.
Impressions and Comments (1914) 31 July 1912

5 All civilization has from time to time become a thin crust over a volcano of revolution.
Little Essays of Love and Virtue (1922)

Ben Elton 1959–

British writer and comedian

6 People who get through life dependent on other people's possessions are always the first to lecture you on how little possessions count.
Stark (1989)

7 Uncool people never hurt anybody—all they do is collect stamps, read science-fiction books and stand on the end of railway platforms staring at trains.
in *Radio Times* 18/24 April 1998

Paul Éluard 1895–1952

French poet

8 *Adieu tristesse*
Bonjour tristesse.
Farewell sadness
Good-day sadness.
'À peine défigurée' (1932)

Odysseus Elytis 1911–96

Greek poet

9 Greek the language they gave me;
poor the house on Homer's shores.
My only care my language on Homer's shores.
There bream and perch
windbeaten verbs,
green sea currents in the blue.
'The Axion Esti' (1959)

Buchi Emecheta 1944–

Nigerian writer

10 I am a woman and a woman of Africa. I am a daughter of Nigeria and if she is in shame, I shall stay and mourn with her in shame.
Destination Biafra (1982)

11 The whole world seemed so unequal, so unfair. Some people were created with all the good things ready-made for them, others were just created like mistakes. God's mistakes.
Second-Class Citizen (1974)

Tracey Emin 1963–

British artist

12 I'm not an outsider at all. I'm on every bloody A-list there is in the art world.
in *Independent* 22 July 2000

13 If you're vivacious and a bit wild, they call you mad. That's the thing about being a woman and successful. If you were a bloke you would just be eccentric.
in *Observer* 24 September 2000

William Empson 1906–84

English poet and literary critic

14 There is a Supreme God in the ethnological section;
A hollow toad shape, faced with a blank shield.
He needs his belly to include the Pantheon,

Which is inserted through a hole behind.
At the navel, at the points formally
stressed, at the organs of sense,
Lice glue themselves, dolls, local deities,
His smooth wood creeps with all the
creeds of the world.

'Homage to the British Museum' (1935)

1 Just a smack at Auden.

title of poem, 1940

2 Waiting for the end, boys, waiting for the end.

'Just a smack at Auden' (1940)

3 You don't want madhouse and the whole thing there.

'Let it Go' (1955)

4 Slowly the poison the whole blood stream fills.
It is not the effort nor the failure tires.
The waste remains, the waste remains and kills.

'Missing Dates' (1935)

5 Seven types of ambiguity.

title of book (1930)

Nora Ephron 1941–

American writer and journalist

6 We have lived through the era when happiness was a warm puppy, and the era when happiness was a dry martini, and now we have come to the era when happiness is 'knowing what your uterus looks like'.

Crazy Salad (1975) 'Vaginal Politics'; see **Advertising slogans** 3:22, **Lennon** 196:1, **Schulz** 291:11

7 The anecdote is a particularly dehumanising sort of descriptive narrative.

Scribble, Scribble (1978)

8 I am continually fascinated at the difficulty intelligent people have in distinguishing what is controversial from what is merely offensive.

in *Esquire* January 1976

■ Epitaphs

see box opposite

Jacob Epstein 1880–1959

British sculptor

9 Why don't they stick to murder and leave art to us?

on hearing that his statue of Lazarus in New College chapel, Oxford, kept ***Khrushchev*** *awake at night*

attributed

Ludwig Erhard 1897–1977

German statesman, Chancellor of West Germany (1963–6)

10 Without Britain Europe would remain only a torso.

remark on West German television, 27 May 1962

Susan Ertz 1894–1985

American writer

11 Millions long for immortality who don't know what to do with themselves on a rainy Sunday afternoon.

Anger in the Sky (1943)

Lord Esher 1913–

English architect and planner

12 When politicians and civil servants hear the word 'culture' they feel for their blue pencils.

speech, House of Lords, 2 March 1960; see **Johst** 172:4

13 Who would guess that those gloomy bunkers were built to celebrate the pleasures of the senses?

of the Hayward Gallery complex, London

A Broken Wave (1987)

Linda Evangelista 1965–

Canadian supermodel

14 I don't get out of bed for less than $10,000 a day.

attributed

Epitaphs

1 Alan died suddenly at Saltwood on Sunday 5th September. He said he would like it to be stated that he regarded himself as having gone to join Tom and the other dogs.

announcement of the death of Alan **Clark**

in *The Times* 8 September 1999

2 Commander Jacques-Yves Cousteau has rejoined the world of silence.

announcement by the Cousteau Foundation, Paris, 25 June 1997; **Cousteau** (1910–97) *published* The Silent World *in 1953*

in *Daily Telegraph* 26 June 1997

3 Even amidst fierce flames the golden lotus can be planted.

on the gravestone of Sylvia **Plath**

Monkey, poem by the Chinese poet Wu Cheng-en (*c.*1500–82)

4 Excuse My Dust.

Dorothy **Parker**'s suggested epitaph for herself (1925); Alexander Woollcott *While Rome Burns* (1934) 'Our Mrs Parker'

5 Free at last, free at last
Thank God almighty
We are free at last.

epitaph of Martin Luther **King**, *Atlanta, Georgia*

anonymous spiritual, with which he ended his 'I have a dream' speech; see **King** 181:6

6 God damn you all: I told you so.

H. G. **Wells**' *suggestion for his own epitaph, in conversation with Ernest Barker, 1939*

Ernest Barker *Age and Youth* (1953)

7 He encouraged us.

the epitaph Tony **Benn** *would like for himself*

Anthony Clare *In the Psychiatrist's Chair 111* (1998)

8 He helped people see God in the ordinary things of life, and he made children laugh.

Revd W. **Awdry**'s preferred epitaph; in *Independent* 22 March 1997, obituary

9 Hereabouts died a very gallant gentleman, Captain L. E. G. Oates of the Inniskilling Dragoons. In March 1912, returning from the Pole, he walked willingly to his death in a blizzard to try and save his comrades, beset by hardships.

epitaph on cairn erected in the Antarctic, 15 November 1912 by E. L. Atkinson (1882–1929) and Apsley Cherry-Garrard (1882–1959)

Apsley Cherry-Garrard *Worst Journey in the World* (1922); see **Last words** 190:6

10 Here lies Groucho Marx—and lies and lies and lies. P.S. He never kissed an ugly girl.

his own suggestion for his epitaph

B. Norman *The Movie Greats* (1981)

11 Here lies W. C. Fields. I would rather be living in Philadelphia.

suggested epitaph for himself, in *Vanity Fair* June 1925

12 He was an average guy who could carry a tune.

Bing **Crosby**'s *suggested epitaph for himself*

in *Newsweek* 24 October 1977

13 His foe was folly and his weapon wit.

inscription for W. S. Gilbert's memorial on the Victoria Embankment, London (1915), by Anthony Hope (1863–1933)

14 I will return. And I will be millions.

inscription on the tomb of Eva **Perón**, Buenos Aires

15 John Le Mesurier wishes it to be known that he conked out on November 15th. He sadly misses family and friends.

obituary notice on the death of John Le Mesurier (1912–83), in *The Times* 16 November 1983

16 Poor G.K.C., his day is past—
Now God will know the truth at last.

mock epitaph for G. K. **Chesterton**, *by E. V. Lucas (1868–1938)*

Dudley Barker *G. K. Chesterton* (1973)

17 Rest in peace. The mistake shall not be repeated.

inscription on the cenotaph at Hiroshima, Japan

18 She did it the hard way.

epitaph of Bette Davis, chosen by herself

James Spada *More Than a Woman* (1993)

▶

▸ Epitaphs continued

1 A soldier of the Great War known unto God.

standard epitaph for the unidentified dead of World War One

adopted by the War Graves Commission

2 Their name liveth for evermore.

*standard inscription on the Stone of Sacrifice in each military cemetery of World War One, proposed by Rudyard **Kipling** as a member of the War Graves Commission*

Charles Carrington *Rudyard Kipling* (rev. ed. 1978); see below

Their bodies are buried in peace; but their name liveth for evermore.

Bible (Apocrypha) Ecclesiasticus

3 Timothy has passed . . .

*message on his Internet web page announcing the death of Timothy **Leary**, 31 May 1996*

in *Guardian* 1 June 1996

4 When you go home, tell them of us and say,
'For your tomorrow we gave our today.'

Kohima memorial to the Burma campaign of the Second World War; in recent years used at Remembrance Day parades in the UK (see **Binyon** 35:12); see below

When you go home, tell them of us and say,
'For your tomorrows these gave their today.'

John Maxwell Edmonds (1875–1958) *Inscriptions Suggested for War Memorials* (1919)

5 Without you, Heaven would be too dull to bear,
And Hell would not be Hell if you are there.

*epitaph for Maurice **Bowra** by John **Sparrow***

in *Times Literary Supplement* 30 May 1975

Gavin Ewart 1916–95

British poet

6 So the last date slides into the bracket,
that will appear in all future anthologies—
And in quiet Cornwall and in London's ghastly racket
We are now Betjemanless.

'In Memoriam, Sir John Betjeman (1906–84)' (1985)

7 Is it Colman's smile
That makes life worth while
Or Crawford's significant form?
Is it Lombard's lips
Or Mae West's hips
That carry you through the storm?

'Verse from an Opera' (1939)

William Norman Ewer 1885–1976

British writer

8 I gave my life for freedom—This I know:
For those who bade me fight had told me so.

'Five Souls' (1917)

9 How odd
Of God
To choose
The Jews.

The Week-End Book (1924); see **Browne** 46:3

Winifred Ewing 1929–

Scottish Nationalist politician

10 The Scottish Parliament which adjourned on 25 March in the year 1707 is hereby reconvened.

opening speech, as oldest member of the new Parliament

in Scottish Parliament 12 May 1999

11 I am an expert in being a minority. I was alone in the House of Commons for three years and alone in the European Parliament for nineteen years, but we are all minorities now.

in Scottish Parliament 12 May 1999

Richard Eyre 1943-

English theatre director

1 We exercise the ultimate sanction of switching off only in an extreme case, like a heroin addict rejecting the needle in the face of death.

on television as an agent of cultural destruction

attributed, 1995

Clifton Fadiman 1904-

American critic

2 Milk's leap toward immortality.

of cheese

Any Number Can Play (1957)

3 The mama of dada.

of Gertrude ***Stein***

Party of One (1955)

Frantz Fanon 1925-61

French West Indian psychoanalyst and writer

4 Leave this Europe where they are never done talking of Man, yet murder men everywhere they find them.

The Wretched of the Earth (1961)

5 The shape of Africa resembles a revolver, and Zaire is the trigger.

attributed

Wallace Fard 1891?-1934

American religious leader, founder of the Nation of Islam

6 The blue-eyed devil white man.

Malcolm X with Alex Haley *The Autobiography of Malcolm X* (1965); see **Malcolm X** 214:3

Eleanor Farjeon 1881-1965

English writer for children

7 Morning has broken
Like the first morning,
Blackbird has spoken
Like the first bird.

'A Morning Song (for the First Day of Spring)' (1957)

Herbert Farjeon 1887-1945

English writer and theatre critic

8 For I've danced with a man.
I've danced with a man
Who—well, you'll never guess.
I've danced with a man who's danced with a girl
Who's danced with the Prince of Wales!

'I've danced with a man who's danced with a girl'; first written for Elsa Lanchester and sung at private parties; later sung on stage (1928) by Mimi Crawford

King Farouk 1920-65

King of Egypt, 1936-52

9 Soon there will be only five Kings left—the King of England, the King of Spades, the King of Clubs, the King of Hearts and the King of Diamonds.

said to Lord Boyd-Orr at a conference in Cairo, 1948; Lord Boyd-Orr *As I Recall* (1966)

Mia Farrow 1945-

American actress

10 He had polyester sheets and I wanted to get cotton sheets. He discussed it with his shrink many times before he made the switch.

of the dependence of her former partner, Woody ***Allen****, on psychotherapists*

in *Independent* 8 February 1997

William Faulkner 1897-1962

American novelist

see also **Film lines** 117:1, **Film titles** 118:9

11 Maybe the only thing worse than having to give gratitude constantly all the time, is having to accept it.

Requiem for a Nun (1951)

12 He made the books and he died.

his own 'sum and history of my life'

letter to Malcolm Cowley, 11 February 1949

13 He [the writer] must teach himself that the basest of all things is to be afraid and, teaching himself that, forget it forever, leaving no room in his workshop for anything but the old verities and truths of the heart, the old universal truths

lacking which any story is ephemeral and doomed—love and honor and pity and pride and compassion and sacrifice.
Nobel Prize speech, Stockholm, 10 December 1950

1 The poet's voice need not merely be the record of man; it can be one of the props, the pillars, to help him endure and prevail.
Nobel prize acceptance speech, Stockholm, 10 December 1950

2 The writer's only responsibility is to his art. He will be completely ruthless if he is a good one. . . . If a writer has to rob his mother, he will not hesitate; the *Ode on a Grecian Urn* is worth any number of old ladies.
in *Paris Review* Spring 1956

3 A man shouldn't fool with booze until he's fifty; then he's a damn fool if he doesn't.
James M. Webb and A. Wigfall Green *William Faulkner of Oxford* (1965)

Dianne Feinstein 1933–

American Democratic politician, Mayor of San Francisco

4 Toughness doesn't have to come in a pinstripe suit.
in *Time* 4 June 1984

5 There was a time when you could say the least government was the best—but not in the nation's most populous state.
campaign speech, 15 March 1990

Vanessa Feltz 1962–

British television presenter

6 Marriage 2001-style, as I know to my cost, is entirely expendable, more easily disposable than a McDonald's wrapper.
in *Sunday Times* 15 April 2001

James Fenton 1949–

English poet

7 It is not what they built. It is what they knocked down.
It is not the houses. It is the spaces between the houses.
It is not the streets that exist. It is the streets that no longer exist.
German Requiem (1981)

8 'I didn't exist at Creation
I didn't exist at the Flood,
And I won't be around for Salvation
To sort out the sheep from the cud—

'Or whatever the phrase is. The fact is
In soteriological terms
I'm a crude existential malpractice
And you are a diet of worms.'
'God, A Poem' (1983)

9 Yes
You have come upon the fabled lands where myths
Go when they die.
'The Pitt-Rivers Museum' (1983)

10 Windbags can be right. Aphorists can be wrong. It is a tough world.
in *Times* 21 February 1985

Edna Ferber 1887–1968

American writer

11 Being an old maid is like death by drowning, a really delightful sensation after you cease to struggle.
R. E. Drennan *Wit's End* (1973)

Enrico Fermi 1901–54

Italian-born American atomic physicist

12 If I could remember the names of all these particles I'd be a botanist.
R. L. Weber *More Random Walks in Science* (1973)

13 Whatever Nature has in store for mankind, unpleasant as it may be, men must accept, for ignorance is never better than knowledge.
Laura Fermi *Atoms in the Family* (1955)

Kathleen Ferrier

see **Last words** 191:2

Paul Feyerabend 1924–94

Austrian philosopher

1 The time is overdue for adding the separation of state and science to the by now customary separation of state and church. Science is only *one* of the many instruments man has invented to cope with his surroundings. It is not the only one, it is not infallible, and it has become too powerful, too pushy, and too dangerous to be left on its own.

Against Method (1975)

Richard Phillips Feynman 1918–88

American theoretical physicist

2 For a successful technology, reality must take precedence over public relations, for nature cannot be fooled.

Appendix to the *Rogers Commission Report on the Space Shuttle Challenger Accident* 6 June 1986

3 What I cannot create, I do not understand.

attributed

Frank Field 1942–

British Labour politician

4 The archbishop is usually to be found nailing his colours to the fence.

of Archbishop ***Runcie****; a similar comment has been recorded on A. J.* ***Balfour****, c.1904*

attributed in *Crockfords 1987/88* (1987)

Helen Fielding 1958–

British writer

5 Head is full of moony fantasies about . . . being trendy Smug Married instead of sheepish Singleton.

Bridget Jones's Diary (1996)

6 Wish to be like Tina Brown, though not, obviously, quite so hardworking.

Bridget Jones's Diary (1996)

Dorothy Fields 1905–74

American songwriter

7 The minute you walked in the joint,
I could see you were a man of distinction,
A real big spender . . .
Hey! big spender, spend a little time with me.

'Big Spender' (1966 song)

8 A fine romance with no kisses.
A fine romance, my friend, this is.

'A Fine Romance' (1936 song)

9 Grab your coat, and get your hat,
Leave your worry on the doorstep,
Just direct your feet
To the sunny side of the street.

'On the Sunny Side of the Street' (1930 song)

10 Pick yourself up,
Dust yourself off,
Start all over again.

'Pick Yourself Up' (1936 song)

W. C. Fields 1880–1946

American humorist

on Fields: see **Rosten** 279:14*; see also* **Epitaphs** 109:11, **Film lines** 116:8

11 Some weasel took the cork out of my lunch.

You Can't Cheat an Honest Man (1939 film)

12 Never give a sucker an even break.

title of a W. C. Fields film (1941); the catch-phrase (Fields's own) is said to have originated in the musical comedy *Poppy* (1923)

13 It ain't a fit night out for man or beast.

adopted by Fields but claimed by him not to be original; letter, 8 February 1944

14 Hell, I never vote *for* anybody. I always vote *against*.

R. L. Taylor *W. C. Fields* (1950)

15 The funniest thing about comedy is that you never know why people laugh. I know *what* makes them laugh but trying to get your hands on the *why* of it is like trying to pick an eel out of a tub of water.

R. J. Anobile *A Flask of Fields* (1972)

16 If at first you don't succeed, try, try again. Then quit. No use being a damn fool about it.

attributed

1 Last week, I went to Philadelphia, but it was closed.

R. J. Anobile *Godfrey Daniels* (1975)

Zlata Filipovic 1980–

Bosnian child writer

2 Why is politics making us unhappy, separating us, when we ourselves know who is good and who isn't? We mix with the good, not with the bad. And among the good there are Serbs and Croats and Muslims, just as there are among the bad. I simply don't understand it.

Zlata's Diary: A Child's Life in Sarajevo (1993) 19 November 1992

■ Film lines

see box opposite

see also Woody **Allen**, W. C. **Fields**, Greta **Garbo**, Stan **Laurel**, **Taglines for films** 314:1, Mae **West**

■ Film titles

see box on page 118

Michael Fish 1944–

British weather forecaster

3 A woman rang to say she heard there was a hurricane on the way. Well don't worry, there isn't.

weather forecast on the night before serious gales in southern England

BBC TV, 15 October 1987

Carrie Fisher 1956–

American actress and writer

4 Here's how men think. Sex, work—and those are reversible, depending on age—sex, work, food, sports and lastly, begrudgingly, relationships. And here's how women think. Relationships, relationships, relationships, work, sex, shopping, weight, food.

Surrender the Pink (1990)

H. A. L. Fisher 1856–1940

English historian

5 Purity of race does not exist. Europe is a continent of energetic mongrels.

A History of Europe (1935)

Lord Fisher 1841–1920

British admiral

6 Sack the lot!

on government overmanning and overspending

letter to *The Times*, 2 September 1919

7 Never contradict. Never explain. Never apologize.

letter to *The Times*, 5 September 1919

Marve Fisher

American songwriter

8 I like Chopin and Bizet, and the voice of
Doris Day,
Gershwin songs and old forgotten carols.
But the music that excels is the sound of
oil wells
As they slurp, slurp, slurp into the
barrels.

'An Old-Fashioned Girl' (1954 song)

9 I want an old-fashioned house
With an old-fashioned fence
And an old-fashioned millionaire.

'An Old-Fashioned Girl' (1954 song)

R. A. Fisher 1890–1962

English statistician and geneticist

10 The best causes tend to attract to their support the worst arguments.

Statistical Methods and Scientific Inference (1956)

11 It was Darwin's chief contribution, not only to Biology but to the whole of natural science, to have brought to light a process by which contingencies *a priori* improbable are given, in the process of time, an increasing probability, until it is their non-occurrence, rather than their

▶▶

Film lines

1 Anyway, Ma, I made it . . . Top of the world!

White Heat (1949 film) written by Ivan Goff (1910–) and Ben Roberts (1916–84); last lines—spoken by James Cagney

2 EUNICE GRAYSON: Mr—?
SEAN CONNERY: Bond. James Bond.

Dr No (1962 film, written by Richard Maibaum, Johanna Harwood, and Berkely Mather, and based on the novel by Ian **Fleming**)

3 Cancel the kitchen scraps for lepers and orphans. No more merciful beheadings. And call off Christmas!

Robin Hood, Prince of Thieves (1991 film), written by Pen Densham and John Watson; spoken by Alan Rickman

4 Don't let's ask for the moon! We have the stars!

Now, Voyager (1942 film), from the novel (1941) by Olive Higgins Prouty (1882–1974); spoken by Bette Davis

5 Either he's dead, or my watch has stopped.

A Day at the Races (1937 film) written by Robert Pirosh, George Seaton, and George Oppenheimer; spoken by Groucho **Marx**

6 E.T. phone home.

E.T. (1982 film) written by Melissa Mathison (1950–)

7 Fasten your seat-belts, it's going to be a bumpy night.

All About Eve (1950 film) written by Joseph L. Mankiewicz (1909–); spoken by Bette Davis

8 Figures you wouldn't know how to work it, if it's got a computer.

Strange Brew (1983 film), directed and written by Dave **Thomas** and Rick Moranis (1953–); spoken by Dave Thomas as Doug McKenzie to his brother Bob (Rick Moranis)

9 Frankly, my dear, I don't give a damn!

Gone with the Wind (1939 film) written by Sidney Howard; spoken by Clark Gable; see **Mitchell** 228:3

10 Go ahead, make my day.

Sudden Impact (1983 film) written by Joseph C. Stinson (1947–); spoken by Clint Eastwood

11 Greed—for lack of a better word—is good. Greed is right. Greed works.

Wall Street (1987 film) written by Stanley Weiser and Oliver Stone (1946–); see **Boesky** 39:4

12 Here's looking at you, kid.

Casablanca (1942 film) written by Julius J. Epstein (1909–2001), Philip G. Epstein (1909–52), and Howard Koch (1902–); spoken by Humphrey Bogart to Ingrid Bergman; see **Film lines** 115:17, 116:14, 117:5

13 I ate his liver with some fava beans and a nice chianti.

The Silence of the Lambs (1991 film, based on the novel by Thomas Harris), written by Thomas Harris (1940–) and Ted Tally (1952–); spoken by Anthony **Hopkins** as Hannibal Lecter

14 I could have had class. I could have been a contender.

On the Waterfront (1954 film) written by Budd Schulberg (1914–); spoken by Marlon Brando

15 I do wish we could chat longer, but I'm having an old friend for dinner.

The Silence of the Lambs (1991 film, based on the novel by Thomas Harris), written by Thomas Harris (1940–) and Ted Tally (1952–); spoken by Anthony **Hopkins** as Hannibal Lecter

16 I fear all we have done is awaken a sleeping giant and fill him with a terrible resolve.

Tora! Tora! Tora! (1970 film, written by Larry Forrester, Hideo Oguni, and Ryuzo Kikushima); see **Yamamoto** 346:5

17 If she can stand it, I can. Play it!

usually quoted as 'Play it again, Sam'

Casablanca (1942 film) written by Julius J. Epstein (1909–2001), Philip G. Epstein (1909–52), and Howard Koch (1902–); spoken by Humphrey Bogart; see **Film lines** 115:12, 116:14, 117:5, **Misquotations** 226:13

▶

▸ Film lines continued

1 If you can't leave in a taxi you can leave in a huff. If that's too soon, you can leave in a minute and a huff.

Duck Soup (1933 film) written by Bert Kalmar (1884–1947), Harry Ruby (1895–1974), Arthur Sheekman (1891–1978), and Nat Perrin; spoken by Groucho **Marx**; see **Film lines** 117:8, 117:14

2 If you carry a 00 number it means you're licensed to kill, not get killed.

Dr No (1962 film, written by Richard Maibaum, Johanna Harwood, and Berkely Mather, and based on the novel by Ian **Fleming**), spoken by Bernard Lee as 'M'; see **Fleming** 120:6

3 I'll be back.

The Terminator (1984 film) written by James Cameron (1954–) and Gale Anne Hurd; spoken by Arnold Schwarzenegger; see **Taglines for films** 314:4

4 I love the smell of napalm in the morning. It smells like victory.

Apocalypse Now (1979 film) written by John Milius and Francis Ford Coppola (1939–); spoken by Robert Duvall

Julius Caesar of his assassins:

5 Infamy, infamy, they've all got it in for me!

Carry on, Cleo (1964 film, written by Talbot Rothwell, 1916–74); according to Frank Muir's letter to the *Guardian*, 22 July 1995, the line had actually been written by him and Denis Norden for a radio sketch for 'Take It From Here', and was later used by Rothwell with their permission

6 In Italy for thirty years under the Borgias they had warfare, terror, murder, bloodshed—they produced Michelangelo, Leonardo da Vinci and the Renaissance. In Switzerland they had brotherly love, five hundred years of democracy and peace and what did that produce . . . ? The cuckoo clock.

The Third Man (1949 film); words added by Orson **Welles** to Graham **Greene**'s screenplay

7 I see dead people.

The Sixth Sense (1999 film, written by Manoj Night Shyamalan), spoken by Haley Joel Osment

8 It's a funny old world—a man's lucky if he gets out of it alive.

You're Telling Me (1934 film), written by Walter de Leon and Paul M. Jones; spoken by W. C. **Fields**; see **Thatcher** 317:16

9 DRIFTWOOD (Groucho Marx): It's all right. That's—that's in every contract. That's—that's what they call a sanity clause.
FIORELLO (Chico Marx): You can't fool me. There ain't no Sanity Claus.

Night at the Opera (1935 film) written by George S. Kaufman (1889–1961) and Morrie Ryskind (1895–1985)

10 Let's get out of these wet clothes and into a dry Martini.

line coined in the 1920s by Robert **Benchley**'s press agent and adopted by Mae **West** in *Every Day's a Holiday* (1937 film)

11 Let's go to work.

Reservoir Dogs (1992 film) written and directed by Quentin Tarantino; spoken by Lawrence Tierney

12 Lunch is for wimps.

Wall Street (1987 film) written by Stanley Weiser and Oliver Stone (1946–)

13 Madness! Madness!

The Bridge on the River Kwai (1957 film of the novel by Pierre Boulle) written by Carl Foreman (1914–), closing line

14 Major Strasser has been shot. Round up the usual suspects.

Casablanca (1942 film) written by Julius J. Epstein (1909–2001), Philip G. Epstein (1909–52), and Howard Koch (1902–); spoken by Claude Rains; see **Film lines** 115:12, 115:17, 117:5

15 Man your ships, and may the force be with you.

Star Wars (1977 film) written by George Lucas (1944–)

16 Marriage isn't a word . . . it's a *sentence*!

The Crowd (1928 film) written by King Vidor (1895–1982)

▸

▸ Film lines continued

1 Maybe just whistle. You know how to whistle, don't you, Steve? You just put your lips together and blow.

To Have and Have Not (1944 film) written by Jules Furthman (1888–1960) and William **Faulkner**; spoken by Lauren **Bacall**

2 Mr Kane was a man who got everything he wanted, and then lost it. Maybe Rosebud was something he couldn't get or something he lost. Anyway, it wouldn't have explained anything. I don't think any word can explain a man's life. No, I guess Rosebud is just a piece in a jigsaw puzzle, a missing piece.

Citizen Kane (1941 film) written by Herman J. Mankiewicz (1897–1953) and Orson **Welles**

3 My momma always said life was like a box of chocolates . . . you never know what you're gonna get.

Forrest Gump (1994 film), written by Eric Ross, based on the novel (1986) by Winston Groom; spoken by Tom Hanks

4 Nature, Mr Allnutt, is what we are put into this world to rise above.

The African Queen (1951 film) written by James Agee 1909–55; not in the novel by C. S. Forester

5 Of all the gin joints in all the towns in all the world, she walks into mine.

Casablanca (1942 film) written by Julius J. Epstein (1909–2001), Philip G. Epstein (1909–52), and Howard Koch (1902–); spoken by Humphrey Bogart; see **Film lines** 115:12, 115:17, 116:14

6 Oh no, it wasn't the aeroplanes. It was Beauty killed the Beast.

King Kong (1933 film) written by James Creelman (1901–41) and Ruth Rose

7 The pellet with the poison's in the vessel with the pestle. The chalice from the palace has the brew that is true.

The Court Jester (1955 film) written by Norman Panama (1914–) and Melvin Frank (1913–88); spoken by Danny Kaye

8 Remember, you're fighting for this woman's honour . . . which is probably more than she ever did.

Duck Soup (1933 film) written by Bert Kalmar (1884–1947), Harry Ruby (1895–1974), Arthur Sheekman (1891–1978), and Nat Perrin; spoken by Groucho **Marx**; see **Film lines** 116:1, 117:14

9 The son of a bitch stole my watch!

The Front Page (1931 film), from the play (1928) by Charles MacArthur (1895–1956) and Ben Hecht (1894–1964)

10 This movie was shot in 3B, three beers and it looks good, eh?

Strange Brew (1983 film), directed and written by Dave **Thomas** and Rick Moranis (1953–); spoken by Rick Moranis as Bob McKenzie

11 GERRY: We can't get married at all....I'm a man.

OSGOOD: Well, nobody's perfect.

Some Like It Hot (1959 film) written by Billy **Wilder** and I. A. L. Diamond; closing words spoken by Jack Lemmon and Joe E. Brown

12 What a dump!

Beyond the Forest (1949 film) written by Lenore Coffee (?1897–1984); line spoken by Bette Davis, entering a room

13 What have the Romans ever done for us?

Monty Python's Life of Brian (1983 film) written by John Cleese, Graham Chapman, Eric Idle, Michael Palin, Terry Gilliam, and Terry Jones

14 Why, a four-year-old child could understand this report. Run out and find me a four-year-old child. I can't make head or tail of it.

Duck Soup (1933 film) written by Bert Kalmar (1884–1947), Harry Ruby (1895–1974), Arthur Sheekman (1891–1978), and Nat Perrin; spoken by Groucho **Marx**; see **Film lines** 116:1, 117:8

15 You finally, really did it—you maniacs! You blew it up! Damn you! Damn you all to hell!

Planet of the Apes (1968 film, written by Michael Wilson and Rod Serling); spoken by Charlton **Heston**

▶

▸ Film lines continued

1 You're going out a youngster but you've *got* to come back a star.

42nd Street (1933 film) written by James Seymour and Rian James

2 JOE GILLIS: You used to be in pictures. You used to be big.
NORMA DESMOND: I am big. It's the pictures that got small.

Sunset Boulevard (1950 film) written by Charles Brackett (1892–1969), Billy **Wilder**, and D. M. Marshman Jr.

Film titles

3 Back to the future.

written by Robert Zemeckis and Bob Gale, 1985

4 Close encounters of the third kind.

written by Steven Spielberg (1947–), 1977

5 The discreet charm of the bourgeoisie.

written by Luis **Buñuel**, 1972

6 The Empire strikes back.

written by George Lucas (1944–), 1980; the sequel to *Star Wars*

7 Every which way but loose.

written by Jeremy Joe Kronsberg, 1978; starring Clint Eastwood

8 The good, the bad, and the ugly.

written by Age Scarpelli, Luciano Vincenzoni (1926–), and Sergio Leone (1921–), 1966

9 The long hot summer.

written by Irving Ravetch and Harriet Frank, 1958; based on stories by William **Faulkner**

10 Naughty but nice.

written by Jerry Wald (1911–62) and Richard Macaulay, 1939

11 Never on Sunday.

written by Jules Dassin (1911–), 1959

12 Rebel without a cause.

written by R. M. Lindner (1914–56), 1959, based on his book (1944); starring James Dean

13 Sunday, bloody Sunday.

written by Penelope Gilliatt, 1971

14 Sweet smell of success.

written by Ernest Lehman, 1957

15 Take the money and run.

written by Mickey Rose and Woody **Allen**, 1969

▸▸ R. A. Fisher continued

occurrence, which becomes highly probable.

sometimes quoted as 'Natural selection is a mechanism for generating an exceedingly high degree of improbability'

'Retrospect of the criticisms of the Theory of Natural Selection' in Julian Huxley *Evolution as a Process* (1954)

Gerry Fitt 1926–

Northern Irish politician

16 People [in Northern Ireland] don't march as an alternative to jogging. They do it to assert their supremacy. It is pure tribalism, the cause of troubles all over the world.

referring to the 'marching season' in Northern Ireland, leading up to the anniversary of the Battle of the Boyne on 12 July, when parades by Orange communities traditionally take place

in *The Times* 5 August 1994

F. Scott Fitzgerald 1896–1940

American novelist

17 Let me tell you about the very rich. They are different from you and me.

to which Ernest ***Hemingway*** *replied, 'Yes, they have more money'*

All the Sad Young Men (1926) 'Rich Boy'

18 The beautiful and damned.

title of novel (1922)

1 At eighteen our convictions are hills from which we look; at forty-five they are caves in which we hide.

'Bernice Bobs her Hair' (1920)

2 Her voice is full of money.

of Daisy

The Great Gatsby (1925)

3 They were careless people, Tom and Daisy—they smashed up things and creatures and then retreated back into their money or their vast carelessness, or whatever it was that kept them together, and let other people clean up the mess they had made.

The Great Gatsby (1925)

4 See that little stream—we could walk to it in two minutes. It took the British a month to walk it—a whole empire walking very slowly, dying in front and pushing forward behind. And another empire walked very slowly backward a few inches a day, leaving the dead like a million bloody rugs.

Tender is the Night (1934)

5 The test of a first-rate intelligence is the ability to hold two opposed ideas in the mind at the same time, and still retain the ability to function.

in *Esquire* February 1936 'The Crack-Up'

6 In a real dark night of the soul it is always three o'clock in the morning.

'dark night of the soul' being a translation of the Spanish title of a work (1578–80) by St John of the Cross

'Handle with Care' in *Esquire* March 1936

7 No grand idea was ever born in a conference, but a lot of foolish ideas have died there.

Edmund Wilson (ed.) *The Crack-Up* (1945) 'Note-Books E'

8 Show me a hero and I will write you a tragedy.

Edmund Wilson (ed.) *The Crack-Up* (1945) 'Note-Books E'

9 There are no second acts in American lives.

Edmund Wilson (ed.) *The Last Tycoon* (1941) 'Hollywood, etc.'

Penelope Fitzgerald 1916–2000

English novelist and biographer

10 Why read when you can pick up a spade and find out for yourself?

of archaeology

The Golden Child (1977)

11 Duty is what no-one else will do at the moment.

Offshore (1979)

Lorna Fitzsimons 1962–

British Labour politician

12 The art of politics is to get someone to change their mind without humiliating them.

in *Independent* 24 February 2001

Bud Flanagan 1896–1968

British comedian

13 Underneath the Arches,
I dream my dreams away,
Underneath the Arches,
On cobble-stones I lay.

'Underneath the Arches' (1932 song)

Michael Flanders 1922–75 and Donald Swann 1923–94

English songwriters

14 Have some Madeira, m'dear.

title of song (c.1956)

15 Mud! Mud! Glorious mud!
Nothing quite like it for cooling the blood.

'The Hippopotamus' (1952 song)

16 Eating people is wrong!

'The Reluctant Cannibal' (1956 song)

17 That monarch of the road,
Observer of the Highway Code,
That big six-wheeler
Scarlet-painted
London Transport
Diesel-engined
Ninety-seven horse power
Omnibus!

'A Transport of Delight' (c.1956 song)

James Elroy Flecker
1884–1915

English poet

1 West of these out to seas colder than the Hebrides
I must go
Where the fleet of stars is anchored and the young
Star captains glow.

'The Dying Patriot' (1913)

2 The dragon-green, the luminous, the dark, the serpent-haunted sea.

'The Gates of Damascus' (1913)

3 We are the Pilgrims, master: we shall go
Always a little further: it may be
Beyond that last blue mountain barred with snow,
Across that angry or that glimmering sea.

The Golden Journey to Samarkand (1913) pt. 1, 'Epilogue'

4 For lust of knowing what should not be known,
We take the Golden Road to Samarkand.

The Golden Journey to Samarkand (1913) pt. 1, 'Epilogue'

5 I have seen old ships sail like swans asleep
Beyond the village which men still call Tyre,
With leaden age o'ercargoed, dipping deep
For Famagusta and the hidden sun
That rings black Cyprus with a lake of fire.

'Old Ships' (1915)

Ian Fleming 1908–64

English thriller writer
see also **Film lines** 116:2

6 The licence to kill for the Secret Service, the double-o prefix, was a great honour.

Dr No (1958); see **Film lines** 116:2

7 A medium Vodka dry Martini—with a slice of lemon peel. Shaken and not stirred.

Dr No (1958)

8 From Russia with love.

title of novel (1957)

9 Live and let die.

title of novel (1954)

Peter Fleming 1907–71

English journalist and travel writer

10 São Paulo is like Reading, only much farther away.

Brazilian Adventure (1933)

11 Last night we went to a Chinese dinner at six and a French dinner at nine, and I can feel the sharks' fins navigating unhappily in the Burgundy.

letter from Yunnanfu, 20 March 1938

Dario Fo 1926–

Italian dramatist

12 *Non si paga, non si paga.*

We won't pay, we won't pay.

title of play (1975; translated by Lino Pertile in 1978 as 'We Can't Pay? We Won't Pay!' and performed in London in 1981 as *'Can't Pay? Won't Pay!'*); see **Political sayings and slogans** 261:10

Ferdinand Foch 1851–1929

French general

13 My centre is giving way, my right is retreating, situation excellent, I am attacking.

message during the first Battle of the Marne, September 1914

R. Recouly *Foch* (1919)

14 This is not a peace treaty, it is an armistice for twenty years.

at the signing of the Treaty of Versailles, 1919

P. Reynaud *Mémoires* (1963)

J. Foley 1906–1970

British songwriter

15 Old soldiers never die,
They simply fade away.

'Old Soldiers Never Die' (1920 song); copyrighted by Foley but possibly a folk-song from the First World War; see **MacArthur** 206:3

Jane Fonda 1937–

American actress

1 A man has every season, while a woman has only the right to spring.

in *Daily Mail* 13 September 1989

2 Ted needs someone to be there 100% of the time. He thinks that's love. It's not love—it's babysitting.

on the breakdown of her marriage to Ted Turner

in *Sunday Times* 15 April 2001

Michael Foot 1913–

British Labour politician

3 A speech from Ernest Bevin on a major occasion had all the horrific fascination of a public execution. If the mind was left immune, eyes and ears and emotions were riveted.

Aneurin Bevan (1962)

4 Think of it! A second Chamber selected by the Whips. A seraglio of eunuchs.

speech in the House of Commons, 3 February 1969

5 It is not necessary that every time he rises he should give his famous imitation of a semi-house-trained polecat.

of Norman ***Tebbit***

speech in the House of Commons, 2 March 1978

Anna Ford 1943–

English journalist and broadcaster

6 Let's face it, there are no plain women on television.

in *Observer* 23 September 1979

Gerald Ford 1909–

American Republican statesman, 38th President of the US, 1974–7

on Ford: see **Abzug** 1:4

7 I am a Ford, not a Lincoln.

on taking the vice-presidential oath, 6 December 1973

8 Our long national nightmare is over. Our Constitution works; our great Republic is a Government of laws and not of men.

on being sworn in as President, 9 August 1974; see below

A government of laws, and not of men.

John Adams (1735–1826) in *Boston Gazette* (1774)

9 If the Government is big enough to give you everything you want, it is big enough to take away everything you have.

J. F. Parker *If Elected* (1960)

Henry Ford 1863–1947

American car manufacturer

10 Any customer can have a car painted any colour that he wants so long as it is black.

on the Model T Ford, 1909

My Life and Work (with Samuel Crowther, 1922)

11 History is more or less bunk.

in *Chicago Tribune* 25 May 1916

12 What we call evil is simply ignorance bumping its head in the dark.

in *Observer* 16 March 1930

Lena Guilbert Ford 1870–1916

English songwriter

13 Keep the Home-fires burning,
While your hearts are yearning,
Though your lads are far away
They dream of Home.
There's a silver lining
Through the dark cloud shining;
Turn the dark cloud inside out,
Till the boys come Home.

'Till the Boys Come Home!' (1914 song); music by Ivor Novello

Howell Forgy 1908–83

American naval chaplain

14 Praise the Lord and pass the ammunition.

at Pearl Harbor, 7 December 1941, while sailors passed ammunition by hand to the deck

in *New York Times* 1 November 1942 (later title of song by Frank Loesser, 1942)

E. M. Forster 1879–1970

English novelist

1 Yes—oh dear yes—the novel tells a story.
Aspects of the Novel (1927)

2 How can I tell what I think till I see what I say?
Aspects of the Novel (1927); see **Wallas** 329:9

3 It is a period between two wars—the long week-end it has been called.
The Development of English Prose between 1918 and 1939 (1945)

4 Railway termini. They are our gates to the glorious and the unknown. Through them we pass out into adventure and sunshine, to them, alas! we return.
Howards End (1910)

5 It will be generally admitted that Beethoven's Fifth Symphony is the most sublime noise that has ever penetrated into the ear of man.
Howards End (1910)

6 To trust people is a luxury in which only the wealthy can indulge; the poor cannot afford it.
Howards End (1910)

7 She felt that those who prepared for all the emergencies of life beforehand may equip themselves at the expense of joy.
Howards End (1910)

8 Personal relations are the important thing for ever and ever, and not this outer life of telegrams and anger.
Howards End (1910)

9 Only connect! . . . Only connect the prose and the passion, and both will be exalted, and human love will be seen at its height.
Howards End (1910)

10 Death destroys a man: the idea of death saves him.
Howards End (1910)

11 The sick had no rights . . . one could lie to them remorselessly.
Howards End (1910)

12 It's the worst thing that can ever happen to you in all your life, and you've got to mind it . . . They'll come saying, 'Bear up—trust to time.' No, no; they're wrong. Mind it.
The Longest Journey (1907)

13 There is much good luck in the world, but it is luck. We are none of us safe. We are children, playing or quarrelling on the line.
The Longest Journey (1907)

14 The so-called white races are really pinko-grey.
A Passage to India (1924)

15 Nothing in India is identifiable, the mere asking of a question causes it to disappear or to merge in something else.
A Passage to India (1924)

16 Pathos, piety, courage—they exist, but are identical, and so is filth. Everything exists, nothing has value.
A Passage to India (1924)

17 Where there is officialism every human relationship suffers.
A Passage to India (1924)

18 God si [is] Love. Is this the final message of India?
A Passage to India (1924)

19 Think before you speak is criticism's motto; speak before you think creation's.
Two Cheers for Democracy (1951) 'Raison d'être of Criticism'

20 If I had to choose between betraying my country and betraying my friend, I hope I should have the guts to betray my country.
Two Cheers for Democracy (1951) 'What I Believe'

21 So Two cheers for Democracy: one because it admits variety and two because it permits criticism. Two cheers are quite enough: there is no occasion to give three. Only Love the Beloved Republic deserves that.
Two Cheers for Democracy (1951) 'What I Believe'; see below

Even love, the beloved Republic, that
feeds upon freedom lives.

Algernon Charles Swinburne (1837–1909) 'Hertha' (1871)

Margaret Forster 1938–

English novelist

1 But that perhaps is the point of any memoir—to walk with the dead and yet see them with our eyes, from our vantage point.

Hidden Lives: A Family Memoir (1995)

Frederick Forsyth 1938–

English novelist

2 Everyone seems to remember with great clarity what they were doing on November 22nd, 1963, at the precise moment they heard President Kennedy was dead.

The Odessa File (1972)

Harry Emerson Fosdick 1878–1969

American Baptist minister

3 I renounce war for its consequences, for the lies it lives on and propagates, for the undying hatred it arouses, for the dictatorships it puts in the place of democracy, for the starvation that stalks after it.

Armistice Day Sermon in New York, 1933

Allan Fotheringham 1932–

Canadian journalist

4 In the Maritimes, politics is a disease, in Quebec a religion, in Ontario a business, on the Prairies a protest and in British Columbia entertainment.

in 1975; *Last Page First* (1999)

5 Canada is ten independent personalities, united only by a common suspicion of Ottawa.

in *Maclean's* 11 February 1985

6 The voters don't know who he is. And . . . neither does he.

predicting electoral defeat for the Canadian Alliance leader, Stockwell Day

26 November 2000, prior to the federal election

Gene Fowler 1890–1960

American screenwriter

7 Will Hays is my shepherd, I shall not want, He maketh me to lie down in clean postures.

on the establishment of the 'Hays Office' in 1922 to monitor the Hollywood film industry

Clive Marsh and Gaye Ortiz (eds.) *Explorations in Theology and Film* (1997); see below

The Lord's my shepherd, I'll not want.
He makes me down to lie
In pastures green.

Bible Psalm 23 (Scottish Metrical Psalms, 1650)

H. W. Fowler 1858–1933

English lexicographer and grammarian

8 The English speaking world may be divided into (1) those who neither know nor care what a split infinitive is; (2) those who do not know, but care very much; (3) those who know and condemn; (4) those who know and approve; and (5) those who know and distinguish. Those who neither know nor care are the vast majority and are a happy folk, to be envied by most of the minority classes.

Modern English Usage (1926)

Norman Fowler 1938–

British Conservative politician

9 I have a young family and for the next few years I should like to devote more time to them.

often quoted as 'spend more time with my family'

resignation letter to the Prime Minister, in *Guardian* 4 January 1990; see **Thatcher** 317:13

Michael J. Fox 1961–

Canadian actor

10 It's all about losing your brain without losing your mind.

on his fight against Parkinson's disease

in *Times Weekend* 16 September 2000

Terry Fox 1958–81

Canadian runner, whose right leg was amputated because of cancer

1 I'm not a dreamer . . . but I believe in miracles. I have to.

planning a fund-raising run across Canada; he completed two thirds of his 'Marathon of Hope'

letter to the Canadian Cancer Society, 15 October 1979

Theodore Fox 1899–1989

English doctor

2 We shall have to learn to refrain from doing things merely because we know how to do them.

speech to Royal College of Physicians, 18 October 1965

Janet Frame 1924–

New Zealand writer

3 For your own good is a persuasive argument that will eventually make a man agree to his own destruction.

Faces in the Water (1961), ch. 4

Anatole France 1844–1924

French writer

4 Imitation lies at the root of most human actions. A respectable person is one who conforms to custom. People are called good when they do as others do.

Crainquebille (1923)

5 Without lies humanity would perish of despair and boredom.

La Vie en fleur (1922)

6 Make hatred hated!

to public school teachers

speech in Tours, August 1919; Carter Jefferson *Anatole France: The Politics of Scepticism* (1965)

7 You think you are dying for your country; you die for the industrialists.

in *L'Humanité* 18 July 1922

Anne Frank 1929–45

German-born Jewish diarist

8 I want to go on living even after death!

diary, 4 April 1944

Felix Frankfurter 1882–1965

American lawyer

9 It is a fair summary of history to say that the safeguards of liberty have been forged in controversies involving not very nice people.

dissenting opinion in *United States v. Rabinowitz* 1950

Lord Franks 1905–92

British philosopher and administrator

10 The Pentagon, that immense monument to modern man's subservience to the desk.

in *Observer* 30 November 1952

11 A secret in the Oxford sense: you may tell it to only one person at a time.

in *Sunday Telegraph* 30 January 1977

Dawn Fraser 1937–

Australian swimmer

12 I hated the easy assumption that girls had to be slower than boys.

attributed; Colin Jarman *Guinness Dictionary of Sports Quotations* (1990)

Malcolm Fraser 1930–

Australian Liberal statesman, Prime Minister 1975–83

on Fraser: see **Keating** 176:5

13 Life is not meant to be easy.

5th Alfred Deakin Lecture, 20 July 1971; see **Shaw** 295:6

Arthur Freed 1894–1973

American songwriter

14 Singin' in the rain.

title of song (1929)

Cathy Freeman 1973–

Australian athlete

1 I was so angry because they were denying they had done anything wrong, denying that a whole generation was stolen.

of official response to concerns about the 'stolen generation' of Aboriginal children forcibly removed from their families

interview in *Daily Telegraph* 16 July 2000

2 Running's like breathing. It's something that comes really naturally.

interview in *Daily Telegraph* 16 July 2000

3 Sport is this great arena for drama; it's a reflection of life. Sometimes favourites don't win.

after winning a gold medal at the Sydney Olympics

in *Daily Telegraph* 26 September 2000

Marilyn French 1929–

American writer

4 Whatever they may be in public life, whatever their relations with men, in their relations with women, all men are rapists, and that's all they are. They rape us with their eyes, their laws, and their codes.

The Women's Room (1977)

5 'I hate discussions of feminism that end up with who does the dishes,' she said. So do I. But at the end, there are always the damned dishes.

The Women's Room (1977)

Sigmund Freud 1856–1939

Austrian psychiatrist; originator of psychoanalysis

on Freud: see **Auden** 17:5, **Dodd** 93:6

6 We are so made, that we can only derive intense enjoyment from a contrast, and only very little from a state of things.

Civilization and its Discontents (1930)

7 Anatomy is destiny.

Collected Writings (1924) vol. 5

8 The interpretation of dreams is the royal road to a knowledge of the unconscious activities of the mind.

The Interpretation of Dreams (2nd ed., 1909); see **Misquotations** 226:4

9 Intolerance of groups is often, strangely enough, exhibited more strongly against small differences than against fundamental ones.

Moses and Monotheism (1938)

10 Analogies decide nothing, that is true, but they can make one feel more at home.

New Introductory Lectures on Psychoanalysis (1933)

11 The great question that has never been answered and which I have not yet been able to answer, despite my thirty years of research into the feminine soul, is 'What does a woman want?'

letter to Marie Bonaparte, in E. Jones *Sigmund Freud* (1955)

12 All that matters is love and work.

attributed

13 Frozen anger.

his definition of depression

attributed

14 Yes, America is gigantic, but a gigantic mistake.

Peter Gay *Freud: A Life for Our Time* (1988)

Nancy Friday 1937–

American writer

15 The older I get the more of my mother I see in myself.

My Mother, My Self (1977)

16 It was the promise of men, that around each corner there was yet another man, more wonderful than the last, that sustained me. You see, I had men confused with life . . . You can't get what I wanted from a man, not in this life.

My Mother, My Self (1977)

Betty Friedan 1921–

American feminist

17 The problem that has no name.

being the fact that American women are kept from growing to their full human capacities

The Feminine Mystique (1963); see 126:2

1 It is easier to live through someone else than to become complete yourself.
The Feminine Mystique (1963)

2 Today the problem that has no name is how to juggle work, love, home and children.
The Second Stage (1987); see 125:17

Milton Friedman 1912–

American economist and exponent of monetarism; policy adviser to President **Reagan** 1981–9
see also **Sayings** 290:9

3 There is an invisible hand in politics that operates in the opposite direction to the invisible hand in the market. In politics, individuals who seek to promote only the public good are led by an invisible hand to promote special interests that it was no part of their intention to promote.
Bright Promises, Dismal Performance: An Economist's Protest (1983)

4 History suggests that capitalism is a necessary condition for political freedom. Clearly it is not a sufficient condition for it.
Capitalism and Freedom (1962)

5 A society that puts equality—in the sense of equality of outcome—ahead of freedom will end up with neither equality nor freedom.
Free to Choose (1980)

6 Inflation is the one form of taxation that can be imposed without legislation.
in *Observer* 22 September 1974

7 Thank heavens we do not get all of the government that we are made to pay for.
attributed; quoted in the House of Lords, 24 November 1994

Brian Friel 1929–

Irish writer

8 Do you want the whole countryside to be laughing at us?—women of our years?—mature women, *dancing?*
Dancing at Lughnasa (1990)

Max Frisch 1911–91

Swiss novelist and dramatist

9 Technology . . . the knack of so arranging the world that we need not experience it.
Homo Faber (1957)

Charles Frohman

see **Last words** 191:8

Erich Fromm 1900–80

American philosopher and psychologist

10 Man's main task in life is to give birth to himself, to become what he potentially is. The most important product of his effort is his own personality.
Man for Himself (1947)

11 In the nineteenth century the problem was that *God is dead*; in the twentieth century the problem is that *man is dead.* In the nineteenth century inhumanity meant cruelty; in the twentieth century it means schizoid self-alienation. The danger of the past was that men became slaves. The danger of the future is that men may become robots.
The Sane Society (1955)

David Frost 1939–

English broadcaster and writer
on Frost: see **Muggeridge** 234:3; *see also* **Catch-phrases** 59:1, 60:2

12 Having one child makes you a parent; having two you are a referee.
in *Independent* 16 September 1989

Robert Frost 1874–1963

American poet

13 I'd like to get away from earth awhile
And then come back to it and begin over.
May no fate wilfully misunderstand me
And half grant what I wish and snatch me away
Not to return. Earth's the right place for love:

I don't know where it's likely to go
better.
'Birches' (1916)

1 Most of the change we think we see in
life
Is due to truths being in and out of
favour.
'The Black Cottage' (1914)

2 Forgive, O Lord, my little jokes on Thee
And I'll forgive Thy great big one on me.
'Cluster of Faith' (1962)

3 And nothing to look backward to with
pride,
And nothing to look forward to with
hope.
'The Death of the Hired Man' (1914)

4 'Home is the place where, when you
have to go there,
They have to take you in.'
'I should have called it
Something you somehow haven't to
deserve.'
'The Death of the Hired Man' (1914)

5 They cannot scare me with their empty
spaces
Between stars—on stars where no
human race is.
I have it in me so much nearer home
To scare myself with my own desert
places.
'Desert Places' (1936)

6 Some say the world will end in fire,
Some say in ice.
From what I've tasted of desire
I hold with those who favour fire.
But if it had to perish twice,
I think I know enough of hate
To say that for destruction ice
Is also great
And would suffice.
'Fire and Ice' (1923)

7 The land was ours before we were the
land's.
'The Gift Outright' (1942)

8 Happiness makes up in height for what it
lacks in length.
title of poem (1942)

9 Never ask of money spent
Where the spender thinks it went.
Nobody was ever meant
To remember or invent
What he did with every cent.
'The Hardship of Accounting' (1936)

10 And were an epitaph to be my story
I'd have a short one ready for my own.
I would have written of me on my stone:
I had a lover's quarrel with the world.
'The Lesson for Today' (1942)

11 Something there is that doesn't love a
wall,
That sends the frozen-ground-swell under
it.
'Mending Wall' (1914)

12 My apple trees will never get across
And eat the cones under his pines, I tell
him.
He only says, 'Good fences make good
neighbours.'
'Mending Wall' (1914)

13 Before I built a wall I'd ask to know
What I was walling in or walling out,
And to whom I was like to give offence.
'Mending Wall' (1914)

14 I never dared be radical when young
For fear it would make me conservative
when old.
'Precaution' (1936)

15 No memory of having starred
Atones for later disregard,
Or keeps the end from being hard.
'Provide Provide' (1936)

16 Two roads diverged in a wood, and I—
I took the one less travelled by,
And that has made all the difference.
'The Road Not Taken' (1916)

17 We dance round in a ring and suppose,
But the Secret sits in the middle and
knows.
'The Secret Sits' (1942)

18 I've broken Anne of gathering bouquets.
It's not fair to the child. It can't be helped
though:
Pressed into service means pressed out of
shape.
'The Self-Seeker' (1914)

19 The best way out is always through.
'A Servant to Servants' (1914)

20 Whose woods these are I think I know.
His house is in the village though;

He will not see me stopping here
To watch his woods fill up with snow.

'Stopping by Woods on a Snowy Evening' (1923); see **O'Rourke** 248:10

1 The woods are lovely, dark and deep.
But I have promises to keep,
And miles to go before I sleep.

'Stopping by Woods on a Snowy Evening' (1923)

2 It should be of the pleasure of a poem itself to tell how it can. The figure a poem makes. It begins in delight and ends in wisdom. The figure is the same as for love.

Collected Poems (1939) 'The Figure a Poem Makes'

3 Like a piece of ice on a hot stove the poem must ride on its own melting. A poem may be worked over once it is in being, but may not be worried into being.

Collected Poems (1939) 'The Figure a Poem Makes'

4 Poetry is a way of taking life by the throat.

E. S. Sergeant *Robert Frost* (1960)

5 I'd as soon write free verse as play tennis with the net down.

E. Lathem *Interviews with Robert Frost* (1966)

6 Poetry is what is lost in translation. It is also what is lost in interpretation.

L. Untermeyer *Robert Frost* (1964)

Barbara Frum 1937–92

Canadian journalist

7 I don't care if I'm understood. I just don't want to be misunderstood.

her view of journalism

interview in Paul McLaughlin *Asking Questions: the Art of the Media Interview* (1986)

Christopher Fry 1907–

English dramatist

8 The dark is light enough.

title of play (1954)

9 The lady's not for burning.

title of play (1949); see **Thatcher** 316:15

10 What after all
Is a halo? It's only one more thing to keep clean.

The Lady's not for Burning (1949)

11 Where in this small-talking world can I find
A longitude with no platitude?

The Lady's not for Burning (1949)

12 The best
Thing we can do is to make wherever we're lost in
Look as much like home as we can.

The Lady's not for Burning (1949)

Roger Fry 1866–1934

English art critic

13 Art is significant deformity.

Virginia Woolf *Roger Fry* (1940)

14 Bach almost persuades me to be a Christian.

Virginia Woolf *Roger Fry* (1940)

Stephen Fry 1957–

English actor and writer

15 Nudity is a deep worry if you have a body like a bin bag full of yoghurt, which I have.

in *Observer* 12 March 2000

Carlos Fuentes 1928–

Mexican novelist and writer

16 To be a gringo in Mexico . . . ah, that is euthanasia.

The Old Gringo (1985)

17 High on the agenda for the 21st century will be the need to restore some kind of tragic consciousness.

Rushworth M. Kidder *An Agenda for the 21st Century* (1987)

Francis Fukuyama 1952–

American historian

18 What we may be witnessing is not just the end of the Cold War but the end of history as such: that is, the end point of man's ideological evolution and the

universalism of Western liberal democracy.
in *Independent* 20 September 1989

J. William Fulbright 1905–95

American politician

1 The Soviet Union has indeed been our greatest menace, not so much because of what it has done, but because of the excuses it has provided us for our failures.
in *Observer* 21 December 1958

John Fuller 1937–

English poet

2 You and I, when our days are done, must say
Without exactly saying it, good-bye.
'Pyrosymphonie' (1996)

R. Buckminster Fuller 1895–1983

American designer and architect

3 God, to me, it seems,
is a verb
not a noun,
proper or improper.
untitled poem written in 1940, in *No More Secondhand God* (1963)

4 Now there is one outstandingly important fact regarding Spaceship Earth, and that is that no instruction book came with it.
Operating Manual for Spaceship Earth (1969)

5 Either war is obsolete or men are.
in *New Yorker* 8 January 1966

Sam Fuller 1912–

American film director

6 When you're in the battlefield, survival is all there is. Death is the only great emotion.
in *Guardian* 26 February 1991

Alfred Funke *b.* 1869

German writer

7 *Gott strafe England!*
God punish England!
Schwert und Myrte (1914); see **Squire** 305:6

Will Fyffe 1885–1947

Scottish comedian

8 I belong to Glasgow
Dear Old Glasgow town!
But what's the matter wi' Glasgow?
For it's going round and round.
I'm only a common old working chap,
As anyone can see,
But when I get a couple of drinks on a Saturday,
Glasgow belongs to me.
'I Belong to Glasgow' (1920 song)

Rose Fyleman 1877–1957

English writer for children

9 There are fairies at the bottom of our garden!
'The Fairies' (1918)

Clark Gable

see **Film lines** 115:9

Zsa Zsa Gabor 1919–

Hungarian-born film actress

10 I never hated a man enough to give him diamonds back.
in *Observer* 25 August 1957

11 A man in love is incomplete until he has married. Then he's finished.
in *Newsweek* 28 March 1960

12 You mean apart from my own?
when asked how many husbands she had had
K. Edwards *I Wish I'd Said That* (1976)

Hugh Gaitskell 1906–63

British Labour politician
on Gaitskell: see **Bevan** 34:10, **Crossman** 82:1

1 There are some of us . . . who will fight and fight and fight again to save the Party we love.
speech at Labour Party Conference, 5 October 1960

2 It means the end of a thousand years of history.
on a European federation
speech at Labour Party Conference, 3 October 1962

3 The subtle terrorism of words.
in a warning given to his Party, c.1957
Harry Hopkins *The New Look* (1963); attributed

J. K. Galbraith 1908–

Canadian-born American economist

4 The affluent society.
title of book (1958)

5 The conventional wisdom.
ironic term for 'the beliefs that are at any time assiduously, solemnly and mindlessly traded between the conventionally wise'
The Affluent Society (1958)

6 In a community where public services have failed to keep abreast of private consumption things are very different. Here, in an atmosphere of private opulence and public squalor, the private goods have full sway.
The Affluent Society (1958)

We have public poverty and private opulence.
Sallust (86–35 BC) *Catiline*

7 It is not necessary to advertise food to hungry people, fuel to cold people, or houses to the homeless.
American Capitalism (1952)

8 The salary of the chief executive of the large corporation is not a market reward for achievement. It is frequently in the nature of a warm personal gesture by the individual to himself.
Annals of an Abiding Liberal (1979)

9 Trickle-down theory—the less than elegant metaphor that if one feeds the horse enough oats, some will pass through to the road for the sparrows.
The Culture of Contentment (1992)

of the defeat of Germany in World War Two:
10 That they were defeated is conclusive testimony to the inherent inefficiencies of dictatorship, the inherent efficiencies of freedom.
in *Fortune* December 1945

11 Politics is not the art of the possible. It consists in choosing between the disastrous and the unpalatable.
letter to President Kennedy, 2 March 1962; see below; see **Butler** 50:3

Politics is the art of the possible.
Bismarck (1815–98), conversation with Meyer von Waldeck, 11 August 1867

12 If all else fails, immortality can always be assured by a spectacular error.
attributed

Noel Gallagher 1967–

English pop singer

13 We are lads. We have burgled houses and nicked car stereos, and we like girls and swear and go to the football and take the piss.
interview in *Melody Maker* 30 March 1996

John Galsworthy 1867–1933

English novelist

14 He was afflicted by the thought that where Beauty was, nothing ever ran quite straight, which, no doubt, was why so many people looked on it as immoral.
In Chancery (1920)

15 A man of action forced into a state of thought is unhappy until he can get out of it.
Maid in Waiting (1931)

16 I know nothing—nobody tells me anything.
A Man of Property (1906)

Ray Galton 1930– and Alan Simpson 1929–

English scriptwriters

1 I came in here in all good faith to help my country. I don't mind giving a reasonable amount [of blood], but a pint . . . why that's very nearly an armful.

Hancock's Half Hour 'The Blood Donor' (1961 television programme); words spoken by Tony Hancock

George Gamow 1904–68

Russian-born American physicist

2 We do not know why they [elementary particles] have the masses they do; we do not know why they transform into another the way they do; we do not know anything! The one concept that stands like the Rock of Gibraltar in our sea of confusion is the Pauli [exclusion] principle.

in *Scientific American* July 1959

3 With five free parameters, a theorist could fit the profile of an elephant.

attributed; in *Nature* 21 June 1990

Peter Ganci 1938–2001

American firefighter, Chief of the New York City Fire Department

4 Sometimes in this job, goodbye is really goodbye.

at the funeral of a firefighter killed on duty; a week later, Ganci died in the collapse of the northern tower of the World Trade Center, 11 September 2001

in *Times* 14 September 2001, obituary

Mahatma Gandhi 1869–1948

Indian statesman

on Gandhi: see **Naidu** 236:13, **Nehru** 238:11

5 What difference does it make to the dead, the orphans and the homeless, whether the mad destruction is wrought under the name of totalitarianism or the holy name of liberty or democracy?

Non-Violence in Peace and War (1942) vol. 1

6 The moment the slave resolves that he will no longer be a slave, his fetters fall. He frees himself and shows the way to others. Freedom and slavery are mental states.

Non-Violence in Peace and War (1949) vol. 2

7 Non-violence is the first article of my faith. It is also the last article of my creed.

speech on a charge of sedition

at Shahi Bag, 18 March 1922

8 In my humble opinion, non-cooperation with evil is as much a duty as is cooperation with good.

speech in Ahmadabad, 23 March 1922

on being asked what he thought of modern civilization:

9 That would be a good idea.

while visiting England in 1930

E. F. Schumacher *Good Work* (1979)

Greta Garbo 1905–90

Swedish film actress

on Garbo: see **Taglines for films** 314:3

10 I want to be alone.

Grand Hotel (1932 film)

11 I tank I go home.

on being refused a pay rise by Louis B. Mayer

Norman Zierold *Moguls* (1969)

Federico García Lorca

see **Lorca**

Gabriel García Márquez 1928–

Colombian novelist

12 The world must be all fucked up when men travel first class and literature goes as freight.

One Hundred Years of Solitude (1967)

13 A famous writer who wants to continue writing has to be constantly defending himself against fame.

in *Writers at Work* (6th series, 1984)

Ed Gardner 1901–63

American radio comedian

1 Opera is when a guy gets stabbed in the back and, instead of bleeding, he sings.
Duffy's Tavern (US radio programme, 1940s)

John Nance Garner 1868–1967

American Democratic politician, vice-president 1933–41

2 The vice-presidency isn't worth a pitcher of warm piss.
O. C. Fisher *Cactus Jack* (1978)

Bill Gates 1955–

American computer entrepreneur
on Gates: see **Stross** 311:1

3 If they want we will give them a sleeping bag, but there is something romantic about sleeping under the desk. They want to do it.
on his young software programmers
in *Independent* 18 November 1995 'Quote Unquote'

Noel Gay 1898–1954

British songwriter

4 I'm leaning on a lamp-post at the corner
of the street,
In case a certain little lady comes by.
'Leaning on a Lamp-Post' (1937); sung by George Formby

Eric Geddes 1875–1937

British politician and administrator

5 The Germans . . . are going to be squeezed as a lemon is squeezed—until the pips squeak.
speech at Cambridge, 10 December 1918

Bob Geldof 1954–

Irish rock musician

6 Most people get into bands for three very simple rock and roll reasons: to get laid, to get fame, and to get rich.
in *Melody Maker* 27 August 1977

Bob Geldof 1954– and Midge Ure 1953–

Irish rock musician; Scottish rock musician

7 Feed the world
Feed the world.
Feed the world
Let them know it's Christmas time again.
'Do They Know it's Christmas?' (1984 song)

Martha Gellhorn 1908–98

American journalist

8 I believed that all one did about a war was go to it, as a gesture of solidarity, and get killed, or survive if lucky until the war was over . . . I had no idea you could be what I became, an unscathed tourist of wars.
The Face of War (1959)

of the defeat of the Spanish Republic:

9 I daresay we all became more competent press tourists because of it, since we never again cared so much. You can only love one war; afterward, I suppose, you do your duty.
The Honeyed Peace (1953)

10 Never believe governments, not any of them, not a word they say; keep an untrusting eye on all they do.
in obituary, *Daily Telegraph* 17 February 1998

Jean Genet 1910–86

French novelist, poet, and dramatist

11 What we need is hatred. From it our ideas are born.
The Blacks (1959); epigraph

12 Are you there . . . Africa of the millions of royal slaves, deported Africa, drifting continent, are you there? Slowly you vanish, you withdraw into the past, into the tales of castaways, colonial museums, the works of scholars.
The Blacks (1959)

13 Anyone who hasn't experienced the ecstasy of betrayal knows nothing about ecstasy at all.
Prisoner of Love (1986)

George V 1865–1936

King of Great Britain and Ireland from 1910
on George V: see **Nicolson** 241:10*; see also* **Last words** 190:1, 190:5

1 Wake up, England.
title of 1911 reprint of speech below

I venture to allude to the impression which seemed generally to prevail among their brethren across the seas, that the Old Country must wake up if she intends to maintain her old position of pre-eminence in her Colonial trade against foreign competitors.
speech at Guildhall, 5 December 1901

2 I pray that my coming to Ireland today may prove to be the first step towards an end of strife among her people, whatever their race or creed. In that hope I appeal to all Irishmen to pause, to stretch out the hand of forbearance and conciliation, to forgive and forget, and to join with me in making for the land they love a new era of peace, contentment and goodwill.
speech to the new Ulster Parliament at Stormont, 22 June 1921

3 I have many times asked myself whether there can be more potent advocates of peace upon earth through the years to come than this massed multitude of silent witnesses to the desolation of war.
message read at Terlincthun Cemetery, Boulogne, 13 May 1922

4 After I am dead, the boy will ruin himself in twelve months.
of his son, the future ***Edward VIII***
K. Middlemas and J. Barnes *Baldwin* (1969)

on H. G. ***Wells****'s comment on 'an alien and uninspiring court':*

5 I may be uninspiring, but I'll be damned if I'm an alien!
Sarah Bradford *George VI* (1989); attributed

6 My father was frightened of his mother; I was frightened of my father, and I am damned well going to see to it that my children are frightened of me.
attributed in Randolph S. Churchill *Lord Derby* (1959), but said by Kenneth Rose in *George V* (1983) to be almost certainly apocryphal; see **Morshead** 232:11

George VI 1895–1952

King of Great Britain and Northern Ireland from 1936
see also **Haskins** 148:10

7 I feel happier now that we have no allies to be polite to and to pamper.
to Queen Mary, 27 June 1940
J. Wheeler-Bennett *King George VI* (1958)

8 Abroad is bloody.
W. H. Auden *A Certain World* (1970) 'Royalty'; see **Mitford** 228:6

9 The family firm.
description of the British monarchy
attributed

Daniel George

English writer

10 O Freedom, what liberties are taken in thy name!
The Perpetual Pessimist (1963); see below

O liberty! what crimes are committed in thy name!
Mme Roland (1754–93) in A. de Lamartine *Histoire des Girondins* (1847)

Ira Gershwin 1896–1983

American songwriter
see also **Heyward**

11 I got rhythm,
I got music,
I got my man
Who could ask for anything more?
'I Got Rhythm' (1930 song)

12 Lady, be good!
title of musical (1924)

13 You like potato and I like po-tah-to,
You like tomato and I like to-mah-to;
Potato, po-tah-to, tomato, to-mah-to—
Let's call the whole thing off!
'Let's Call the Whole Thing Off' (1937 song)

14 In time the Rockies may crumble,
Gibraltar may tumble,
They're only made of clay,
But our love is here to stay.
'Love is Here to Stay' (1938 song)

15 Holding hands at midnight
'Neath a starry sky,

Nice work if you can get it,
And you can get it if you try.
'Nice Work If You Can Get It' (1937 song)

1 The way you wear your hat,
The way you sip your tea,
The mem'ry of all that—
No, no! They can't take that away from me!
'They Can't Take That Away from Me' (1937 song)

J. Paul Getty 1892–1976

American industrialist

2 If you can actually count your money, then you are not really a rich man.
in *Observer* 3 November 1957

Stella Gibbons 1902–89

English novelist

3 Something nasty in the woodshed.
Cold Comfort Farm (1932)

Wolcott Gibbs 1902–58

American critic

4 Backward ran sentences until reeled the mind.
satirizing the style of Time *magazine*
in *New Yorker* 28 November 1936 'Time . . . Fortune . . . Life . . . Luce'

Kahlil Gibran 1883–1931

Syrian writer and painter

5 Are you a politician who says to himself: 'I will use my country for my own benefit'? . . . Or are you a devoted patriot, who whispers in the ear of his inner self: 'I love to serve my country as a faithful servant.'
The New Frontier (1931); see **Kennedy** 178:7

6 Your children are not your children.
They are the sons and daughters of Life's longing for itself.
They came through you but not from you
And though they are with you yet they belong not to you.
The Prophet (1923) 'On Children'

7 Work is love made visible. And if you cannot work with love but only with distaste, it is better that you should leave your work and sit at the gate of the temple and take alms of those who work with joy.
The Prophet (1923) 'On Work'

8 An exaggeration is a truth that has lost its temper.
Sand and Foam (1926)

Ben Gill 1950–

British farmer, President of the National Farmers' Union from 1998

9 Our farms should be starting to jump to life with new-born lambs and calves. Instead, many will feel that spring has been cancelled.
on the foot and mouth epidemic
in *Independent* 16 March 2001

Eric Gill 1882–1940

English sculptor, engraver, and typographer

10 That state is a state of slavery in which a man does what he likes to do in his spare time and in his working time that which is required of him.
Art-nonsense and Other Essays (1929) 'Slavery and Freedom'

Penelope Gilliatt 1933–93

see **Film titles** 118:13

Hermione Gingold 1897–1987

English actress

11 Contrary to popular belief, English women do not wear tweed nightgowns.
in *Saturday Review* 16 April 1955

Newton Gingrich 1943–

American Republican politician

12 No society can survive, no civilization can survive, with 12-year-olds having babies, with 15-year-olds killing each other, with 17-year-olds dying of Aids,

with 18-year-olds getting diplomas they can't read.

in December 1994, after the Republican electoral victory

in *The Times* 9 February 1995

Allen Ginsberg 1926–97

American poet and novelist
see also **Last words** 190:9

1 What if someone gave a war & Nobody came?

'Graffiti' (1972); see **Sandburg** 286:10

2 I saw the best minds of my generation destroyed by madness, starving hysterical naked.
dragging themselves through the negro streets at dawn looking for an angry fix,
angelheaded hipsters burning for the ancient heavenly connection to the starry dynamo in the machinery of the night.

Howl (1956)

3 What thoughts I have of you tonight, Walt Whitman, for I walked
down the sidestreets under the trees with a headache self-
conscious looking at the full moon.

'A Supermarket in California' (1956)

4 What peaches and what penumbras!
Whole families shopping at night! Aisles
full of husbands! Wives in the avocados,
babies in the tomatoes!—and you, Garcia
Lorca what were you doing down by the
watermelons?

'A Supermarket in California' (1956)

5 Ah, dear father, graybeard, lonely old courage-teacher, what
America did you have when Charon quit poling his ferry and you
got out on a smoking bank and stood watching the boat
disappear on the black waters of Lethe?

'A Supermarket in California' (1956)

Nikki Giovanni 1943–

American poet

6 Mistakes are a fact of life
It is the response to error that counts.

'Of Liberation' (1970)

George Gipp 1895–1920

American footballer

7 Win just one for the Gipper.

attributed; the catch-phrase later became associated with Ronald **Reagan**, who uttered the immortal words in the 1940 film *Knute Rockne, All American*

Jean Giraudoux 1882–1944

French dramatist

8 As soon as war is declared it will be impossible to hold the poets back. Rhyme is still the most effective drum.

La Guerre de Troie n'aura pas lieu (1935); tr. Christopher Fry as *Tiger at the Gates*, 1955

9 No poet ever interpreted nature as freely as a lawyer interprets the truth.

La Guerre de Troie n'aura pas lieu (1935)

Rudolph Giuliani 1944–

American Republican politician, Mayor of New York 1993–2001
on Giuliani: see **Letterman** 197:11

10 The number of casualties will be more than any of us can bear.

in the aftermath of the terrorist attacks which destroyed the World Trade Center in New York, and damaged the Pentagon, 11 September 2001

in *Times* 12 September 2001

11 People should remain calm—we're just being tested one more time and we're going to pass this test, too.

following the crash of a commercial jet aircraft into a residential New York neighbourhood

in *The Times* 13 November 2001

Edna Gladney 1886–1961

American philanthropist

12 There are no illegitimate children, only illegitimate parents.

during her successful lobbying of the Texas legislature to expunge the word 'illegitimate' from birth certificates; MGM paid her a large sum for the line for the 1941 film based on her life, 'Blossoms in the Dust'

A. Loos *Kiss Hollywood Good-Bye* (1978)

George Glass 1910–84

American film producer

1 An actor is a kind of a guy who if you ain't talking about him ain't listening.

Bob Thomas *Brando* (1973); said to be often quoted by Marlon Brando, as in *Observer* 1 January 1956

David Glencross 1936–

British television executive

2 It is unlikely that the government reaches for a revolver when it hears the word culture. The more likely response is to search for a dictionary.

Royal Television Society conference on the future of television, 26–27 November 1988; see **Johst** 172:4

Victoria Glendinning 1937–

English biographer and novelist

3 There's no greater bliss in life than when the plumber eventually comes to unblock your drains. No writer can give that sort of pleasure.

in *Observer* 3 January 1993

Jean-Luc Godard 1930–

French film director

4 Photography is truth. The cinema is truth 24 times per second.

Le Petit Soldat (1960 film)

5 *Ce n'est pas une image juste, c'est juste une image.*

This is not a just image, it is just an image.

Colin MacCabe *Godard: Images, Sounds, Politics* (1980)

6 GEORGES FRANJU: Movies should have a beginning, a middle and an end.
JEAN-LUC GODARD: Certainly, but not necessarily in that order.

in *Time* 14 September 1981

A. D. Godley 1856–1925

English classicist

7 What is this that roareth thus?
Can it be a Motor Bus?
Yes, the smell and hideous hum
Indicat Motorem Bum!

letter, 10 January 1914, in *Reliquiae* (1926)

Joseph Goebbels 1897–1945

German Nazi leader

8 We can manage without butter but not, for example, without guns. If we are attacked we can only defend ourselves with guns not with butter.

speech in Berlin, 17 January 1936; see **Goering** 136:10

9 Making noise is an effective means of opposition.

Ernest K. Bramsted *Goebbels and National Socialist Propaganda 1925–45* (1965)

Hermann Goering 1893–1946

German Nazi leader

see also **Johst** 172:4

10 Would you rather have butter or guns? . . . preparedness makes us powerful. Butter merely makes us fat.

speech at Hamburg, 1936, in W. Frischauer *Goering* (1951); see **Goebbels** 136:8

11 I herewith commission you to carry out all preparations with regard to . . . a *total solution* of the Jewish question in those territories of Europe which are under German influence.

instructions to Reinhard **Heydrich**, 31 July 1941; W. L. Shirer *Rise and Fall of the Third Reich* (1962); see **Heydrich** 154:12

William Golding 1911–93

English novelist

12 Nothing is so impenetrable as laughter in a language you don't understand.

An Egyptian Journal (1985)

13 Anyone who moved through those years without understanding that man produces evil as a bee produces honey, must have been blind or wrong in the head.

of the Second World War

The Hot Gates (1965) 'Fable'

1 Sleep is when all the unsorted stuff comes flying out as from a dustbin upset in a high wind.
Pincher Martin (1956)

Barry Goldwater 1909–98

American Republican politician

2 I would remind you that extremism in the defence of liberty is no vice! And let me remind you also that moderation in the pursuit of justice is no virtue!
accepting the presidential nomination, 16 July 1964; see **Johnson** 171:12

Sam Goldwyn 1882–1974

American film producer
on Goldwyn: see **Hand** 145:5, **Hecht** 151:10; *see also* **Shaw** 297:1

3 Gentlemen, include me out.
resigning from the Motion Picture Producers and Distributors of America, October 1933
M. Freedland *The Goldwyn Touch* (1986)

4 A verbal contract isn't worth the paper it is written on.
Alva Johnston *The Great Goldwyn* (1937)

5 'I can answer you in two words, "im-possible" ' is almost the cornerstone of the Goldwyn legend, but Sam did not say it. It was printed late in 1925 in a humorous magazine and credited to an anonymous Potash or Perlmutter.
Alva Johnston *The Great Goldwyn* (1937)

6 That's the way with these directors, they're always biting the hand that lays the golden egg.
Alva Johnston *The Great Goldwyn* (1937)

7 Why should people go out and pay to see bad movies when they can stay at home and see bad television for nothing?
in *Observer* 9 September 1956

8 I'll give you a definite maybe.
attributed

9 Let's have some new clichés.
attributed, perhaps apocryphal

10 Pictures are for entertainment, messages should be delivered by Western Union.
A. Marx *Goldwyn* (1976); see **Behan** 27:3

11 What we need is a story that starts with an earthquake and works its way up to a climax.
attributed, perhaps apocryphal

Amy Goodman 1957–

American journalist

12 Go to where the silence is and say something.
accepting an award from Columbia University for her coverage of the 1991 massacre in East Timor by Indonesian troops
in *Columbia Journalism Review* March/April 1994

Mikhail Sergeevich Gorbachev 1931–

Soviet statesman, General Secretary of the Communist Party of the USSR 1985–91 and President 1988–91
on Gorbachev: see **Gromyko** 141:8, **Thatcher** 317:7

13 The guilt of Stalin and his immediate entourage before the Party and the people for the mass repressions and lawlessness they committed is enormous and unforgivable.
speech on the seventieth anniversary of the Russian Revolution, 2 November 1987

14 The idea of restructuring [perestroika] . . . combines continuity and innovation, the historical experience of Bolshevism and the contemporaneity of socialism.
speech on the seventieth anniversary of the Russian Revolution, 2 November 1987

15 After leaving the Kremlin . . . my conscience was clear. The promise I gave to the people when I started the process of perestroika was kept: I gave them freedom.
Memoirs (1995)

Mack Gordon 1904–59

American songwriter

16 Pardon me boy is that the Chattanooga
Choo-choo,
Track twenty nine,
Boy you can gimme a shine.
'Chattanooga Choo-choo' (1941 song)

Albert Gore Jr. 1948–

American Democratic politician, Vice-President 1993–2001; presidential candidate in 2000

1 GEORGE W. BUSH: You're calling me back to retract your concession?
ALBERT GORE JR.: There's no need to get snippy.
on election night, retracting a premature concession
in *Daily Telegraph* 14 November 2000

2 I am Al Gore, and I used to be the next president of the United States of America.
addressing Bocconi University in Milan
in *Newsweek* 19 March 2001; see **Carter** 55:1

Maxim Gorky 1868–1936

Russian writer and revolutionary

3 The proletarian state must bring up thousands of excellent 'mechanics of culture', 'engineers of the soul'.
speech at the Writers' Congress 1934; see **Kennedy** 178:14, **Stalin** 305:8

Stuart Gorrell 1902–63

American songwriter

4 Georgia, Georgia, no peace I find,
Just an old sweet song keeps Georgia on my mind.
'Georgia on my Mind' (1930 song)

Luke Goss 1968–

British pop singer, member of Bros

5 Fame has a bloody long sell-by date. You reach a certain level and it is pumped with preservatives, like long-life milk. But success is like fresh fruit: it perishes every day.
in *Observer* 11 March 2001

Stephen Jay Gould 1941–

American palaeontologist

6 A man does not attain the status of Galileo merely because he is persecuted; he must also be right.
Ever since Darwin (1977)

7 Science is an integral part of culture. It's not this foreign thing, done by an arcane priesthood. It's one of the glories of human intellectual tradition.
in *Independent* 24 January 1990

Lew Grade 1906–98

British television producer and executive

8 All my shows are great. Some of them are bad. But they are all great.
in *Observer* 14 September 1975

D. M. Graham 1911–99

British television producer

9 That this House will in no circumstances fight for its King and Country.
motion worded by Graham for a debate at the Oxford Union, 9 February 1933

Bernie Grant 1944–2000

British Labour politician

10 The police were to blame for what happened on Sunday night and what they got was a bloody good hiding.
after a riot in which a policeman was killed
speech as leader of Haringey Council, 8 October 1985

Cary Grant

see **Telegrams** 316:6

Robert Graves 1895–1985

English poet

11 There's a cool web of language winds us in,
Retreat from too much joy or too much fear.
'The Cool Web' (1927)

12 Truth-loving Persians do not dwell upon
The trivial skirmish fought near Marathon.
'The Persian Version' (1945)

1 Love is a universal migraine.
A bright stain on the vision
Blotting out reason.
'Symptoms of Love'

2 Goodbye to all that.
title of autobiography (1929)

3 If there's no money in poetry, neither is there poetry in money.
speech at London School of Economics, 6 December 1963

4 LSD reminds me of the minks that escape from mink-farms and breed in the forest and become dangerous and destructive. It has escaped from the drug factory and gets made in college laboratories.
George Plimpton (ed.) *The Writer's Chapbook* (1989)

Muriel Gray 1959–

Scottish writer and broadcaster

5 Of course I want political autonomy but not cultural autonomy. You just have to watch the Scottish Baftas to want to kill yourself.
explaining her preference for devolution rather than full independence
in *Scotland on Sunday* 14 January 1996

Jimmy Greaves 1940–

English footballer

6 The thing about sport, any sport, is that swearing is very much part of it.
attributed, 1989

Graham Greene 1904–91

English novelist
see also **Film lines** 116:6

7 Catholics and Communists have committed great crimes, but at least they have not stood aside, like an established society, and been indifferent. I would rather have blood on my hands than water like Pilate.
The Comedians (1966)

8 He gave her a bright fake smile; so much of life was a putting-off of unhappiness for another time. Nothing was ever lost by delay.
The Heart of the Matter (1948)

9 They had been corrupted by money, and he had been corrupted by sentiment. Sentiment was the more dangerous, because you couldn't name its price. A man open to bribes was to be relied upon below a certain figure, but sentiment might uncoil in the heart at a name, a photograph, even a smell remembered.
The Heart of the Matter (1948)

10 Despair is the price one pays for setting oneself an impossible aim.
Heart of the Matter (1948)

11 Here you could love human beings nearly as God loved them, knowing the worst; you didn't love a pose, a pretty dress, a sentiment artfully assumed.
The Heart of the Matter (1948)

12 He felt the loyalty we all feel to unhappiness—the sense that that is where we really belong.
The Heart of the Matter (1948)

13 Any victim demands allegiance.
The Heart of the Matter (1948)

14 His hilarity was like a scream from a crevasse.
The Heart of the Matter (1948)

15 Goodness has only once found a perfect incarnation in a human body and never will again, but evil can always find a home there. Human nature is not black and white but black and grey.
The Lost Childhood and Other Essays (1951) title essay

16 There is always one moment in childhood when the door opens and lets the future in.
The Power and the Glory (1940)

17 Innocence always calls mutely for protection, when we would be so much wiser to guard ourselves against it: innocence is like a dumb leper who has lost his bell, wandering the world meaning no harm.
The Quiet American (1955)

18 For a writer, success is always temporary, success is only a delayed failure. And it is incomplete.
A Sort of Life (1971)

Alan Greenspan 1926–

American economist, Chairman of the Federal Reserve Fund

1 How do we know when irrational exuberance has unduly escalated asset values?

speech in Washington, 5 December 1996

2 We're still standing and that's good news.

reporting to the House of Representatives Financial Services Committee, 18 July 2001

Germaine Greer 1939–

Australian feminist

3 Women have very little idea of how much men hate them.

The Female Eunuch (1971)

4 You can now see the Female Eunuch the world over . . . spreading herself wherever blue jeans and Coca-Cola may go. Wherever you see nail varnish, lipstick, brassieres, and high heels, the Eunuch has set up her camp.

The Female Eunuch (20th anniversary ed., 1991) foreword

5 I didn't fight to get women out from behind the vacuum cleaner to get them onto the board of Hoover.

in *Guardian* 27 October 1986

6 The World Wide Web is fantasyland. There is no way that anyone can find anything on the Web without having to adopt the thought patterns of a weirdo.

in *Independent* 27 January 2001

Hubert Gregg 1914–

English songwriter

7 Maybe it's because I'm a Londoner
That I love London so.

'Maybe It's Because I'm a Londoner' (1947 song)

Dick Gregory 1932–

American comedian

8 You gotta say this for the white race—its self-confidence knows no bounds. Who else could go to a small island in the South Pacific where there's no poverty, no crime, no unemployment, no war and no worry—and call it a 'primitive society'?

From the Back of the Bus (1962)

9 Wouldn't it be a hell of a thing if all this was burnt cork and you people were being tolerant for nothing?

Nigger (1965)

10 Baseball is very big with my people. It figures. It's the only way we can get to shake a bat at a white man without starting a riot.

D. H. Nathan (ed.) *Baseball Quotations* (1991)

Joyce Grenfell 1910–79

English comedy actress and writer

11 George—don't do that.

recurring line in monologues about a nursery school

from the 1950s; *George—Don't Do That* (1977)

12 So gay the band,
So giddy the sight,
Full evening dress is a must,
But the zest goes out of a beautiful waltz
When you dance it bust to bust.

'Stately as a Galleon' (1978 song)

Julian Grenfell 1888–1915

English soldier and poet

13 And Life is Colour and Warmth and Light
And a striving evermore for these;
And he is dead, who will not fight;
And who dies fighting has increase.

'Into Battle' in *The Times* 28 May 1915

Wayne Gretzky 1961–

Canadian ice-hockey player

14 I skate to where the puck is going to be, not where it's been.

attributed, 1985; John Robert Colombo *Colombo's New Canadian Quotations* (1987)

Clifford Grey 1887–1941

English songwriter

15 If you were the only girl in the world

And I were the only boy.
'If You Were the Only Girl in the World' (1916 song)

Lord Grey of Fallodon
1862–1933

British Liberal politician

1 The lamps are going out all over Europe; we shall not see them lit again in our lifetime.
on the eve of the First World War
25 Years (1925)

Mervyn Griffith-Jones
1909–79

British lawyer

2 Is it a book you would even wish your wife or your servants to read?
of D. H. ***Lawrence****'s* Lady Chatterley's Lover, *while appearing for the prosecution at the Old Bailey*
in *The Times* 21 October 1960

John Grigg 1924–

British writer and journalist, who as Lord Altrincham disclaimed his hereditary title in 1963

3 The personality conveyed by the utterances which are put into her mouth is that of a priggish schoolgirl, captain of the hockey team, a prefect, and a recent candidate for confirmation. It is not thus that she will be able to come into her own as an independent and distinctive character.
of Queen ***Elizabeth II***
in *National and English Review* August 1958

4 Autobiography is now as common as adultery and hardly less reprehensible.
in *Sunday Times* 28 February 1962

Geoffrey Grigson 1905–85

English critic

5 The old ideas of nobility and sacrifice have become a howitzer squatting at Hyde Park like a petrified toad, and the hero has become a cabinet minister on a pedestal in bronze boots.
on modern sculpture
Henry Moore (1944)

Joseph ('Jo') Grimond
1913–93

British Liberal politician, Leader of the Liberal Party (1956–67)

6 In bygone days, commanders were taught that when in doubt, they should march their troops towards the sound of gunfire. I intend to march my troops towards the sound of gunfire.
speech to the Liberal Party Assembly, 14 September 1963

on the chance of a pact with the Labour Government:
7 Our teeth are in the real meat.
speech to the Liberal Party Assembly, 1965

Andrei Gromyko 1909–89

Soviet statesman, President of the USSR 1985–8

8 Comrades, this man has a nice smile, but he's got iron teeth.
of Mikhail ***Gorbachev***
speech to Soviet Communist Party Central Committee, 11 March 1985

Andrew Grove 1936–

American businessman

9 Only the paranoid survive.
dictum on which he has long run his company, the Intel Corporation
in *New York Times* 18 December 1994

Philip Guedalla 1889–1944

British historian and biographer

10 Any stigma, as the old saying is, will serve to beat a dogma.
Masters and Men (1923) 'Ministers of State'

11 The little ships, the unforgotten Homeric catalogue of *Mary Jane* and *Peggy IV*, of *Folkestone Belle*, *Boy Billy*, and *Ethel Maud*, of *Lady Haig* and *Skylark* . . . the

little ships of England brought the Army home.

on the evacuation of Dunkirk

Mr Churchill (1941)

1 The cheerful clatter of Sir James Barrie's cans as he went round with the milk of human kindness.

Supers and Supermen (1920) 'Some Critics'

2 The work of Henry James has always seemed divisible by a simple dynastic arrangement into three reigns: James I, James II, and the Old Pretender.

Supers and Supermen (1920) 'Some Critics'

Ernesto ('Che') Guevara 1928–67

Argentinian revolutionary and guerrilla leader

3 The Revolution is made by man, but man must forge his revolutionary spirit from day to day.

Socialism and Man in Cuba (1968)

Alec Guinness 1914–2000

English actor

on Guinness: see **le Carré** 194:13

4 I just couldn't go on speaking those bloody awful, banal lines. I'd had enough of the mumbo-jumbo.

of his refusal to play Obi-Wan Kenobi in Star Wars *sequels*

attributed, September 1998

Nubar Gulbenkian 1896–1972

British industrialist and philanthropist

5 The best number for a dinner party is two—myself and a dam' good head waiter.

in *Daily Telegraph* 14 January 1965

Thom Gunn 1929–

English poet

6 My thoughts are crowded with death
and it draws so oddly on the sexual
that I am confused
confused to be attracted
by, in effect, my own annihilation.

'In Time of Plague' (1992)

7 Their relationship consisted
In discussing if it existed.

'Jamesian' (1992)

Alan Guth 1947–

American physicist

8 It is often said that there is no such thing as a free lunch. The Universe, however, is a free lunch.

in *Harpers* November 1994; see **Sayings** 290:9

Woody Guthrie 1912–67

American folksinger and songwriter

9 This land is your land, this land is my land,
From California to the New York Island.
From the redwood forest to the Gulf Stream waters
This land was made for you and me.

'This Land is Your Land' (1956 song)

William Hague 1961–

British Conservative politician, Leader of the Conservative Party 1997–2001

10 Feather-bedding, pocket-lining, money-grabbing cronies.

during the debate on lobbyists' influence and 'cronyism'

in the House of Commons, 8 July 1998

11 This is a candidate of probity and integrity—I am going to back him to the full.

of Jeffrey Archer as candidate for Mayor of London

at the Conservative party conference, October 1999

12 Let me take you on a journey to a foreign land—to Britain after a second term of Tony Blair.

speech to Conservative Party spring conference, Harrogate, 4 March 2001

13 Debating with him at the Dispatch Box has been exciting, fascinating, fun, an enormous challenge and, from my point of view, wholly unproductive.

during his final Prime Minister's Question Time as Leader of the Opposition

in the House of Commons, 18 July 2001

Lord Haig 1861–1928

British soldier, Commander of British armies in France, 1915–18

1 A very weak-minded fellow I am afraid, and, like the feather pillow, bears the marks of the last person who has sat on him!

describing the 17th Earl of Derby

letter to Lady Haig, 14 January 1918

2 Every position must be held to the last man: there must be no retirement. With our backs to the wall, and believing in the justice of our cause, each one of us must fight on to the end.

order to British troops, 12 April 1918; A. Duff Cooper *Haig* (1936)

Lord Hailsham (Quintin Hogg) 1907–2001

British Conservative politician

3 Conservatives do not believe that the political struggle is the most important thing in life . . . The simplest of them prefer fox-hunting—the wisest religion.

The Case for Conservatism (1947)

4 We are a democratically governed republic with a wholly admirable head of state.

Values: Collapse and Cure (1994)

5 A great party is not to be brought down because of a scandal by a woman of easy virtue and a proved liar.

BBC television interview on the Profumo affair; in *The Times* 14 June 1963

6 The elective dictatorship.

title of the Dimbleby Lecture, 19 October 1976

7 The English and, more latterly, the British, have the habit of acquiring their institutions by chance or inadvertence, and shedding them in a fit of absent-mindedness.

'The Granada Guildhall Lecture 1987' 10 November 1987; see below

We seem . . . to have conquered and peopled half the world in a fit of absence of mind.

John Seeley (1834–95) *The Expansion of England* (1883)

J. B. S. Haldane 1892–1964

Scottish mathematical biologist

8 Now, my own suspicion is that the universe is not only queerer than we suppose, but queerer than we *can* suppose.

Possible Worlds (1927)

9 If my mental processes are determined wholly by the motions of atoms in my brain, I have no reason for supposing that my beliefs are true. They may be sound chemically, but that does not make them sound logically. And hence I have no reason for supposing my brain to be composed of atoms.

Possible Worlds (1927) 'When I am Dead'

10 I wish I had the voice of Homer
To sing of rectal carcinoma,
Which kills a lot more chaps, in fact,
Than were bumped off when Troy was sacked.

'Cancer's a Funny Thing'; Ronald Clark *J. B. S.* (1968)

11 The Creator, if He exists, has a special preference for beetles.

on observing that there are 400,000 species of beetles on this planet, but only 8,000 species of mammals

in *Journal of the British Interplanetary Society* (1951)

12 I'd lay down my life for two brothers or eight cousins.

attributed; in *New Scientist* 8 August 1974

H. R. Haldeman 1929–93

Presidential assistant to Richard Nixon

1 Once the toothpaste is out of the tube, it is awfully hard to get it back in.
on the Watergate affair
to John Dean, 8 April 1973, in *Hearings Before the Select Committee on Presidential Campaign Activities of US Senate: Watergate and Related Activities* (1973)

Radclyffe Hall 1883–1943

English novelist

2 The well of loneliness.
title of novel (1928)

3 You're neither unnatural, nor abominable, nor mad; you're as much a part of what people call nature as anyone else; only you're unexplained as yet—you've not got your niche in creation.
The Well of Loneliness (1928)

Margaret Halsey 1910–

American writer

4 Englishwomen's shoes look as if they had been made by someone who had often heard shoes described but had never seen any.
With Malice Toward Some (1938)

5 The English never smash in a face. They merely refrain from asking it to dinner.
With Malice Toward Some (1938)

W. F. ('Bull') Halsey 1882–1959

American admiral

6 The Third Fleet's sunken and damaged ships have been salvaged and are retiring at high speed toward the enemy.
on hearing claims that the Japanese had virtually annihilated the US fleet
report, 14 October 1944; E. B. Potter *Bull Halsey* (1985)

Oscar Hammerstein II 1895–1960

American songwriter

7 Fish got to swim and birds got to fly
I got to love one man till I die,
Can't help lovin' dat man of mine.
'Can't Help Lovin' Dat Man of Mine' (1927 song)

8 Climb ev'ry mountain, ford ev'ry stream
Follow ev'ry rainbow, till you find your dream!
'Climb Ev'ry Mountain' (1959 song)

9 June is bustin' out all over.
title of song (1945)

10 The last time I saw Paris
Her heart was warm and gay,
I heard the laughter of her heart in ev'ry street café.
'The Last Time I saw Paris' (1941 song)

11 The corn is as high as an elephant's eye.
'Oh, What a Beautiful Mornin' ' (1943 song)

12 Oh, what a beautiful mornin',
Oh, what a beautiful day!
I got a beautiful feelin'
Ev'rything's goin' my way.
'Oh, What a Beautiful Mornin' ' (1943 song)

13 Ol' man river, dat ol' man river,
He must know sumpin', but don't say nothin',
He jus' keeps rollin',
He jus' keeps rollin' along.
'Ol' Man River' (1927 song)

14 Some enchanted evening,
You may see a stranger,
You may see a stranger,
Across a crowded room.
'Some Enchanted Evening' (1949 song)

15 The hills are alive with the sound of music,
With songs they have sung for a thousand years.
The hills fill my heart with the sound of music,
My heart wants to sing ev'ry song it hears.
'The Sound of Music' (1959 song)

16 There is nothin' like a dame.
title of song (1949)

17 I'm as corny as Kansas in August,

High as a flag on the Fourth of July!
'A Wonderful Guy' (1949 song)

1 You'll never walk alone.
title of song (1945)

Christopher Hampton 1946–

English dramatist

2 Masturbation is the thinking man's television.
Philanthropist (1970)

3 A definition of capitalism . . . the process whereby American girls turn into American women.
Savages (1974)

Learned Hand 1872–1961

American judge

4 No plagiarist can excuse the wrong by showing how much of his work he did not pirate.
in *Sheldon v. Metro-Goldwyn Pictures Corp.* 1936

5 A self-made man may prefer a self-made name.
on Samuel Goldfish's changing his name to Samuel ***Goldwyn***
Bosley Crowther *Lion's Share* (1957)

Carol Hanisch

see **Political sayings and slogans** 261:26

Brian Hanrahan 1949–

British journalist

6 I counted them all out and I counted them all back.
on the number of British aeroplanes joining the raid on Port Stanley
BBC broadcast report, 1 May 1982

Lorraine Hansberry 1930–65

American dramatist

7 Though it be a thrilling and marvellous thing to be merely young and gifted in such times, it is doubly so, doubly dynamic—to be young, gifted and *black*.
To be young, gifted and black: Lorraine Hansberry in her own words (1969) adapted by Robert Nemiroff; see **Irvine** 165:14

Rick Hansen 1957–

Canadian wheelchair athlete

8 You have to be the best with what you have.
in *Globe and Mail* 3 November 1986

Pauline Hanson

Australian politician, founder of the One Nation party

in response to the question, 'Are you xenophobic?':
9 Please explain!
interview on *60 Minutes*, 20 October 1996

Otto Harbach 1873–1963

American songwriter

10 Now laughing friends deride tears I
cannot hide,
So I smile and say 'When a lovely flame
dies,
Smoke gets in your eyes.'
'Smoke Gets in your Eyes' (1933 song)

E. Y. ('Yip') Harburg 1898–1981

American songwriter

11 Brother can you spare a dime?
title of song (1932)

12 Say, it's only a paper moon,
Sailing over a cardboard sea.
'It's Only a Paper Moon' (1933 song, with Billy Rose)

13 Wanna cry, wanna croon.
Wanna laugh like a loon.
It's that Old Devil Moon in your eyes.
'Old Devil Moon' (1946 song)

14 Somewhere over the rainbow
Way up high,
There's a land that I heard of
Once in a lullaby.
'Over the Rainbow' (1939 song)

15 When our organs have been transplanted

And the new ones made happy to lodge
in us,
Let us pray one wish be granted—
We retain our zones erogenous.
'Seated One Day at the Organ' (1965)

1 Follow the yellow brick road.
'We're Off to See the Wizard' (1939 song); see below; see **John** 171:1

The road to the City of Emeralds is paved with yellow brick.
L. Frank Baum (1856–1919) *The Wonderful Wizard of Oz* (1900)

D. W. Harding 1906–

British psychologist and critic

2 Regulated hatred.
title of an article on the novels of Jane Austen in *Scrutiny* March 1940

Godfrey Harold Hardy 1877–1947

English mathematician

3 Beauty is the first test: there is no permanent place in the world for ugly mathematics.
A Mathematician's Apology (1940)

Thomas Hardy 1840–1928

English novelist and poet

4 'Peace upon earth!' was said. We sing it,
And pay a million priests to bring it.
After two thousand years of mass
We've got as far as poison-gas.
'Christmas: 1924' (1928)

5 In a solitude of the sea
Deep from human vanity
And the Pride of Life that planned her,
stilly couches she.
on the loss of the Titanic
'Convergence of the Twain' (1914)

6 The Immanent Will that stirs and urges
everything.
'Convergence of the Twain' (1914)

7 And as the smart ship grew
In stature, grace, and hue,
In shadowy silent distance grew the
Iceberg too . . .
Till the Spinner of the Years
Said 'Now!' And each one hears,
And consummation comes, and jars two
hemispheres.
'Convergence of the Twain' (1914)

8 An aged thrush, frail, gaunt, and small,
In blast-beruffled plume.
'The Darkling Thrush' (1902)

9 So little cause for carollings
Of such ecstatic sound
Was written on terrestrial things
Afar or nigh around,
That I could think there trembled
through
His happy good-night air
Some blessed Hope, whereof he knew
And I was unaware.
'The Darkling Thrush' (1902)

10 If way to the Better there be, it exacts a
full look at the worst.
'De Profundis' (1902)

11 I am the family face;
Flesh perishes, I live on,
Projecting trait and trace
Through time to times anon,
And leaping from place to place
Over oblivion.
'Heredity' (1917)

12 Yes; quaint and curious war is!
You shoot a fellow down
You'd treat if met where any bar is,
Or help to half-a-crown.
'The Man he Killed' (1909)

13 What of the faith and fire within us
Men who march away
Ere the barn-cocks say
Night is growing grey,
To hazards whence no tears can win us;
What of the faith and fire within us
Men who march away?
'Men Who March Away' (1914)

14 In the third-class seat sat the journeying
boy
And the roof-lamp's oily flame
Played down on his listless form and face,
Bewrapt past knowing to what he was
going,

Or whence he came.
'Midnight on the Great Western' (1917)

1 Woman much missed, how you call to me, call to me.
'The Voice' (1914)

2 When I set out for Lyonnesse,
A hundred miles away,
The rime was on the spray,
And starlight lit my lonesomeness.
'When I set out for Lyonnesse' (1914)

3 War makes rattling good history; but
Peace is poor reading.
The Dynasts (1904)

4 A local thing called Christianity.
The Dynasts (1904)

David Hare 1947–

English actor and dramatist

5 Being taken no notice of in 10 million homes.
of appearing on television
Amy's View (1997)

6 To portray only what you would like to be true is the beginning of censorship.
The History Plays (1984)

7 If Christ were to return today, the Church of England would ask him to set out his ideas on a single sheet of A4.
Racing Demon (1990)

W. F. Hargreaves 1846–1919

British songwriter

8 I'm Burlington Bertie
I rise at ten thirty and saunter along like a toff,
I walk down the Strand with my gloves on my hand,
Then I walk down again with them off.
'Burlington Bertie from Bow' (1915 song)

9 I acted so tragic the house rose like magic,
The audience yelled 'You're sublime.'
They made me a present of Mornington Crescent
They threw it a brick at a time.
'The Night I Appeared as Macbeth' (1922 song)

Lord Harlech 1918–85

British diplomat

10 Britain will be honoured by historians more for the way she disposed of an empire than for the way in which she acquired it.
in *New York Times* 28 October 1962; see **Hailsham** 143:7

Charles Eustace Harman 1894–1970

British judge

11 Accountants are the witch-doctors of the modern world and willing to turn their hands to any kind of magic.
speech, February 1964, in A. Sampson *The New Anatomy of Britain* (1971)

Jimmy Harper et al.

12 The biggest aspidistra in the world.
title of song (1938); popularized by Gracie Fields

Michael Harrington 1928–89

American writer and sociologist

13 For the urban poor the police are those who arrest you. In almost any slum there is a vast conspiracy against the forces of law and order.
The Other America: Poverty in the United States (1962)

Arthur Harris 1892–1984

British Air Force Marshal

14 I would not regard the whole of the remaining cities of Germany as worth the bones of one British Grenadier.
supporting the continued strategic bombing of German cities
letter to Norman Bottomley, deputy Chief of Air Staff, 29 March 1945; Max Hastings *Bomber Command* (1979); see below

Not worth the healthy bones of a single Pomeranian grenadier.
Bismarck (1815–98) in G. O. Kent *Bismarck and his Times* (1978)

Paul Harrison 1936–

American dramatist and director

1 The poor tread lightest upon the earth. The higher our income, the more resources we control and the more havoc we wreak.
in *Guardian* 1 May 1992

Josephine Hart 1942–

Irish novelist

2 Damaged people are dangerous. They know they can survive.
Damage (1991); see **Starkie** 305:13

Lorenz Hart 1895–1943

American songwriter

3 Bewitched, bothered, and bewildered am I.
'Bewitched' (1941 song)

4 When love congeals
It soon reveals
The faint aroma of performing seals.
'I Wish I Were in Love Again' (1937 song)

5 I get too hungry for dinner at eight.
I like the theatre, but never come late.
I never bother with people I hate.
That's why the lady is a tramp.
'The Lady is a Tramp' (1937 song)

6 In a mountain greenery
Where God paints the scenery—
Just two crazy people together.
'Mountain Greenery' (1926 song)

7 Thou swell! Thou witty!
Thou sweet! Thou grand!
Wouldst kiss me pretty?
Wouldst hold my hand?
'Thou Swell' (1927 song)

Moss Hart 1904–61 and George S. Kaufman 1889–1961

American songwriter; American dramatist

8 You can't take it with you.
title of play (1936)

L. P. Hartley

see **Opening lines** 247:16

F. W. Harvey *b.* 1888

English poet

9 From troubles of the world
I turn to ducks
Beautiful comical things.
'Ducks' (1919)

Minnie Louise Haskins 1875–1957

English teacher and writer

10 And I said to the man who stood at the gate of the year: 'Give me a light that I may tread safely into the unknown.'
And he replied:
'Go out into the darkness and put your hand into the Hand of God. That shall be to you better than light and safer than a known way.'
quoted by **George VI** *in his Christmas broadcast, 1939*
Desert (1908) 'God Knows'

Václav Havel 1936–

Czech dramatist and statesman; President of Czechoslovakia 1989–92 and of the Czech Republic since 1993

11 Hope is definitely not the same thing as optimism. It is not the conviction that something will turn out well, but the certainty that something makes sense, regardless of how it turns out.
Disturbing the Peace (1986)

12 That special time caught me up in its wild vortex and—in the absence of leisure to reflect on the matter—compelled me to do what had to be done.
on his election to the Presidency
Summer Meditations (1992)

13 Let us teach ourselves and others that politics can be not only the art of the possible, especially if this means the art of speculation, calculation, intrigue, secret deals, and pragmatic manoeuvring, but that it can even be the art of the impossible, namely, the art of improving ourselves and the world.

speech, Prague, 1 January 1990; see **Butler** 50:3

1 Even a purely moral act that has no hope of any immediate and visible political effect can gradually and indirectly, over time, gain in political significance.

letter to Alexander Dubček, August 1969

2 The Gypsies are a litmus test not of democracy but of civil society.

attributed

Jacquetta Hawkes 1910–96

English archaeologist and writer

3 I was conscious of this vanished being and myself as part of an unbroken stream of consciousness . . . With an imaginative effort it is possible to see the eternal present in which all days, all the seasons of the plain, stand in enduring unity.

discovering a Neanderthal skeleton

in *New York Times Biographical Service* 21 March 1996

Stephen Hawking 1942–

English theoretical physicist

4 Someone told me that each equation I included in the book would halve the sales.

A Brief History of Time (1988)

5 In effect, we have redefined the task of science to be the discovery of laws that will enable us to predict events up to the limits set by the uncertainty principle.

A Brief History of Time (1988)

6 What is it that breathes fire into the equations and makes a universe for them to describe . . . Why does the universe go to all the bother of existing?

A Brief History of Time (1988)

7 If we find the answer to that [why it is that we and the universe exist], it would be the ultimate triumph of human reason—for then we would know the mind of God.

A Brief History of Time (1988)

8 By 2600, the world population would be standing shoulder to shoulder and the electricity consumed would make the earth glow red-hot.

on what will happen if the population continues to increase at the present rate

in *The Times* 17 February 2001

Ian Hay 1876–1952

Scottish novelist and dramatist

9 War is hell, and all that, but it has a good deal to recommend it. It wipes out all the small nuisances of peace-time.

The First Hundred Thousand (1915)

10 What do you mean, funny? Funny-peculiar or funny ha-ha?

The Housemaster (1938)

Bill Hayden 1933–

Australian Labor politician

11 I am not convinced the Labor Party could not win under my leadership. I believe a drover's dog could lead the Labor Party to victory the way the country is.

Hayden had resigned as Opposition leader in 1983 as Malcolm ***Fraser*** *was in the process of calling the election*

John Stubbs *Hayden* (1989)

Alfred Hayes 1911–85

American songwriter

12 I dreamed I saw Joe Hill last night
Alive as you and me.
Says I, 'But Joe, you're ten years dead.'
'I never died,' says he.

'I Dreamed I Saw Joe Hill Last Night' (1936 song)

Lee Hazlewood 1929–

American singer and songwriter

13 These boots are made for walkin'.

title of song (1966)

Bessie Head 1937–86

South African-born writer

14 And if the white man thought that Asians were a low, filthy nation, Asians could still smile with relief—at least, they were not Africans. And if the white man thought that Africans were a low, filthy nation, Africans in southern Africa could still smile—at least, they were not bushmen. They all have their monsters.

Maru (1971) pt. 1

1 Love is mutually feeding each other, not one living on another like a ghoul.

A Question of Power (1973)

Denis Healey 1917–

British Labour politician

2 I warn you there are going to be howls of anguish from the 80,000 people who are rich enough to pay over 75% [tax] on the last slice of their income.

speech at Labour Party Conference, 1 October 1973

3 Like being savaged by a dead sheep.

on being criticized by Geoffrey ***Howe*** *in the House of Commons*

in the House of Commons, 14 June 1978

4 While the rest of Europe is marching to confront the new challenges, the Prime Minister is shuffling along in the gutter in the opposite direction, like an old bag lady, muttering imprecations at anyone who catches her eye.

of Margaret ***Thatcher***

in the House of Commons, 22 February 1990

Edna Healey 1918–

British writer

5 She has no hinterland; in particular she has no sense of history.

of Margaret ***Thatcher***

Denis Healey *The Time of My Life* (1989)

Seamus Heaney 1939–

Irish poet

6 All agog at the plasterer on his ladder
Skimming our gable and writing our name there
With his trowel point, letter by strange letter.

'Alphabets' (1987)

7 And found myself thinking: if it were nowadays,
This is how Death would summon Everyman.

'A Call' (1996)

8 How culpable was he
That last night when he broke
Our tribe's complicity?
'Now you're supposed to be
An educated man,'
I hear him say. 'Puzzle me
The right answer to that one.'

'Casualty' (1979)

9 History says, *Don't hope*
On this side of the grave.
But then, once in a lifetime
The longed-for tidal wave
Of justice can rise up
And hope and history rhyme.

The Cure at Troy (version of Sophocles' *Philoctetes*, 1990)

10 Between my finger and my thumb
The squat pen rests.
I'll dig with it.

'Digging' (1966)

11 Me waiting until I was nearly fifty
To credit marvels.

'Fosterling' (1991)

12 The annals say: when the monks of Clonmacnoise
Were all at prayers inside the oratory
A ship appeared above them in the air.

'Lightenings viii' (1991)

13 Don't be surprised
If I demur, for, be advised
My passport's green.
No glass of ours was ever raised
To toast *The Queen.*

rebuking the editors of The Penguin Book of Contemporary British Poetry *for including him among its authors*

Open Letter (1983)

14 Who would connive
in civilised outrage
yet understand the exact
and tribal, intimate revenge.

'Punishment' (1975)

15 My heart besieged by anger, my mind a gap of danger,
I walked among their old haunts, the home ground where they bled;
And in the dirt lay justice like an acorn in the winter

Till its oak would sprout in Derry where
the thirteen men lay dead.

of Bloody Sunday, Londonderry, 30 January 1972

'The Road to Derry'

1 HERE IS THE NEWS,
Said the absolute speaker. Between him
and us
A great gulf was fixed where
pronunciation
Reigned tyrannically.

'A Sofa in the Forties' (1996)

2 The famous
Northern reticence, the tight gag of place
And times: yes, yes. Of the 'wee six' I
sing
Where to be saved you only must save
face
And whatever you say, you say nothing.

'Whatever You Say Say Nothing' (1975)

3 If revolution is the kicking down of a rotten door, evolution is more like pushing the stone from the mouth of the tomb. There is an Easter energy about it, a sense of arrival rather than wreckage.

in *Observer* 12 April 1998

4 No death outside my immediate family has left me more bereft. No death in my lifetime has hurt poets more.

funeral oration for Ted **Hughes**, 3 November 1998

Edward Heath 1916–

British Conservative statesman; Prime Minister, 1970–4

on Heath: see **Jenkins** 169:11

5 This would, at a stroke, reduce the rise in prices, increase production and reduce unemployment.

press release from Conservative Central Office, 16 June 1970, never actually spoken by Heath

6 The unpleasant and unacceptable face of capitalism.

on the Lonrho affair

in the House of Commons, 15 May 1973

7 Rejoice, rejoice, rejoice.

telephone call to his office on hearing of Margaret ***Thatcher****'s fall from power in 1990*

attributed; in *Daily Telegraph* 24 September 1998 (online edition)

Fred Heatherton

British songwriter

8 I've got a loverly bunch of coconuts,
There they are a-standing in a row.

'I've Got a Lovely Bunch of Coconuts' (1944 song; revised version 1948)

John Heath-Stubbs 1918–

English poet

9 Venerable Mother Toothache
Climb down from the white battlements,
Stop twisting in your yellow fingers
The fourfold rope of nerves.

'A Charm Against the Toothache' (1954)

Ben Hecht 1894–1964

American screenwriter

see also **Film lines** 117:9

10 [Goldwyn] filled the room with wonderful panic and beat at your mind like a man in front of a slot machine, shaking it for a jackpot.

A. Scott Berg *Goldwyn* (1989)

Tippi Hedren 1935–

American actress

11 [Alfred Hitchcock] thought of himself as looking like Cary Grant. That's tough, to think of yourself one way and look another.

interview in California, 1982; P. F. Boller and R. L. Davis *Hollywood Anecdotes* (1988)

Amanda Heggs

British sufferer from Aids

12 Sometimes I have a terrible feeling that I am dying not from the virus, but from being untouchable.

of Aids

in *Guardian* 12 June 1989

Werner Heisenberg 1901–76

German mathematical physicist

13 An expert is someone who knows some of the worst mistakes that can be made in

his subject and who manages to avoid them.

Der Teil und das Ganze (1969); tr. A. J. Pomerans as *Physics and Beyond*, 1971

on Felix Bloch's stating that space was the field of linear operations:

1 Nonsense. Space is blue and birds fly through it.

Felix Bloch 'Heisenberg and the early days of quantum mechanics' in *Physics Today* December 1976

Joseph Heller 1923–99

American novelist

2 There was only one catch and that was Catch-22, which specified that a concern for one's own safety in the face of dangers that were real and immediate was the process of a rational mind . . . Orr would be crazy to fly more missions and sane if he didn't, but if he was sane he had to fly them. If he flew them he was crazy and didn't have to; but if he didn't want to he was sane and had to.

Catch-22 (1961)

3 Some men are born mediocre, some men achieve mediocrity, and some men have mediocrity thrust upon them. With Major Major it had been all three.

Catch-22 (1961); see below

Some men are born great, some achieve greatness, and some have greatness thrust upon them.

William Shakespeare (1564–1616) *Twelfth Night* (1601)

4 When I read something saying I've not done anything as good as *Catch-22* I'm tempted to reply, 'Who has?'

in *The Times* 9 June 1993

Lillian Hellman 1905–84

American dramatist

on Hellman: see **McCarthy** 206:11

5 Cynicism is an unpleasant way of saying the truth.

The Little Foxes (1939)

6 I cannot and will not cut my conscience to fit this year's fashions.

letter to John S. Wood, 19 May 1952

Leona Helmsley *c.*1920–

American hotelier

7 Only the little people pay taxes.

comment made to her housekeeper in 1983, and reported at her trial for tax evasion

in *New York Times* 12 July 1989

Ernest Hemingway 1899–1961

American novelist

on Hemingway: see **Vidal** 328:2; *see also* **Fitzgerald** 118:17, **Stein** 306:11

8 Where do the noses go? I always wondered where the noses would go.

For Whom the Bell Tolls (1940)

9 But did thee feel the earth move?

For Whom the Bell Tolls (1940)

10 Cowardice, as distinguished from panic, is almost always simply a lack of ability to suspend the functioning of the imagination.

Men at War (1942)

11 Paris is a movable feast.

A Movable Feast (1964) epigraph

12 A man can be destroyed but not defeated.

The Old Man and the Sea (1952)

13 The sun also rises.

title of novel (1926)

14 Grace under pressure.

when asked what he meant by 'guts' in an interview with Dorothy ***Parker***

in *New Yorker* 30 November 1929

15 The most essential gift for a good writer is a built-in, shock-proof shit detector. This is the writer's radar and all great writers have had it.

in *Paris Review* Spring 1958

Jimi Hendrix 1942–70

American rock musician

16 Purple haze is in my brain
Lately things don't seem the same.

'Purple Haze' (1967 song)

17 A musician, if he's a messenger, is like a child who hasn't been handled too many times by man, hasn't had too many fingerprints across his brain.

in *Life Magazine* (1969)

Arthur W. D. Henley

1 Nobody loves a fairy when she's forty.
title of song (1934)

Tim Henman 1974–

British tennis player
on Henman: see **McEnroe** 208:8

2 Someone in the locker room said my matches should come with a health warning. But to come through a match with that much drama feels pretty satisfying.
after the match in which he defeated Roger Federer for a place in the Wimbledon semi-final
in *Guardian* 5 July 2001

Peter Hennessy 1947–

British historian and writer

3 The model of a modern Prime Minister would be a kind of grotesque composite freak—someone with the dedication to duty of a Peel, the physical energy of a Gladstone, the detachment of a Salisbury, the brains of an Asquith, the balls of a Lloyd George, the word-power of a Churchill, the administrative gifts of an Attlee, the style of a Macmillan, the managerialism of a Heath, and the sleep requirements of a Thatcher. Human beings do not come like that.
The Hidden Wiring (1995)

Barbara Hepworth 1903–75

English sculptor

4 Carving is interrelated masses conveying an emotion: a perfect relationship between the mind and the colour, light and weight which is the stone, made by the hand which feels.
Herbert Read (ed.) *Unit One* (1934)

A. P. Herbert 1890–1971

English writer and humorist

5 Don't let's go to the dogs tonight,
For mother will be there.
'Don't Let's Go to the Dogs Tonight' (1926)

6 The Farmer will never be happy again;
He carries his heart in his boots;
For either the rain is destroying his grain
Or the drought is destroying his roots.
'The Farmer' (1922)

7 Let's find out what everyone is doing,
And then stop everyone from doing it.
'Let's Stop Somebody from Doing Something!' (1930)

8 As my poor father used to say
In 1863,
Once people start on all this Art
Goodbye, moralitee!
'Lines for a Worthy Person' (1930)

9 This high official, all allow,
Is grossly overpaid;
There wasn't any Board, and now
There isn't any Trade.
'The President of the Board of Trade' (1922)

10 Nothing is wasted, nothing is in vain:
The seas roll over but the rocks remain.
Tough at the Top (operetta c.1949)

11 Holy deadlock.
title of novel (1934)

12 People must not do things for fun. We are not here for fun. There is no reference to fun in any Act of Parliament.
Uncommon Law (1935) 'Is it a Free Country?'

13 'Was the cow crossed?'
'No, your worship, it was an open cow.'
on an attempt to write a cheque on a cow
Uncommon Law (1935) 'The Negotiable Cow'

Michael Heseltine 1933–

British Conservative politician

14 I knew that, 'He who wields the knife never wears the crown.'
in *New Society* 14 February 1986

15 The market has no morality.
on *Panorama*, BBC1 TV, 27 June 1988

16 Polluted rivers, filthy streets, bodies bedded down in doorways are no advertisement for a prosperous or caring society.
speech at Conservative Party Conference 10 October 1989

17 If I have to intervene to help British companies . . . I'll intervene—before breakfast, before lunch, before tea and before dinner. And I'll get up the next morning and I'll start all over again.

of his role as President of the Board of Trade

to the Conservative Party Conference, 7 October 1992

1 You can't wield a handbag from an empty chair.

at the launch of Britain in Europe, 14 October 1999

2 The fundamental question is is the Conservative Party leadable?

in the aftermath of disastrous electoral defeat

in *Daily Telegraph* 9 June 2001 (electronic edition)

Hermann Hesse 1877–1962

German novelist and poet

3 If you hate a person, you hate something in him that is part of yourself. What isn't part of ourselves doesn't disturb us.

Demian (1919)

4 The bourgeois prefers comfort to pleasure, convenience to liberty, and a pleasant temperature to the deathly inner consuming fire.

Der Steppenwolf (1927) 'Tractat vom Steppenwolf'

Charlton Heston 1924–

American actor

5 It's not the guns that kill, it's the maladjusted kids.

in *Independent* on 22 April 2000

Lord Hewart 1870–1943

British lawyer and politician

6 Justice should not only be done, but should manifestly and undoubtedly be seen to be done.

Rex v. *Sussex Justices*, 9 November 1923

Dorothy Hewett 1923–

Australian poet

7 Clancy and Dooley and Don McLeod
Walked by the wurlies when the wind was loud,
And their voice was new as the fresh sap running,
And we keep on fighting and we keep on coming.

'Clancy and Dooley and Don McLeod'

8 I had a tremendous world in my head and more than three-quarters of it will be buried with me.

The Chapel Perilous (1973)

Robert Hewison 1943–

British historian

9 The turn of the century raises expectations. The end of a millennium promises apocalypse and revelation. But at the close of the twentieth century the golden age seems behind us, not ahead. The end game of the 1990s promises neither nirvana nor Armageddon, but entropy.

Future Tense (1990)

John Hewitt 1907–87

Northern Irish poet

10 We would be strangers in the Capitol;
this is our country also, no-where else;
and we shall not be outcast on the world.

'The Colony' (1950)

11 I'm an Ulsterman, of planter stock. I was born in the island of Ireland, so secondarily I'm an Irishman. I was born in the British archipelago and English is my native tongue, so I am British. The British archipelago consists of offshore islands to the continent of Europe, so I'm European. This is my hierarchy of values and so far as I am concerned, anyone who omits one step in that sequence of values is falsifying the situation.

in *The Irish Times* 4 July 1974

Reinhard Heydrich 1904–42

German Nazi leader

12 Now the rough work has been done we begin the period of finer work. We need to work in harmony with the civil administration. We count on you

gentlemen as far as the final solution is concerned.

on the planned mass murder of eleven million European Jews

speech in Wannsee, 20 January 1942; see **Goering** 136:11

Du Bose Heyward 1885–1940 and **Ira Gershwin** 1896–1983

American songwriters

1 It ain't necessarily so,
De t'ings dat yo' li'ble
To read in de Bible
It ain't necessarily so.

'It ain't necessarily so' (1935 song)

2 Summer time an' the livin' is easy,
Fish are jumpin' an' the cotton is high.

'Summertime' (1935 song)

3 A woman is a sometime thing.

title of song (1935)

J. R. Hicks 1904–

British economist

4 The best of all monopoly profits is a quiet life.

Econometrica (1935) 'The Theory of Monopoly'

Seymour Hicks 1871–1949

English actor-manager and author

5 You will recognize, my boy, the first sign of old age: it is when you go out into the streets of London and realize for the first time how young the policemen look.

C. R. D. Pulling *They Were Singing* (1952)

David Hilbert 1862–1943

German mathematician

6 The importance of a scientific work can be measured by the number of previous publications it makes it superfluous to read.

attributed; Lewis Wolpert *The Unnatural Nature of Science* (1993)

Christopher Hill 1912–

British historian

7 Only very slowly and late have men come to realize that unless freedom is universal it is only extended privilege.

Century of Revolution (1961)

Damon Hill 1960–

English motor-racing driver

8 Winning is everything. The only ones who remember you when you come second are your wife and your dog.

in *Sunday Times* 18 December 1994

Geoffrey Hill 1932–

English poet

9 Poetry
Unearths from among the speechless dead

Lazarus mystified, common man
Of death. The lily rears its gouged face
From the provided loam.

'History as Poetry' (1968)

10 She kept the siege. And every day
We watched her brooding over death
Like a strong bird above its prey.
The room filled with the kettle's breath.

Damp curtains glued against the pane
Sealed time away. Her body froze
As if to freeze us all, and chain
Creation to a stunned repose.

'In Memory of Jane Fraser' (1959)

11 I love my work and my children. God
Is distant, difficult. Things happen.
Too near the ancient troughs of blood
Innocence is no earthly weapon.

'Ovid in the Third Reich' (1968)

Joe Hill 1879–1915

American labour leader and songwriter

on Hill: see **Hayes** 149:12

12 Work and pray, live on hay,
You'll get pie in the sky when you die.

'Preacher and the Slave' (1911 song)

1 I will die like a true-blue rebel. Don't waste any time in mourning—organize.
before his death by firing squad
farewell telegram to Bill Haywood, 18 November 1915

Pattie S. Hill 1868–1946

American educationist

2 Happy birthday to you.
title of song (1935)

Edmund Hillary 1919–

New Zealand mountaineer

3 Well, we knocked the bastard off!
on conquering Mount Everest, 1953
Nothing Venture, Nothing Win (1975)

Fred Hillebrand 1893–

4 Home James, and don't spare the horses.
title of song (1934)

James Hilton 1900–54

English novelist

5 Nothing really wrong with him—only anno domini, but that's the most fatal complaint of all, in the end.
Goodbye, Mr Chips (1934)

Emperor Hirohito 1901–89

Emperor of Japan from 1926

6 The war situation has developed not necessarily to Japan's advantage.
announcing Japan's surrender, in a broadcast to his people after atom bombs had destroyed Hiroshima and Nagasaki
on 15 August 1945

Damien Hirst 1965–

English artist

7 It's amazing what you can do with an E in A-level art, twisted imagination and a chainsaw.
after winning the 1995 Turner Prize
in *Observer* 3 December 1995

Ian Hislop 1960–

English satirical journalist

8 If this is justice, I am a banana.
on the libel damages awarded against Private Eye *to Sonia Sutcliffe, wife of the Yorkshire Ripper*
comment, 24 May 1989

Alfred Hitchcock 1899–1980

British-born film director
on Hitchcock: see **Hedren** 151:11

9 Actors are cattle.
in *Saturday Evening Post* 22 May 1943

10 Television has brought back murder into the home—where it belongs.
in *Observer* 19 December 1965

11 There is no terror in a bang, only in the anticipation of it.
Leslie Halliwell (ed.) *Halliwell's Filmgoer's Companion* (1984); attributed

Adolf Hitler 1889–1945

German dictator
on Hitler: see **Buchman** 47:6, **Chamberlain** 61:12

12 The night of the long knives.
referring to the massacre of Ernst Roehm and his associates by Hitler on 29–30 June 1934 (subsequently associated with Harold **Macmillan***'s Cabinet dismissals of 13 July 1962)*
S. H. Roberts *The House Hitler Built* (1937)

13 I go the way that Providence dictates with the assurance of a sleepwalker.
speech in Munich, 15 March 1936

14 It is the last territorial claim which I have to make in Europe.
on the Sudetenland
speech in Berlin, 26 September 1938

15 Is Paris burning?
on 5 August 1944; L. Collins and D. Lapierre *Is Paris Burning?* (1965)

16 The broad mass of a nation . . . will more easily fall victim to a big lie than to a small one.
Mein Kampf (1925)

Eric Hobsbawm 1917-

British historian

1 For 80 per cent of humanity the Middle Ages ended suddenly in the 1950s; or perhaps better still, they were *felt* to end in the 1960s.

Age of Extremes (1994)

2 This was the kind of war which existed in order to produce victory parades.

*of the **Falklands** War*

in *Marxism Today* January 1983

David Hockney 1937-

British artist

3 All you can do with most ordinary photographs is stare at them—they stare back, blankly—and presently your concentration begins to fade. They stare you down. I mean, photography is all right if you don't mind looking at the world from the point of view of a paralysed cyclops—*for a split second.*

as told to Lawrence Weschler, *Cameraworks* (1984)

4 All painting, no matter what you're painting, is abstract in that it's got to be organized.

David Hockney (1976)

5 The thing with high-tech is that you always end up using scissors.

in *Observer* 10 July 1994

Dorothy Hodgkin 1910-94

British chemist and Nobel prize-winner

6 Nobody who lived through the first year or two of the trials of penicillin in Oxford could possibly not care about what it was. But also it's difficult not to enjoy just growing the crystals.

Lewis Wolpert & Alison Richards *A Passion for Science* (1988)

Howard Hodgkin 1932-

British painter and printmaker

7 Mostly painting is like putting a message in a bottle and flinging it into the sea.

in *Observer* 10 June 2001

Ralph Hodgson 1871-1962

English poet

8 'Twould ring the bells of Heaven
The wildest peal for years,
If Parson lost his senses
And people came to theirs,
And he and they together
Knelt down with angry prayers
For tamed and shabby tigers
And dancing dogs and bears,
And wretched, blind, pit ponies,
And little hunted hares.

'Bells of Heaven' (1917)

Eric Hoffer 1902-83

American philosopher

9 When people are free to do as they please, they usually imitate each other. Originality is deliberate and forced, and partakes of the nature of a protest.

Passionate State of Mind (1955)

Al Hoffman 1902-60 and Dick Manning 1912-91

American songwriters

10 Takes two to tango.

title of song (1952)

Gerard Hoffnung 1925-59

English humorist

11 Standing among savage scenery, the hotel offers stupendous revelations. There is a French widow in every bedroom, affording delightful prospects.

supposedly quoting a letter from a Tyrolean landlord

in speech at the Oxford Union, 4 December 1958

Lancelot Hogben 1895-1975

English scientist

12 This is not the age of pamphleteers. It is the age of the engineers. The spark-gap is mightier than the pen.

Science for the Citizen (1938) epilogue

Billie Holiday 1915–59

American singer
see also **Opening lines** 247:14

1 Mama may have, papa may have,
But God bless the child that's got his own!

'God Bless the Child' (1941 song, with Arthur Herzog Jnr)

2 Southern trees bear strange fruit,
Blood on the leaves and blood at the root,
Black bodies swinging in the Southern breeze,
Strange fruit hanging from the poplar trees.

'Strange Fruit' (1939)

3 You can be up to your boobies in white satin, with gardenias in your hair and no sugar cane for miles, but you can still be working on a plantation.

Lady Sings the Blues (1956, with William Duffy)

4 In this country, don't forget, a habit is no damn private hell. There's no solitary confinement outside of jail. A habit is hell for those you love.

of a drug habit

Lady Sings the Blues (1956, with William Duffy)

John H. Holmes 1879–1964

American Unitarian minister

5 This, now, is the judgement of our scientific age—the third reaction of man upon the universe! This universe is not hostile, nor yet is it friendly. It is simply indifferent.

The Sensible Man's View of Religion (1932)

Oliver Wendell Holmes Jr. 1841–1935

American lawyer
see also **Misquotations** 226:15

6 I have long thought that if you knew a column of advertisements by heart, you could achieve unexpected felicities with them. You can get a happy quotation anywhere if you have the eye.

letter to Harold Laski, 31 May 1923

Miroslav Holub 1923–

Czech poet and pathologist

7 Here in the Lord's bosom rest
the tongues of beggars,
the lungs of generals,
the eyes of informers,
the skins of martyrs

in the absolute
of the microscope's lenses.

I leaf through Old Testament slices of liver,
in the white monuments of brain I read
the hieroglyphs of decay . . .

And out of the tricolours of mortal suffering
we day after day
pull
threads of wisdom.

'Pathology' (1967)

8 But above all
we have
the ability
to sort peas,
to cup water in our hands,
to seek
the right screw
under the sofa
for hours.

'Wings' (1967)

Alec Douglas-Home, Lord Home 1903–95

British Conservative statesman; Prime Minister, 1963–4

9 When I have to read economic documents I have to have a box of matches and start moving them into position to simplify and illustrate the points to myself.

in *Observer* 16 September 1962

10 As far as the fourteenth earl is concerned, I suppose Mr Wilson, when you come to think of it, is the fourteenth Mr Wilson.

replying to Harold **Wilson***'s remark (on Home's becoming leader of the Conservative party) that 'the whole* [democratic] *process has ground to a halt with a fourteenth Earl'*

in *Daily Telegraph* 22 October 1963

Herbert Hoover 1874–1964

American Republican statesman, 31st President of the US, 1929–33

1 Our country has deliberately undertaken a great social and economic experiment, noble in motive and far-reaching in purpose.

on the Eighteenth Amendment enacting Prohibition

letter to Senator W. H. Borah, 23 February 1928

2 The American system of rugged individualism.

speech, 22 October 1928

3 The slogan of progress is changing from the full dinner pail to the full garage.

sometimes paraphrased as, 'a car in every garage and a chicken in every pot'

speech, 22 October 1928; see below

I want there to be no peasant in my kingdom so poor that he is unable to have a chicken in his pot every Sunday.

Henri IV, King of France (1553–1610) in Hardouin de Péréfixe *Histoire de Henry le Grand* (1681)

4 The grass will grow in the streets of a hundred cities, a thousand towns.

on proposals 'to reduce the protective tariff to a competitive tariff for revenue'

speech, 31 October 1932

5 Older men declare war. But it is youth who must fight and die.

speech at the Republican National Convention, Chicago, 27 June 1944

A. D. Hope 1907–

Australian poet

6 And her five cities, like teeming sores,
Each drains her: a vast parasite robber-
state
Where second-hand Europeans pullulate
Timidly on the edge of alien shores.

'Australia' (1939)

Anthony Hope 1863–1933

English novelist
see also **Epitaphs** 109:13

7 Oh, for an hour of Herod!

at the first night of Peter Pan *in 1904*

D. Mackail *Story of JMB* (1941)

Bob Hope 1903–

American comedian

8 A bank is a place that will lend you money if you can prove that you don't need it.

Alan Harrington *Life in the Crystal Palace* (1959) 'The Tyranny of Farms'

9 Well, I'm still here.

after erroneous reports of his death, marked by tributes paid to him in Congress

in *Mail on Sunday* 7 June 1998

Anthony Hopkins 1937–

Welsh actor

10 I live in Mickey Mouse land, in La La land, you know, and that's what I like. I'm a beach bum by heart. I've got no need to prove to myself that I can do Shakespeare. I've done it.

in *Observer* 11 February 2001

11 We are fascinated by the darkness in ourselves.

on his new film Hannibal

in *The Times* 17 February 2001

Nick Hornby 1957–

British writer

12 The natural state of the football fan is bitter disappointment, no matter what the score.

Fever Pitch (1992)

13 If your main cultural interests are not-getting-mugged and commuting it's the place to be.

on Maidenhead, where he grew up

in *Sunday Times* 3 June 2001

John Lee Hooker 1917–2001

American blues singer and guitarist

1 When Adam and Eve first saw each other, that's when the blues started. No matter what anybody says, it all comes down to the same thing: a man and a woman, a broken heart and a broken home.

in *The Healer* (1989 album); in *Independent* 23 June 2001, obituary

2 When I die they'll bury the blues with me. But the blues will never die.

in conversation, *c.*1991; Charles Shaar Murray 'The death of the Boogie Man: an Appreciation' (online obituary, salon.com, 2001)

A. E. Housman 1859–1936

English poet

on Housman: see **Kingsmill** 182:1, 182:2; *see also* **Last words** 191:4

3 The Grizzly Bear is huge and wild;
He has devoured the infant child.
The infant child is not aware
He has been eaten by the bear.

'Infant Innocence' (1938)

4 And how am I to face the odds
Of man's bedevilment and God's?
I, a stranger and afraid
In a world I never made.

Last Poems (1922) no. 12

5 Their shoulders held the sky suspended;
They stood, and earth's foundations stay;
What God abandoned, these defended,
And saved the sum of things for pay.

Last Poems (1922) no. 37 'Epitaph on an Army of Mercenaries'

6 For nature, heartless, witless nature,
Will neither care nor know
What stranger's feet may find the meadow
And trespass there and go,
Nor ask amid the dews of morning
If they are mine or no.

Last Poems (1922) no. 40

7 Life, to be sure, is nothing much to lose;
But young men think it is, and we were young.

More Poems (1936) no. 36

8 A year or two ago . . . I received from America a request that I would define poetry. I replied that I could no more define poetry than a terrier can define a rat, but that I thought we both recognized the object by the symptoms which it provokes in us.

The Name and Nature of Poetry (1933)

9 Experience has taught me, when I am shaving of a morning, to keep watch over my thoughts, because, if a line of poetry strays into my memory, my skin bristles so that the razor ceases to act . . . The seat of this sensation is the pit of the stomach.

The Name and Nature of Poetry (1933)

10 Whence came the intrusive comma on p. 4? It did not fall from the sky.

letter to the Richards Press, 3 July 1930

Geoffrey Howe 1926–

British Conservative politician

on Howe: see **Healey** 150:3

11 It is rather like sending your opening batsmen to the crease only for them to find the moment that the first balls are bowled that their bats have been broken before the game by the team captain.

on the difficulties caused him as Foreign Secretary by Margaret Thatcher's anti-European views

resignation speech as Deputy Prime Minister, in the House of Commons, 13 November 1990

12 The time has come for others to consider their own response to the tragic conflict of loyalties with which I have myself wrestled for perhaps too long.

in the House of Commons, 13 November 1990

Frankie Howerd 1922–92

British comedian

13 Such cruel glasses.

of Robin ***Day***

That Was The Week That Was (BBC television series, from 1963)

14 It's television, you see. If you are not on the thing every week, the public think you are either dead or deported.

attributed

Fred Hoyle 1915-2001

English astrophysicist

1 Space isn't remote at all. It's only an hour's drive away if your car could go straight upwards.

in *Observer* 9 September 1979

2 When I was young, the old regarded me as an outrageous young fellow, and now that I'm old the young regard me as an outrageous old fellow.

in *Scientific American* March 1995

3 There is a coherent plan to the universe, though I don't know what it's a plan for.

attributed

Elbert Hubbard 1859-1915

American writer

4 Life is just one damned thing after another.

in *Philistine* December 1909; often attributed to Frank Ward O'Malley; see **Millay** 223:12

Howard Hughes Jr. 1905-76

American industrialist, aviator, and film producer

5 That man's ears make him look like a taxi-cab with both doors open.

of Clark Gable

Charles Higham and Joel Greenberg *Celluloid Muse* (1969)

Jimmy Hughes and **Frank Lake**

British writers

6 Bless 'em all! Bless 'em all! The long and the short and the tall.

'Bless 'Em All' (1940 song)

Langston Hughes 1902-67

American writer and poet

7 I, too, sing America.

I am the darker brother.
They send me to eat in the kitchen
When company comes.

'I, Too' (1925)

8 That Justice is a blind goddess
Is a thing to which we black are wise.
Her bandage hides two festering sores
That once perhaps were eyes.

'Justice'

9 Sometimes a crumb falls
From the tables of joy,
Sometimes a bone
Is flung.

To some people
Love is given,
To others
Only heaven.

'Luck'

10 I've known rivers:
I've known rivers ancient as the world and older than the flow of human blood in human veins.

'The Negro Speaks of Rivers' (1921)

11 I bathed in the Euphrates when dawns were young.
I built my hut near the Congo and it lulled me to sleep.
I looked upon the Nile and raised the pyramids above it.
I heard the singing of the Mississippi when Abe Lincoln went down to New Orleans, and I've seen its muddy bosom turn all golden in the sunset.

'The Negro Speaks of Rivers' (1921)

12 'It's powerful,' he said.
'What?'
'That one drop of Negro blood—because just *one* drop of black blood makes a man coloured. *One* drop—you are a Negro!'

Simple Takes a Wife (1953)

13 I got the Weary Blues
And I can't be satisfied.

'Weary Blues' (1926)

Robert Hughes 1938-

Australian writer

14 What the convict system bequeathed to later Australian generations was not the sturdy, skeptical independence . . . but an intense concern with social and political respectability. The idea of the 'convict stain', a moral blot soaked into our

fabric, dominated all argument about Australian selfhood by the 1840s.
The Fatal Shore (1987), introduction

1 Would Australians have done anything differently if their country had not been settled as the jail of infinite space? Certainly they would. They would have remembered more of their own history. The obsessive cultural enterprise of Australians a hundred years ago was to forget it entirely, to sublimate it, to drive it down into unconsulted recesses.
The Fatal Shore (1987) ch. 17

Ted Hughes 1930–98

English poet
on Hughes: see **Heaney** 151:4

2 Daylong this tomcat lies stretched flat
As an old rough mat, no mouth and no eyes,
Continual wars and wives are what
Have tattered his ears and battered his head.
'Esther's Tomcat' (1960)

3 At that time
I had not understood
How the death hurtling to and fro
Inside your head, had to alight somewhere
And again somewhere, and had to be kept moving.
And had to be rested
Temporarily somewhere.
Birthday Letters (1998) 'The 59th Bear' (1998)

4 It took the whole of Creation
To produce my foot, my each feather:
Now I hold Creation in my foot.
'Hawk Roosting' (1960)

5 Fourteen centuries have learned,
From charred remains, that what took place
When Alexandria's library burned
Brain-damaged the human race.
'Hear it Again' (1997)

6 I saw the horses:
Huge in the dense grey—ten together—
Megalith-still.
'The Horses' (1957)

7 Adam ate the apple.
Eve ate Adam.
The serpent ate Eve.
This is the dark intestine.
'Theology' (1967)

8 . . . With a sudden sharp hot stink of fox,
It enters the dark hole of the head.
'The Thought-Fox' (1957)

9 Ten years after your death
I meet on a page of your journal, as never before,
The shock of your joy.
'Visit' (1998)

10 Grape is my mulatto mother
In this frozen whited country.
'Wino' (1967)

William Morris 'Billy' Hughes 1864–1952

British-born Australian statesman, Prime Minister of Australia 1917–23

11 Oh well, I suppose it's right that the members of these old families should stick together nowadays. After all, their ancestors in those days were probably chained together.
of support for a political rival in North Sydney, 1931
John Thompson *On the Lips of Living Men* (1962)

12 If you paved the way from here to Broken Hill with Bibles, and if that man Hitler swore an oath on every one of them, I wouldn't believe a goddam bloody word he said.
John Thompson *On the Lips of Living Men* (1962)

13 I don't want justice, I want mercy.
on having his portrait painted
John Thompson *On the Lips of Living Men* (1962)

14 He couldn't lead a flock of homing pigeons.
of Robert ***Menzies***
Howard Beale *This Inch of Time . . .* (1977)

Josephine Hull ?1886–1957

American actress

15 Shakespeare is so tiring. You never get a chance to sit down unless you're a king.
in *Time* 16 November 1953

Basil Hume 1923–99

British Catholic priest, Cardinal-Archbishop of Westminster

1 I have received two wonderful graces. First, I have been given time to prepare for a new future. Secondly, I find myself—uncharacteristically—calm and at peace.

breaking the news of his imminent death from cancer

letter to priests of Westminster diocese, 16 April 1999

2 It is harder for some people to believe that God loves them than to believe that he exists.

in *Guardian* 18 June 1999

Hubert Humphrey 1911–78

American Democratic politician

3 There are not enough jails, not enough policemen, not enough courts to enforce a law not supported by the people.

speech at Williamsburg, 1 May 1965

4 Here we are the way politics ought to be in America, the politics of happiness, the politics of purpose and the politics of joy.

speech in Washington, 27 April 1968

Robert Hunter 1941–

Canadian journalist and environmentalist

5 The word *Greenpeace* had a ring to it—it conjured images of Eden; it said ecology and antiwar in two syllables; it fit easily into even a one-column headline.

Warriors of the Rainbow (1979); see **Darnell** 84:4

Herman Hupfeld 1894–1951

American songwriter

6 You must remember this, a kiss is still a kiss,
A sigh is just a sigh;
The fundamental things apply,
As time goes by.

'As Time Goes By' (1931 song)

Douglas Hurd 1930–

British Conservative politician; Foreign Secretary

7 One of the principal props which have allowed Britain to punch above its weight in the world.

of American support for Nato

speech at Chatham House; in *Financial Times* 4 February 1993

8 Silence is often a good policy on some subjects in politics, but silence is regarded as a sort of sin now, and it has to be filled with a lot of gossip and sound bites.

in *Independent* 23 April 2001

Saddam Hussein 1937–

Iraqi statesman, President since 1979

9 The mother of battles.

popular interpretation of his description of the approaching Gulf War; in The Times *7 January 1991 it was reported that he was ready for the 'mother of all wars'*

speech in Baghdad, 6 January 1991

Aldous Huxley 1894–1963

English novelist

10 The sexophones wailed like melodious cats under the moon.

Brave New World (1932)

11 That men do not learn very much from the lessons of history is the most important of all the lessons that history has to teach.

Collected Essays (1959) 'Case of Voluntary Ignorance'

12 The proper study of mankind is books.

Crome Yellow (1921); see below

The proper study of mankind is man.

Alexander Pope (1688–1744) *An Essay on Man* (1733)

13 The end cannot justify the means, for the simple and obvious reason that the means employed determine the nature of the ends produced.

Ends and Means (1937)

1 So long as men worship the Caesars and Napoleons, Caesars and Napoleons will duly arise and make them miserable.
Ends and Means (1937)

2 There is no substitute for talent. Industry and all the virtues are of no avail.
Point Counter Point (1928)

3 Those who believe that they are exclusively in the right are generally those who achieve something.
Proper Studies (1927) 'Note on Dogma'

4 Facts do not cease to exist because they are ignored.
Proper Studies (1927) 'Note on Dogma'

5 Most human beings have an almost infinite capacity for taking things for granted.
Themes and Variations (1950) 'Variations on a Philosopher'

6 A million million spermatozoa,
All of them alive:
Out of their cataclysm but one poor Noah
Dare hope to survive.

And among that billion minus one
Might have chanced to be
Shakespeare, another Newton, a new
  Donne—
But the One was Me.
'Fifth Philosopher's Song' (1920); see below

And a thousand thousand slimy things
Lived on; and so did I.
Samuel Taylor Coleridge (1772–1834) 'The Rime of the Ancient Mariner' (1798) pt. 1

7 Beauty for some provides escape,
Who gain a happiness in eyeing
The gorgeous buttocks of the ape
Or Autumn sunsets exquisitely dying.
'Ninth Philosopher's Song' (1920)

8 Even if I could be Shakespeare, I think I should still choose to be Faraday.
in 1925, attributed; Walter M. Elsasser *Memoirs of a Physicist in the Atomic Age* (1978)

Julian Huxley 1887–1975

English biologist

9 Operationally, God is beginning to resemble not a ruler but the last fading smile of a cosmic Cheshire cat.
Religion without Revelation (1957 ed.)

Henry Hyde 1924–

American Republican politician, leader of the prosecution for the impeachment of President **Clinton**

10 We hoped that the public would move from its total indifference to concern. That hope was unrequited.
in *Times* 13 February 1999

Nicholas Hytner 1956–

English theatre and film director

11 If you gave him a good script, actors and technicians, Mickey Mouse could direct a movie.
in an interview, *Daily Telegraph* 24 February 1994

Dolores Ibarruri ('La Pasionaria') 1895–1989

Spanish Communist leader

12 It is better to die on your feet than to live on your knees.
speech in Paris, 3 September 1936; also attributed to Emiliano **Zapata**

13 *No pasarán.*
They shall not pass.
radio broadcast, Madrid, 19 July 1936; see **Sayings** 289:22

Ice Cube 1970–

American rap musician

14 If I'm more of an influence to your son as a rapper than you are as a father . . . you got to look at yourself as a parent.
to Mike Sager in *Rolling Stone* 4 October 1990

Ice-T 1958–

American rap musician

15 When they call you articulate, that's another way of saying 'He talks good for a black guy'.
in *Independent* 30 December 1995

Francis Iles

see **Opening lines** 247:9

Ivan Illich 1926–

American sociologist

1 In a consumer society there are inevitably two kinds of slaves: the prisoners of addiction and the prisoners of envy.

Tools for Conviviality (1973)

Mick Imlah 1956–

British poet

2 Oh, foolish boys!
The English elephant
Never lies!

'Tusking' (1988)

Dean Inge 1860–1954

English writer; Dean of St. Paul's, 1911–34

3 The enemies of Freedom do not argue; they shout and they shoot.

End of an Age (1948)

4 It takes in reality only one to make a quarrel. It is useless for the sheep to pass resolutions in favour of vegetarianism, while the wolf remains of a different opinion.

Outspoken Essays: First Series (1919) 'Patriotism'

5 The nations which have put mankind and posterity most in their debt have been small states—Israel, Athens, Florence, Elizabethan England.

Outspoken Essays: Second Series (1922) 'State, visible and invisible'

6 A man may build himself a throne of bayonets, but he cannot sit on it.

Philosophy of Plotinus (1923); see **Yeltsin** 349:1

Bernard Ingham 1932–

British journalist and public relations specialist, Chief Press Secretary to the Prime Minister, 1979–90

7 Many journalists have fallen for the conspiracy theory of government. I do assure you that they would produce more accurate work if they adhered to the cock-up theory.

in *Observer* 17 March 1985

8 Blood sport is brought to its ultimate refinement in the gossip columns.

speech, 5 February 1986

Richard Ingrams 1937–

English satirical journalist, editor of Private Eye

9 My motto is publish and be sued.

on BBC Radio 4, 4 May 1977

Eugène Ionesco 1912–94

Romanian-born French dramatist

10 A civil servant doesn't make jokes.

The Killer (1958)

11 If God exists, why write literature?
And if he doesn't, why write literature?

Non (1934)

12 Living is abnormal.

The Rhinoceros (1959)

13 You can only predict things after they have happened.

The Rhinoceros (1959)

Weldon J. Irvine

American musician

14 Young, gifted and black.

title of song (1969), music by Nina Simone; see **Hansberry** 145:7

Christopher Isherwood 1904–86

English novelist

see also **Auden** 16:16

15 The common cormorant (or shag)
Lays eggs inside a paper bag,

You follow the idea, no doubt?
It's to keep the lightning out.
But what these unobservant birds
Have never thought of, is that herds
Of wandering bears might come with
buns
And steal the bags to hold the crumbs.

'The Common Cormorant' (written *c.*1925)

1 I am a camera with its shutter open, quite passive, recording, not thinking.

Goodbye to Berlin (1939) 'Berlin Diary' Autumn 1930

Hastings Lionel ('Pug') Ismay 1887–1965

British general and Secretary to the Committee of Imperial Defence; first Secretary-General of Nato

2 NATO exists for three reasons—to keep the Russians out, the Americans in and the Germans down.

to a group of British Conservative backbenchers in 1949

Peter Hennessy *Never Again* (1992); oral tradition

Alec Issigonis

British engineer

3 A camel is a horse designed by a committee.

on his dislike of working in teams

in *Guardian* 14 January 1991 'Notes and Queries'; attributed

Goran Ivanisevic 1971–

Croatian tennis player

4 I have never enjoyed playing tennis more than that. I don't care now if I never win a match in my life again.

interviewed after winning the Wimbledon Men's Singles, 9 July 2001

in *Times* 10 July 2001 (electronic edition)

Charles Ives 1874–1954

American composer

5 Beauty in music is too often confused with something that lets the ears lie back in an easy chair.

Joseph Machlis *Introduction to Contemporary Music* (1963)

Molly Ivins 1944– and Lou Dubose

American journalists

6 Young political reporters are always told there are three ways to judge a politician. The first is to look at the record. The second is to look at the record. And third, look at the record.

Molly Ivins and Lou Dubose *Shrub* (2000)

7 If you think his daddy had trouble with 'the vision thing', wait till you meet this one.

of presidential candidate George W. ***Bush***

Molly Ivins and Lou Dubose *Shrub* (2000)

Alija Izetbegović 1925–

Bosnian statesman; President of Bosnia and Herzegovina since 1990

8 And to my people I say, this may not be a just peace, but it is more just than a continuation of war.

after signing the Dayton accord with representatives of Serbia and Croatia

in Dayton, Ohio, 21 November 1995

Eddie Izzard 1962–

British comedian

9 'Cake or death?' 'Cake, please.'

imagining how a Church of England Inquisition might have worked

Dress to Kill (stage show, San Francisco, 1998)

10 I want to succeed in America where, unlike Britain, they do not regard ambition as being the same as eating babies.

in *The Times* 20 January 2001

Glenda Jackson 1936–

British Labour politician and actress

11 If I am one of Blair's babes, well I've been called a damn sight worse.

in *Independent on Sunday* 8 August 1999

Jesse Jackson 1941–

American Democratic politician and clergyman

1 When I look out at this convention, I see the face of America, red, yellow, brown, black, and white. We are all precious in God's sight—the real rainbow coalition.

speech at Democratic National Convention, Atlanta, 19 July 1988

Michael Jackson 1958–

American pop singer

2 Before you judge me, try hard to love me,
look within your heart
Then ask,—have you seen my
childhood?

'Childhood' (1995 song)

3 My father was a management genius.
But what I really wanted was a dad.

speech at the Oxford Union, on his children's 'Bill of Rights', in *Independent on Sunday* 11 March 2001

Robert H. Jackson 1892–1954

American lawyer and judge

4 That four great nations, flushed with victory and stung with injury, stay the hands of vengeance and voluntarily submit their captive enemies to the judgement of the law, is one of the most significant tributes that Power has ever paid to Reason.

opening statement for the prosecution at Nuremberg

before the International Military Tribunal in Nuremberg, 21 November 1945

Joe Jacobs 1896–1940

American boxing manager

5 We was robbed!

after Jack Sharkey beat Max Schmeling (of whom Jacobs was manager) in the heavyweight title fight, 21 June 1932

P. Heller *In This Corner* (1975)

6 I should of stood in bed.

after leaving his sick-bed to attend the World Baseball Series in Detroit, 1935, and betting on the losers

J. Lardner *Strong Cigars* (1951)

Mick Jagger 1943–

English rock musician

7 We don't look like a bunch of schoolmasters, I admit, but at least we try to educate people in American blues music.

Pete Goodman *In: Our Own Story by the Rolling Stones* (1964)

Mick Jagger 1943– and Keith Richards 1943–

English rock musicians

8 Get off of my cloud.

title of song (1966)

9 And though she's not really ill,
There's a little yellow pill:
She goes running for the shelter
Of a mother's little helper.

'Mother's Little Helper' (1966 song)

10 I can't get no satisfaction
I can't get no girl reaction.

'(I Can't Get No) Satisfaction' (1965 song)

11 Ev'rywhere I hear the sound of
marching, charging feet, boy,
'Cause summer's here and the time is
right for fighting in the street, boy.

'Street Fighting Man' (1968 song)

12 There's just no place for a street fighting man!

'Street Fighting Man' (1968 song)

Clive James 1939–

Australian critic and writer

13 Television is simultaneously blamed, often by the same people, for worsening the world and for being powerless to change it.

Glued to the Box (1981)

Henry James 1843–1916

American novelist

on James: see **Guedalla** 142:2

14 The deep well of unconscious cerebration.

The American (1909 ed.) preface

1 The house of fiction has in short not one window, but a million . . . but they are, singly or together, as nothing without the posted presence of the watcher.
The Portrait of a Lady (1908 ed.) preface

2 Life being all inclusion and confusion, and art being all discrimination and selection.
The Spoils of Poynton (1909 ed.) preface

3 The war has used up words.
in *New York Times* 21 March 1915

4 So here it is at last, the distinguished thing!
on experiencing his first stroke
Edith Wharton *A Backward Glance* (1934)

5 Summer afternoon—summer afternoon . . . the two most beautiful words in the English language.
Edith Wharton *A Backward Glance* (1934)

P. D. James 1920–

English crime writer

6 What the detective story is about is not murder but the restoration of order.
in *Face* December 1986

7 I believe that political correctness can be a form of linguistic fascism, and it sends shivers down the spine of my generation who went to war against fascism.
in *Paris Review* 1995

Randall Jarrell 1914–65

American poet

8 From my mother's sleep I fell into the State,
And I hunched in its belly till my wet fur froze.
Six miles from earth, loosed from its dream of life,
I woke to black flak and the nightmare fighters.
When I died they washed me out of the turret with a hose.
'The Death of the Ball Turret Gunner' (1945)

9 The firelight of a long, blind, dreaming story
Lingers upon your lips; and I have seen
Firm, fixed forever in your closing eyes,
The Corn King beckoning to his Spring Queen.
'A Girl in a Library' (1951)

10 In bombers named for girls, we burned
The cities we had learned about in school—
Till our lives wore out; our bodies lay among
The people we had killed and never seen.
When we lasted long enough they gave us medals;
When we died they said, 'Our casualties were low.'
'Losses' (1963)

11 To Americans, English manners are far more frightening than none at all.
Pictures from an Institution (1954)

12 It is better to entertain an idea than to take it home to live with you for the rest of your life.
Pictures from an Institution (1954)

13 One of the most obvious facts about grown-ups, to a child, is that they have forgotten what it is like to be a child.
introduction to Christina Stead *The Man Who Loved Children* (1965)

Antony Jay

see Jonathan **Lynn** and Antony Jay

Douglas Jay 1907–96

British Labour politician
see also **Political sayings and slogans** 261:12

14 In the case of nutrition and health, just as in the case of education, the gentleman in Whitehall really does know better what is good for people than the people know themselves.
The Socialist Case (1939)

Margaret Jay 1939–

British Labour politician, daughter of James **Callaghan**

15 We're simply saying that what may have

been right 800 or even 200 years ago is not right now.
on the abolition of the hereditary right to sit in the House of Lords
in *Guardian* 12 November 1999

1 Any proposal totally to elect the second chamber under the mistaken view that it would increase the democratic base of parliament would in fact undermine democracy.
in the House of Lords, 7 March 2000

Marianne Jean-Baptiste

British actress

2 The old men running the industry just have not got a clue . . . Britain is no longer totally a white place where people ride horses, wear long frocks and drink tea. The national dish is no longer fish and chips, it's curry.
having been excluded from the group of actors invited to promote British talent at Cannes
in *Observer* 18 May 1997

James Jeans 1877–1946

English astronomer, physicist, and mathematician

3 If we assume that the last breath of, say, Julius Caesar has by now become thoroughly scattered through the atmosphere, then the chances are that each of us inhales one molecule of it with every breath we take.
An Introduction to the Kinetic Theory of Gases (1940); see also **Misquotations** 226:5

4 Life exists in the universe only because the carbon atom possesses certain exceptional properties.
The Mysterious Universe (1930)

5 From the intrinsic evidence of his creation, the Great Architect of the Universe now begins to appear as a pure mathematician.
The Mysterious Universe (1930)

Patrick Jenkin 1926–

British Conservative politician

6 People can clean their teeth in the dark, use the top of the stove instead of the oven, all sorts of savings, but they must use less electricity.
asking the public to save electricity as a miners' strike reduced supplies
radio broadcast, 15 January 1974

David Jenkins 1925–

English theologian and Anglican bishop

7 I am not clear that God manoeuvres physical things . . . After all, a conjuring trick with bones only proves that it is as clever as a conjuring trick with bones.
on the Resurrection
in 'Poles Apart' (BBC radio, 4 October 1984)

Roy Jenkins 1920–

British politician; co-founder of the Social Democratic Party, 1981

8 The politics of the left and centre of this country are frozen in an out-of-date mould which is bad for the political and economic health of Britain and increasingly inhibiting for those who live within the mould. Can it be broken?
speech to Parliamentary Press Gallery, 9 June 1980

9 A dead or dying beast lying across a railway line and preventing other trains from getting through.
of the Labour Party
in *Guardian* 16 May 1987

10 A First Minister whose self-righteous stubbornness has not been equalled, save briefly by Neville Chamberlain, since Lord North.
of Margaret ***Thatcher***
in *Observer* 11 March 1990

11 A great lighthouse which stands there, flashing out beams of light, indifferent to the waves which beat against him.
of Edward ***Heath***
in *Independent* 22 September 1990

12 Nearly all Prime Ministers are dissatisfied with their successors, perhaps even more so if they come from their own party.
Gladstone (1995)

Elizabeth Jennings 1926–2001

English poet

1 I hate a word like 'pets': it sounds so much
Like something with no living of its own.
'My Animals' (1966)

2 Do they know they're old,
These two who are my father and my mother
Whose fire from which I came, has now grown cold?
'One Flesh' in *Collected Poems* (1967)

Paul Jennings 1918–89

English writer

3 Resistentialism is concerned with what Things think about men.
Even Oddlier (1952) 'Developments in Resistentialism'

C. E. M. Joad 1891–1953

English philosopher
see also **Catch-phrases** 59:12

4 It will be said of this generation that it found England a land of beauty and left it a land of 'beauty spots'.
The Horrors of the Countryside (1931)

John XXIII 1881–1963

Italian cleric, Pope from 1958

5 If civil authorities legislate for or allow anything that is contrary to that order and therefore contrary to the will of God, neither the laws made or the authorizations granted can be binding on the consciences of the citizens, since God has more right to be obeyed than man.
Pacem in Terris (1963)

6 The social progress, order, security and peace of each country are necessarily connected with the social progress, order, security and peace of all other countries.
Pacem in Terris (1963)

7 I want to throw open the windows of the Church so that we can see out and the people can see in.
attributed

8 Signora, do you believe my blessing cannot pass through plastic?
to a pilgrim who asked him to bless again some medals and rosaries which he had blessed before she had time to remove them from her purse, 1959
Laureano López Rodó *Memorias* (1990)

Elton John 1947–

English pop singer and songwriter

9 It's the only song I've ever written where I get goose bumps every time I play it.
of 'Candle in the Wind'
in *Daily Telegraph* 9 September 1997

10 I'm not a nest-egg person.
giving evidence in court on his average monthly expenditure
in *Sunday Times* 19 November 2000

Elton John 1947– and Bernie Taupin 1950–

English pop singer and songwriter; songwriter

11 Goodbye Norma Jean . . .

It seems to me you lived your life
Like a candle in the wind.
Never knowing who to cling to
When the rain set in.
And I would have liked to have known you
But I was just a kid
The candle burned out long before
Your legend ever did.
of Marilyn ***Monroe***
'Candle in the Wind' (song, 1973)

12 Even when you died
Oh the press still hounded you.
'Candle in the Wind' (song, 1973)

13 Goodbye England's rose;
May you ever grow in our hearts.
rewritten for and sung at the funeral of ***Diana****, Princess of Wales, 7 September 1997*
'Candle in the Wind' (song, revised version, 1997)

14 And it seems to me you lived your life
Like a candle in the wind:
Never fading with the sunset
When the rain set in.
And your footsteps will always fall here
On England's greenest hills;

Your candle's burned out long before
Your legend ever will.

'Candle in the Wind' (song, revised version, 1997)

1 Goodbye yellow brick road.

title of song (1973); see **Harburg** 146:1

John Paul II 1920–

Polish cleric, Pope since 1978

2 It would be simplistic to say that Divine Providence caused the fall of communism. It fell by itself as a consequence of its own mistakes and abuses. It fell by itself because of its own inherent weaknesses.

when asked by the Italian writer Vittorio Missori if the fall of the USSR could be ascribed to God

Carl Bernstein and Marco Politi *His Holiness: John Paul II and the Hidden History of our Time* (1996)

Amryl Johnson 1944–2001

Trinidadian poet

3 for . . . I am
Black
And I am
Angry
My name is
Midnight
Without
Pity.

'Midnight Without Pity' (1982)

Lyndon Baines Johnson 1908–73

American Democratic statesman, 36th President of the US, 1963–9
on Johnson: see **Political sayings and slogans** 261:2, 261:14, **White** 336:10

to a reporter who had queried his embracing Richard ***Nixon*** *on the vice-president's return from a controversial tour of South America in 1958:*

4 Son, in politics you've got to learn that overnight chicken shit can turn to chicken salad.

Fawn Brodie *Richard Nixon* (1983)

5 I am a free man, an American, a United States Senator, and a Democrat, in that order.

in *Texas Quarterly* Winter 1958

6 All I have I would have given gladly not to be standing here today.

following the assassination of J. F. ***Kennedy***

first speech to Congress as President, 27 November 1963

7 We have talked long enough in this country about equal rights. We have talked for a hundred years or more. It is time now to write the next chapter, and to write it in the books of law.

speech to Congress, 27 November 1963

8 This administration today, here and now declares unconditional war on poverty in America.

State of the Union address to Congress, 8 January 1964

9 In your time we have the opportunity to move not only toward the rich society and the powerful society, but upward to the Great Society.

speech at University of Michigan, 22 May 1964

10 We still seek no wider war.

speech on radio and television, 4 August 1964

11 We are not about to send American boys 9 or 10,000 miles away from home to do what Asian boys ought to be doing for themselves.

speech at Akron University, 21 October 1964; see **Roosevelt** 278:3

12 Extremism in the pursuit of the Presidency is an unpardonable vice. Moderation in the affairs of the nation is the highest virtue.

speech in New York, 31 October 1964; see **Goldwater** 137:2

13 Better to have him inside the tent pissing out, than outside pissing in.

of J. Edgar Hoover

D. Halberstam *The Best and the Brightest* (1972)

14 I don't want loyalty. I want *loyalty*. I want him to kiss my ass in Macy's window at high noon and tell me it

smells like roses. I want his pecker in my pocket.

discussing a prospective assistant

D. Halberstam *The Best and the Brightest* (1972)

1 So dumb he can't fart and chew gum at the same time.

of Gerald ***Ford***

R. Reeves *A Ford, not a Lincoln* (1975)

Philander Chase Johnson 1866–1939

American journalist

2 Cheer up! the worst is yet to come!

in *Everybody's Magazine* May 1920

Philip Johnson 1906–

American architect

3 Architecture is the art of how to waste space.

in *New York Times* 27 December 1964

Hanns Johst 1890–1978

German dramatist

4 Whenever I hear the word culture . . . I release the safety-catch of my Browning!

often attributed to Hermann ***Goering****, and quoted 'Whenever I hear the word culture, I reach for my pistol!'*

Schlageter (1933)

Al Jolson 1886–1950

American singer

5 You think that's noise—you ain't heard nuttin' yet!

first said in a café, competing with the din from a neighbouring building site, in 1906; subsequently an aside in the 1927 film The Jazz Singer

M. Abramson *Real Story of Al Jolson* (1950); also the title of a Jolson song, 1919, 'You Ain't Heard Nothing Yet'

Ieuan Wyn Jones 1949–

Welsh nationalist politician, president of Plaid Cymru

6 The priority for us now is for Wales to gain the same powers as Scotland.

speech to the Plaid Cymru Party Conference

in *Guardian* 23 September 2000

Barry Owen Jones 1932–

Australian Labor politician

7 The sheer incompetence of Australia's current management is for the time being an asset in maintaining high employment levels. But we cannot count on that incompetence for ever.

Sleepers, Wake! (1982) preface

8 Academic economists have about the status and reliability of astrologers or the readers of Tarot cards. If the medical profession was as lacking in resources . . . we would not have advanced very far beyond the provision of splints for broken arms.

John Wilkes (ed.) *The Future of Work* (1981)

Steve Jones 1944–

English geneticist

9 The Admiralty sent the *Beagle* to South America with Darwin on board not because they were interested in evolution but because they knew that the first step to understanding (and, with luck, controlling) the world was to make a map of it. The same is true of the genes.

The Language of the Genes (1993)

10 Sex and taxes are in many ways the same. Tax does to cash what males do to genes. It dispenses assets among the population as a whole. Sex, not death, is the great leveller.

speech to the Royal Society; in *Independent* 25 January 1997

Erica Jong 1942–

American writer

11 The zipless fuck is the purest thing there

is. And it is rarer than the unicorn. And I have never had one.

Fear of Flying (1973)

Janis Joplin 1943–70

American singer

1 Oh, Lord, won't you buy me a Mercedes Benz
My friends all drive Porsches,
I must make amends.

'Mercedes Benz' (1970 song)

2 Fourteen heart attacks and he had to die in my week. In MY week.

when ex-President ***Eisenhower****'s death prevented her photograph appearing on the cover of* Newsweek

in *New Musical Express* 12 April 1969

3 Onstage I make love to twenty-five thousand people, then I go home alone.

in *New Yorker* 14 August 1971

Jenny Joseph 1932–

English poet

4 When I am an old woman I shall wear purple
With a red hat which doesn't go, and doesn't suit me.
And I shall spend my pension on brandy and summer gloves
And satin sandals, and say we've got no money for butter.

'Warning' (1974)

James Joyce 1882–1941

Irish novelist

on Joyce: see **Lawrence** 192:19, **Woolf** 345:7; *see also* **Opening lines** 247:15, 247:17, 247:19

5 His soul swooned slowly as he heard the snow falling faintly through the universe and faintly falling, like the descent of their last end, upon all the living and the dead.

Dubliners (1914) 'The Dead'

6 That ideal reader suffering from an ideal insomnia.

Finnegans Wake (1939)

7 All moanday, tearsday, wailsday, thumpsday, frightday, shatterday till the fear of the Law.

Finnegans Wake (1939)

8 Three quarks for Muster Mark!

Finnegans Wake (1939)

9 A portrait of the artist as a young man.

title of novel, 1916

10 When the soul of a man is born in this country, there are nets flung at it to hold it back from flight. You talk to me of nationality, language, religion. I shall try to fly by those nets.

A Portrait of the Artist as a Young Man (1916)

11 Ireland is the old sow that eats her farrow.

A Portrait of the Artist as a Young Man (1916)

12 Pity is the feeling which arrests the mind in the presence of whatsoever is grave and constant in human sufferings and unites it with the human sufferer. Terror is the feeling which arrests the mind in the presence of whatsoever is grave and constant in human sufferings and unites it with the secret cause.

A Portrait of the Artist as a Young Man (1916)

13 The artist, like the God of the creation, remains within or behind or beyond or above his handiwork, invisible, refined out of existence, indifferent, paring his fingernails.

A Portrait of the Artist as a Young Man (1916)

14 I will not serve that in which I no longer believe whether it call itself my home, my fatherland or my church: and I will try to express myself in some mode of life or art as freely as I can and as wholly as I can, using for my defence the only arms I allow myself to use, silence, exile, and cunning.

A Portrait of the Artist as a Young Man (1916)

15 The snotgreen sea. The scrotumtightening sea.

Ulysses (1922)

16 It is a symbol of Irish art. The cracked lookingglass of a servant.

Ulysses (1922)

17 I fear those big words, Stephen said, which make us so unhappy.

Ulysses (1922)

1 History, Stephen said, is a nightmare from which I am trying to awake.
Ulysses (1922)

2 A man of genius makes no mistakes. His errors are volitional and are the portals of discovery.
Ulysses (1922)

3 Greater love than this, he said, no man hath that a man lay down his wife for his friend.
Ulysses (1922); see below

Greater love hath no man than this, that a man lay down his life for his friends.
Bible St John; see **Thorpe** 320:4

4 The heaventree of stars hung with humid nightblue fruit.
Ulysses (1922)

5 When a young man came up to him in Zurich and said, 'May I kiss the hand that wrote *Ulysses?*' Joyce replied, somewhat like King Lear, 'No, it did lots of other things too.'
Richard Ellmann *James Joyce* (1959); see below

GLOUCESTER: O! let me kiss that hand!
LEAR: Let me wipe it first; it smells of mortality.
William Shakespeare (1564–1616) *King Lear* (1605–6)

William Joyce (Lord Haw-Haw) 1906–46

wartime broadcaster from Nazi Germany, executed for treason

6 Germany calling! Germany calling!
habitual introduction to propaganda broadcasts to Britain during the Second World War

Juan Carlos I 1938–

King of Spain from 1975

7 The Crown, the symbol of the permanence and unity of Spain, cannot tolerate any actions by people attempting to disrupt by force the democratic process.
on the occasion of the attempted coup in 1981
television broadcast at 1.15 a.m., 24 February 1981

8 I will neither abdicate the Crown nor leave Spain. Whoever rebels will provoke a new civil war and will be responsible.
television broadcast, 24 February 1981

Jack Judge 1878–1938 and Harry Williams 1874–1924

British songwriters

9 It's a long way to Tipperary,
It's a long way to go;
It's a long way to Tipperary,
To the sweetest girl I know!
'It's a Long Way to Tipperary' (1912 song)

Carl Gustav Jung 1875–1961

Swiss psychologist

10 A man who has not passed through the inferno of his passions has never overcome them.
Memories, Dreams, Reflections (1962)

11 As far as we can discern, the sole purpose of human existence is to kindle a light in the darkness of mere being.
Memories, Dreams, Reflections (1962)

12 Every form of addiction is bad, no matter whether the narcotic be alcohol or morphine or idealism.
Memories, Dreams, Reflections (1962)

13 The meeting of two personalities is like the contact of two chemical substances: if there is any reaction, both are transformed.
Modern Man in Search of a Soul (1933)

14 The afternoon of human life must also have a significance of its own and cannot be merely a pitiful appendage to life's morning.
The Stages of Life (1930)

15 Where love rules, there is no will to power, and where power predominates, love is lacking. The one is the shadow of the other.
'Über die Psychologie des Unbewussten' (1917)

16 I do not believe . . . I know.
L. van der Post *Jung and the Story of our Time* (1976)

John Junor 1919–97

British journalist and editor
see also **Catch-phrases** 60:1

1 Such a graceful exit. And then he had to go and do this on the doorstep.
on Harold **Wilson**'s *'Lavender List' (the honours list he drew up on resigning the British premiership in 1976)*
in *Observer* 23 January 1990

Donald Justice 1925–

American poet

2 Men at forty
Learn to close softly
The doors to rooms they will not be
Coming back to.
'Men at Forty' (1967)

Pauline Kael 1919–2001

American film critic

3 The words 'Kiss Kiss Bang Bang' which I saw on an Italian movie poster, are perhaps the briefest statement imaginable of the basic appeal of movies.
Kiss Kiss Bang Bang (1968) 'Note on the Title'

Franz Kafka 1883–1924

Czech novelist
see also **Opening lines** 247:18, 248:3

4 You may object that it is not a trial at all; you are quite right, for it is only a trial if I recognize it as such.
The Trial (1925)

5 It's often better to be in chains than to be free.
The Trial (1925)

Gus Kahn 1886–1941 and **Raymond B. Egan** 1890–1952

American songwriters

6 There's nothing surer,
The rich get rich and the poor get children.
In the meantime, in between time,
Ain't we got fun.
'Ain't We Got Fun' (1921 song)

Sarah Kane 1971–99

British dramatist

7 I write the truth and it kills me.
Crave (1998)

George S. Kaufman 1889–1961

American dramatist
see also **Film lines** 116:9, **Hart** 148:8

8 Satire is what closes Saturday night.
Scott Meredith *George S. Kaufman and his Friends* (1974)

Gerald Kaufman 1930–

British Labour politician

9 The longest suicide note in history.
on the Labour Party manifesto New Hope for Britain (1983)
Denis Healey *The Time of My Life* (1989)

Paul Kaufman and **Mike Anthony**

American songwriters

10 Poetry in motion.
title of song (1960)

Kenneth Kaunda 1924–

Zambian statesman, President 1964–91

11 Westerners have aggressive problem-solving minds; Africans experience people.
attributed, 1990

Patrick Kavanagh 1904–67

Irish poet

12 Cassiopeia was over
Cassidy's hanging hill,
I looked and three whin bushes rode across

The horizon—the Three Wise Kings.
'A Christmas Childhood' (1947)

1 Clay is the word and clay is the flesh
Where the potato-gatherers like
mechanized scarecrows move
Along the side-fall of the hill—Maguire
and his men.
'The Great Hunger' (1947)

2 Who bent the coin of my destiny
That it stuck in the slot?
'The Great Hunger' (1947)

3 That was how his life happened.
No mad hooves galloping in the sky,
But the weak, washy way of true
tragedy—
A sick horse nosing around the meadow
for a clean place to die.
'The Great Hunger' (1947)

4 I hate what every poet hates in spite
Of all the solemn talk of contemplation.
Oh, Alexander Selkirk knew the plight
Of being king and government and
nation.
A road, a mile of kingdom, I am king
Of banks and stones and every blooming
thing.
'Inniskeen Road: July Evening' (1936); see below

I am monarch of all I survey . . .
Better dwell in the midst of alarms,
Than reign in this horrible place.
William Cowper (1731–1800) 'Verses Supposed to be Written by Alexander Selkirk' (1782)

Danny Kaye

see **Film lines** 117:7

Paul Keating 1944–

Australian Labor statesman, Prime Minister 1991–6

5 You look like an Easter Island statue with an arse full of razor blades.

in the Australian Parliament to Malcolm ***Fraser****, 1983*

Michael Gordon *A Question of Leadership* (1993)

6 This is a recession that Australia had to have.

speaking as Federal Treasurer, 29 November 1990

7 Even as it [Great Britain] walked out on you and joined the Common Market, you were still looking for your MBEs and your knighthoods, and all the rest of the regalia that comes with it. You would take Australia right back down the time tunnel to the cultural cringe where you have always come from.

addressing Australian Conservative supporters of Great Britain

speech, House of Representatives (Australia) 27 February 1992; see **Phillips** 257:13

8 Leadership is not about being nice. It's about being right and being strong.

in *Time* 9 January 1995

John Keats 1920–

see also **Nader** 236:11

9 The automobile changed our dress, manners, social customs, vacation habits, the shape of our cities, consumer purchasing patterns, common tastes and positions in intercourse.

The Insolent Chariots (1958)

John Keegan 1934–

British military historian

10 It now does look as if air power has prevailed in the Balkans and that the time to redefine how victory in war may be won has come.

in *Daily Telegraph* 4 June 1999

Garrison Keillor 1942–

American humorous writer and broadcaster

11 Years ago, manhood was an opportunity for achievement, and now it is a problem to be overcome.

The Book of Guys (1994)

12 Ronald Reagan, the President who never told bad news to the American people.

We Are Still Married (1989)

Helen Keller 1880–1968

American writer and social reformer, blind and deaf from the age of 19 months

1 Science may have found a cure for most evils; but it has found no remedy for the worst of them all—the apathy of human beings.

My Religion (1927)

2 The mystery of language was revealed to me. I knew then that 'w-a-t-e-r' meant the wonderful cool something that was flowing over my hand. That living word awakened my soul, gave it light, joy, set it free!

The Story of My Life (1902)

Walt Kelly

see **Cartoons** 56:10

Jaan Kenbrovin and **William Kellette**

American songwriters

3 I'm forever blowing bubbles.

title of song (1919)

Charles Kennedy 1959–

British Liberal Democrat politician, Party Leader from 1999

4 War is not the word; nor is crusade. Resolve is.

of the appropriate response to the danger of world terrorism

speech to the Liberal Democrat Party Conference, 24 September 2001

Florynce Kennedy 1916–2000

American lawyer

5 If men could get pregnant, abortion would be a sacrament.

in *Ms.* March 1973

6 When you want to get to the suites, start in the streets.

her rule for political activism

attributed; in *Los Angeles Times* 28 December 2000 (obituary)

7 Freedom is like taking a bath: You got to keep doing it every day.

attributed; in *Madison Capital Times* 28 December 2000 (obituary)

Jacqueline Kennedy

see Jacqueline Kennedy **Onassis**

James B. Kennedy and **John W. Bratton**

British songwriters

8 If you go down in the woods today
You're sure of a big surprise
If you go down in the woods today
You'd better go in disguise
For every Bear that ever there was
Will gather there for certain because,
Today's the day the Teddy Bears have
their Picnic.

'Teddy Bear's Picnic' (1932 song)

Jimmy Kennedy 1902–84 and **Michael Carr** 1904–68

British songwriters

9 We're gonna hang out the washing on the Siegfried Line.

title of song (1939)

John Fitzgerald Kennedy 1917–63

American Democratic statesman, 35th President of the US, 1961–3; son of Joseph and Rose **Kennedy**, brother of Robert **Kennedy**, and first husband of Jacqueline Kennedy **Onassis**

on Kennedy: see **Bentsen** 30:11, **Kennedy** 178:16

10 Don't buy a single vote more than necessary. I'll be damned if I'm going to pay for a landslide.

telegraphed message from his father, read at a Gridiron dinner in Washington, 15 March 1958, and almost certainly JFK's invention

1 We stand today on the edge of a new frontier.
speech accepting the Democratic nomination, 15 July 1960; see **Schlossberg** 291:3

2 The torch has been passed to a new generation of Americans—born in this century, tempered by war, disciplined by a hard and bitter peace.
inaugural address, 20 January 1961

3 We shall pay any price, bear any burden, meet any hardship, support any friend, oppose any foe to assure the survival and the success of liberty.
inaugural address, 20 January 1961

4 If a free society cannot help the many who are poor, it cannot save the few who are rich.
inaugural address, 20 January 1961

5 Let us never negotiate out of fear. But let us never fear to negotiate.
inaugural address, 20 January 1961

6 All this will not be finished in the first 100 days. Nor will it be finished in the first 1,000 days, nor in the life of this Administration, nor even perhaps in our lifetime on this planet. But let us begin.
inaugural address, 20 January 1961

7 And so, my fellow Americans: ask not what your country can do for you—ask what you can do for your country.
inaugural address, 20 January 1961; see **Gibran** 134:5

8 I believe that this Nation should commit itself to achieving the goal, before this decade is out, of landing a man on the Moon and returning him safely to earth.
Supplementary State of the Union message to Congress, 25 May 1961

9 Mankind must put an end to war or war will put an end to mankind.
speech to United Nations General Assembly, 25 September 1961

10 Those who make peaceful revolution impossible will make violent revolution inevitable.
speech at the White House, 13 March 1962

11 Probably the greatest concentration of talent and genius in this house except for perhaps those times when Thomas Jefferson ate alone.
of a dinner for Nobel Prizewinners at the White House
in *New York Times* 30 April 1962

12 There are no 'white' or 'coloured' signs on the foxholes or graveyards of battle.
on proposed Civil Rights Bill
message to Congress, 19 June 1963

13 *Ich bin ein Berliner.*
I am a Berliner.
speech in West Berlin, 26 June 1963

14 In free society art is not a weapon . . . Artists are not engineers of the soul.
speech at Amherst College, Mass., 26 October 1963; see **Gorky** 138:3

15 It was involuntary. They sank my boat.
on being asked how he became a war hero
A. M. Schlesinger Jr. *A Thousand Days* (1965)

Joseph P. Kennedy 1888–1969

American financier and diplomat; husband of Rose **Kennedy**, father of John Fitzgerald and Robert **Kennedy**
see also **Sayings and slogans** 290:15

16 We're going to sell Jack like soapflakes.
when his son John made his bid for the Presidency
John H. Davis *The Kennedy Clan* (1984)

Robert Kennedy 1925–68

American Democratic politician, son of Joseph and Rose **Kennedy**, brother of John Fitzgerald **Kennedy**

17 One-fifth of the people are against everything all the time.
speech, University of Pennsylvania, 6 May 1964

Rose Kennedy 1890–1995

wife of Joseph **Kennedy**, mother of John Fitzgerald and Robert **Kennedy**

18 It's our money, and we're free to spend it any way we please . . . If you have money you spend it, and win.
in response to criticism of overlavish funding of her son Robert's 1968 presidential campaign
in *Daily Telegraph* 24 January 1995 (obituary)

1 Now Teddy must run.
to her daughter, on hearing of the assassination of Robert ***Kennedy***
in *The Times* 24 January 1995 (obituary); attributed, perhaps apocryphal

Jomo Kenyatta 1891–1978

Kenyan statesman, Prime Minister of Kenya 1963 and President 1964–78

2 The African is conditioned, by the cultural and social institutions of centuries, to a freedom of which Europe has little conception, and it is not in his nature to accept serfdom forever. He realizes that he must fight unceasingly for his own emancipation; for without this he is doomed to remain the prey of rival imperialisms.
Facing Mount Kenya (1938); conclusion

Jack Kerouac 1922–69

Amerian novelist
on Kerouac: see **Burroughs** 48:11

3 The beat generation.
phrase coined in the course of a conversation; in *Playboy* June 1959

4 It is not my fault that certain so-called bohemian elements have found in my writings something to hang their peculiar beatnik theories on.
in *New York Journal-American* 8 December 1960

Jean Kerr 1923–

American writer

5 I feel about airplanes the way I feel about diets. It seems to me that they are wonderful things for other people to go on.
The Snake Has All the Lines (1958)

John Maynard Keynes 1883–1946

English economist

6 I work for a Government I despise for ends I think criminal.
letter to Duncan Grant, 15 December 1917

7 Lenin was right. There is no subtler, no surer means of overturning the existing basis of society than to debauch the currency.
Economic Consequences of the Peace (1919)

8 I do not know which makes a man more conservative—to know nothing but the present, or nothing but the past.
The End of Laissez-Faire (1926)

9 The important thing for Government is not to do things which individuals are doing already, and to do them a little better or a little worse; but to do those things which at present are not done at all.
The End of Laissez-Faire (1926)

10 This extraordinary figure of our time, this syren, this goat-footed bard, this half-human visitor to our age from the hag-ridden magic and enchanted woods of Celtic antiquity.
Essays in Biography (1933) 'Mr Lloyd George'

11 If the Treasury were to fill old bottles with banknotes, bury them at suitable depths in disused coalmines which are then filled up to the surface with town rubbish, and leave it to private enterprise on well-tried principles of *laissez-faire* to dig the notes up again . . . there need be no more unemployment and, with the help of the repercussions, the real income of the community, and its capital wealth also, would probably become a good deal greater than it actually is.
General Theory (1936)

12 Practical men, who believe themselves to be quite exempt from any intellectual influences, are usually the slaves of some defunct economist. Madmen in authority, who hear voices in the air, are distilling their frenzy from some academic scribbler of a few years back.
General Theory (1947 ed.)

13 *In the long run* we are all dead.
A Tract on Monetary Reform (1923)

14 I evidently knew more about economics than my examiners.
explaining why he performed badly in the Civil Service examinations
Roy Harrod *Life of John Maynard Keynes* (1951)

1 LADY VIOLET BONHAM-CARTER: What do you think happens to Mr Lloyd George when he is alone in the room?
KEYNES: When he is alone in the room there is nobody there.
Lady Violet Bonham-Carter *Impact of Personality in Politics* (Romanes Lecture, 1963)

2 We threw good housekeeping to the winds. But we saved ourselves and helped save the world.
of Britain in the Second World War
A. J. P. Taylor *English History, 1914–1945* (1965)

Ruhollah Khomeini 1900–89

Iranian Shiite Muslim leader

3 If laws are needed, Islam has established them all. There is no need . . . after establishing a government, to sit down and draw up laws.
Islam and Revolution: Writings and Declarations of Imam Khomeini (1981) 'Islamic Government'

4 I would like to inform all the intrepid Muslims in the world that the author of the book entitled *The Satanic Verses*, which has been compiled, printed and published in opposition to Islam, the Prophet and the Qur'an, as well as those publishers who were aware of its contents, have been declared *madhur el dam* [those whose blood must be shed]. I call on all zealous Muslims to execute them quickly, wherever they find them, so that no-one will dare to insult Islam again. Whoever is killed in this path will be regarded as a martyr.
fatwa against Salman **Rushdie**, issued 14 February 1989; see **Wesker** 334:5

Nikita Khrushchev 1894–1971

Soviet statesman; Premier, 1958–64
on Khrushchev: see **Epstein** 108:9

5 If anyone believes that our smiles involve abandonment of the teaching of Marx, Engels and Lenin he deceives himself. Those who wait for that must wait until a shrimp learns to whistle.
speech in Moscow, 17 September 1955

6 Comrades! We must abolish the cult of the individual decisively, once and for all.
speech to secret session of 20th Congress of the Communist Party, 25 February 1956

7 If you don't like us, don't accept our invitations and don't invite us to come to see you. Whether you like it or not, history is on our side. We will bury you.
speech to Western diplomats in Moscow, 18 November 1956

8 If one cannot catch the bird of paradise, better take a wet hen.
in *Time* 6 January 1958

9 If you start throwing hedgehogs under me, I shall throw a couple of porcupines under you.
in *New York Times* 7 November 1963

Joyce Kilmer 1886–1918

American poet

10 I think that I shall never see
A poem lovely as a tree.
'Trees' (1914)

11 Poems are made by fools like me,
But only God can make a tree.
'Trees' (1914)

Lord Kilmuir (David Maxwell Fyfe) 1900–67

British Conservative politician and lawyer

12 Loyalty is the Tory's secret weapon.
Anthony Sampson *Anatomy of Britain* (1962)

Anthony King 1934–

British political scientist

13 It is an asteroid hitting the planet and destroying practically all life on earth.
of the scale of the Conservatives' electoral defeat
on 'Election Night' (BBC1) 2 May 1997

Martin Luther King 1929–68

American civil rights leader
see also: **Epitaphs** 109:5

1 I want to be the white man's brother, not his brother-in-law.
in *New York Journal-American* 10 September 1962

2 Judicial decrees may not change the heart; but they can restrain the heartless.
speech in Nashville, Tennessee, 27 December 1962

3 Injustice anywhere is a threat to justice everywhere.
letter from Birmingham Jail, Alabama, 16 April 1963

4 The Negro's great stumbling block in the stride toward freedom is not the White Citizens Councillor or the Ku Klux Klanner but the white moderate who is more devoted to order than to justice; who prefers a negative peace which is the absence of tension to a positive peace which is the presence of justice.
letter from Birmingham Jail, Alabama, 16 April 1963

5 If a man hasn't discovered something he will die for, he isn't fit to live.
speech in Detroit, 23 June 1963

6 I have a dream that one day on the red hills of Georgia the sons of former slaves and the sons of former slave owners will be able to sit down together at the table of brotherhood.
speech at Civil Rights March in Washington, 28 August 1963

7 I have a dream that my four little children will one day live in a nation where they will not be judged by the colour of their skin but by the content of their character.
speech at Civil Rights March in Washington, 28 August 1963

8 We must learn to live together as brothers or perish together as fools.
speech at St Louis, 22 March 1964

9 I just want to do God's will. And he's allowed me to go up to the mountain. And I've looked over, and I've seen the promised land . . . So I'm happy tonight. I'm not worried about anything. I'm not fearing any man.
on the day before his assassination
speech in Memphis, 3 April 1968

10 Nothing in all the world is more dangerous than sincere ignorance and conscientious stupidity.
Strength to Love (1963)

11 The means by which we live have outdistanced the ends for which we live. Our scientific power has outrun our spiritual power. We have guided missiles and misguided men.
Strength to Love (1963)

12 A riot is at bottom the language of the unheard.
Where Do We Go From Here? (1967)

Oona King 1967–

British Labour politician

13 To say that change at Westminster happens at a snail's pace is to insult the pace of snails.
in *The Times* 25 November 2000

Stephen King 1947–

American writer

14 Terror . . . often arises from a pervasive sense of disestablishment; that things are in the unmaking.
Danse Macabre (1981)

William Lyon Mackenzie King 1874–1950

Canadian Liberal statesman, Prime Minister 1921–6, 1926–30, and 1935–48

15 If some countries have too much history, we have too much geography.
speech, Canadian House of Commons, 18 June 1936

16 Not necessarily conscription, but conscription if necessary.
speech, Canadian House of Commons, 7 July 1942

Hugh Kingsmill 1889–1949

English man of letters

1 What still alive at twenty-two,
A clean upstanding chap like you?
Sure, if your throat 'tis hard to slit,
Slit your girl's, and swing for it.

'Two Poems, after A. E. Housman' (1933) no. 1

2 But bacon's not the only thing
That's cured by hanging from a string.

'Two Poems, after A. E. Housman' (1933) no. 1

Miles Kington 1941–

English humorist

3 There are those who think that Britain is a class-ridden society, and those who think it doesn't matter either way as long as you know your place in the set-up.

Welcome to Kington (1989)

Neil Kinnock 1942–

British Labour politician

to a heckler who said that Mrs ***Thatcher*** *'showed guts' during the Falklands War*

4 It's a pity others had to leave theirs on the ground at Goose Green to prove it.

television interview, 6 June 1983

5 If Margaret Thatcher wins on Thursday, I warn you not to be ordinary, I warn you not to be young, I warn you not to fall ill, and I warn you not to grow old.

on the prospect of a Conservative re-election

speech at Bridgend, 7 June 1983

6 The grotesque chaos of a Labour council hiring taxis to scuttle round the city handing out redundancy notices to its own workers.

of the actions of the city council in Liverpool

speech at the Labour Party Conference, 1 October 1985

7 I would die for my country but I could never let my country die for me.

speech at Labour Party Conference, 30 September 1986

8 Why am I the first Kinnock in a thousand generations to be able to get to a university?

later plagiarized by the American politician Joe Biden

speech in party political broadcast, 21 May 1987

9 There are lots of ways to get socialism, but I think trying to fracture the Labour party by incessant contest cannot be one of them.

in *Guardian* 29 January 1988

Alfred Kinsey 1894–1956

American zoologist and sex researcher

10 The only unnatural sex act is that which you cannot perform.

in *Time* 21 January 1966

Rudyard Kipling 1865–1936

English writer and poet

see also **Epitaphs** 110:2

11 Foot—foot—foot—foot—sloggin' over
Africa—
(Boots—boots—boots—boots—movin'
up and down again!)

'Boots' (1903)

12 If any question why we died,
Tell them, because our fathers lied.

'Epitaphs of the War: Common Form' (1919)

13 I could not dig: I dared not rob:
Therefore I lied to please the mob.
Now all my lies are proved untrue
And I must face the men I slew.
What tale shall serve me here among
Mine angry and defrauded young?

'Epitaphs of the War: A Dead Statesman' (1919)

14 My son was killed while laughing at
some jest. I would I knew
What it was, and it might serve me in a
time when jests are few.

'Epitaphs of the War: A Son' (1919)

15 The female of the species is more deadly
than the male.

'The Female of the Species' (1919)

1 For all we have and are,
For all our children's fate,
Stand up and take the war.
The Hun is at the gate!
For All We Have and Are (1914)

2 The Garden called Gethsemane
In Picardy it was.
'Gethsemane' (1918)

3 And all the time we halted there
I prayed my cup might pass.

It didn't pass—it didn't pass—
It didn't pass from me.
I drank it when we met the gas
Beyond Gethsemane!
'Gethsemane' (1918); see below

If it be possible, let this cup pass from me.
Bible St Matthew

4 Our England is a garden, and such gardens are not made
By singing:—'Oh, how beautiful!' and sitting in the shade,
While better men than we go out and start their working lives
At grubbing weeds from gravel paths with broken dinner-knives.
'The Glory of the Garden' (1911)

5 If you can keep your head when all about you
Are losing theirs and blaming it on you.
'If—' (1910)

6 If you can meet with Triumph and Disaster
And treat those two impostors just the same.
'If—' (1910)

7 If you can talk with crowds and keep your virtue,
Or walk with Kings—nor lose the common touch . . .
If you can fill the unforgiving minute
With sixty seconds' worth of distance run,
Yours is the Earth and everything that's in it,
And—which is more—you'll be a Man, my son!
'If—' (1910)

8 Then ye returned to your trinkets; then ye contented your souls
With the flannelled fools at the wicket or the muddied oafs at the goals.
'The Islanders' (1903)

9 They shall not return to us, the resolute, the young,
The eager and whole-hearted whom we gave:
But the men who left them thriftily to die in their own dung,
Shall they come with years and honour to the grave?
'Mesopotamia' (1917)

10 Dawn off the Foreland—the young flood making
Jumbled and short and steep—
Black in the hollows and bright where it's breaking—
Awkward water to sweep.
'Mines reported in the fairway,
'Warn all traffic and detain.
' 'Sent up *Unity*, *Claribel*, *Assyrian*, *Stormcock*, and *Golden Gain*.'
'Mine Sweepers' (1915)

11 'Have you news of my boy Jack?'
Not this tide.
'When d'you think that he'll come back?
Not with this wind blowing, and this tide.
'My Boy Jack' (1916)

12 Brothers and Sisters, I bid you beware
Of giving your heart to a dog to tear.
'The Power of the Dog' (1909)

13 Five and twenty ponies,
Trotting through the dark—
Brandy for the Parson,
'Baccy for the Clerk;
Laces for a lady, letters for a spy,
Watch the wall, my darling, while the Gentlemen go by!
'A Smuggler's Song' (1906)

14 Of all the trees that grow so fair,
Old England to adorn,
Greater are none beneath the Sun,
Than Oak, and Ash, and Thorn.
'A Tree Song' (1906)

15 What answer from the North?
One Law, one Land, one Throne.
'Ulster' (1912)

16 They shut the road through the woods
Seventy years ago.
Weather and rain have undone it again,
And now you would never know

There was once a road through the woods.
'The Way through the Woods' (1910)

1 And that is called paying the Dane-geld;
But we've proved it again and again,
That if once you have paid him the Dane-geld
You never get rid of the Dane.
'What Dane-geld means' (1911)

2 Human nature seldom walks up to the word 'cancer'.
Debits and Credits (1926) 'The Wish House'

3 But the wildest of all the wild animals was the Cat. He walked by himself, and all places were alike to him.
Just So Stories (1902) 'The Cat that Walked by Himself'

4 An Elephant's Child—who was full of 'satiable curtiosity.
Just So Stories (1902) 'The Elephant's Child'

5 Go to the banks of the great grey-green, greasy Limpopo River, all set about with fever-trees, and find out.
Just So Stories (1902) 'The Elephant's Child'

6 Little Friend of all the World.
Kim's nickname
Kim (1901)

7 'Tisn't beauty, so to speak, nor good talk necessarily. It's just It. Some women'll stay in a man's memory if they once walked down a street.
Traffics and Discoveries (1904) 'Mrs Bathurst'

8 Words are, of course, the most powerful drug used by mankind.
speech, 14 February 1923

9 Power without responsibility: the prerogative of the harlot throughout the ages.
summing up Lord ***Beaverbrook****'s political standpoint* vis-à-vis *the* Daily Express, *and quoted by Stanley* ***Baldwin****, 18 March 1931*
in *Kipling Journal* December 1971

Henry Kissinger 1923–

American Republican politician and diplomat

10 The management of a balance of power is a permanent undertaking, not an exertion that has a foreseeable end.
White House Years (1979)

11 The conventional army loses if it does not win. The guerrilla wins if he does not lose.
in *Foreign Affairs* January 1969

12 There cannot be a crisis next week. My schedule is already full.
in *New York Times Magazine* 1 June 1969

13 Power is the great aphrodisiac.
in *New York Times* 19 January 1971

14 We are the President's men.
M. and B. Kalb *Kissinger* (1974)

15 For other nations, Utopia is a blessed past never to be recovered; for Americans it is just beyond the horizon.
attributed

Lord Kitchener 1850–1916

British soldier and politician
on Kitchener: see **Asquith** 15:6

16 Do your duty bravely. Fear God. Honour the King.
message to soldiers of the British Expeditionary Force (1914)
in *The Times* 19 August 1914

17 I don't mind your being killed, but I object to your being taken prisoner.
to the Prince of Wales during the First World War
Journals and Letters of Viscount Esher (1938) vol. 3, 18 December 1914

Paul Klee 1879–1940

Swiss painter

18 Art does not reproduce the visible; rather, it makes visible.
Inward Vision (1958) 'Creative Credo' (1920)

19 An active line on a walk, moving freely without a goal. A walk for walk's sake. The agent is a point which moves around.
Pedagogical Sketchbook (1925)

20 Colour has taken hold of me; no longer do I have to chase after it. I know that it has hold of me for ever. That is the significance of this blessed moment.
on a visit to Tunis in 1914
Herbert Read *A Concise History of Modern Painting* (1968)

Bill Knapp

American Democratic media consultant

1 This is when compassion runs head-on into conservatism.
on Missouri Senator John Ashcroft's nomination to be US attorney general
in *Newsweek* 8 January 2001

Charles Knight and Kenneth Lyle

British songwriters

2 When there's trouble brewing,
When there's something doing,
Are we downhearted?
No! Let 'em all come!
'Here we are! Here we are again!!' (1914 song)

Frank H. Knight 1885–1973

American economist

3 Costs merely register competing attractions.
Risk, Uncertainty and Profit (1921)

Ronald Knox 1888–1957

English writer and Roman Catholic priest

4 When suave politeness, tempering bigot zeal,
Corrected *I believe* to *One does feel.*
'Absolute and Abitofhell' (1913)

5 There once was a man who said, 'God
Must think it exceedingly odd
If he finds that this tree
Continues to be
When there's no one about in the Quad.'
L. Reed *Complete Limerick Book* (1924), to which came the anonymous reply:

Dear Sir,
Your astonishment's odd:
I am always about in the Quad.
And that's why the tree
Will continue to be,
Since observed by
Yours faithfully,
God.

6 It is stupid of modern civilization to have given up believing in the devil, when he is the only explanation of it.
Let Dons Delight (1939)

7 The baby doesn't understand English and the Devil knows Latin.
on being asked to perform a baptism in English
Evelyn Waugh *Ronald Knox* (1959)

8 A loud noise at one end and no sense of responsibility at the other.
definition of a baby
attributed

Ted Koehler

American songwriter

9 Stormy weather,
Since my man and I ain't together.
'Stormy Weather' (1933 song)

Arthur Koestler 1905–83

Hungarian-born writer

10 One may not regard the world as a sort of metaphysical brothel for emotions.
Darkness at Noon (1940) 'The Second Hearing'

11 Behaviourism is indeed a kind of flat-earth view of the mind . . . it has substituted for the erstwhile anthropomorphic view of the rat, a ratomorphic view of man.
The Ghost in the Machine (1967)

12 God seems to have left the receiver off the hook, and time is running out.
The Ghost in the Machine (1967)

13 The most persistent sound which reverberates through man's history is the beating of war drums.
Janus (1978)

14 Man can leave the earth and land on the moon, but cannot cross from East to West Berlin. Prometheus reaches for the stars with an insane grin on his face and a totem-symbol in his hand.
Janus (1978)

Helmut Kohl 1930–

German statesman, Chancellor of West Germany (1982–90) and of Germany (1990–98)

1 We Germans now have the historic chance to realize the unity of our fatherland.

on the reunification of Germany

in *Guardian* 15 February 1990

2 The policy of European integration is in reality a question of war and peace in the 21st century.

speech at Louvain University, 2 February 1996

Vojislav Kostunica 1944–

Yugoslav statesman, President from 2000

3 Yugoslavia is running the victory lap and along that track there is no Milosevic.

in *Newsweek* 31 October 2000

Karl Kraus 1874–1936

Austrian satirist

4 How is the world ruled and how do wars start? Diplomats tell lies to journalists and then believe what they read.

Aphorisms and More Aphorisms (1909)

Jiddu Krishnamurti *d.* 1986

Indian spiritual philosopher

5 Religion is the frozen thought of men out of which they build temples.

in *Observer* 22 April 1928

6 Truth is a pathless land, and you cannot approach it by any path whatsoever, by any religion, by any sect.

speech in Holland, 3 August 1929

7 Happiness is a state of which you are unconscious, of which you are not aware. The moment you are aware that you are happy, you cease to be happy . . . You want to be consciously happy; the moment you are consciously happy, happiness is gone.

Penguin Krishnamurti Reader (1970) 'Questions and Answers'

Kris Kristofferson 1936–

American actor

8 Freedom's just another word for nothin' left to lose,
Nothin' ain't worth nothin', but it's free.

'Me and Bobby McGee' (1969 song, with Fred Foster)

Joseph Wood Krutch 1893–1970

American critic and naturalist

9 The most serious charge which can be brought against New England is not Puritanism but February.

The Twelve Seasons (1949)

10 Cats seem to go on the principle that it never does any harm to ask for what you want.

Twelve Seasons (1949)

Stanley Kubrick 1928–99

American film director

11 The great nations have always acted like gangsters, and the small nations like prostitutes.

in *Guardian* 5 June 1963

Satish Kumar 1937–

Indian writer

12 Lead me from death to life, from falsehood to truth.
Lead me from despair to hope, from fear to trust.
Lead me from hate to love, from war to peace.
Let peace fill our heart, our world, our universe.

'Prayer for Peace' (1981); adapted from the Upanishads

Milan Kundera 1929–

Czech novelist

13 *I think, therefore I am* is the statement of an intellectual who underrates toothaches.

Immortality (1991)

1 The unbearable lightness of being.
title of novel (1984)

2 Mankind's true moral test, its fundamental test (which lies deeply buried from view) consists of its attitudes towards those who are at its mercy: animals.
The Unbearable Lightness of Being (1984)

3 A man able to think isn't defeated—even when he is defeated.
in *Sunday Times* 20 May 1984

Christian Lacroix 1951–

French couturier

4 Haute Couture should be fun, foolish and almost unwearable.
in *Observer* 27 December 1987

Fiorello La Guardia 1882–1947

American politician

5 When I make a mistake, it's a beaut!
on the appointment of Herbert O'Brien as a judge in 1936
William Manners *Patience and Fortitude* (1976)

John Lahr 1941–

American critic

6 Society drives people crazy with lust and calls it advertising.
in *Guardian* 2 August 1989

7 Momentum was part of the exhilaration and the exhaustion of the twentieth century which Coward decoded for the British but borrowed wholesale from the Americans.
in *New Yorker* 9 September 1996

8 I know in an existential sense that life can change on a dime . . . something has instantly and inexorably changed in American life.
in the aftermath of the terrorist attacks which destroyed the World Trade Center in New York, and damaged the Pentagon
'Forever Changed', online correspondence with August Wilson in *Slate*, posted 11 September 2001

R. D. Laing 1927–89

Scottish psychiatrist

9 The divided self.
title of book on schizophrenia, 1960

10 The brotherhood of man is evoked by particular men according to their circumstances. But it seldom extends to all men. In the name of our freedom and our brotherhood we are prepared to blow up the other half of mankind and to be blown up in turn.
The Politics of Experience (1967)

11 The experience and behaviour that gets labelled schizophrenic is a special strategy that a person invents in order to live in an unlivable situation.
Politics of Experience (1967)

12 Madness need not be all breakdown. It may also be break-through.
The Politics of Experience (1967)

Constant Lambert 1905–51

English composer

13 The whole trouble with a folk song is that once you have played it through there is nothing much you can do except play it over again and play it rather louder.
Music Ho! (1934)

Eleanor Lambert 1904–

American fashion consultant and publicist

14 Someone who is to be remembered for dressing well does not remove her clothes in public.
the compiler of the Best-Dressed List on Nicole Kidman
in *Observer* January 2001

George Lamming 1927–

Barbados-born novelist and poet

15 In the castle of my skin.
title of novel (1953)

Norman Lamont 1942–

British Conservative politician
see also **Misquotations** 226:8

1 Rising unemployment and the recession have been the price that we've had to pay to get inflation down. [Labour shouts] That is a price well worth paying.
speech in the House of Commons, 16 May 1991

2 We give the impression of being in office but not in power.
as a backbencher
speech in the House of Commons, 9 June 1993

Giuseppe di Lampedusa 1896–1957

Italian writer

3 If we want things to stay as they are, things will have to change.
The Leopard (1957)

4 Love. Of course, love. Flames for a year, ashes for thirty.
The Leopard (1957)

Osbert Lancaster 1908–86

English writer and cartoonist

5 For self-revelation, whether it be a Tudor villa on the by-pass or a bomb-proof chalet at Berchtesgaden, there's no place like home.
Homes Sweet Homes (1939)

Julia Lang

see **Catch-phrases** 58:5

Susanne Langer 1895–1985

American philosopher

6 Art is the objectification of feeling, and the subjectification of nature.
Mind (1967) vol. 1

Ring Lardner Jr. 1915–2000

American writer

of the question, 'Are you now, or have you ever been . . . ':

7 HUAC CHAIRMAN: It is a very simple question. Any real American would be proud to answer it.
RING LARDNER JR.: I could answer the question exactly the way you want, but if I did, I would hate myself in the morning.
testimony before the House Un-American Activities Committee, 30 October 1947 (see **Political sayings and slogans** 261:3)

Philip Larkin 1922–85

English poet

8 Sexual intercourse began
In nineteen sixty-three
(Which was rather late for me)—
Between the end of the *Chatterley* ban
And the Beatles' first LP.
'Annus Mirabilis' (1974)

9 Time has transfigured them into
Untruth. The stone fidelity
They hardly meant has come to be
Their final blazon, and to prove
Our almost-instinct almost true:
What will survive of us is love.
'An Arundel Tomb' (1964)

10 Life is first boredom, then fear.
Whether or not we use it, it goes,
And leaves what something hidden from us chose,
And age, and then the only end of age.
'Dockery & Son' (1964)

11 And that will be England gone,
The shadows, the meadows, the lanes,
The guildhalls, the carved choirs.
There'll be books; it will linger on
In galleries; but all that remains
For us will be concrete and tyres.
'Going, Going' (1974)

12 Nothing, like something, happens anywhere.
'I Remember, I Remember' (1955)

13 Perhaps being old is having lighted rooms
Inside your head, and people in them, acting.

People you know, yet can't quite name.
'The Old Fools' (1974)

1 They fuck you up, your mum and dad.
They may not mean to, but they do.
They fill you with the faults they had
And add some extra, just for you.
'This Be The Verse' (1974)

2 Man hands on misery to man.
It deepens like a coastal shelf.
Get out as early as you can,
And don't have any kids yourself.
'This Be The Verse' (1974)

3 Why should I let the toad *work*
Squat on my life?
Can't I use my wit as a pitchfork
And drive the brute off?
'Toads' (1955)

4 Give me your arm, old toad;
Help me down Cemetery Road.
'Toads Revisited' (1964)

5 I thought of London spread out in the sun,
Its postal districts packed like squares of wheat.
'The Whitsun Weddings' (1964)

6 I listen to money singing. It's like looking down
From long french windows at a provincial town,
The slums, the canal, the churches ornate and mad
In the evening sun. It is intensely sad.
'Money' (1974)

7 Deprivation is for me what daffodils were for Wordsworth.
Required Writing (1983)

8 The notion of expressing sentiments in short lines having similar sounds at their ends seems as remote as mangoes on the moon.
letter to Barbara Pym, 22 January 1975

Harold Laski 1893–1950

British Labour politician and writer
on Laski: see **Attlee** 16:2

9 I respect fidelity to colleagues even though they are fit for the hangman.
letter to Oliver Wendell **Holmes** Jr., 4 December 1926

10 It was like watching someone organize her own immortality. Every phrase and gesture was studied. Now and again, when she said something a little out of the ordinary, she wrote it down herself in a notebook.
of Virginia ***Woolf***
letter to Oliver Wendell **Holmes** Jr., 30 November 1930

■ Last words

see box overleaf

Harry Lauder 1870–1950

Scottish music-hall entertainer

11 Keep right on to the end of the road,
Keep right on to the end.
Tho' the way be long, let your heart be strong,
Keep right on round the bend.
'The End of the Road' (1924 song)

12 I love a lassie, a bonnie, bonnie lassie,
She's as pure as the lily in the dell.
She's as sweet as the heather, the bonnie bloomin' heather—
Mary, ma Scotch Bluebell.
'I Love a Lassie' (1905 song)

13 Roamin' in the gloamin'.
title of song (1911)

Stan Laurel 1890–1965

British-born American film comedian

14 Another nice mess you've gotten me into.
often 'another fine mess'
Another Fine Mess (1930 film) and many other Laurel and Hardy films; spoken by Oliver Hardy

15 Why don't you do something to *help* me?
Drivers' Licence Sketch (1947); spoken by Oliver Hardy

Last words

1 Bugger Bognor.

*King **George V** (1865–1936) on his deathbed in 1936, when someone remarked 'Cheer up, your Majesty, you will soon be at Bognor again'; alternatively, a comment made in 1929, when it was proposed that the town be named Bognor Regis on account of the king's convalescence there after a serious illness*

K. Rose *King George V* (1983); see **Last words** 190:5

2 Come closer, boys. It will be easier for you.

*Erskine **Childers** (1870–1922) to the firing squad at his execution*

Burke Wilkinson *The Zeal of the Convert* (1976)

3 Farewell, my friends. I go to glory.

last words of Isadora Duncan (1878–1927) before her scarf caught in a car wheel, breaking her neck

Mary Desti *Isadora Duncan's End* (1929)

4 For God's sake look after our people.

*Robert Falcon **Scott** (1868–1912)*

last diary entry, 29 March 1912

5 How's the Empire?

*said by King **George** V (1865–1936) to his private secretary on the morning of his death*

K. Rose *King George V* (1983); see **Last words** 190:1

6 I am just going outside and may be some time.

last words of Captain Lawrence Oates (1880–1912)

Robert Falcon **Scott** diary entry, 16–17 March 1912; see **Epitaphs** 109:9

7 If this is dying, then I don't think much of it.

*Lytton **Strachey** (1880–1932) on his deathbed*

M. Holroyd *Lytton Strachey* (1968) vol. 2

8 I'm stuck in this building . . . I just wanted you to know that I love you. Bye bye.

final recorded message for her husband from Melissa Hughes in the World Trade Center, 11 September 2001; 'I love you' was the final telephone message from many of those trapped in the buildings and planes involved in the day's terrorist attacks

in *Guardian* 14 September 2001; see also **Last words** 191:6, **McEwan** 208:14

9 I'm tired, and I have to go to sleep.

*Allen **Ginsberg** (1912–97), before lapsing into a final coma*

in *Athens News* 9 April 1997

10 In this life there's nothing new in dying,
But nor, of course, is living any newer.

*the final poem of Sergei **Yesenin** (1895–1925), written in his own blood the day before he hanged himself in his Leningrad hotel room*

'Goodbye, my Friend, Goodbye' (1925)

11 It is dark for writing but I will try to by touch. It looks as though there is no chance.

final written message from Dmitry Kolesnikov, one of those lost in the Russian nuclear submarine Kursk

in *Daily Telegraph* 3 November 2000

12 I've got the bows up . . . I'm going . . . I'm on my back . . . I've gone. Oh.

last recorded words of Donald Campbell (1921-67), killed while trying to break his own water speed record; the wreckage of his boat Bluebird, with Campbell's body, was found and raised in March 2001

in *Times* 9 March 2001

13 Let's do it!

Gary Gilmore (1941–77) to the firing squad at his execution; after his conviction for murder, Gilmore had refused to appeal, and petitioned the Supreme Court that the execution should be carried out

Norman Mailer *The Executioner's Song* (1979)

14 Lord take my soul, but the struggle continues.

Ken Saro-Wiwa (1941–95), just before he was hanged

in *Daily Telegraph* 13 November 1995

15 The love boat has crashed against the everyday. You and I, we are quits, and

▶

▸ Last words continued

there is no point in listing mutual pains, sorrows, and hurts.
from an unfinished poem found among Vladimir ***Mayakovsky****'s papers, a variant of which he quoted in his suicide letter*
letter, 12 April 1930

1 Love? What is it? Most natural painkiller. What there is . . . LOVE.
final entry in the journal of William S. ***Burroughs****, 1 August 1997, the day before he died*
in *New Yorker* 18 August 1997

2 Now I'll have eine kleine Pause.
last words of Kathleen Ferrier (1912–53)
Gerald Moore *Am I Too Loud?* (1962)

3 Tell them I've had a wonderful life.
Ludwig ***Wittgenstein*** *(1889–1951) to his doctor's wife, before losing consciousness, 28 April 1951*
Ray Monk *Ludwig Wittgenstein* (1990)

4 That is indeed very good. I shall have to repeat that on the Golden Floor!
said by A. E. ***Housman*** *(1859–1936) to his physician who had told him a risqué story*
attributed

5 We are putting passengers off in small boats . . . Engine room getting flooded . . . CQ.
CQD was the original SOS call for shipping
last signals sent from the *Titanic*, 15 April 1912

6 What do I tell the pilot to do?
American lawyer Barbara Olson (1955–2001), in a final telephone conversation to her husband, the US Solicitor-General, from the hijacked plane which crashed into the Pentagon, 11 September 2001
in *Daily Telegraph* 14 September 2001, obituary; see also **Last words** 190:8

7 'What *is* the answer?' No answer came. She laughed and said, 'In that case what is the question?'
Gertrude ***Stein*** *(1874–1946)*
Donald Sutherland *Gertrude Stein, A Biography of her Work* (1951)

8 Why fear death? It is the most beautiful adventure in life.
the American theatrical manager Charles Frohman (1860–1915) before drowning in the Lusitania*, 7 May 1915*
I. F. Marcosson and D. Frohman *Charles Frohman* (1916); see **Barrie** 24:2

9 Why not? Why not? Why not? Yeah.
Timothy ***Leary*** *(1920–96)*
in *Independent* 1 June 1996

10 Yes, I believe in God.
reply to gunman
attributed to the American schoolgirl Cassie Bernall (1981–99), Columbine High School, Littleton, Colorado, 20 April 1999; the words have also been attributed to a survivor

William L. Laurence
1888–1977

American journalist

11 At first it was a giant column that soon took the shape of a supramundane mushroom.
on the first atomic explosion in New Mexico, 16 July 1945
in *New York Times* 26 September 1945

D. H. Lawrence 1885–1930

English novelist and poet
on Lawrence: see **Griffith-Jones** 141:2, **Robinson** 275:12

12 To the Puritan all things are impure, as somebody says.
Etruscan Places (1932) 'Cerveteri'; see below
Unto the pure all things are pure.
Bible Titus

13 It was in 1915 the old world ended.
Kangaroo (1923)

14 John Thomas says good-night to Lady Jane, a little droopingly, but with a hopeful heart.
Lady Chatterley's Lover (1928)

1 Pornography is the attempt to insult sex, to do dirt on it.
Phoenix (1936) 'Pornography and Obscenity'

2 The novel is the one bright book of life.
Phoenix (1936) 'Why the novel matters'

3 The bridge to the future is the phallus.
Sex, Literature and Censorship (1955)

4 Never trust the artist. Trust the tale. The proper function of a critic is to save the tale from the artist who created it.
Studies in Classic American Literature (1923)

5 Be a good animal, true to your instincts.
The White Peacock (1911)

6 Don't you find it a beautiful clean thought, a world empty of people, just uninterrupted grass, and a hare sitting up?
Women in Love (1920)

7 How beastly the bourgeois is
Especially the male of the species.
'How Beastly the Bourgeois Is' (1929)

8 While we have sex in the mind, we truly have none in the body.
'Leave Sex Alone' (1929)

9 Men! The only animal in the world to fear!
'Mountain Lion' (1923)

10 I never saw a wild thing
Sorry for itself.
'Self-Pity' (1929)

11 A snake came to my water-trough
On a hot, hot day, and I in pyjamas for the heat,
To drink there.
'Snake' (1923)

12 And so, I missed my chance with one of the lords
Of life.
And I have something to expiate:
A pettiness.
'Snake' (1923)

13 Not I, not I, but the wind that blows through me!
'Song of a Man who has Come Through' (1917)

14 When I read Shakespeare I am struck with wonder
That such trivial people should muse and thunder
In such lovely language.
'When I Read Shakespeare' (1929)

15 Curse the blasted, jelly-boned swines, the slimy, the belly-wriggling invertebrates, the miserable sodding rotters, the flaming sods, the snivelling, dribbling, dithering, palsied, pulse-less lot that make up England today. They've got white of egg in their veins, and their spunk is that watery it's a marvel they can breed. They *can* nothing but frog-spawn—the gibberers! God, how I hate them!
letter to Edward Garnett, 3 July 1912

16 Tragedy ought really to be a great kick at misery.
letter to A. W. McLeod, 6 October 1912

17 The dead don't die. They look on and help.
letter to J. Middleton Murry, 2 February 1923

18 I want to go south, where there is no autumn, where the cold doesn't crouch over one like a snow-leopard waiting to pounce. The heart of the North is dead, and the fingers of cold are corpse fingers.
letter to J. Middleton Murry, 3 October 1924

19 My God, what a clumsy *olla putrida* James Joyce is! Nothing but old fags and cabbage-stumps of quotations from the Bible and the rest, stewed in the juice of deliberate, journalistic dirty-mindedness.
letter to Aldous and Maria Huxley, 15 August 1928

T. E. Lawrence 1888–1935

English soldier and writer
on Lawrence: see **Berners** 31:17

20 Many men would take the death-sentence without a whimper to escape the life-sentence which fate carries in her other hand.
The Mint (1955)

21 I loved you, so I drew these tides of men into my hands and wrote my will across the sky in stars.
To earn you freedom, the seven pillared worthy house, that your eyes might be shining for me
When we came.
Seven Pillars of Wisdom (1926) dedication

1 The trouble with Communism is that it accepts too much of today's furniture. I hate furniture.

letter to Cecil Day Lewis, 20 December 1934

2 Surely the sex business isn't worth all this damned fuss? I've met only a handful of people who cared a biscuit for it.

on reading Lady Chatterley's Lover

Christopher Hassall *Edward Marsh* (1959)

Nigel Lawson 1932–

British Conservative politician, Chancellor 1983–9

3 It represented the tip of a singularly ill-concealed iceberg, with all the destructive potential that icebergs possess.

of an article by Alan Walters, Margaret ***Thatcher****'s economic adviser, criticizing the Exchange Rate Mechanism*

in the House of Commons following his resignation as Chancellor, 31 October 1989

Irving Layton 1912–

Canadian poet

4 An aphorism
should be
like a burr:
sting,
stick,
and leave
a little soreness
afterwards.

The Whole Bloody Bird (1969) 'Aphs'

5 We love in another's soul
whatever of ourselves
we can deposit in it;
the greater the deposit,
the greater the love.

The Whole Bloody Bird (1969) 'Aphs'

6 I would like to live forever, but I'll settle for another seventy years.

on his seventieth birthday

in *The Globe and Mail* 13 March 1982

Edmund Leach 1910–89

English anthropologist

7 Far from being the basis of the good society, the family, with its narrow privacy and tawdry secrets, is the source of all our discontents.

BBC Reith Lectures, 1967, in *Listener* 30 November 1967

Stephen Leacock 1869–1944

British-born Canadian humorist

8 When Rutherford was done with the atom all the solidity was pretty well knocked out of it.

The Boy I Left Behind Me (1947)

9 The parent who could see his boy as he really is, would shake his head and say: 'Willie, is no good; I'll sell him.'

Essays and Literary Studies (1916) 'Lot of a Schoolmaster'

10 Advertising may be described as the science of arresting human intelligence long enough to get money from it.

Garden of Folly (1924) 'The Perfect Salesman'

11 A sportsman is a man who, every now and then, simply has to get out and kill something. Not that he's cruel. He wouldn't hurt a fly. It's not big enough.

My Remarkable Uncle (1942)

Timothy Leary 1920–96

American psychologist

on Leary: see **Epitaphs** 110:3*; see also* **Last words** 191:9

12 If you take the game of life seriously, if you take your nervous system seriously, if you take your sense organs seriously, if you take the energy process seriously, you must turn on, tune in and drop out.

The Politics of Ecstasy (1968)

13 The PC is the LSD of the '90s.

remark made in the early 1990s; in *Guardian* 1 June 1996

on abandoning his plan to have his head preserved by the cryonics movement:

14 They have no sense of humour. I was

worried I would wake up in 50 years surrounded by people with clipboards.
in *Daily Telegraph* 10 May 1996

F. R. Leavis 1895–1978

English literary critic

1 The common pursuit.
title of book (1952)

2 The great tradition.
title of book (1948)

3 It is well to start by distinguishing the few really great—the major novelists who count in the same way as the major poets, in the sense that they not only change the possibilities of the art for practitioners and readers, but that they are significant in terms of the human awareness they promote; awareness of the possibilities of life.
The Great Tradition (1948)

4 Self-contempt, well-grounded.
on the foundation of T. S. ***Eliot****'s work*
in *Times Literary Supplement* 21 October 1988

Fran Lebowitz 1946–

American humorist

5 Modern science was largely conceived of as an answer to the servant problem.
Metropolitan Life (1978)

6 If people don't want to listen to *you*, what makes you think they want to hear from your sweater?
of slogans on clothing
Metropolitan Life (1978)

7 The opposite of talking isn't listening. The opposite of talking is waiting.
Social Studies (1981)

8 Remember that as a teenager you are at the last stage in your life when you will be happy to hear that the phone is for you.
Social Studies (1981)

9 The best fame is a writer's fame: it's enough to get a table at a good restaurant, but not enough that you get interrupted when you eat.
in *Observer* 30 May 1993

Stanislaw Lec 1909–66

Polish writer

10 Is it progress if a cannibal uses knife and fork?
Unkempt Thoughts (1962)

11 One has to multiply thoughts to the point where there aren't enough policemen to control them.
Unkempt Thoughts (1962)

John le Carré 1931–

English thriller writer

12 The spy who came in from the cold.
title of novel (1963)

13 He gives his trust slowly and with the greatest care. And he is ready at any time to take it back.
of Alec ***Guinness***
in *Daily Telegraph* 7 August 2000

Le Corbusier 1887–1965

French architect

14 A house is a machine for living in.
Vers une architecture (1923)

15 This frightful word [function] was born under other skies than those I have loved—those where the sun reigns supreme.
Stephen Gardiner *Le Corbusier* (1974)

Gypsy Rose Lee 1914–70

American striptease artiste

16 God is love, but get it in writing.
attributed

Harper Lee 1926–

American novelist

17 Shoot all the bluejays you want, if you can hit 'em, but remember it's a sin to kill a mockingbird.
To Kill a Mockingbird (1960)

Laurie Lee 1914–97

English writer

1 I was set down from the carrier's cart at the age of three; and there with a sense of bewilderment and terror my life in the village began.

Cider with Rosie (1959)

2 Quiet incest flourished where roads were bad.

Guardian 15 May 1997; obituary

Ursula K. Le Guin 1929–

American writer

3 He had grown up in a country run by politicians who sent the pilots to man the bombers to kill the babies to make the world safer for children to grow up in.

The Lathe of Heaven (1971) ch. 6

4 Love doesn't just sit there, like a stone, it has to be made, like bread; remade all the time, made new.

The Lathe of Heaven (1971) ch. 10

5 We like to think we live in daylight, but half the world is always dark; and fantasy, like poetry, speaks the language of the night.

in *World Magazine* 21 November 1979

Tom Lehrer 1928–

American humorist

6 Plagiarize! Let no one else's work evade
your eyes,
Remember why the good Lord made your
eyes.

'Lobachevski' (1953 song)

7 Poisoning pigeons in the park.

song title, 1953

Vivien Leigh 1913–67

English actress

8 Shaw is like a train. One just speaks the words and sits in one's place. But Shakespeare is like bathing in the sea—one swims where one wants.

letter from Harold Nicolson to Vita Sackville-West, 1 February 1956

Curtis E. LeMay 1906–90

American air-force officer

9 We're going to bomb them back into the Stone Age.

on the North Vietnamese

Mission with LeMay (1965)

John Le Mesurier

see **Epitaphs** 109:15

Lenin 1870–1924

Russian revolutionary

10 Imperialism is the monopoly stage of capitalism.

Imperialism as the Last Stage of Capitalism (1916)

11 No, Democracy is *not* identical with majority rule. Democracy is a *State* which recognizes the subjection of the minority to the majority, that is, an organization for the systematic use of *force* by one class against the other, by one part of the population against another.

State and Revolution (1919)

12 While the State exists, there can be no freedom. When there is freedom there will be no State.

State and Revolution (1919)

13 What is to be done?

title of pamphlet (1902); originally the title of a novel (1863) by N. G. Chernyshevsky

14 A good man fallen among Fabians.

of George Bernard ***Shaw***

A. Ransome *Six Weeks in Russia in 1919* (1919) 'Notes of Conversations with Lenin'

15 Communism is Soviet power plus the electrification of the whole country.

report to 8th Congress, 1920

16 Who? Whom?

definition of political science, meaning 'Who will outstrip whom?'

in *Polnoe Sobranie Sochinenii* vol. 44 (1970) 17 October 1921 and elsewhere

17 Liberty is precious—so precious that it must be rationed.

Sidney and Beatrice Webb *Soviet Communism* (1936)

John Lennon 1940–80

English pop singer and songwriter
see also **Lennon and McCartney, Ono** 246:13

1 Happiness is a warm gun.
title of song (1968); see **Advertising slogans** 3:22, **Ephron** 108:6, **Schulz** 291:11

2 Will the people in the cheaper seats clap your hands? All the rest of you, if you'll just rattle your jewellery.
at the Royal Variety Performance, 4 November 1963

3 We're more popular than Jesus now; I don't know which will go first—rock 'n' roll or Christianity.
of The Beatles
interview in *Evening Standard* 4 March 1966

John Lennon 1940–80 and Paul McCartney 1942–

English pop singers and songwriters
see also **Lennon, Macartney**

4 All you need is love.
title of song (1967)

5 For I don't care too much for money,
For money can't buy me love.
'Can't Buy Me Love' (1964 song)

6 All the lonely people, where do they all come from?
'Eleanor Rigby' (1966 song)

7 Give peace a chance.
title of song (1969)

8 It's been a hard day's night,
And I've been working like a dog.
'A Hard Day's Night' (1964 song)

9 Strawberry fields forever.
title of song (1967)

10 She's got a ticket to ride, but she don't care.
'Ticket to Ride' (1965 song)

11 Will you still need me, will you still feed me,
When I'm sixty four?
'When I'm Sixty Four' (1967 song)

12 Oh I get by with a little help from my friends,
Mm, I get high with a little help from my friends.
'With a Little Help From My Friends' (1967 song)

13 Yesterday, all my troubles seemed so far away,
Now it looks as though they're here to stay.
Oh I believe in yesterday.
'Yesterday' (1965 song)

Jay Leno 1950–

American comedian

14 This Ken Starr report is now posted on the Internet. I'll bet Clinton's glad he put a computer in every classroom.
in *Sunday Times* 20 September 1998

Alan Jay Lerner 1918–86

American songwriter

15 Don't let it be forgot
That once there was a spot
For one brief shining moment that was known
As Camelot.
now particularly associated with the White House of John Fitzgerald **Kennedy** (*see* **Onassis** 246:2)
'Camelot' (1960 song)

16 I'm getting married in the morning,
Ding! dong! the bells are gonna chime.
Pull out the stopper;
Let's have a whopper;
But get me to the church on time!
'Get Me to the Church on Time' (1956 song)

17 Why can't a woman be more like a man?
Men are so honest, so thoroughly square;
Eternally noble, historically fair.
'A Hymn to Him' (1956)

18 We met at nine.
We met at eight.
I was on time.
No, you were late.
Ah yes! I remember it well.
'I Remember it Well' (1958 song)

19 I've grown accustomed to the trace
Of something in the air;
Accustomed to her face.
'I've Grown Accustomed to her Face' (1956 song)

1 On a clear day (you can see forever).
title of song (1965)

2 The rain in Spain stays mainly in the plain.
'The Rain in Spain' (1956)

3 Thank heaven for little girls!
For little girls get bigger every day.
'Thank Heaven for Little Girls' (1958 song)

4 All I want is a room somewhere,
Far away from the cold night air,
With one enormous chair;
Oh, wouldn't it be loverly?
'Wouldn't it be Loverly' (1956 song)

5 Oozing charm from every pore,
He oiled his way around the floor.
'You Did It' (1956)

Doris Lessing 1919–

English writer

6 There's only one real sin, and that is to persuade oneself that the second-best is anything but the second-best.
Golden Notebook (1962)

7 When old settlers say 'One has to understand the country,' what they mean is, 'You have to get used to our ideas about the native.'
The Grass is Singing (1950)

8 What of October, that ambiguous month, the month of tension, the unendurable month?
Martha Quest (1952)

9 What is charm then? . . . something extra, superfluous, unnecessary, essentially a power thrown away.
Particularly Cats (1967)

10 We do not know which of our silver products will be judged as gold by our successors, nor does it matter.
on the possibility that work by British novelists since the Second World War might prove to be a 'silver age'
in London, accepting the David Cohen prize for a lifetime of excellence in writing; in *Guardian* 21 March 2001

David Letterman 1947–

American broadcaster

11 If you didn't know how to behave, all you had to do at any moment was watch the mayor.
of Rudolph ***Giuliani****'s leadership after the terrorist destruction of the World Trade Center, 11 September 2001*
on *The Late Show* (CBS), 17 September 2001

Winifred Mary Letts 1882–1972

English writer

12 I saw the spires of Oxford
As I was passing by,
The grey spires of Oxford
Against a pearl-grey sky;
My heart was with the Oxford men
Who went abroad to die.
'The Spires of Oxford' (1916)

Oscar Levant 1906–72

American pianist

13 Underneath this flabby exterior is an enormous lack of character.
Memoirs of an Amnesiac (1965)

14 Epigram: a wisecrack that played Carnegie Hall.
in *Coronet* September 1958

Lord Leverhulme 1851–1925

English industrialist and philanthropist

15 Half the money I spend on advertising is wasted, and the trouble is I don't know which half.
David Ogilvy *Confessions of an Advertising Man* (1963)

Denise Levertov 1923–

English-born American poet

16 Images
split the truth
in fractions.
'A Sequence' (1961)

17 two by two in the ark of

the ache of it.
'The Ache of Marriage' (1964)

René Lévesque 1922–87

Canadian politician, founder of Parti Québecois

1 Outside Quebec, I don't find two great cultures. I feel like a foreigner. First and foremost, I am a Québecois, and second—with a rather growing sense of doubt—a Canadian.
in *Toronto Star* 1 June 1963

2 A nation is judged by how it treats its minorities.
attributed, 1978; John Robert Colombo *Colombo's New Canadian Quotations* (1987)

Primo Levi 1919–87

Italian novelist and poet

3 Our language lacks words to express this offence, the demolition of a man.
of a year spent in Auschwitz
If This is a Man (1958)

Bernard Levin 1928–

British journalist

4 Between them, then, Walrus and Carpenter, they divided up the Sixties.
of the Harolds, ***Macmillan*** *and* ***Wilson***
The Pendulum Years (1970)

5 I have heard tell of a Professor of Economics who has a sign on the wall of his study, reading 'the future is not what it was'. The sentiment was admirable; unfortunately, the past is not getting any better either.
in *Sunday Times* 22 May 1977; see **Berra** 32:5

6 Whom the mad would destroy, they first make gods.
of ***Mao*** *Zedong in 1967*
Levin quoting himself in *The Times* 21 September 1987; see below

Whom God would destroy He first sends mad.

James Duport (1606–79) *Homeri Gnomologia* (1660), ultimately representing the scholiastic annotation to Sophocles's *Antigone* 'Whenever God prepares evil for a man, He first damages his mind, with which he deliberates'

Claude Lévi-Strauss 1908–

French social anthropologist

7 Language is a form of human reason, and has its reasons which are unknown to man.
The Savage Mind (1962) ch. 9

8 The purpose of myth is to provide a logical model capable of overcoming a contradiction (an impossible achievement if, as it happens, the contradiction is real).
Structural Anthropology (1968) ch. 11

C. S. Lewis 1898–1963

English literary scholar

9 No one ever told me that grief felt so like fear.
A Grief Observed (1961)

10 She's the sort of woman who lives for others—you can always tell the others by their hunted expression.
The Screwtape Letters (1942)

11 A young man who wishes to remain a sound atheist cannot be too careful of his reading.
Surprised by Joy (1955)

12 For twenty years I've stared my level best
To see if evening—any evening—would
 suggest
A patient etherized upon a table;
In vain. I simply wasn't able.
on contemporary poetry
'A Confession' (1964); see **Eliot** 104:2

13 Often when I pray I wonder if I am not posting letters to a non-existent address.
letter to Arthur Greeves, 24 December 1930

14 Courage is not simply *one* of the virtues but the form of every virtue at the testing point.
Cyril Connolly *The Unquiet Grave* (1944); see **Barrie** 24:6

15 He that but looketh on a plate of ham and eggs to lust after it, hath already committed breakfast with it in his heart.
letter, 10 March 1954

Jerry Lee Lewis 1935–

American singer

1 Elvis was the greatest, but I'm the best.
in *The Face* May 1989

Sam M. Lewis 1885–1959 and **Joe Young** 1889–1939

American songwriters

2 How 'ya gonna keep 'em down on the farm (after they've seen Paree)?
title of song (1919)

Sinclair Lewis 1885–1951

American novelist

3 Our American professors like their literature clear and cold and pure and very dead.
The American Fear of Literature (Nobel Prize Address, 12 December 1930)

4 To George F. Babbitt, as to most prosperous citizens of Zenith, his motor car was poetry and tragedy, love and heroism. The office was his pirate ship but the car his perilous excursion ashore.
Babbitt (1922)

5 She did her work with the thoroughness of a mind which reveres details and never quite understands them.
Babbitt (1922)

Willmott Lewis 1877–1950

British journalist

6 I think it well to remember that, when writing for the newspapers, we are writing for an elderly lady in Hastings who has two cats of which she is passionately fond. Unless our stuff can successfully compete for her interest with those cats, it is no good.
Claud Cockburn *In Time of Trouble* (1957)

Wyndham Lewis 1882–1957

English novelist, painter, and critic

7 Gertrude Stein's prose-song is a cold, black suet-pudding . . . Cut it at any point, it is the same thing . . . all fat, without nerve.
of Three Lives (1909)
Time and Western Man (1927)

8 Angels in jumpers.
describing the figures in Stanley ***Spencer****'s paintings*
attributed

Liberace 1919–87

American showman

9 I cry all the way to the bank.
on bad reviews (from the mid-1950s)
Autobiography (1973)

Helen Liddell 1950–

British Labour politician, Secretary of State for Scotland

10 Good girls come in wee bulks.
describing her height (1.6 m) measured in the metric system
in *Independent on Sunday* 21 January 2001

Joseph Lieberman 1942

American Democratic politician

11 His wrongdoing in this sordid saga does not justify making him the first president to be ousted from office in our history.
voting to acquit President ***Clinton***
at the trial for impeachment, 11 February 1999

A. J. Liebling 1904–63

American writer

12 Freedom of the press is guaranteed only to those who own one.
'The Wayward Press: Do you belong in Journalism?' (1960)

Vachel Lindsay 1879–1931

American poet

13 Then I saw the Congo, creeping through
the black,
Cutting through the forest with a golden
track.
'The Congo' pt. 1 (1914)

1 Booth led boldly with his big bass drum—
(Are you washed in the blood of the Lamb?)
'General William Booth Enters into Heaven' (1913); see below

. . . Have washed their robes, and made them white in the blood of the Lamb.
Bible Revelation

2 Booth died blind and still by faith he trod,
Eyes still dazzled by the ways of God.
'General William Booth Enters into Heaven' (1913)

Gary Lineker 1960–

English footballer

3 The nice aspect about football is that, if things go wrong, it's the manager who gets the blame.
remark before his first match as captain of England
in *Independent* 12 September 1990

4 Coaching a football team is not rocket science and most of the advice is blindingly obvious.
in *Independent* 21 October 2000

Eric Linklater 1899–1974

Scottish novelist

5 'There won't be any revolution in America,' said Isadore. Nikitin agreed. 'The people are all too clean. They spend all their time changing their shirts and washing themselves. You can't feel fierce and revolutionary in a bathroom.'
Juan in America (1931)

Walter Lippmann 1889–1974

American journalist

6 The final test of a leader is that he leaves behind him in other men the conviction and the will to carry on.
in *New York Herald Tribune* 14 April 1945

Joan Littlewood 1914– and Charles Chilton 1914–

British theatre director; British writer

7 Oh what a lovely war.
title of stage show (1963)

Maxim Litvinov 1876–1951

Soviet diplomat

8 Peace is indivisible.
note to the Allies, 25 February 1920; A. U. Pope *Maxim Litvinoff* (1943)

Penelope Lively 1933–

English novelist

9 Language tethers us to the world; without it we spin like atoms.
Moon Tiger (1987)

10 We are walking lexicons. In a single sentence of idle chatter we preserve Latin, Anglo-Saxon, Norse; we carry a museum inside our heads, each day we commemorate peoples of whom we have never heard.
Moon Tiger (1987)

Ken Livingstone 1945–

British Labour politician, Mayor of London since 2000

11 If voting changed anything, they'd abolish it.
title of book, 1987; recorded earlier as a saying

12 I feel like Galileo going before the Inquisition to explain that the sun doesn't revolve around the earth. I hope I have more success.
at Millbank, prior to appearing before the Labour Party's selection panel for the Mayor of London
in *Guardian* 17 November 1999

13 Every year the international finance system kills more people than the Second World War. But at least Hitler was mad, you know.
in *Sunday Times* 16 April 2000

Richard Llewellyn 1907–83

Welsh novelist and dramatist

1 How green was my valley.

title of book (1939)

David Lloyd George 1863–1945

British Liberal statesman; Prime Minister, 1916–22

on Lloyd George: see **Anonymous** 11:12, **Clemenceau** 71:2, **Keynes** 179:10, 180:1

2 A mastiff? It is the Right Hon. Gentleman's poodle.

on the House of Lords and A. J. ***Balfour*** *respectively*

in the House of Commons, 26 June 1907

3 A fully-equipped duke costs as much to keep up as two Dreadnoughts; and dukes are just as great a terror and they last longer.

speech at Newcastle, 9 October 1909

4 The great peaks of honour we had forgotten—Duty, Patriotism, and—clad in glittering white—the great pinnacle of Sacrifice, pointing like a rugged finger to Heaven.

speech at Queen's Hall, London, 19 September 1914

5 At eleven o'clock this morning came to an end the cruellest and most terrible war that has ever scourged mankind. I hope we may say that thus, this fateful morning, came to an end all wars.

speech in the House of Commons, 11 November 1918

6 What is our task? To make Britain a fit country for heroes to live in.

speech at Wolverhampton, 23 November 1918

7 Unless I am mistaken, by the steps we have taken [in Ireland] we have murder by the throat.

speech at the Mansion House, 9 November 1920

on being asked what place Arthur ***Balfour*** *would have in history:*

8 He will be just like the scent on a pocket handkerchief.

Thomas Jones diary, 9 June 1922

9 Death is the most convenient time to tax rich people.

Lord Riddell diary, 23 April 1919

10 The world is becoming like a lunatic asylum run by lunatics.

in *Observer* 8 January 1933; see **Rowland** 280:9

11 A politician was a person with whose politics you did not agree. When you did agree, he was a statesman.

speech at Central Hall, Westminster, 2 July 1935

12 Negotiating with de Valera . . . is like trying to pick up mercury with a fork.

to which de Valera replied, 'Why doesn't he use a spoon?'

M. J. MacManus *Eamon de Valera* (1944)

13 Sufficient conscience to bother him, but not sufficient to keep him straight.

of Ramsay ***MacDonald***

A. J. Sylvester *Life with Lloyd George* (1975)

David Lodge 1935–

English novelist

14 Literature is mostly about having sex and not much about having children. Life is the other way round.

The British Museum is Falling Down (1965)

15 Four times, under our educational rules, the human pack is shuffled and cut—at eleven-plus, sixteen-plus, eighteen-plus and twenty-plus—and happy is he who comes top of the deck on each occasion, but especially the last. This is called Finals, the very name of which implies that nothing of importance can happen after it.

Changing Places (1975)

Frank Loesser 1910–69

American songwriter

16 See what the boys in the back room will
have

And tell them I'm having the same.
'Boys in the Back Room' (1939 song); see **Beaverbrook** 25:6

1 Isn't it grand! Isn't it fine! Look at the cut, the style, the line!
The suit of clothes is altogether, but altogether it's altogether
The most remarkable suit of clothes that I have ever seen.
'The King's New Clothes' (1952 song)

Frederick Loewe 1904–88

American composer

2 I don't like my music, but what is my opinion against that of millions of others.
Nat Shapiro (ed.) *An Encyclopedia of Quotations about Music* (1978)

Christopher Logue 1926–

English poet

3 Come to the edge.
We might fall.
Come to the edge.
It's too high!
COME TO THE EDGE!
And they came
and he pushed
and they flew . . .
on ***Apollinaire***
'Come to the edge' (1969)

4 I, Christopher Logue, was baptized the year
Many thousands of Englishmen,
Fists clenched, their bellies empty,
Walked day and night on the capital city.
'The Song of Autobiography' (1996)

Jack London 1876–1916

American novelist

5 The call of the wild.
title of novel (1903)

Huey Long 1893–1935

American Democratic politician

6 For the present you can just call me the Kingfish.
Every Man a King (1933)

7 Oh hell, say that I am *sui generis* and let it go at that.
to journalists attempting to analyse his political personality
T. Harry Williams *Huey Long* (1969)

Michael Longley 1939–

Irish poet

8 Astrologers or three wise men
Who may shortly be setting out
For a small house up the Shankill
Or the Falls, should pause on their way
To buy gifts at Jim Gibson's shop,
Dates and chestnuts and tambourines.
'The Greengrocer' (1979)

9 I am travelling from one April to another.
It is the same train between the same embankments.
Gorse fires are smoking, but primroses burn
And celandines and white may and gorse flowers.
'Gorse Fires' (1991)

Alice Roosevelt Longworth 1884–1980

daughter of Theodore **Roosevelt**
see also **Anonymous** 12:8

10 If you haven't got anything good to say about anyone come and sit by me.
maxim embroidered on a cushion in her home
Michael Teague *Mrs L: Conversations with Alice Roosevelt Longworth* (1981)

Anita Loos 1893–1981

American writer

11 Gentlemen prefer blondes.
title of book (1925)

12 So I really think that American gentlemen are the best after all, because kissing your hand may make you feel very very good but a diamond and safire bracelet lasts forever.
Gentlemen Prefer Blondes (1925); see **Advertising slogans** 3:12, **Robin** 275:6

13 Fun is fun but no girl wants to laugh all of the time.
Gentlemen Prefer Blondes (1925)

1 I'm furious about the women's liberationists. They keep getting up on soap boxes and proclaiming that women are brighter than men. That's true, but it should be kept very quiet or it ruins the whole racket.
attributed

Federico García Lorca 1899–1936

Spanish poet and dramatist

2 *A las cinco de la tarde.*
Eran las cinco en punto de la tarde.
Un niño trajo la blanca sábana
a las cinco de la tarde.

At five in the afternoon.
It was exactly five in the afternoon.
A boy brought the white sheet
at five in the afternoon.
Llanto por Ignacio Sánchez Mejías (1935) 'La Cogida y la muerte'

3 *Verde que te quiero verde.*
Verde viento. Verdes ramas.
El barco sobre la mar
y el caballo en la montaña.

Green how I love you green.
Green wind.
Green boughs.
The ship on the sea
and the horse on the mountain.
Romance sonámbulo (1924–7)

Edward N. Lorenz 1917–

American meteorologist

4 Predictability: Does the flap of a butterfly's wings in Brazil set off a tornado in Texas?
title of paper given to the American Association for the Advancement of Science, Washington, 29 December 1979; James Gleick *Chaos* (1988)

Konrad Lorenz 1903–89

Austrian zoologist

5 It is a good morning exercise for a research scientist to discard a pet hypothesis every day before breakfast.
On Aggression (1966)

Joe Louis 1914–81

American boxer

6 He can run. But he can't hide.
of Billy Conn, his opponent, before a heavyweight title fight, 19 June 1946
Louis: My Life Story (1947)

Courtney Love 1965–

American rock singer, wife of Kurt **Cobain**

7 When . . . you're first famous and you're flush with your influence and you say something whimsical, at a party or something to be cool, it gets reported for real.
interview in *Guardian* 28 February 1997

Bernard Lovell 1913–

British astronomer

8 The pursuit of the good and evil are now linked in astronomy as in almost all science . . . The fate of human civilization will depend on whether the rockets of the future carry the astronomer's telescope or a hydrogen bomb.
The Individual and the Universe (1959)

9 Youth is vivid rather than happy, but memory always remembers the happy things.
in *The Times* 20 August 1993

James Lovell 1928–

American astronaut

10 Houston, we've had a problem.
on Apollo 13 space mission, 14 April 1970
in *The Times* 15 April 1970

James Lovelock 1919–

English scientist, originator of the Gaia hypothesis

11 I always think it grossly unfair that people accept the selfish gene as a metaphor—and I think it's a lovely metaphor—but they won't accept Gaia or the living Earth.
of the response to his hypothesis that the living and non-living components of earth collectively

define and regulate the material conditions necessary for the continuance of life

in *New Scientist* 9 September 2000; see **Dawkins** 85:11

David Low 1891–1963

New Zealand-born political cartoonist

1 I have never met anyone who wasn't against war. Even Hitler and Mussolini were, according to themselves.

in *New York Times Magazine* 10 February 1946

Amy Lowell 1874–1925

American poet

2 All books are either dreams or swords,
You can cut, or you can drug, with words.

'Sword Blades and Poppy Seed' (1914); see **Kipling** 184:8

3 Do we want laurels for ourselves most,
Or most that no one else shall have any?

'La Ronde du Diable' (1925)

Robert Lowell 1917–77

American poet

4 Terrible that old life of decency
without unseemly intimacy
or quarrels, when the unemancipated woman
still had her Freudian papa and maids!

'During Fever' (1959)

5 The aquarium is gone. Everywhere,
giant finned cars nose forward like fish;
a savage servility
slides by on grease.

'For the Union Dead' (1964)

6 Their monument sticks like a fishbone
in the city's throat.

'For the Union Dead' (1964)

7 These are the tranquillized *Fifties*,
and I am forty. Ought I to regret my seed-time?

'Memories of West Street and Lepke' (1956)

8 At forty-five,
What next, what next?
At every corner,
I meet my Father,
my age, still alive.

'Middle Age' (1964)

9 This is death.
To die and know it. This is the Black Widow, death.

'Mr Edwards and the Spider' (1950)

10 After fifty
the clock can't stop,
each saving breath
takes something.

'Our Afterlife I' (1977)

11 The Lord survives the rainbow of His will.

'The Quaker Graveyard in Nantucket' (1950)

12 We feel the machine slipping from our hands
As if someone else were steering;
If we see light at the end of the tunnel,
It's the light of the oncoming train.

'Since 1939' (1977)

13 But I suppose even God was born
too late to trust the old religion

'Tenth Muse' (1964)

14 The present, yes,
we are in it,
it's the infection
of things gone.

'We Took Our Paradise' (1977)

L. S. Lowry 1887–1976

English painter

15 I'm a simple man, and I use simple materials.

Mervyn Levy *Paintings of L. S. Lowry* (1975)

Malcolm Lowry 1909–57

English novelist

16 How alike are the groans of love to those of the dying.

Under the Volcano (1947)

Mina Loy 1882–1966

British-born American poet and painter

17 [Be] *Brave* and deny at the outset—that pathetic clap-trap war cry *Woman is the equal of man* for She is NOT! . . . Leave off looking to men to find out what you are *not*—Seek within yourselves to find out what you *are*.

'Feminist Manifesto' (1914, unpublished) in Virginia M. Kovidis *Mina Loy* (1980)

Clare Booth Luce 1903–87

American diplomat, politician, and writer

1 Much of . . . his global thinking is, no matter how you slice it, still globaloney.

speech to the House of Representatives, February 1943

2 But if God had wanted us to think just with our wombs, why did He give us a brain?

in *Life* 16 October 1970

Alison Lurie 1926–

American novelist

3 Clothes which make a woman's life difficult and handicap her in competition with men are always felt to be sexually attractive

The Language of Clothes (1981)

4 As with most couples, they are like two people jumping out of an aeroplane clasped together, each believing the other to be a parachute.

Love and Friendship (1962)

5 There's a rule, I think. You get what you want in life, but not your second choice too.

Real People (1969)

Rosa Luxemburg 1871–1919

German revolutionary

6 Freedom is always and exclusively freedom for the one who thinks differently.

Die Russische Revolution (1918)

7 The revolution will 'raise itself again clashing', and to your horror it will proclaim to the sound of trumpets, *I was, I am, I shall be*!

quoting lines from 19th-century German poet and radical Ferdinand Freiligrath (1810–76)

'Order Reigns in Berlin' in *Die Rote Fahne* [The Red Flag] 14 January 1919

Jonathan Lynn 1943– and Antony Jay 1930–

English writers

8 'We went in,' he said, 'to screw the French by splitting them off from the Germans. The French went in to protect their inefficient farmers from commercial competition. The Germans went in to cleanse themselves of genocide and apply for readmission to the human race.'

of the European Community

Yes Minister (1982) vol. 2

9 I think it will be a clash between the political will and the administrative won't.

Yes Prime Minister (1987) vol. 2

Mary McAleese 1951–

Irish stateswoman; President from 1997

10 People ask me what does the Celtic Tiger look like; it looks like this place.

visiting Clonaslee in Co. Laois

in *Irish Times* 13 April 1998

11 The day of the dinosaurs is over. The future belongs to the bridge-builders, not the wreckers.

on the election to the Northern Ireland Assembly

in *Irish Times* 27 June 1998

12 Those whom we commemorate . . . fell victim to a war against oppression in Europe. Their memory, too, fell victim to a war for independence at home in Ireland . . . Respect for the memory of one set of heroes was often at the expense of respect for the memory of another.

at the Armistice Day commemorations in Belgium

in *Irish Times* 14 November 1998

Alexander McArthur and H. Kingsley Long

13 Battles and sex are the only free diversions in slum life. Couple them with drink, which costs money, and you have the three principal outlets for that escape complex which is for ever working in the tenement dweller's subconscious mind.

No Mean City (1935)

Douglas MacArthur
1880–1964

American general
on MacArthur: see **Truman** 323:14

1 I came through and I shall return.
on reaching Australia, having broken through Japanese lines en route from Corregidor
statement in Adelaide, 20 March 1942

2 In war, indeed, there can be no substitute for victory.
address to a Joint Meeting of Congress, 19 April 1951

3 I still remember the refrain of one of the most popular barracks ballads of that day, which proclaimed most proudly that old soldiers never die; they just fade away. I now close my military career and just fade away.
address to a Joint Meeting of Congress, 19 April 1951; see **Foley** 120:15

Rose Macaulay

see **Opening lines** 247:20

Anthony McAuliffe 1898–1975

American general

4 Nuts!
replying to the German demand for surrender
at Bastogne, Belgium, 22 December 1944

Norman McCaig 1910–96

Scottish poet

5 Who owns this landscape?
The millionaire who bought it or
the poacher staggering downhill in the early morning
with a deer on his back?
'A Man in Assynt' (1969)

John McCain 1936–

American Republican politician and presidential candidate

6 I will not take the low road to the highest office in the land. I want the presidency in the best way, not the worst way.
conceding victory in the South Carolina primary to George W. ***Bush***
in *Guardian* 24 February 2000

Joseph McCarthy 1908–57

American politician and anti-Communist agitator
on McCarthy: see **Cartoons** 56:13, **Eisenhower** 101:8, **Murrow** 236:1, **Welch** 333:1

7 I have here in my hand a list of two hundred and five [people] that were known to the Secretary of State as being members of the Communist Party and who nevertheless are still working and shaping the policy of the State Department.
speech at Wheeling, West Virginia, 9 February 1950

8 McCarthyism is Americanism with its sleeves rolled.
speech in Wisconsin, 1952; Richard Rovere *Senator Joe McCarthy* (1973)

Mary McCarthy 1912–89

American novelist

9 The immense popularity of American movies abroad demonstrates that Europe is the unfinished negative of which America is the proof.
On the Contrary (1961) 'America the Beautiful'

10 If someone tells you he is going to make a 'realistic decision', you immediately understand that he has resolved to do something bad.
On the Contrary (1961) 'American Realist Playwrights'

11 Every word she writes is a lie, including 'and' and 'the'.
on Lillian ***Hellman***
quoting herself, in *New York Times* 16 February 1980

Paul McCartney 1942–

English pop singer and songwriter
see also **Lennon and McCartney**

1 Ballads and babies. That's what happened to me.
on reaching the age of fifty
in *Time* 8 June 1992

2 You cannot reheat a soufflé.
discounting rumours of a Beatles reunion
attributed; L. Botts *Loose Talk* (1980)

Ewen MacColl 1915–89

English folksinger and songwriter

3 I found my love by the gasworks crofts
Dreamed a dream by the old canal
Kissed my girl by the factory wall
Dirty old town, dirty old town.
'Dirty Old Town' (1950 song)

4 And I used to sleep standing on my feet
As we hunted for the shoals of herring.
'The Shoals of Herring' (1960 song, from the BBC Radio broadcast *Singing the Fishing*)

David McCord 1897–1997

American poet

5 By and by
God caught his eye.
'Remainders' (1935); epitaph for a waiter

Horace McCoy 1897–1955

American novelist

6 They shoot horses don't they.
title of novel (1935)

John McCrae 1872–1918

Canadian poet and military physician

7 In Flanders fields the poppies blow
Between the crosses, row on row.
'In Flanders Fields' (1915)

Carson McCullers 1917–67

American writer

8 The heart is a lonely hunter.
title of novel (1940); see below

My heart is a lonely hunter that hunts on a lonely hill.
Fiona McLeod (1855–1905) 'The Lonely Hunter' (1896)

Derek McCulloch

see **Catch-phrases** 58:21

Colleen McCullough 1937–

Australian writer

9 The lovely thing about being forty is that you can appreciate twenty-five-year-old men more.
attributed

Hugh MacDiarmid 1892–1978

Scottish poet and nationalist

10 I'll ha'e nae hauf-way hoose, but aye be whaur
Extremes meet—it's the only way I ken
To dodge the curst conceit o' bein' richt
That damns the vast majority o' men.
A Drunk Man Looks at the Thistle (1926)

11 He's no a man ava',
And lacks a proper pride,
Gin less than a' the world
Can ser' him for a bride!
A Drunk Man Looks at the Thistle (1926)

12 The rose of all the world is not for me.
I want for my part
Only the little white rose of Scotland
That smells sharp and sweet—and breaks the heart.
'The Little White Rose' (1934)

13 I must be a Bolshevik
Before the Revolution, but I'll cease to be one quick
When Communism comes to rule the roost,
For real literature can exist only when it's produced
By madmen, hermits, heretics,
Dreamers, rebels, sceptics,
—And such a door of utterance has been given to me
As none may close whosoever they be.
'Talking with Five Thousand People in Edinburgh' (1972)

1 Scotland small? Our multiform, our infinite Scotland *small?*
Only as a patch of hillside may be a cliché corner
To a fool who cries 'Nothing but heather!' . . .
Direadh 1 (1974)

Dwight Macdonald 1906–82

American writer and film critic

2 Götterdämmerung without the gods.
of the use of atomic bombs against the Japanese
in *Politics* September 1945 'The Bomb'

Ramsay MacDonald 1866–1937

British Labour statesman; Prime Minister, 1924, 1931–5
on MacDonald: see **Churchill** 66:5, **Lloyd George** 201:13

3 We hear war called murder. It is not: it is suicide.
in *Observer* 4 May 1930

4 Tomorrow every Duchess in London will be wanting to kiss me!
after forming the National Government, 25 August 1931
Viscount Snowden *An Autobiography* (1934)

Trevor McDonald 1939–

West Indian-born broadcaster

5 I am a West Indian peasant who has drifted into this business and who has survived. If I knew the secret, I would bottle it and sell it.
in *Independent* 20 April 1996

John McEnroe 1959–

American tennis player

6 You cannot be serious!
said to tennis umpire at Wimbledon, early 1980s

7 It's a fabulous place, I'll never forget it, and the right guy won.
after defeating Bjorn Borg in a charity tennis match in the grounds of Buckingham Palace
in *Guardian* 5 July 2000

8 He doesn't make it easy for you guys.
to British fans, while commentating on the Tim ***Henman****–Roger Federer match, 4 July 2001*
in *Guardian* 5 July 2001

Ian McEwan 1948–

English novelist

9 Shakespeare would have grasped wave functions, Donne would have understood complementarity and relative time. They would have been excited. What richness! They would have plundered this new science for their imagery. And they would have educated their audiences too. But you 'arts' people, you're not only ignorant of these magnificent things, you're rather proud of knowing nothing.
The Child in Time (1987)

10 The committee divided between the theorists, who had done all their thinking long ago, or had had it done for them, and the pragmatists, who hoped to discover what it was they thought in the process of saying it.
The Child in Time (1987)

11 Mostly, we are good when it makes sense. A good society is one that makes sense of being good.
Enduring Love (1998)

12 Conflicts, like living organisms, had a natural lifespan. The trick was to know when to let them die.
Enduring Love (1998)

13 I've never outgrown that feeling of mild pride, of acceptance, when children take your hand.
Enduring Love (1998)

14 I love you . . . That is what they were all saying down their phones, from the hijacked planes and the burning towers. There is only love, and then oblivion. Love was all they had to set against the hatred of their murderers.
of the last messages received from those trapped by terrorist attack in buildings and planes, 11 September 2001
in *Guardian* 15 September 2001; see **Last words** 190:8

Patrick McGoohan 1928– , **George Markstein**, and **David Tomblin**

American actor and screenwriters

1 I am not a number, I am a free man!
Number Six, in *The Prisoner* (TV series 1967–68); additional title sequence from the second episode onwards

Roger McGough 1937–

English poet

2 You will put on a dress of guilt
and shoes with broken high ideals.
'Comeclose and Sleepnow' (1967)

3 I wanna be the leader
I wanna be the leader
Can I be the leader?
Can I? Can I?
Promise? Promise?
Yippee, I'm the leader
I'm the leader.
Ok what shall we do now?
'I Wanna be the Leader'

4 Let me die a youngman's death
Not a clean & in-between-
The-sheets, holy-water death.
'Let Me Die a Youngman's Death' (1967)

George McGovern 1922–

American Democratic politician, presidential candidate in 1972

5 Sometimes, when they say you're ahead of your time, it's just a polite way of saying you have a real bad sense of timing.
in *Observer* 18 March 1990

Jimmie McGregor 1932–

Scottish singer and songwriter

6 Oh, he's football crazy, he's football mad
And the football it has robbed him o' the wee bit sense he had.
And it would take a dozen skivvies, his clothes to wash and scrub,
Since our Jock became a member of that terrible football club.
'Football Crazy' (1960 song)

Lord McGregor 1921–

British sociologist

7 An odious exhibition of journalists dabbling their fingers in the stuff of other people's souls.
on Press coverage of the marital difficulties of the Prince and Princess of Wales, speaking as Chairman of the Press Complaints Commission
in *The Times* 9 June 1992

Dennis McHarrie

British poet

8 'He died who loved to live,' they'll say,
'Unselfishly so we might have today!'
Like hell! He fought because he had to fight;
He died that's all. It was his unlucky night.
'Luck' (1980); see **Epitaphs** 110:4

Compton Mackenzie 1883–1972

English novelist

9 Love makes the world go round? Not at all. Whisky makes it go round twice as fast.
Whisky Galore (1947)

Kelvin Mackenzie 1946–

British journalist and media executive

10 We are surfing food.
of cable television
in *Trouble at the Top* (BBC2) 12 February 1997

Alistair Maclean 1922–1987

Scottish thriller writer

11 Where eagles dare.
title of novel (1967)

Don McLean 1945–

American songwriter

12 Something touched me deep inside
The day the music died.
on the death of Buddy Holly
'American Pie' (1972 song)

1 So, bye, bye, Miss American Pie,
Drove my Chevy to the levee
But the levee was dry.
Them good old boys was drinkin'
whiskey and rye
Singin' 'This'll be the day that I die.'
'American Pie' (1972 song)

Archibald MacLeish
1892–1982

American poet, later public official

2 A poem should not mean
But be.
'Ars Poetica' (1926)

Henry McLeish 1948–

Scottish Labour politician, First Minister 2000–1

3 This was a muddle, it was certainly not a fiddle.
of his claiming office expenses while receiving income from sub-letting the premises; McLeish resigned as First Minister 8 November 2001
in *Scotsman* 7 November 2001

Iain Macleod 1913–70

British Conservative politician
on Macleod: see **Salisbury** 285:11

4 It is some measure of the tightness of the magic circle on this occasion that neither the Chancellor of the Exchequer nor the Leader of the House of Commons had any inkling of what was happening.
*of the 'evolvement' of Alec Douglas-**Home** as Conservative leader after the resignation of Harold **Macmillan***
in *The Spectator* 17 January 1964

5 The Conservative Party always in time forgives those who were wrong. Indeed often, in time, they forgive those who were right.
in *The Spectator* 21 February 1964

Marshall McLuhan 1911–80

Canadian communications scholar

6 The new electronic interdependence recreates the world in the image of a global village.
The Gutenberg Galaxy (1962); see **Debord** 87:9

7 When this circuit learns your job, what are you going to do?
The Medium is the Massage (1967)

8 The medium is the message.
Understanding Media (1964)

9 The car has become the carapace, the protective and aggressive shell, of urban and suburban man.
Understanding Media (1964)

10 Television brought the brutality of war into the comfort of the living room. Vietnam was lost in the living rooms of America—not the battlefields of Vietnam.
in *Montreal Gazette* 16 May 1975

11 Gutenberg made everybody a reader. Xerox makes everybody a publisher.
in *Guardian Weekly* 12 June 1977

Harold Macmillan 1894–1986

British Conservative statesman; Prime Minister, 1957–63
on Macmillan: see **Levin** 198:4, **Thorpe** 320:4; *see also* **Hitler** 156:12, **Misquotations** 226:14, **Stockton** 309:3

12 We . . . are Greeks in this American empire . . . We must run the Allied Forces HQ as the Greeks ran the operations of the Emperor Claudius
*to Richard **Crossman** in 1944*
in *Sunday Telegraph* 9 February 1964

13 There ain't gonna be no war.
following the Geneva summit
at a London press conference, 24 July 1955

14 Let us be frank about it: most of our people have never had it so good.
'You Never Had It So Good' was the Democratic Party slogan during the 1952 US election campaign
speech at Bedford, 20 July 1957

15 I thought the best thing to do was to settle up these little local difficulties, and then turn to the wider vision of the Commonwealth.
on leaving for a Commonwealth tour, following the resignation of the Chancellor of the Exchequer and others
statement at London airport 7 January 1958

1 The wind of change is blowing through this continent, and, whether we like it or not, this growth of [African] national consciousness is a political fact.

speech at Cape Town, 3 February 1960; *Pointing the Way* (1972)

2 I was determined that no British government should be brought down by the action of two tarts.

comment on the Profumo affair, July 1963

A. Sampson *Macmillan* (1967)

3 Power? It's like a Dead Sea fruit. When you achieve it, there is nothing there.

Anthony Sampson *The New Anatomy of Britain* (1971)

4 There are three bodies no sensible man directly challenges: the Roman Catholic Church, the Brigade of Guards and the National Union of Mineworkers.

in *Observer* 22 February 1981; see **Baldwin** 21:13

5 Events, dear boy. Events.

when asked what his biggest problem was

attributed

on the appointment of Michael Ramsey to succeed Geoffrey Fisher as Archbishop of Canterbury:

6 We have had enough of Martha and it is time for some Mary.

attributed

Robert McNamara 1916–

American Democratic politician, Secretary of Defense during the Vietnam War

7 I don't object to it's being called 'McNamara's War' . . . It is a very important war and I am pleased to be identified with it and do whatever I can to win it.

in *New York Times* 25 April 1964

8 We . . . acted according to what we thought were the principles and traditions of this nation. We were wrong. We were terribly wrong.

of the conduct of the Vietnam War by the ***Kennedy*** *and* ***Johnson*** *administrations*

in *Daily Telegraph* (electronic edition) 10 April 1995

Louis MacNeice 1907–63

British poet, born in Belfast

9 Better authentic mammon than a bogus god.

Autumn Journal (1939)

10 It's no go the merrygoround, it's no go the rickshaw,
All we want is a limousine and a ticket for the peepshow.

'Bagpipe Music' (1938)

11 It's no go the picture palace, it's no go the stadium,
It's no go the country cot with a pot of pink geraniums,
It's no go the Government grants, it's no go the elections,
Sit on your arse for fifty years and hang your hat on a pension.

'Bagpipe Music' (1938)

12 The glass is falling hour by hour, the glass will fall for ever,
But if you break the bloody glass you won't hold up the weather.

'Bagpipe Music' (1938)

13 So they were married—to be the more together—
And found they were never again so much together,
Divided by the morning tea,
By the evening paper,
By children and tradesmen's bills.

'Les Sylphides' (1941)

14 Time was away and somewhere else,
There were two glasses and two chairs
And two people with the one pulse.

'Meeting Point' (1941)

15 I am not yet born; O fill me
With strength against those who would freeze my
humanity.

'Prayer Before Birth' (1944)

16 Let them not make me a stone and let them not spill me,
Otherwise kill me.

'Prayer Before Birth' (1944)

17 The sunlight on the garden
Hardens and grows cold,
We cannot cage the minute
Within its net of gold.

'Sunlight on the Garden' (1938)

1 By a high star our course is set,
Our end is Life. Put out to sea.
'Thalassa' (1964)

Robert McNeil 1931–

Canadian journalist and writer

2 Canadians feel that any people can live where the climate is gentle. It takes a special people to prosper where nature makes it so hard.
in *Travel and Leisure* June 1978 'Notes of a Native Son'

William Macpherson of Cluny 1926–

Scottish lawyer

3 For the purposes of our Inquiry the concept of institutional racism which we apply consists of:
The collective failure of an organisation to provide an appropriate and professional service to people because of their colour, culture, or ethnic origin. It can be seen or detected in processes, attitudes and behaviour which amount to discrimination through unwitting prejudice, ignorance, thoughtlessness and racist stereotyping with disadvantage minority ethnic people.
The Stephen Lawrence Inquiry: Report (February 1999)

Candia McWilliam 1955–

English novelist

4 With the birth of each child, you lose two novels.
in *Guardian* 5 May 1993

Salvador de Madariaga 1886–1978

Spanish writer and diplomat

5 Since, in the main, it is not armaments that cause wars but wars (or the fears thereof) that cause armaments, it follows that every nation will at every moment strive to keep its armament in an efficient state as required by its fear, otherwise styled security.
Morning Without Noon (1974)

Madonna 1958–

American pop singer and actress

6 Being blonde is definitely a different state of mind. I can't really put my finger on it, but the artifice of being blonde has some incredible sort of sexual connotation.
in *Rolling Stone* 23 March 1989

7 Many people see Eva Perón as either a saint or the incarnation of Satan. That means I can definitely identify with her.
on playing the starring role in the film Evita
in *Newsweek* 5 February 1996

John Gillespie Magee 1922–41

American airman, member of the Royal Canadian Airforce

8 Oh! I have slipped the surly bonds of earth
And danced the skies on laughter-silvered wings.
quoted by Ronald ***Reagan*** *following the explosion of the space shuttle* Challenger, *January 1986*
'High Flight' (1943); see **Reagan** 271:14

9 And, while with silent lifting mind I've trod
The high, untrespassed sanctity of space,
Put out my hand and touched the face of God.
'High Flight' (1943); see **Reagan** 271:14

Derek Mahon 1941–

Northern Irish poet

10 'I am just going outside and may be some time.'
The others nod, pretending not to know.
At the heart of the ridiculous, the sublime.
'Antarctica' (1985); see **Last words** 190:6

11 Somewhere beyond the scorched gable end and the burnt-out buses
there is a poet indulging
his wretched rage for order.
'Rage for Order' (1978)

1 Even now there are places where a
thought might grow—
Peruvian mines, worked out and
abandoned
To a slow clock of condensation,
An echo trapped for ever, and a flutter
Of wildflowers in the lift-shaft . . .
And in a disused shed in Co. Wexford.

'A Disused Shed in Co. Wexford' (1978)

Margaret Mahy 1936–

New Zealand writer for children

2 Canadians are Americans with no Disneyland.

The Changeover (1984)

Norman Mailer 1923–

American novelist and essayist

3 So we think of Marilyn who was every man's love affair with America, Marilyn Monroe who was blonde and beautiful and had a sweet little rinky-dink of a voice and all the cleanliness of all the clean American backyards.

Marilyn (1973)

4 Society is built on many people hurting many people, it is just who does the hurting, which is forever in dispute.

Miami and the Siege of Chicago (1968)

5 The world stood like a playing card on edge . . . One looked at the buildings one passed and wondered if one was to see them again.

looking back at the week of the Cuban Missile Crisis

The Presidential Papers (1964)

6 Hip is the sophistication of the wise primitive in a giant jungle.

Voices of Dissent (1959) 'The White Negro'

7 Once a newspaper touches a story, the facts are lost forever, even to the protagonists.

in *Esquire* June 1960

8 All the security around the American president is just to make sure the man who shoots him gets caught.

in *Sunday Telegraph* 4 March 1990

John Major 1943–

British Conservative statesman; Prime Minister, 1990–7

on Major: see **Cranborne** 79:14

9 If the policy isn't hurting, it isn't working.

on controlling inflation

speech in Northampton, 27 October 1989; see **Political sayings and slogans** 262:8

10 Society needs to condemn a little more and understand a little less.

interview with *Mail on Sunday* 21 February 1993

11 Fifty years on from now, Britain will still be the country of long shadows on county [cricket] grounds, warm beer, invincible green suburbs, dog lovers, and—as George Orwell said—old maids bicycling to Holy Communion through the morning mist.

speech to the Conservative Group for Europe, 22 April 1993; see **Orwell** 249:16

12 It is time to get back to basics: to self-discipline and respect for the law, to consideration for others, to accepting responsibility for yourself and your family, and not shuffling it off on the state.

speech to the Conservative Party Conference, 8 October 1993

13 In retrospect, I think her behaviour was intolerable, and I hope none of my successors are treated in that way.

*of Margaret **Thatcher***

in *Daily Telegraph* 11 August 1999

Bernard Malamud 1914–86

American novelist and short-story writer

14 The past exudes legend: one can't make pure clay of time's mud. There is no life that can be recaptured wholly; as it was. Which is to say that all biography is ultimately fiction.

Dubin's Lives (1979)

15 Levin wanted friendship and got friendliness; he wanted steak and they offered spam.

A New Life (1961)

16 There comes a time in a man's life when to get where he has to go—if there are no doors or windows—he walks through a wall.

Rembrandt's Hat (1972)

Malcolm X 1925-65

American civil rights campaigner

1 If you're born in America with a black skin, you're born in prison.

in an interview, June 1963

2 You can't separate peace from freedom because no one can be at peace unless he has his freedom.

speech in New York, 7 January 1965

3 The white man was *created* a devil, to bring chaos upon this earth.

speech, *c.*1953; Malcolm X with Alex Haley *The Autobiography of Malcolm X* (1965); see **Fard** 111:6

4 We are not speaking of any *individual* white man. We are speaking of the *collective* white man's *historical* record.We are speaking of the collective white man's cruelties, and evils, and greeds, that have seen him *act* like a devil toward the non-white man.

Malcolm X with Alex Haley *The Autobiography of Malcolm X* (1965)

George Leigh Mallory 1886–1924

British mountaineer

5 Because it's there.

on being asked why he wanted to climb Mount Everest (Mallory disappeared on Everest in the following year; his body was discovered in May 1999)

in *New York Times* 18 March 1923

Ruth Mallory

British wife of George Leigh **Mallory**

6 Whether he got to the top of the mountain or not, whether he lived or died, makes no difference to my admiration for him.

letter written shortly after her husband was lost on Everest

David Robertson *George Mallory* (1969)

André Malraux 1901–76

French novelist, essayist, and art critic

7 There are not fifty ways of fighting, there's only one, and that's to win. Neither revolution nor war consists in doing what one pleases.

L'Espoir (1937)

8 Man knows that the world is not made on a human scale; and he wishes that it were.

Les Noyers d'Altenburg (1945)

9 *L'art est un anti-destin.*

Art is a revolt against fate.

Les Voix du silence (1951)

Lord Mancroft 1914–87

British Conservative politician

10 Cricket—a game which the English, not being a spiritual people, have invented in order to give themselves some conception of eternity.

Bees in Some Bonnets (1979)

Nelson Mandela 1918–

South African statesman, President since 1994; former husband of Winnie Madikizela-**Mandela**

11 I have dedicated my life to this struggle of the African people. I have fought against white domination, and I have fought against black domination. I have cherished the ideal of a democratic and free society in which all persons live together in harmony with equal opportunities. It is an ideal which I hope to live for, and to see realized. But my lord, if needs be, it is an ideal for which I am prepared to die.

speech in Pretoria, 20 April 1964, which he quoted on his release in Cape Town, 11 February 1990

12 I stand here before you not as a prophet but as a humble servant of you, the people. Your tireless and heroic sacrifices have made it possible for me to be here today. I therefore place the remaining years of my life in your hands.

speech in Cape Town, 11 February 1990

1 Through its imperialist system Britain brought about untold suffering of millions of people. And this is an historical fact. To be able to admit this would increase the respect, you know, which we have for British institutions.
in *Guardian* 2 April 1990

2 No one is born hating another person because of the colour of his skin, or his background, or his religion. People must learn to hate, and if they can learn to hate, they can be taught to love, for love comes more naturally to the human heart than its opposite.
Long Walk to Freedom (1994)

3 True reconciliation does not consist in merely forgetting the past.
speech, 7 January 1996

4 We close the century with most people still languishing in poverty, subjected to hunger, preventable disease, illiteracy and insufficient shelter.
speaking at a ceremony at his former prison cell on Robben Island
in *Observer* on 2 January 2000

5 One of the things I learnt when I was negotiating was that until I changed myself I could not change others.
in *Sunday Times* 16 April 2000

Winnie Madikizela-Mandela 1934–

South African political activist; former wife of Nelson **Mandela**

6 With that stick of matches, with our necklace, we shall liberate this country.
speech in black townships, 14 April 1986

7 Maybe there is no rainbow nation after all because it does not have the colour black.
at the funeral of a black child reportedly shot dead by a white farmer
in *Irish Times* 25 April 1998

Peter Mandelson 1953–

British Labour politician
on Mandelson: see **Blair** 37:8, **Campbell** 51:13, **Parris** 254:10

8 Few politicians are good at taking the high ground and throwing themselves off it.
of Tony ***Blair*** *and the revision of Clause Four; see also* **Blair** 37:3
in *New Yorker* 5 February 1996

9 Before this campaign started, it was said that I was facing political oblivion, my career in tatters . . . They underestimated me, because I am a fighter and not a quitter.
on winning back his Hartlepool seat in the General Election
speech, 8 June 2001

Nadezhda Mandelstam d. 1980

wife of Osip **Mandelstam**

10 He was as helpless as everybody else, but at least he tried to do something for others.
of the Russian writer and journalist Ilya Ehrenburg (1891–1967)
Hope Abandoned (1974)

Osip Mandelstam 1892–1938

Russian poet; husband of Nadezhda **Mandelstam**

11 The age is rocking the wave
with human grief
to a golden beat, and an adder
is breathing in time with it in the grass.
'The Age' (1923)

12 Perhaps my whisper was already born
before my lips.
'Poems Published Posthumously' (written 1934)

Herbie Mann 1930–

American jazz musician

13 If you're in jazz and more than ten people like you, you're labelled commercial.
Henry Pleasants *Serious Music and all that Jazz!* (1969)

Thomas Mann 1875–1955

German novelist

1 Death in Venice.
title of novella (1912)

2 Time has no divisions to mark its passage, there is never a thunderstorm or blare of trumpets to announce the beginning of a new month or year. Even when a new century begins it is only we mortals who ring bells and fire off pistols.
The Magic Mountain (1924)

3 We come out of the dark and go into the dark again, and in between lie the experiences of our life.
The Magic Mountain (1924)

4 A man's dying is more the survivors' affair than his own.
The Magic Mountain (1924)

5 Speech is civilization itself. The word, even the most contradictory word, preserves contact—it is silence which isolates.
The Magic Mountain (1924)

Mao Zedong 1893–1976

Chinese statesman; chairman of the Communist Party of the Chinese People's Republic from 1949
on Mao: see **Levin** 198:6

6 Politics is war without bloodshed while war is politics with bloodshed.
lecture, 1938; *Selected Works* (1965) vol. 2

7 Every Communist must grasp the truth, 'Political power grows out of the barrel of a gun'.
speech, 6 November 1938

8 The atom bomb is a paper tiger which the United States reactionaries use to scare people. It looks terrible, but in fact it isn't . . . All reactionaries are paper tigers.
interview, 1946; *Selected Works* (1961) vol. 4

9 Letting a hundred flowers blossom and a hundred schools of thought contend is the policy for promoting progress in the arts and the sciences and a flourishing socialist culture in our land.
speech in Peking, 27 February 1957

Diego Maradona 1960–

Argentine football player

10 The goal was scored a little bit by the hand of God, another bit by head of Maradona.
on his controversial goal against England in the 1986 World Cup
in *Guardian* 1 July 1986

John Marchi 1948–

American Republican politician

11 We ought not to permit a cottage industry in the God business.
on hearing that British scientists had successfully cloned a lamb (Dolly)
in *Guardian* 28 February 1997

Princess Margaret 1930–2002

British princess, sister of **Elizabeth II**

12 Mindful of the Church's teaching that Christian marriage is indissoluble, and conscious of my duty to the Commonwealth, I have resolved to put these considerations before any others.
announcing her decision not to marry a divorced man, Group Captain Peter Townsend
statement from Clarence House, 31 October 1955

13 My children are not royal, they just happen to have the Queen as their aunt.
Elizabeth Longford (ed.) *The Oxford Book of Royal Anecdotes* (1989)

Miriam Margolyes 1941–

English actress

14 Life, if you're fat, is a minefield—you have to pick your way, otherwise you blow up.
in *Observer* 9 June 1991

Lynn Margulis 1938–

American biologist

15 Gaia is a tough bitch. People think the earth is going to die and they have to save it, that's ridiculous . . . There's no doubt that Gaia can compensate for our output of greenhouse gases, but the environment that's left will not be happy for any people.

in *New York Times Biographical Service* January 1996

Johnny Marks 1909–85

American songwriter

1 Rudolph, the Red-Nosed Reindeer
Had a very shiny nose,
And if you ever saw it,
You would even say it glows.

'Rudolph, the Red-Nosed Reindeer' (1949 song)

Bob Marley 1945–81

Jamaican reggae musician and songwriter

2 Get up, stand up
Stand up for your rights
Get up, stand up
Never give up the fight.

'Get up, Stand up' (1973 song)

3 I shot the sheriff
But I swear it was in self-defence
I shot the sheriff
And they say it is a capital offence.

'I Shot the Sheriff' (1974 song)

Don Marquis 1878–1937

American poet and journalist

4 procrastination is the
art of keeping
up with yesterday.

archy and mehitabel (1927) 'certain maxims of archy'

5 an optimist is a guy
that has never had
much experience.

archy and mehitabel (1927) 'certain maxims of archy'

6 it s cheerio
my deario that
pulls a lady through.

archy and mehitabel (1927) 'cheerio, my deario'

7 I have got you out here
in the great open spaces
where cats are cats.

archy and mehitabel (1927) 'mehitabel has an adventure'

8 but wotthehell archy wotthehell
jamais triste archy jamais triste
that is my motto.

archy and mehitabel (1927) 'mehitabel sees paris'

9 boss there is always
a comforting thought
in time of trouble when
it is not our trouble.

archy does his part (1935) 'comforting thoughts'

10 did you ever
notice that when
a politician
does get an idea
he usually
gets it all wrong.

archys life of mehitabel (1933) 'archygrams'

11 now and then
there is a person born
who is so unlucky
that he runs into accidents
which started to happen
to somebody else.

archys life of mehitabel (1933) 'archy says'

12 Prohibition makes you want to cry into your beer and denies you the beer to cry into.

Sun Dial Time (1936)

13 The art of newspaper paragraphing is to stroke a platitude until it purrs like an epigram.

E. Anthony *O Rare Don Marquis* (1962)

14 Writing a book of poetry is like dropping a rose petal down the Grand Canyon and waiting for the echo.

E. Anthony *O Rare Don Marquis* (1962)

Anthony Marriott 1931– and Alistair Foot

British writers

15 No sex please—we're British.

title of play (1971)

Arthur Marshall 1910–89

British journalist and former schoolmaster

1 What, knocked a tooth out? Never mind, dear, laugh it off, laugh it off; it's all part of life's rich pageant.

The Games Mistress (recorded monologue, 1937)

Thomas R. Marshall 1854–1925

American politician

2 What this country needs is a really good 5-cent cigar.

in *New York Tribune* 4 January 1920

Thurgood Marshall 1908–93

American Supreme Court judge

3 We must never forget that the only real source of power that we as judges can tap is the respect of the people.

in *Chicago Tribune* 15 August 1981

Dean Martin 1917–95

American singer and actor

4 You're not drunk if you can lie on the floor without holding on.

Paul Dickson *Official Rules* (1978)

Holt Marvell 1901–69

English songwriter

5 These foolish things remind me of you.

title of song (1935)

6 A cigarette that bears a lipstick's traces,
An airline ticket to romantic places.

'These Foolish Things Remind Me of You' (1935 song)

Chico Marx 1891–1961

American film comedian

7 I wasn't kissing her, I was just whispering in her mouth.

on being discovered by his wife with a chorus girl

Groucho Marx and Richard J. Anobile *Marx Brothers Scrapbook* (1973)

Groucho Marx 1895–1977

American film comedian

see also **Epitaphs** 109:10, **Film lines** 115:5, 116:1, 116:9, 117:8, 117:14

8 PLEASE ACCEPT MY RESIGNATION. I DON'T WANT TO BELONG TO ANY CLUB THAT WILL ACCEPT ME AS A MEMBER.

Groucho and Me (1959)

9 I never forget a face, but in your case I'll be glad to make an exception.

Leo Rosten *People I have Loved, Known or Admired* (1970) 'Groucho'

10 I've been around so long, I knew Doris Day before she was a virgin.

Max Wilk *The Wit and Wisdom of Hollywood* (1972)

Queen Mary 1867–1953

Queen Consort of **George V**

11 Well, Mr Baldwin! *this* is a pretty kettle of fish!

after ***Edward VIII*** *had told her he was prepared to give up the throne to marry Mrs Simpson*

said on 17 November 1936; James Pope-Hennessy *Life of Queen Mary* (1959)

12 I do not think you have ever realised the shock, which the attitude you took up caused your family and the whole nation. It seemed inconceivable to those who had made such sacrifices during the war that you, as their King, refused a lesser sacrifice.

letter to the Duke of Windsor (formerly **Edward VIII**), July 1938; James Pope-Hennessy *Queen Mary* (1959)

Eric Maschwitz 1901–69

British writer

13 A nightingale sang in Berkeley Square.

title of song (1940)

Donald Mason 1913–

American naval officer

14 Sighted sub, sank same.

on sinking a Japanese submarine in the Atlantic region (the first US naval success in the war)

radio message, 28 January 1942; in *New York Times* 27 February 1942

Nick Mason 1944–

English drummer and percussionist

1 In the 1960s, the record companies seemed to sign anything with long hair; if it was a sheepdog, so what.

N. Shaffner *A Saucerful of Secrets: the Pink Floyd Odyssey*

Leonard Matlovich *d.* 1988

American Air Force Sergeant

2 When I was in the military, they gave me a medal for killing two men and a discharge for loving one.

attributed

Cerys Matthews 1969–

Welsh pop singer

3 Every day when I wake up, I thank the Lord I'm Welsh.

in *Sunday Times* 4 March 2001

W. Somerset Maugham 1874–1965

English novelist

4 You can't learn too soon that the most useful thing about a principle is that it can always be sacrificed to expediency.

The Circle (1921)

5 It is not true that suffering ennobles the character; happiness does that sometimes, but suffering, for the most part, makes men petty and vindictive.

The Moon and Sixpence (1919)

6 A woman can forgive a man for the harm he does her, but she can never forgive him for the sacrifices he makes on her account.

The Moon and Sixpence (1919)

7 Money is like a sixth sense without which you cannot make a complete use of the other five.

Of Human Bondage (1915)

8 I [Death] was astonished to see him in Baghdad, for I had an appointment with him tonight in Samarra.

Sheppey (1933)

9 I am told that today rather more than 60 per cent of the men who go to the universities go on a Government grant. This is a new class that has entered upon the scene . . . They are scum.

in *Sunday Times* 25 December 1955

to a friend who had said that he hated English food:

10 All you have to do is eat breakfast three times a day.

Ted Morgan *Somerset Maugham* (1980)

11 Dying is a very dull, dreary affair. And my advice to you is to have nothing whatever to do with it.

to his nephew Robin, in 1965

Robin Maugham *Conversations with Willie* (1978)

Bill Mauldin

see **Cartoons** 56:3

André Maurois 1885–1967

French writer

12 Growing old is no more than a bad habit which a busy man has no time to form.

The Art of Living (1940)

James Maxton 1885–1946

British Labour politician

13 All I say is, if you cannot ride two horses you have no right in the circus.

opposing disaffiliation of the Scottish Independent Labour Party from the Labour Party; usually quoted as, '. . . no right in the bloody circus'

in *Daily Herald* 12 January 1931

Glyn Maxwell 1962–

English poet

14 May his anorak grow big with jotters,
Noting the numbers of trains he saw.

'Curse on a Child' (1995)

Vladimir Mayakovsky 1893–1930

Russian poet
see also **Last words** 190:15

1 If you wish—
. . . I'll be irreproachably tender;
not a man, but—a cloud in trousers!
'The Cloud in Trousers' (1915)

2 Not a sound. The universe sleeps, resting a huge ear on its paw with mites of stars.
'The Cloud in Trousers' (1915)

3 In our language rhyme is a barrel. A barrel of dynamite. The line is a fuse. The line smoulders to the end and explodes; and the town is blown sky-high in a stanza.
'Conversation with an Inspector of Taxes about Poetry' (1926)

4 The poet is always indebted to the universe, paying interest and fines on sorrow.
'Conversation with an Inspector of Taxes about Poetry' (1926)

5 Oh for just
one
more conference
regarding the eradication of all
conferences!
'In Re Conferences'; Herbert Marshall (ed.) *Mayakovsky* (1965)

6 To us love says humming that the heart's stalled motor has begun working again.
'Letter from Paris to Comrade Kostorov on the Nature of Love' (1928)

Louis B. Mayer 1885–1957

Russian-born American film executive, head of MGM

7 We've got more stars than there are in the heavens, all of them except for that damned Mouse over at Disney.
Sheridan Morley and Ruth Leon *Gene Kelly* (1996)

Percy Mayfield 1920–84

American songwriter

8 Hit the road, Jack.
title of song (1961)

Charles H. Mayo 1865–1939

American doctor, co-founder of the Mayo Clinic

9 The definition of a specialist as one who 'knows more and more about less and less' is good and true.
in *Modern Hospital* September 1938; see **Butler** 50:1

Margaret Mead 1901–78

American anthropologist

10 The knowledge that the personalities of the two sexes are socially produced is congenial to every programme that looks forward towards a planned order of society. It is a two-edged sword.
Sex and Temperament in Three Primitive Societies (1935)

Shepherd Mead 1914–

American advertising executive

11 How to succeed in business without really trying.
title of book (1952)

Hughes Mearns 1875–1965

American writer

12 As I was walking up the stair
I met a man who wasn't there.
He wasn't there again today.
I wish, I wish he'd stay away.
lines written for an amateur play *The Psycho-ed* (1910) and set to music in 1939 as 'The Little Man Who Wasn't There'

Peter Medawar 1915–87

English immunologist and author

13 A bishop wrote gravely to the *Times* inviting all nations to destroy 'the formula' of the atomic bomb. There is no simple remedy for ignorance so abysmal.
The Hope of Progress (1972)

14 If politics is the art of the possible, research is surely the art of the soluble.

Both are immensely practical-minded affairs.

in *New Statesman* 19 June 1964; see **Butler** 50:3, **Galbraith** 130:11

1 During the 1950s, the first great age of molecular biology, the English Schools of Oxford and particularly of Cambridge produced more than a score of graduates of quite outstanding ability—much more brilliant, inventive, articulate and dialectically skilful than most young scientists; right up in the Watson class. But Watson had one towering advantage over all of them: in addition to being extremely clever he had something important to be clever *about*.

review of James D. **Watson**'s *The Double Helix* in *New York Review of Books* 28 March 1968

Golda Meir 1898–1978

Israeli stateswoman, Prime Minister 1969–74

2 Those that perished in Hitler's gas chambers were the last Jews to die without standing up to defend themselves.

speech to United Jewish Appeal Rally, New York, 11 June 1967

3 Women's Liberation is just a lot of foolishness. It's the men who are discriminated against. They can't bear children. And no-one's likely to do anything about that.

in *Newsweek* 23 October 1972

David Mellor 1949–

British Conservative politician

4 I do believe the popular press is drinking in the last chance saloon.

interview on *Hard News* (Channel 4), 21 December 1989

H. L. Mencken 1880–1956

American journalist and literary critic

5 Love is the delusion that one woman differs from another.

Chrestomathy (1949)

6 Puritanism. The haunting fear that someone, somewhere, may be happy.

Chrestomathy (1949)

7 Democracy is the theory that the common people know what they want, and deserve to get it good and hard.

A Little Book in C major (1916)

8 Conscience: the inner voice which warns us that someone may be looking.

A Little Book in C major (1916)

9 It is now quite lawful for a Catholic woman to avoid pregnancy by a resort to mathematics, though she is still forbidden to resort to physics and chemistry.

Notebooks (1956) 'Minority Report'

10 No one in this world, so far as I know—and I have searched the records for years, and employed agents to help me—has ever lost money by underestimating the intelligence of the great masses of the plain people.

in *Chicago Tribune* 19 September 1926

11 If there had been any formidable body of cannibals in the country he would have promised to provide them with free missionaries fattened at the taxpayer's expense.

*of Harry **Truman** in the 1948 presidential campaign*

in *Baltimore Sun* 7 November 1948

Elsie Mendl 1865–1950

American socialite and fashionable decorator

explaining her dislike of soup:

12 I do not believe in building a meal on a lake.

Elsie de Wolfe *After All* (1935)

13 It's just my colour: it's *beige*!

her first view of the Parthenon

Osbert Sitwell *Rat Week: An Essay on the Abdication* (1986)

Yehudi Menuhin 1916–99

American-born British violinist

14 It is only in our advanced and synthetic civilization that mothers no longer sing to the babies they are carrying.

in *Observer* 4 January 1987

Robert Gordon Menzies 1894–1978

Australian Liberal statesman, Prime Minister 1939–41 and 1949–66
on Menzies: see **Curtin** 83:3

1 What Great Britain calls the Far East is to us the near north.
in *Sydney Morning Herald* 27 April 1939

David Mercer 1928–80

English dramatist

2 A suitable case for treatment.
title of television play (1962); later filmed as *Morgan–A Suitable Case for Treatment* (1966)

Johnny Mercer 1909–76

American songwriter

3 You've got to ac-cent-tchu-ate the positive
Elim-my-nate the negative
Latch on to the affirmative
Don't mess with Mister In-between.
'Ac-cent-tchu-ate the Positive' (1944 song)

4 Jeepers Creepers—where you get them peepers?
'Jeepers Creepers' (1938 song)

5 We're drinking my friend,
To the end of a brief episode,
Make it one for my baby
And one more for the road.
'One For My Baby' (1943 song)

6 That old black magic.
title of song (1942)

Rick Mercer 1969–

Canadian comedian

7 America is our neighbour, our ally, our trading partner, and our friend. Still, sometimes you'd like to give them such a smack.
This Hour Has 22 Minutes (CBC television, 11 November 1996)

Bob Merrill 1921–98

American songwriter and composer

8 How much is that doggie in the window?
title of song (1953)

9 People who need people are the luckiest people in the world.
'People who Need People' (1964 song)

James Merrill 1926–95

American poet

10 Each thirteenth year he married. When he died
There were already several chilled wives
In sable orbit—rings, cars, permanent waves.
We'd felt him warming up for a green bride.

He could afford it. He was 'in his prime'
And three score ten. But money was not time.
'The Broken Home' (1966)

11 Always that same old story—
Father Time and Mother Earth,
a marriage on the rocks.
'The Broken Home' (1966)

W. S. Merwin 1927–

American poet

12 Sometimes it is inconceivable that I should be the age I am.
'The Child' (1968)

13 This is the black sea-brute bulling through wave-wrack,
Ancient as ocean's shifting hills.
'Leviathan' (1956)

14 The sea curling
Star-climbed, wind-combed, cumbered with itself still
As at first it was, is the hand not yet contented
Of the Creator. And he waits for the world to begin.
'Leviathan' (1956)

Anthony Meyer 1920–

British Conservative politician

1 I question the right of that great Moloch, national sovereignty, to burn its children to save its pride.
speaking against the Falklands War, 1982
in *Listener* 27 September 1990

Bette Midler 1945–

American actress

2 When it's three o'clock in New York, it's still 1938 in London.
attributed

George Mikes 1912–

Hungarian-born writer

3 An Englishman, even if he is alone, forms an orderly queue of one.
How to be an Alien (1946)

Edna St Vincent Millay 1892–1950

American poet

4 Childhood is the kingdom where nobody
dies.
Nobody that matters, that is.
'Childhood is the Kingdom where Nobody dies' (1934)

5 Down, down, down into the darkness of
the grave
Gently they go, the beautiful, the tender,
the kind;
Quietly they go, the intelligent, the witty,
the brave.
I know. But I do not approve. And I am
not resigned.
'Dirge Without Music' (1928)

6 My candle burns at both ends;
It will not last the night;
But ah, my foes, and oh, my friends—
It gives a lovely light.
A Few Figs From Thistles (1920) 'First Fig'

7 Euclid alone
Has looked on Beauty bare. Fortunate
they
Who, though once only and then but far
away,
Have heard her massive sandal set on
stone.
The Harp-Weaver and Other Poems (1923)
sonnet 22

8 Justice denied in Massachusetts.
relating to the trial of Sacco and ***Vanzetti*** *and their execution on 22 August 1927*
title of poem (1928)

9 The sun that warmed our stooping backs
and withered the weeds uprooted—
We shall not feel it again.
We shall die in darkness, and be buried
in the rain.
'Justice Denied in Massachusetts' (1928)

10 Death devours all lovely things;
Lesbia with her sparrow
Shares the darkness—presently
Every bed is narrow.
'Passer Mortuus Est' (1921)

11 After all, my erstwhile dear,
My no longer cherished,
Need we say it was not love,
Now that love is perished?
'Passer Mortuus Est' (1921)

12 It's not true that life is one damn thing after another—it's one damn thing over and over.
letter to Arthur Davison Ficke, 24 October 1930; see **Hubbard** 161:4

Alice Duer Miller 1874–1942

American writer

13 I am American bred,
I have seen much to hate here—much to
forgive,
But in a world where England is finished
and dead,
I do not wish to live.
The White Cliffs (1940)

Arthur Miller 1915–

American dramatist
on Miller: see **Newspaper headlines** 240:5

14 A suicide kills two people, Maggie, that's what it's for!
After the Fall (1964)

15 All organization is and must be grounded on the idea of exclusion and prohibition

just as two objects cannot occupy the same space.
The Crucible (1953)

1 Death of a salesman
title of play (1949)

2 The world is an oyster, but you don't crack it open on a mattress.
Death of a Salesman (1949)

3 Willy Loman never made a lot of money. His name was never in the paper. He's not the finest character that ever lived. But he's a human being, and a terrible thing is happening to him. So attention must be paid.
Death of a Salesman (1949)

4 For a salesman, there is no rock bottom to the life. He don't put a bolt to a nut, he don't tell you the law or give you medicine. He's a man way out there in the blue, riding on a smile and a shoeshine. And when they start not smiling back—that's an earthquake . . . A salesman is got to dream, boy. It comes with the territory.
Death of a Salesman (1949) 'Requiem'

5 The car, the furniture, the wife, the children—everything has to be disposable. Because you see the main thing today is—shopping.
The Price (1968)

6 The ultimate human mystery may not be anything more than the claims on us of clan and race, which may yet turn out to have the power, because they defy the rational mind, to kill the world.
Timebends (1987)

7 A good newspaper, I suppose, is a nation talking to itself.
in *Observer* 26 November 1961

Henry Miller 1891–1980

American novelist

8 Even before the music begins there is that bored look on people's faces. A polite form of self-imposed torture, the concert.
Tropic of Cancer (1934)

9 Every man with a bellyful of the classics is an enemy to the human race.
Tropic of Cancer (1934)

Jonathan Miller 1934–

English writer and director

10 I'm not really a *Jew*. Just Jew-*ish*. Not the whole hog, you know.
Beyond the Fringe (1960 revue) 'Real Class'

Spike Milligan 1918–2002

British comedian and writer
see also **Catch-phrases** 59:5, 60:16, 60:18

11 Money couldn't buy friends but you got a better class of enemy.
Puckoon (1963)

A. J. Mills, Fred Godfrey, and **Bennett Scott**

British songwriters

12 Take me back to dear old Blighty.
title of song (1916)

Irving Mills 1894–1985

American songwriter

13 It don't mean a thing
If it ain't got that swing.
'It Don't Mean a Thing' (1932 song; music by Duke Ellington)

John Mills 1908–

British actor

14 I have worked with more submarines than leading ladies.
in *The Times* 12 February 2000

15 Never let the sun set on your wrath and avoid silences at all costs. You've got to keep talking.
recipe for a happy marriage, on his diamond wedding anniversary
in *Sunday Telegraph* 21 January 2001

A. A. Milne 1882–1956

English writer for children
on Milne: see **Parker** 253:11

1 The more he looked inside the more
Piglet wasn't there.
The House at Pooh Corner (1928)

2 I am a Bear of Very Little Brain, and long words Bother me.
Winnie-the-Pooh (1926)

3 Time for a little something.
Winnie-the-Pooh (1926)

4 My spelling is Wobbly. It's good spelling but it Wobbles, and the letters get in the wrong places.
Winnie-the-Pooh (1926)

5 Owl hasn't exactly got Brain, but he
Knows Things.
Winnie-the-Pooh (1926)

6 They're changing guard at Buckingham Palace—
Christopher Robin went down with Alice.
Alice is marrying one of the guard.
'A soldier's life is terrible hard,'
Says Alice.
'Buckingham Palace' (1924)

7 James James
Morrison Morrison
Weatherby George Dupree
Took great
Care of his Mother,
Though he was only three.
James James
Said to his Mother,
'Mother,' he said, said he;
'You must never go down to the end of the town, if you don't go down with me.'
'Disobedience' (1924)

8 King John was not a good man—
He had his little ways.
And sometimes no one spoke to him
For days and days and days.
'King John's Christmas' (1927)

9 The King asked
The Queen, and
The Queen asked
The Dairymaid:
'Could we have some butter for
The Royal slice of bread?'
'The King's Breakfast' (1924)

10 *What* is the matter with Mary Jane?
She's perfectly well and she hasn't a pain,
And it's lovely rice pudding for dinner again!
What *is* the matter with Mary Jane?
'Rice Pudding' (1924)

11 Hush! Hush! Whisper who dares!
Christopher Robin is saying his prayers.
'Vespers' (1924); see **Morton** 232:15

■ **Misquotations**

see box overleaf

Adrian Mitchell 1932–

English poet, novelist, and dramatist

12 Most people ignore most poetry
because
most poetry ignores most people.
Poems (1964) p. 8

George Mitchell 1933–

American politician

13 Although he is regularly asked to do so, God does not take sides in American politics.
comment during the hearing of the Senate Select Committee on the Iran-Contra affair, July 1987

14 Nobody ever said it would be easy—and that was an understatement.
on the Northern Irish peace talks
in *Times* 19 February 1998

15 Peace, political stability and reconciliation are not too much to ask for. They are the minimum that a decent society provides.
in *Irish Post* 18 April 1998

John Mitchell 1913–88

American lawyer and US Attorney-General to the Nixon administration

16 Katie Graham's gonna get her tit caught in a big fat wringer if that's published.
on hearing that Katherine Graham's Washington Post *was to reveal the connection between*

▸▸

Misquotations

1 Beam me up, Scotty.

supposedly the form in which Captain Kirk habitually requested to be returned from a planet to the Starship Enterprise; *in fact the nearest equivalent found is*

Beam us up, Mr Scott.

Gene Roddenberry *Star Trek* (1966 onwards) 'Gamesters of Triskelion'

2 Come with me to the Casbah.

often attributed to Charles Boyer (1898–1978) in the film Algiers *(1938), but apocryphal*

L. Swindell *Charles Boyer* (1983)

3 Crisis? What crisis?

in *Sun* headline, 11 January 1979; summarizing James **Callaghan**'s remark

I don't think other people in the world would share the view there is mounting chaos.

at London Airport, 10 January 1979

4 Dreams are the royal road to the unconscious.

summary of **Freud**'s view; see **Freud** 125:8

5 The dying breath of Socrates.

usual formulation of the proposition set out by James **Jeans**: see **Jeans** 169:3

6 Elementary, my dear Watson, elementary.

remark attributed to Sherlock Holmes, but not found in this form in any book by Arthur Conan **Doyle**, *first found in P.G. Wodehouse* Psmith Journalist *(1915)*

attributed

7 A good day to bury bad news.

popular misquotation of Jo **Moore**'s email of 11 September 2001; see **Moore** 230:5

8 The green shoots of recovery.

popular version of the Chancellor's view of the economic situation

The green shoots of economic spring are appearing once again.

Norman Lamont, speech at Conservative Party Conference, 9 October 1991

9 I paint with my prick.

attributed to Pierre Auguste Renoir (1841–1919); possibly an inversion of

It's with my brush I make love.

A. André *Renoir* (1919)

when asked what jazz is:

10 Man, if you gotta ask you'll never know.

frequently quoted version of Louis **Armstrong**'s response

If you still have to ask . . . shame on you.

Max Jones et al. *Salute to Satchmo* (1970)

11 Me Tarzan, you Jane.

Johnny Weissmuller summing up his role in Tarzan, the Ape Man *(1932 film); the words occur neither in the film nor the original, by Edgar Rice Burroughs*

in *Photoplay Magazine* June 1932

12 My lips are sealed.

misquotation from Stanley **Baldwin**'s speech on the Abyssinian crisis

I shall be but a short time tonight. I have seldom spoken with greater regret, for my lips are not yet unsealed.

speech in the House of Commons, 10 December 1935

13 Play it again, Sam.

in the film Casablanca, *written by Julius J. Epstein et al., Humphrey Bogart says, 'If she can stand it, I can. Play it!'; earlier in the film Ingrid Bergman says, 'Play it, Sam. Play* As Time Goes By.*'*

Casablanca (1942 film); see **Film lines** 115:17

14 Selling off the family silver.

summary of Harold **Macmillan**'s attack on privatization

First of all the Georgian silver goes, and then all that nice furniture that used to be in the saloon. Then the Canalettos go.

speech to the Tory Reform Group, 8 November 1985

15 Shouting fire in a crowded theatre.

popular summary of Oliver Wendell **Holmes** Jr.'s definition of the limits of free speech; see below

▶

▸ Misquotations continued

The most stringent protection of free speech would not protect a man falsely shouting fire in a theatre and causing a panic.

in *Schenck v. United States* (1919)

1 The soft under-belly of Europe.

popular version of Winston **Churchill**'s phrase

We make this wide encircling movement in the Mediterranean, having for its primary object the recovery of the command of that vital sea, but also having for its object the exposure of the under-belly of the Axis, especially Italy, to heavy attack.

speech in the House of Commons, 11 November 1942

2 Something must be done.

popular summary of King **Edward VIII**'s words at the derelict Dowlais Iron and Steel Works, 18 November 1936

These works brought all these people here. Something should be done to get them at work again.

in *Western Mail* 19 November 1936

3 We are the masters now.

from Hartley Shawcross's assertion of Labour's strength after winning the 1945 election, '"But," said Alice, "the question is whether you can make a word mean different things." "Not so," said Humpty-Dumpty, "the question is which is to be master. That's all." We are the masters at the moment, and not only at the moment, but for a very long time to come.'

in the House of Commons, 2 April 1946; see below; see **Blair** 37:5

'When *I* use a word,' Humpty Dumpty said in a rather scornful tone, 'it means just what I choose it to mean—neither more nor less.'

Lewis Carroll (1832–98) *Through the Looking-Glass* (1872)

4 The white heat of technology.

phrase deriving from Harold **Wilson**'s speech

The Britain that is going to be forged in the white heat of this revolution will be no place for restrictive practices or for outdated methods on either side of industry.

speech at the Labour Party Conference, 1 October 1963

5 Why don't you come up and see me sometime?

alteration of Mae **West**'s invitation

Why don't you come up sometime, and see me?

She Done Him Wrong (1933 film)

6 You dirty rat!

associated with James Cagney (1899–1986), but not used by him in any film; in a speech at the American Film Institute banquet, 13 March 1974, Cagney said, 'I never said "Mmm, you dirty rat!"'

Cagney by Cagney (1976)

▸▸ John Mitchell continued

Watergate and the campaign funding for the Committee to Re-Elect the President

in 1973; Katherine Graham *Personal History* (1997)

Joni Mitchell 1945–

Canadian singer and songwriter

7 They paved paradise
And put up a parking lot.

'Big Yellow Taxi' (1970 song)

8 I've looked at life from both sides now,
From win and lose and still somehow
It's life's illusions I recall;
I really don't know life at all.

'Both Sides Now' (1967 song)

9 We are stardust,
We are golden,
And we got to get ourselves
Back to the garden.

'Woodstock' (1969 song)

Margaret Mitchell 1900–49

American novelist

1 Providing you have enough courage—or money—you can do without a reputation.

said by Rhett Butler

Gone with the Wind (1936)

2 Death and taxes and childbirth! There's never any convenient time for any of them.

Gone with the Wind (1936)

3 I wish I could care what you do or where you go but I can't . . . My dear, I don't give a damn.

Gone with the Wind (1936); see **Film lines** 115:9

4 After all, tomorrow is another day.

Gone with the Wind (1936); closing words, spoken by Scarlett O'Hara

Warren Mitchell 1926–

British actor

5 You don't retire in this business. You just notice the phone has not rung for 10 years.

in *Guardian* 30 December 2000

Nancy Mitford 1904–73

English writer

6 Abroad is unutterably bloody and foreigners are fiends.

The Pursuit of Love (1945); see **George VI** 133:8

François Mitterrand 1916–96

French socialist statesman; President of France 1981–95

7 She has the eyes of Caligula, but the mouth of Marilyn Monroe.

of Margaret ***Thatcher****, briefing his new European Minister Roland Dumas*

in *Observer* 25 November 1990

Wilson Mizner 1876–1933

American dramatist

8 Be nice to people on your way up because you'll meet 'em on your way down.

A. Johnston *The Legendary Mizners* (1953)

9 If you steal from one author, it's plagiarism; if you steal from many, it's research.

A. Johnston *The Legendary Mizners* (1953)

10 A trip through a sewer in a glass-bottomed boat.

of Hollywood

A. Johnston *The Legendary Mizners* (1953)

Ariane Mnouchkine 1934–

French theatre director

11 A cultural Chernobyl.

of Euro Disney

in *Harper's Magazine* July 1992; see **Ballard** 22:4

Emilio Mola 1887–1937

Spanish nationalist general

12 Fifth column.

an extra body of supporters claimed by General Mola in a broadcast as being within Madrid when he besieged the city with four columns of Nationalist forces

in *New York Times* 16 and 17 October 1936

Gebhardt von Moltke 1938–

German diplomat

13 One has the impression sometimes that the teaching of history in this country stops at 1945. I regret and am deeply concerned by the lack of interest and curiosity I detect among young British people, not only with regard to learning German but also with travelling to Germany.

as outgoing German Ambassador to Britain

article in *Initiative*, magazine of the German-British Chamber of Industry and Commerce; in *Daily Telegraph* 12 October 1999

Walter Mondale 1928–

American Democratic politician

1 When I hear your new ideas I'm reminded of that ad, 'Where's the beef?'
in a televised debate with Gary Hart, 11 March 1984; see **Advertising slogans** 4:31

Piet Mondrian 1872–1944

Dutch painter

2 The essence of painting has actually always been to make it [the universal] plastically perceptible through colour and line.
'Natural Reality and Abstract Reality' (written 1919)

3 In order to approach the spiritual in art, one employs reality as little as possible . . . This explains logically why primary forms are employed. Since these forms are abstract, an abstract art comes into being.
Sketchbook II (1914)

Jean Monnet 1888–1979

French economist and diplomat; founder of the European Community

4 Europe has never existed. It is not the addition of national sovereignties in a conclave which creates an entity. One must genuinely *create* Europe.
Anthony Sampson *The New Europeans* (1968)

5 I did not understand the politics of Versailles, only the economics.
of the Treaty of Versailles
in an interview in 1971; François Duchêne *Jean Monnet* (1994)

6 Britain did not have to exorcize its history.
Memoirs (1978)

7 We should not create a nation Europe instead of a nation France.
François Duchêne *Jean Monnet* (1994)

Marilyn Monroe 1926–62

American actress
on Monroe: see **Curtis** 83:4, **John** 170:11, **Mailer** 213:3, **Newspaper headlines** 240:5, **Wilder** 338:12; *see also* **Mitterrand** 228:7

when asked if she really had nothing on in a calendar photograph:

8 I had the radio on.
in *Time* 11 August 1952

on being asked what she wore in bed:

9 Chanel No. 5.
Pete Martin *Marilyn Monroe* (1956)

John Montague 1929–

Irish poet and writer

10 To grow
a second tongue, as
harsh a humiliation
as twice to be born.
'A Grafted Tongue' (1972)

11 Like dolmens round my childhood, the old people.
'Like Dolmens Round my Childhood' (1972)

Lord Montgomery of Alamein 1887–1976

British field marshal
on Montgomery: see **Churchill** 68:8

12 *Here* we will stand and fight; there will be no further withdrawal. I have ordered that all plans and instructions dealing with further withdrawal are to be burnt, and at once. We will stand and fight *here*. If we can't stay here alive, then let us stay here dead.
speech in Cairo, 13 August 1942

13 Rule 1, on page 1 of the book of war, is: 'Do not march on Moscow' . . . [Rule 2] is: 'Do not go fighting with your land armies in China.'
speech in the House of Lords, 30 May 1962

14 I have heard some say . . . [homosexual] practices are allowed in France and in other NATO countries. We are not

French, and we are not other nationals.
We are British, thank God!
on the 2nd reading of the Sexual Offences Bill
speech in the House of Lords, 24 May 1965

Monty Python's Flying Circus 1969–74

BBC TV programme, written by Graham Chapman (1941–89), John **Cleese** (1939–), Terry Gilliam (1940–), Eric Idle (1943–), Terry Jones (1942–), and Michael Palin (1943–)
see also **Catch-phrases** 58:2

1 Your wife interested in . . . *photographs?* Eh? Know what I mean—*photographs?* He asked him knowingly . . . nudge nudge, snap snap, grin grin, wink wink, say no more.
Monty Python's Flying Circus (1969)

2 It's *not* pining—it's passed on! This parrot is no more! It has ceased to be! It's expired and gone to meet its maker! This is a late parrot! It's a stiff! Bereft of life it rests in peace—if you hadn't nailed it to the perch it would be pushing up the daisies! It's rung down the curtain and joined the choir invisible! THIS IS AN EX-PARROT!
Monty Python's Flying Circus (1969)

3 Nobody expects the Spanish Inquisition!
Monty Python's Flying Circus (1970)

Henry Moore 1898–1986

English sculptor and draughtsman

4 The first hole made through a piece of stone is a revelation.
in *Listener* 18 August 1937

Jo Moore

British government adviser

5 It is now a very good day to get out anything we want to bury.
email sent in the aftermath of the terrorist action in America, 11 September 2001
in *Daily Telegraph* 10 October 2001; see **Misquotations** 226:7

Marianne Moore 1887–1972

American poet

6 O to be a dragon,
a symbol of the power of Heaven—of silkworm
size or immense; at times invisible.
Felicitous phenomenon!
'O To Be a Dragon' (1959)

7 I, too, dislike it: there are things that are important beyond all this fiddle.
Reading it, however, with a perfect contempt for it, one discovers in it, after all, a place for the genuine.
'Poetry' (1935)

8 Nor till the poets among us can be
'literalists of
the imagination'—above
insolence and triviality and can present
for inspection, imaginary gardens with real toads in them, shall we have
it.
'Poetry' (1935)

9 My father used to say,
'Superior people never make long visits,
have to be shown Longfellow's grave
or the glass flowers at Harvard.'
'Silence' (1935)

Jeanne Moreau 1928–

French actress

10 The rhythm hammers us, hits us and possesses us, making us prisoners of noise. It's like a drug.
of popular music
in *Guardian* 13 August 1997

Larry Morey 1905–71

11 Heigh-ho, heigh-ho,
It's off to work we go.
'Heigh-Ho' (1937 song)

12 Whistle while you work.
title of song (1937)

Rhodri Morgan 1939–

British Labour politician

1 I thought you were the original professor of rotational medicine.

*to Bernard **Ingham**, who was appearing before the Commons public administration select committee*

in *Mail on Sunday* 7 June 1998

2 Nice try, but no deal.

on his party's suggestion that he should stand as deputy to Alun Michael as leader of the new Welsh assembly

in *Mirror* 6 November 1998

3 We cannot allow the culling of First Secretaries to become Wales's own annual blood sport. My number one target as First Secretary is to survive until the half-term recess at the end of this week.

on succeeding Alun Michael as First Secretary for Wales

in *Observer* 20 February 2000

Robin Morgan 1941–

American feminist

4 Sisterhood is powerful.

title of book (1970)

Christopher Morley 1890–1957

American writer

5 Life is a foreign language: all men mispronounce it.

Thunder on the Left (1925)

Bill Morris 1938–

British trade unionist

6 In this foreign land, I do not fear the racist on our street, I fear the words of our politicians—which are sometimes taken by the racists as a licence to attack anyone who does not look or speak like them.

in *Independent* 28 April 2001; see **Hague** 142:12

Desmond Morris 1928–

English anthropologist

7 The city is not a concrete jungle, it is a human zoo.

The Human Zoo (1969) introduction

8 There are one hundred and ninety-three living species of monkeys and apes. One hundred and ninety-two of them are covered with hair. The exception is a naked ape self-named *Homo sapiens*.

The Naked Ape (1967) introduction

Blake Morrison 1950–

British poet and critic

9 Only a culture without hope cannot forgive—a culture that doesn't believe in progress or redemption. Have we so little faith in ourselves we can't accept the possibility of maturation, change, cure?

on the killing of the child James Bulger by two young boys

As If (1997)

Herbert 'Herb' Morrison d. 1989

American radio announcer

10 It's bursting into flames . . . Oh, the humanity, and all the passengers!

eyewitness account of the Hindenburg airship bursting into flames

recorded broadcast, 6 May 1937

11 Listen folks, I'm going to have to stop for a minute, because I've lost my voice—This is the worst thing I've ever witnessed.

eyewitness account of the Hindenburg disaster

recorded broadcast, 6 May 1937

Herbert Morrison 1888–1965

British Labour politician

12 Work is the call. Work at war speed. Good-night—and go to it.

broadcast as Minister of Supply, 22 May 1940

13 Socialism is what the Labour Government does.

attributed

Jim Morrison 1943–71

American rock singer and songwriter

1 C'mon, baby, light my fire.
'Light My Fire' (1967 song, with Robby Krieger)

2 We want the world and we want it now!
'When the Music's Over' (1967 song)

3 I'm interested in anything about revolt, disorder, chaos, especially activity that appears to have no meaning. It seems to me to be the road toward freedom.
in *Time* 24 January 1968

4 When you make your peace with authority, you become an authority.
Andrew Doe and John Tobler *In Their Own Words: The Doors* (1988)

Toni Morrison 1931–

American novelist

5 At some point in life the world's beauty becomes enough. You don't need to photograph, paint or even remember it. It is enough.
Tar Baby (1981)

6 The unending problem of growing old was not how he changed, but how things did.
Tar Baby (1981)

7 There are no 'mixed' marriages. It just looks that way. People don't mix races; they abandon them or pick them.
Tar Baby (1981)

Van Morrison 1945–

Irish singer, songwriter, and musician

8 Music is spiritual. The music business is not.
in *The Times* 6 July 1990

Morrissey 1959–

English singer and songwriter

9 I was looking for a job, and then I found
a job
And heaven knows I'm miserable now.
'Heaven Knows I'm Miserable Now' (1984 song)

Wayne Lyman Morse 1900–74

American Democratic politician

10 I believe that history will record that we have made a great mistake.
in the Senate debate on the Tonkin Gulf Resolution, which committed the United States to intervention in Vietnam; Morse was the only Senator to vote against the resolution
in *Congressional Record* 6–7 August 1964

Owen Morshead 1893–1977

English librarian

11 The House of Hanover, like ducks, produce bad parents—they trample on their young.
as Royal Librarian, in conversation with Harold ***Nicolson****, biographer of* ***George V***
Harold Nicolson, letter to Vita Sackville-West, 7 January 1949

John Mortimer 1923–

English novelist, barrister, and dramatist

12 No power on earth, however, can abolish the merciless class distinction between those who are physically desirable and the lonely, pallid, spotted, silent, unfancied majority.
Clinging to the Wreckage (1982)

13 At school I never minded the lessons. I just resented having to work terribly hard at playing.
A Voyage Round My Father (1971)

14 The worst fault of the working classes is telling their children they're not going to succeed, saying: 'There is life, but it's not for you.'
in *Daily Mail* 31 May 1988

J. B. Morton ('Beachcomber') 1893–1975

British journalist

15 Hush, hush,
Nobody cares!
Christopher Robin
Has
Fallen

Down-
Stairs.

By the Way (1931); see **Milne** 225:11

1 Dr Strabismus (Whom God Preserve) of Utrecht has patented a new invention. It is an illuminated trouser-clip for bicyclists who are using main roads at night.

Morton's Folly (1933)

Jelly Roll Morton 1885–1941

American jazz pianist, composer, and bandleader

2 Jazz music is to be played sweet, soft, plenty rhythm.

Mister Jelly Roll (1950)

Rogers Morton 1914–79

American public relations officer

3 I'm not going to rearrange the furniture on the deck of the Titanic.

having lost five of the last six primaries as President ***Ford****'s campaign manager*

in *Washington Post* 16 May 1976

Edwin Moses 1955–

American athlete

4 I don't really see the hurdles. I sense them like a memory.

attributed

Oswald Mosley 1896–1980

British politician and Fascist leader

5 I am not, and never have been, a man of the right. My position was on the left and is now in the centre of politics.

letter to *The Times* 26 April 1968

Kate Moss 1974–

British model

6 It's a sin to be tired.

on life in the world of fashion

in *The Times* 17 February 2001

Andrew Motion 1952–

English poet

7 Beside the river, swerving under ground.
your future tracked you, snapping at
your heels:
Diana, breathless, hunted by your own
quick hounds.

'Mythology' (1997)

Earl Mountbatten of Burma 1900–79

British sailor, soldier, and statesman

on Mountbatten: see **Ziegler** 350:9

8 Right, now I understand people think you're the Forgotten Army on the Forgotten Front. I've come here to tell you you're quite wrong. You're not the Forgotten Army on the Forgotten Front. No, make no mistake about it. Nobody's ever *heard* of you.

encouragement to troops when taking over as Supreme Allied Commander South-East Asia in late 1943

R. Hough *Mountbatten* (1980)

Marjorie ('Mo') Mowlam 1949–

British Labour politician

9 It takes courage to push things forward.

on her decision to visit Loyalist prisoners in The Maze

in *Guardian* 8 January 1998

Daniel P. Moynihan 1927–

American Democratic politician

10 Welfare became a term of opprobrium—a contentious, often vindictive area of political conflict in which liberals and conservatives clashed and children were lost sight of.

in *The Washington Post* 25 November 1994

Lord Moynihan 1865–1936

British surgeon

11 Lord Dawson of Penn
Has killed lots of men.

So that's why we sing
God save the King.
Kenneth Rose *King George V* (1983)

Robert Mugabe 1924–

African statesman; Prime Minister of Zimbabwe, 1980–7, President since 1987

1 Cricket civilizes people and creates good gentlemen. I want everyone to play cricket in Zimbabwe; I want ours to be a nation of gentlemen.
in *Sunday Times* 26 February 1984

2 Our present state of mind is that you are now our enemies.
to white farmers in Zimbabwe
television broadcast, 18 April 2000

Kitty Muggeridge

British wife of Malcolm **Muggeridge**

3 David Frost has risen without trace.
said c.1965 to Malcolm Muggeridge

Malcolm Muggeridge 1903–90

British journalist; husband of Kitty **Muggeridge**

4 Something beautiful for God.
title of book (1971); see **Teresa** 315:6

5 The orgasm has replaced the Cross as the focus of longing and the image of fulfilment.
Tread Softly (1966)

6 He was not only a bore; he bored for England.
of Anthony ***Eden***
Tread Softly (1966)

7 On television I feel like a man playing a piano in a brothel; every now and again he solaces himself by playing 'Abide with Me' in the hope of edifying both the clients and the inmates.
interview on *Parkinson*, BBC1 TV, 23 September 1972

Edwin Muir 1887–1959

Scottish poet

8 And without fear the lawless roads
Ran wrong through all the land.
'Hölderlin's Journey' (1937)

9 Barely a twelvemonth after
The seven days war that put the world to sleep,
Late in the evening the strange horses came.
'The Horses' (1956)

Frank Muir 1920–98

English writer and broadcaster

10 The thinking man's crumpet.
of Joan ***Bakewell***
attributed

Paul Muldoon 1951–

Irish poet

11 I thought of you tonight, *a leanbh*, lying there in your long barrow,
colder and dumber than a fish by Francisco de Herrera.
'Incantata' (1994)

12 The Volkswagen parked in the gap,
But gently ticking over.
You wonder if it's lovers
And not men hurrying back
Across two fields and a river.
'Ireland' (1980)

H. J. Muller 1890–1967

American geneticist

13 To say, for example, that a man is made up of certain chemical elements is a satisfactory description only for those who intend to use him as a fertilizer.
Science and Criticism (1943)

Herbert J. Muller 1905–

American writer

14 Few have heard of Fra Luca Pacioli, the inventor of double-entry book-keeping; but he has probably had much more influence on human life than has Dante or Michelangelo.

Uses of the Past (1957)

Lewis Mumford 1895-

American sociologist

1 Every generation revolts against its fathers and makes friends with its grandfathers.

The Brown Decades (1931)

2 Our national flower is the concrete cloverleaf.

in *Quote Magazine* 8 October 1961

Alice Munro 1931-

Canadian writer

3 Moments of kindness and reconciliation are worth having, even if the parting has to come sooner or later.

The Progress of Love (1986)

4 Any woman who tells the truth about herself is a feminist.

in *Toronto Star* 6 May 1979; attributed

Iris Murdoch 1919-99

English novelist

on Murdoch: see **Bayley** 25:3

5 Dora Greenfield left her husband because she was afraid of him. She decided six months later to return to him for the same reason.

The Bell (1958)

6 All our failures are ultimately failures in love.

The Bell (1958)

7 The chief requirement of the good life, is to live without any image of oneself.

The Bell (1958)

8 Only in our virtues are we original, because virtue is difficult . . . Vices are general, virtues are particular.

Nuns and Soldiers (1980)

9 One doesn't have to get anywhere in a marriage. It's not a public conveyance.

A Severed Head (1961)

10 Love is the extremely difficult realisation that something other than oneself is real. Love, and so art and morals, is the discovery of reality.

'The Sublime and the Good' in *Chicago Review* 13 (1959)

11 I'm just wandering, I think of things and then they go away for ever.

in September 1996 on her inability to write; the following February it was announced that she was suffering from Alzheimer's disease

in *Times* 5 February 1997

Rupert Murdoch 1931-

Australian-born American publisher and media entrepeneur

asked why he had allowed Page 3 to develop:

12 I don't know. The editor did it when I was away.

in *Guardian* 25 February 1994

13 I'd say our newspapers paid far too much for them.

of buying paparazzi pictures

in *Daily Telegraph* 8 October 1997

Les Murray 1938-

Australian poet

14 In a place where 'please' is pronounced 'I
s'pose you couldn't'
it is rare to meet with any belief in help.

The Boys Who Stole the Funeral (1989)

15 Nothing's said till it's dreamed out in
words
And nothing's true that figures in words
only.

The Daylight Moon (1987) 'Poetry and Religion'

16 Men must have legends, else they will die
of strangeness.

The Ilex Tree (1965) 'The Noonday Axeman'

17 Waiting for the Australian republic is like waiting for the other shoe to drop. We all know it is coming; according to one's convictions, the waiting is therefore either a sour and uncreative delaying operation or a sort of null interregnum in which all energies are frustrated.

'The Coming Republic' in *Quadrant* April 1976

Ed Murrow 1908–65

American broadcaster and journalist

1 No one can terrorize a whole nation, unless we are all his accomplices.

of Joseph ***McCarthy***

'See It Now', broadcast, 7 March 1954

2 He mobilized the English language and sent it into battle to steady his fellow countrymen and hearten those Europeans upon whom the long dark night of tyranny had descended.

of Winston ***Churchill***

broadcast, 30 November 1954; *In Search of Light* (1967)

3 Anyone who isn't confused doesn't really understand the situation.

on the Vietnam War

Walter Bryan *The Improbable Irish* (1969)

Benito Mussolini 1883–1945

Italian Fascist dictator

on Mussolini: see **Taylor** 313:14

4 We must leave exactly on time . . . From now on everything must function to perfection.

to a station-master

Giorgio Pini *Mussolini* (1939); see Infanta Eulalia of Spain *Courts and Countries after the War* (1925): 'The first benefit of Benito Mussolini's direction in Italy begins to be felt when one crosses the Italian Frontier and hears "*Il treno arriva all'orario* [the train is arriving on time]" '

A. J. Muste 1885–1967

American pacifist

5 If I can't love Hitler, I can't love at all.

at a Quaker meeting 1940; in *New York Times* 12 February 1967

6 There is no way to peace. Peace is the way.

in *New York Times* 16 November 1967

Vladimir Nabokov 1899–1977

Russian novelist

see also **Opening lines** 247:12

7 You can always count on a murderer for a fancy prose style.

Lolita (1955)

8 Life is a great surprise. I do not see why death should not be an even greater one.

Pale Fire (1962)

9 The cradle rocks above an abyss, and common sense tells us that our existence is but a brief crack of light between two eternities of darkness.

Speak, Memory (1951)

10 That life-quickening atmosphere of a big railway station where everything is something trembling on the brink of something else.

Spring in Fialta and other stories (1956) 'Spring in Fialta'

Ralph Nader 1934–

American consumer protectionist

on Nader: see **Vidal** 328:11

11 Unsafe at any speed.

title of book (1965); the phrase was used earlier by John **Keats** in *The Insolent Chariots* (1958)

12 Only Al Gore can beat Al Gore. And he's been doing a pretty good job of that.

responding to claims that his candidacy could split the liberal vote and cost Gore the election

in *Newsweek* 6 November 2000

Sarojini Naidu 1879–1949

Indian politician

13 If only Bapu knew the cost of setting him up in poverty!

of ***Gandhi***

A. Campbell-Johnson *Mission with Mountbatten* (1951)

Shiva Naipaul 1945–85

Trinidadian writer

14 Hopeless doomed continent! Only lies flourished here. Africa was swaddled in lies—the lies of an aborted European

civilisation; the lies of liberation. Nothing but lies.

North of South (1978)

1 The Third World is an artificial construction of the West—an ideological empire on which the sun is always setting.

An Unfinished Journey (1986)

Tom Nairn

Scottish writer

2 As far as I am concerned, Scotland will be reborn when the last minister is strangled with the last copy of the *Sunday Post*.

'The Dreams of Scottish Nationalism'; Karl Miller (ed.) *Memoirs of a Modern Scotland* (1970)

Fridtjof Nansen 1861–1930

Norwegian polar explorer

3 Never stop because you are afraid—you are never so likely to be wrong. Never keep a line of retreat: it is a wretched invention. The difficult is what takes a little time; the impossible is what takes a little longer.

in *Listener* 14 December 1939; see **Sayings** 289:12

Ogden Nash 1902–71

American humorist

4 The turtle lives 'twixt plated decks
Which practically conceal its sex.
I think it clever of the turtle
In such a fix to be so fertile.

'Autres Bêtes, Autres Moeurs' (1931)

5 A bit of talcum
Is always walcum.

'The Baby' (1931)

6 The cow is of the bovine ilk;
One end is moo, the other, milk.

'The Cow' (1931)

7 A door is what a dog is perpetually on the wrong side of.

'A Dog's Best Friend is his Illiteracy' (1953)

8 Let us pause to consider the English,
Who when they pause to consider themselves they get all reticently thrilled and tinglish,
Because every Englishman is convinced of one thing, viz.:
That to be an Englishman is to belong to the most exclusive club there is.

'England Expects' (1938)

9 One would be in less danger
From the wiles of the stranger
If one's own kin and kith
Were more fun to be with.

'Family Court' (1931)

10 Parsley
Is gharsley.

'Further Reflections on Parsley' (1942)

11 I believe a little incompatibility is the spice of life, particularly if he has income and she is pattable.

'I Do, I Will, I Have' (1949)

12 The trouble with a kitten is
THAT
Eventually it becomes a
CAT.

'The Kitten' (1940)

13 Beneath this slab
John Brown is stowed.
He watched the ads,
And not the road.

'Lather as You Go' (1942)

14 Do you think my mind is maturing late,
Or simply rotted early?

'Lines on Facing Forty' (1942)

15 Good wine needs no bush,
And perhaps products that people really want need no hard-sell or soft-sell TV push.
Why not?
Look at pot.

'Most Doctors Recommend or Yours For Fast, Fast, Fast Relief' (1972)

16 Children aren't happy with nothing to ignore,
And that's what parents were created for.

'The Parent' (1933)

17 He tells you when you've got on too much lipstick,
And helps you with your girdle when your hips stick.

'The Perfect Husband' (1949)

1 Any kiddie in school can love like a fool,
But hating, my boy, is an art.
'Plea for Less Malice Toward None' (1933)

2 Candy
Is dandy
But liquor
Is quicker.
'Reflections on Ice-breaking' (1931)

3 I test my bath before I sit,
And I'm always moved to wonderment
That what chills the finger not a bit
Is so frigid upon the fundament.
'Samson Agonistes' (1942)

4 I think that I shall never see
A billboard lovely as a tree.
Perhaps, unless the billboards fall,
I'll never see a tree at all.
'Song of the Open Road' (1933); see **Kilmer** 180:10

5 Sure, deck your lower limbs in pants;
Yours are the limbs, my sweeting.
You look divine as you advance—
Have you seen yourself retreating?
'What's the Use?' (1940)

6 Life is not having been told that the man has just waxed the floor.
'You and Me and P. B. Shelley' (1942)

Terry Nation

see **Catch-phrases** 58:18

Robert J. Natter 1945–

American admiral, Commander of the US Atlantic Fleet

7 We have been attacked like we haven't since Pearl Harbor.
after terrorist attacks destroyed the World Trade Center in New York, and damaged the Pentagon, 11 September 2001
in *Times* 12 September 2001

James Ball Naylor 1860–1945

8 King David and King Solomon
Led merry, merry lives,
With many, many lady friends,
And many, many wives;
But when old age crept over them—
With many, many qualms!—
King Solomon wrote the Proverbs
And King David wrote the Psalms.
'King David and King Solomon' (1935)

Jawaharlal Nehru 1889–1964

Indian statesman, Prime Minister 1947–64

9 There is no easy walk-over to freedom anywhere, and many of us will have to pass through the valley of the shadow again and again before we reach the mountain-tops of our desire.
'From Lucknow to Tripuri' (1939)

10 At the stroke of the midnight hour, while the world sleeps, India will awake to life and freedom.
immediately prior to Independence
speech to the Indian Constituent Assembly, 14 August 1947

11 The light has gone out of our lives and there is darkness everywhere.
*following **Gandhi**'s assassination*
broadcast, 30 January 1948

12 I may lose many things including my temper, but I do not lose my nerve.
at a press conference in Delhi, 4 June 1958

A. S. Neill 1883–1973

Scottish teacher and educationist

13 If we have to have an exam at 11, let us make it one for humour, sincerity, imagination, character—and where is the examiner who could test such qualities.
letter to *Daily Telegraph* 1957; in *Daily Telegraph* 25 September 1973

Howard Nemerov 1920–91

American poet and novelist

14 praise without end the go-ahead zeal
of whoever it was invented the wheel;
but never a word for the poor soul's sake
that thought ahead, and invented the brake.
'To the Congress of the United States, Entering Its Third Century' 26 February 1989

Pablo Neruda 1904–73

Chilean poet

1 Forgive me.
If you are not living,
If you, beloved, my love,
If you have died
All the leaves will fall on my breast
It will rain on my soul, all night, all day
My feet will want to march to where you are sleeping
But I shall go on living.

'The Dead Woman'

2 Night, snow, and sand make up the form of my thin country,
all silence lies in its long line,
all foam flows from its marine beard,
all coal covers it with mysterious kisses.

'Discoverers of Chile' (1950)

3 I have gone marking the blank atlas of your body
with crosses of fire.
My mouth went across: a spider, trying to hide.
In you, behind you, timid, driven by thirst.

'I Have Gone Marking' (1924), translated 1969 by W. S. Merwin

4 The typewriter separated me from a deeper intimacy with poetry, and my hand brought me closer to that intimacy again.

in *Writers at Work* (5th series, 1981)

Edith Nesbit 1858–1924

English novelist and children's writer

5 The affection you get back from children is sixpence given as change for a sovereign.

Julia Briggs *A Woman of Passion* (1987)

Susan Ness

American Federal Communications Commissioner

6 You've got approval.

mimicking AOL's YOU'VE GOT MAIL *message when giving final approval for the company's merger with Time-Warner*

in *Newsweek* 22 January 2001

John von Neumann 1903–57

Hungarian-born American mathematician and computer pioneer

7 In mathematics you don't understand things. You just get used to them.

Gary Zukav *The Dancing Wu Li Masters* (1979)

Allan Nevins 1890–1971

American historian

8 The former Allies had blundered in the past by offering Germany too little, and offering even that too late.

in *Current History* (New York) May 1935

Anthony Newley 1931–

English singer, songwriter, and actor

and Leslie Bricusse 1931–

English songwriter and composer

9 Stop the world, I want to get off.

title of musical (1961)

■ Newspaper headlines and leaders

see box overleaf

see also **Cockburn** 72:9

Huey Newton 1942–

American political activist

10 I suggested [in 1966] that we use the panther as our symbol and call our political vehicle the Black Panther Party. The panther is a fierce animal, but he will not attack until he is backed into a corner; then he will strike out.

Revolutionary Suicide (1973)

Chester Nez

American Navajo Indian

11 Back in the '20s and '30s, we were told 'Don't speak Navajo.' . . . Then Uncle

▸▸

Newspaper headlines and leaders

1 Believe it or not.

title of syndicated newspaper feature (from 1918), written by Robert L. Ripley (1893–1949)

2 Bush Wins It.

original headline in the Miami Herald *for 8 November 2000; changed in final edition to 'It's Not Over Yet'*

in *Daily Telegraph* 9 November 2000

3 Crisis? What Crisis?

summarizing an interview with James ***Callaghan***

headline in *Sun*, 11 January 1979; see **Misquotations** 226:3

4 Dewey defeats Truman.

anticipating the result of the Presidential election, which ***Truman*** *won against expectation*

in *Chicago Tribune* 3 November 1948

5 Egghead weds hourglass.

on the marriage of Arthur ***Miller*** *and Marilyn* ***Monroe***

headline in *Variety* 1956; attributed

6 The filth and the fury.

following a notorious interview with the Sex Pistols broadcast live on Thames Television

headline in *Daily Mirror*, 2 December 1976

7 Freddie Starr ate my hamster.

headline in *Sun* 13 March 1986

8 GOTCHA!

on the sinking of the General Belgrano

headline in *Sun* 4 May 1982

9 If Kinnock wins today will the last person to leave Britain please turn out the lights.

on election day, showing Neil Kinnock's head inside a light bulb

headline in *Sun* 9 April 1992

10 It *is* a moral issue.

leader following the resignation of Profumo

in *The Times* 11 June 1963; see **Hailsham** 143:5, **Macmillan** 211:2

11 It's that man again . . . ! At the head of a cavalcade of seven black motor cars Hitler swept out of his Berlin Chancellery last night on a mystery journey.

the acronym ITMA became the title of a BBC radio show, from September 1939 (see individual entries at **Catch-phrases***)*

headline in *Daily Express* 2 May 1939

12 It's The Sun Wot Won It.

following the 1992 general election

headline in *Sun* 11 April 1992

13 King's Moll Reno'd in Wolsey's Home Town.

on Wallis Simpson's divorce proceedings in Ipswich

US newspaper headline; F. Donaldson *Edward VIII* (1974)

14 Named Shamed.

headline announcing a campaign to publish names and addresses said to identify convicted paedophiles

in *News of the World* 23 July 2000

15 Only a sentence, but what a sentence!

on Prince Charles' speech referring to the Falklands

in *La Nación* (Buenos Aires) 11 March 1999

16 Outside the G.O.P.'s big tent, hoping he's let back in.

of the former Republican Robert C. Smith, whose independent campaign for the presidential nomination had failed; G.O.P. = 'Grand Old Party'

headline in *New York Times* 1 November 1999; see **Political sayings and slogans** 261:7

17 Sawdust Caesars: Mods v. Rockers battles flare again.

Daily Express 19 May 1964

18 Sticks nix hick pix.

on the lack of enthusiasm for farm dramas among rural populations

headline in *Variety* 17 July 1935

19 The Sun backs Blair.

the day after the announcement of the general election

headline in *Sun* 18 March 1997

▶

▸ Newspaper headlines and leaders continued

1 Wall St. lays an egg.
on the Wall St. crash
headline in *Variety* 30 October 1929

2 Who breaks a butterfly on a wheel?
defending Mick ***Jagger*** *after his arrest for cannabis possession*
leader in *The Times* 1 June 1967, written by William Rees-Mogg; see below

Who breaks a butterfly upon a wheel?
Alexander Pope (1688–1744) 'An Epistle to Dr Arbuthnot' (1735)

3 Whose finger do you want on the trigger?
referring to the atom bomb
in *Daily Mirror* 21 September 1951

4 Winter of discontent.
headline in *Sun* 30 April 1979; see below; see **Callaghan** 51:5

Now is the winter of our discontent
Made glorious summer by this sun of York.
William Shakespeare (1564–1616) *Richard III* (1591)

▸▸ Chester Nez

Sam came along and told us to use our language in World War II.
one of the 29 'Navajo Code Talkers', who constructed an unbreakable code from the Navajo language to use against the Japanese in the Pacific
in *Los Angeles Times* 26 July 2001

Nancy Nicholson *d.* 1977

daughter of English artist William Nicholson

5 God is a man, so it must be all rot.
reading the marriage service for the first time, on the morning of her wedding to Robert ***Graves***
R. Graves *Goodbye to All That* (1929)

Norman Nicholson 1914–87

British poet and writer

6 Flowers are for wrapping in cellophane to present as a bouquet;
Flowers are for prize arrangements in vases and silver tea-pots;
Flowers are for plaiting into funeral wreaths.
You can keep your flowers.
Give me weeds.
'Weeds' (1981)

Vivian Nicholson 1936–

British pools winner

7 I want to spend, and spend, and spend.
said to reporters on arriving to collect her husband's football pools winnings of £152,000
in *Daily Herald* 28 September 1961

Harold Nicolson 1886–1968

English diplomat, politician, and writer; husband of Vita **Sackville-West** and father of Nigel **Nicolson**

8 To be a good diarist one must have a little snouty, sneaky mind.
diary, 9 November 1947

9 I do not think it is quite fair to say that the British businessman has trampled on the faces of the poor. But he has sometimes not been very careful where he put his feet.
replying to a heckler in the North Croydon by-election, 1948
Nigel Nicolson (ed.) *Diaries and Letters of Harold Nicolson 1945–1962* vol. 3 (1968)

10 For seventeen years he did nothing at all but kill animals and stick in stamps.
of King ***George V***
diary, 17 August 1949

11 Suez—a smash and grab raid that was all smash and no grab.
in conversation with Antony Jay, November 1956; see also letter to Vita Sackville-West, 8 November 1956, 'Our smash-and-grab raid got stuck at the smash'

Nigel Nicolson 1917–

British Conservative politician and writer; son of Harold **Nicolson**

1 One final tip to rebels: always have a second profession in reserve.

on the Maastricht Treaty vote in the House of Commons, having lost his own seat after abstaining on the Suez Crisis in 1956

in *The Spectator* 7 November 1992

Reinhold Niebuhr 1892–1971

American theologian

2 Man's capacity for justice makes democracy possible, but man's inclination to injustice makes democracy necessary.

Children of Light and Children of Darkness (1944)

3 Our gadget-filled paradise suspended in a hell of international insecurity.

Pious and Secular America (1957)

4 God, give us the serenity to accept what cannot be changed;
Give us the courage to change what should be changed;
Give us the wisdom to distinguish one from the other.

prayer said to have been first published in 1951

Richard Wightman Fox *Reinhold Niebuhr* (1985)

Martin Niemöller 1892–1984

German theologian

5 Ask the first man you meet what he means by defending freedom, and he'll tell you privately he means defending the standard of living.

address at Augsburg, January 1958; James Bentley *Martin Niemöller* (1984)

6 In Germany they came first for the Communists, and I didn't speak up because I wasn't a Communist; and then they came for the trade unionists, and I didn't speak up because I wasn't a trade unionist; and then they came for the Jews, and I didn't speak up because I wasn't a Jew; and then . . . they came for me . . . and by that time there was no-one left to speak up.

quoted in many versions since the Second World War; this version was approved by Niemöller as the original (in *'Quote Unquote' Newsletter* April 2001)

Richard Nixon 1913–94

American Republican statesman, 37th President of the US, 1969–74

on Nixon: see **Abzug** 1:4, **Political sayings and slogans** 262:7, **Stevenson** 308:10, 308:13, **Ziegler** 350:10

7 She's pink right down to her underwear.

in 1950, accusing Helen Gahagan Douglas, his opponent for a Senate seat, of Communist sympathies

Stephen E. Ambrose *Nixon: The Education of a Politician* (1987); see **Roosevelt** 277:11

8 You won't have Nixon to kick around any more because, gentlemen, this is my last press conference.

after losing the election for Governor of California

to the press, 5 November 1962

9 This is the greatest week in the history of the world since the Creation.

welcoming the return of the first men to land on the moon

speech 24 July 1969

10 The great silent majority.

broadcast, 3 November 1969

11 There can be no whitewash at the White House.

on Watergate

television speech 30 April 1973

12 People have got to know whether or not their President is a crook. Well, I'm not a crook.

speech, 17 November 1973

13 I brought myself down. I gave them a sword. And they stuck it in.

television interview, 19 May 1977; David Frost *I Gave Them a Sword* (1978)

14 When the President does it, that means that it is not illegal.

David Frost *I Gave Them a Sword* (1978)

Kwame Nkrumah 1900–72

Ghanaian statesman, Prime Minister 1957–60, President 1960–6

1 Freedom is not something that one people can bestow on another as a gift. They claim it as their own and none can keep it from them.

speech in Accra, 10 July 1953

2 We face neither East nor West: we face forward.

conference speech, Accra, 7 April 1960; *Axioms of Kwame Nkrumah* (1967)

Christopher Nolan 1965–

Irish writer

3 My real motive is to describe how my brain-damaged life is as normal for me as my friends' able-bodied life is to them. My mind is just like a spin-dryer at full speed; my thoughts fly around my skull while millions of beautiful words cascade down into my lap. Images gunfire across my consciousness and while trying to discipline them I jump in awe at the soulfilled bounty of my mind's expanse. Try then to imagine how frustrating it is to give expression to that avalanche in efforts of one great nod after the other.

of his reasons for writing The Eye of the Clock

in *Observer* 8 November 1987

Steven Norris 1945–

British Conservative politician

4 You have your own company, your own temperature control, your own music—and don't have to put up with dreadful human beings sitting alongside you.

on cars compared to public transport

comment to Commons Environment Select Committee, in *Daily Telegraph* 9 February 1995

Lord Northcliffe 1865–1922

British newspaper proprietor

5 The power of the press is very great, but not so great as the power of suppress.

office message, *Daily Mail* 1918; R. Rose and G. Harmsworth *Northcliffe* (1959)

6 When I want a peerage, I shall buy it like an honest man.

Tom Driberg *Swaff* (1974)

Lord Nuffield 1877–1963

British motor manufacturer and philanthropist

on seeing the Morris Minor prototype in 1945:

7 It looks like a poached egg—we can't make that.

attributed

Sam Nunn 1938–

American Democratic politician

8 Don't ask, don't tell.

summary of the **Clinton** *administration's compromise policy on homosexuals serving in the armed forces*

in *New York Times* 12 May 1993

Simon Nye 1958–

British writer

9 Twenty years ago when we had no respect for women they just used to say, 'You're chucked.' And now we do respect them we have to lie to them sensitively.

Men Behaving Badly (ITV, series 1, 1992) 'Intruders'

10 GARY: She put me right on a few technical details, yes.
DERMOT: She said it was like sleeping with a badly-informed labrador.

Men Behaving Badly (ITV, series 1, 1992) 'Intruders'

Julius Nyerere 1922–99

Tanzanian statesman, President of Tanganyika 1962–4 and of Tanzania 1964–85

11 Should we really let our people starve so we can pay our debts?

in *Guardian* 21 March 1985

Lawrence Oates

see **Last words** 190:6

Conor Cruise O'Brien 1917–

Irish politician, writer, and journalist

1 If I saw Mr Haughey buried at midnight at a crossroads, with a stake driven through his heart—politically speaking—I should continue to wear a clove of garlic round my neck, just in case.

in *Observer* 10 October 1982

Edna O'Brien 1936–

Irish novelist and short-story writer

2 August is a wicked month.

title of novel (1965)

Flann O'Brien 1911–66

Irish novelist and journalist

3 The conclusion of your syllogism, I said lightly, is fallacious, being based upon licensed premises.

At Swim-Two-Birds (1939)

4 A pint of plain is your only man.

At Swim-Two-Birds (1939)

5 Waiting for the German verb is surely the ultimate thrill.

The Hair of the Dogma (1977)

Sean O'Casey 1880–1964

Irish dramatist

6 I killin' meself workin', an' he sthruttin' about from mornin' till night like a paycock!

Juno and the Paycock (1925)

7 He's an oul' butty o' mine—oh, he's a darlin' man, a daarlin' man.

Juno and the Paycock (1925)

8 The whole worl's in a state o' chassis!

Juno and the Paycock (1925)

9 It's my rule never to lose me temper till it would be dethrimental to keep it.

The Plough and the Stars (1926)

10 English literature's performing flea.

of P. G. ***Wodehouse***

P. G. Wodehouse *Performing Flea* (1953)

Bernard O'Donoghue 1945–

Irish poet and academic

11 We were terribly lucky to catch
The Ceauşescus' execution, being
By sheer chance that Christmas Day
In the only house for twenty miles
With satellite TV. We sat,
Cradling brandies, by the fire
Watching those two small, cranky autocrats
Lying in snow against a blood-spattered wall,
Hardly able to believe our good fortune.

'Carolling' (1995)

12 The reporter told us how
The cross woman's peasant origins
Came out at the last, shouting
At her executioners 'I have been
A mother to you and this is how
You thank me for it.'

'Carolling' (1995)

■ Official advice

see box opposite

David Ogilvy 1911–99

British-born advertising executive

13 The consumer isn't a moron; she is your wife.

Confessions of an Advertising Man (1963)

John O'Hara 1905–70

American writer

14 George [Gershwin] died on July 11, 1937, but I don't have to believe that if I don't want to.

in *Newsweek* 15 July 1940

15 An artist is his own fault.

The Portable F. Scott Fitzgerald (1945) introduction

Abraham Okpik *d.* 1997

Canadian Inuit spokesman

16 There are very few Eskimos, but millions of Whites, just like mosquitoes. It is

▸▸

Official advice

1 Careless talk costs lives.
wartime security slogan, 1940s

2 Clunk, click, every trip.
road safety campaign promoting the use of seat-belts, 1971

3 Coughs and sneezes spread diseases. Trap the germs in your handkerchief.
Second World War health slogan, 1942

4 Dig for victory.
radio broadcast by Reginald Dorman-Smith (1899–1977), Minister for Agriculture, 3 October 1939

5 Don't ask a man to drink and drive.
UK road safety slogan, from 1964

6 Don't die of ignorance.
Aids publicity campaign, 1987

7 Duck and cover.
US advice in the event of a missile attack, c.1950; associated particularly with children's cartoon character 'Bert the Turtle'

8 Is your journey *really* necessary?
slogan coined to discourage Civil Servants from going home for Christmas, 1939

9 Just say no.
motto of the Nancy Reagan Drug Abuse Fund, founded 1985

10 Keep Britain tidy.
issued by the Central Office of Information, 1950s

11 Make do and mend.
wartime slogan, 1940s

12 Slip, slop, slap.
sun protection slogan, meaning slip *on a T-shirt,* slop *on some suncream,* slap *on a hat*
Australian health education programme, 1980s

13 Smoking can seriously damage your health.
government health warning now required by British law to be printed on cigarette packets
from early 1970s, in form 'Smoking can damage your health'

14 Stop-look-and-listen.
road safety slogan, current in the US from 1912

15 *Taisez-vous! Méfiez-vous! Les oreilles ennemies vous écoutent.*
Keep your mouth shut! Be on your guard! Enemy ears are listening to you.
official notice in France, 1915

16 Whenever possible, remember that you are still free and that there is still beauty in the world. It's OK to smile.
flier distributed by the American Red Cross to survivors in the week following the destruction of the World Trade Center, 11 September 2001

▸▸ Abraham Okpik continued

something very special and wonderful to be an Eskimo—they are like the snow geese. If an Eskimo forgets his language and Eskimo ways, he will be nothing but just another mosquito.
attributed, 1966

Bruce Oldfield 1950–

English fashion designer

17 Fashion is more usually a gentle progression of revisited ideas.
in *Independent* 9 September 1989

Laurence Olivier 1907–89

English actor and director

18 The tragedy of a man who could not make up his mind.
introduction to his 1948 screen adaptation of *Hamlet*

19 Shakespeare—the nearest thing in incarnation to the eye of God.
in *Kenneth Harris Talking To* (1971) 'Sir Laurence Olivier'

20 Acting is a masochistic form of exhibitionism. It is not quite the occupation of an adult.
in *Time* 3 July 1978

Jacqueline Kennedy Onassis 1929–94

wife of John Fitzgerald **Kennedy**, First Lady of the US 1961–3

1 The one thing I do not want to be called is First Lady. It sounds like a saddle horse.
Peter Colier and David Horowitz *The Kennedys* (1984)

2 There'll be great Presidents again—and the Johnsons are wonderful, they've been wonderful to me—but there'll never be another Camelot again.
in *Life* 6 December 1963; see **Lerner** 196:15

Michael Ondaatje 1943–

Canadian writer

3 The heart is an organ of fire.
The English Patient (1992)

4 We die containing a richness of lovers and tribes, tastes we have swallowed, bodies we have plunged into and swum up as if rivers of wisdom, characters we have climbed into as if trees, fears we have hidden as if in caves.
The English Patient (1992)

Eugene O'Neill 1888–1953

American dramatist

5 For de little stealin' dey gits you in jail soon or late. For de big stealin' dey makes you Emperor and puts you in de Hall o' Fame when you croaks.
The Emperor Jones (1921)

6 The iceman cometh.
title of play (1946)

7 A long day's journey into night.
title of play (written 1940–1)

8 Mourning becomes Electra
title of play (1931)

9 The sea hates a coward!
Mourning becomes Electra (1931)

10 What beastly incidents our memories insist on cherishing! . . . the ugly and disgusting . . . the beautiful things we have to keep diaries to remember!
Strange Interlude (1928)

11 The only living life is in the past and future . . . the present is an interlude . . . strange interlude in which we call on past and future to bear witness we are living.
Strange Interlude (1928)

Paul O'Neill 1935–

American businessman and Republican politician, Treasury Secretary from 2001

12 If you set aside Three Mile Island and Chernobyl, the safety record of nuclear is really very good.
in *Wall Street Journal* 25 May 2001

Yoko Ono 1933–

Japanese poet and songwriter

13 Woman is the nigger of the world.
interview for *Nova* magazine (1968); adopted by her husband John **Lennon** as song title (1972)

■ Opening lines

see box opposite

J. Robert Oppenheimer 1904–67

American physicist

14 I remembered the line from the Hindu scripture, the *Bhagavad Gita* . . . 'I am become death, the destroyer of worlds.'
on the explosion of the first atomic bomb near Alamogordo, New Mexico, 16 July 1945
Len Giovannitti and Fred Freed *The Decision to Drop the Bomb* (1965)

15 The physicists have known sin; and this is a knowledge which they cannot lose.
lecture at Massachusetts Institute of Technology, 25 November 1947

16 When you see something that is technically sweet, you go ahead and do it and you argue about what to do about it only after you have had your technical success. That is the way it was with the atomic bomb.
in *In the Matter of J. Robert Oppenheimer, USAEC Transcript of Hearing Before Personnel Security Board* (1954)

Opening lines

1 At the age of fifteen my grandmother became the concubine of a warlord general.

Jung Chang *Wild Swans* (1991)

2 *Aujourd'hui, maman est morte. Ou peut-être hier, je ne sais pas.*

Mother died today. Or perhaps it was yesterday, I don't know.

Albert **Camus** *L'Étranger* (1944)

3 If I am out of my mind, it's all right with me, thought Moses Herzog.

Saul **Bellow** *Herzog* (1961)

4 If I should die, think only this of me:
That there's some corner of a foreign field
That is for ever England.

Rupert **Brooke** 'The Soldier' (1914)

5 In a hole in the ground there lived a hobbit.

J. R. R. **Tolkien** *The Hobbit* (1937)

6 In my beginning is my end.

T. S. **Eliot** *Four Quartets* 'East Coker' (1940)

7 'Is there anybody there?' said the Traveller,
Knocking on the moonlit door.

Walter **de la Mare** 'The Listener' (1912)

8 It was a bright cold day in April, and the clocks were striking thirteen.

George **Orwell** *Nineteen Eighty-Four* (1949)

9 It was not until several weeks after he had decided to murder his wife that Dr Bickleigh took any active steps in the matter. Murder is a serious business.

Francis Iles *Malice Aforethought* (1931)

10 It was the afternoon of my eighty-first birthday, and I was in bed with my catamite when Ali announced that the archbishop had come to see me.

Anthony **Burgess** *Earthly Powers* (1980)

11 Last night I dreamt I went to Manderley again.

Daphne Du Maurier *Rebecca* (1938)

12 Lolita, light of my life, fire of my loins. My sin, my soul. Lo-lee-ta: the tip of the tongue taking a trip of three steps down the palate to tap, at three, on the teeth. Lo. Lee. Ta.

Vladimir **Nabokov** *Lolita* (1955)

13 Long ago in 1945 all the nice people in England were poor, allowing for exceptions.

Muriel **Spark** *The Girls of Slender Means* (1963)

14 Mom and Pop were just a couple of kids when they got married. He was eighteen, she was sixteen, and I was three.

Billie **Holiday** *Lady Sings the Blues* (1956)

15 Once upon a time and a very good time it was there was a moocow coming down along the road and this moocow that was down along the road met a nicens little boy named baby tuckoo.

James **Joyce** *A Portrait of the Artist as a Young Man* (1916)

16 The past is a foreign country: they do things differently there.

L. P. **Hartley** *The Go-Between* (1953)

17 riverrun, past Eve and Adam's, from swerve of shore to bend of bay, brings us by a commodious vicus of recirculation back to Howth Castle and Environs.

James **Joyce** *Finnegans Wake* (1939)

18 Someone must have traduced Joseph K., for without having done anything wrong he was arrested one fine morning.

Franz **Kafka** *The Trial* (1925)

19 Stately, plump Buck Mulligan came from the stairhead, bearing a bowl of lather on which a mirror and a razor lay crossed.

James **Joyce** *Ulysses* (1922)

20 'Take my camel, dear,' said my aunt Dot, as she climbed down from this animal on her return from High Mass.

Rose Macaulay *The Towers of Trebizond* (1956)

▶

Opening lines continued

1 To begin at the beginning: It is spring, moonless night in the small town, starless and bible-black.
Dylan **Thomas** *Under Milk Wood* (1954)

2 *Toute ma vie, je me suis fait une certaine idée de la France.*
All my life I have thought of France in a certain way.
Charles **de Gaulle** *War Memoirs* (1955) vol. 1

3 When Gregor Samsa awoke one morning from uneasy dreams he found himself transformed in his bed into a gigantic insect.
Franz **Kafka** *The Metamorphosis* (1915)

Susie Orbach 1946–

American psychotherapist

4 Fat is a feminist issue.
title of book (1978)

Roy Orbison 1936–88 and Joe Melson

American singer and songwriter; American songwriter

5 Only the lonely (know the way I feel).
title of song (1960)

Tony O'Reilly 1936–

Irish newspaper entrepreneur

6 You grab a paper and there is a rush, there is adrenalin. Good God—look what we said today! It's more than you can get out of baked beans.
in *Guardian* 7 September 1998

P. J. O'Rourke 1947–

American humorous writer

7 That happy sense of purpose people have when they are standing up for a principle they haven't really been knocked down for yet.
Give War a Chance (1992)

8 You can't shame or humiliate modern celebrities. What used to be called shame and humiliation is now called publicity.
Give War a Chance (1992)

9 Every government is a parliament of whores. The trouble is, in a democracy the whores are us.
Parliament of Whores (1991)

10 Whose woods are whose everybody knows exactly, and everybody knows who got them rezoned for a shopping mall and who couldn't get the financing to begin construction and why it was he couldn't get it.
on a traditional New England community
Parliament of Whores (1991); see **Frost** 127:20

11 Anybody can have one kid. But going from one kid to two is like going from owning a dog to running a zoo.
in *Observer* 9 September 2001

José Ortega y Gasset 1883–1955

Spanish writer and philosopher

12 I am I plus my surroundings, and if I do not preserve the latter I do not preserve myself.
Meditaciones del Quijote (1914)

13 Civilization is nothing more than the effort to reduce the use of force to the last resort.
La Rebelión de las Masas (1930)

Joe Orton 1933–67

English dramatist

14 I'd the upbringing a nun would envy and that's the truth. Until I was fifteen I was more familiar with Africa than my own body.
Entertaining Mr Sloane (1964)

15 KATH: Can he be present at the birth of his child? . . .

ED: It's all any reasonable child can expect if the dad is present at the conception.

Entertaining Mr Sloane (1964)

1 Every luxury was lavished on you—atheism, breast-feeding, circumcision.

Loot (1967)

2 Reading isn't an occupation we encourage among police officers. We try to keep the paper work down to a minimum.

Loot (1967)

3 You were born with your legs apart. They'll send you to the grave in a Y-shaped coffin.

What the Butler Saw (1969)

George Orwell 1903–50

English novelist

4 Man is the only creature that consumes without producing.

Animal Farm (1945)

5 Four legs good, two legs bad.

Animal Farm (1945)

6 All animals are equal but some animals are more equal than others.

Animal Farm (1945)

7 The creatures outside looked from pig to man, and from man to pig, and from pig to man again, but already it was impossible to say which was which.

Animal Farm (1945); closing words

8 Good prose is like a window-pane.

Collected Essays (1968) vol. 1 'Why I Write'

9 I'm fat, but I'm thin inside. Has it ever struck you that there's a thin man inside every fat man, just as they say there's a statue inside every block of stone?

Coming up For Air (1939); see **Connolly** 75:9

10 Roast beef and Yorkshire, or roast pork and apple sauce, followed up by suet pudding and driven home, as it were, by a cup of mahogany-brown tea, have put you in just the right mood . . . In these blissful circumstances, what is it that you want to read about? Naturally, about a murder.

Decline of the English Murder and other essays (1965) title essay, written 1946

11 Down and out in Paris and London

title of book (1933)

12 There was much in it that I did not understand, in some ways I did not even like it, but I recognized it immediately as a state of affairs worth fighting for.

Homage to Catalonia (1938)

13 Down here it was still the England I had known in my childhood: the railway cuttings smothered in wild flowers . . . the red buses, the blue policemen—all sleeping the deep, deep sleep of England, from which I sometimes fear that we shall never wake till we are jerked out of it by the roar of bombs.

Homage to Catalonia (1938)

14 Keep the aspidistra flying.

title of novel (1936)

15 England is not the jewelled isle of Shakespeare's much-quoted passage, nor is it the inferno depicted by Dr Goebbels. More than either it resembles a family, a rather stuffy Victorian family, with not many black sheep in it but with all its cupboards bursting with skeletons . . . A family with the wrong members in control.

The Lion and the Unicorn (1941) pt. 1 'England Your England'

16 Old maids biking to Holy Communion through the mists of the autumn mornings . . . these are not only fragments, but *characteristic* fragments, of the English scene.

The Lion and the Unicorn (1941) pt. 1 'England Your England'; see **Major** 213:11

17 Probably the battle of Waterloo *was* won on the playing-fields of Eton, but the opening battles of all subsequent wars have been lost there.

The Lion and the Unicorn (1941) pt. 1 'England Your England'; see below

The battle of Waterloo was won on the playing fields of Eton.

Duke of Wellington (1769–1852) oral tradition, but not found in this form of words

1 It was a bright cold day in April, and the clocks were striking thirteen.
Nineteen Eighty-Four (1949)

2 BIG BROTHER IS WATCHING YOU.
Nineteen Eighty-Four (1949)

3 Who controls the past controls the future: who controls the present controls the past.
Nineteen Eighty-Four (1949)

4 Freedom is the freedom to say that two plus two make four. If that is granted, all else follows.
Nineteen Eighty-Four (1949)

5 The Lottery, with its weekly pay-out of enormous prizes, was the one public event to which the proles paid serious attention . . . It was their delight, their folly, their anodyne, their intellectual stimulant . . . the prizes were largely imaginary. Only small sums were actually paid out, the winners of the big prizes being non-existent persons.
Nineteen Eighty-Four (1949)

6 *Doublethink* means the power of holding two contradictory beliefs in one's mind simultaneously, and accepting both of them.
Nineteen Eighty-Four (1949)

7 Power is not a means, it is an end. One does not establish a dictatorship in order to safeguard a revolution; one makes the revolution in order to establish the dictatorship.
Nineteen Eighty-Four (1949)

8 If you want a picture of the future, imagine a boot stamping on a human face—for ever.
Nineteen Eighty-Four (1949)

9 The road to Wigan Pier.
title of book (1937)

10 To the ordinary working man, the sort you would meet in any pub on Saturday night, Socialism does not mean much more than better wages and shorter hours and nobody bossing you about.
The Road to Wigan Pier (1937)

11 Political language . . . is designed to make lies sound truthful and murder respectable, and to give an appearance of solidity to pure wind.
Shooting an Elephant (1950) 'Politics and the English Language'

12 [Serious sport] is war minus the shooting.
Shooting an Elephant (1950) 'The Sporting Spirit'

13 Whatever is funny is subversive, every joke is ultimately a custard pie . . . A dirty joke is a sort of mental rebellion.
in *Horizon* September 1941 'The Art of Donald McGill'

14 The Catholic and the Communist are alike in assuming that an opponent cannot be both honest and intelligent.
in *Polemic* January 1946 'The Prevention of Literature'

15 The quickest way of ending a war is to lose it.
in *Polemic* May 1946 'Second Thoughts on James Burnham'

16 At 50, everyone has the face he deserves.
last words in his notebook, 17 April 1949; *Collected Essays, Journalism and Letters . . .* (1968)

17 Advertising is the rattling of a stick inside a swill bucket.
attributed

John Osborne 1929–94

English dramatist; former husband of Jill **Bennett**

18 Don't clap too hard—it's a very old building.
The Entertainer (1957)

19 But I have a go, lady, don't I? I 'ave a go. I do.
The Entertainer (1957)

20 Look back in anger.
title of play (1956)

21 I don't think one 'comes down' from Jimmy's university. According to him, it's not even red brick, but white tile.
Look Back in Anger (1956)

22 There aren't any good, brave causes left. If the big bang does come, and we all get killed off, it won't be in aid of the old-fashioned, grand design. It'll just be for the Brave New-nothing-very-much-

thank-you. About as pointless and inglorious as stepping in front of a bus.
Look Back in Anger (1956)

1 Royalty is the gold filling in a mouthful of decay.
'They call it cricket' in T. Maschler (ed.) *Declaration* (1957)

2 This is a letter of hate. It is for you my countrymen, I mean those men of my country who have defiled it. The men with manic fingers leading the sightless, feeble, betrayed body of my country to its death . . . damn you England.
in *Tribune* 18 August 1961

David Owen 1938–

British Social Democratic politician

3 We are fed up with fudging and mudging, with mush and slush. We need courage, conviction, and hard work.
speech to his supporters at Labour Party Conference in Blackpool, 2 October 1980

Wilfred Owen 1893–1918

English poet

4 My subject is War, and the pity of War.
The Poetry is in the pity.
Poems (1963) preface (written 1918)

5 All a poet can do today is warn.
Poems (1963) preface (written 1918)

6 What passing-bells for these who die as cattle?
Only the monstrous anger of the guns.
'Anthem for Doomed Youth' (written 1917)

7 The shrill, demented choirs of wailing shells;
And bugles calling for them from sad shires.
'Anthem for Doomed Youth' (written 1917)

8 The pallor of girls' brows shall be their pall;
Their flowers the tenderness of patient minds,
And each slow dusk a drawing-down of blinds.
'Anthem for Doomed Youth' (written 1917)

9 If you could hear, at every jolt, the blood
Come gargling from the froth-corrupted lungs,
Obscene as cancer, bitter as the cud
Of vile, incurable sores on innocent tongues,—
My friend, you would not tell with such high zest
To children ardent for some desperate glory,
The old Lie: Dulce et decorum est
Pro patria mori.
'Dulce et Decorum Est' (1963 ed.); see below

Dulce et decorum est pro patria mori.
Lovely and honourable it is to die for one's country.
Horace (65–8 BC) *Odes*; see **Pound** 263:13

10 Was it for this the clay grew tall?
'Futility' (written 1918)

11 'Strange friend,' I said, 'here is no cause to mourn.'
'None,' said that other, 'save the undone years,
The hopelessness. Whatever hope is yours,
Was my life also.'
'Strange Meeting' (written 1918)

12 Courage was mine, and I had mystery,
Wisdom was mine, and I had mastery.
'Strange Meeting' (written 1918)

13 I am the enemy you killed, my friend.
I knew you in this dark.
'Strange Meeting' (written 1918)

14 Let us sleep now.
'Strange Meeting' (written 1918)

Vance Packard 1914–97

American writer and journalist

15 The hidden persuaders.
title of a study of the advertising industry (1957)

Ignacy Jan Paderewski 1860–1941

Polish pianist, composer, and statesman

16 What a terrible revenge by the culture of the Negroes on that of the whites!
of jazz
Nat Shapiro (ed.) *An Encyclopedia of Quotations about Music* (1978)

Camille Paglia 1947–

American author and critic

1 Modern body building is ritual, religion, sport, art, and science, awash in Western chemistry and mathematics. Defying nature, it surpasses it.

Sex, Art, and American Culture (1992)

2 Television is actually closer to reality than anything in books. The madness of TV is the madness of human life.

in *Harper's Magazine* March 1991

3 There is no female Mozart because there is no female Jack the Ripper.

in *International Herald Tribune* 26 April 1991

4 He tried to lecture *me* on how women felt when they were raped.

having walked out of an interview with Jonathan Dimbleby

in *Daily Telegraph* 25 June 1998

Marcel Pagnol 1895–1974

French dramatist and film-maker

5 Honour is like a match, you can only use it once.

Marius (1946)

6 It's better to choose the culprits than to seek them out.

Topaze (1930)

Leroy ('Satchel') Paige 1906–82

American baseball player

7 Don't look back. Something may be gaining on you.

in *Collier's* 13 June 1953

Ian Paisley 1926–

Presbyterian minister and Northern Irish politician

8 I would rather be British than just.

remark to Bernadette Devlin, October 1969, reported by *Sunday Times* Insight Team in *Ulster* (1972)

9 The mother of all treachery.

on the Good Friday agreement

in *Times* 16 April 1998

10 She has become a parrot.

on the perceived readiness of the Queen to repeat the views of her Prime Minister

in *Daily Telegraph* 27 May 1998

Christabel Pankhurst 1880–1958

English suffragette; daughter of Emmeline Pankhurst

see also **Political sayings and slogans** 262:5

11 Never lose your temper with the Press or the public is a major rule of political life.

Unshackled (1959)

12 We are here to claim our right as women, not only to be free, but to fight for freedom. That it is our right as well as our duty.

speech in London, 23 March 1911

Emmeline Pankhurst 1858–1928

English suffragette leader; founder of the Women's Social and Political Union, 1903

see also **Political sayings and slogans** 262:5

13 There is something that Governments care far more for than human life, and that is the security of property, and so it is through property that we shall strike the enemy . . . I say to the Government: You have not dared to take the leaders of Ulster for their incitement to rebellion. Take me if you dare.

speech at Albert Hall, 17 October 1912

14 The argument of the broken window pane is the most valuable argument in modern politics.

G. Dangerfield *The Strange Death of Liberal England* (1936)

Mitchell Parish 1900–93

American songwriter

15 When the deep purple falls over sleepy garden walls.

'Deep Purple' (1939 song)

Charlie Parker 1920–55

American jazz saxophonist

1 Music is your own experience, your thoughts, your wisdom. If you don't live it, it won't come out of your horn.
Nat Shapiro and Nat Hentoff *Hear Me Talkin' to Ya* (1955)

Dorothy Parker 1893–1967

American critic and humorist
on Parker: see **Benchley** 28:13, **Woollcott** 345:11; *see also* **Epitaphs** 109:4, **Telegrams** 316:3

2 Oh, life is a glorious cycle of song,
A medley of extemporanea;
And love is a thing that can never go wrong;
And I am Marie of Roumania.
'Comment' (1937)

3 Four be the things I'd been better without:
Love, curiosity, freckles, and doubt.
'Inventory' (1937)

4 Men seldom make passes
At girls who wear glasses.
'News Item' (1937)

5 Why is it no one ever sent me yet
One perfect limousine, do you suppose?
Ah no, it's always just my luck to get
One perfect rose.
'One Perfect Rose' (1937)

6 Whose love is given over-well
Shall look on Helen's face in hell
Whilst they whose love is thin and wise
Shall see John Knox in Paradise.
'Partial Comfort' (1937)

7 If, with the literate, I am
Impelled to try an epigram,
I never seek to take the credit;
We all assume that Oscar said it.
'A Pig's-Eye View of Literature' (1937)

8 Guns aren't lawful;
Nooses give;
Gas smells awful;
You might as well live.
'Résumé' (1937)

9 Where's the man could ease a heart like a satin gown?
'The Satin Dress' (1937)

10 By the time you say you're his,
Shivering and sighing
And he vows his passion is
Infinite, undying—
Lady, make a note of this:
One of you is lying.
'Unfortunate Coincidence' (1937)

11 And it is that word 'hummy', my darlings, that marks the first place in 'The House at Pooh Corner' at which Tonstant Weader fwowed up.
in *New Yorker* 20 October 1928 (review by Dorothy Parker as 'Constant Reader')

12 *House Beautiful* is play lousy.
New Yorker review (1933); P. Hartnoll *Plays and Players* (1984)

13 She ran the whole gamut of the emotions from A to B.
of Katharine Hepburn at a Broadway first night, 1933
attributed

14 That woman speaks eighteen languages, and can't say No in any of them.
Alexander Woollcott *While Rome Burns* (1934) 'Our Mrs Parker'

15 And there was that wholesale libel on a Yale prom. If all the girls attending it were laid end to end, Mrs Parker said, she wouldn't be at all surprised.
Alexander Woollcott *While Rome Burns* (1934) 'Our Mrs Parker'

16 There's a hell of a distance between wise-cracking and wit. Wit has truth in it; wise-cracking is simply callisthenics with words.
in *Paris Review* Summer 1956

17 How do they know?
on being told that Calvin ***Coolidge*** *had died*
M. Cowley *Writers at Work* 1st Series (1958)

18 Hollywood money isn't money. It's congealed snow, melts in your hand, and there you are.
Malcolm Cowley *Writers at Work* 1st Series (1958)

19 It serves me right for putting all my eggs in one bastard.
on her abortion
J. Keats *You Might as well Live* (1970)

20 One more drink and I'd have been under the host.
Howard Teichmann *George S. Kaufman* (1972)

1 You can lead a horticulture, but you can't make her think.
J. Keats *You Might as well Live* (1970)

Ross Parker 1914–74 and **Hugh Charles** 1907–

British songwriters

2 There'll always be an England
While there's a country lane,
Wherever there's a cottage small
Beside a field of grain.
'There'll always be an England' (1939 song)

3 We'll meet again, don't know where,
Don't know when,
But I know we'll meet again some sunny day.
'We'll Meet Again' (1939 song)

C. Northcote Parkinson 1909–93

English writer

4 Expenditure rises to meet income.
The Law and the Profits (1960)

5 Work expands so as to fill the time available for its completion.
Parkinson's Law (1958)

6 Perfection of planned layout is achieved only by institutions on the point of collapse.
Parkinson's Law (1958)

7 The man who is denied the opportunity of taking decisions of importance begins to regard as important the decisions he is allowed to take.
Parkinson's Law (1958)

Rosa Parks 1913–

American civil rights activist

8 Our mistreatment was just not right, and I was tired of it.
of her refusal, in December 1955, to surrender her seat on a segregated bus in Alabama to a white man
Quiet Strength (1994)

Matthew Parris 1949–

British journalist and former politician

9 Being an MP feeds your vanity and starves your self-respect.
in *The Times* 9 February 1994

10 My name is Mandy: Peter B.,
I'm back in charge—don't mess with me.
My cheeks are drawn, my face is bony,
The line I take comes straight from Tony.
on Peter ***Mandelson****'s return to government*
in *Times* 21 October 1999, parodying a 19th-century poem on Lord **Curzon**

Tony Parsons 1953–

English critic and writer

11 I never saw a beggar yet who would recognise guilt if it bit him on his unwashed ass.
Dispatches from the Front Line of Popular Culture (1994)

Dolly Parton 1946–

American singer and actress

12 It costs a lot of money to look this cheap.
attributed, perhaps apocryphal

Frances Partridge 1900–

English writer and diarist

13 Thirty years is a very long time to live alone and life doesn't get any nicer.
on widowhood, at the age of 92
G. Kinnock and F. Miller (eds.) *By Faith and Daring* (1993)

Boris Pasternak 1890–1960

Russian novelist and poet

14 Man is born to live, not to prepare for life.
Doctor Zhivago (1958)

15 Most people experience love, without noticing that there is anything remarkable about it.
Doctor Zhivago (1958)

16 I don't like people who have never fallen or stumbled. Their virtue is lifeless and it

isn't of much value. Life hasn't revealed its beauty to them.
Doctor Zhivago (1958)

1 The whole human way of life has been destroyed and ruined. All that's left is the bare, shivering human soul, stripped to the last shred, the naked force of the human psyche for which nothing has changed because it was always cold and shivering and reaching out to its nearest neighbour, as cold and lonely as itself.
Doctor Zhivago (1958)

2 In time to come, I tell them, we'll be equal
to any living now. If cripples, then
no matter; we shall just have been run over
by 'New Man' in the wagon of his 'Plan'.
'When I Grow Weary' (1932)

Alan Paton 1903–

South African writer

3 Cry, the beloved country.
title of novel (1948)

Leslie Paul 1905–85

Irish writer

4 Angry young man.
title of book (1951); the phrase subsequently associated with John **Osborne**'s play *Look Back in Anger* (1956)

Wolfgang Pauli 1900–58

Austrian-born American physicist who worked chiefly in Switzerland
on Pauli: see **Weisskopf** 332:13

5 I don't mind your thinking slowly: I mind your publishing faster than you think.
attributed

Tom Paulin 1949–

English poet and critic

6 That stretch of water, it's always
There for you to cross over
To the other shore, observing
The light of cities on blackness.
'States' (1977)

7 Now dream
of that sweet
equal republic
where the juniper
talks to the oak,
the thistle,
the bandaged elm,
and the jolly jolly chestnut.
'The Book of Juniper' (1983)

8 The owl of Minerva in a hired car.
'Desertmartin' (1983)

Jeremy Paxman 1950–

British journalist and broadcaster

9 No government in history has been as obsessed with public relations as this one . . . Speaking for myself, if there is a message I want to be off it.
after criticism from Alastair ***Campbell*** *of his interviewing tactics*
in *Daily Telegraph* 3 July 1998

Octavio Paz 1914–98

Mexican poet, critic, and diplomat

10 Surrealism has been the drunken flame that guides the steps of the sleepwalker who tiptoes along the edge of the shadow that the blade of the guillotine casts on the neck of the condemned.
'This and This and This' (1988)

11 Love is one of the answers humankind invented to stare death in the face: time ceases to be a measure, and we can briefly know paradise.
The Double Flame (1995)

Mervyn Peake 1911–68

British novelist, poet, and artist

12 To live at all is miracle enough.
The Glassblower (1950)

13 Each day I live in a glass room
Unless I break it with the thrusting
Of my senses and pass through
The splintered walls to the great landscape.
'Each day I live in a glass room' (1967)

Norman Vincent Peale 1898–1993

American religious broadcaster and writer

1 The power of positive thinking.
title of book (1952)

Patrick Pearse 1879–1916

Irish nationalist leader; executed after the Easter Rising

2 The fools, the fools, the fools, they have left us our Fenian dead, and while Ireland holds these graves Ireland unfree shall never be at peace.
oration over the grave of the Fenian Jeremiah O'Donovan Rossa, 1 August 1915

Hesketh Pearson 1887–1964

English actor and biographer

3 Misquotation is, in fact, the pride and privilege of the learned. A widely-read man never quotes accurately, for the rather obvious reason that he has read too widely.
Common Misquotations (1934)

Lester Pearson 1897–1972

Canadian diplomat and Liberal statesman, Prime Minister 1963–8

4 The grim fact is that we prepare for war like precocious giants and for peace like retarded pygmies.
speech in Toronto, 14 March 1955

Pelé 1940–

Brazilian footballer

5 Football? It's the beautiful game.
attributed

Roger Penrose 1931–

British mathematician and theoretical physicist

6 Consciousness . . . is the phenomenon whereby the universe's very existence is made known.
The Emperor's New Mind (1989)

S. J. Perelman 1904–79

American humorist

7 Crazy like a fox.
title of book (1944)

Shimon Peres 1923–

Israeli statesman

8 Television has made dictatorship impossible, but democracy unbearable.
at a Davos meeting, in *Financial Times* 31 January 1995

Anthony Perkins 1932–92

American actor

9 I have learned more about love, selflessness and human understanding in this great adventure in the world of Aids than I ever did in the cut-throat, competitive world in which I spent my life.
posthumous statement, in *Independent on Sunday* 20 September 1992

Eva Perón 1919–52

wife of Juan **Perón**

on Perón: see **Epitaphs** 109:14, **Madonna** 212:7

10 Keeping books on charity is capitalist nonsense! I just use the money for the poor. I can't stop to count it.
Fleur Cowles *Bloody Precedent: the Peron Story* (1952)

Juan Perón 1895–1974

Argentine soldier and statesman, President 1946–55 and 1973–4; husband of Eva **Perón**

11 If I had not been born Perón, I would have liked to be Perón.
in *Observer* 21 February 1960

H. Ross Perot 1930–

American businessman; independent presidential candidate in the 1992 election

12 An activist is the guy who cleans the

river, not the guy who concludes it's dirty.

a favourite saying; Ken Gross *Ross Perot* (1992)

Jimmy Perry

British songwriter

1 Who do you think you are kidding, Mister Hitler?

theme song of *Dad's Army*, BBC television (1968–77)

Ted Persons

2 Things ain't what they used to be.

title of song (1941)

Max Perutz 1914–

Austrian-born scientist

3 The priest persuades humble people to endure their hard lot; the politician urges them to rebel against it; and the scientist thinks of a method that does away with the hard lot altogether.

Is Science Necessary (1989)

Marshal Pétain 1856–1951

French soldier and statesman

see also **Sayings** 289:22

4 To write one's memoirs is to speak ill of everybody except oneself.

in *Observer* 26 May 1946

Laurence J. Peter 1919–90

Canadian writer

5 In a hierarchy every employee tends to rise to his level of incompetence.

The Peter Principle (1969)

Mike Peters

American cartoonist

6 When I go into the voting booth, do I vote for the person who is the best President? Or the slime bucket who will make my life as a cartoonist wonderful?

in *Wall Street Journal* 20 January 1993

Jamie Petrie and Peter Cunnah

British singers and songwriters

7 Things can only get better.

title of song (1994); see **Political sayings and slogans** 262:3

Kim Philby 1912–88

British intelligence officer and Soviet spy

8 To betray, you must first belong.

in *Sunday Times* 17 December 1967

Prince Philip, Duke of Edinburgh 1921–

husband of **Elizabeth II**

9 Gentlemen, I think it is about time we 'pulled our fingers out' . . . If we want to be more prosperous we've simply got to get down to it and work for it. The rest of the world does not owe us a living.

speech in London, 17 October 1961

10 If you stay here much longer you'll all be slitty-eyed.

remark to Edinburgh University students in Peking, 16 October 1986

11 Tolerance is the one essential ingredient . . . You can take it from me that the Queen has the quality of tolerance in abundance.

his recipe for a successful marriage, during celebrations for their golden wedding anniversary

in *The Times* 20 November 1997

12 I can only assume that it is largely due to the accumulation of toasts to my health over the years that I am still enjoying a fairly satisfactory state of health and have reached such an unexpectedly great age.

speech to the Corporation of the City of London, 6 June 2001

Arthur Angell Phillips 1900–85

Australian critic and editor

13 Above our writers—and other artists—looms the intimidating mass of Anglo-

Saxon culture. Such a situation almost inevitably produces the characteristic Australian Cultural Cringe—appearing either as the Cringe Direct, or as the Cringe Inverted, in the attitude of the Blatant Blatherskite, the God's-Own-Country and I'm-a-better-man-than-you-are Australian bore.

Meanjin (1950) 'The Cultural Cringe'; see **Keating** 176:7

Morgan Phillips 1902–63

British Labour politician

1 The Labour Party owes more to Methodism than to Marxism.

James Callaghan *Time and Chance* (1987)

Pablo Picasso 1881–1973

Spanish painter

2 The fact that for a long time Cubism has not been understood and that even today there are people who cannot see anything in it, means nothing. I do not read English, an English book is a blank book to me. This does not mean that the English language does not exist.

interview with Marius de Zayas, 1923; Herschel B. Chipp *Theories of Modern Art* (1968)

3 No, painting is not made to decorate apartments. It's an offensive and defensive weapon against the enemy.

interview with Simone Téry, 24 March 1945

4 When I was the age of these children I could draw like Raphael: it took me many years to learn how to draw like these children.

to Herbert ***Read****, when visiting an exhibition of children's drawings*

quoted in letter from Read to *The Times* 27 October 1956

5 I paint objects as I think them, not as I see them.

John Golding *Cubism* (1959)

6 God is really only another artist. He invented the giraffe, the elephant, and the cat. He has no real style. He just goes on trying other things.

F. Gilot and C. Lake *Life With Picasso* (1964)

7 Every positive value has its price in negative terms . . . The genius of Einstein leads to Hiroshima.

F. Gilot and C. Lake *Life With Picasso* (1964)

8 We all know that Art is not truth. Art is a lie that makes us realize truth.

Dore Ashton *Picasso on Art* (1972) 'Two statements by Picasso'

John Pilger 1939–

Australian journalist

9 I used to see Vietnam as a war, rather than a country.

in *Sunday Times* 1 December 1996

Ben Pimlott 1945–

English historian and royal biographer

10 If you have a Royal Family you have to make the best of whatever personalities the genetic lottery comes up with.

in *Independent* 13 September 1997

Harold Pinter 1930–

English dramatist

11 If only I could get down to Sidcup! I've been waiting for the weather to break. He's got my papers, this man I left them with, it's got it all down there, I could prove everything.

The Caretaker (1960)

12 Apart from the known and the unknown, what else is there?

The Homecoming (1965)

13 The weasel under the cocktail cabinet.

on being asked what his plays were about

J. Russell Taylor *Anger and After* (1962)

Luigi Pirandello 1867–1936

Italian dramatist and novelist

14 Six characters in search of an author.

title of play (1921)

Armand J. Piron 1888–1943

American jazz musician

1 I wish I could shimmy like my sister
Kate,
She shivers like the jelly on a plate.
'Shimmy like Kate' (1919 song)

Robert M. Pirsig 1928–

American writer

2 Zen and the art of motorcycle maintenance.
title of book (1974)

3 That's the classical mind at work, runs fine inside but looks dingy on the surface.
Zen and the Art of Motorcycle Maintenance (1974)

Walter B. Pitkin 1878–1953

American writer

4 Life begins at forty.
title of book (1932)

Pius XII 1876–1958

Italian cleric; Pope from 1939

5 One Galileo in two thousand years is enough.
on being asked to proscribe the works of ***Teilhard de Chardin***
attributed; Stafford Beer *Platform for Change* (1975)

Max Planck 1858–1947

German physicist

6 A new scientific truth does not triumph by convincing its opponents and making them see the light, but rather because its opponents eventually die, and a new generation grows up that is familiar with it.
A Scientific Autobiography (1949)

Sylvia Plath 1932–63

American poet

7 Is there no way out of the mind?
'Apprehensions' (1971)

8 Every woman adores a Fascist,
The boot in the face, the brute
Brute heart of a brute like you.
'Daddy' (1963)

9 I am the ghost of an infamous suicide,
My own blue razor rusting in my throat.
O pardon the one who knocks for pardon at
Your gate, father—your hound-bitch, daughter, friend.
It was my love that did us both to death.
'Electra on Azalea Path' (1959)

10 The blood jet is poetry,
There is no stopping it.
'Kindness' (1965)

11 Dying,
Is an art, like everything else.
'Lady Lazarus' (1963)

12 Out of the ash
I rise with my red hair
And I eat men like air.
'Lady Lazarus' (1963)

13 Love set you going like a fat gold watch.
'Morning Song' (1965)

14 Widow. The word consumes itself.
'Widow' (1971)

William Plomer 1903–73

British poet

15 Out of that bungled, unwise war
An alp of unforgiveness grew.
'The Boer War' (1960)

16 With first-rate sherry flowing into
second-rate whores,
And third-rate conversation without one
single pause:
Just like a young couple
Between the wars.
'Father and Son: 1939' (1945)

17 On a sofa upholstered in panther skin
Mona did researches in original sin.
'Mews Flat Mona' (1960)

John C. Polanyi 1929–

German-born Canadian scientist

1 When . . . we fear science, we really fear ourselves. Human dignity is better served by embracing knowledge.

accepting the Nobel Prize for Chemistry, 10 December 1986

Political sayings and slogans

see box opposite

Harry Pollitt 1890–1960

British Communist politician

on being asked by Stephen ***Spender*** *in the 1930s how best a poet could serve the Communist cause:*

2 Go to Spain and get killed. The movement needs a Byron.

attributed, perhaps apocryphal

Jackson Pollock 1912–56

American painter

3 There was a reviewer a while back who wrote that my pictures didn't have any beginning or any end. He didn't mean it as a compliment, but it was. It was a fine compliment.

Francis V. O'Connor *Jackson Pollock* (1967)

John Pope-Hennessy 1913–94

British art historian

4 I still recall, with something of a shock the moment, at the end of the first sitting, when I looked at what had been a lump of clay, and found that a third person was in the room.

on sitting to Elizabeth Frink

Learning to Look (1991)

Karl Popper 1902–94

Austrian-born British philosopher

5 I shall certainly admit a system as empirical or scientific only if it is capable of being *tested* by experience. These considerations suggest that not the *verifiability* but the *falsifiability* of a system is to be taken as a criterion of demarcation . . . *It must be possible for an empirical scientific system to be refuted by experience.*

The Logic of Scientific Discovery (1934)

6 We may become the makers of our fate when we have ceased to pose as its prophets.

The Open Society and its Enemies (1945)

7 We should therefore claim, in the name of tolerance, the right not to tolerate the intolerant.

The Open Society and Its Enemies (1945)

8 There is no history of mankind, there are only many histories of all kinds of aspects of human life. And one of these is the history of political power. This is elevated into the history of the world.

The Open Society and its Enemies (1945)

9 Science must begin with myths, and with the criticism of myths.

'The Philosophy of Science' in C. A. Mace (ed.) *British Philosophy in the Mid-Century* (1957)

10 For this, indeed, is the true source of our ignorance—the fact that our knowledge can only be finite, while our ignorance must necessarily be infinite.

lecture to British Academy, 20 January 1960

Cole Porter 1891–1964

American songwriter

11 But I'm always true to you, darlin', in
my fashion.
Yes I'm always true to you, darlin', in
my way.

'Always True to You in my Fashion' (1949 song)

12 In olden days a glimpse of stocking
Was looked on as something shocking
Now, heaven knows,
Anything goes.

'Anything Goes' song (1934)

13 When they begin the Beguine
It brings back the sound of music so
tender,

▸▸

Political sayings and slogans

1 All power to the Soviets.
workers in Petrograd, 1917

2 All the way with LBJ.
US Democratic Party campaign slogan, 1960

3 Are you now, or have you ever been, a member of the Communist Party?
from 1947, the question habitually put by the House Un-American Activities Committee (HUAC) to those appearing before it, now particularly associated with the McCarthy period of the 1950s; see **Lardner** 188:7

4 Ban the bomb.
US anti-nuclear slogan, adopted by the Campaign for Nuclear Disarmament, 1953 onwards

5 A bayonet is a weapon with a worker at each end.
British pacifist slogan, 1940

6 Better red than dead.
slogan of nuclear disarmament campaigners, late 1950s

7 The big tent.
slogan used by the Republican Party to denote a policy of inclusiveness
recorded from 1990; see also **Newspaper headlines** 240:16

8 Black is beautiful.
slogan of American civil rights campaigners, mid-1960s

9 Burn, baby, burn.
black extremist slogan, Los Angeles riots, August 1965

10 Can't pay, won't pay.
anti-Poll Tax slogan, *c.*1990; see **Fo** 120:12

11 *Ein Reich, ein Volk, ein Führer.*
One realm, one people, one leader.
Nazi Party slogan, early 1930s

12 Fair shares for all, is Labour's call.
slogan for the North Battersea by-election, 1946, coined by Douglas ***Jay***
Douglas Jay *Change and Fortune* (1980)

13 Free by '93.
Scottish National Party, general election campaign, 1992

14 Hey, hey, LBJ, how many kids did you kill today?
anti-Vietnam marching slogan, 1960s

15 I like Ike.
used when General ***Eisenhower*** *was first seen as a potential presidential nominee*
US button badge, 1947; coined by Henry D. Spalding (d. 1990)

16 It'll play in Peoria.
catch-phrase of the **Nixon** administration (early 1970s) meaning 'it will be acceptable to middle America', but originating in a standard music hall joke of the 1930s

17 It's morning again in America.
Ronald **Reagan**'s 1984 election campaign slogan; coined by Hal Riney (1932–)

18 It's Scotland's oil.
Scottish National Party, 1972

19 It's the economy, stupid.
on a sign put up at the 1992 **Clinton** presidential campaign headquarters by campaign manager James Carville

20 Keep the bastards honest.
coined by the Australian politician Don Chipp (1925–), on leaving the Liberal Party to form the Australian Democrats

21 *Kraft durch Freude.*
Strength through joy.
German Labour Front slogan, from 1933; coined by Robert Ley (1890–1945)

22 Labour isn't working.
on poster showing a long queue outside an unemployment office
Conservative Party slogan 1978–9

23 Labour's double whammy.
Conservative Party election slogan 1992

24 Life's better with the Conservatives. Don't let Labour ruin it.
Conservative Party election slogan, 1959

25 New Labour, new danger.
Conservative slogan, 1996

26 The personal is political.
1970s feminist slogan, attributed to Carol Hanisch (1945–)

▶

▸ Political sayings and slogans continued

1 Power to the people.
slogan of the Black Panther movement, from c.1968; see **Newton** 239:10

2 Save the pound.
slogan for those opposed to the single currency, used particularly in the Conservative campaign for the 2001 British General Election

3 Things can only get better.
Labour campaign slogan, 1997; see **Petrie** 257:7

4 Thirteen years of Tory misrule.
unofficial Labour party election slogan, also in the form 'Thirteen wasted years', 1964

5 Votes for women.
*adopted when it proved impossible to use a banner with the longer slogan 'Will the Liberal Party Give Votes for Women?' made by Emmeline **Pankhurst** (1858–1928), Christabel **Pankhurst** (1880–1958), and Annie Kenney (1879–1953)*
slogan of the women's suffrage movement, from 13 October 1905; Emmeline Pankhurst *My Own Story* (1914)

6 War will cease when men refuse to fight.
pacifist slogan, often quoted 'Wars will cease . . . ', from c.1936

7 Would you buy a used car from this man?
campaign slogan directed against Richard **Nixon**, 1968

8 Yes it hurt, yes it worked.
Conservative Party slogan, 1996; see **Major** 213:9

9 Yesterday's men (they failed before!).
Labour Party slogan, referring to the Conservatives, 1970; coined by David Kingsley, Dennis Lyons, and Peter Lovell-Davis

▸▸ Cole Porter continued

It brings back a night of tropical splendour,
It brings back a memory ever green.
'Begin the Beguine' (1935 song)

10 Oh, give me land, lots of land
Under starry skies above
DON'T FENCE ME IN.
'Don't Fence Me In' (1934 song)

11 There's no love song finer,
But how strange the change from major to minor
Every time we say goodbye.
'Every Time We Say Goodbye' (1944 song)

12 I get no kick from champagne,
Mere alcohol doesn't thrill me at all.
'I Get a Kick Out of You' song (1934)

13 I've got you under my skin.
title of song (1936)

14 Night and day, you are the one,
Only you beneath the moon and under the sun.
'Night and Day' (1932 song)

15 So goodbye dear, and Amen,
Here's hoping we meet now and then,
It was great fun,
But it was just one of those things.
'Just One of Those Things' (1935 song)

16 Birds do it, bees do it,
Even educated fleas do it.
Let's do it, let's fall in love.
'Let's Do It' (1954 song; words added to the 1928 original)

17 Miss Otis regrets (she's unable to lunch today).
title of song (1934)

18 My heart belongs to Daddy.
title of song (1938)

19 SHE: Have you heard it's in the stars,
Next July we collide with Mars?
HE: WELL, DID YOU EVAH! What a swell party this is.
'Well, Did You Evah?' (1956 song)

20 Who wants to be a millionaire?
title of song (1956)

Michael Portillo 1953-

British Conservative politician

1 A truly terrible night for the Conservatives.

after losing Enfield South to Labour in the General Election of 1997

comment, 2 May 1997; Brian Cathcart *Were You Still Up for Portillo?* (1997)

Dennis Potter 1935-94

English television dramatist

2 Below my window . . . the blossom is out in full now . . . I *see* it is the whitest, frothiest, blossomiest blossom that there ever could be, and I can see it. . . . The nowness of everything is absolutely wondrous.

on his heightened awareness of things, in the face of his imminent death

interview with Melvyn Bragg on Channel 4, March 1994

3 Religion to me has always been the wound, not the bandage.

interview with Melvyn Bragg on Channel 4, March 1994

Stephen Potter 1900-69

British writer

4 A good general rule is to state that the bouquet is better than the taste, and vice versa.

on wine-tasting

One-Upmanship (1952)

5 *How to be one up*—how to make the other man feel that something has gone wrong, however slightly.

Lifemanship (1950)

6 'Yes, but not in the South', with slight adjustments, will do for any argument about any place, if not about any person.

Lifemanship (1950)

7 The theory and practice of gamesmanship or The art of winning games without actually cheating.

title of book (1947)

Ezra Pound 1885-1972

American poet

8 Winter is icummen in,
Lhude sing Goddamm,
Raineth drop and staineth slop,
And how the wind doth ramm!
Sing: Goddamm.

'Ancient Music' (1917); see below

Sumer is icumen in,
Lhude sing cuccu!
Groweth sed, and bloweth med,
And springeth the wude nu.

Anonymous 'Cuckoo Song' (c.1250)

9 With usura hath no man a house of good stone
each block cut smooth and well fitting.

Cantos (1954) no. 45

10 Tching prayed on the mountain and
wrote MAKE IT NEW
on his bath tub.

Cantos (1954) no. 53

11 And even I can remember
A day when the historians left blanks in their writings,
I mean for things they didn't know.

Draft of XXX Cantos (1930) no. 13

12 Christ follows Dionysus,
Phallic and ambrosial
Made way for macerations;
Caliban casts out Ariel.

Hugh Selwyn Mauberley (1920) 'E. P. *Ode* . . .' pt. 3

13 Died some, pro patria,
non 'dulce' non 'et decor' . . .
walked eye-deep in hell
believing in old men's lies, the unbelieving
came home, home to a lie.

Hugh Selwyn Mauberley (1920) 'E. P. *Ode* . . .' pt. 4; see below

Dulce et decorum est pro patria mori.

Lovely and honourable it is to die for one's country.

Horace (65-8 BC) *Odes*; see **Owen** 251:9

14 There died a myriad,
And of the best, among them,

For an old bitch gone in the teeth,
For a botched civilization.

Hugh Selwyn Mauberley (1920) 'E. P. *Ode . . .*' pt. 5

1 The tip's a good one, as for literature
It gives no man a sinecure.

And no one knows, at sight, a
masterpiece.
And give up verse, my boy,
There's nothing in it.

Hugh Selwyn Mauberley (1920) 'Mr Nixon'

2 The ant's a centaur in his dragon world.

Pisan Cantos (1948) no. 81

3 Music begins to atrophy when it departs too far from the dance . . . poetry begins to atrophy when it gets too far from music.

The ABC of Reading (1934) 'Warning'

4 One of the pleasures of middle age is to *find out* that one WAS right, and that one was much righter than one knew at say 17 or 23.

ABC of Reading (1934)

5 Literature is news that STAYS news.

The ABC of Reading (1934)

6 Great literature is simply language charged with meaning to the utmost possible degree.

How To Read (1931)

Anthony Powell 1905–2000

English novelist

7 He fell in love with himself at first sight and it is a passion to which he has always remained faithful.

The Acceptance World (1955)

8 Dinner at the Huntercombes' possessed 'only two dramatic features—the wine was a farce and the food a tragedy'.

The Acceptance World (1955)

9 Books do furnish a room.

title of novel (1971)

10 Parents—especially step-parents—are sometimes a bit of a disappointment to their children. They don't fufil the promise of their early years.

A Buyer's Market (1952)

11 A dance to the music of time.

title of novel sequence (1951–75), after *Le 4 stagioni che ballano al suono del tempo* (title given by Giovanni Pietro Bellori to a painting by Nicolas Poussin)

12 He's so wet you could shoot snipe off him.

A Question of Upbringing (1951)

13 Growing old is like being increasingly penalized for a crime you haven't committed.

Temporary Kings (1973)

14 She was the sort of woman who, if she had been taken in adultery, would have caught the first stone and thrown it back.

A Writer's Notebook (2001)

Colin Powell 1937–

American general and Republican politician, Secretary of State from 2001

15 First, we are going to cut it off, and then, we are going to kill it.

strategy for dealing with the Iraqi Army in the Gulf War

at a press conference, 23 January 1991

16 Some in our party miss no opportunity to roundly and loudly condemn affirmative action that helped a few thousand black kids get an education, but hardly a whimper is heard from them over affirmative action for lobbyists who load our federal tax codes with preferences for special interest.

speech at the Republican Convention, 31 August 2000

17 Nato is the bedrock of Europe. It is sacrosanct.

in *Independent on Sunday* 21 January 2001

18 To save a lot of cable traffic now, I have no food preferences, no drink preferences; a cheeseburger will be fine. I like Holiday Inns.

in *Newsweek* 5 February 2001

19 A great tragedy has struck our country. It will not affect the nature of our society.

after the terrorist attacks on the World Trade Center and the Pentagon, 11 September 2001

in *Times* 12 September 2001

Enoch Powell 1912–98

British Conservative politician

1 History is littered with the wars which everybody knew would never happen.
speech to Conservative Party Conference, 19 October 1967

2 Those whom the gods wish to destroy, they first make mad. We must be mad, literally mad, as a nation to be permitting the annual inflow of some 50,000 dependents, who are for the most part the material of the future growth of the immigrant descended population. It is like watching a nation busily engaged in heaping up its own funeral pyre.
speech at Annual Meeting of West Midlands Area Conservative Political Centre, Birmingham, 20 April 1968

3 As I look ahead, I am filled with foreboding. Like the Roman, I seem to see 'the River Tiber foaming with much blood'.
speech at Birmingham, 20 April 1968; see below

I see wars, horrible wars, and the Tiber foaming with much blood.
Virgil (70–19 BC) *Aeneid*

4 Judas was paid! I am sacrificing my whole political life.
response to a heckler's call of 'Judas', having advised Conservatives to vote Labour at the coming general election
speech at Bull Ring, Birmingham, 23 February 1974

5 To write a diary every day is like returning to one's own vomit.
interview in *Sunday Times* 6 November 1977

6 For a politician to complain about the press is like a ship's captain complaining about the sea.
in *Guardian* 3 December 1984

7 ANNE BROWN: How would you like to be remembered?
ENOCH POWELL: I should like to have been killed in the war.
in a radio interview, 13 April 1986

8 To be and to remain a member of the House of Commons was the overriding and undiscussable motivation of my life as a politician.
'Theory and Practice' 1990

9 All political lives, unless they are cut off in midstream at a happy juncture, end in failure, because that is the nature of politics and of human affairs.
Joseph Chamberlain (1977)

Vince Powell and **Harry Driver**

British writers

10 Never mind the quality, feel the width.
title of ITV comedy series, 1967–9

Terry Pratchett 1948–

English science fiction writer

11 Personal isn't the same as important.
Men at Arms (1993)

12 Most modern fantasy just rearranges the furniture in Tolkien's attic.
Stan Nicholls (ed.) *Wordsmiths of Wonder* (1993)

13 [The Internet is] a whining Californian mall rat, forever demanding that the real world be redefined to suit its whims.
in *Bookseller* 15 September 2000

John Prescott 1938–

British Labour politician

14 People like me were branded, pigeon-holed, a ceiling put on our ambitions.
on failing his 11-plus
speech at Ruskin College, Oxford, 13 June 1996

15 We did it! Let's wallow in our victory!
on Tony ***Blair****'s warning that the Labour Party should not be triumphalist in victory*
speech to the Labour Party Conference, 29 September 1997

16 The wife does not like her hair blown about.
explaining why he had driven from his hotel to the conference centre at the Labour Party Conference
in *Daily Telegraph* 1 October 1999

Keith Preston 1884–1927

American poet

17 Of all the literary scenes

Saddest this sight to me:
The graves of little magazines
Who died to make verse free.
'The Liberators'

Jacques Prévert 1900–77

French poet and screenwriter

1 *C'est tellement simple, l'amour.*

It's so simple, love.
Les Enfants du Paradis (1945 film)

Anthony Price 1928–

English thriller writer and editor

2 The Devil himself had probably redesigned Hell in the light of information he had gained from observing airport layouts.
The Memory Trap (1989)

Gerald Priestland 1927–91

English writer and journalist

3 Journalists belong in the gutter because that is where the ruling classes throw their guilty secrets.
on Radio London 19 May 1988

J. B. Priestley 1894–1984

English novelist, dramatist, and critic

4 I never read the life of any important person without discovering that he knew more and could do more than I could ever hope to know or to do in half a dozen lifetimes.
Apes and Angels (1928)

5 The first fall of snow is not only an event, but it is a magical event. You go to bed in one kind of world and wake up to find yourself in another quite different, and if this is not enchantment, then where is it to be found?
Apes and Angels (1928) 'First Snow'

6 To say that these men paid their shillings to watch twenty-two hirelings kick a ball is merely to say that a violin is wood and catgut, that *Hamlet* is so much paper and ink. For a shilling the Bruddersford United AFC offered you Conflict and Art.
Good Companions (1929)

7 First you take their faces from 'em by calling 'em the masses and then you accuse 'em of not having any faces.
Saturn Over the Water (1961)

8 Our great-grand-children, when they learn how we began this war by snatching glory out of defeat, and then swept on to victory, may also learn how the little holiday steamers made an excursion to hell and came back glorious.
on the evacuation of Dunkirk
radio broadcast, 5 June 1940

9 The weakness of American civilization, and perhaps the chief reason why it creates so much discontent, is that it is so curiously abstract. It is a bloodless extrapolation of a satisfying life . . . You dine off the advertiser's 'sizzling' and not the meat of the steak.
in *New Statesman* 10 December 1971

V. S. Pritchett 1900–97

English writer and critic

10 The principle of procrastinated rape is said to be the ruling one in all the great best-sellers.
The Living Novel (1946) 'Clarissa'

11 The detective novel is the art-for-art's-sake of our yawning Philistinism, the classic example of a specialized form of art removed from contact with the life it pretends to build on.
in *New Statesman* 16 June 1951 'Books in General'

Romano Prodi 1939–

Italian statesman, President of the European Commission

12 The pillars of the nation state are the sword and the currency, and we changed that. The euro-decision changed the concept of the nation state.
in *Daily Telegraph* 7 April 1999

Marcel Proust 1871–1922

French novelist

1 *A la recherche du temps perdu.*

In search of lost time.

translated by C. K. Scott-Moncrieff and S. Hudson, 1922–31, as Remembrance of things past

title of novel (1913–27); see below

When to the sessions of sweet silent
thought
I summon up remembrance of things
past.

William Shakespeare (1564–1616) sonnet 30

2 I have a horror of sunsets, they're so romantic, so operatic.

Cities of the Plain (1922)

3 Everything we think of as great has come to us from neurotics. It is they and they alone who found religions and create great works of art. The world will never realise how much it owes to them and what they have suffered in order to bestow their gifts on it.

Guermantes Way (1921)

4 And suddenly the memory revealed itself. The taste was that of the little piece of madeleine which . . . my aunt Léonie used to give me, dipping it first in her own cup of tea or tisane.

Swann's Way (1913)

5 The true paradises are the paradises that we have lost.

Time Regained (1926)

6 For if unhappiness develops the forces of the mind, happiness alone is salutary to the body.

Time Regained (1926)

7 One becomes moral as soon as one is unhappy.

Within a Budding Grove (1918)

Pu Yi 1906–67

Emperor of China 1908–12; Japan's puppet emperor of Manchuria 1934–45

8 For the past 40 years I had never folded my own quilt, made my own bed, or poured out my own washing. I had never even washed my own feet or tied my shoes.

From Emperor to Citizen (1964)

John Pudney 1909–77

English poet and writer

9 Do not despair
For Johnny-head-in-air;
He sleeps as sound
As Johnny underground.

'For Johnny' (1942)

10 And keep your tears
For him in after years.

Better by far
For Johnny-the-bright-star,
To keep your head,
And see his children fed.

'For Johnny' (1942)

Al Purdy 1918–2000

Canadian poet and writer

11 Look here
You've never seen this country
it's not the way you thought it was
Look again.

of Canada

'The Country of the Young' (1976)

12 Looking into his eyes
it is possible to see the first hunters
(if you have your own vision)
after the last ice age.

'Inuit' (1967)

Mario Puzo 1920–99

American novelist

13 I'll make him an offer he can't refuse.

The Godfather (1969)

14 A lawyer with his briefcase can steal more than a hundred men with guns.

The Godfather (1969)

Barbara Pym 1913–80

English novelist

15 She experienced all the cosiness and irritation which can come from living with thoroughly nice people with whom one has nothing in common.

Less than Angels (1955)

Mary Quant 1934-

English fashion designer

1 It was she who established the fact that this latter half of the twentieth century belongs to Youth.

of her invention, the Chelsea Girl

Quant by Quant (1966)

2 Being young is greatly overestimated . . . Any failure seems so total. Later on you realize you can have another go.

interview in *Observer* 5 May 1996

Dan Quayle 1947-

American Republican politician

on Quayle: see **Bentsen** 30:11

3 Space is almost infinite. As a matter of fact, we think it is infinite.

in *Daily Telegraph* 8 March 1989

4 What a waste it is to lose one's mind, or not to have a mind. How true that is.

speech to the United Negro College Fund, whose slogan is 'a mind is a terrible thing to waste'; in *The Times* 26 May 1989

Arthur Quiller-Couch 1863-1944

English writer and academic

5 All the old statues of Victory have wings: but Grief has no wings. She is the unwelcome lodger that squats on the hearthstone between us and the fire and will not move or be dislodged.

Armistice Day anniversary sermon, Cambridge, November 1923

W. V. O. Quine 1908-

American philosopher

6 On the doctrinal side, I do not see that we are farther along today than where [David] Hume left us. The Humean predicament is the human predicament.

Ontological Relativity and Other Essays (1969)

7 It is the tension between the scientist's laws and his own attempted breaches of them that powers the engines of science and makes it forge ahead.

Quiddities (1987)

8 Students of the heavens are separable into astronomers and astrologers as readily as are the minor domestic ruminants into sheep and goats, but the separation of philosophers into sages and cranks seems to be more sensitive to frames of reference.

Theories and Things (1981)

9 Different persons growing up in the same language are like different bushes trimmed and trained to take the shape of identical elephants. The anatomical details of twigs and branches will fulfill the elephantine shape differently from bush to bush, but the overall outward results are alike.

Word and Object (1960)

Yitzhak Rabin 1922-95

Israeli statesman and military leader, Prime Minister 1974-7 and 1992-5

10 We say to you today in a loud and a clear voice: enough of blood and tears. Enough.

to the Palestinians, at the signing of the Israel–Palestine Declaration

in Washington, 13 September 1993

Lord Radcliffe 1899-1977

British lawyer and public servant

11 Society has become used to the standing armies of power—the permanent Civil Service, the police force, the tax-gatherer—organized on a scale which was unknown to earlier centuries.

Power and the State (BBC Reith Lectures, 1951)

12 Governments always tend to want not really a free press but a managed or well-conducted one.

in 1967; Peter Hennessy *What the Papers Never Said* (1985)

James Rado 1939– and **Gerome Ragni** 1942–

American songwriters

1 When the moon is in the seventh house,
And Jupiter aligns with Mars,
Then peace will guide the planets,
And love will steer the stars;
This is the dawning of the age of
Aquarius.

'Aquarius' (1967 song)

John Rae 1931–

English writer

2 War is, after all, the universal perversion. We are all tainted: if we cannot experience our perversion at first hand we spend our time reading war stories, the pornography of war; or seeing war films, the blue films of war; or titillating our senses with the imagination of great deeds, the masturbation of war.

The Custard Boys (1960)

Hasan Abdel Rahman

Palestinian Authority representative to Washington

3 We are not looking for a pretext to say no. We are looking for a reason to proceed.

on the prospects of a Middle East peace deal
in *Newsweek* 8 January 2001

Craig Raine 1944–

English poet

4 In homes, a haunted apparatus sleeps,
that snores when you pick it up.

If the ghost cries, they carry it
to their lips and soothe it to sleep

with sounds. And yet, they wake it up
deliberately, but tickling it with a finger.

'A Martian sends a Postcard Home' (1979)

Claude Rains

see **Film lines** 116:14

Walter Raleigh 1861–1922

English lecturer and critic

5 In examinations those who do not wish to know ask questions of those who cannot tell.

Laughter from a Cloud (1923) 'Some Thoughts on Examinations'

6 I wish I loved the Human Race;
I wish I loved its silly face;
I wish I liked the way it walks;
I wish I liked the way it talks;
And when I'm introduced to one
I wish I thought *What Jolly Fun!*

'Wishes of an Elderly Man' (1923)

7 An anthology is like all the plums and orange peel picked out of a cake.

letter to Mrs Robert Bridges, 15 January 1915

Srinivasa Ramanujan 1887–1920

Indian mathematician

replying to G. H. Hardy's suggestion that the number of a taxi-cab (1729) *was 'dull':*

8 No, it is a very interesting number; it is the smallest number expressible as a sum of two cubes in two different ways.

the two ways being 1^3+12^3 *and* 9^3+10^3
in *Proceedings of the London Mathematical Society* 26 May 1921

Ayn Rand 1905–82

American writer

9 Civilization is the progress toward a society of privacy. The savage's noble existence is public, ruled by the laws of his tribe. Civilization is the process of setting man free from men.

The Fountainhead (1947)

John Crowe Ransom 1888–1974

American poet and critic

10 Two evils, monstrous either one apart,
Possessed me, and were long and loath at
going:
A cry of Absence, Absence, in the heart,

And in the wood the furious winter
blowing.
'Winter Remembered' (1945)

Arthur Ransome

see **Telegrams** 316:2

Frederic Raphael 1931–

British novelist and screenwriter

1 'So this is the city of dreaming spires,' Sheila said. 'Theoretically speaking that's Oxford,' Adam said. 'This is the city of perspiring dreams.'

of Cambridge

The Glittering Prizes (1976); see below

And that sweet City with her dreaming spires.

Matthew Arnold (1822–88) 'Thyrsis' (1866)

2 I come from suburbia . . . and I don't ever want to go back. It's the one place in the world that's further away than anywhere else.

The Glittering Prizes (1976) 'A Sex Life'

Gerald Ratner 1949–

English businessman

3 We even sell a pair of earrings for under £1, which is cheaper than a prawn sandwich from Marks & Spencers. But I have to say the earrings probably won't last as long.

speech to the Institute of Directors, Albert Hall, 23 April 1991

Terence Rattigan 1911–77

English dramatist

4 Let us invent a character, a nice respectable, middle-class, middle-aged, maiden lady, with time on her hands and the money to help her pass it. She enjoys pictures, books, music, and the theatre and though to none of these arts (or rather, for consistency's sake, to none of these three arts and the one craft) does she bring much knowledge or discernment, at least, as she is apt to tell her cronies, she 'does know what she likes'. Let us call her Aunt Edna . . . Aunt Edna is universal, and to those who may feel that all the problems of the modern theatre might be solved by her liquidation, let me add that I have no doubt at all that she is also immortal.

Collected Plays (1953) vol. 2, preface

5 French without tears.

title of play (1937)

6 Do you know what 'le vice Anglais'—the English vice—really is? Not flagellation, not pederasty—whatever the French believe it to be. It's our refusal to admit our emotions. We think they demean us, I suppose.

In Praise of Love (1973)

7 You can be in the Horseguards and still be common, dear.

Separate Tables (1954) 'Table Number Seven'

Irina Ratushinskaya 1954–

Russian poet

8 Russian literature saved my soul. When I was a young girl in school and I asked what is good and what is evil, no one in that corrupt system could show me.

in *Observer* 15 October 1989

Derek Raymond 1931–94

English thriller writer

9 The psychopath is the furnace that gives no heat.

The Hidden Files (1992)

Claire Rayner 1931–

English journalist

10 I always say I don't think everyone has the right to happiness or to be loved. Even the Americans have written into their constitution that you have the right to the 'pursuit of happiness'. You have the right to try but that is all.

G. Kinnock and F. Miller (eds.) *By Faith and Daring* (1993)

Herbert Read 1893–1968

English art historian

1 Do not judge this movement kindly. It is not just another amusing stunt. It is defiant—the desperate act of men too profoundly convinced of the rottenness of our civilization to want to save a shred of its respectability.

International Surrealist Exhibition Catalogue, New Burlington Galleries, London, 11 June–4 July 1936, introduction

2 Art is . . . pattern informed by sensibility.

The Meaning of Art (1955)

3 Lorca was killed, singing,
and Fox who was my friend.
The rhythm returns: the song
which has no end.

'The Heart Conscripted' (1938)

4 I saw him stab
And stab again
A well-killed Boche.

This is the happy warrior,
This is he . . .

Naked Warriors (1919) 'The Scene of War, 4. The Happy Warrior'

Piers Paul Read 1941–

English novelist

5 Sins become more subtle as you grow older. You commit sins of despair rather than lust.

in *Daily Telegraph* 3 October 1990

Nancy Reagan 1923–

American actress and wife of Ronald **Reagan**, First Lady of the US, 1981–9
see also **Official advice** 245:9

6 A woman is like a teabag—only in hot water do you realize how strong she is.

in *Observer* 29 March 1981

7 If the President has a bully pulpit, then the First Lady has a white glove pulpit . . . more refined, restricted, ceremonial, but it's a pulpit all the same.

in *New York Times* 10 March 1988; see **Roosevelt** 279:3

Ronald Reagan 1911–

American Republican statesman; 40th President of the US, 1981–9; husband of Nancy **Reagan**
on Reagan: see **Keillor** 176:12, **Schroeder** 291:9, **Vidal** 328:6, **Warner** 330:5; *see also* **Dempsey** 89:14, **Gipp** 135:7

8 I paid for this microphone.

in 1980, debating for the Republican nomination against George ***Bush****; the moderator had ordered Reagan's microphone turned off when he asked for the participation of other candidates, and the refusal to allow this was held to be very damaging to Bush*

Lou Cannon *Ronald Reagan* (1982)

President Carter had described a proposal for a national health insurance plan

9 JIMMY CARTER: Governor Reagan, again, typically is against such a proposal.
RONALD REAGAN: There you go again!

as Republican challenger debating with President Carter in the 1980 presidential campaign; in *Times* 30 October 1980

10 Politics is supposed to be the second oldest profession. I have come to realize that it bears a very close resemblance to the first.

at a conference in Los Angeles, 2 March 1977

11 You can tell a lot about a fellow's character by his way of eating jellybeans.

in *New York Times* 15 January 1981

12 My fellow Americans, I am pleased to tell you I just signed legislation which outlaws Russia forever. The bombing begins in five minutes.

said during radio microphone test, 11 August 1984

13 We are especially not going to tolerate these attacks from outlaw states run by the strangest collection of misfits, Looney Tunes, and squalid criminals since the advent of the Third Reich.

following the hijack of a US plane

speech, 8 July 1985

14 We will never forget them, nor the last time we saw them this morning, as they prepared for the journey and waved goodbye and 'slipped the surly bonds of earth' to 'touch the face of God.'

after the loss of the space shuttle Challenger *with all its crew*

broadcast from the Oval Office, 28 January 1986; see **Magee** 212:8, 212:9

1 I now begin the journey that will lead me into the sunset of my life.

statement to the American people revealing that he had Alzheimer's disease

in *Daily Telegraph* 5 January 1995

Henry Reed 1914–86

English poet and dramatist

2 Today we have naming of parts.
 Yesterday,
We had daily cleaning. And tomorrow
 morning,
We shall have what to do after firing. But
 today,
Today we have naming of parts.

'Lessons of the War: 1, Naming of Parts' (1946)

3 They call it easing the Spring: it is
 perfectly easy
If you have any strength in your thumb:
 like the bolt,
And the breech, and the cocking-piece,
 and the point of balance,
Which in our case we have not got.

'Lessons of the War: 1, Naming of Parts' (1946)

4 And the sooner the tea's out of the way, the sooner we can get out the gin, eh?

Private Life of Hilda Tablet (1954 radio play)

5 Modest? My word, no . . . He was an all-the-lights-on man.

A Very Great Man Indeed (1953 radio play)

6 I have known her pass the whole evening without mentioning a single book, or *in fact anything unpleasant*, at all.

A Very Great Man Indeed (1953 radio play)

John Reed 1887–1920

American journalist and revolutionary

7 Ten days that shook the world.

title of book (1919)

Keith Reid 1946–

English pop singer and songwriter

8 Her face, at first . . . just ghostly
Turned a whiter shade of pale.

'A Whiter Shade of Pale' (1967 song)

Lord Reith 1889–1971

British administrator and politician, first general manager (1922–7) and first director-general (1927–8) of the BBC

9 By the time the civil service has finished drafting a document to give effect to a principle, there may be little of the principle left.

Into the Wind (1949)

10 When people feel deeply, impartiality is bias.

Into the Wind (1949)

Erich Maria Remarque 1898–1970

German novelist

11 All quiet on the western front.

English title of *Im Westen nichts Neues* (1929 novel)

Montague John Rendall 1862–1950

Member of the first BBC Board of Governors

12 Nation shall speak peace unto nation.

motto of the BBC (1927); see below

Nation shall not lift up sword against nation.

Bible Isaiah

Jean Renoir 1894–1979

French film director

13 Is it possible to succeed without any act of betrayal?

My Life and My Films (1974) 'Nana'

14 Don't think that this is a letter. It is only a small eruption of a disease called friendship.

letter to Janine Bazin, 12 June 1974

Pierre Auguste Renoir

see **Misquotations** 226:9

David Reuben 1933–

American psychiatrist

1 Everything you always wanted to know about sex, but were afraid to ask.
title of book (1969)

Walter Reuther 1907–70

American labour leader

2 If it looks like a duck, walks like a duck and quacks like a duck, then it just may be a duck.
as a test, during the **McCarthy** *era, of Communist affiliations*
attributed

Charles Revson 1906–75

American businessman

3 In the factory we make cosmetics; in the store we sell hope.
A. Tobias *Fire and Ice* (1976)

Malvina Reynolds 1900–78

American songwriter

4 Little boxes on the hillside,
Little boxes made of ticky-tacky,
Little boxes on the hillside,
Little boxes all the same.
on the tract houses in the hills to the south of San Francisco
'Little Boxes' (1962 song)

Jean Rhys c.1890–1979

British novelist and short-story writer

5 We can't all be happy, we can't all be rich, we can't all be lucky—and it would be so much less fun if we were . . . Some must cry so that others may be able to laugh the more heartily.
Good Morning, Midnight (1939)

6 The perpetual hunger to be beautiful and that thirst to be loved which is the real curse of Eve.
The Left Bank (1927) 'Illusion'

7 A doormat in a world of boots.
describing herself
in *Guardian* 6 December 1990

Grantland Rice 1880–1954

American sports writer

8 For when the One Great Scorer comes to
mark against your name,
He writes—not that you won or lost—
but how you played the Game.
'Alumnus Football' (1941)

9 All wars are planned by old men
In council rooms apart.
'The Two Sides of War' (1955)

10 Outlined against a blue-grey October sky, the Four Horsemen rode again. In dramatic lore they were known as Famine, Pestilence, Destruction, and Death. These are only aliases. Their real names are Stuhldreher, Miller, Crowley, and Layden. They formed the crest of the South Bend cyclone before which another fighting Army football team was swept over the precipice.
report of football match between US Military Academy at West Point NY and University of Notre Dame, in *New York Tribune* 19 October 1924

Tim Rice 1944–

English songwriter

11 Don't cry for me Argentina.
title of song (1976) from the musical *Evita*, based on the life of Eva **Perón**

12 Prove to me that you're no fool
Walk across my swimming pool.
Jesus Christ Superstar (1970) 'Herod's Song'

Mandy Rice-Davies 1944–

English model and showgirl

13 He would, wouldn't he?
on hearing that Lord Astor denied her allegations, concerning himself and his house parties at Cliveden
at the trial of Stephen Ward, 29 June 1963

Adrienne Rich 1923–

American poet and critic

1 The thing I came for:
the wreck and not the story of the wreck
the thing itself and not the myth.

'Diving into the Wreck' (1973)'

2 Memory says: Want to do right? Don't
count on me.

'Eastern War Time' (1991)

3 I'm accused of child-death of drinking
blood . . .
there is spit on my sleeve there are
phonecalls in the night . . .

'Eastern War Time' (1991)

4 Our friends were not unearthly beautiful.
Nor spoke with tongues of gold; our
lovers blundered
Now and again when most we sought
perfection,
Or hid in cupboards when the heavens
thundered.
The human rose to haunt us everywhere,
Raw, flawed, and asking more than we
could bear.

'Ideal Landscape' (1955)

Ann Richards 1933–

American Democratic politician

5 Poor George, he can't help it—he was born with a silver foot in his mouth.

of George ***Bush***

keynote speech at the Democratic convention, 1988; in *Independent* 20 July 1988

I. A. Richards 1893–1979

English literary critic

6 We believe a scientist because he can substantiate his remarks, not because he is eloquent and forcible in his enunciation. In fact, we distrust him when he seems to be influencing us by his manner.

Science and Poetry (1926)

7 It [poetry] is capable of saving us; it is a perfectly possible means of overcoming chaos.

Science and Poetry (1926)

Keith Richards 1943–

English rock musician

see also **Jagger**

8 Sure thing, man. I used to be a laboratory myself once.

on being asked to autograph a fan's school chemistry book

in *Independent on Sunday* 7 August 1994

Justin Richardson 1900–75

British poet

9 People who have three daughters try
once more
And then it's fifty-fifty they'll have four.
Those with a son or sons will let things
be.
Hence all these surplus women. Q.E.D.

'Note for the Scientist' (1959)

10 For years a secret shame destroyed my
peace—
I'd not read Eliot, Auden or MacNeice.
But then I had a thought that brought
me hope—
Neither had Chaucer, Shakespeare,
Milton, Pope.

'Take Heart, Illiterates' (1966)

Ralph Richardson 1902–83

English actor

11 Acting is merely the art of keeping a large group of people from coughing.

in *New York Herald Tribune* 19 May 1946

Mordecai Richler 1931–

Canadian writer

12 I'm world famous, Dr Parks said, all over Canada.

The Incomparable Atuk (1963)

Laura Riding 1901–91

American poet and novelist

13 Without dressmakers to connect
The good-will of the body
With the purpose of the head,
We should be two worlds
Instead of a world and its shadow

The flesh.
'Because of Clothes' (1938)

Nicholas Ridley 1929–93

British Conservative politician

of the European community:

1 This is all a German racket, designed to take over the whole of Europe.
in *Spectator* 14 July 1990

Rainer Maria Rilke 1875–1926

German poet

2 We live our lives, for ever taking leave.
Duineser Elegien (1948) no. 8

César Ritz 1850–1918

Swiss hotel proprietor

3 *Le client n'a jamais tort.*
The customer is never wrong.
R. Nevill and C. E. Jerningham *Piccadilly to Pall Mall* (1908)

Joan Riviere 1883–1962

British psychoanalyst

4 Civilization and its discontents.
title given to her translation of Sigmund Freud's *Das Unbehagen in der Kultur* (1930)

Lord Robbins 1898–1984

British economist

5 Economics is the science which studies human behaviour as a relationship between ends and scarce means which have alternative uses.
Essay on the Nature and Significance of Economic Science (1932)

Leo Robin 1900–84

American songwriter

6 A kiss on the hand may be quite continental,
But diamonds are a girl's best friend.
'Diamonds are a Girl's Best Friend' (1949 song); from the film *Gentlemen Prefer Blondes*; see **Loos** 202:12

7 Thanks for the memory.
title of song (with Ralph Rainger, 1937)

Anne Robinson 1944–

British television presenter
see also **Catchphrases** 60:12

8 What are they for? They are always so pleased with themselves.
of the Welsh; a dismissive comment, made on BBC2's Room 101 *programme, which roused a storm of protest*
in *Daily Telegraph* 7 March 2001

Edwin Arlington Robinson 1869–1935

American poet

9 I shall have more to say when I am dead.
'John Brown' (1920)

10 So on we worked, and waited for the light,
And went without meat, and cursed the bread;
And Richard Cory, one calm summer night,
Went home and put a bullet through his head.
'Richard Cory' (1897)

John Robinson 1919–83

English theologian; Bishop of Woolwich, 1959–69

11 Honest to God.
title of book (1963)

12 I think Lawrence tried to portray this [sex] relation as in a real sense an act of holy communion. For him flesh was sacramental of the spirit.
as defence witness in the case against Penguin Books for publishing Lady Chatterley's Lover
comment, 27 October 1960; see **Griffith-Jones** 141:2

Mary Robinson 1944–

Irish Labour stateswoman; President 1990–97

1 Instead of rocking the cradle, they rocked the system.

in her victory speech, paying tribute to the women of Ireland

in *The Times* 10 November 1990

Sugar Ray Robinson 1920–89

American boxer

when asked by the coroner if he had intended to 'get Doyle in trouble':

2 Mister, it's my *business* to get him in trouble.

following the death of Jimmy Doyle from his injuries after fighting Robinson, 24 June 1947

Sugar Ray Robinson with Dave Anderson *Sugar Ray* (1970)

Gene Roddenberry 1921–91

American film producer

see also **Misquotations** 226:1

3 These are the voyages of the starship *Enterprise*. Its five-year mission . . . to boldly go where no man has gone before.

Star Trek (television series, from 1966)

Anita Roddick 1942–

English businesswoman

4 I think that business practices would improve immeasurably if they were guided by 'feminine' principles—qualities like love and care and intuition.

Body and Soul (1991)

5 Running a company on market research is like driving while looking in the rear view mirror.

in *Independent* 22 August 1997

6 There is nothing on God's planet that will take away 30 years of arguing with your husband and 40 years of environmental abuse . . . You would be better off spending the money on a good bottle of pinot noir.

of 'anti-ageing' creams

in *Sunday Times* 22 October 2000

Almiro Rodrigues 1932–

Portuguese judge, presiding at the War Crimes Tribunal in The Hague

7 Individually you agreed to evil.

sentencing the Bosnian Serb General Radislav Krstic for his part in the massacre of Bosnian Muslims at Srebenica in July 1995

at The Hague, 2 August 2001

Sue Rodriguez 1951–94

Canadian activist for the legalization of assisted suicide

8 If I cannot give consent to my own death, then whose body is this? Who owns my life?

appealing to a subcomittee of the Canadian Commons, November 1992, as the victim of a terminal illness

in *Globe and Mail* 5 December 1992

Theodore Roethke 1908–63

American poet

9 Thought does not crush to stone.
The great sledge drops in vain.
Truth never is undone;
Its shafts remain.

'The Adamant' (1941)

10 I have known the inexorable sadness of pencils,
Neat in their boxes, dolour of pad and paper-weight,
All the misery of manilla folders and mucilage,
Desolation in immaculate public places.

'Dolour' (1948)

11 The body and the soul know how to play
In that dark world where gods have lost their way.

'Four for Sir John Davies' (1953) no. 2

12 O who can be
Both moth and flame? The weak moth blundering by.
Whom do we love? I thought I knew the truth;
Of grief I died, but no one knew my death.

'The Sequel' (1964)

13 I wake to sleep, and take my waking slow.

I feel my fate in what I cannot fear.
I learn by going where I have to go.
The Waking (1953)

Will Rogers 1879–1935

American actor and humorist

1 There is only one thing that can kill the movies, and that is education.
Autobiography of Will Rogers (1949)

2 Income Tax has made more Liars out of the American people than Golf.
The Illiterate Digest (1924) 'Helping the Girls with their Income Taxes'

3 Well, all I know is what I read in the papers.
in *New York Times* 30 September 1923

4 Heroing is one of the shortest-lived professions there is.
newspaper article, 15 February 1925, in Paula McSpadden Grove *The Will Rogers Book* (1961)

5 Communism is like prohibition, it's a good idea but it won't work.
Weekly Articles (1981); first published 1927

6 You can't say civilization don't advance, however, for in every war they kill you in a new way.
in *New York Times* 23 December 1929

7 Half our life is spent trying to find something to do with the time we have rushed through life trying to save.
letter in *New York Times* 29 April 1930

Mies van der Rohe 1886–1969

German-born architect and designer

8 Less is more.
P. Johnson *Mies van der Rohe* (1947); see **Venturi** 327:6

9 God is in the details.
in *New York Times* 19 August 1969

Eleanor Roosevelt 1884–1962

American humanitarian and diplomat; wife of Franklin **Roosevelt**
on Roosevelt: see **Stevenson** 308:12

10 I cannot believe that war is the best solution. No one won the last war, and no one will win the next war.
letter to Harry Truman, 22 March 1948

11 I have always felt that anyone who wanted an election so much that they would use those methods did not have the character that I really admired in public life.
on the tactics used by Richard **Nixon** *in his 1950 Senatorial campaign against the actress and politician Helen Gahagan Douglas (see* **Nixon** 242:7)
on 'Meet the Press' (NBC TV), 16 September 1956

12 No one can make you feel inferior without your consent.
in *Catholic Digest* August 1960

Franklin D. Roosevelt 1882–1945

American Democratic statesman, 32nd President of the US, 1933–45; husband of Eleanor **Roosevelt**

13 These unhappy times call for the building of plans that . . . build from the bottom up and not from the top down, that put their faith once more in the forgotten man at the bottom of the economic pyramid.
radio address, 7 April 1932

14 I pledge you, I pledge myself, to a new deal for the American people.
speech to the Democratic Convention in Chicago, 2 July 1932, accepting the presidential nomination

15 The only thing we have to fear is fear itself.
inaugural address, 4 March 1933

16 In the field of world policy I would dedicate this Nation to the policy of the good neighbour.
inaugural address, 4 March 1933

17 We face the arduous days that lie before us in the warm courage of national unity.
inaugural address, 4 March 1933; see **Bush** 49:13

18 I have seen war. I have seen war on land and sea. I have seen blood running from the wounded. I have seen men coughing out their gassed lungs. I have seen the dead in the mud. I have seen cities destroyed. I have seen 200 limping, exhausted men come out of line—the survivors of a regiment of 1,000 that went forward 48 hours before. I have seen children starving. I have seen the agony of mothers and wives. I hate war.

speech at Chautauqua, NY, 14 August 1936

1 I see one-third of a nation ill-housed, ill-clad, ill-nourished.

second inaugural address, 20 January 1937

2 I am reminded of four definitions: A Radical is a man with both feet firmly planted—in the air. A Conservative is a man with two perfectly good legs who, however, has never learned to walk forward. A Reactionary is a somnambulist walking backwards. A Liberal is a man who uses his legs and his hands at the behest—at the command—of his head.

radio address to *New York Herald Tribune* Forum, 26 October 1939

3 I have said this before, but I shall say it again and again and again: Your boys are not going to be sent into any foreign wars.

speech in Boston, 30 October 1940; see **Johnson** 171:11

4 We must be the great arsenal of democracy.

broadcast, 29 December 1940

5 We look forward to a world founded upon four essential human freedoms. The first is freedom of speech and expression—everywhere in the world. The second is freedom of every person to worship God in his own way—everywhere in the world. The third is freedom from want . . . The fourth is freedom from fear.

message to Congress, 6 January 1941

6 Yesterday, December 7, 1941—a date which will live in infamy—the United States of America was suddenly and deliberately attacked by naval and air forces of the Empire of Japan.

address to Congress, 8 December 1941

7 Books can not be killed by fire. People die, but books never die. No man and no force can abolish memory. No man and no force can put thought in a concentration camp forever. No man and no force can take from the world the books that embody man's eternal fight against tyranny of every kind. In this war, we know, books are weapons. And it is a part of your dedication always to make them weapons for man's freedom.

'Message to the Booksellers of America' 6 May 1942

8 It is fun to be in the same decade with you.

acknowledging congratulations on his 60th birthday

cabled reply to Winston **Churchill**, in W. S. Churchill *The Hinge of Fate* (1950)

9 The work, my friend, is peace. More than an end of this war—an end to the beginnings of all wars.

undelivered address for Jefferson Day, 13 April 1945 (the day after Roosevelt died)

Theodore Roosevelt

1858–1919

American Republican statesman, 26th President of the US, 1901–9

10 Speak softly and carry a big stick; you will go far.

quoting an 'old adage'

speech in Chicago, 3 April 1903

11 A man who is good enough to shed his blood for the country is good enough to be given a square deal afterwards.

speech at the Lincoln Monument, Springfield, Illinois, 4 June 1903

12 The men with the muck-rakes are often indispensable to the well-being of society; but only if they know when to stop raking the muck.

speech in Washington, 14 April 1906

13 It is not the critic who counts; not the man who points out how the strong man stumbles, or where the doer of deeds could have done better. The credit belongs to the man who is actually in the arena.

speech at the Sorbonne, Paris, 23 April 1910

14 We stand at Armageddon, and we battle for the Lord.

speech at the Republican National Convention, 18 June 1912

1 There is no room in this country for hyphenated Americanism.

speech in New York, 12 October 1915

2 One of our defects as a nation is a tendency to use what have been called 'weasel words'. When a weasel sucks eggs the meat is sucked out of the egg. If you use a 'weasel word' after another, there is nothing left of the other.

speech in St Louis, 31 May 1916

3 I have got such a bully pulpit!

his personal view of the presidency

in *Outlook* (New York) 27 February 1909; see **Reagan** 271:7

4 Foolish fanatics . . . the men who form the lunatic fringe in all reform movements.

Autobiography (1913)

Lord Rootes 1894–1964

English motor-car manufacturer

5 No other man-made device since the shields and lances of ancient knights fulfils a man's ego like an automobile.

attributed, 1958

Billy Rose 1899–1966 and **Marty Bloom**

American songwriters

6 Does the spearmint lose its flavour on the bedpost overnight?

revived in 1959 by Lonnie Donegan with the title 'Does your chewing-gum lose its flavour on the bedpost overnight?'

title of song (1924)

Ethel Rosenberg 1916–53 and **Julius Rosenberg** 1918–53

American couple convicted of spying for the Russians, and executed for espionage

7 We are innocent, as we have proclaimed and maintained from the time of our arrest. This is the whole truth. To forsake this truth is to pay too high a price even for the priceless gift of life—for life thus purchased we could not live out in dignity and self-respect.

petition for executive clemency, filed 9 January 1953

8 Ethel wants it made known that we are the first victims of American Fascism.

letter from Julius to Emanuel Bloch before the execution, 19 June 1953

Harold Ross 1892–1951

American journalist and editor

9 The *New Yorker* will be the magazine which is not edited for the old lady in Dubuque.

James Thurber *The Years with Ross* (1959)

10 Who he?

frequent comment on manuscripts and proofs

Dale Kramer *Ross and The New Yorker* (1952)

Jean Rostand 1894–1977

French biologist

11 The biologist passes, the frog remains.

sometimes quoted as 'Theories pass. The frog remains'

Inquiétudes d'un Biologiste (1967)

12 To be adult is to be alone.

Pensées d'un biologiste (1954)

13 Kill a man, and you are an assassin. Kill millions of men, and you are a conqueror. Kill everyone, and you are a god.

Pensées d'un biologiste (1939)

Leo Rosten 1908–97

American writer and social scientist

14 Any man who hates dogs and babies can't be all bad.

of W. C. ***Fields****, and often attributed to him*

speech at Masquers' Club dinner, 16 February 1939; letter in *Times Literary Supplement* 24 January 1975

Philip Roth 1933–

American novelist

15 A Jewish man with parents alive is a

fifteen-year-old boy, and will remain a fifteen-year-old boy until *they die*!

Portnoy's Complaint (1967)

1 Doctor, my doctor, what do you say, LET'S PUT THE ID BACK IN YID!

Portnoy's Complaint (1967)

Lord Rothschild 1910–90

British administrator and scientist

2 The promises and panaceas that gleam like false teeth in the party manifestoes.

Meditations of a Broomstick (1977)

Johnny Rotten 1956–

English singer and songwriter, member of the Sex Pistols

on Rotten: see **Newspaper headlines** 240:6

3 I am an Anti-Christ
I am an anarchist.

'Anarchy in the UK' (1976 song)

4 We're so pretty, oh so pretty
We're vacant.

'Pretty Vacant' (1977 song)

5 If you accept the forms that be, then you're doomed to your own ultimate blandness.

R. Palmer *Dancing in the Street; a rock and roll history* (1996)

Matthew Rowbottom, Richard Stannard, and The Spice Girls

English songwriters, and English pop singers (Melanie Brown, Victoria Adams, Geri Halliwell, Emma Bunton, and Melanie Chisholm)

see also **Chisholm**

6 Yo I'll tell you what I want, what I really really want
so tell me what you want, what you really really want.

'Wannabe' (1996 song)

Helen Rowland 1875–1950

American writer

7 A husband is what is left of a lover, after the nerve has been extracted.

A Guide to Men (1922)

8 The follies which a man regrets most, in his life, are those which he didn't commit when he had the opportunity.

A Guide to Men (1922)

Richard Rowland *c.*1881–1947

American film producer

9 The lunatics have taken charge of the asylum.

on the take-over of United Artists by Charles ***Chaplin*** *and others*

T. Ramsaye *A Million and One Nights* (1926)

Maude Royden 1876–1956

English religious writer

10 The Church [of England] should go forward along the path of progress and be no longer satisfied only to represent the Conservative Party at prayer.

in *The Times* 17 July 1917

Mike Royko 1932–97

American journalist

11 No self-respecting fish would be wrapped in a Murdoch newspaper.

resigning from the Chicago Sun-Times *in 1984 when the paper was sold to Rupert* ***Murdoch***

Karl E. Meyer (ed.) *Pundits, Poets, and Wits* (1990)

Paul Alfred Rubens 1875–1917

English songwriter

12 Oh! we don't want to lose you but we think you ought to go
For your King and your Country both need you so.

'Your King and Country Want You' (1914 song)

Carol Rumens 1944–

British poet

1 A slow psalm of two nations
Mourning a common pain
—Hebrew and Arabic mingling
Their silver-rooted vine;
Olives and roses falling
To sweeten Palestine.
'A New Song' (1993)

2 It's simple, isn't it?
Never say the yes
you don't mean, but the no
you always meant, say that,
even if it's too late,
even if it kills you.
'A Woman of a Certain Age' (1993)

Donald Rumsfeld 1932–

American Republican politician and businessman, Defense Secretary from 2001

3 Learn to say, 'I don't know.' If used when appropriate, it will be often.
'Rumsfeld's Rules'; interview in *Wall Street Journal* 29 January 2001

4 If you are not criticized, you may not be doing much.
'Rumsfeld's Rules'; interview in *Wall Street Journal* 29 January 2001

Robert Runcie 1921–99

English Protestant clergyman; Archbishop of Canterbury
on Runcie: see **Field** 113:4

5 People are mourning on both sides of this conflict. In our prayers we shall quite rightly remember those who are bereaved in our own country and the relations of the young Argentinian soldiers who were killed. Common sorrow could do something to reunite those who were engaged in this struggle. A shared anguish can be a bridge of reconciliation. Our neighbours are indeed like us.
service of thanksgiving at the end of the Falklands war, St. Paul's Cathedral, London, 26 July 1982

6 In the middle ages people were tourists because of their religion, whereas now they are tourists because tourism is their religion.
speech in London, 6 December 1988

7 I have done my best to die before this book is published. It now seems possible that I may not succeed.
letter to Humphrey Carpenter, July 1996, in H. Carpenter *Robert Runcie* (1996)

Damon Runyon 1884–1946

American writer

8 'My boy,' he says, 'always try to rub up against money, for if you rub up against money long enough, some of it may rub off on you.'
in *Cosmopolitan* August 1929, 'A Very Honourable Guy'

9 I do see her in tough joints more than somewhat.
in *Collier's* 22 May 1930, 'Social Error'

10 I long ago come to the conclusion that all life is 6 to 5 against.
in *Collier's* 8 September 1934, 'A Nice Price'

Salman Rushdie 1947–

Indian-born British novelist

11 Most of what matters in your life takes place in your absence.
Midnight's Children (1981)

12 Family history, of course, has its proper dietary laws. One is supposed to swallow and digest only the permitted parts of it, the halal portions of the past, drained of their redness, their blood.
Midnight's Children (1981)

13 What is freedom of expression? Without the freedom to offend, it ceases to exist.
in *Weekend Guardian* 10 February 1990

14 One of the things a writer is for is to say the unsayable, speak the unspeakable and ask difficult questions.
in *Independent on Sunday* 10 September 1995

Dean Rusk 1909–94

American politician; Secretary of State, 1961–9

1 We're eyeball to eyeball, and I think the other fellow just blinked.
on the Cuban missile crisis
24 October 1962; in *Saturday Evening Post* 8 December 1962

2 Scratch any American and underneath you'll find an isolationist.
Tony Benn, diary, 12 January 1968

Bertrand Russell 1872–1970

British philosopher and mathematician

3 Three passions, simple but overwhelmingly strong, have governed my life: the longing for love, the search for knowledge, and unbearable pity for the suffering of mankind.
Autobiography (1967)

4 I was told that the Chinese said they would bury me by the Western Lake and build a shrine to my memory. I have some slight regret that this did not happen as I might have become a god, which would have been very *chic* for an atheist.
Autobiography (1968)

5 One of the symptoms of approaching nervous breakdown is the belief that one's work is terribly important, and that to take a holiday would bring all kinds of disaster.
The Conquest of Happiness (1930)

6 One should as a rule respect public opinion in so far as is necessary to avoid starvation and to keep out of prison, but anything that goes beyond this is voluntary submission to an unnecessary tyranny.
The Conquest of Happiness (1930)

7 A sense of duty is useful in work, but offensive in personal relations. People wish to be liked, not to be endured with patient resignation.
The Conquest of Happiness (1930)

8 Of all forms of caution, caution in love is perhaps the most fatal to true happiness.
The Conquest of Happiness (1930)

9 To be able to fill leisure intelligently is the last product of civilization.
The Conquest of Happiness (1930)

10 Aristotle maintained that women have fewer teeth than men; although he was twice married, it never occurred to him to verify this statement by examining his wives' mouths.
Impact of Science on Society (1952)

11 Work is of two kinds: first, altering the position of matter at or near the earth's surface relatively to other such matter; second, telling other people to do so. The first kind is unpleasant and ill paid; the second is pleasant and highly paid.
In Praise of Idleness and Other Essays (1986) title essay (1932)

12 The fact that an opinion has been widely held is no evidence whatever that it is not utterly absurd; indeed in view of the silliness of the majority of mankind, a widespread belief is more likely to be foolish than sensible.
Marriage and Morals (1929)

13 Mathematics may be defined as the subject in which we never know what we are talking about, nor whether what we are saying is true.
Mysticism and Logic (1918)

14 Mathematics, rightly viewed, possesses not only truth, but supreme beauty—a beauty cold and austere, like that of sculpture.
Philosophical Essays (1910)

15 The man who has fed the chicken every day throughout its life at last wrings its neck instead, showing that a more refined view as to the uniformity of nature would have been useful to the chicken.
The Problems of Philosophy (1912)

16 Every man, wherever he goes, is encompassed by a cloud of comforting convictions, which move with him like flies on a summer day.
Sceptical Essays (1928) 'Dreams and Facts'

17 We have, in fact, two kinds of morality side by side: one which we preach but do not practise, and another which we practise but seldom preach.

Sceptical Essays (1928) 'Eastern and Western Ideals of Happiness'

1 The fundamental defect of fathers, in our competitive society, is that they want their children to be a credit to them.

Sceptical Essays (1928) 'Freedom versus Authority in Education'

2 Machines are worshipped because they are beautiful, and valued because they confer power; they are hated because they are hideous, and loathed because they impose slavery.

Sceptical Essays (1928) 'Machines and Emotions'

3 The infliction of cruelty with a good conscience is a delight to moralists. That is why they invented Hell.

Sceptical Essays (1928) 'On the Value of Scepticism'

4 It is obvious that 'obscenity' is not a term capable of exact legal definition; in the practice of the Courts, it means 'anything that shocks the magistrate'.

Sceptical Essays (1928) 'The Recrudescence of Puritanism'

5 Man is a credulous animal, and must believe *something*; in the absence of good grounds for belief, he will be satisfied with bad ones.

Unpopular Essays (1950) 'Outline of Intellectual Rubbish'

6 Fear is the main source of superstition, and one of the main sources of cruelty.

Unpopular Essays (1950) 'An Outline of Intellectual Rubbish'

7 'Change' is scientific, 'progress' is ethical; change is indubitable, whereas progress is a matter of controversy.

Unpopular Essays (1950) 'Philosophy and Politics'

8 The linguistic philosophy, which cares only about language, and not about the world, is like the boy who preferred the clock without the pendulum because, although it no longer told the time, it went more easily than before and at a more exhilarating pace.

foreword to Ernest Gellner *Words and Things* (1959)

Dora Russell 1894–1986

English feminist

9 We want better reasons for having children than not knowing how to prevent them.

Hypatia (1925)

Ernest Rutherford 1871–1937

New Zealand physicist

on Rutherford: see **Bullard** 47:9, **Leacock** 193:8

10 All science is either physics or stamp collecting.

J. B. Birks *Rutherford at Manchester* (1962)

11 If your experiment needs statistics, you ought to have done a better experiment.

Norman T. J. Bailey *The Mathematical Approach to Biology and Medicine* (1967)

12 It was quite the most incredible event that has ever happened to me in my life. It was almost as incredible as if you fired a 15-inch shell at a piece of tissue paper and it came back and hit you.

on the back-scattering effect of metal foil on alpha-particles

E. N. da C. Andrade *Rutherford and the Nature of the Atom* (1964)

13 We haven't got the money, so we've got to think!

in *Bulletin of the Institute of Physics* (1962) vol. 13

Sue Ryder 1923–2000

British charity worker

14 I don't look for reward. Surely, according to God's judgement, our reward is when we die. We are all pilgrims on this earth.

after her peerage was awarded in 1979

in *Daily Telegraph* 3 November 2000; obituary

15 Each place had its own individuality, atmosphere and tradition—all foul, of course.

of Nazi concentration camps

in *Daily Telegraph* 3 November 2000; obituary

Gilbert Ryle 1900–76

English philosopher

1 A myth is, of course, not a fairy story. It is the presentation of facts belonging to one category in the idioms appropriate to another. To explode a myth is accordingly not to deny the facts but to re-allocate them.

The Concept of Mind (1949)

2 Philosophy is the replacement of category-habits by category-disciplines.

The Concept of Mind (1949)

3 The dogma of the Ghost in the Machine.

the mind viewed as distinct from the body

The Concept of Mind (1949)

Jonathan Sacks 1948–

British Chief Rabbi

4 Modernity is the transition from fate to choice.

'The Persistence of Faith' (Reith Lecture, 1990)

5 When television presents moral issues, it chooses extreme spokesmen . . . creating a tragic view of the moral life, in which the rudest voice wins.

in *Daily Telegraph* 6 September 2001

Vita Sackville-West 1892–1962

English writer and gardener; wife of Harold **Nicolson**

6 The greater cats with golden eyes
Stare out between the bars.

The King's Daughter (1929)

Anwar al-Sadat 1918–81

Egyptian statesman, President 1970–81

7 Peace is much more precious than a piece of land.

speech in Cairo, 8 March 1978

Carl Sagan 1934–96

American scientist and writer

8 If you wish to make an apple pie from scratch, you must first invent the universe.

Cosmos (1980)

9 Extraordinary claims require extraordinary evidence.

interview in *Nova* 1996

on an image of the earth seen from deep space:

10 This distant image . . . underscores our responsibility to deal more kindly and compassionately with one another and to preserve and cherish that pale blue dot, the only home we've ever known.

commencement address, 11 May 1996

Françoise Sagan 1935–

French novelist

11 To jealousy, nothing is more frightful than laughter.

La Chamade (1965)

Antoine de Saint-Exupéry 1900–44

French writer and aviator

12 Grown-ups never understand anything for themselves, and it is tiresome for children to be always and forever explaining things to them.

Le Petit Prince (1943)

13 Experience shows us that love does not consist in gazing at each other but in looking together in the same direction.

Wind, Sand and Stars (1939)

Lord St John of Fawsley 1929–

British Conservative politician and author

14 The monarchy has become our only truly popular institution at a time when the House of Commons has declined in public esteem and the Lords is a matter of controversy. The monarchy is, in a real sense, underpinning the other two estates of the realm.

in *The Times* 1 February 1982

Yves Saint Laurent 1936–

French couturier

1 I don't really like knees.

in *Observer* 3 August 1958

Andrei Sakharov 1921–89

Russian nuclear physicist

2 Every day I saw the huge material, intellectual and nervous resources of thousands of people being poured into the creation of a means of total destruction, something capable of annihilating all human civilization. I noticed that the control levers were in the hands of people who, though talented in their own ways, were cynical.

Sakharov Speaks (1974)

Saki 1870–1916

British writer

3 'I must be going,' said Mrs Eggelby, in a tone which had been thoroughly sterilised of even perfunctory regret.

Beasts and Super-Beasts (1914) 'Clovis on Parental Responsibilities'

4 Waldo is one of those people who would be enormously improved by death.

Beasts and Super-Beasts (1914) 'The Feast of Nemesis'

5 The people of Crete unfortunately make more history than they can consume locally.

Chronicles of Clovis (1911) 'The Jesting of Arlington Stringham'

6 The cook was a good cook, as cooks go; and as cooks go, she went.

Reginald (1904) 'Reginald on Besetting Sins'

7 Whenever I feel in the least tempted to be methodical or business-like or even decently industrious, I go to Kensal Green and look at the graves of those who died in business.

The Square Egg (1924)

J. D. Salinger 1919–

American novelist and short-story writer

8 The catcher in the rye.

title of novel (1951)

9 What really knocks me out is a book that, when you're all done reading it, you wish the author that wrote it was a terrific friend of yours and you could call him up on the phone whenever you felt like it.

The Catcher in the Rye (1951)

10 Sex is something I really don't understand too hot. You never know *where* the hell you are. I keep making up these sex rules for myself, and then I break them right away.

The Catcher in the Rye (1951)

Lord Salisbury 1893–1972

British Conservative politician

11 Too clever by half.

*of Iain **Macleod**, Colonial Secretary; the term 'too clever by half' had been applied by an earlier Lord Salisbury (1830–1903) to Disraeli's amendment on Disestablishment, 30 March 1868*

in the House of Lords, 7 March 1961

Alex Salmond 1954–

Scottish Nationalist politician

12 Nobody ever celebrated Devolution Day.

asserting his belief in full independence

in *Independent* 2 April 1992

13 I do not want to be separate from anything. I want for my country to be joined in co-operation and mutual respect—on a footing of equality—with all the nations of Europe.

in *Scotsman* 27 November 1998

14 The Scottish parliament is our passport to independence.

outgoing speech as party leader to the Scottish Nationalist Party Conference

in *Guardian* 23 September 2000

Anthony Sampson 1926–

British author and journalist

1 A secret tome of *The Great and the Good* is kept, listing everyone who has the right, safe qualifications of worthiness, soundness and discretion; and from this tome came the stage army of committee people.

Anatomy of Britain Today (1965)

2 Of all the legacies of empire, the most dangerous is surely an immobile bureaucracy which can perpetuate its own interests and values, like those ancient hierarchies which presided over declining civilizations . . . As the British mandarins reinforce their defences, awarding each other old imperial honours, do they hear any echoes from Castile or Byzantium?

The Changing Anatomy of Britain (1982)

Lord Samuel 1870–1963

British Liberal politician

3 A library is thought in cold storage.

A Book of Quotations (1947)

Paul A. Samuelson 1915–

American economist

4 The consumer, so it is said, is the king . . . each is a voter who uses his money as votes to get the things done that he wants done.

Economics (8th ed., 1970)

Carl Sandburg 1878–1967

American poet

5 Hog Butcher for the World,
Tool Maker, Stacker of Wheat,
Player with Railroads and the Nation's
Freight Handler;
Stormy, husky, brawling,
City of the Big Shoulders.

'Chicago' (1916)

6 When Abraham Lincoln was shovelled
into the tombs,
he forgot the copperheads and the
assassin . . .
in the dust, in the cool tombs.

'Cool Tombs' (1918)

7 The fog comes
on little cat feet.

It sits looking
over harbour and city
on silent haunches
and then moves on.

'Fog' (1916)

8 Pile the bodies high at Austerlitz and
Waterloo.
Shovel them under and let me work—
I am the grass; I cover all.

'Grass' (1918)

9 I tell you the past is a bucket of ashes.

'Prairie' (1918)

10 Little girl . . . Sometime they'll give a war and nobody will come.

The People, Yes (1936); 'Suppose They Gave a War and No One Came?' was the title of a piece by Charlotte Keyes in *McCall's* October 1966; 'Suppose They Gave a War and Nobody Came?' was the title of a 1970 film; see **Ginsberg** 135:1

11 Poetry is the achievement of the synthesis of hyacinths and biscuits.

in *Atlantic Monthly* March 1923 'Poetry Considered'

12 Slang is a language that rolls up its sleeves, spits on its hands and goes to work.

in *New York Times* 13 February 1959

Henry 'Red' Sanders 1905–58

American football coach

13 Sure, winning isn't everything. It's the only thing.

in *Sports Illustrated* 26 December 1955; often attributed to Vince Lombardi

George Santayana 1863–1952

Spanish-born philosopher and critic

14 Fanaticism consists in redoubling your effort when you have forgotten your aim.

The Life of Reason (1905)

15 Those who cannot remember the past are condemned to repeat it.

The Life of Reason (1905)

John Singer Sargent
1856–1925

American painter

1 Every time I paint a portrait I lose a friend.
N. Bentley and E. Esar *Treasury of Humorous Quotations* (1951)

Leslie Sarony 1897–1985

British songwriter

2 Ain't it grand to be blooming well dead?
title of song (1932)

Ken Saro-Wiwa

see **Last words** 190:14

Nathalie Sarraute 1902–

French novelist

3 Radio and television, to which we devote so many of the leisure hours once spent listening to parlour chatter and parlour music, have succeeded in lifting the manufacture of banality out of the sphere of handicraft and placed it in that of a major industry.
in *Times Literary Supplement* 10 June 1960

Jean-Paul Sartre 1905–80

French philosopher, novelist, dramatist, and critic
on Sartre: see **de Gaulle** 88:16

4 When the rich wage war it's the poor who die.
Le Diable et le bon Dieu (1951)

5 Nothingness haunts being.
L'Être et le néant (1943)

6 I am condemned to be free.
L'Être et le néant (1943)

7 Hell is other people.
Huis Clos (1944)

8 Like all dreamers, I mistook disenchantment for truth.
Les Mots (1964) 'Écrire'

9 I confused things with their names: that is belief.
Les Mots (1964) 'Écrire'

10 The poor don't know that their function in life is to exercise our generosity.
Les Mots (1964) 'Lire'

11 She believed in nothing; only her scepticism kept her from being an atheist.
Les Mots (1964) 'Lire'

12 Human life begins on the far side of despair.
Les Mouches (1943)

13 Three o'clock is always too late or too early for anything you want to do.
La Nausée (Nausea, 1938) 'Vendredi'

14 I hate victims who respect their executioners.
Les Séquestrés d'Altona (1960)

15 A writer must refuse, therefore, to allow himself to be transformed into an institution.
refusing the Nobel Prize
declaration read at Stockholm, 22 October 1964

16 The whole question boils down to knowing whether one is interested in talking about the flight of butterflies or the condition of the Jews.
attributed

Siegfried Sassoon 1886–1967

English poet

17 If I were fierce, and bald, and short of
breath,
I'd live with scarlet Majors at the Base,
And speed glum heroes up the line to
death.
'Base Details' (1918)

18 Does it matter?—losing your sight? . . .
There's such splendid work for the blind;
And people will always be kind,
As you sit on the terrace remembering
And turning your face to the light.
'Does it Matter?' (1918)

19 You are too young to fall asleep for ever;
And when you sleep you remind me of
the dead.
'The Dug-Out' (1919)

1 Everyone suddenly burst out singing;
And I was filled with such delight
As prisoned birds must find in freedom.

'Everyone Sang' (1919)

2 The song was wordless; the singing will never be done.

'Everyone Sang' (1919)

3 'He's a cheery old card,' grunted Harry to Jack
As they slogged up to Arras with rifle and pack.

But he did for them both by his plan of attack.

'The General' (1918)

4 Here was the world's worst wound. And here with pride
'Their name liveth for ever' the Gateway claims.
Was ever an immolation so belied
As these intolerably nameless names?

'On Passing the New Menin Gate' (1928); see **Epitaphs** 110:2

5 You smug-faced crowds with kindling eye
Who cheer when soldier lads march by,
Sneak home and pray you'll never know
The hell where youth and laughter go.

'Suicide in the Trenches' (1918)

6 I am making this statement as an act of wilful defiance of military authority, because I believe that the War is being deliberately prolonged by those who have the power to end it.

'A Soldier's Declaration' addressed to his commanding officer and sent to the *Bradford Pioneer* July 1917; Stanley Jackson *The Sassoons* (1968)

Cicely Saunders 1916–

English founder of St Christopher's Hospice, London

7 Deception is not as creative as truth. We do best in life if we look at it with clear eyes, and I think that applies to coming up to death as well.

of the Hospice movement

in *Time* 5 September 1988

Dorothy L. Sayers 1893–1957

English writer of detective fiction

8 I admit it is better fun to punt than to be punted, and that a desire to have all the fun is nine-tenths of the law of chivalry.

Gaudy Night (1935)

9 I always have a quotation for everything—it saves original thinking.

Have His Carcase (1932)

10 As I grow older and older,
And totter towards the tomb,
I find that I care less and less
Who goes to bed with whom.

'That's Why I Never Read Modern Novels', in Janet Hitchman *Such a Strange Lady* (1975)

11 Those who prefer their English sloppy have only themselves to thank if the advertisement writer uses his mastery of vocabulary and syntax to mislead their weak minds . . . The moral of all this . . . is that we have the kind of advertising we deserve.

in *Spectator* 19 November 1937 'The Psychology of Advertising'

12 Perhaps it is no wonder that women were first at the Cradle and the Cross. They had never known a man like this man—there has never been such another . . . who never made jokes about them, never treated them either as 'The women, God help us', or 'The ladies, God bless them!'

J. Morley and H. Ward (eds.) *Celebrating Women* (1986); attributed

■ Sayings and slogans

see box opposite

see also **Advertising slogans, Official advice, Political sayings and slogans**

Gerald Scarfe 1936–

English caricaturist

13 I find a particular delight in taking the caricature as far as I can. It satisfies me to stretch the human frame about and recreate it and yet keep a likeness.

Scarfe by Scarfe (1986)

Sayings and slogans

1 Action this day.
annotation as used by Winston Churchill at the Admiralty in 1940

2 Are we downhearted? No!
expression much taken up by British soldiers during the First World War

3 Been there, done that, got the T-shirt.
'been there, done that' recorded from 1980s, expanded form from 1990s

4 Burn your bra.
feminist slogan, 1970s

5 Business is like a car: it will not run by itself except downhill.
American saying

6 Children: one is one, two is fun, three is a houseful.
American

7 A committee is a group of the unwilling, chosen from the unfit, to do the unnecessary.
various attributions (origin unknown)

8 A conservative is a liberal who's been mugged.
American saying, 1980s; see **Wolfe** 343:16

9 Crime doesn't pay.
a slogan of the FBI and the cartoon detective Dick Tracy

10 Daddy, what did you do in the Great War?
daughter to father in First World War recruiting poster

11 [Death is] nature's way of telling you to slow down.
life insurance proverb; in *Newsweek* 25 April 1960

12 The difficult we do immediately, the impossible takes a little longer.
US Armed Forces slogan

13 A dog is for life, not just for Christmas.
slogan of the National Canine Defence League

14 Do not fold, spindle or mutilate.
instruction on punched cards (1950s, and in differing forms from the 1930s)

15 The family that prays together stays together.
motto devised by Al Scalpone for the Roman Catholic Family Rosary Crusade, 1947

16 Fifty million Frenchmen can't be wrong.
saying popular with American servicemen during the First World War; later associated with Mae **West** and Texas Guinan (1884–1933), it was also the title of a 1927 song by Billy Rose and Willie Raskin

17 Garbage in, garbage out.
in computing, incorrect or faulty input will always cause poor output; origin of the acronym GIGO

18 Go to jail. Go directly to jail. Do not pass go. Do not collect £200.
instructions on 'Community Chest' card in the game 'Monopoly'; invented by Charles Brace Darrow (1889–1967) in 1931

19 If it ain't broke, don't fix it.
Bert Lance (1931–), in *Nation's Business* May 1977

20 If it moves, salute it; if it doesn't move, pick it up; and if you can't pick it up, paint it.
1940s saying; P. Dickson *The Official Rules* (1978)

21 If you pay peanuts, you get monkeys.
recorded from the mid 1960s, and most commonly associated with pay negotiations

22 *Ils ne passeront pas.*
They shall not pass.
slogan of the French army at the defence of Verdun 1916; variously attributed to Marshal **Pétain** and to General Robert Nivelle, and taken up by the Republicans in the Spanish Civil War; see **Ibarruri** 164:13

23 I'm backing Britain.
slogan coined by workers at the Colt factory, Surbiton, Surrey and subsequently used in a national campaign, in *The Times* 1 January 1968

▶

▸ Sayings and slogans continued

1 It takes 40 dumb animals to make a fur coat, but only one to wear it.
slogan of an anti-fur campaign poster, 1980s; sometimes attributed to David **Bailey**

2 Lions led by donkeys.
associated with British soldiers during the First World War
attributed to Max Hoffman (1869–1927) in Alan Clark *The Donkeys* (1961); this attribution has not been traced elsewhere, and the phrase was well-known by the 1870s

3 Lousy but loyal.
London East End slogan at **George V**'s Jubilee (1935)

4 Make love not war.
student slogan, 1960s

5 The opera ain't over 'til the fat lady sings.
Dan Cook, in *Washington Post* 3 June 1978

6 Pile it high, sell it cheap.
slogan coined by John Cohen (1898–1979), founder of Tesco

7 Save the whale.
environmental slogan associated with alarm over the rapidly declining whale population which led in 1985 to a moratorium on commercial whaling

8 There is one thing stronger than all the armies in the world; and that is an idea whose time has come.
in *Nation* 15 April 1943

9 There's no such thing as a free lunch.
colloquial axiom in US economics from the 1960s, much associated with Milton **Friedman**; recorded in form 'there ain't no such thing as a free lunch' from 1938, which gave rise to the acronym TANSTAAFL in Robert Heinlein's *The Moon is a Harsh Mistress* (1966)

10 Think globally, act locally.
Friends of the Earth slogan, *c.*1985

11 To err is human but to really foul things up requires a computer.
Farmers' Almanac for 1978 'Capsules of Wisdom'; see below

To err is human; to forgive, divine.
Alexander Pope (1688–1744) *An Essay on Criticism* (1711)

12 We shall not be moved.
title of labour and civil rights song (1931) adapted from an earlier gospel hymn

13 We shall overcome.
title of song, originating from before the American Civil War, adapted as a Baptist hymn ('I'll Overcome Some Day', 1901) by C. A. Tindley; revived in 1946 as a protest song by black tobacco workers, and in 1963 during the black Civil Rights Campaign

14 What you see is what you get.
often shortened to the acronym *wysiwyg*, especially in Computing

15 When the going gets tough, the tough get going.
attributed to Joseph P. **Kennedy** (1888–1969), and also to Knute Rockne

16 Who dares wins.
motto of the British Special Air Service regiment, from 1942

17 Your King and Country need you.
recruitment slogan for First World War, coined by Eric Field; *Advertising* (1959)

Arthur Scargill 1938–

British trades-union leader

18 Parliament itself would not exist in its present form had people not defied the law.
evidence to House of Commons Select Committee on Employment, 2 April 1980

19 I wouldn't vote for Ken Livingstone if he were running for Mayor of Toytown.
in *Observer* 7 May 2000

Lord Scarman 1911–

British judge

20 A government above the law is a menace to be defeated.
Why Britain Needs a Written Constitution (1992)

Arthur M. Schlesinger Jr.

1917–

American historian

1 The answer to the runaway Presidency is not the messenger-boy Presidency. The American democracy must discover a middle way between making the President a czar and making him a puppet.

The Imperial Presidency (1973); preface

Moritz Schlick 1882–1936

German philosopher

2 The meaning of a proposition is the method of its verification.

in *Philosophical Review* (1936) vol. 45

Caroline Kennedy Schlossberg 1958–

American writer, daughter of John F. **Kennedy**

3 Now it is our turn to prove that the New Frontier was not a place in time but a timeless call.

speech at the Democratic Convention, 15 August 2000; see **Kennedy** 178:1

Artur Schnabel 1882–1951

Austrian-born pianist

4 I know two kinds of audiences only—one coughing, and one not coughing.

My Life and Music (1961)

5 Applause is a receipt, not a note of demand.

in *Saturday Review of Literature* 29 September 1951

6 The notes I handle no better than many pianists. But the pauses between the notes—ah, that is where the art resides!

in *Chicago Daily News* 11 June 1958

Arnold Schoenberg

1874–1951

Austrian-born American composer and musical theorist

7 If it is art, it is not for the masses. 'If it is for the masses it is not art' is a topic which is rather similar to a word of yourself.

letter to W. S. Schlamm, 1 July 1945

8 I am delighted to add another unplayable work to the repertoire. I want the Concerto to be difficult and I want the little finger to become longer. I can wait.

of his Violin Concerto

Joseph Machlis *Introduction to Contemporary Music* (1963)

Patricia Schroeder 1940–

American Democratic politician

9 Ronald Reagan . . . is attempting a great breakthrough in political technology—he has been perfecting the Teflon-coated Presidency. He sees to it that nothing sticks to him.

speech in the US House of Representatives, 2 August 1983

Budd Schulberg 1914–

American writer

see also **Film lines** 115:14

10 What makes Sammy run?

title of book (1941)

Charles Monroe Schulz

1922–2000

American cartoonist

11 Happiness is a warm puppy.

title of book (1962); see **Advertising slogans** 3:22, **Ephron** 108:6, **Lennon** 196:1

E. F. Schumacher 1911–77

German-born economist

12 It was not the power of the Spaniards that destroyed the Aztec Empire but the disbelief of the Aztecs in themselves.

Roots of Economic Growth (1962)

1 Small is beautiful. A study of economics as if people mattered.
title of book (1973)

2 Call a thing immoral or ugly, soul-destroying or a degradation of man, a peril to the peace of the world or to the well-being of future generations: as long as you have not shown it to be 'uneconomic' you have not really questioned its right to exist, grow, and prosper.
Small is Beautiful (1973)

J. A. Schumpeter 1883–1950

American economist

3 The cold metal of economic theory is in Marx's pages immersed in such a wealth of steaming phrases as to acquire a temperature not naturally its own.
Capitalism, Socialism and Democracy (1942)

4 One servant is worth a thousand gadgets.
J. K. Galbraith *A Life in our Times* (1981)

Delmore Schwartz 1913–66

American poet

5 Dogs are Shakespearean, children are strangers.
Let Freud and Wordsworth discuss the child,
Angels and Platonists shall judge the dog.
'Dogs are Shakespearean, Children are Strangers' (1938)

6 The heavy bear who goes with me,
A manifold honey to smear his face,
Clumsy and lumbering here and there,
The central ton of every place,
The hungry beating brutish one
In love with candy, anger, and sleep,
Crazy factotum, dishevelling all,
Climbs the building, kicks the football,
Boxes his brother in the hate-ridden city.
'The Heavy Bear Who Goes With Me' (1958)

H. Norman Schwarzkopf 1934–

American general, Commander-in-chief of Allied forces in the Gulf War

7 Seven months ago I could give a single command and 541,000 people would immediately obey it. Today I can't get a plumber to come to my house.
in *Newsweek* 11 November 1991; see **Truman** 323:13

Albert Schweitzer 1875–1965

Franco-German missionary

8 'Hullo! friend,' I call out, 'Won't you lend us a hand?' 'I am an intellectual and don't drag wood about,' came the answer. 'You're lucky,' I reply. 'I too wanted to become an intellectual, but I didn't succeed.'
More from the Primeval Forest (1931)

9 Late on the third day, at the very moment when, at sunset, we were making our way through a herd of hippopotamuses, there flashed upon my mind, unforeseen and unsought, the phrase, 'Reverence for Life'.
My Life and Thought (1933)

Kurt Schwitters 1887–1948

German painter

10 I am a painter and I nail my pictures together.
R. Hausmann *Am Anfang war Dada* (1972)

C. P. Scott 1846–1932

British journalist; editor of the *Manchester Guardian*, 1872–1929

11 Comment is free, but facts are sacred.
in *Manchester Guardian* 5 May 1921; see **Stoppard** 309:13

12 *Television?* The word is half Greek, half Latin. No good can come of it.
Asa Briggs *The BBC: the First Fifty Years* (1985)

Robert Falcon Scott
1868–1912

English polar explorer
see also **Last words** 190:4

1 Great God! this is an awful place.
of the South Pole
diary, 17 January 1912

2 We took risks, we knew we took them; things have come out against us, and therefore we have no cause for complaint.
'The Last Message' in *Scott's Last Expedition* (1913)

Alan Seeger 1888–1916

American poet

3 I have a rendezvous with Death
At some disputed barricade.
'I Have a Rendezvous with Death' (1916)

Pete Seeger 1919–

American folk singer and songwriter

4 Where have all the flowers gone?
title of song (1961)

Erich Segal

see **Taglines for films** 314:8

Rony Seikaly

American basketball player

5 The NBA players are smart enough to know you get the virus from unprotected sex, and we're not going to have unprotected sex on the basketball court.
on the return of Earvin 'Magic' Johnson, who is HIV-positive
in *San Francisco Chronicle* 8 February 1996

Arthur Seldon 1916–

British economist

6 Government of the busy by the bossy for the bully.
on over-government
Capitalism (1990)

W. C. Sellar 1898–1951 and R. J. Yeatman 1898–1968

British writers

7 1066 and all that.
title of book (1930)

8 History is not what you thought. *It is what you can remember.*
1066 and All That (1930) 'Compulsory Preface'

9 The Cavaliers (Wrong but Wromantic) and the Roundheads (Right but Repulsive).
1066 and All That (1930)

10 The National Debt is a very Good Thing and it would be dangerous to pay it off, for fear of Political Economy.
1066 and All That (1930)

11 [Gladstone] spent his declining years trying to guess the answer to the Irish Question; unfortunately whenever he was getting warm, the Irish secretly changed the Question.
1066 and All That (1930)

12 AMERICA was thus clearly top nation, and History came to a .
1066 and All That (1930)

Gitta Sereny 1923–

Hungarian-born British writer and journalist

to Albert Speer, who having always denied knowledge of the Holocaust had said that he was at fault in having 'looked away':

13 You cannot look away from something you don't know. If you looked away, then you knew.
recalled on BBC2 *Reputations*, 2 May 1996

Nicholas Serota 1946–

British art expert, Director of the Tate Gallery

14 This is a plea for patience. Your scepticism will gradually diminish and your fear will turn to love . . . All art was modern once.
to critics of modern art
in *Independent* 26 November 2000

Robert W. Service 1874–1958

Canadian poet

1 A promise made is a debt unpaid, and the
trail has its own stern code.

'The Cremation of Sam McGee' (1907)

2 Ah! the clock is always slow;
It is later than you think.

'It Is Later Than You Think' (1921)

3 This is the law of the Yukon, that only
the Strong shall thrive;
That surely the Weak shall perish, and
only the Fit survive.

'The Law of the Yukon' (1907)

4 Back of the bar, in a solo game, sat
Dangerous Dan McGrew,
And watching his luck was his light-
o'-love, the lady that's known as Lou.

'The Shooting of Dan McGrew' (1907)

Vikram Seth 1952–

Indian writer

5 I do need your help. Getting you married is not easy.

A Suitable Boy (1993)

6 A pity that the blubbering blobs
Come unequipped with volume knobs.

on babies

The Golden Gate (1986)

Anne Sexton 1928–74

American poet

7 I was tired of being a woman,
tired of the spoons and the pots,
tired of my mouth and my breasts
tired of the cosmetics and silks . . .
I was tired of the gender of things.

'Consorting with angels' (1967)

8 God owns heaven
but He craves the earth.

'The Earth' (1975)

9 My sleeping pill is white.
It is a splendid pearl;
it floats me out of myself,
my stung skin as alien
as a loose bolt of cloth.

'Lullaby' (1960)

10 In a dream you are never eighty.

'Old' (1962)

11 But suicides have a special language.
Like carpenters they want to know *which*
tools.
They never ask *why build*.

'Wanting to Die' (1966)

Peter Shaffer 1926–

English dramatist

12 The Normal is the good smile in a child's eyes—all right. It is also the dead stare in a million adults. It both sustains and kills—like a God. It is the Ordinary made beautiful; it is also the Average made lethal.

Equus (1983 ed.)

Bill Shankly 1914–81

Scottish footballer and club manager

13 Some people think football is a matter of life and death . . . I can assure them it is much more serious than that.

in *Sunday Times* 4 October 1981

Robert Shapiro 1942–

American lawyer

14 Not only did we play the race card, we played it from the bottom of the deck.

on the defence team's change of strategy at the trial of O. J. Simpson

in *The Times* 5 October 1995

Robert B. Shapiro 1938–

American lawyer and businessman, formerly Chief Executive of Monsanto

of his first view of corporate life:

15 It was the best game I'd ever seen. It has so many moving parts and so many different skills you had to have to make it work. It took me a while to realise that this is not a game. This is one of the realest things you get to do in life.

in *Sunday Telegraph* 14 May 2000

1 We painted a big bull's-eye on our chest, and we went over the top of the hill.
of Monsanto's development of GM technology
in *Sunday Telegraph* 14 May 2000

Ariel Sharon 1928–

Israeli Likud statesman, Prime Minister from 2001

2 I'm not going to make any compromise whatsoever.
on relations with the Palestinians
in *Sunday Times* 12 August 2001

William Shatner 1931–

American actor, 'Captain Kirk' in Star Trek

3 Get a life!
to Star Trek fans on Saturday Night Live, *1986*
William Shatner *Get a Life!* (1999)

George Bernard Shaw 1856–1950

Irish dramatist and writer
on Shaw: see **Agate** 12:2, **Leigh** 195:8, **Lenin** 195:14, **Taylor** 313:13; *see also* **Catch-phrases** 58:3

4 You see things; and you say 'Why?' But I dream things that never were; and I say 'Why not?'
Back to Methuselah (1921)

5 I enjoy convalescence. It is the part that makes illness worth while.
Back to Methuselah (1921)

6 Life is not meant to be easy, my child; but take courage: it can be delightful.
Back to Methuselah (rev. ed., 1930); see also **Fraser** 124:13

7 The British soldier can stand up to anything except the British War Office.
The Devil's Disciple (1901)

8 There is at bottom only one genuinely scientific treatment for all diseases, and that is to stimulate the phagocytes.
The Doctor's Dilemma (1911)

9 All professions are conspiracies against the laity.
The Doctor's Dilemma (1911)

10 Parentage is a very important profession, but no test of fitness for it is ever imposed in the interest of the children.
Everybody's Political What's What? (1944)

11 A government which robs Peter to pay Paul can always depend on the support of Paul.
Everybody's Political What's What? (1944)

12 The captain is in his bunk, drinking bottled ditch-water; and the crew is gambling in the forecastle. She will strike and sink and split. Do you think the laws of God will be suspended in favour of England because you were born in it?
Heartbreak House (1919)

13 The greatest of evils and the worst of crimes is poverty.
Major Barbara (1907) preface

14 I am a Millionaire. That is my religion.
Major Barbara (1907)

15 I can't talk religion to a man with bodily hunger in his eyes.
Major Barbara (1907)

16 Wot prawce Selvytion nah?
Major Barbara (1907)

17 Alcohol is a very necessary article . . . It enables Parliament to do things at eleven at night that no sane person would do at eleven in the morning.
Major Barbara (1907)

18 Nothing is ever done in this world until men are prepared to kill one another if it is not done.
Major Barbara (1907)

19 But a lifetime of happiness! No man alive could bear it: it would be hell on earth.
Man and Superman (1903)

20 Of all human struggles there is none so treacherous and remorseless as the struggle between the artist man and the mother woman.
Man and Superman (1903)

21 Hell is full of musical amateurs: music is the brandy of the damned.
Man and Superman (1903)

22 Englishmen never will be slaves: they are free to do whatever the Government and public opinion allow them to do.
Man and Superman (1903)

1 In the arts of peace Man is a bungler.
Man and Superman (1903)

2 When the military man approaches, the world locks up its spoons and packs off its womankind.
Man and Superman (1903)

3 There are two tragedies in life. One is not to get your heart's desire. The other is to get it.
Man and Superman (1903)

4 The golden rule is that there are no golden rules.
Man and Superman (1903) 'Maxims for Revolutionists: The Golden Rule'

5 Democracy substitutes election by the incompetent many for appointment by the corrupt few.
Man and Superman (1903) 'Maxims: Democracy'

6 Liberty means responsibility. That is why most men dread it.
Man and Superman (1903) 'Maxims: Liberty and Equality'

7 He who can, does. He who cannot, teaches.
Man and Superman (1903) 'Maxims: Education'

8 Marriage is popular because it combines the maximum of temptation with the maximum of opportunity.
Man and Superman (1903) 'Maxims: Marriage'

9 If you strike a child take care that you strike it in anger, even at the risk of maiming it for life. A blow in cold blood neither can nor should be forgiven.
Man and Superman (1903) 'Maxims: How to Beat Children'

10 Youth, which is forgiven everything, forgives itself nothing: age, which forgives itself everything, is forgiven nothing.
Man and Superman (1903) 'Maxims: Stray Sayings'

11 Take care to get what you like or you will be forced to like what you get.
Man and Superman (1903) 'Maxims: Stray Sayings'

12 Anarchism is a game at which the police can beat you.
Misalliance (1914)

13 You'll never have a quiet world till you knock the patriotism out of the human race.
O'Flaherty V.C. (1919)

14 A perpetual holiday is a good working definition of hell.
Parents and Children (1914) 'Children's Happiness'

15 It is impossible for an Englishman to open his mouth without making some other Englishman hate or despise him.
Pygmalion (1916) preface

16 Remember that you are a human being with a soul and the divine gift of articulate speech: that your native language is the language of Shakespeare and Milton and The Bible; and don't sit there crooning like a bilious pigeon.
Pygmalion (1916)

17 I don't want to talk grammar, I want to talk like a lady.
Pygmalion (1916)

18 I'm one of the undeserving poor . . . up agen middle-class morality all the time . . . What is middle-class morality? Just an excuse for never giving me anything.
Pygmalion (1916)

19 Gin was mother's milk to her.
Pygmalion (1916)

20 Walk! Not bloody likely.
Pygmalion (1916)

21 No Englishman is ever fairly beaten.
Saint Joan (1924)

22 Must then a Christ perish in torment in every age to save those that have no imagination?
Saint Joan (1924)

23 Assassination is the extreme form of censorship.
The Showing-Up of Blanco Posnet (1911) 'Limits to Toleration'

24 The photographer is like the cod which produces a million eggs in order that one may reach maturity.
introduction to the catalogue for Alvin Langdon Coburn's exhibition at the Royal Photographic Society, 1906; Bill Jay and Margaret Moore *Bernard Shaw and Photography* (1989)

1 The trouble, Mr Goldwyn, is that you are only interested in art and I am only interested in money.

telegraphed version of the outcome of a conversation between Shaw and Sam ***Goldwyn***

A. Johnson *The Great Goldwyn* (1937)

replying to a lady's proposal 'You have the greatest brain in the world, and I have the most beautiful body; so we ought to produce the most perfect child':

2 What if the child inherits my body and your brains?

Hesketh Pearson *Bernard Shaw* (1942)

3 [Dancing is] a perpendicular expression of a horizontal desire.

in *New Statesman* 23 March 1962; attributed

4 England and America are two countries divided by a common language.

attributed in this and other forms, but not found in Shaw's published writings

Hartley Shawcross 1902–

British Labour politician and lawyer

see also **Misquotations** 227:3

5 I don't think it was right. It was victors' justice.

of the Nuremberg trials, at which he appeared for the prosecution

interviewed on his 95th birthday, in *Daily Telegraph* 10 February 1997

Patrick Shaw-Stewart 1888–1917

English poet

6 I saw a man this morning
Who did not wish to die;
I ask and cannot answer
If otherwise wish I.

written 1916; M. Baring *Have You Anything to Declare?* (1936)

7 Stand in the trench, Achilles,
Flame-capped, and shout for me.

written 1916; M. Baring *Have You Anything to Declare?* (1936)

Burt Shevelove 1915–82 and Larry Gelbart ?1928–

American writers

8 A funny thing happened on the way to the Forum.

title of musical (1962)

Carol Shields 1935–

Canadian novelist

9 To be like everyone else. Isn't that what we all want in the end?

Larry's Party (1997)

10 Unless your life is going well you don't dream of giving a party. Unless you can look in the mirror and see a benign and generous and healthy human being, you shrink from acts of hospitality.

Larry's Party (1997)

11 Canada is . . . a country always dressed in its Sunday go-to-meeting clothes. A country you wouldn't ask to dance a second waltz. Clean. Christian. Dull. Quiescent. But growing.

The Stone Diaries (1993)

12 When we say a thing or an event is real, never mind how suspect it sounds, we honour it. But when a thing is made up—regardless of how true and just it seems—we turn up our noses.

The Stone Diaries (1995)

Emanuel Shinwell 1884–1986

British Labour politician

13 We know that the organized workers of the country are our friends. As for the rest, they don't matter a tinker's cuss.

speech to the Electrical Trades Union conference at Margate, 7 May 1947

Mikhail Sholokhov 1905–84

Russian novelist

14 And quiet flows the Don.

title of novel (1934)

Clare Short 1946–

British Labour politician

contrasting political advisers with elected politicians:

1 I sometimes call them the people who live in the dark. Everything they do is in hiding . . . Everything we do is in the light. They live in the dark.

in *New Statesman* 9 August 1996

2 It will be golden elephants next.

suggesting that the government of Montserrat was 'talking mad money' in claiming assistance for evacuating the island

in *Observer* 24 August 1997

Alexandra Shulman 1957–

British journalist

3 I long for the day when a new generation of Anita Roddicks can address the AGM in a bright pink dress and strappy sandals.

in *Sunday Times* 23 May 1999

Jean Sibelius 1865–1957

Finnish composer

4 Remember, a statue has never been set up in honour of a critic!

Bengt de Törne *Sibelius: A Close-Up* (1937)

Maurice Sigler 1901–61 and Al Hoffman 1902–60

American songwriters

5 Little man, you've had a busy day.

title of song (1934)

Jim Sillars 1937–

Scottish Nationalist politician

6 I think the greatest problem we have is that we will sing Flower of Scotland at Hampden or Murrayfield, and that we have too many 90-minute patriots.

interview on Scottish Television, 23 April 1992

Alan Sillitoe 1928–

English writer

7 The loneliness of the long-distance runner.

title of novel (1959)

Frank Silver 1892–1960 and Irving Cohn 1898–1961

8 Yes! we have no bananas,
We have no bananas today.

'Yes! We Have No Bananas' (1923 song)

Georges Simenon 1903–89

Belgian novelist

9 Writing is not a profession but a vocation of unhappiness.

interview in *Paris Review* Summer 1955

Neil Simon 1927–

American dramatist

10 I *love* living. I have some problems with my *life*, but living is the best thing they've come up with so far.

Last of the Red Hot Lovers (1970)

Paul Simon 1942–

American singer and songwriter

11 Like a bridge over troubled water
I will lay me down.

'Bridge over Troubled Water' (1970 song)

12 And here's to you, Mrs Robinson
Jesus loves you more than you will know.

'Mrs Robinson' (1967 song, from the film *The Graduate*)

13 People talking without speaking
People hearing without listening . . .
'Fools,' said I, 'You do not know
Silence like a cancer grows.'

'Sound of Silence' (1964 song)

14 Still crazy after all these years.

title of song (1975)

15 Improvisation is too good to leave to chance.

in *International Herald Tribune* 12 October 1990

John Simpson 1944–

British journalist

1 I'm sick to death of the 'I'm going to tell you everything about me and what I think' school of journalism. You don't watch the BBC for polemic.

interview in *Radio Times* 9 August 1997

Kirke Simpson 1881–1972

American journalist

2 [Warren] Harding of Ohio was chosen by a group of men in a smoke-filled room early today as Republican candidate for President.

often attributed to Harry Daugherty, one of Harding's supporters, who appears merely to have concurred with this version of events, when pressed for comment by Simpson

news report, filed 12 June 1920; W. Safire *New Language of Politics* (1968)

O. J. Simpson 1947–

American football player and actor

3 Fame vaporizes, money goes with the wind, and all that's left is character.

Juice: O.J. Simpson's Life (1977)

C. H. Sisson 1914–

English poet

4 Here lies a civil servant. He was civil
To everyone, and servant to the devil.

The London Zoo (1961)

Edith Sitwell 1887–1964

English poet and critic

on Sitwell: see **Bowen** 41:14

5 Jane, Jane,
Tall as a crane,
The morning light creaks down again.

Façade (1923) 'Aubade'

6 The fire was furry as a bear.

Façade (1923) 'Dark Song'

7 Still falls the Rain—
Dark as the world of man, black as our loss—
Blind as the nineteen hundred and forty nails
Upon the Cross.

'Still Falls the Rain' (1942)

8 I enjoyed talking to her, but thought *nothing* of her writing. I considered her 'a beautiful little knitter'.

of Virginia ***Woolf***

letter to Geoffrey Singleton, 11 July 1955

Osbert Sitwell 1892–1969

English writer

9 The British Bourgeoise
Is not born,
And does not die,
But, if it is ill,
It has a frightened look in its eyes.

At the House of Mrs Kinfoot (1921)

10 On the coast of Coromandel
Dance they to the tunes of Handel.

'On the Coast of Coromandel' (1943)

11 *Educ*: during the holidays from Eton.

entry in *Who's Who* (1929)

'Red' Skelton 1913–

American comedian

12 Well, it only proves what they always say—give the public something they want to see, and they'll come out for it.

on crowds attending the funeral of Harry Cohn

comment, on 2 March 1958; Bob Thomas *King Cohn* (1967)

B. F. Skinner 1904–90

American psychologist

13 The real question is not whether machines think but whether men do.

Contingencies of Reinforcement (1969)

14 Education is what survives when what has been learned has been forgotten.

in *New Scientist* 21 May 1964

Gillian Slovo 1952–

South African writer

1 In most families it is the children who leave home. In mine it was the parents.

of her anti-apartheid activist parents, Joe Slovo and Ruth First

Every Secret Thing (1997)

Alfred Emanuel Smith 1873–1944

American politician

2 All the ills of democracy can be cured by more democracy.

speech in Albany, 27 June 1933

3 No sane local official who has hung up an empty stocking over the municipal fireplace, is going to shoot Santa Claus just before a hard Christmas.

on the New Deal

in *New Outlook* December 1933

Delia Smith

English cookery expert

4 A hen's egg is, simply, a work of art, a masterpiece of design, construction, and brilliant packaging.

Delia Smith's How to Cook (1998)

Dodie Smith 1896–1990

English novelist and dramatist

5 The family—that dear octopus from whose tentacles we never quite escape.

Dear Octopus (1938)

F. E. Smith, Lord Birkenhead 1872–1930

British Conservative politician and lawyer

on Smith: see **Chesterton** 63:8

6 The world continues to offer glittering prizes to those who have stout hearts and sharp swords.

Rectorial Address, Glasgow University, 7 November 1923

7 JUDGE: You are extremely offensive, young man.
SMITH: As a matter of fact, we both are, and the only difference between us is that I am trying to be, and you can't help it.

2nd Earl of Birkenhead *Earl of Birkenhead* (1933)

Godfrey Smith 1926–

English journalist and columnist

8 In a world full of audio visual marvels, may words matter to you and be full of magic.

letter to a new grandchild, in *Sunday Times* 5 July 1987

Iain Duncan Smith 1954–

British Conservative politician

9 I am not trying to make people say 'Wow!' . . . I'm not going to play Hollywood lookalikes.

of his candidacy for the Conservative leadership

in *Independent* 21 July 2001

Ian Smith 1919–

Rhodesian statesman; Prime Minister, 1964–79

10 I don't believe in black majority rule in Rhodesia—not in a thousand years.

broadcast speech, 20 March 1976

Logan Pearsall Smith 1865–1946

American-born man of letters

11 What music is more enchanting than the voices of young people, when you can't hear what they say?

Afterthoughts (1931) 'Age and Death'

12 A best-seller is the gilded tomb of a mediocre talent.

Afterthoughts (1931) 'Art and Letters'

13 People say that life is the thing, but I prefer reading.

Afterthoughts (1931) 'Myself'

Stevie Smith 1902–71

English poet and novelist

1 Oh I am a cat that likes to
Gallop about doing good.
'The Galloping Cat' (1972)

2 Why does my Muse only speak when she is unhappy?
She does not, I only listen when I am unhappy
When I am happy I live and despise writing
For my Muse this cannot but be dispiriting.
'My Muse' (1964)

3 I was much too far out all my life
And not waving but drowning.
'Not Waving but Drowning' (1957)

4 People who are always praising the past
And especially the times of faith as best
Ought to go and live in the Middle Ages
And be burnt at the stake as witches and sages.
'The Past' (1957)

5 This Englishwoman is so refined
She has no bosom and no behind.
'This Englishwoman' (1937)

6 I long for the Person from Porlock
To bring my thoughts to an end,
I am growing impatient to see him
I think of him as a friend.
'Thoughts about the "Person from Porlock" ' (1962); see below

At this moment he was unfortunately called out by a person on business from Porlock.
Samuel Taylor Coleridge (1772–1834) 'Kubla Khan' (1816) preliminary note

7 A good time was had by all.
title of book (1937)

8 If there wasn't death, I think you couldn't go on.
in *Observer* 9 November 1969

Jan Christiaan Smuts 1870–1950

South African soldier and statesman, Prime Minister 1919–24 and 1939–48

9 Mankind is once more on the move. The very foundations have been shaken and loosened, and things are again fluid. The tents have been struck, and the great caravan of humanity is once more on the march.
on the setting up of the League of Nations, in the wake of the First World War
W. K. Hancock *Smuts* (1968)

John Snagge 1904–96

English sports commentator

10 I can't see who's in the lead but it's either Oxford or Cambridge.
commentary on the 1949 Boat Race
C. Dodd *Oxford and Cambridge Boat Race* (1983)

C. P. Snow 1905–80

English novelist and scientist

11 The official world, the corridors of power.
Homecomings (1956)

12 The two cultures and the scientific revolution.
title of The Rede Lecture (1959)

Alexander Solzhenitsyn 1918–

Russian novelist

13 If decade after decade the truth cannot be told, each person's mind begins to roam irretrievably. One's fellow countrymen become harder to understand than Martians.
Cancer Ward (1968)

14 You only have power over people as long as you don't take *everything* away from them. But when you've robbed a man of *everything* he's no longer in your power—he's free again.
The First Circle (1968)

1 The Gulag archipelago.
title of book (1973–5)

2 Work was like a stick. It had two ends. When you worked for the knowing you gave them quality; when you worked for a fool you simply gave him eyewash.
One Day in the Life of Ivan Denisovich (1962)

3 How can you expect a man who's warm to understand one who's cold?
One Day in the Life of Ivan Denisovich (1962)

4 After the suffering of decades of violence and oppression, the human soul longs for higher things, warmer and purer than those offered by today's mass living habits, introduced as by a calling card by the revolting invasion of commercial advertising, by TV stupor and by intolerable music.
speech in Cambridge, Massachusetts, 8 June 1978

5 The clock of communism has stopped striking. But its concrete building has not yet come crashing down. For that reason, instead of freeing ourselves, we must try to save ourselves being crushed by the rubble.
in *Komsomolskaya Pravda* 18 September 1990

6 The Iron Curtain did not reach the ground and under it flowed liquid manure from the West.
speaking at Far Eastern Technical University, Vladivostok, 30 May 1994; see **Churchill** 67:14

Anastasio Somoza 1925–80

Nicaraguan dictator

7 You won the elections, but I won the count.
replying to an accusation of ballot-rigging
in *Guardian* 17 June 1977

Stephen Sondheim 1930–

American songwriter

8 I like to be in America!
OK by me in America!
Ev'rything free in America
For a small fee in America!
'America' (1957 song)

9 Everything's coming up roses.
title of song (1959)

10 A toast to that invincible bunch
The dinosaurs surviving the crunch
Let's hear it for the ladies who lunch.
'The Ladies who Lunch' (1970)

11 Send in the clowns.
title of song (1973)

Susan Sontag 1933–

American writer

12 Societies need to have one illness which becomes identified with evil, and attaches blame to its 'victims'.
AIDS and its Metaphors (1989)

13 What pornography is really about, ultimately, isn't sex but death.
in *Partisan Review* Spring 1967

14 The white race *is* the cancer of human history, it is the white race, and it alone—its ideologies and inventions—which eradicates autonomous civilizations wherever it spreads, which has upset the ecological balance of the planet, which now threatens the very existence of life itself.
in *Partisan Review* Winter 1967

15 The camera makes everyone a tourist in other people's reality, and eventually in one's own.
in *New York Review of Books* 18 April 1974

16 Illness is the night-side of life, a more onerous citizenship. Everyone who is born holds dual citizenship, in the kingdom of the well and in the kingdom of the sick.
in *New York Review of Books* 26 January 1978

Charles Hamilton Sorley 1895–1915

English poet

17 I do wish people would not deceive themselves by talk of a just war. There is no such thing as a just war. What we are doing is casting out Satan by Satan.
letter to his mother from Aldershot, March 1915

John Philip Sousa 1854–1932

American composer and conductor

1 Jazz will endure, just as long as people hear it through their feet instead of their brains.

Nat Shapiro (ed.) *An Encyclopedia of Quotations about Music* (1978)

Wole Soyinka 1934–

Nigerian writer

2 Books and all forms of writing have always been objects of terror to those who seek to suppress truth.

The Man Died (1972)

3 The man dies in all who keep silent in the face of tyranny.

The Man Died (1972)

4 Justice is the first condition of humanity.

The Man Died (1972)

Muriel Spark 1918–

British novelist
see also **Opening lines** 247:13

5 I am a hoarder of two things: documents and trusted friends.

Curriculum Vitae (1992)

6 I am putting old heads on your young shoulders . . . all my pupils are the crème de la crème.

The Prime of Miss Jean Brodie (1961)

7 Give me a girl at an impressionable age, and she is mine for life.

The Prime of Miss Jean Brodie (1961)

8 One's prime is elusive. You little girls, when you grow up, must be on the alert to recognise your prime at whatever time of your life it may occur.

The Prime of Miss Jean Brodie (1961)

John Sparrow 1906–92

English barrister and academic, Warden of All Souls College, Oxford, 1952–77
see also **Epitaphs** 110:5

9 That indefatigable and unsavoury engine of pollution, the dog.

letter to *The Times* 30 September 1975

Lord Spencer 1964–

English peer

10 I always believed the press would kill her in the end. But not even I could believe they would take such a direct hand in her death as seems to be the case . . . Every proprietor and editor of every publication that has paid for intrusive and exploitative photographs of her . . . has blood on their hands today.

on the death of his sister, ***Diana****, Princess of Wales, in a car crash while being pursued by photographers, 31 August 1997*

in *Daily Telegraph* 1 September 1997

11 She needed no royal title to continue to generate her particular brand of magic.

tribute at the funeral of his sister, ***Diana****, Princess of Wales, 7 September 1997*

in *Guardian* 8 September 1997

12 We, your blood family, will do all we can to continue the imaginative way in which you were steering these two exceptional young men so that their souls are not simply immersed by duty and tradition but can sing openly as you planned.

of his nephews, Prince William and Prince Harry;

in *Guardian* 8 September 1997

Raine, Countess Spencer 1929–

13 Alas, for our towns and cities. Monstrous carbuncles of concrete have erupted in gentle Georgian Squares.

The Spencers on Spas (1983); see **Charles** 63:3

Stanley Spencer 1891–1959

English painter
on Spencer: see **Lewis** 199:8

14 Painting is saying 'Ta' to God.

letter from Spencer's daughter Shirin, in *Observer* 7 February 1988

Stephen Spender 1909–95

English poet

on Spender: see **Waugh** 331:16; *see also* **Pollitt** 260:2

1 After the first powerful plain manifesto
The black statement of pistons, without more fuss
But gliding like a queen, she leaves the station.
'The Express' (1933)

2 I think continually of those who were truly great.
'I think continually of those who were truly great' (1933)

3 Born of the sun they travelled a short while towards the sun,
And left the vivid air signed with their honour.
'I think continually of those who were truly great' (1933)

4 My parents kept me from children who were rough
And who threw words like stones and who wore torn clothes.
'My parents kept me from children who were rough' (1933)

5 Never being, but always at the edge of Being.
title of poem (1933)

6 Their collected
Hearts wound up with love, like little watch springs.
'The Past Values' (1939)

7 Pylons, those pillars
Bare like nude, giant girls that have no secret.
'The Pylons' (1933)

8 What I had not foreseen
Was the gradual day
Weakening the will
Leaking the brightness away.
'What I expected, was' (1933)

9 Who live under the shadow of a war,
What can I do that matters?
'Who live under the shadow of a war' (1933)

Oswald Spengler 1880–1936

German philosopher

10 Socialism is nothing but the capitalism of the lower classes.
The Hour of Decision (1933)

Spice Girls

see **Chisholm**, **Rowbottom**

Benjamin Spock 1903–

American paediatrician and writer

11 You know more than you think you do.
Common Sense Book of Baby and Child Care (1946) [later *Baby and Child Care*], opening words

12 To win in Vietnam, we will have to exterminate a nation.
Dr Spock on Vietnam (1968)

William Archibald Spooner 1844–1930

English clergyman and scholar; Warden of New College, Oxford, 1903–24

13 Her late husband, you know, a very sad death—eaten by missionaries—poor soul!
William Hayter *Spooner* (1977)

14 You have tasted your worm, you have hissed my mystery lectures, and you must leave by the first town drain.
to an undergraduate
Oxford University What's What (1948); William Hayter in *Spooner* (1977) maintains this saying is apocryphal

Cecil Spring-Rice 1859–1918

British diplomat; Ambassador to Washington from 1912

15 I vow to thee, my country—all earthly things above—
Entire and whole and perfect, the service of my love,
The love that asks no question: the love that stands the test,
That lays upon the altar the dearest and the best:

The love that never falters, the love that pays the price,
The love that makes undaunted the final sacrifice.

'I Vow to Thee, My Country' (written on the eve of his departure from Washington, 12 January 1918)

Bruce Springsteen 1949–

American rock singer and songwriter

1 Born in the USA.

title of song (1984)

2 Born down in a dead man's town
The first kick I took was when I hit the ground.

'Born in the USA' (1984 song)

3 We gotta get out while we're young,
'Cause tramps like us, baby, we were born to run.

'Born to Run' (1974 song)

J. C. Squire 1884–1958

English man of letters

4 I'm not so think as you drunk I am.

'Ballade of Soporific Absorption' (1931)

5 It did not last: the Devil howling 'Ho!
Let Einstein be!' restored the status quo.

'In continuation of Pope on Newton' (1926); see below

Nature, and Nature's laws lay hid in night.
God said, *Let Newton be!* and all was light.

Alexander Pope (1688–1744) 'Epitaph: Intended for Sir Isaac Newton' (1730)

6 God heard the embattled nations sing and shout
'Gott strafe England!' and 'God save the King!'
God this, God that, and God the other thing—
'Good God!' said God, 'I've got my work cut out.'

'The Dilemma' (1916); see **Funke** 129:7

Joseph Stalin 1879–1953

Soviet dictator

7 The State is an instrument in the hands of the ruling class, used to break the resistance of the adversaries of that class.

Foundations of Leninism (1924)

8 There are various forms of production: artillery, automobiles, lorries. You also produce 'commodities', 'works', 'products'. Such things are highly necessary. Engineering things. For people's souls. 'Products' are highly necessary too. 'Products' are very important for people's souls. You are engineers of human souls.

speech to writers at **Gorky**'s house, 26 October 1932; A. Kemp-Welch *Stalin and the Literary Intelligentsia, 1928–39* (1991); see **Gorky** 138:3

9 The Pope! How many divisions has *he* got?

on being asked to encourage Catholicism in Russia by way of conciliating the Pope, 13 May 1935

W. S. Churchill *The Gathering Storm* (1948)

10 One death is a tragedy, a million deaths a statistic.

attributed

Charles E. Stanton 1859–1933

American soldier

11 *Lafayette, nous voilà!*

Lafayette, we are here.

at the tomb of Lafayette in Paris, 4 July 1917

Freya Stark 1893–1993

English writer and traveller

12 The great and almost only comfort about being a woman is that one can always pretend to be more stupid than one is and no one is surprised.

The Valleys of the Assassins (1934)

Enid Starkie 1897–1970

English academic

13 Unhurt people are not much good in the world.

letter, 18 June 1943; Joanna Richardson *Enid Starkie* (1973); see **Hart** 148:2

Joseph Starnes

American Republican politician

1 CONGRESSMAN STARNES: You are quoting from this Marlowe. Is he a Communist?
HALLIE FLANAGAN: I am very sorry. I was quoting from Christopher Marlowe . . . the greatest dramatist in the period immediately preceding Shakespeare.

at the hearing on the Federal Theatre Project by the House Un-American Activities Committee, 6 December 1938

Christina Stead 1902–83

Australian novelist

2 If all the rich people in the world divided up their money among themselves there wouldn't be enough to go round.

House of All Nations (1938)

3 A self-made man is one who believes in luck and sends his son to Oxford.

House of All Nations (1938)

David Steel 1938–

British Liberal politician; Leader of the Liberal Party 1976–88

4 I have the good fortune to be the first Liberal leader for over half a century who is able to say to you at the end of our annual assembly: go back to your constituencies and prepare for government.

speech to the Liberal Party Assembly, 18 September 1981

5 It is the settled will of the majority of people in Scotland that they want not just the symbol, but the substance of the return of democratic control over internal affairs.

on the announcement that the Stone of Destiny would be returned to Scotland

in *Scotsman* 4 July 1996

Lincoln Steffens 1866–1936

American journalist

6 I have seen the future; and it works.

following a visit to the Soviet Union in 1919

letter to Marie Howe, 3 April 1919

Gertrude Stein 1874–1946

American writer

on Stein: see **Fadiman** 111:3, **Lewis** 199:7; *see also* **Last words** 191:7

7 Remarks are not literature.

Autobiography of Alice B. Toklas (1933)

8 'Native' always means people who belong somewhere else, because they had once belonged somewhere. That shows us the white race does not really belong anywhere, because they think of everybody else as native.

Everybody's Autobiography (1937)

9 In the United States there is more space where nobody is than where anybody is. That is what makes America what it is.

The Geographical History of America (1936)

10 Rose is a rose is a rose is a rose, is a rose.

Sacred Emily (1913)

11 You are all a lost generation.

of the young who served in the First World War

subsequently taken by Ernest **Hemingway** as epigraph to *The Sun Also Rises* (1926)

John Steinbeck 1902–68

American novelist

12 All the world's great have been little boys who wanted the moon.

Cup of Gold (1953)

13 Man, unlike any other thing organic or inorganic in the universe, grows beyond his work, walks up the stairs of his concepts, emerges ahead of his accomplishments.

The Grapes of Wrath (1939)

14 I know this—a man got to do what he got to do.

The Grapes of Wrath (1939)

15 Okie use' ta mean you was from Oklahoma. Now it means you're a dirty son-of-a-bitch. Okie means you're scum. Don't mean nothing itself, it's the way they say it.

The Grapes of Wrath (1939)

16 How can you frighten a man whose hunger is not only in his own cramped stomach but in the wretched bellies of his

children? You can't scare him—he has known a fear beyond every other.
The Grapes of Wrath (1939)

1 I guess—what may happen is what keeps us alive. We want to see tomorrow.
letter to Carlton Sheffield, 16 October 1952

Gloria Steinem 1934–

American journalist

2 We are becoming the men we wanted to marry.
in *Ms* July/August 1982

3 A woman without a man is like a fish without a bicycle.
attributed

Casey Stengel 1891–1975

American baseball player and manager

4 All you have to do is keep the five players who hate your guts away from the five who are undecided.
John Samuel (ed.) *The Guardian Book of Sports Quotes* (1985)

James Stephens 1882–1950

Irish poet and writer

5 Finality is death. Perfection is finality. Nothing is perfect. There are lumps in it.
The Crock of Gold (1912)

6 I hear a sudden cry of pain!
There is a rabbit in a snare:
Now I hear the cry again,
But I cannot tell from where . . .
Little one! Oh, little one!
I am searching everywhere.
'The Snare' (1915)

7 People say: 'Of course, they will be beaten.' The statement is almost a query, and they continue, 'but they are putting up a decent fight.' For being beaten does not matter greatly in Ireland, but not fighting does matter.
The Insurrection in Dublin (1916)

8 In my definition they were good men—men, that is, who willed no evil. No person living is the worse off for having known Thomas MacDonagh.
of the leaders of the Easter Rising
The Insurrection in Dublin (1916)

Brooks Stevens 1911–

American industrial designer

9 Our whole economy is based on planned obsolescence.
V. Packard *The Waste Makers* (1960)

Wallace Stevens 1879–1955

American poet

10 The poet is the priest of the invisible.
'Adagia' (1957)

11 Chieftain Iffucan of Azcan in caftan
Of tan with henna hackles, halt!
'Bantams in Pine Woods' (1923)

12 Call the roller of big cigars,
The muscular one, and bid him whip
In kitchen cups concupiscent curds.
'The Emperor of Ice-Cream' (1923)

13 Let be be finale of seem.
The only emperor is the emperor of ice-cream.
'The Emperor of Ice-Cream' (1923)

14 Frogs eat butterflies. Snakes eat frogs.
Hogs eat snakes. Men eat hogs.
title of poem (1923)

15 Poetry is the supreme fiction, madame.
'A High-Toned old Christian Woman' (1923)

16 They said, 'You have a blue guitar,
You do not play things as they are.'

The man replied, 'Things as they are
Are changed upon the blue guitar.'
'The Man with the Blue Guitar' (1937)

17 The inconceivable idea of the sun.

You must become an ignorant man again
And see the sun again with an ignorant eye
And see it clearly in the idea of it.
Notes Toward a Supreme Fiction (1947) 'It Must Be Abstract' no. 1

18 They will get it straight one day at the Sorbonne.
We shall return at twilight from the lecture

Pleased that the irrational is rational.
Notes Toward a Supreme Fiction (1947) 'It Must Give Pleasure' no. 10

1 Music is feeling, then, not sound.
'Peter Quince at the Clavier' (1923)

2 Beauty is momentary in the mind—
The fitful tracing of a portal;
But in the flesh it is immortal.
The body dies; the body's beauty lives.
'Peter Quince at the Clavier' (1923)

3 I do not know which to prefer,
The beauty of inflections
Or the beauty of innuendoes,
The blackbird whistling
Or just after.
'Thirteen Ways of Looking at a Blackbird' (1923)

Adlai Stevenson 1900–65

American Democratic politician

4 I suppose flattery hurts no one, that is, if he doesn't inhale.
television broadcast, 30 March 1952

5 If they [the Republicans] will stop telling lies about the Democrats, we will stop telling the truth about them.
speech during 1952 Presidential campaign; J. B. Martin *Adlai Stevenson and Illinois* (1976)

6 Let's talk sense to the American people. Let's tell them the truth, that there are no gains without pains.
speech of acceptance at the Democratic National Convention, 26 July 1952

7 There is no evil in the atom; only in men's souls.
speech at Hartford, Connecticut, 18 September 1952

8 In America any boy may become President and I suppose it's just one of the risks he takes!
speech in Indianapolis, 26 September 1952

9 A free society is a society where it is safe to be unpopular.
speech in Detroit, 7 October 1952

10 The young man [Richard Nixon] who asks you to set him one heart-beat from the Presidency of the United States.
commonly quoted as 'just a heart-beat away . . . '
speech at Cleveland, Ohio, 23 October 1952

11 We hear the Secretary of State boasting of his brinkmanship—the art of bringing us to the edge of the abyss.
speech in Hartford, Connecticut, 25 February 1956; see **Dulles** 95:8

12 She would rather light a candle than curse the darkness, and her glow has warmed the world.
*on learning of Eleanor **Roosevelt**'s death*
in *New York Times* 8 November 1962

13 The kind of politician who would cut down a redwood tree, and then mount the stump and make a speech on conservation.
*of Richard **Nixon***
Fawn M. Brodie *Richard Nixon* (1983)

Anne Stevenson 1933–

English poet

14 Blackbirds are the cellos of the deep
farms.
'Green Mountain, Black Mountain' (1982)

15 At fifty, menopausal, nervous, thin,
She joined a women's group and studied
Zen.
Her latest book, *The Happy Lesbian*,
Is recommended reading for gay men.
'A Quest' (1993)

Ian Stewart 1945–

British mathematician

16 Genes are not like engineering blueprints; they are more like recipes in a cookbook. They tell us what ingredients to use, in what quantities, and in what order—but they do not provide a complete, accurate plan of the final result.
Life's Other Secret (1998) preface

Sting 1951–

English rock singer, songwriter, and actor

17 If I were a Brazilian without land or money or the means to feed my children, I would be burning the rain forest too.
in *International Herald Tribune* 14 April 1989

1 Arrogance is a highly under-appreciated character trait.
in *Independent* 23 June 2001

Michael Stipe 1960–

American singer and songwriter

2 On the ladder of important things in this world, being in a rock band is probably on a lower rung, but then again, being Secretary of State is probably way down there too.
T. Fletcher *Remarks: the story of REM* (1993)

Lord Stockton 1943–

British peer, grandson of Harold **Macmillan**

3 As an old man he only had nightmares about two things: the trenches in the Great War and what would have happened if the Cuban Missile Crisis had gone wrong.
of Harold ***Macmillan***
in 1998; Peter Hennessy *The Prime Minister: the Office and its Holders since 1945* (2000)

Mervyn Stockwood 1913–95

English Anglican clergyman, Bishop of Southwark 1959–80

4 A psychiatrist is a man who goes to the Folies-Bergère and looks at the audience.
in *Observer* 15 October 1961

Leopold Stokowski 1882–1977

Polish-born American conductor

5 On matters of intonation and technicalities I am more than a martinet—I am a martinetissimo!
Nat Shapiro (ed.) *An Encyclopedia of Quotations about Music* (1978)

I. F. Stone 1907–89

American journalist

6 The difference between burlesque and the newspapers is that the former never pretended to be performing a public service by exposure.
I. F. Stone's Weekly 7 September 1952

Marie Stopes 1880–1958

Scottish pioneer of birth-control clinics

7 An impersonal and scientific knowledge of the structure of our bodies is the surest safeguard against prurient curiosity and lascivious gloating.
Married Love (1918)

Tom Stoppard 1937–

Czechoslovakian-born British dramatist

8 We would never love anybody if we could see past our invention.
The Invention of Love (1997)

9 It's not the voting that's democracy, it's the counting.
Jumpers (1972)

10 The House of Lords, an illusion to which I have never been able to subscribe—responsibility without power, the prerogative of the eunuch throughout the ages.
Lord Malquist and Mr Moon (1966); see **Kipling** 184:9

11 The media. It sounds like a convention of spiritualists.
Night and Day (1978)

12 I'm with you on the free press. It's the newspapers I can't stand.
Night and Day (1978)

13 Comment is free but facts are on expenses.
Night and Day (1978); see **Scott** 292:11

14 Save the gerund and screw the whale.
The Real Thing (1982); see **Sayings and slogans** 290:7

15 I can do you blood and love without the rhetoric, and I can do you blood and rhetoric without the love, and I can do you all three concurrent or consecutive, but I can't do you love and rhetoric without the blood. Blood is compulsory—they're all blood, you see.
Rosencrantz and Guildenstern are Dead (1967)

16 We're *actors*—we're the opposite of people! . . . Think, in your head, *now*, think of the most . . . *private* . . . *secret* . . . *intimate* thing you have ever done secure

in the knowledge of its privacy . . . Are you thinking of it? . . . *Well, I saw you do it!*

Rosencrantz and Guildenstern Are Dead (1967)

1 Eternity's a terrible thought. I mean, where's it all going to end?

Rosencrantz and Guildenstern are Dead (1967)

2 The bad end unhappily, the good unluckily. That is what tragedy means.

Rosencrantz and Guildenstern are Dead (1967)

3 Life is a gamble at terrible odds—if it was a bet, you wouldn't take it.

Rosencrantz and Guildenstern are Dead (1967)

4 Childhood is Last Chance Gulch for happiness. After that, you know too much.

Where Are They Now? (1973)

Lytton Strachey 1880–1932

English biographer

see also **Last words** 190:7

5 CHAIRMAN OF MILITARY TRIBUNAL: What would you do if you saw a German soldier trying to violate your sister?
STRACHEY: I would try to get between them.

otherwise rendered as, 'I should interpose my body'

Robert Graves *Good-bye to All That* (1929)

6 Discretion is not the better part of biography.

M. Holroyd *Lytton Strachey* (1967) vol. 1

William L. Strauss and **A. J. E. Cave**

7 Notwithstanding, if he could be reincarnated and placed in a New York subway—provided that he were bathed, shaved, and dressed in modern clothing—it is doubtful whether he would attract any more attention than some of its other denizens.

of Neanderthal man

in *Quarterly Review of Biology* Winter 1957

Igor Stravinsky 1882–1971

Russian composer

8 My music is best understood by children and animals.

in *Observer* 8 October 1961

9 Academism results when the reasons for the rule change, but not the rule.

attributed

10 Music is, by its very nature, essentially powerless to *express* anything at all . . . music expresses itself.

in *Esquire* December 1972

John Whitaker ('Jack') Straw 1946–

British Labour politician

11 It's not because ageing wrinklies have tried to stop people having fun.

asserting his opposition to the legalization of cannabis

on *Breakfast with Frost*, BBC1 TV, 4 January 1998

12 What you have within the UK is three small nations who've been under the cosh of the English.

in *Sunday Times* 6 January 2000

Janet Street-Porter 1946–

English broadcaster and journalist

13 A terminal blight has hit the TV industry nipping fun in the bud and stunting our growth. This blight is management—the dreaded Four M's: male, middle class, middle-aged and mediocre.

MacTaggart Lecture, Edinburgh Television Festival, 25 August 1995

Barbra Streisand 1942–

American singer and actress

14 We elected a President, not a Pope.

to journalists at the White House, 5 February 1998

reported by James Naughtie, BBC Radio 4, Today programme, 6 February 1998

Randall E. Stross

1 American anti-intellectualism will never again be the same because of Bill Gates. Gates embodies what was supposed to be impossible—the practical intellectual.

The Microsoft Way (1996)

Simeon Strunsky 1879–1948

Russian-born American journalist and writer

2 People who want to understand democracy should spend less time in the library with Aristotle and more time on the buses and in the subway.

No Mean City (1944)

3 Famous remarks are very seldom quoted correctly.

No Mean City (1944)

Jan Struther 1901–53

English-born novelist and hymn-writer

4 Lord of all hopefulness, Lord of all joy,
Whose trust, ever childlike, no cares could destroy,
Be there at our waking, and give us, we pray,
Your bliss in our hearts, Lord, at the break of the day.

'All Day Hymn' (1931)

G. A. Studdert Kennedy 1883–1929

British poet

5 When Jesus came to Birmingham they simply passed Him by,
They never hurt a hair of Him, they only let Him die.

'Indifference' (1921)

6 Waste of Blood, and waste of Tears,
Waste of youth's most precious years,
Waste of ways the saints have trod,
Waste of Glory, waste of God,
War!

'Waste' (1919)

J. W. N. Sullivan 1886–1937

7 It is much easier to make measurements than to know exactly what you are measuring.

comment, 1928; R. L. Weber *More Random Walks in Science* (1982)

Louis Henri Sullivan 1856–1924

American architect

8 Form follows function.

The Tall Office Building Artistically Considered (1896)

John Sulstan 1942–

British biologist

9 We're at a milestone but we're not at the end of the road. We're at the beginning of a new road.

on the deciphering of 90% of the human genome

in *Independent* 27 June 2000

Arthur Hays Sulzberger 1891–1968

American newspaper proprietor

10 We tell the public which way the cat is jumping. The public will take care of the cat.

on journalism

in *Time* 8 May 1950

Edith Summerskill 1901–80

British Labour politician

11 Nagging is the repetition of unpalatable truths.

speech to the Married Women's Association, 14 July 1960

Jacqueline Susann 1921–74

American novelist

12 Valley of the dolls.

title of novel (1966)

David Sutton 1944–

English poet

1 Sorrow in all lands, and grievous omens.
Great anger in the dragon of the hills,
And silent now the earth's green oracles
That will not speak again of innocence.

'Geomancies' (1991)

Hannen Swaffer 1879–1962

English journalist and critic

2 Freedom of the press in Britain means freedom to print such of the proprietor's prejudices as the advertisers don't object to.

Tom Driberg *Swaff* (1974)

Herbert Bayard Swope 1882–1958

American journalist and editor
see also **Baruch** 24:12

3 The First Duty of a newspaper is to be Accurate. If it is Accurate, it follows that it is Fair.

letter to *New York Herald Tribune* 16 March 1958

4 He [Swope] enunciated no rules for success, but offered a sure formula for failure: *Just try to please everyone.*

E. J. Kahn Jr. *World of Swope* (1965)

Thomas Szasz 1920–

Hungarian-born psychiatrist

5 A child becomes an adult when he realizes that he has a right not only to be right but also to be wrong.

The Second Sin (1973) 'Childhood'

6 Happiness is an imaginary condition, formerly often attributed by the living to the dead, now usually attributed by adults to children, and by children to adults.

The Second Sin (1973) 'Emotions'

7 The stupid neither forgive nor forget; the naive forgive and forget; the wise forgive but do not forget.

The Second Sin (1973) 'Personal Conduct'

8 If you talk to God, you are praying; if God talks to you, you have schizophrenia. If the dead talk to you, you are a spiritualist; if God talks to you, you are a schizophrenic.

The Second Sin (1973) 'Schizophrenia'

9 Formerly, when religion was strong and science weak, men mistook magic for medicine; now, when science is strong and religion weak, men mistake medicine for magic.

The Second Sin (1973) 'Science and Scientism'

10 Traditionally, sex has been a very private, secretive activity. Herein perhaps lies its powerful force for uniting people in a strong bond. As we make sex less secretive, we may rob it of its power to hold men and women together.

The Second Sin (1973) 'Sex'

11 Two wrongs don't make a right, but they make a good excuse.

The Second Sin (1973) 'Social Relations'

George Szell 1897–1970

American conductor

12 Conductors must give unmistakable and suggestive signals to the orchestra—not choreography to the audience.

in *Newsweek* 28 January 1963

Albert von Szent-Györgyi 1893–1986

Hungarian-born biochemist

13 Discovery consists of seeing what everybody has seen and thinking what nobody has thought.

I. Good (ed.) *The Scientist Speculates* (1962)

14 Water is life's *mater* and *matrix*, mother and medium. There is no life without water.

in *Perspectives in Biology and Medicine* Winter 1971

Wislawa Szymborska 1923–

Polish poet and critic

15 When the piranha strikes, it feels no
shame.

If snakes had hands, they'd claim their
hands were clean.

A jackal doesn't understand remorse.
Lions and lice don't waver in their
course.
Why should they, when they know
they're right?

'In Praise of Feeling Bad about Yourself' (1976)

1 There's no life
that couldn't be immortal
if only for a moment.

'On Death, without Exaggeration' (1995)

■ Taglines for films

see box overleaf

Rabindranath Tagore 1861–1941

Bengali poet and philosopher

2 Bigotry tries to keep truth safe in its hand
With a grip that kills it.

Fireflies (1928)

3 Man goes into the noisy crowd to drown his own clamour of silence.

'Stray Birds' (1916)

Nellie Talbot

4 Jesus wants me for a sunbeam.

title of hymn (1921)

Sony Labou Tansi 1947–95

African writer

5 What good is an ounce of justice in an ocean of shit?

The Antipeople (1983)

Bernie Taupin

see Elton **John** and Bernie Taupin

R. H. Tawney 1880–1962

British economic historian

6 Those who dread a dead-level of income or wealth . . . do not dread, it seems, a dead-level of law and order, and of security for life and property.

Equality (4th ed., 1931)

7 Private property is a necessary institution, at least in a fallen world; men work more and dispute less when goods are private than when they are common. But it is to be tolerated as a concession to human frailty, not applauded as desirable in itself.

Religion and the Rise of Capitalism (1926)

8 To take usury is contrary to Scripture; it is contrary to Aristotle; it is contrary to nature, for it is to live without labour; it is to sell time, which belongs to God, for the advantage of wicked men.

Religion and the Rise of Capitalism (1926)

A. J. P. Taylor 1906–90

English historian

9 History gets thicker as it approaches recent times.

English History 1914–45 (1965) bibliography

10 The First World War had begun—imposed on the statesmen of Europe by railway timetables.

The First World War (1963)

11 A racing tipster who only reached Hitler's level of accuracy would not do well for his clients.

Origins of the Second World War (1962)

12 The glories of his revolutionary triumph pale before the nobility of his later defeats.

on ***Trotsky***

in *New Statesman and Nation* 20 February 1954

13 The magic of Shaw's words may still bewitch posterity . . . but it will find that he has nothing to say.

in *Observer* 22 July 1956

14 A great showman whose technique improved as the real situation deteriorated.

of ***Mussolini***

in *Observer* 28 February 1982

Taglines for films

1 Be afraid. Be very afraid.
The Fly (1986 film), written by David **Cronenberg**

2 Being the adventures of a young man whose principal interests are rape, ultra-violence and Beethoven.
A Clockwork Orange (1972 film)

3 Garbo talks.
Anna Christie (1930 film), her first talkie

4 He said 'I'll be back!' . . . and he meant it!
Terminator 2: Judgment Day (1991 film); see **Film lines** 116:3

5 In space no one can hear you scream.
Alien (1979 film)

6 Just when you thought it was safe to go back in the water.
publicity for *Jaws 2* (1978 film)

7 A long time ago in a galaxy far, far away . . .
Star Wars (1977)

8 Love means never having to say you're sorry.
Love Story (1970 film); from the novel (1970) by Erich Segal (1937–)

9 The man you love to hate.
anonymous billing for Erich von Stroheim in the film *The Heart of Humanity* (1918)

10 Mean, Moody and Magnificent!
The Outlaw (1946 film) starring Jane Russell

11 Please don't tell the ending. It's the only one we have.
Psycho (1960 film)

12 Somewhere in the universe, there must be something better than Man.
Planet of the Apes (1968 film)

13 They're young . . . they're in love . . . and they kill people.
Bonnie and Clyde (1967 film)

14 We are not alone.
Close Encounters of the Third Kind (1977 film)

15 Where were you in '62?
American Graffiti (1973 film)

John Taylor 1952–

British barrister and Conservative politician

16 If you asked them what reggae is, they'd think you were talking about the Kray brothers.
*on William **Hague**'s advisers*
in *Independent on Sunday* 8 October 2000

Ron Taylor

Scottish headteacher

17 Evil visited us yesterday. We don't know why.
following the murder of sixteen children and their teacher at Dunblane primary school
in *Daily Telegraph* 15 March 1996

Norman Tebbit 1931–

British Conservative politician
on Tebbit: see **Foot** 121:5

18 I grew up in the Thirties with our unemployed father. He did not riot, he got on his bike and looked for work.
speech, 15 October 1981

19 The cricket test—which side do they cheer for? . . . Are you still looking back to where you came from or where you are?
on the loyalties of Britain's immigrant population
interview in *Los Angeles Times*, reported in *Daily Telegraph* 20 April 1990

Pierre Teilhard de Chardin
1881–1955

French Jesuit philosopher and palaeontologist
on Teilhard de Chardin: see **Pius XII** 259:5

1 The history of the living world can be summarised as the elaboration of ever more perfect eyes within a cosmos in which there is always something more to be seen.
The Phenomenon of Man (1959)

■ Telegrams
see box overleaf

William Temple 1881–1944

English theologian; Archbishop of Canterbury from 1942

2 In place of the conception of the power-state we are led to that of the welfare-state.
Citizen and Churchman (1941)

3 Christianity is the most materialistic of all great religions.
Readings in St John's Gospel (1939) vol. 1

4 Personally, I have always looked on cricket as organized loafing.
attributed

Mother Teresa 1910–97

Roman Catholic nun and missionary, born in what is now Macedonia of Albanian parentage

5 We ourselves feel that what we are doing is just a drop in the ocean. But if that drop was not in the ocean, I think the ocean would be less because of that missing drop. I do not agree with the big way of doing things.
A Gift for God (1975)

6 Now let us do something beautiful for God.
letter to Malcolm Muggeridge before making a BBC TV programme about the Missionaries of Charity, 1971; see **Muggeridge** 234:4

7 The biggest disease today is not leprosy or tuberculosis, but rather the feeling of being unwanted, uncared for and deserted by everybody.
in *The Observer* 3 October 1971

8 By blood and origin I am Albanian. My citizenship is Indian. I am a Catholic nun. As to my calling, I belong to the whole world. As to my heart, I belong entirely to the heart of Jesus.
in *Independent* 6 September 1997; obituary

A. S. J. Tessimond 1902–62

9 Cats, no less liquid than their shadows,
Offer no angles to the wind.
Cats (1934)

Margaret Thatcher 1925–

British Conservative stateswoman; Prime Minister, 1979–90
on Thatcher: see **Anonymous** 11:3, **Callaghan** 51:8, **Carrington** 54:6, **Critchley** 81:4, **Healey** 150:4, **Healey** 150:5, **Jenkins** 169:10, **Kinnock** 182:4, **Mitterrand** 228:7, **West** 335:10

10 No woman in my time will be Prime Minister or Chancellor or Foreign Secretary—not the top jobs. Anyway I wouldn't want to be Prime Minister. You have to give yourself 100%.
on her appointment as Shadow Education Spokesman
in *Sunday Telegraph* 26 October 1969

11 In politics if you want anything said, ask a man. If you want anything done, ask a woman.
in *People* (New York) 15 September 1975

12 I stand before you tonight in my red chiffon evening gown, my face softly made up, my fair hair gently waved . . . the Iron Lady of the Western World! Me? A cold war warrior? Well, yes—if that is how they wish to interpret my defence of values and freedoms fundamental to our way of life.
speech at Finchley, 31 January 1976; see **Anonymous** 11:3

13 Where there is discord may we bring
harmony.
Where there is error may we bring truth.

▸▸

Telegrams

1 AM IN MARKET HARBOROUGH. WHERE OUGHT I TO BE?

*sent by G. K. **Chesterton** to his wife in London*

G. K. Chesterton *Autobiography* (1936)

2 BETTER DROWNED THAN DUFFERS IF NOT DUFFERS WONT DROWN.

Arthur Ransome *Swallows and Amazons* (1930)

3 GOOD WORK, MARY. WE ALL KNEW YOU HAD IT IN YOU.

*from Dorothy **Parker** to Mrs Sherwood on the arrival of her baby*

Alexander Woollcott *While Rome Burns* (1934) 'Our Mrs Parker'

4 HOW DARE YOU BECOME PRIME MINISTER WHEN I'M AWAY GREAT LOVE CONSTANT THOUGHT VIOLET.

*from Violet Bonham Carter (1887–1969) to her father, H. H. **Asquith**, 7 April 1908*

Mark Bonham Carter and Mark Pottle (eds.) *Lantern Slides* (1996)

5 NURSE UNUPBLOWN.

*Evelyn **Waugh**'s terse response to the cable request 'Require earliest name life story photograph American nurse upblown Adowa.'*

Waugh in Abyssinia (1936)

in response to a telegraphic enquiry, HOW OLD CARY GRANT?:

6 OLD CARY GRANT FINE. HOW YOU?

from Cary Grant (1904–86)

R. Schickel *Cary Grant* (1983)

7 ON YOUR 100TH BIRTHDAY, ALL THE FAMILY JOIN WITH ME IN SENDING YOU OUR LOVE AND BEST WISHES FOR THIS SPECIAL DAY. LILIBET.

*Queen **Elizabeth II** to the Queen Mother*

in *Daily Telegraph* 5 August 2000

8 STREETS FLOODED. PLEASE ADVISE.

*message sent by Robert **Benchley** on arriving in Venice*

R. E. Drennan (ed.) *Wits End* (1973)

9 UNABLE OBTAIN BIDET. SUGGEST HANDSTAND IN SHOWER.

*from Billy **Wilder** to his wife, who had asked him to send her a bidet from Paris*

Leslie Halliwell *Filmgoer's Book of Quotes* (1973)

10 WELCOME STORIES EX-CHICAGO NOT UNDULY EMPHASISING CRIME.

authorizing the young Times *correspondent in America, Claud Cockburn, to report a murder in Al Capone's Chicago*

Claud Cockburn *In Time of Trouble* (1956)

▸▸ Margaret Thatcher continued

Where there is doubt may we bring faith. Where there is despair may we bring hope.

Downing Street, London, 4 May 1979; see below

Lord, make me an instrument of Your peace!
Where there is hatred let me sow love;
Where there is injury, pardon;
Where there is doubt, faith;
Where there is despair, hope.

St Francis of Assisi (1181–1226) 'Prayer of St Francis' (attributed)

11 Pennies don't fall from heaven. They have to be earned on earth.

in *Observer* 18 November 1979; see **Burke** 48:7

12 No one would remember the Good Samaritan if he'd only had good intentions. He had money as well.

television interview, 6 January 1980

13 I don't mind how much my Ministers talk, as long as they do what I say.

in *Observer* 27 January 1980

14 We have to get our production and our earnings in balance. There's no easy popularity in what we are proposing, but it is fundamentally sound. Yet I believe people accept there is no real alternative.

popularly encapsulated in the acronym TINA

speech at Conservative Women's Conference, 21 May 1980

15 To those waiting with bated breath for that favourite media catch-phrase, the U-turn, I have only this to say. 'You turn if you want; the lady's not for turning.'

speech at Conservative Party Conference in Brighton, 10 October 1980; see **Fry** 128:9

1 Just rejoice at that news and congratulate our armed forces and the Marines. Rejoice!

on the recapture of South Georgia, usually quoted as, 'Rejoice, rejoice!'

to newsmen outside 10 Downing Street, 25 April 1982

2 It is exciting to have a real crisis on your hands, when you have spent half your political life dealing with humdrum issues like the environment.

on the Falklands campaign, 1982

speech to Scottish Conservative Party conference, 14 May 1982; Hugo Young *One of Us* (1990)

3 We have to see that the spirit of the South Atlantic—the real spirit of Britain—is kindled not only by war but can now be fired by peace. We have the first prerequisite. We know that we can do it—we haven't lost the ability. That is the Falklands Factor.

speech in Cheltenham, 3 July 1982

4 Let me make one thing absolutely clear. The National Health Service is safe with us.

speech at Conservative Party Conference, 8 October 1982

5 I was asked whether I was trying to restore Victorian values. I said straight out I was. And I am.

speech to the British Jewish Community, 21 July 1983, referring to an interview with Brian Walden on 17 January 1983

6 Now it must be business as usual.

on the steps of Brighton police station a few hours after the bombing of the Grand Hotel, Brighton; often quoted as 'We shall carry on as usual'

in *The Times* 13 October 1984

7 We can do business together.

of Mikhail ***Gorbachev***

in *The Times* 18 December 1984

8 We must try to find ways to starve the terrorist and the hijacker of the oxygen of publicity on which they depend.

speech, 15 July 1985

9 There is no such thing as society. There are individual men and women, and there are families.

in *Woman's Own* 31 October 1987

10 We have not successfully rolled back the frontiers of the State in Britain only to see them reimposed at European level, with a European super-State exercising a new dominance from Brussels.

speech in Bruges, 20 September 1988

11 We have become a grandmother.

in *The Times* 4 March 1989

12 Advisers advise and ministers decide.

on the respective roles of her personal economic adviser, Alan Walters, and her Chancellor, Nigel ***Lawson*** *(who resigned the following day)*

in the House of Commons, 26 October 1989

13 I am naturally very sorry to see you go, but understand . . . your wish to be able to spend more time with your family.

reply to Norman ***Fowler****'s resignation letter*

in *Guardian* 4 January 1990; see **Fowler** 123:9

14 No! No! No!

making clear her opposition to a single European currency, and more centralized controls from Brussels

in the House of Commons, 30 October 1990

15 I fight on, I fight to win.

having failed to win outright in the first ballot for party leader

comment, 21 November 1990

16 It's a funny old world.

on withdrawing from the contest for leadership of the Conservative party

comment, 22 November 1990; see **Film lines** 116:8

17 I shan't be pulling the levers there but I shall be a very good back-seat driver.

after leaving office as Prime Minister

in *Independent* 27 November 1990

18 Home is where you come to when you have nothing better to do.

in *Vanity Fair* May 1991

of the poll tax:

19 Given time, it would have been seen as one of the most far-reaching and beneficial reforms ever made in the working of local government.

The Downing Street Years (1993)

1 I'm worried about that young man, he's getting awfully bossy.

on Tony ***Blair***

in *Irish Times* 6 February 1999

2 In my lifetime all our problems have come from mainland Europe and all the solutions have come from the English-speaking nations of the world.

in *Times* 6 October 1999

Dave Thomas 1949–

Canadian comic writer and actor

see also **Film lines** 115:8, 117:10

3 We thought, 'Well, they get what they deserve. This is their Canadian content. I hope they like it.'

of the creation of the 'Mckenzie Brothers' to fulfil the requirements of Canadian broadcasting law for the SCTV comedy show

interview on *Film Force* (online ed.), 10 February 2000

Dylan Thomas 1914–53

Welsh poet

see also **Opening lines** 248:1

4 Though lovers be lost love shall not;
And death shall have no dominion.

'And death shall have no dominion' (1936); see below

Christ being raised from the dead dieth no more; death hath no more dominion over him.

Bible Romans

5 Do not go gentle into that good night,
Old age should burn and rave at close of day;
Rage, rage against the dying of the light.

'Do Not Go Gentle into that Good Night' (1952)

6 The force that through the green fuse drives the flower
Drives my green age.

'The force that through the green fuse' (1934)

7 The hand that signed the paper felled a city;
Five sovereign fingers taxed the breath,
Doubled the globe of dead and halved a country;
These five kings did a king to death.

'The hand that signed the paper felled a city' (1936)

8 Light breaks where no sun shines;
Where no sea runs, the waters of the heart
Push in their tides.

'Light breaks where no sun shines' (1934)

9 It was my thirtieth year to heaven.

'Poem in October' (1946)

10 There could I marvel
My birthday
Away but the weather turned around.

'Poem in October' (1946)

11 After the first death, there is no other.

'A Refusal to Mourn the Death, by Fire, of a Child in London' (1946)

12 I can never remember whether it snowed for six days and six nights when I was twelve or whether it snowed for twelve days and twelve nights when I was six.

A Child's Christmas in Wales (1954)

13 Books that told me everything about the wasp, except why.

A Child's Christmas in Wales (1954)

14 Chasing the naughty couples down the grassgreen gooseberried double bed of the wood.

Under Milk Wood (1954)

15 Oh, isn't life a terrible thing, thank God?

Under Milk Wood (1954)

16 I want, above all, to work like a fiend, a *good* fiend.

letter to Edith **Sitwell**, 11 April 1947; *Collected Letters* (1987)

17 The land of my fathers. My fathers can have it.

of Wales

in *Adam* December 1953

18 A man you don't like who drinks as much as you do.

definition of an alcoholic

Constantine Fitzgibbon *Life of Dylan Thomas* (1965)

19 Poetry is not the most important thing in life . . . I'd much rather lie in a hot bath

reading Agatha Christie and sucking sweets.
Joan Wyndham *Love is Blue* (1986) 6 July 1943

Edward Thomas 1878–1917

English poet

1 Yes; I remember Adlestrop—
The name, because one afternoon
Of heat the express-train drew up there
Unwontedly. It was late June.
'Adlestrop' (1917)

2 The past is the only dead thing that smells sweet.
'Early one morning in May I set out' (1917)

3 If I should ever by chance grow rich
I'll buy Codham, Cockridden, and Childerditch,
Roses, Pyrgo, and Lapwater,
And let them all to my elder daughter.
'Household Poems: Bronwen' (1917)

4 I see and hear nothing;
Yet seem, too, to be listening, lying in wait
For what I should, yet never can, remember.
'Old Man' (1917)

5 Out in the dark over the snow
The fallow fawns invisible go.
'Out in the dark' (1917)

6 As well as any bloom upon a flower
I like the dust on the nettles, never lost
Except to prove the sweetness of a shower.
'Tall Nettles' (1917)

Gwyn Thomas 1913–81

Welsh novelist and dramatist

7 I wanted a play that would paint the full face of sensuality, rebellion and revivalism. In South Wales these three phenomena have played second fiddle only to Rugby Union which is a distillation of all three.
introduction to *Jackie the Jumper* (1962)

8 There are still parts of Wales where the only concession to gaiety is a striped shroud.
in *Punch* 18 June 1958

Irene Thomas 1919–2001

British writer and broadcaster

9 Protestant women may take the pill. Roman Catholic women must keep taking The Tablet.
in *Guardian* 28 December 1990

R. S. Thomas 1913–2000

Welsh poet and clergyman

10 Doctors in verse
Being scarce now, most poets
Are their own patients.
'The Cure' (1958)

11 There is no love
For such, only a willed
gentleness.
'They' (1968)

12 There is no present in Wales,
And no future;
There is only the past,
Brittle with relics . . .
And an impotent people,
Sick with inbreeding,
Worrying the carcase of an old song.
'Welsh Landscape' (1955)

E. P. Thompson 1924–

British social historian

13 Humankind must at last grow up. We must recognize that the Other is ourselves.
Beyond the Cold War (1982)

14 This 'going into Europe' will not turn out to be the thrilling mutual exchange supposed. It is more like nine middle-aged couples with failing marriages meeting in a darkened bedroom in a Brussels hotel for a Group Grope.
in *Sunday Times* 27 April 1975

Hunter S. Thompson 1939–

American writer

15 Fear and loathing in Las Vegas.
title of two articles in *Rolling Stone* 11 and 25 November 1971 (under the pseudonym 'Raoul Duke')

Julian Thompson 1934–

British soldier, second-in-command of the land forces during the Falklands campaign.

1 You don't mind dying for Queen and country, but you certainly don't want to die for politicians.

'The Falklands War— the Untold Story' (Yorkshire Television) 1 April 1987; see **France** 124:7, **Graham** 138:9

David Thomson 1941–

British film critic

2 Fiction is the great virus waiting to do away with fact—that is one of the most ominous meanings of the film.

of Citizen Kane

Rosebud: the Story of Orson Welles (1996)

Roy Thomson 1894–1976

Canadian-born British newspaper proprietor

3 Like having your own licence to print money.

on the profitability of commercial television in Britain

R. Braddon *Roy Thomson* (1965)

Jeremy Thorpe 1929–

British Liberal politician

4 Greater love hath no man than this, that he lay down his friends for his life.

on Harold ***Macmillan****'s sacking seven of his Cabinet on 13 July 1962*

D. E. Butler and A. King *General Election of 1964* (1965); see below

Greater love hath no man than this, that a man lay down his life for his friends.

Bible St John

James Thurber 1894–1961

American humorist
see also **Cartoons** 56:1, 56:4, 56:11

5 I suppose that the high-water mark of my youth in Columbus, Ohio, was the night the bed fell on my father.

My Life and Hard Times (1933)

6 Her own mother lived the latter years of her life in the horrible suspicion that electricity was dripping invisibly all over the house.

My Life and Hard Times (1933)

7 The war between men and women.

cartoon series title in *New Yorker* 20 January–28 April 1934

8 Then, with that faint fleeting smile playing about his lips, he faced the firing squad; erect and motionless, proud and disdainful, Walter Mitty, the undefeated, inscrutable to the last.

in *New Yorker* 18 March 1939 'The Secret Life of Walter Mitty'

9 Humour is emotional chaos remembered in tranquillity.

in *New York Post* 29 February 1960; see below

Poetry . . . takes its origin from emotion recollected in tranquillity.

William Wordsworth (1770–1850) *Lyrical Ballads* (2nd ed., 1802)

Anthony Thwaite 1930–

English writer

10 The name is history.
The thick Miljacka flows
Under its bridges through a canyon's breadth
Fretted with minarets and plump with domes,
Cupped in its mountains, caught on a drawn breath.

'Sarajevo: I' (1973)

Lionel Tiger 1937–

American anthropologist

11 Male bonding.

Men in Groups (1969)

Paul Tillich 1886–1965

German-born Protestant theologian

12 Neurosis is the way of avoiding non-being by avoiding being.

The Courage To Be (1952)

Alvin Toffler 1928–

American writer

1 Future shock.
defined by Toffler as 'the dizzying disorientation brought on by the premature arrival of the future' in Horizon *Summer 1965*
title of book (1970)

J. R. R. Tolkien 1892–1973

British philologist and writer
on Tolkien: see **Pratchett** 265:12; *see also* **Opening lines** 247:5

2 One Ring to rule them all, One Ring to find them
One Ring to bring them all and in the darkness bind them.
The Lord of the Rings pt. 1 *The Fellowship of the Ring* (1954) epigraph

Arturo Toscanini 1867–1957

Italian conductor

3 I smoked my first cigarette and kissed my first woman on the same day. I have never had time for tobacco since.
in *Observer* 30 June 1946

Sue Townsend 1946–

English writer

4 The secret diary of Adrian Mole aged $13\frac{3}{4}$.
title of book (1982)

Pete Townshend 1945–

British rock musician and songwriter

5 Hope I die before I get old.
'My Generation' (1965 song)

Arnold Toynbee 1889–1975

English historian

6 The twentieth century will be remembered chiefly, not as an age of political conflicts and technical inventions, but as an age in which human society dared to think of the health of the whole human race as a practical objective.
attributed

Polly Toynbee 1946–

English journalist

7 Feminism is the most revolutionary idea there has ever been. Equality for women demands a change in the human psyche more profound than anything Marx dreamed of. It means valuing parenthood as much as we value banking.
in *Guardian* 19 January 1987

Merle Travis 1917–83

American country singer

8 Sixteen tons, what do you get?
Another day older and deeper in debt.
Say brother, don't you call me 'cause I can't go
I owe my soul to the company store.
'Sixteen Tons' (1947 song)

Herbert Beerbohm Tree 1852–1917

English actor-manager

9 Ladies, just a little more virginity, if you don't mind.
to a motley collection of females, assembled to play ladies-in-waiting to a queen
Alexander Woollcott *Shouts and Murmurs* (1923)

Rose Tremain 1943–

British novelist and dramatist

10 A child, punished by selfish parents, does not feel anger. It goes to its little private corner to weep.
Restoration (1989)

G. M. Trevelyan 1876–1962

English historian

11 Disinterested intellectual curiosity is the life-blood of real civilization.
English Social History (1942)

12 If the French noblesse had been capable of playing cricket with their peasants, their chateaux would never have been burnt.

English Social History (1942)

1 [Education] has produced a vast population able to read but unable to distinguish what is worth reading, an easy prey to sensations and cheap appeals.

English Social History (1942)

John Trevelyan

British film censor

2 We are paid to have dirty minds.

in *Observer* 15 November 1959

William Trevor 1928–

Anglo-Irish novelist and short story writer

3 A disease in the family that is never mentioned.

of the troubles in Northern Ireland

in *Observer* 18 November 1990

Calvin Trillin 1935–

American journalist and writer

4 The shelf life of the modern hardback writer is somewhere between the milk and the yoghurt.

in *Sunday Times* 9 June 1991; attributed

David Trimble 1944–

Northern Irish politician, leader of the Ulster Unionists

5 We are not here to negotiate with them, but to confront them.

on entering the Mitchell talks on Northern Ireland with Sinn Fein

in *Guardian* 18 September 1997

6 The fundamental Act of Union is there, intact.

of the Northern Ireland settlement

in *Daily Telegraph* 11 April 1998

7 Mr Adams, it is over to you. We have jumped, you follow.

after the Ulster Unionist Council had voted to accept the setting up of the Northern Irish executive

in *Sunday Telegraph* 28 November 1999

Tommy Trinder 1909–89

British comedian

8 Overpaid, overfed, oversexed, and over here.

of American troops in Britain during the Second World War

associated with Trinder, but probably not original

Leon Trotsky 1879–1940

Russian revolutionary

on Trotsky: see **Taylor** 313:12

9 You [the Mensheviks] are pitiful isolated individuals; you are bankrupts; your role is played out. Go where you belong from now on—into the dustbin of history!

History of the Russian Revolution (1933)

10 Where force is necessary, there it must be applied boldly, decisively and completely. But one must know the limitations of force; one must know when to blend force with a manoeuvre, a blow with an agreement.

What Next? (1932)

11 It was the supreme expression of the mediocrity of the apparatus that Stalin himself rose to his position.

My Life (1930)

12 Old age is the most unexpected of all things that happen to a man.

diary, 8 May 1935

Pierre Trudeau 1919–2000

Canadian Liberal statesman, Prime Minister, 1968–79 and 1980–4

13 The state has no place in the nation's bedrooms.

interview, Ottawa, 22 December 1967

14 The twentieth century really belongs to those who will build it. The future can be promised to no one.

in 1968; see below

The nineteenth century was the century of the United States. I think we can claim that it is Canada that shall fill the twentieth century.

Wilfrid Laurier (1841–1919) speech, Ottawa, 18 January 1904

1 Living next to you is in some ways like sleeping with an elephant. No matter how friendly and even-tempered the beast, one is affected by every twitch and grunt.
on relations between Canada and the US
speech at National Press Club, Washington D. C., 25 March 1969

François Truffaut 1932–84

French film director

2 I've always had the impression that real militants are like cleaning women, doing a thankless, daily but necessary job.
letter to Jean-Luc Godard, May-June 1973

Harry S. Truman 1884–1972

American Democratic statesman, 33rd President of the US, 1945–53
on Truman: see **Mencken** 221:11; *see also* **Newspaper headlines** 240:4

to reporters the day after his accession to the Presidency on the death of Franklin ***Roosevelt****:*

3 When they told me yesterday what had happened, I felt like the moon, the stars and all the planets had fallen on me.
on 13 April 1945

4 Sixteen hours ago an American airplane dropped one bomb on Hiroshima . . . The force from which the sun draws its power has been loosed against those who brought war to the Far East.
first announcement of the dropping of the atomic bomb
on 6 August 1945

5 Effective, reciprocal, and enforceable safeguards acceptable to all nations.
Declaration on Atomic Energy by President Truman, Clement ***Attlee****, and W. L. Mackenzie* ***King***
on 15 November 1945

6 What we are doing in Korea is this: we are trying to prevent a third world war.
after the recall of ***MacArthur***
address to the nation, 16 April 1951

7 I never give them [the public] hell. I just tell the truth, and they think it is hell.
in *Look* 3 April 1956

8 A statesman is a politician who's been dead 10 or 15 years.
in *New York World Telegram and Sun* 12 April 1958

9 It's a recession when your neighbour loses his job; it's a depression when you lose yours.
in *Observer* 13 April 1958

10 Wherever you have an efficient government you have a dictatorship.
lecture at Columbia University, 28 April 1959

11 Always be sincere, even if you don't mean it.
attributed

12 The buck stops here.
unattributed motto on Truman's desk

13 He'll sit right here and he'll say do this, do that! And nothing will happen. Poor Ike—it won't be a bit like the Army.
of his successor ***Eisenhower***
Harry S. Truman (1973) vol. 2; see **Schwarzkopf** 292:7

14 I didn't fire him [General MacArthur] because he was a dumb son of a bitch, although he was, but that's not against the law for generals. If it was, half to three-quarters of them would be in jail.
Merle Miller *Plain Speaking* (1974)

15 If you can't stand the heat, get out of the kitchen.
attributed by Truman himself to Harry Vaughan, his 'military jester'
in *Time* 28 April 1952

Donald Trump 1946–

American businessman

16 Deals are my art form. Other people paint beautifully on canvas or write wonderful poetry. I like making deals, preferably big deals. That's how I get my kicks.
Donald Trump and Tony Schwartz *The Art of the Deal* (1987)

Morton Tsvangirai

Zimbabwean politician

17 This country is for blacks. But we need the knowledge of the whites to train people and create jobs.
in *Times* 15 April 2000

Marina Tsvetaeva 1892–1941

Russian poet

1 In this
most Christian of worlds all poets
are Jews.

'Poem of the End' (1924)

Sophie Tucker 1884–1966

Russian-born American vaudeville artiste

2 From birth to 18 a girl needs good parents. From 18 to 35, she needs good looks. From 35 to 55, good personality. From 55 on, she needs good cash.

M. Freedland *Sophie* (1978)

3 I've been rich and I've been poor: rich is better.

attributed

Alan Turing 1912–54

English mathematician and codebreaker

4 We are not interested in the fact that the brain has the consistency of cold porridge.

A. P. Hodges *Alan Turing: the Enigma* (1983)

Sherry Turkle 1948–

American sociologist

5 Like the anthropologist returning home from a foreign culture, the voyager in virtuality can return home to a real world better equipped to understand its artifices.

Life on the Screen: Identity in the Age of the Internet (1995)

Walter James Redfern Turner 1889–1946

British writer and critic

6 When I was but thirteen or so
I went into a golden land,
Chimborazo, Cotopaxi
Took me by the hand.

'Romance' (1916)

John Tusa 1936–

British broadcaster and radio journalist

7 Management that wants to change an institution must first show it loves that institution.

in *Observer* 27 February 1994

Desmond Tutu 1931–

South African Anglican clergyman, Archbishop of Cape Town

8 I have struggled against tyranny. I didn't do that in order to substitute one tyranny with another.

on the ANC's attempt to prevent publication of the Truth Commission report

in *Irish Times* 31 October 1998

9 We may be surprised at the people we find in heaven. God has a soft spot for sinners. His standards are quite low.

in *Sunday Times* 15 April 2001

Jill Tweedie 1936–93

British journalist

10 My boredom threshold is low at the best of times but I have spent more time being slowly and excruciatingly bored by children than any other section of the human race.

It's Only Me (1980)

11 I blame the women's movement for ten years in a boiler suit.

attributed, 1989

Twiggy 1949–

English model and actress

12 It always makes me laugh when people ask why anyone would want to do a sitcom in America. If it runs five years, you never have to work again.

in *Independent* 4 October 1997

Kenneth Tynan 1927–80

English theatre critic

13 Oh, I think so, certainly. I doubt if there are very many rational people in this world to whom the word 'fuck' is

particularly diabolical or revolting or totally forbidden.

on 13 November 1965 on a late-night programme called BBC-3

Kathleen Tynan (ed.) *Kenneth Tynan: Letters* (1994)

1 A critic is a man who knows the way but can't drive the car.

in *New York Times Magazine* 9 January 1966

2 'Sergeant Pepper'—a decisive moment in the history of Western Civilization.

in 1967; Howard Elson *McCartney* (1986)

3 A neurosis is a secret you don't know you're keeping.

Kathleen Tynan *Life of Kenneth Tynan* (1987)

Mike Tyson 1966–

American boxer

4 I'm in the hurt business.

in *Independent on Sunday* 24 December 2000

Tracey Ullman 1959–

British actress

5 The most remarkable thing about my mother is that for 30 years she served nothing but leftovers. The original meal was never found.

in *Observer* 23 May 1999

Miguel de Unamuno 1864–1937

Spanish philosopher and writer

6 *La vida es duda,*
y la fe sin la duda es sólo muerte.

Life is doubt,
And faith without doubt is nothing but death.

'Salmo II' (1907)

John Updike 1932–

American novelist and short-story writer

7 A healthy male adult bore consumes *each year* one and a half times his own weight in other people's patience.

Assorted Prose (1965) 'Confessions of a Wild Bore'

8 The heart *prefers* to move against the grain of circumstance; perversity is the soul's very life.

Assorted Prose (1965) 'More Love in the Western World'

9 A soggy little island huffing and puffing to keep up with Western Europe.

of England

Picked Up Pieces (1976) 'London Life' (written 1969)

10 America is a land whose centre is nowhere; England one whose centre is everywhere.

Picked Up Pieces (1976) 'London Life' (written 1969)

11 America is a vast conspiracy to make you happy.

Problems (1980) 'How to love America and Leave it at the Same Time'

12 You shouldn't sit in judgment of your parents. We did the best we could while being people too.

Rabbit at Rest (1990)

13 Without the cold war, what's the point of being an American?

Rabbit at Rest (1990)

14 Celebrity is a mask that eats into the face.

Self-Consciousness: Memoirs (1989)

15 Neutrinos, they are very small
They have no charge and have no mass
And do not interact at all.

'Cosmic Gall ' (1964)

16 I've never much enjoyed going to plays . . . The unreality of painted people standing on a platform saying things they've said to each other for months is more than I can overlook.

George Plimpton (ed.) *Writers at Work* 4th Series (1977)

Peter Ustinov 1921–

Russian-born actor, director, and writer

17 Laughter . . . the most civilized music in the world.

Dear Me (1977)

18 I do not believe that friends are necessarily the people you like best, they are merely the people who got there first.

Dear Me (1977)

1 At the age of four with paper hats and wooden swords we're all Generals. Only some of us never grow out of it.
Romanoff and Juliet (1956)

2 Laughter would be bereaved if snobbery died.
in *Observer* 13 March 1955

3 Toronto is a kind of New York operated by the Swiss.
in *Globe & Mail* 1 August 1987; attributed

Paul Valéry 1871–1945

French poet, critic, and man of letters

4 A poem is never finished; it's always an accident that puts a stop to it—that is to say, gives it to the public.
Littérature (1930)

5 Science means simply the aggregate of all the recipes that are always successful. The rest is literature.
Moralités (1932)

6 God created man and, finding him not sufficiently alone, gave him a companion to make him feel his solitude more keenly.
Tel Quel 1 (1941) 'Moralités'

7 Politics is the art of preventing people from taking part in affairs which properly concern them.
Tel Quel 2 (1943) 'Rhumbs'

Paul Vance and Lee Pockriss

American singer and American songwriter

8 Itsy bitsy teenie weenie, yellow polkadot bikini.
title of song (1960)

Vivian van Damm c.1889–1960

British theatre manager

9 We never closed.
of the Windmill Theatre, London, during the Second World War
Tonight and Every Night (1952)

Laurens van der Post 1906–96

South African explorer and writer

10 Human beings are perhaps never more frightening than when they are convinced beyond doubt that they are right.
Lost World of the Kalahari (1958)

11 I don't think a man who has watched the sun going down could walk away and commit a murder.
in *Daily Telegraph* 17 December 1996; obituary

Henry Van Dyke 1852–1933

American Presbyterian minister and writer

12 Time is
Too slow for those who wait,
Too swift for those who fear,
Too long for those who grieve,
Too short for those who rejoice;
But for those who love,
Time is eternity.
'Time is too slow for those who wait' (1905), read at the funeral of **Diana**, Princess of Wales; Nigel Rees in 'Quote . . . Unquote' October 1997 notes that the original form of the last line is 'Time is not'

Raoul Vaneigem 1934–

Belgian philosopher

13 Never before has a civilization reached such a degree of a contempt for life; never before has a generation, drowned in mortification, felt such a rage to live.
of the 1960s
The Revolution of Everyday Life (1967)

14 The same people who are murdered slowly in the mechanized slaughterhouses of work are also arguing, singing, drinking, dancing, making love, holding the streets, picking up weapons and inventing a new poetry.
The Revolution of Everyday Life (1967)

15 Work to survive, survive by consuming, survive to consume: the hellish cycle is complete.
The Revolution of Everyday Life (1967)

Bartolomeo Vanzetti
1888–1927

American anarchist, born in Italy
see also **Millay** 223:8, 223:9

1 Sacco's name will live in the hearts of the people and in their gratitude when Katzmann's and yours bones will be dispersed by time, when your name, his name, your laws, institutions, and your false god are but a deem rememoring of a cursed past in which man was wolf to the man.

statement disallowed at his trial, with Nicola Sacco, for murder and robbery,; M. D. Frankfurter and G. Jackson *Letters of Sacco and Vanzetti* (1928); see below

A man is a wolf rather than a man to another man, when he hasn't yet found out what he's like.

Plautus (c.250–184 BC) *Asinaria*; often quoted as 'A man is a wolf to another man'

2 If it had not been for these thing, I might have live out my life talking at street corners to scorning men. I might have die, unmarked, unknown, a failure. Now we are not a failure. This is our career and our triumph. Never in our full life could we hope to do such work for tolerance, for joostice, for man's onderstanding of man as now we do by accident.

statement after being sentenced to death, 9 April 1927

Janet-Maria Vaughan
1899–1993

English scientist

3 I am here—trying to do science in hell.

working as a doctor in Belsen at the end of the war

letter to a friend, 12 May 1945; P. A. Adams (ed.) *Janet-Maria Vaughan* (1993)

Ralph Vaughan Williams
1872–1958

English composer

4 I don't know whether I like it, but it's what I meant.

on his 4th symphony

Christopher Headington *Bodley Head History of Western Music* (1974)

on being asked by a reporter, 'What do you think about music?':

5 It's a Rum Go!

Leslie Ayr *The Wit of Music* (1966)

Robert Venturi 1925–

American architect

6 Less is a bore.

Complexity and Contradiction in Architecture (1966); see **Rohe** 277:8

Gianni Versace 1949–96

Italian designer

7 I like to dress egos. If you haven't got an ego today, you can forget it.

in *Guardian* 16 July 1997; obituary

Hendrik Frensch Verwoerd
1901–66

South African statesman; Prime Minister from 1958

8 Up till now he [the Bantu] has been subjected to a school system which drew him away from his own community and practically misled him by showing him the green pastures of the European but still did not allow him to graze there . . . It is abundantly clear that unplanned education creates many problems, disrupts the communal life of the Bantu and endangers the communal life of the European.

speech in South African Senate, 7 June 1954

Sid Vicious 1957–79

British rock musician, member of the Sex Pistols

on Vicious: see **Newspaper headlines** 240:6

1 You just pick a chord, go twang, and you've got music.

attributed

Gore Vidal 1925–

American novelist and critic

2 What other culture could have produced someone like Hemingway and *not* seen the joke?

Pink Triangle and Yellow Star (1982)

3 I'm all for bringing back the birch, but only between consenting adults.

in *Sunday Times Magazine* 16 September 1973

4 Whenever a friend succeeds, a little something in me dies.

in *Sunday Times Magazine* 16 September 1973

5 It is not enough to succeed. Others must fail.

G. Irvine *Antipanegyric for Tom Driberg* 8 December 1976

6 A triumph of the embalmer's art.

of Ronald ***Reagan***

in *Observer* 26 April 1981

on being asked what would have happened in 1963, had ***Khrushchev*** *and not* ***Kennedy*** *been assassinated:*

7 With history one can never be certain, but I think I can safely say that Aristotle Onassis would not have married Mrs Khrushchev.

in *Sunday Times* 4 June 1989

8 A genius with the IQ of a moron.

of Andy ***Warhol***

in *Observer* 18 June 1989

of Truman ***Capote****'s death:*

9 Good career move.

attributed

10 He will lie even when it is inconvenient: the sign of the true artist.

attributed

explaining why he would support Ralph ***Nader*** *for the presidency in preference to his own cousin Al* ***Gore****:*

11 In the long run Gore is thicker than Nader.

in *Daily Telegraph* 18 August 2000

José Antonio Viera Gallo 1943–

Chilean politician

12 Socialism can only arrive by bicycle.

Ivan Illich *Energy and Equity* (1974) epigraph

John Wain 1925–94

English poet and novelist

13 Poetry is to prose as dancing is to walking.

BBC radio broadcast, 13 January 1976

Derek Walcott 1930–

West Indian poet and dramatist

14 I who have cursed
The drunken officer of British rule, how choose
Between this Africa and the English tongue I love?

'A Far Cry From Africa' (1962)

15 Famine sighs like scythe
across the field of statistics and the desert
is a moving mouth.

'The Fortunate Traveller' (1981)

16 The worst crime is to leave a man's hands empty.
Men are born makers, with that primal simplicity
In every maker since Adam.

Omeros 1990

17 I come from a backward place: your duty is supplied by life around you. One guy plants bananas; another plants cocoa; I'm a writer, I plant lines. There's the same clarity of occupation, and the sense of devotion.

in *Guardian* 12 July 1997

Lech Wałęsa 1943–

Polish trade unionist and statesman, President since 1990

1 You have riches and freedom here but I feel no sense of faith or direction. You have so many computers, why don't you use them in the search for love?

in Paris, on his first journey outside the Soviet area, in *Daily Telegraph* 14 December 1988

Alice Walker 1944–

American poet

2 Did this happen to your mother? Did your sister throw up a lot?

title of poem, 1979

3 Expect nothing. Live frugally
on surprise.

'Expect nothing' (1973)

4 The quietly pacifist peaceful
always die
to make room for men
who shout.

'The QPP' (1973)

5 We have a beautiful
mother
Her green lap
immense
Her brown embrace
eternal
Her blue body
everything
we know.

'We Have a Beautiful Mother' (1991)

6 I think it pisses God off if you walk by the colour purple in a field somewhere and don't notice it.

The Colour Purple (1982)

George Wallace 1919–98

American Democratic politician

7 Segregation now, segregation tomorrow and segregation forever!

inaugural speech as Governor of Alabama, January 1963

Henry Wallace 1888–1965

American Democratic politician

8 The century on which we are entering—the century which will come out of this war—can be and must be the century of the common man.

speech, 8 May 1942

Graham Wallas 1858–1932

British politicial scientist

9 The little girl had the making of a poet in her who, being told to be sure of her meaning before she spoke, said, 'How can I know what I think till I see what I say?'

The Art of Thought (1926)

Julie Walters 1950–

British actress

10 I have a rare intolerance to herbs which means I can only drink fermented liquids, such as gin.

in *Observer* 14 March 1999

Barbara Ward 1914–81

British author and educator

11 We cannot cheat on DNA. We cannot get round photosynthesis. We cannot say I am not going to give a damn about phytoplankton. All these tiny mechanisms provide the preconditions of our planetary life. To say we do not care is to say in the most literal sense that 'we choose death'.

Only One Earth (1972)

Andy Warhol 1927–87

American artist

on Warhol: see **Vidal** 328:8

12 In the future everybody will be world famous for fifteen minutes.

Andy Warhol (1968)

13 Being good in business is the most fascinating kind of art.

Philosophy of Andy Warhol (From A to B and Back Again) (1975)

1 An artist is someone who produces things that people don't need to have but that he—for *some reason*—thinks it would be a good idea to give them.

Philosophy of Andy Warhol (From A to B and Back Again) (1975)

2 Isn't life a series of images that change as they repeat themselves?

Victor Bokris *Andy Warhol* (1989)

3 The things I want to show are mechanical. Machines have less problems.

Mike Wrenn *Andy Warhol: In His Own Words* (1991)

Shane Warne 1969–

Australian cricketer

4 I have learnt to think of three words all the time—what, when and why. That means always knowing what I am going to bowl, when I am going to bowl it and to be clear why I have chosen that option.

My Autobiography (2001)

Jack Warner 1892–1978

American film producer

*on hearing that Ronald **Reagan** was seeking nomination as Governor of California:*

5 No, *no. Jimmy Stewart* for governor—Reagan for his best friend.

Max Wilk *The Wit and Wisdom of Hollywood* (1972)

Sylvia Townsend Warner 1893–1978

English writer

6 One need not write in a diary what one is to remember for ever.

diary, 22 October 1930

7 One cannot overestimate the power of a good rancorous hatred on the part of the *stupid*. The stupid have so much more industry and energy to expend on hating. They build it up like coral insects.

diary, 26 September 1954

8 Total grief is like a minefield. No knowing when one will touch the tripwire.

diary, 11 December 1969

Robert Penn Warren 1905–1989

American poet, novelist, and critic

9 Long ago in Kentucky, I, a boy, stood
By a dirt road, in first dark, and heard
The great geese hoot northward.

Audubon (1969) 'Tell Me a Story'

10 Ages to our construction went,
Dim architecture, hour by hour:
And violence, forgot now, lent
The present stillness all its power.

'Bearded Oaks' (1942)

11 They were human, they suffered, wore long black coat and gold watch chain.
They stare from daguerrotype with severe reprehension,
Or from genuine oil, and you'd never guess any pain
In those merciless eyes that now remark our own time's sad declension.

'Promises' (1957)

Ned Washington 1901–76

American songwriter

12 Hi diddle dee dee (an actor's life for me).

title of song from the film *Pinocchio* (1940)

13 The night is like a lovely tune,
Beware my foolish heart!
How white the ever-constant moon,
Take care, my foolish heart!

'My Foolish Heart' (1949 song)

Keith Waterhouse 1929–

English novelist, dramatist, and screenwriter

14 Jeffery Bernard is unwell.

from the Spectator*'s habitual explanation for the non-appearance of Jeffery **Bernard**'s column*

title of play (1989)

James D. Watson 1928–

American biologist
see also **Crick and Watson**

1 No *good* model ever accounted for *all* the facts, since some data was bound to be misleading if not plain wrong.
Francis Crick *Some Mad Pursuit* (1988)

2 Some day a child is going to sue its parents for being born. They will say, my life is so awful with these terrible genetic defects and you just callously didn't find out.
on the question of genetic screening of foetuses
interview in *Sunday Telegraph* 16 February 1997

Thomas Watson Snr. 1874–1956

American businessman; Chairman of IBM 1914–52

3 Clothes don't make the man . . . but they go a long way toward making a businessman.
Robert Sobel *IBM: Colossus in Transition* (1981)

4 You cannot be a success in any business without believing that it is the greatest business in the world . . . You have to put your heart in the business and the business in your heart.
Robert Sobel *IBM: Colossus in Transition* (1981)

Evelyn Waugh 1903–66

English novelist

5 Charm is the great English blight. It does not exist outside these damp islands. It spots and kills anything it touches. It kills love, it kills art.
Brideshead Revisited (1945)

6 The sound of English county families baying for broken glass.
Decline and Fall (1928); see **Belloc** 28:1

7 I expect you'll be becoming a schoolmaster, sir. That's what most of the gentlemen does, sir, that gets sent down for indecent behaviour.
Decline and Fall (1928)

8 Any one who has been to an English public school will always feel comparatively at home in prison. It is the people brought up in the gay intimacy of the slums, Paul learned, who find prison so soul-destroying.
Decline and Fall (1928)

9 Only when one has lost all curiosity about the future has one reached the age to write an autobiography.
A Little Learning (1964)

10 In the dying world I come from quotation is a national vice. No one would think of making an after-dinner speech without the help of poetry. It used to be the classics, now it's lyric verse.
The Loved One (1948)

11 He abhorred plastics, Picasso, sunbathing and jazz—everything in fact that had happened in his own lifetime.
The Ordeal of Gilbert Pinfold (1957)

12 *The Beast* stands for strong mutually antagonistic governments everywhere . . . Self-sufficiency at home, self-assertion abroad.
Scoop (1938)

13 Up to a point, Lord Copper.
Scoop (1938)

14 Feather-footed through the plashy fen passes the questing vole.
Scoop (1938)

15 Other nations use 'force'; we Britons alone use 'Might'.
Scoop (1938)

16 To see him fumbling with our rich and delicate language is to experience all the horror of seeing a Sèvres vase in the hands of a chimpanzee.
of Stephen ***Spender***
in *The Tablet* 5 May 1951

17 I do not aspire to advise my sovereign in her choice of servants.
on why he did not vote
in *Spectator* 2 October 1959

18 A typical triumph of modern science to find the only part of Randolph that was not malignant and remove it.
on hearing that Randolph Churchill's lung, when removed, proved non-malignant
diary, March 1964

1 You have no idea how much nastier I would be if I was not a Catholic. Without supernatural aid I would hardly be a human being.
Noel Annan *Our Age* (1990)

Frederick Weatherly
1848–1929

English songwriter

2 Roses are flowering in Picardy,
But there's never a rose like you.
'Roses of Picardy' (1916 song)

Beatrice Webb 1858–1943

English socialist

3 I never visualised labour as separate men and women of different sorts and kinds . . . labour was an abstraction, which seemed to denote an arithmetically calculable mass of human beings, each individual a repetition of the other.
My Apprenticeship (1926)

4 If I ever felt inclined to be timid as I was going into a room full of people, I would say to myself, 'You're the cleverest member of one of the cleverest families in the cleverest class of the cleverest nation in the world, why should you be frightened?'
Bertrand Russell *Autobiography* (1967)

Sidney Webb 1859–1947

English socialist

5 The inevitability of gradualness.
Presidential address to the annual conference of the Labour Party, 26 June 1923

6 Marriage is the waste-paper basket of the emotions.
Bertrand Russell *Autobiography* (1967)

Simone Weil 1909–43

French essayist and philosopher

7 An obligation which goes unrecognized by anybody loses none of the full force of its existence. A right which goes unrecognized by anybody is not worth very much.
L'Enracinement (1949) 'Les Besoins de l'âme'

8 All sins are attempts to fill voids.
La Pesanteur et la grâce (1948)

9 The authentic and pure values—truth, beauty, and goodness—in the activity of a human being are the result of one and the same act, a certain application of the full attention to the object.
La Pesanteur et la grâce (1948)

10 A work of art has an author and yet, when it is perfect, it has something which is essentially anonymous about it.
La Pesanteur et la grâce (1948)

11 What a country calls its vital economic interests are not the things which enable its citizens to live, but the things which enable it to make war.
W. H. Auden *A Certain World* (1971)

Max Weinreich 1894–1969

12 A language is a dialect with an army and a navy.
Steven Pinker *The Language Instinct* (1994)

Victor Weisskopf 1908–

American physicist

13 It was absolutely marvellous working for Pauli. You could ask him anything. There was no worry that he would think a particular question was stupid, since he thought *all* questions were stupid.
in *American Journal of Physics* 1977

Johnny Weissmuller

see **Misquotations** 226:11

Chaim Weizmann 1874–1952

Russian-born Israeli statesman, President 1949–52

14 Something had been done for us which, after two thousand years of hope and yearning, would at last give us a resting-place in this terrible world.
of the Balfour declaration
speech in Jerusalem, 25 November 1936

Joseph Welch 1890–1960

American lawyer

1 Until this moment, Senator, I think I never really gauged your cruelty or your recklessness . . . Have you no sense of decency, sir? At long last, have you left no sense of decency?

to Joseph ***McCarthy****, 9 June 1954, defending the US Army against allegations of harbouring subversive activities; the televised confrontation was deeply damaging to McCarthy*

in *American National Biography* (online edition) 'Joseph McCarthy'

Fay Weldon 1931–

British novelist and scriptwriter
see also **Advertising slogans** 3:20

2 Natalie had left the wives and joined the women.

Heart of the Country (1987)

3 The life and loves of a she-devil.

title of novel (1984)

4 Every time you open your wardrobe, you look at your clothes and you wonder what you are going to wear. What you are really saying is 'Who am I going to be today?'

in *New Yorker* 26 June 1995

5 It's very unfashionable to say this, but rape actually isn't the worst thing that can happen to a woman if you're safe, alive and unmarked after the event.

in *Radio Times* 4 July 1998

Colin Welland 1934–

English actor and scriptwriter

6 The British are coming.

speech accepting an Oscar for his *Chariots of Fire* screenplay, 30 March 1982

Orson Welles 1915–85

American actor and film director
see also **Film lines** 116:6

7 The biggest electric train set any boy ever had!

of the RKO studios

Peter Noble *The Fabulous Orson Welles* (1956)

8 I hate television. I hate it as much as peanuts. But I can't stop eating peanuts.

in *New York Herald Tribune* 12 October 1956

9 There are only two emotions in a plane: boredom and terror.

interview to celebrate his 70th birthday, in *The Times* 6 May 1985

H. G. Wells 1866–1946

English novelist and political writer
see also **Epitaphs** 109:6

10 'Sesquippledan,' he would say. 'Sesquippledan verboojuice.'

The History of Mr Polly (1909)

11 'I'm a Norfan, both sides,' he would explain, with the air of one who had seen trouble.

Kipps (1905)

12 I was thinking jest what a Rum Go everything is.

Kipps (1905)

13 The Social Contract is nothing more or less than a vast conspiracy of human beings to lie to and humbug themselves and one another for the general Good. Lies are the mortar that bind the savage individual man into the social masonry.

Love and Mr Lewisham (1900)

14 Human history becomes more and more a race between education and catastrophe.

The Outline of History (1920)

15 The shape of things to come.

title of book (1933)

16 The war that will end war.

title of book (1914); see **Lloyd George** 201:5

17 In England we have come to rely upon a comfortable time-lag of fifty years or a century intervening between the perception that something ought to be done and a serious attempt to do it.

The Work, Wealth and Happiness of Mankind (1931)

Irvine Welsh 1957–

Scottish novelist

1 It's nae good blamin' it oan the English fir colonising us. Ah don't hate the English. They're just wankers. We can't even pick a decent vibrant, healthy culture to be colonised by.

Trainspotting (1994)

Eudora Welty 1909–

American writer

2 I am a writer who came of a sheltered life. A sheltered life can be a daring life as well. For all serious daring starts from within.

One Writer's Beginnings (1984)

Arnold Wesker 1932–

English dramatist

3 Chips with every damn thing. You breed babies and you eat chips with everything.

Chips with Everything (1962)

4 A journalist is somebody who possesses himself of a fantasy and lures the truth towards it.

Journey into Journalism (1977)

5 The Khomeini cry for the execution of Rushdie is an infantile cry. From the beginning of time we have seen that. To murder the thinker does not murder the thought.

in *Weekend Guardian* 3 June 1989; see **Khomeini** 180:4

Mary Wesley 1912–

English novelist

6 When people discussed tonics, pick-me-ups after a severe illness, she kept to herself the prescription of a quick dip in bed with someone you liked but were not in love with. A shock of sexual astonishment which could make you feel astonishingly well and high spirited.

Not That Sort of Girl (1987)

Mae West 1892–1980

American film actress

see also **Misquotations** 227:5, **Sayings and slogans** 289:16

7 It's better to be looked over than overlooked.

Belle of the Nineties (1934 film)

8 A man in the house is worth two in the street.

Belle of the Nineties (1934 film)

9 I always say, keep a diary and some day it'll keep you.

Every Day's a Holiday (1937 film)

10 Beulah, peel me a grape.

I'm No Angel (1933 film)

11 I've been things and seen places.

I'm No Angel (1933 film)

12 When I'm good, I'm very, very good, but when I'm bad, I'm better.

I'm No Angel (1933 film)

13 It's not the men in my life that counts—it's the life in my men.

I'm No Angel (1933 film)

14 Give a man a free hand and he'll try to put it all over you.

Klondike Annie (1936 film)

15 Between two evils, I always pick the one I never tried before.

Klondike Annie (1936 film)

16 'Goodness, what beautiful diamonds!' 'Goodness had nothing to do with it.'

Night After Night (1932 film)

17 I've been in *Who's Who*, and I know what's what, but it'll be the first time I ever made the dictionary.

letter to the RAF, early 1940s, on having an inflatable life jacket named after her

Fergus Cashin *Mae West* (1981)

18 Is that a gun in your pocket, or are you just glad to see me?

usually quoted as, 'Is that a pistol in your pocket . . .'

J. Weintraub *Peel Me a Grape* (1975)

19 I used to be Snow White . . . but I drifted.

Joseph Weintraub *Peel Me a Grape* (1975)

1 A hard man is good to find.
attributed

2 It's not what I do, but the way I do it. It's not what I say, but the way I say it.
G. Eells and S. Musgrove *Mae West* (1989)

Rebecca West 1892–1983

English novelist and journalist

3 Were I to . . . take a peasant by the shoulders and whisper to him, 'In your lifetime, have you known peace?' wait for his answer, shake his shoulders and transform him into his father, and ask him the same question, and transform him in his turn to his father, I would never hear the word 'Yes', if I carried my questioning of the dead back for a thousand years.
of Yugoslavia in the 1930s
Black Lamb and Grey Falcon (1941) vol. 1

4 There is no such thing as conversation. It is an illusion. There are intersecting monologues, that is all.
'The Harsh Voice' (1935)

5 Having watched the form of our traitors for a number of years, I cannot think that espionage can be recommended as a technique for building an impressive civilization. It's a lout's game.
The Meaning of Treason (1982 ed.)

6 The point is that nobody likes having salt rubbed into their wounds, even if it is the salt of the earth.
The Salt of the Earth (1935)

7 I myself have never been able to find out precisely what feminism is: I only know that people call me a feminist whenever I express sentiments that differentiate me from a doormat or a prostitute.
in *The Clarion* 14 November 1913

8 Just how difficult it is to write biography can be reckoned by anybody who sits down and considers just how many people know the truth about his or her love affairs.
in *Vogue* 1 November 1952

9 There is, of course, no reason for the existence of the male sex except that sometimes one needs help with moving the piano.
in *Sunday Telegraph* 28 June 1970

10 Whatever happens, never forget that people would rather be led to *perdition* by a man, than to *victory* by a woman.
in conversation in 1979, just before Margaret ***Thatcher****'s first election victory*
in *Sunday Telegraph* 17 January 1988

Loelia, Duchess of Westminster 1902–93

English aristocrat

11 Anybody seen in a bus over the age of thirty has been a failure in life.
Cocktails and Laughter (1983); habitual remark

William C. Westmoreland 1914–

American general

12 Vietnam was the first war ever fought without censorship. Without censorship, things can get terribly confused in the public mind.
attributed, 1982

R. P. Weston 1878–1936 and **Bert Lee** 1880–1947

British songwriters

13 Good-bye-ee!—Good-bye-ee!
Wipe the tear, baby dear, from your eye-ee.
Tho' it's hard to part, I know,
I'll be tickled to death to go.
Don't cry-ee—don't sigh-ee!
There's a silver lining in the sky-ee!
Bonsoir, old thing! cheerio! chin-chin!
Nahpoo! Toodle-oo! Good-bye-ee!
'Good-bye-ee!' (c.1915 song)

Alan Wharton 1923–

English cricketer

14 It's a well-known fact that, when I'm on 99, I'm the best judge of a run in all the bloody world.
to Cyril Washbrook; Freddie Trueman *You Nearly Had Me That Time* (1978)

Edith Wharton 1862–1937

American novelist

1 Mrs Ballinger is one of the ladies who pursue Culture in bands, as though it were dangerous to meet it alone.

Xingu and Other Stories (1916) 'Xingu'

2 To your generation, I must represent the literary equivalent of tufted furniture and gas chandeliers.

letter to F. Scott Fitzgerald, 8 June 1925

E. B. White 1899–1985

American humorist

see also **Cartoons** 56:5

3 The so-called science of poll-taking is not a science at all but a mere necromancy. People are unpredictable by nature, and although you can take a nation's pulse, you can't be sure that the nation hasn't just run up a flight of stairs.

in *New Yorker* 13 November 1948

4 Commuter—one who spends his life
In riding to and from his wife;
A man who shaves and takes a train,
And then rides back to shave again.

'The Commuter' (1982)

Edmund White 1940–

American writer and critic

5 The Aids epidemic has rolled back a big rotting log and revealed all the squirming life underneath it, since it involves, all at once, the main themes of our existence: sex, death, power, money, love, hate, disease and panic. No American phenomenon has been so compelling since the Vietnam War.

States of Desire: Travels in Gay America (afterword to 1986 edition)

Patrick White 1912–90

Australian novelist

6 Conversation is imperative if gaps are to be filled, and old age, it is the last gap but one.

The Tree of Man (1955)

7 So that, in the end, there was no end.

The Tree of Man (1955); closing words

8 In all directions stretched the great Australian Emptiness, in which the mind is the least of possessions.

The Vital Decade (1968) 'The Prodigal Son'

T. H. White 1906–64

English novelist

9 The once and future king.

taken from Sir Thomas Malory Le Morte d'Arthur: 'Hic iacet Arthurus, rex quondam rexque futurus'

title of novel (1958)

Theodore H. White 1915–86

American writer and journalist

10 Johnson's instinct for power is as primordial as a salmon's going upstream to spawn.

of Lyndon ***Johnson***

The Making of the President (1964)

11 The flood of money that gushes into politics today is a pollution of democracy.

in *Time* 19 November 1984

Alfred North Whitehead 1861–1947

English philosopher and mathematician

12 Life is an offensive, directed against the repetitious mechanism of the Universe.

Adventures of Ideas (1933)

13 It is more important that a proposition be interesting than that it be true. This statement is almost a tautology. For the energy of operation of a proposition in an occasion of experience is its interest, and is its importance. But of course a true proposition is more apt to be interesting than a false one.

Adventures of Ideas (1933)

14 There are no whole truths; all truths are half-truths. It is trying to treat them as whole truths that plays the devil.

Dialogues (1954) prologue

1 Intelligence is quickness to apprehend as distinct from ability, which is capacity to act wisely on the thing apprehended.
Dialogues (1954) 15 December 1939

2 What is morality in any given time or place? It is what the majority then and there happen to like, and immorality is what they dislike.
Dialogues (1954) 30 August 1941

3 Art is the imposing of a pattern on experience, and our aesthetic enjoyment is recognition of the pattern.
Dialogues (1954) 10 June 1943

4 Civilization advances by extending the number of important operations which we can perform without thinking about them.
Introduction to Mathematics (1911)

5 No more impressive warning can be given to those who would confine knowledge and research to what is apparently useful, than the reflection that conic sections were studied for eighteen hundred years merely as an abstract science, without regard to any utility other than to satisfy the craving for knowledge on the part of mathematicians, and that then at the end of this long period of abstract study, they were found to be the necessary key with which to attain the knowledge of the most important laws of nature.
Introduction to Mathematics (1911)

6 The safest general characterization of the European philosophical tradition is that it consists of a series of footnotes to Plato.
Process and Reality (1929)

Katharine Whitehorn 1928–

English journalist

7 Children and zip fasteners do not respond to force . . . Except occasionally.
Observations (1970)

8 In our society mothers take the place elsewhere occupied by the Fates, the System, Negroes, Communism or Reactionary Imperialist Plots; mothers go on getting blamed until they're eighty, but shouldn't take it personally.
Observations (1970)

9 Being young is not having any money; being young is not minding not having any money.
Observations (1970)

10 An office party is not, as is sometimes supposed, the Managing Director's chance to kiss the tea-girl. It is the tea-girl's chance to kiss the Managing Director.
Roundabout (1962) 'The Office Party'

11 I wouldn't say when you've seen one Western you've seen the lot; but when you've seen the lot you get the feeling you've seen one.
Sunday Best (1976) 'Decoding the West'

Gough Whitlam 1916–

Australian Labor statesman, Prime Minister 1972–5

12 Well may he say 'God Save the Queen'. But after this nothing will save the Governor-General.
having been dismissed from office by the Governor-General, Sir John Kerr
speech in Canberra, 11 November 1975

Charlotte Whitton 1896–1975

Canadian writer and politician

13 Whatever women do they must do twice as well as men to be thought half as good.
in *Canada Month* June 1963

William H. Whyte 1917–

American writer

14 This book is about the organization man . . . I can think of no other way to describe the people I am talking about. They are not the workers, nor are they the white-collar people in the usual, clerk sense of the word. These people only work for the Organization. The ones I am talking about *belong* to it as well.
The Organization Man (1956)

Ann Widdecombe 1947–

British Conservative politician

1 He has something of the night in him.
of Michael Howard as a contender for the Conservative leadership
in *Sunday Times* 11 May 1997 (electronic edition)

Elie Wiesel 1928–

Romanian-born American writer and Nobel Prize winner; Auschwitz survivor

2 The opposite of love is not hate, it's indifference. The opposite of art is not ugliness, it's indifference. The opposite of faith is not heresy, it's indifference. And the opposite of life is not death, it's indifference.
in *U.S. News and World Report* 27 October 1986

3 Take sides. Neutrality helps the oppressor, never the victim. Silence encourages the tormentor, never the tormented.
accepting the Nobel Peace Prize
in *New York Times* 11 December 1986

4 God of forgiveness, do not forgive those murderers of Jewish children here.
at an unofficial ceremony at Auschwitz on 26 January 1995, commemorating the 50th anniversary of its liberation
in *The Times* 27 January 1995

Richard Wilbur 1921–

American poet

5 Spare us all word of the weapons, their
force and range,
The long numbers that rocket the mind.
'Advice to a Prophet' (1961)

6 We milk the cow of the world, and as we
do
We whisper in her ear, 'You are not
true.'
'Epistemology' (1950)

7 Mind in its purest play is like some bat
That beats about in caverns all alone,
Contriving by a kind of senseless wit
Not to conclude against a wall of stone.
'Mind' (1956)

8 The good grey guardians of art
Patrol the halls on spongy shoes.
'Museum Piece' (1950)

Billy Wilder 1906–2002

American screenwriter and director
see also **Film lines** 117:11, 118:2

9 It used to be that we in films were the lowest form of art. Now we have something to look down on.
of television
A. Madsen *Billy Wilder* (1968)

10 What they [critics] call dirty in our pictures, they call lusty in foreign films.
A. Madsen *Billy Wilder* (1968)

11 Hindsight is always twenty-twenty.
J. R. Columbo *Wit and Wisdom of the Moviemakers* (1979)

on Marilyn ***Monroe****'s unpunctuality:*
12 My Aunt Minnie would always be punctual and never hold up production, but who would pay to see my Aunt Minnie?
P. F. Boller and R. L. Davis *Hollywood Anecdotes* (1988)

Thornton Wilder 1897–1975

American novelist and dramatist

13 Even memory is not necessary for love. There is a land of the living and a land of the dead and the bridge is love, the only survival, the only meaning.
The Bridge of San Luis Rey (1927), closing words

14 Marriage is a bribe to make a housekeeper think she's a householder.
The Merchant of Yonkers (1939)

15 Literature is the orchestration of platitudes.
in *Time* 12 January 1953

Robert Wilensky 1951–

American academic

16 We've all heard that a million monkeys banging on a million typewriters will eventually reproduce the entire works of

Shakespeare. Now, thanks to the Internet, we know this is not true.
in *Mail on Sunday* 16 February 1997 'Quotes of the Week'; see **Eddington** 98:8

Geoffrey Willans 1911–58 and Ronald Searle 1920–

English humorous writers

1 As any fule kno.
Down with Skool! (1953)

2 There is no better xsample of a goody-goody than fotherington-tomas in the world in space. You kno he is the one who sa Hullo Clouds Hullo Sky and skip about like a girly.
How To Be Topp (1954)

Heathcote Williams 1941–

British dramatist and poet

3 Whales play, in an amniotic paradise.
Their light minds shaped by buoyancy,
unrestricted by gravity,
Somersaulting.
Like angels, or birds;
Like our own lives, in the womb.
Whale Nation (1988)

Kenneth Williams 1926–88

English actor

4 The nice thing about quotes is that they give us a nodding acquaintance with the originator which is often socially impressive.
Acid Drops (1980)

R. J. P. Williams 1926–

English chemist

5 Biology is the search for the chemistry that works.
lecture in Oxford, June 1996

Shirley Williams 1930–

British Labour and Social Democrat politician

6 No test tube can breed love and affection. No frozen packet of semen ever read a story to a sleepy child.
in *Daily Mirror* 2 March 1978

7 The Catholic Church has never really come to terms with women. What I object to is being treated either as Madonnas or Mary Magdalenes.
in *Observer* 22 March 1981

Tennessee Williams 1911–83

American dramatist

8 We're all of us guinea pigs in the laboratory of God. Humanity is just a work in progress.
Camino Real (1953)

9 What is the victory of a cat on a hot tin roof?—I wish I knew . . . Just staying on it, I guess, as long as she can.
Cat on a Hot Tin Roof (1955)

10 I'm not living with you. We occupy the same cage.
Cat on a Hot Tin Roof (1955)

11 BRICK: Well, they say nature hates a vacuum, Big Daddy.
BIG DADDY: That's what they say, but sometimes I think that a vacuum is a hell of a lot better than some of the stuff that nature replaces it with.
Cat on a Hot Tin Roof (1955)

12 I didn't go to the moon, I went much further—for time is the longest distance between two places.
The Glass Menagerie (1945)

13 We're all of us sentenced to solitary confinement inside our own skins, for life!
Orpheus Descending (1958)

14 Turn that off! I won't be looked at in this merciless glare!
A Streetcar Named Desire (1947)

15 BLANCHE: I don't want realism.
MITCH: Naw, I guess not.
BLANCHE: I'll tell you what I want. Magic!
A Streetcar Named Desire (1947)

16 I have always depended on the kindness of strangers.
A Streetcar Named Desire (1947)

William Carlos Williams
1883–1963

American poet

1 Minds like beds always made up,
(more stony than a shore)
unwilling or unable.

Paterson (1946)

2 so much depends
upon
a red wheel
barrow
glazed with rain
water
beside the white
chickens.

'The Red Wheelbarrow' (1923)

3 I have eaten
the plums
that were in
the icebox

and which
you were probably
saving
for breakfast

Forgive me
they were delicious
so sweet
and so cold.

'This is Just to Say'

4 Is it any better in Heaven, my friend Ford,
Than you found it in Provence?

'To Ford Madox Ford in Heaven' (1944)

Marianne Williamson 1953–

American writer and philanthropist

5 Our deepest fear is not that we are inadequate. Our deepest fear is that we are powerful beyond measure. It is our light, not our darkness, that most frightens us.

A Return to Love (1992)

Roy Williamson 1936–90

Scottish folksinger and musician

6 O flower of Scotland, when will we see your like again,
that fought and died for your bit hill and glen
and stood against him, proud Edward's army,
and sent him homeward tae think again.

unofficial Scottish Nationalist anthem

'O Flower of Scotland' (1968)

Wendell Willkie 1892–1944

American lawyer and politician

7 The constitution does not provide for first and second class citizens.

An American Programme (1944)

Angus Wilson 1913–91

English novelist and short-story writer

8 Once a Catholic always a Catholic.

The Wrong Set (1949)

Charles E. Wilson 1890–1961

American industrialist; President of General Motors, 1941–53

on Wilson: see **Anonymous** 10:2

9 For years I thought what was good for our country was good for General Motors and vice versa.

testimony to the Senate Armed Services Committee on his proposed nomination for Secretary of Defence, 15 January 1953

Edward O. Wilson 1929–

American sociobiologist

10 Every human brain is born not as a blank tablet (a *tabula rasa*) waiting to be filled in by experience but as 'an exposed negative waiting to be slipped into developer fluid'.

on the nature v. nurture debate

attributed; Tom Wolfe in *Independent on Sunday* 2 February 1997

Harold Wilson 1916–95

British Labour statesman; Prime Minister, 1964–70, 1974–6
on Wilson: see **Home** 158:10, **Junor** 175:1, **Levin** 198:4; *see also* **Misquotations** 227:4

1 All these financiers, all the little gnomes in Zurich.

speech, House of Commons, 12 November 1956

2 I myself have always deprecated . . . in crisis after crisis, appeals to the Dunkirk spirit as an answer to our problems.

in the House of Commons, 26 July 1961

3 This party is a moral crusade or it is nothing.

speech at the Labour Party Conference, 1 October 1962

4 If I had the choice between smoked salmon and tinned salmon, I'd have it tinned. With vinegar.

in *Observer* 11 November 1962

5 The university of the air.

an early term for the Open University

in *Glasgow Herald* 9 September 1963

6 A week is a long time in politics.

probably first said at the time of the 1964 sterling crisis

Nigel Rees *Sayings of the Century* (1984)

7 [Labour is] the natural party of government.

in 1965; Anthony Sampson *The Changing Anatomy of Britain*

8 From now the pound abroad is worth 14 per cent or so less in terms of other currencies. It does not mean, of course, that the pound here in Britain, in your pocket or purse or in your bank, has been devalued.

often quoted as 'the pound in your pocket'

ministerial broadcast, 19 November 1967

9 Get your tanks off my lawn, Hughie.

to the trade union leader Hugh **Scanlon**, *at Chequers in June 1969*

Peter Jenkins *The Battle of Downing Street* (1970); see **Clarke** 70:7

Sandy Wilson 1924–

English songwriter

10 We've got to have
We plot to have
For it's so dreary not to have
That certain thing called the Boy Friend.

The Boyfriend (1954) title song

Woodrow Wilson 1856–1924

American Democratic statesman, 28th President of the US, 1913–21
on Wilson: see **Clemenceau** 71:2

11 It is like writing history with lightning. And my only regret is that it is all so terribly true.

on seeing D. W. Griffith's film The Birth of a Nation

at the White House, 18 February 1915

12 No nation is fit to sit in judgement upon any other nation.

speech in New York, 20 April 1915

13 There is such a thing as a man being too proud to fight.

speech in Philadelphia, 10 May 1915

14 We have stood apart, studiously neutral.

speech to Congress, 7 December 1915

15 It must be a peace without victory . . . Only a peace between equals can last.

speech to US Senate, 22 January 1917

16 Armed neutrality is ineffectual enough at best.

speech to Congress, 2 April 1917

17 The world must be made safe for democracy.

speech to Congress, 2 April 1917

18 Once lead this people into war and they will forget there ever was such a thing as tolerance.

John Dos Passos *Mr Wilson's War* (1917)

19 Open covenants of peace, openly arrived at.

first of Fourteen Points

speech to Congress, 8 January 1918

Walter Winchell 1897–1972

American journalist

1 Good evening, Mr and Mrs North America and all the ships at sea. Let's go to press! Flash!

habitual introduction to network radio spot, 1931–56

Barbara Windsor 1937–

British actress

2 They say an actor is only as good as his parts. Well, my parts have done me pretty well, darling.

in *The Times* 13 February 1999

Duchess of Windsor (Wallis Simpson) 1896–1986

wife of the former **Edward VIII**
see also **Anonymous** 10:12

3 You can never be too rich or too thin.

attributed

Duke of Windsor

see **Edward VIII**

Yvor Winters 1900–68

American poet and critic

4 The young are quick of speech.
Grown middle-aged, I teach
Corrosion and distrust,
Exacting what I must.

'On Teaching the Young' (1934)

Ludwig Wittgenstein 1889–1951

Austrian-born philosopher
see also **Last words** 191:3

5 Philosophy is a battle against the bewitchment of our intelligence by means of language.

Philosophische Untersuchungen (1953)

6 What is your aim in philosophy?—To show the fly the way out of the fly-bottle.

Philosophische Untersuchungen (1953)

7 What can be said at all can be said clearly; and whereof one cannot speak thereof one must be silent.

Tractatus Logico-Philosophicus (1922)

8 The world is everything that is the case.

Tractatus Logico-Philosophicus (1922)

9 The limits of my language mean the limits of my world.

Tractatus Logico-Philosophicus (1922)

10 Death is not an event of life.

Tractatus Logico-Philosophicus (1922)

P. G. Wodehouse 1881–1975

English writer; an American citizen from 1955
on Wodehouse: see **O'Casey** 244:10

11 Chumps always make the best husbands . . . All the unhappy marriages come from the husbands having brains.

The Adventures of Sally (1920)

12 It is never difficult to distinguish between a Scotsman with a grievance and a ray of sunshine.

Blandings Castle and Elsewhere (1935) 'The Custody of the Pumpkin'

13 There was another ring at the front door. Jeeves shimmered out and came back with a telegram.

Carry On, Jeeves! (1925) 'Jeeves Takes Charge'

14 He spoke with a certain what-is-it in his voice, and I could see that, if not actually disgruntled, he was far from being gruntled.

The Code of the Woosters (1938)

15 Slice him where you like, a hellhound is always a hellhound.

The Code of the Woosters (1938)

16 It is no use telling me that there are bad aunts and good aunts. At the core, they are all alike. Sooner or later, out pops the cloven hoof.

The Code of the Woosters (1938)

17 Roderick Spode? Big chap with a small moustache and the sort of eye that can open an oyster at sixty paces?

The Code of the Woosters (1938)

18 To my daughter Leonora without whose never-failing sympathy and encouragement this book would have been finished in half the time.

The Heart of a Goof (1926) dedication

1 For the first time since sudden love had thrown them into each other's arms, she had found herself beginning to wonder if her Blair was quite the godlike superman she had supposed. There even flashed through her mind a sinister speculation as to whether, when you came right down to it, he wasn't something of a pill.

Hot Water (1932)

2 I turned to Aunt Agatha, whose demeanour was now rather like that of one who, picking daisies on the railway, has just caught the down express in the small of the back.

The Inimitable Jeeves (1923)

3 When Aunt is calling to Aunt like mastodons bellowing across primeval swamps.

The Inimitable Jeeves (1923)

4 It was my Uncle George who discovered that alcohol was a food well in advance of medical thought.

The Inimitable Jeeves (1923)

5 She fitted into my biggest armchair as if it had been built round her by someone who knew they were wearing armchairs tight about the hips that season.

My Man Jeeves (1919) 'Jeeves and the Unbidden Guest'

6 Ice formed on the butler's upper slopes.

Pigs Have Wings (1952)

7 The Right Hon. was a tubby little chap who looked as if he had been poured into his clothes and had forgotten to say 'When!'

Very Good, Jeeves (1930) 'Jeeves and the Impending Doom'

Terry Wogan 1938–

Irish broadcaster

8 Television contracts the imagination and radio expands it.

in *Observer* 30 December 1984

Naomi Wolf 1962–

American feminist and writer

9 To ask women to become unnaturally thin is to ask them to relinquish their sexuality.

The Beauty Myth (1990)

Humbert Wolfe 1886–1940

British poet

10 You cannot hope
to bribe or twist,
thank God! the
British journalist.

But, seeing what
the man will do
unbribed, there's
no occasion to.

'Over the Fire' (1930)

Thomas Wolfe 1900–38

American novelist

11 Which of us has not remained forever prison-pent? Which of us is not forever a stranger and alone?

foreword to *Look Homeward, Angel* (1929)

12 Most of the time we think we're sick, it's all in the mind.

Look Homeward, Angel (1929)

13 'Where they got you stationed now, Luke?' . . . 'In Norfolk at the Navy base,' Luke answered, 'm-m-making the world safe for hypocrisy.'

Look Homeward, Angel (1929); see **Wilson** 341:17

14 You can't go home again.

title of book, 1940

Tom Wolfe 1931–

American writer

15 The bonfire of the vanities.

title of novel (1987); deriving from Savonarola's 'burning of the vanities' in Florence, 1497

16 A liberal is a conservative who has been arrested.

The Bonfire of the Vanities (1987); see **Sayings and slogans** 289:8

1 Electric Kool-Aid Acid test.
title of novel on hippy culture (1968)

2 By day, Structuralists constructed the structure of meaning and pondered the meaning of structure. By night, Deconstructionists pulled the cortical edifice down. And the next day the Structuralists started in again.
From Bauhaus to Our House (1981)

3 We are now in the Me Decade—seeing the upward roll of . . . the third great religious wave in American history . . . and this one has the mightiest, holiest roll of all, the beat that goes . . . *Me . . . Me . . . Me . . . Me.*
Mauve Gloves and Madmen (1976) 'The Me Decade'

4 Radical Chic . . . is only radical in Style; in its heart it is part of Society and its tradition—Politics, like Rock, Pop, and Camp, has its uses.
in *New York* 8 June 1970

Lewis Wolpert 1929–

English biologist

5 If Watson and Crick had not discovered the nature of DNA, one can be virtually certain that other scientists would eventually have determined it. With art—whether painting, music or literature—it is quite different. If Shakespeare had not written *Hamlet*, no other playwright would have done so.
The Unnatural Nature of Science (1993)

Kenneth Wolstenholme

English sports commentator

6 They think it's all over—it is now.
television commentary in closing moments of the World Cup Final, 30 July 1966

Victoria Wood 1953–

British writer and comedienne

7 JACKIE: (*very slowly*) Take Tube A and apply to Bracket D.
VICTORIA: Reading it slower does not make it any easier to do.
Mens Sana in Thingummy Doodah (1990)

8 It will be a very traditional Christmas, with presents, crackers, doors slamming and people bursting into tears, but without the big dead thing in the middle.
of a vegetarian Christmas
in *Sunday Times* 24 December 2000

George Woodcock 1912–95

Canadian writer

9 Canadians do not like heroes, and so they do not have them.
Canada and the Canadians (1970)

Thomas Woodrooffe 1899–1978

British naval officer

10 The whole Fleet's lit up. When I say 'lit up', I mean lit up by fairy lamps.
live outside broadcast, Spithead Review, 20 May 1937
Asa Briggs *History of Broadcasting in the UK* (1965) vol. 2

Harry Woods 1896–1970

American songwriter

11 Oh we ain't got a barrel of money,
Maybe we're ragged and funny,
But we'll travel along
Singin' a song,
Side by side.
'Side by Side' (1927 song)

Tiger Woods 1975–

American golfer

12 Growing up, I came up with this name: I'm a Cablinasian.
explaining his rejection of 'African-American' as the term to describe his Caucasian, Afro-American, Native American, Thai, and Chinese ancestry
interviewed by Oprah Winfrey, 21 April 1997

Virginia Woolf 1882–1941

English novelist
on Woolf: see **Laski** 189:10, **Sitwell** 299:8

13 On or about December 1910 human nature changed . . . All human relations have shifted—those between masters and servants, husbands and wives, parents and children. And when human relations change there is at the same time a change in religion, conduct, politics, and literature.

'Mr Bennett and Mrs Brown' (1924)

1 A woman must have money and a room of her own if she is to write fiction.

A Room of One's Own (1929)

2 This is an important book, the critic assumes, because it deals with war. This is an insignificant book because it deals with the feelings of women in a drawing room.

A Room of One's Own (1929)

3 So that is marriage, Lily thought, a man and a woman looking at a girl throwing a ball.

To the Lighthouse (1927)

4 I have lost friends, some by death . . . others through sheer inability to cross the street.

The Waves (1931)

5 The vast events now shaping across the Channel are towering over us too closely and too tremendously to be worked into fiction without a painful jolt in the perspective.

in *Times Literary Supplement* 1 March 1917

6 What sort of diary should I like mine to be? . . . I should like it to resemble some deep old desk, or capacious hold-all, in which one flings a mass of odds and ends without looking them through.

diary, 20 April 1919

7 The scratching of pimples on the body of the bootboy at Claridges.

of James ***Joyce****'s* Ulysses

letter to Lytton Strachey, 24 April 1922

8 As an experience, madness is terrific . . . and in its lava I still find most of the things I write about.

letter to Ethel Smyth, 22 June 1930

9 And now with some pleasure I find that it's seven; and must cook dinner. Haddock and sausage meat. I think it is true that one gains a certain hold on sausage and haddock by writing them down.

diary, 8 March 1941

Alexander Woollcott
1887–1943

American writer

10 She was like a sinking ship firing on the rescuers.

of Mrs Patrick ***Campbell***

While Rome Burns (1944) 'The First Mrs Tanqueray'

11 She is so odd a blend of Little Nell and Lady Macbeth. It is not so much the familiar phenomenon of a hand of steel in a velvet glove as a lacy sleeve with a bottle of vitriol concealed in its folds.

of Dorothy ***Parker***

While Rome Burns (1934) 'Our Mrs Parker'

12 All the things I really like to do are either illegal, immoral, or fattening.

R. E. Drennan *Wit's End* (1973)

Terry Worrall

spokesman for British Rail

13 It was the wrong kind of snow.

explaining disruption on British Rail

in *The Independent* 16 February 1991

Frank Lloyd Wright
1867–1959

American architect

14 The physician can bury his mistakes, but the architect can only advise his client to plant vines—so they should go as far as possible from home to build their first buildings.

in *New York Times* 4 October 1953

15 The modern city is a place for banking and prostitution and very little else.

Robert C. Twombly *Frank Lloyd Wright* (1973)

Kenyon Wright 1932–

Scottish Methodist minister, Chairman of the Scottish Constitutional Convention

16 What if that other single voice we know so well responds by saying, 'We say No and we are the State.' Well, we say Yes and we are the People!

*of Margaret **Thatcher** as Prime Minister*

speech at the inaugural meeting of the Scottish Constitutional Convention, 30 March 1989

James Wright 1927–80

American poet

1 Suddenly I realize
That if I stepped out of my body I would break
Into blossom.

'A Blessing' (1963)

2 Between two cold white shadows,
But I dreamed they would rise
Together,
My black Ohioan swan.

'Three Sentences for a Dead Swan' (1968)

Harry Wu

Chinese-born American political activist

3 I want to see the word *laogai* in every dictionary in every language in the world. I want to see the laogai ended. Before 1974, the word 'gulag' did not appear in any dictionary. Today, this single word conveys the meaning of Soviet political violence and its labour camp system. 'Laogai' also deserves a place in our dictionaries.

the laogai *are Chinese labour camps*

in *Washington Post* 26 May 1996

Tammy Wynette 1942–98 and Billy Sherrill *c.*1938–

American singer and American songwriter

4 Stand by your man.

title of song (1968)

Isoroku Yamamoto 1884–1943

Japanese admiral, Commander-in-Chief responsible for planning the Japanese attack on Pearl Harbor

5 A military man can scarcely pride himself on having 'smitten a sleeping enemy'; in fact, to have it pointed out is more a matter of shame.

letter, 9 January 1942; Hirosuki Asawa *The Reluctant Admiral* (1979, tr. John Bester); see **Film lines** 115:16

Minoru Yamasaki 1912–88

American architect, designer of the World Trade Center (1973; destroyed by terrorist attack in September 2001)

6 The World Trade Center should, because of its importance, become a living representation of man's belief in humanity, his need for individual dignity, his belief in the co-operation of men, and through this co-operation his ability to find greatness.

Paul Heyer *Architects on Architecture* (1967)

John Yates 1925–

English theologian; Bishop of Gloucester from 1975

7 There is a lot to be said in the Decade of Evangelism for believing more and more in less and less.

in *Gloucester Diocesan Gazette* August 1991

W. B. Yeats 1865–1939

Irish poet

on Yeats: see **Auden** 17:8

8 O body swayed to music, O brightening glance,
How can we know the dancer from the dance?

'Among School Children' (1928)

9 Only God, my dear,
Could love you for yourself alone
And not your yellow hair.

'Anne Gregory' (1932)

10 The unpurged images of day recede;
The Emperor's drunken soldiery are abed.

'Byzantium' (1933)

11 Those images that yet
Fresh images beget,
That dolphin-torn, that gong-tormented sea.

'Byzantium' (1933)

12 Now that my ladder's gone

I must lie down where all the ladders start,
In the foul rag-and-bone shop of the heart.
'The Circus Animals' Desertion' (1939)

1 We were the last romantics—chose for theme
Traditional sanctity and loveliness.
'Coole and Ballylee, 1931' (1933)

2 The intellect of man is forced to choose
Perfection of the life, or of the work,
And if it take the second must refuse
A heavenly mansion, raging in the dark.
'Coole Park and Ballylee, 1932' (1933)

3 A woman can be proud and stiff
When on love intent;
But Love has pitched his mansion in
The place of excrement;
For nothing can be sole or whole
That has not been rent.
'Crazy Jane Talks with the Bishop' (1932)

4 Nor dread nor hope attend
A dying animal;
A man awaits his end
Dreading and hoping all.
'Death' (1933)

5 All changed, changed utterly:
A terrible beauty is born.
'Easter, 1916' (1921)

6 Too long a sacrifice
Can make a stone of the heart.
'Easter, 1916' (1921)

7 I write it out in a verse—
MacDonagh and MacBride
And Connolly and Pearse
Now and in time to be,
Wherever green is worn,
Are changed, changed utterly:
A terrible beauty is born.
'Easter, 1916' (1921)

8 The fascination of what's difficult
Has dried the sap of my veins, and rent
Spontaneous joy and natural content
Out of my heart.
'The Fascination of What's Difficult' (1910)

9 Never to have lived is best, ancient writers say;
Never to have drawn the breath of life, never to have looked into the eye of day;
The second best's a gay goodnight and quickly turn away.
'From *Oedipus at Colonus*' (1928); see below

Not to be born is, past all prizing, best.
Sophocles (*c.*496–406 BC) *Oedipus Coloneus*

10 The ghost of Roger Casement
Is beating on the door.
'The Ghost of Roger Casement' (1939)

11 The innocent and the beautiful
Have no enemy but time.
'In Memory of Eva Gore-Booth and Con Markiewicz' (1933)

12 My country is Kiltartan Cross;
My countrymen Kiltartan's poor.
'An Irish Airman Foresees his Death' (1919)

13 Nor law, nor duty bade me fight,
Nor public men, nor cheering crowds.
'An Irish Airman Foresees his Death' (1919)

14 A shudder in the loins engenders there
The broken wall, the burning roof and tower
And Agamemnon dead.
'Leda and the Swan' (1928)

15 Did that play of mine send out
Certain men the English shot?
'The Man and the Echo' (1939)

16 We had fed the heart on fantasies,
The heart's grown brutal from the fare.
'Meditations in Time of Civil War' no. 6 'The Stare's Nest by my Window' (1928)

17 Think where man's glory most begins and ends
And say my glory was I had such friends.
'The Municipal Gallery Re-visited' (1939)

18 I think it better that at times like these
A poet's mouth be silent, for in truth
We have no gift to set a statesman right;
He has had enough of meddling who can please
A young girl in the indolence of her youth
Or an old man upon a winter's night.
'On being asked for a War Poem' (1919)

19 Where, where but here have Pride and Truth,
That long to give themselves for wage,
To shake their wicked sides at youth

Restraining reckless middle-age?
'On hearing that the Students of our New University have joined the Agitation against Immoral Literature' (1910)

1 An intellectual hatred is the worst,
So let her think opinions are accursed.
'A Prayer for My Daughter' (1920)

2 Out of Ireland have we come.
Great hatred, little room,
Maimed us at the start.
'Remorse for Intemperate Speech' (1933)

3 That is no country for old men. The young
In one another's arms, birds in the trees—
Those dying generations—at their song.
'Sailing to Byzantium' (1928)

4 An aged man is but a paltry thing,
A tattered coat upon a stick, unless
Soul clap its hands and sing, and louder sing
For every tatter in its mortal dress.
'Sailing to Byzantium' (1928)

5 And therefore I have sailed the seas and come
To the holy city of Byzantium.
'Sailing to Byzantium' (1928)

6 All shuffle there; all cough in ink;
All wear the carpet with their shoes;
All think what other people think;
All know the man their neighbour knows.
Lord, what would they say
Did their Catullus walk that way?
'The Scholars' (1919)

7 Things fall apart; the centre cannot hold;
Mere anarchy is loosed upon the world,
The blood-dimmed tide is loosed, and everywhere
The ceremony of innocence is drowned;
The best lack all conviction, while the worst
Are full of passionate intensity.
'The Second Coming' (1921)

8 And what rough beast, its hour come round at last,
Slouches towards Bethlehem to be born?
'The Second Coming' (1921)

9 Romantic Ireland's dead and gone,
It's with O'Leary in the grave.
'September, 1913' (1914)

10 O, who could have foretold
That the heart grows old?
'A Song' (1919)

11 You think it horrible that lust and rage
Should dance attendance upon my old age;
They were not such a plague when I was young;
What else have I to spur me into song?
'The Spur' (1939)

12 Swift has sailed into his rest;
Savage indignation there
Cannot lacerate his breast.
'Swift's Epitaph' (1933); see below

Ubi saeva indignatio ulterius cor lacerare nequit.

Where fierce indignation can no longer tear his heart.

Jonathan Swift (1667–1745) epitaph

13 Was there ever dog that praised his fleas?
'To a Poet, Who would have Me Praise certain bad Poets, Imitators of His and of Mine' (1910)

14 Michaelangelo left a proof
On the Sistine Chapel roof,
Where but half-awakened Adam
Can disturb globe-trotting Madam.
'Under Ben Bulben' (1939)

15 Irish poets, learn your trade,
Sing whatever is well made.
'Under Ben Bulben' (1939)

16 Cast your mind on other days
That we in coming days may be
Still the indomitable Irishry.
'Under Ben Bulben' (1939)

17 Cast a cold eye
On life, on death.
Horseman, pass by!
'Under Ben Bulben' (1939)

of the Anglo-Irish:

18 We . . . are no petty people. We are one of the great stocks of Europe. We are the people of Burke; we are the people of Swift, the people of Emmet, the people of Parnell. We have created most of the modern literature of this country. We have created the best of its political intelligence.
speech in the Irish Senate, 11 June 1925, in the debate on divorce

Boris Yeltsin 1931–

Russian statesman, President of the Russian Federation since 1991

1 You can make a throne of bayonets, but you can't sit on it for long.
from the top of a tank, during the attempted military coup against ***Gorbachev***
in *Independent* 24 August 1991; see **Inge** 165:6

2 Europe is in danger of plunging into a cold peace.
at the summit meeting of the Conference on Security and Co-operation in Europe
in *Newsweek* 19 December 1994; see **Baruch** 24:12

3 Today is the last day of an era past.
at a Berlin ceremony to end the Soviet military presence
in *Guardian* 1 September 1994

Sergei Yesenin 1895–1925

Russian poet
see also **Last words** 190:10

4 It's always the good feel rotten.
Pleasure's for those who are bad.
'Pleasure's for the Bad' (1923)

Yevgeny Yevtushenko 1933–

Russian poet

5 Over Babiy Yar
There are no memorials.
The steep hillside like a rough inscription.
'Babiy Yar' (1961)

6 So on and on
we walked without thinking of rest
passing craters, passing fire,
under the rocking sky of '41
tottering crazy on its smoking columns.
'The Companion' (1954)

7 Life is a rainbow which also includes black.
in *Guardian* 11 August 1987

Shoichi Yokoi 1915–97

Japanese soldier

8 It is a terrible shame for me—I came back, still alive, without having won the war.
on returning to Japan after surviving for 28 years in the jungles of Guam before surrendering to the Americans in 1972
in *Independent* 26 September 1997

Sarah, Duchess of York 1959–

9 I think it's a fresh, clean page. I think I go onwards and upwards.
the day before her divorce was made absolute
in an interview on *Sky News* 29 May 1996; in *Daily Telegraph* 30 May 1996

Andrew Young 1932–

American clergyman and diplomat

10 Nothing is illegal if one hundred well-placed business men decide to do it.
Morris K. Udall *Too Funny to be President* (1988)

G. M. Young 1882–1959

English historian

11 Being published by the Oxford University Press is rather like being married to a duchess: the honour is almost greater than the pleasure.
Rupert Hart-Davis, letter to George Lyttelton, 29 April 1956

Neil Young 1945– and Jeff Blackburn

Canadian singer and songwriter

12 It's better to burn out
Than to fade away.
quoted by Kurt ***Cobain*** *in his suicide note, 8 April 1994*
'My My, Hey Hey (Out of the Blue)' (1978 song)

Yevgeny Zamyatin 1884–1937

Russian writer

1 Heretics are the only bitter remedy against the entropy of human thought.

'Literature, Revolution and Entropy' quoted in *The Dragon and other Stories* (1967) introduction

2 Yesterday there was a tsar and there were slaves; today there is no tsar, but the slaves remain; tomorrow there will be only tsars . . . We have lived through the epoch of suppression of the masses; we are living in an epoch of suppression of the individual in the name of the masses; tomorrow will bring the liberation of the individual—in the name of man.

'Tomorrow' (1919) in *A Soviet Heretic* (1970)

Israel Zangwill 1864–1926

Jewish spokesman and writer

3 America is God's Crucible, the great Melting-Pot where all the races of Europe are melting and re-forming!

The Melting Pot (1908)

Emiliano Zapata 1879–1919

Mexican revolutionary

see also **Ibarruri** 164:12

4 Many of them, so as to curry favour with tyrants, for a fistful of coins, or through bribery or corruption, are shedding the blood of their brothers.

on the maderistas *who, in Zapata's view, had betrayed the revolutionary cause*

Plan de Ayala 28 November 1911

Frank Zappa 1940–93

American rock musician and songwriter

5 A drug is neither moral or immoral—it's a chemical compound. The compound itself is not a menace to society until a human being treats it as if consumption bestowed a temporary licence to act like an asshole.

The Real Frank Zappa Book (1989)

6 Rock journalism is people who can't write interviewing people who can't talk for people who can't read.

L. Botts *Loose Talk* (1980)

Benjamin Zephaniah 1958–

British poet

7 I think poetry should be alive. You should be able to dance it.

in *Sunday Times* 23 August 1987

Mikhail Zhvanetsky 1934–

Russian writer

8 We enjoyed . . . his slyness. He mastered the art of walking backward into the future. He would say 'After me'. And some people went ahead, and some went behind, and he would go backward.

of Mikhail ***Gorbachev***

in *Time* 12 September 1994; attributed

Philip Ziegler 1929–

British historian

9 Remember. In Spite of Everything, He Was A Great Man.

notice kept on his desk while working on his biography of ***Mountbatten*** *(published 1985)*

Andrew Roberts *Eminent Churchillians* (1994)

Ronald L. Ziegler 1939–

American government spokesman

10 [Mr Nixon's latest statement] is the Operative White House Position . . . and all previous statements are inoperative.

at the time of the Watergate Affair

in *Boston Globe* 18 April 1973

Grigori Zinoviev 1883–1936

Soviet politician

11 Armed warfare must be preceded by a struggle against the inclinations to compromise which are embedded among the majority of British workmen, against the ideas of evolution and peaceful extermination of capitalism. Only then will it be possible to count upon complete success of an armed insurrection.

letter to the British Communist Party, 15 September 1924; the 'Zinoviev Letter', said by some to be a forgery

Hiller B. Zobel

American judge

1 Asking the ignorant to use the incomprehensible to decide the unknowable.

'The Jury on Trial' in *American Heritage* July–August 1995

2 Judges must follow their oaths and do their duty, heedless of editorials, letters, telegrams, threats, petitions, panellists and talk shows.

In this country, we do not administer justice by plebiscite. A judge . . . is a public servant who must follow his conscience, whether or not he counters the manifest wishes of those he serves; whether or not his decision seems a surrender to prevalent demands.

judicial ruling reducing the conviction of Louise Woodward from murder to manslaughter, 10 November 1997

Keyword Index

advertisers a. don't object to SWAF 312:2
advertising A. is the most DELL 89:12
A. is the rattling ORWE 250:17
A. may be described LEAC 193:10
a. we deserve SAYE 288:11
invasion of a. SOLZ 302:4
lust and calls it a. LAHR 187:6
money I spend on a. LEVE 197:15
advice integrated a. ANON 10:16
unsolicited a. COOL 76:11
advise Advisers a. THAT 317:12
aspire to a. WAUG 331:17
PLEASE A. TELE 316:8
advisers political a. SHOR 298:1
aeroplane jumping out of an a. LURI 205:4
aeroplanes it wasn't the a. FILM 117:6
aesthetic a. enjoyment WHIT 337:3
degree of my a. emotion BELL 27:6
affairs his or her love a. WEST 335:8
taking part in a. VALÉ 326:7
affection a. you get back NESB 239:5
affirmative condemn a. action POWE 264:16
affluence A. was a question DRAB 95:1
affluent a. society GALB 130:4
so-called a. society BEVA 34:11
afraid a. of the big bad wolf CHUR 65:12
a. of Virginia Woolf ALBE 5:12
Be a. TAGL 314:1
because she was a. of him MURD 235:5
I, a stranger and a. HOUS 160:4
not a. to die ALLE 6:16
to be a. FAUL 111:13
were a. to ask REUB 273:1
Africa A. than my own body ORTO 248:14
A. was swaddled in lies NAIP 236:14
choose between this A. WALC 328:14
deported A. GENE 132:12
shape of A. FANO 111:5
sloggin' over A. KIPL 182:11
African A. is conditioned KENY 179:2
A. national consciousness MACM 211:1
struggle of the A. people MAND 214:11
Africans A. experience people KAUN 175:11
A. were a low, filthy nation HEAD 149:14
after A. the first death THOM 318:11
A. you, Claude CATC 58:1
one damned thing a. another HUBB 161:4
afternoon a. of human life JUNG 174:14
At five in the a. LORC 203:2
lose the war in an a. CHUR 68:17
summer a. JAME 168:5
again déjà vu all over a. BERR 32:7
go through it all again BARE 23:3
I'll see you a. COWA 78:11
against a. everything KENN 178:17
always vote *a.* FIEL 113:14
anyone who wasn't a. war LOW 204:1
He was a. it COOL 76:12
life is 6 to 5 a. RUNY 281:10
vote a. somebody ADAM 1:14
Agamemnon And A. dead YEAT 347:14
When A. cried aloud ELIO 104:18
age a. is rocking the wave MAND 215:11
a. shall not weary them BINY 35:12
a., which forgives itself SHAW 296:10
be the a. I am MERW 222:12
dawning of the a. of Aquarius RADO 269:1
old a. always fifteen years BARU 24:13
Old a. is the most unexpected TROT 322:12
unexpectedly great a. PHIL 257:12
aged a. man is but a paltry thing YEAT 348:4
learn how to be a. BLYT 39:2
ages A. to our construction went WARR 330:10
AGM address the A. SHUL 298:3
agnosticism all a. means DARR 84:5
agony it was a., Ivy CATC 58:14
most extreme a. BETT 34:2
agreed you a. to evil RODR 276:7
agreement blow with an a. TROT 322:10
ahead a. of your time MCGO 209:5
get a., get a hat ADVE 3:26
aids adventure in the world of A. PERK 256:9
A. epidemic has rolled WHIT 336:5
seventeen-year-olds dying of A. GING 134:12
aim forgotten your a. SANT 286:14
ain't a. necessarily so HEYW 155:1
air a. power has prevailed KEEG 176:10
death of a. ELIO 103:4
lands hatless from the a. BETJ 33:7
university of the a. WILS 341:5
air conditioning respectability and a. BARA 23:1
airline a. ticket to romantic MARV 218:6
airplanes feel about a. KERR 179:5
airport observing a. layouts PRIC 266:2
Alamein Before A. we never had CHUR 68:16
Alan A. died suddenly EPIT 109:1
alas A. but cannot pardon AUDE 18:13
Albert Went there with young A. EDGA 99:3
alcohol A. a necessary article SHAW 295:17
A. didn't cause BOAZ 39:3
a. doesn't thrill me PORT 262:12
a. or morphine JUNG 174:12
a. was a food WODE 343:4
taken more out of a. CHUR 68:7
Aldershot burnish'd by A. sun BETJ 33:14
Alexandria A.'s library burned HUGH 162:5
alibi always has an a. ELIO 104:12
Alice Pass the sick bag, A. CATC 60:1
went down with A. MILN 225:6
alien a. people clutching ELIO 104:1
damned if I'm an a. GEOR 133:5
alike all places were a. to him KIPL 184:3
human beings are more a. ANGE 9:3

A-list on every bloody A. EMIN 107:12
alive a. and well ANON 11:6
a. and working on ANON 10:11
came back, still a. YOKO 349:8
gets out of it a. FILM 116:8
If we can't stay here a. MONT 229:12
Not while I'm a. BEVI 35:6
poetry should be a. ZEPH 350:7
still a. at twenty-two KING 182:1
ways of being a. DAWK 85:9
what keeps us a. STEI 307:1
what keeps you a. CAST 57:5
all 1066 and a. that SELL 293:7
a. shall be well ELIO 103:9
Evening, a. CATC 58:15
allegiance Any victim demands a. GREE 139:13
you have pledged a. BALD 21:6
alley rats' a. ELIO 105:1
allies no a. to be polite to GEOR 133:7
alone adult is to be a. ROST 279:12
a. against smiling enemies BOWE 41:13
dangerous to meet it a. WHAR 336:1
go home a. JOPL 173:3
I want to be a. GARB 131:10
long time to live a. PART 254:13
never a. with a Strand ADVE 4:32
not sufficiently a. VALÉ 326:6
stranger and a. WOLF 343:11
We are not a. TAGL 314:14
When he is a. in the room KEYN 180:1
You'll never walk a. HAMM 145:1
alp a. of unforgiveness PLOM 259:15
altar high a. on the move BOWE 41:14
alternative Considering the a. CHEV 65:1
no real a. THAT 316:14
alternatives decide between a. BONH 40:6
exhausted other a. EBAN 98:6
ignorance of a. ANGE 8:14
always a. be an England PARK 254:2
I a. shall be LUXE 205:7
Alzheimer from A.'s disease BAYL 25:3
he had A.'s disease REAG 272:1
on A.'s disease MURD 235:11
amateur a. is a man who can't AGAT 2:11
amateurs Hell full of musical a. SHAW 295:21
rule by a. ATTL 16:6
ambiguity Seven types of a. EMPS 108:5
ambition do not regard a. IZZA 166:10
ambitions ceiling put on our a. PRES 265:14
fulfilling your a. DE B 87:6
America A. is a land whose UPDI 325:10
A. is a vast conspiracy UPDI 325:11
A. is gigantic FREU 125:14
A. is God's Crucible ZANG 350:3
A. is our friend MERC 222:7
A. is the proof MCCA 206:9
A. thus top nation SELL 293:12
Australia looks to A. CURT 83:2
born in A. MALC 214:1
do a sitcom in A. TWIG 324:12
England and A. divided SHAW 297:4
God bless A. BERL 31:2
I like to be in A. SOND 302:8
impresses me about A. EDWA 99:5
in the living rooms of A. MCLU 210:10
I, too, sing A. HUGH 161:7
love affair with A. MAIL 213:3
makes A. what it is STEI 306:9
morning again in A. POLI 261:17
next to god a. CUMM 82:5
what A. did you have GINS 135:5
American A. as cherry pie BROW 46:1
A. culture COLO 73:13
A. Express ADVE 3:4
A. friends BLAI 37:10
A. people have spoken CLIN 72:5
A. white man to find BALD 21:4
business of the A. people COOL 76:9
changed in A. life LAHR 187:8
controlling A. soil DYLA 97:16
free man, an A. JOHN 171:5
Greeks in this A. empire MACM 210:12
I am A. bred MILL 223:13
in A. politics MITC 225:13
in love with A. names BENÉ 28:15
justice and the A. way ANON 10:8
knocking the A. system CAPO 53:8
Miss A. Pie MCLE 210:1
point of being an A. UPDI 325:13
process whereby A. girls HAMP 145:3
Scratch any A. RUSK 282:2
second acts in A. lives FITZ 119:9
send A. boys JOHN 171:11
tenth A. muse BRON 44:9
weakness of A. civilization PRIE 266:9
Americanism A. with its sleeves MCCA 206:8
hyphenated A. ROOS 279:1
Americans A. with no Disneyland MAHY 213:2
borrowed from the A. LAHR 187:7
for A. it is just beyond KISS 184:15
keep the A. in ISMA 166:2
my fellow A. KENN 178:7
new generation of A. KENN 178:2
Amis cocoa for Kingsley A. COPE 77:4
ammunition pass the a. FORG 121:14
amniotic in an a. paradise WILL 339:3
amour *c'est l'a.* BOUS 41:8
amuse talent to a. COWA 78:10
amused a. by its presumption CART 56:4
analogies A. decide nothing FREU 125:10
anarchism A. is a game SHAW 296:12
anarchist I am an a. ROTT 280:3
anarchy Mere a. is loosed YEAT 348:7
anatomy A. is destiny FREU 125:7

ancient rivers a. as the world HUGH 161:10
and including 'a.' MCCA 206:11
Andromache kissed his sad A. CORN 77:10
anecdote a. dehumanizing EPHR 108:7
angels A. in jumpers LEWI 199:8
Blake saw a treefull of a. BENÉ 29:1
herald a. sing ANON 10:12
anger Frozen a. FREU 125:13
Great a. in the dragon SUTT 312:1
life of telegrams and a. FORS 122:8
Look back in a. OSBO 250:20
monstrous a. of the guns OWEN 251:6
strike it in a. SHAW 296:9
angles Offer no a. TESS 315:9
Anglo-Irishman He was an A. BEHA 27:1
angry A. young man PAUL 255:4
anguish going to be howls of a. HEAL 150:2
animal attend a dying a. YEAT 347:4
Be a good a. LAWR 192:5
only a. in the world to fear LAWR 192:9
animals All a. are equal ORWE 249:6
at its mercy: a. KUND 187:2
not over-fond of a. ATTE 15:13
soft little a. pottering CASS 57:4
takes 40 dumb a. SAYI 290:1
animation too old for a. DISN 93:2
annihilating a. all civilization SAKH 285:2
annihilation by my own a. GUNN 142:6
anno domini only a. HILT 156:5
annoy a. with what you write AMIS 8:6
annus a. horribilis ELIZ 106:3
anonymous essentially a. WEIL 332:10
anorak a. grow big with jotters MAXW 219:14
another a. fine mess LAUR 189:14
answer a. the phone CART 56:11
a. to the Irish Question SELL 293:11
way to a pertinent a. BRON 44:7
What *is* the a. LAST 191:7
answered no one a. DE L 89:6
answers Love is one of the a. PAZ 255:11
ant a.'s a centaur POUN 264:2
like an a. which has foreseen BART 24:9
Antarctica A. was circled EISE 101:6
anthology a. is like all RALE 269:7
anthropomorphic a. view of rat KOES 185:11
anti I am an A.-Christ ROTT 280:3
anti-Christ a. of Communism BUCH 47:6
anticipation only in the a. of it HITC 156:11
anti-Fascist premature a. ANON 12:16
antiwar ecology and a. HUNT 163:5
anybody Is there a. there DE L 89:5
Is there a. there OPEN 247:7
anything A. goes PORT 260:12
A. you can do BERL 30:13
believe in a. CHES 64:18
nobody tells me a. GALS 130:16
anywhere get a. in a marriage MURD 235:9
apart a., studiously neutral WILS 341:14
apathy a. of human beings KELL 177:1
ape gorgeous buttocks of the a. HUXL 164:7
naked a. MORR 231:8
aphorism a. should be like a burr LAYT 193:4
aphorists A. can be wrong FENT 112:10
aphrodisiac Power is the great a. KISS 184:13
apologize Never a. FISH 114:7
apparatus haunted a. sleeps RAIN 269:4
mediocrity of the a. TROT 322:11
appearing Television is for a. on COWA 79:11
applause A. is a receipt SCHN 291:5
apple make an a. pie SAGA 284:8
shaking an a. tree COLL 73:12
apples moon-washed a. of wonder DRIN 95:3
appointment a. at the end DINE 92:8
a. by the corrupt few SHAW 296:5
a. with him tonight MAUG 219:8
apprenticeship a. for freedom BARA 23:2
appropriate that was not a. CLIN 72:2
used when a. RUMS 281:3
approval You've got a. NESS 239:6
April A. is the cruellest month ELIO 104:19
bright cold day in A. OPEN 247:8
bright cold day in A. ORWE 250:1
one A. to another LONG 202:9
aquarium a. is gone LOWE 204:5
Aquarius dawning of the age of A. RADO 269:1
Arab A. world together ARAF 13:6
Arabia spell of far A. DE L 89:2
Arabic Hebrew and A. mingling RUME 281:1
Arbeit *A. macht frei* ANON 9:12
arch triumphant a. COMM 74:2
archaeological a. eye EISE 101:5
archbishop a. had come to see me OPEN 247:10
arches Underneath the A. FLAN 119:13
archipelago Gulag a. SOLZ 302:1
architect a. can only advise WRIG 345:14
A. of the Universe JEAN 169:5
architecture A. acts most slowly DIMN 92:7
A. is the art JOHN 172:3
Dim a. WARR 330:10
fall of English a. BETJ 34:1
are A. you now POLI 261:3
arena actually in the a. ROOS 278:13
Argentina Don't cry for me A. RICE 273:11
Argentinian young A. soldiers RUNC 281:5
argument a. of the broken window PANK 252:14
This is a rotten a. ANON 12:7
arguments attract the worst a. FISH 114:10
arias Clear a. of light DAY- 86:7
Ariel Caliban casts out A. POUN 263:12
Aristotle A. maintained that RUSS 282:10
ark two by two in the a. LEVE 197:17
arm did not put your a. around it BLAC 36:13

Armageddon County Road or A. DYLA 97:15
We stand at A. ROOS 278:14
armaments not a. that cause wars MADA 212:5
armchairs a. tight about the hips WODE 343:5
armed a. conflict EDEN 99:1
A. neutrality WILS 341:16
A. warfare must be preceded ZINO 350:11
Armenteers Mademoiselle from A. ANON 11:13
armful very nearly an a. GALT 131:1
armies standing a. of power RADC 268:11
armistice a. for twenty years FOCH 120:14
arms a. not spending money alone EISE 101:7
army contemptible little a. ANON 10:7
dialect with an a. WEIN 332:12
Forgotten A. MOUN 233:8
little ships brought the A. GUED 141:11
won't be a bit like the A. TRUM 323:13
aroma a. of performing seals HART 148:4
arrange French a. CATH 57:10
arrested a. one fine morning OPEN 247:18
conservative been a. WOLF 343:16
arrive a. where we started ELIO 103:6
arrived a. and to prove it CATC 59:14
arrogance A. a highly under-appreciated STIN 309:1
arrow time's a. EDDI 98:7
arse a. full of razor blades KEAT 176:5
politician is an a. upon CUMM 82:6
Sit on your a. MACN 211:11
arsenal great a. of democracy ROOS 278:4
arses Massing of A. CONN 75:11
art All a. was modern once SERO 293:14
A. and Religion are two roads BELL 27:5
A. a revolt against fate MALR 214:9
A. for art's sake DIET 92:5
a. has an author WEIL 332:10
A. is born of humiliation AUDE 19:2
A. is meant to disturb BRAQ 42:13
A. is not a *brassière* BARN 23:10
a. is not a weapon KENN 178:14
A. is not truth PICA 258:8
A. is pattern informed by READ 271:2
A. is significant deformity FRY 128:13
A. is the imposing of pattern WHIT 337:3
A. is the objectification LANG 188:6
a. is the only thing BOWE 41:11
A. is vice DEGA 88:3
A. not reproduce the visible KLEE 184:18
a. of the impossible HAVE 148:13
a. of the soluble MEDA 220:14
Deals are my a. form TRUM 323:16
Dying is an a. PLAT 259:11
E in A-level a. HIRS 156:7
enemy of good a. CONN 75:7
example of modern a. CHUR 69:3
fascinating kind of a. WARH 329:13
films the lowest form of a. WILD 338:9
good grey guardians of a. WILB 338:8
great religious a. CLAR 70:1
in the a. world EMIN 107:12
it is not a. SCHO 291:7
novel is a.-for-art's-sake PRIT 266:11
offered you Conflict and A. PRIE 266:6
only interested in a. SHAW 297:1
people start on all this A. HERB 153:8
responsibility is to his a. FAUL 112:2
stick to murder and leave a. EPST 108:9
symbol of Irish a. JOYC 173:16
what great a. removes BOLA 39:12
where the a. resides SCHN 291:6
articulate made a. all that I saw BROW 45:10
When they call you a. ICE- 164:15
artificial a. respiration BURG 48:5
artisan give employment to the a. BELL 27:18
artist a. is his own fault O'HA 244:15
a. is someone who WARH 330:1
a. man and mother woman SHAW 295:20
a. remains within JOYC 173:13
a. will be judged CONN 75:12
God is only another a. PICA 258:6
Never trust the a. LAWR 192:4
portrait of the a. JOYC 173:9
sign of a true a. VIDA 328:10
artists A. are not engineers KENN 178:14
arts interested in the a. AYCK 19:12
you 'a.' people MCEW 208:9
ash a. on an old man's sleeve ELIO 103:3
empty a. can CRAN 80:1
Oak, and A., and Thorn KIPL 183:14
Out of the a. PLAT 259:12
ashen Your a. hair Shulamith CELA 61:5
ashes a. for thirty LAMP 188:4
past is a bucket of a. SAND 286:9
Asia not in A. ARDR 13:12
Asian A. boys ought to be JOHN 171:11
Asians A. could still smile HEAD 149:14
ask a. and cannot answer SHAW 297:6
a. not what your country KENN 178:7
could a. him anything WEIS 332:13
Don't a., don't tell NUNN 243:8
Don't let's a. for the moon FILM 115:4
if you gotta a. MISQ 226:10
never does any harm to a. KRUT 186:10
To a. the hard question AUDE 18:14
were afraid to a. REUB 273:1
Would this man a. why AUDE 17:1
asking mere a. of a question FORS 122:15
asphalt a. road ELIO 104:14
aspidistra biggest a. HARP 147:12
Keep the a. flying ORWE 249:14
aspirin a. for a brain tumour CHAN 62:2
ass kiss my a. in Macy's window JOHN 171:14

ass (*cont.*):
on his unwashed a. PARS 254:11
assassin copperheads and the a. SAND 286:6
you are an a. ROST 279:13
assassination A. is extreme form SHAW 296:23
asteroid a. hitting the planet KING 180:13
astonish A. me DIAG 91:6
astonished rightly a. by events BART 24:9
astonishment Your a.'s odd KNOX 185:5
astounded merely a. by them ATTE 15:13
astrologers A. or three wise men LONG 202:8
astronomers and a. QUIN 268:8
reliability of a. JONE 172:8
astronomers a. and astrologers QUIN 268:8
astronomy linked in a. LOVE 203:8
asylum lunatic a. run by lunatics LLOY 201:10
taken charge of the a. ROWL 280:9
ate Freddie Starr a. my hamster NEWS 240:7
atheism a., breast-feeding ORTO 249:1
atheist a. is a man BUCH 47:3
chic for an a. RUSS 282:4
from being an a. SART 287:11
I am still an a. BUÑU 48:1
remain a sound a. LEWI 198:11
atheists no a. in the foxholes CUMM 82:13
atlas blank a. of your body NERU 239:3
Look in the a. AUDE 18:3
atom a. has changed everything EINS 100:12
carbon a. possesses JEAN 169:4
done with the a. LEAC 193:8
grasped mystery of the a. BRAD 42:7
leads through the a. EDDI 98:11
no evil in the a. STEV 308:7
atomic win an a. war BRAD 42:6
atoms motions of a. in my brain HALD 143:9
attack by his plan of a. SASS 288:3
attacked We have been a. NATT 238:7
attacking I am a. FOCH 120:13
attendant a. lord ELIO 104:7
attention a. must be paid MILL 224:3
a. to the object WEIL 332:9
attic furniture in Tolkien's a. PRAT 265:12
attractions register competing a. KNIG 185:3
attractive sexually a. LURI 205:3
audacity tactful in a. COCT 72:11
Auden Just a smack at A. EMPS 108:1
audience looks at the a. STOC 309:4
audiences two kinds of a. SCHN 291:4
audio visual full of a. marvels SMIT 300:8
august A. is a wicked month O'BR 244:2
aunt Aunt is calling to A. WODE 343:3
have the Queen as their a. MARG 216:13
pay to see my a. Minnie WILD 338:12
aunts bad a. and good aunts WODE 342:16
Auschwitz saved one Jew from A. AUDE 19:5
write a poem after A. ADOR 2:9
year spent in A. LEVI 198:3
Austerlitz A. and Waterloo SAND 286:8
Australia A. looks to America CURT 83:2
recession that A. had to have KEAT 176:6
take A. right back down KEAT 176:7
Australian A. republic MURR 235:17
A. selfhood HUGH 161:14
great A. Emptiness WHIT 336:8
Australians A. wouldn't give ADVE 3:6
Would A. have done HUGH 162:1
Austria Don John of A. CHES 64:1
author art has an a. WEIL 332:10
a. made a mistake DIRA 93:1
a. of *The Satanic Verses* KHOM 180:4
in search of an a. PIRA 258:14
wish the a. was a friend SALI 285:9
authority make your peace with a. MORR 232:4
solely on a. AYER 19:13
autobiography age to write an a. WAUG 331:9
a. is an obituary CRIS 81:2
A. is now as common GRIG 141:4
automobile a. changed our dress KEAT 176:9
like an a. ROOT 279:5
autonomy political a. GRAY 139:5
autumn a. arrives BOWE 41:9
mists of the a. mornings ORWE 249:16
available I'm the best a. CLAR 69:14
average a. guy who could carry EPIT 109:12
A. made lethal SHAF 294:12
averages from th' law of a. CART 56:3
avoiding a. being TILL 320:12
awakening moment of a. COET 72:15
aware a. that you are happy KRIS 186:7
awareness signs of his a. BLUN 38:9
away go a. for ever MURD 235:11
WHEN I'M A. TELE 316:4
awful this is an a. place SCOT 293:1
awfully a. big adventure BARR 24:2
awhile leave you here a. ANON 11:1
awoke a. one morning OPEN 248:3
axes no a. being ground BROU 45:8
axis sword the a. of the world DE G 88:14
Aztec destroyed the A. Empire SCHU 291:12

babes one of Blair's b. JACK 166:11
babies Ballads and b. MCCA 207:1
hates dogs and b. ROST 279:14
If men had to have b. DIAN 91:9
no longer sing to the b. MENU 221:14
putting milk into b. CHUR 67:11
same as eating b. IZZA 166:10
twelve-year-olds having b. GING 134:12
Babiy Yar Over B. there are no YEVT 349:5
baby b. doesn't understand KNOX 185:7
B. in an ox's stall BETJ 33:4

Burn, b., burn POLI 261:9
one for my b. MERC 222:5
Who loves ya, b. CATC 60:11
babysitting not love—it's b. FOND 121:2
Bach B. almost persuades me FRY 128:14
of J. S. B. BEEC 26:18
back b. him to the full HAGU 142:11
B. to the future FILM 118:3
b. to the wall CHRÉ 65:9
boys in the b. room LOES 201:16
boys in the b. rooms BEAV 25:6
counted them all b. HANR 145:6
Don't look b. PAIG 252:7
go b. in the water TAGL 314:6
I'll be b. FILM 116:3
in the small of the b. WODE 343:2
on my b. LAST 190:12
said 'I'll be b.!' TAGL 314:4
time to get b. to basics MAJO 213:12
very good b.-seat driver THAT 317:17
Winston is b. ANON 12:14
backing b. into the limelight BERN 31:17
I'm b. Britain SAYI 289:23
backside weight of the b. ADAM 2:3
backward B. ran sentences GIBB 134:4
walking b. into future ZHVA 350:8
backyards clean American b. MAIL 213:3
bacon b.'s not the only thing KING 182:2
bad b. against the worse DAY- 86:9
b. aunts and good aunts WODE 342:16
b. end unhappily STOP 310:2
b. times just around COWA 79:5
B. women never take the blame BROO 45:1
good, the b., and the ugly FILM 118:8
no such thing as b. publicity BEHA 27:4
when I'm b., I'm better WEST 334:12
where roads were b. LEE 195:2
badly worth doing b. CHES 64:16
bag Lays eggs inside a paper b. ISHE 165:15
like an old b. lady HEAL 150:4
baked b. cookies and had teas CLIN 71:8
get out of b. beans O'RE 248:6
balance b. of power KISS 184:10
bald b., and short of breath SASS 287:17
Can't act. Slightly b. ANON 10:3
fight between two b. men BORG 41:5
Balfour of the B. declaration WEIZ 332:14
Balkans prevailed in the B. KEEG 176:10
ball Every b. is BRAD 42:11
girl throwing a b. WOOL 345:3
ballads B. and babies MCCA 207:1
balls B. will be lost always BERR 32:10
great b. of fire BLAC 37:1
ban B. the bomb POLI 261:4
banal awful b. lines GUIN 142:4
banality b. of evil AREN 14:1
manufacture of b. SARR 287:3
banana I am a b. HISL 156:8
bananas Yes! we have no b. SILV 298:8
bandage wound, not the b. POTT 263:3
bands people get into b. GELD 132:6
bang bigger b. for a buck ANON 10:2
If the big b. does come OSBO 250:22
Kiss Kiss B. Bang KAEL 175:3
no terror in a b. HITC 156:11
Not with a b. but a whimper ELIO 103:16
bank b. will lend you money if HOPE 159:8
cry all the way to the b. LIBE 199:9
deposit at a Swiss b. ALLE 7:3
robbing a b. BREC 43:12
banker as a Scotch b. DAVI 84:10
banking as much as we value b. TOYN 321:7
b. and prostitution WRIG 345:15
banknotes old bottles with b. KEYN 179:11
Bantu [B.] has been subjected VERW 327:8
bar treat if met where any b. is HARD 146:12
Barabbas always save B. COCT 72:13
barbarians b. are to arrive today CAVA 61:1
without the b. CAVA 61:2
barbarous b. to write a poem ADOR 2:9
bard goat-footed b. KEYN 179:10
bark heard a seal b. CART 56:1
barrel ain't got a b. of money WOOD 344:11
out of the b. of a gun MAO 216:7
barricade some disputed b. SEEG 293:3
barrow there in your long b. MULD 234:11
baseball B. is very big GREG 140:10
basics time to get back to b. MAJO 213:12
basketball sex on the b. court SEIK 293:5
bastard all my eggs in one b. PARK 253:19
we knocked the b. off HILL 156:3
bastards Keep the b. honest POLI 261:20
Bastille Voltaire in the B. DE G 88:16
bat couldn't b. for the time COMP 74:3
shake a b. at a white man GREG 140:10
bath Freedom is like taking a b. KENN 177:7
rather lie in a hot b. THOM 318:19
test my b. before I sit NASH 238:3
bathroom revolutionary in a b. LINK 200:5
bats b. have been broken HOWE 160:11
batsmen opening b. HOWE 160:11
battery Rock is like a b. CLAP 69:10
battle B. of Britain CHUR 66:12
France has lost a b. DE G 88:4
we b. for the Lord ROOS 278:14
battles B. and sex MCAR 205:13
b. of subsequent wars ORWE 249:17
mother of all b. HUSS 163:9
bayonet b. is a weapon POLI 261:5
bayonets throne of b. INGE 165:6
throne of b. YELT 349:1
BBC don't watch B. for polemic SIMP 299:1
be Let b. be finale of seem STEV 307:13
poem should not mean but b. MACL 210:2

beach On the b. CHES 64:7
beaches fight on the b. CHUR 66:11
beam B. me up, Scotty MISQ 226:1
beans B. meanz Heinz ADVE 3:7
get out of baked b. O'RE 248:6
bear any of us can b. GIUL 135:10
asking more than we could b. RICH 274:4
B. of Very Little Brain MILN 225:2
Cannot b. very much reality ELIO 102:10
embrace the Russian b. CHAN 62:12
fire was furry as a b. SITW 299:6
Grizzly B. is huge and wild HOUS 160:3
heavy b. who goes with me SCHW 292:6
so b. ourselves that CHUR 66:12
bears b. might come with buns ISHE 165:15
b. the marks of the last HAIG 143:1
Teddy B. have their Picnic KENN 177:8
beast Beauty killed the B. FILM 117:6
dead or dying b. JENK 169:9
fit night out for man or b. FIEL 113:13
What rough b. YEAT 348:8
beastly b. the bourgeois is LAWR 192:7
b. to the Germans COWA 78:9
beat b. generation KERO 179:3
can b. Al Gore NADE 236:12
beaten being b. does not matter STEP 307:7
No Englishman is fairly b. SHAW 296:21
Beatles B.' first LP LARK 188:8
beatnik peculiar b. theories KERO 179:4
beats b. as it sweeps ADVE 3:29
beautiful b. and damned FITZ 118:18
B.! beautiful! ALDR 6:4
b. game PELÉ 256:5
Black is b. POLI 261:8
hunger to be b. RHYS 273:6
innocent and the b. YEAT 347:11
Small is b. SCHU 292:1
Something b. for God MUGG 234:4
something b. for God TERE 315:6
what a b. mornin' HAMM 144:12
beauty b. cold and austere RUSS 282:14
B. for some provides HUXL 164:7
B. in music IVES 166:5
B. killed the Beast FILM 117:6
B. momentary in the mind STEV 308:2
b. of inflections STEV 308:3
B. vanishes DE L 89:3
b. without vanity DUNC 95:9
have b. in one's equations DIRA 92:11
land of 'b. spots' JOAD 170:4
looked on B. bare MILL 223:7
terrible b. is born YEAT 347:5
there is still b. OFFI 245:16
Where B. was GALS 130:14
world's b. becomes enough MORR 232:5
Beaverbrook mind of Lord B. ATTL 16:1
because B. I do not hope to turn ELIO 102:2
B. it's there MALL 214:5
bed b. fell on my father THUR 320:5
don't get out of b. for less EVAN 108:14
gooseberried double b. THOM 318:14
in b. with my catamite OPEN 247:10
never made my own b. PU 267:8
on the lawn I lie in b. AUDE 18:1
prescription of a quick dip in b. WESL 334:6
should of stood in b. JACO 167:6
Who goes to b. with whom SAYE 288:10
wore in b. MONR 229:9
bedpost on the b. overnight ROSE 279:6
bedrock b. of Europe POWE 264:17
bedroom French widow in every b. HOFF 157:11
what you do in the b. CAMP 52:3
bedrooms in the nation's b. TRUD 322:13
beds Minds like b. always made up WILL 340:1
bee b. produces honey GOLD 136:13
sting like a b. ALI 6:8
beef love British b. BAKE 21:1
Where's the b. ADVE 4:31
Where's the b. MOND 229:1
been B. there, done that SAYI 289:3
b. things and seen places WEST 334:11
beer denies you the b. to cry into MARQ 217:12
only here for the b. ADVE 3:28
warm b., invincible suburbs MAJO 213:11
beers other b. cannot reach ADVE 3:24
three b. and it looks good FILM 117:10
bees b. do it PORT 262:16
Beethoven B.'s Fifth Symphony FORS 122:5
rape, ultra-violence and B. TAGL 314:2
Roll over, B. BERR 32:9
beetles special preference for b. HALD 143:11
beggar b. would recognise guilt PARS 254:11
begin b. at the beginning OPEN 248:1
b. the Beguine PORT 260:13
But let us b. KENN 178:6
Then I'll b. CATC 58:5
beginning begin at the b. OPEN 248:1
b. is often the end ELIO 103:7
b. of a new road SULS 311:9
end of the b. CHUR 67:9
In my b. is my end ELIO 102:13
In my b. is my end OPEN 247:6
Movies should have a b. GODA 136:6
pictures didn't have b. POLL 260:3
begins glory most b. and ends YEAT 347:17
Beguine begin the B. PORT 260:13
begun already b. before CALV 51:9
behave how to b. LETT 197:11
behaviour b. was intolerable MAJO 213:13
studies human b. ROBB 275:5
behaviourism B. a flat-earth view KOES 185:11
B. works AUDE 18:16
behind no bosom and no b. SMIT 301:5

beige just my colour: it's *b.* MEND 221:13
being at the edge of B. SPEN 304:5
avoiding b. TILL 320:12
darkness of mere b. JUNG 174:11
may not be worried into b. FROS 128:3
Nothingness haunts b. SART 287:5
unbearable lightness of b. KUND 187:1
Belgrano sinking of the *B.* DALY 84:2
belief that is b. SART 287:9
widespread b. more likely RUSS 282:12
believe b. in life DU B 95:6
b. in miracles FOX 124:1
b. in the life to come BECK 25:10
b. is not necessarily true BELL 27:7
B. it or not NEWS 240:1
b. that he exists HUME 163:2
b. what isn't happening COLE 73:2
don't have to b. that O'HA 244:14
even if you don't b. BOHR 39:9
he couldn't b. it CUMM 82:7
I b. in yesterday LENN 196:13
I do not b. . . . I know JUNG 174:16
I don't *b.* it CATC 59:23
If you b., clap your hands BARR 24:3
must b. *something* RUSS 283:5
really b. in themselves CHES 64:10
We b. a scientist RICH 274:6
Yes, I b. LAST 191:10
believing b. more and more YATE 346:7
stop b. in God CHES 64:18
bellies fire in women's b. CAST 57:6
their b. empty LOGU 202:4
bellow b. ultra-right clichés BLAC 36:10
bells floating many b. down CUMM 82:4
ring the b. of Heaven HODG 157:8
belong *b.* to it as well WHYT 337:14
betray, you must first b. PHIL 257:8
don't want to b. to any club MARX 218:8
I b. to Glasgow FYFF 129:8
man doesn't b. out there BRAU 43:1
where we really b. GREE 139:12
belonged once b. somewhere STEI 306:8
belongs moon b. to everyone DE S 90:8
twentieth century b. TRUD 322:14
beloved Cry, the b. country PATO 255:3
bend right on round the b. LAUD 189:11
beneath married b. me ASTO 15:9
benediction clouds in b. DAY- 86:7
bereaved b. if snobbery died USTI 326:2
Berkeley sang in B. Square MASC 218:13
Berlin cross from East to West B. KOES 185:14
Berliner *Ich bin ein B.* KENN 178:13
Bernard Jeffery B. is unwell WATE 330:14
Bertie Burlington B. HARG 147:8
best b. lack all conviction YEAT 348:7
b. of all possible worlds CABE 50:5
b. Prime Minister we have BUTL 50:2
b. things in life are free DE S 90:8
b. way out is always through FROS 127:19
be the b. HANS 145:8
did the b. we could UPDI 325:12
I'm the b. LEWI 199:1
I'm the b. available CLAR 69:14
we will do our b. CHUR 67:5
best-seller b. is the gilded tomb SMIT 300:12
best-sellers all the great b. PRIT 266:10
bet You b. your sweet bippy CATC 60:13
Bethlehem Slouches towards B. YEAT 348:8
Betjemanless We are now B. EWAR 110:6
betray b., you must first belong PHIL 257:8
guts to b. my country FORS 122:20
betrayal any act of b. RENO 272:13
ecstasy of b. GENE 132:13
better b. than Man TAGL 314:12
b. to be looked over WEST 334:7
can only get b. PETR 257:7
can only get b. POLI 262:3
Every day, I am getting b. COUÉ 78:4
Fail b. BECK 26:9
for b. or for worse ARCH 13:10
go b. with Coke ADVE 4:25
I can do b. BERL 30:13
If way to the B. there be HARD 146:10
nothing b. to do THAT 317:18
when I'm bad, I'm b. WEST 334:12
between try to get b. them STRA 310:5
beware B. my foolish heart WASH 330:13
bid you b. KIPL 183:12
bewildered bothered, and b. HART 148:3
to the utterly b. CAPP 53:10
bewitched B., bothered HART 148:3
bewrapt B. past knowing HARD 146:14
bias impartiality is b. REIT 272:10
biases critic is a bundle of b. BALL 22:5
Bible starless and b.-black OPEN 248:1
bible read in de B. HEYW 155:1
bibles Broken Hill with b. HUGH 162:12
bicycle arrive by b. VIER 328:12
fish without a b. STEI 307:3
so is a b. repair kit CONN 75:2
bicycle-pump b. the human heart AMIS 8:4
bicycling old maids b. MAJO 213:11
bicyclists trouser-clip for b. MORT 233:1
bidet UNABLE OBTAIN B. TELE 316:9
big b. enough to take away FORD 121:9
b. spender FIEL 113:7
b. tent POLI 261:7
b. way of doing things TERE 315:5
born with b. bones BINC 35:10
fall victim to a b. lie HITL 156:16
G.O.P.'s b. tent NEWS 240:16
I am b. FILM 118:2
bigamy B. is one husband too many ANON 10:1

biggest b. electric train set WELL 333:7
bigotry B. tries to keep truth TAGO 313:2
bike got on his b. TEBB 314:18
Mind my b. CATC 59:20
bikini b. made me a success ANDR 8:13
yellow polkadot b. VANC 326:8
bill b., drafted in Brussels BURF 48:3
billboard b. lovely as a tree NASH 238:4
biography better part of b. STRA 310:6
B. is about Chaps BENT 30:7
b. ultimately fiction MALA 213:14
forthcoming b. BELL 28:9
to write b. WEST 335:8
biologist b. passes ROST 279:11
biology B. is the search for WILL 339:5
bippy You bet your sweet b. CATC 60:13
birch bringing back the b. VIDA 328:3
bird catch the b. of paradise KHRU 180:8
It's a b. ANON 10:8
birds b. fly throught it HEIS 152:1
b. got to fly HAMM 144:7
b. trying to communicate AUDE 19:3
prisoned b. must find SASS 288:1
Birmingham B. by way of Beachy Head CHES 64:2
B. Six released DENN 90:6
When Jesus came to B. STUD 311:5
birth B., and copulation ELIO 104:15
b. of each child MCWI 212:4
present at the b. ORTO 248:15
seen b. and death ELIO 103:18
birthday eighty-first b. OPEN 247:10
Happy b. to you HILL 156:2
marvel my b. away THOM 318:10
your 100th b. TELE 316:7
biscuit cared a b. for it LAWR 193:2
biscuits hyacinths and b. SAND 286:11
bisexuality b. doubles your chances ALLE 7:4
bishop make a b. kick a hole CHAN 62:1
bitch Gaia a tough b. MARG 216:15
old b. gone in the teeth POUN 263:14
bits swallowed their b. BETJ 33:9
black b. against may BUNT 47:12
B. is beautiful POLI 261:8
b. kids get an education POWE 264:16
b. majority rule SMIT 300:10
B. Panther Party NEWT 239:10
B. Power CARM 54:4
but b. and grey GREE 139:15
Creature from the B. Lagoon CRON 81:6
growth of b. consciousness BIKO 35:8
I am B. JOHN 171:3
not b. and white BOY 42:4
not have the colour b. MAND 215:7
old b. magic MERC 222:6
one drop of b. blood HUGH 161:12
rainbow which includes b. YEVT 349:7
so long as it is b. FORD 121:10
talks good for a b. guy ICE- 164:15
with a b. skin MALC 214:1
young, gifted and b. HANS 145:7
Young, gifted and b. IRVI 165:14
blackbird B. has spoken FARJ 111:7
b. whistling STEV 308:3
blackbirds B. are the cellos STEV 308:14
Blackpool seaside place called B. EDGA 99:3
blacks country is for b. TSVA 323:17
black widow This is the B., death LOWE 204:9
Blair if her B. was quite WODE 343:1
one of B.'s babes JACK 166:11
Sun backs B. NEWS 240:19
Blake B. saw a treefull of angels BENÉ 29:1
blame Bad women never take the b. BROO 45:1
manager who gets the b. LINE 200:3
blamed mothers go on getting b. WHIT 337:8
blaming b. it on you KIPL 183:5
b. on his boots BECK 26:2
blandness ultimate b. ROTT 280:5
blanket b. of ocean CAUS 60:19
with the b. over his head BABE 20:2
blast In b.-beruffled plume HARD 146:8
blatherskite Blatant B. PHIL 257:13
bleeding instead of b., he sings GARD 132:1
bleeper do not wear a b. CLAR 70:8
Blenheim still fighting B. BEVA 34:5
bless B. 'em all HUGH 161:6
blessing b. cannot pass through JOHN 170:8
blew You b. it up FILM 117:15
blight great English b. WAUG 331:5
Blighty back to dear old B. MILL 224:12
blind *b.* watchmaker DAWK 85:8
Booth died b. LIND 200:2
Justice is a b. goddess HUGH 161:8
splendid work for the b. SASS 287:18
without science is b. EINS 100:1
blinds drawing-down of b. OWEN 251:8
blinked other fellow just b. RUSK 282:1
bliss Your b. in our hearts STRU 311:4
blithering B. economic nonsense CLAR 70:9
blitz b. of a boy CAUS 60:21
blobs blubbering b. SETH 294:6
block each b. cut smooth POUN 263:9
bloke if you were a b. EMIN 107:13
blonde Being b. is definitely MADO 212:6
b. to make a bishop kick CHAN 62:1
blondes b. and switchblades COOP 77:1
Gentlemen prefer b. LOOS 202:11
blood b. and love without STOP 309:15
b. come gargling OWEN 251:9
b. jet is poetry PLAT 259:10
b. on their hands SPEN 303:10
B. sport brought to INGH 165:8

b., toil, tears and sweat CHUR 66:8
by b. Albanian TERE 315:8
enough of b. and tears RABI 268:10
flow of human b. HUGH 161:10
foaming with much b. POWE 265:3
for cooling the b. FLAN 119:15
one drop of black b. HUGH 161:12
rather have b. on my hands GREE 139:7
show business with b. BRUN 46:9
washed in the b. of the Lamb LIND 200:1
We, your b. family SPEN 303:12
blood-dimmed b. tide is loosed YEAT 348:7
bloodshed war without b. MAO 216:6
bloody Abroad is b. GEOR 133:8
b. curtain ELIS 105:16
B. men like bloody buses COPE 77:3
Not b. likely SHAW 296:20
sang within the b. wood ELIO 104:18
Sunday, b. Sunday FILM 118:13
under the b. past AHER 5:3
blooming b. well dead SARO 287:2
blossom break Into b. WRIG 346:1
frothiest, blossomiest b. POTT 263:2
hundred flowers b. MAO 216:9
blow B. out, you bugles BROO 44:10
b. up the other half LAIN 187:10
b. with an agreement TROT 322:10
blowing answer is b. in the wind DYLA 97:4
I'm forever b. bubbles KENB 177:3
blubbering b. blobs SETH 294:6
blue b.-eyed devil white man FARD 111:6
b. guitar STEV 307:16
b. of the night CROS 81:9
Her b. body WALK 329:5
last b. mountain FLEC 120:3
pale b. dot SAGA 284:10
Space is b. HEIS 152:1
bluebell Mary, ma Scotch B. LAUD 189:12
bluebirds There'll be b. over BURT 49:3
blueprints Genes not like b. STEW 308:16
blues bury the b. with me HOOK 160:2
go back to b. CLAP 69:10
got the Weary B. HUGH 161:13
in American b. JAGG 167:7
when the b. started HOOK 160:1
blunder so grotesque a b. BENT 30:8
board There wasn't any B. HERB 153:9
boat sank my b. KENN 178:15
sewer in a glass-bottomed b. MIZN 228:10
boats passengers off in small b. LAST 191:5
bodies B. never lie DE M 89:13
Pile the b. high SAND 286:8
structure of our b. STOP 309:7
body Africa than my own b. ORTO 248:14
b. and the soul know ROET 276:11
b. building is ritual PAGL 252:1
b. like a bin bag FRY 128:15
b. swayed to music YEAT 346:8
good-will of the b. RIDI 274:13
i like my b. CUMM 82:11
interpose my b. STRA 310:5
my b. and your brains SHAW 297:2
my useless b. BROW 45:10
none in the b. LAWR 192:8
salutary to the b. PROU 267:6
stepped out of my b. WRIG 346:1
whose b. is this RODR 276:8
bog b.-standard comprehensive CAMP 51:14
recognize the term b.-standard BLUN 38:8
Bognor Bugger B. LAST 190:1
bogus b. god MACN 211:9
bohemian so-called b. elements KERO 179:4
boiler ten years in a b. suit TWEE 324:11
boldly to b. go RODD 276:3
Bolshevik I must be a B. MACD 207:13
bomb atom b. is a paper tiger MAO 216:8
Ban the b. POLI 261:4
b. on Hiroshima TRUM 323:4
b. them back into Stone Age LEMA 195:9
defence against the atom b. ANON 9:13
'formula' of the atomic b. MEDA 220:13
bombed glad we've been b. ELIZ 106:8
bomber b. will always get through BALD 21:10
bombers b. named for girls JARR 168:10
bombing b. begins in five minutes REAG 271:12
bombs Come, friendly b. BETJ 33:13
bond B. James Bond. FILM 115:2
bonding male b. TIGE 320:11
bonds surly b. of earth MAGE 212:8
surly b. of earth REAG 271:14
boneless b. wonder CHUR 66:5
bones b. of one British Grenadier HARR 147:14
conjuring trick with b. JENK 169:7
dead men lost their b. ELIO 105:1
bonfire b. of the vanities WOLF 343:15
bonjour *B. tristesse* ÉLUA 107:8
book before this b. is published RUNC 281:7
b. would have been finished WODE 342:18
b. you would wish your wife GRIF 141:2
insignificant b. because WOOL 345:2
knocks me out is a b. SALI 285:9
mentioning a single b. REED 272:6
one bright b. of life LAWR 192:2
book-keeping double-entry b. MULL 234:14
books B. and all forms of writing SOYI 303:2
b. are either dreams LOWE 204:2
b. are weapons ROOS 278:7
B. do furnish a room POWE 264:9
B. from Boots' BETJ 33:11
B. say: she did this because BARN 23:11
b. undeservedly forgotten AUDE 19:1
his b. were read BELL 28:4
If my b. had been any worse CHAN 62:4
Keeping b. on charity PERÓ 256:10

books (*cont.*):
made the b. and he died FAUL 111:12
read any good b. lately CATC 58:22
study of mankind is b. HUXL 163:12
boot b. in the face PLAT 259:8
b. stamping on a human face ORWE 250:8
bootboy b. at Claridges WOOL 345:7
Booth B. led boldly LIND 200:1
boots blaming on his b. BECK 26:2
Books from B.' BETJ 33:11
b. are made for walkin' HAZL 149:13
boots—b.—movin' KIPL 182:11
doormat in a world of b. RHYS 273:7
on a pedestal in bronze b. GRIG 141:5
booze fool with b. until he's 50 FAUL 112:3
boozes tell a man who "b." BURT 49:1
bop Playing 'B.' ELLI 107:1
border Night Mail crossing the B. AUDE 17:16
bore healthy male adult b. UPDI 325:7
Less is a b. VENT 327:6
bored b. by children TWEE 324:10
b. for England MUGG 234:6
I'd get b. and fall over COMP 74:3
works and is not b. CASA 55:9
boredom b. and terror WELL 333:9
first b., then fear LARK 188:10
perish of despair and b. FRAN 124:5
Borgias Italy under the B. FILM 116:6
boring b. kind of guy BUSH 49:6
Life, friends, is b. BERR 32:12
born already b. before my lips MAND 215:12
because you were b. in it SHAW 295:12
B. in the USA SPRI 305:1
B. of the sun SPEN 304:3
b. three thousand years old DELA 89:10
b. to run SPRI 305:3
b. with your legs apart ORTO 249:3
for being b. WATS 331:2
human beings are b. free ANON 9:10
I am not yet b. MACN 211:15
Man is b. to live PAST 254:14
not to be b. is best AUDE 16:15
One is not b. a woman DE B 87:3
bosom no b. and no behind SMIT 301:5
boss b. there is always MARQ 217:9
bossing nobody b. you ORWE 250:10
bossy by the b. for the bully SELD 293:6
getting awfully b. THAT 318:1
botanist I'd be a b. FERM 112:12
botch I make a b. BELL 28:3
bother conscience to b. him LLOY 201:13
long words B. me MILN 225:2
young whom I hope to b. AUDE 18:8
bothered Bewitched, b. HART 148:3
bottle bothers to buy a b. DWOR 97:3
b. it and sell it MCDO 208:5
b. of pinot noir RODD 276:6
putting a message in a b. HODG 157:7
way out of the fly-b. WITT 342:6
bottles old b. with banknotes KEYN 179:11
bottom at the b. of our garden FYLE 129:9
forgotten man at the b. ROOS 277:13
from the b. of the deck SHAP 294:14
bought b. the company ADVE 3:27
bouquet b. better than the taste POTT 263:4
bourgeois beastly the b. is LAWR 192:7
b. prefers comfort HESS 154:4
bourgeoise British B. is not born SITW 299:9
bourgeoisie charm of the b. FILM 118:5
Bovril B. prevents ADVE 3:8
bowl when I am going to bowl WARN 330:4
bows got the b. up LAST 190:12
box life like a b. of chocolates FILM 117:3
boxes Little b. on the hillside REYN 273:4
boxing B.'s just showbusiness BRUN 46:9
boy any b. may become President STEV 308:8
b. brought in the white sheet LORC 203:2
b. will ruin himself GEOR 133:4
Mad about the b. COWA 78:13
remain a fifteen-year-old b. ROTH 279:15
sat the journeying b. HARD 146:14
You silly twisted b. CATC 60:18
boy friend thing called the B. WILS 341:10
boys b. in the back room LOES 201:16
b. in the back rooms BEAV 25:6
b. not going to be sent ROOS 278:3
see if the b. are still there BARU 24:15
send American b. JOHN 171:11
slower than b. FRAS 124:12
bra Burn your b. SAYI 289:4
I want a b. BLUM 38:3
bracket date slides into the b. EWAR 110:6
brain Bear of Very Little B. MILN 225:2
b. has the consistency TURI 324:4
b.? my second favourite ALLE 6:15
dry b. in a dry season ELIO 103:12
fingerprints across his b. HEND 152:17
hasn't exactly got B. MILN 225:5
losing your b. FOX 123:10
motions of atoms in my b. HALD 143:9
why did He give us a b. LUCE 205:2
brains feet instead of their b. SOUS 303:1
my body and your b. SHAW 297:2
brake invented the b. NEME 238:14
brandy B. for the parson KIPL 183:13
b. of the damned SHAW 295:21
brassière Art is not a *b.* BARN 23:10
Brazilian If I were a B. STIN 308:17
bread made, like b. LE G 195:4
Royal slice of b. MILN 225:9
break at the b. of the day STRU 311:4
b. Into blossom WRIG 346:1
Can it be b. JENK 169:8
give a sucker an even b. FIEL 113:12

Have a b. ADVE 3:23
if you b. the bloody glass MACN 211:12
breakdown Madness need not be b. LAIN 187:12
nervous b. RUSS 282:5
breakers b. cliffward leaping CRAN 79:17
breakfast b. three times MAUG 219:10
committed b. with it LEWI 198:15
embarrassment and b. BARN 23:9
intervene—before b. HESE 153:17
breath drawn the b. of life YEAT 347:9
dying b. of Socrates MISQ 226:5
each saving b. LOWE 204:10
last b. of Julius Caesar JEAN 169:3
breathing Running's like b. FREE 125:2
brew b. that is true FILM 117:7
bribe cannot hope to b. or twist WOLF 343:10
Marriage is a b. WILD 338:14
bribes open to b. GREE 139:9
brick b. at a time HARG 147:9
Follow the yellow b. road HARB 146:1
Goodbye yellow b. road JOHN 171:1
bride ser' him for a b. MACD 207:11
bridge b. and the Bradman ANON 10:10
b. is love WILD 338:13
b. over troubled water SIMO 298:11
b. to the future LAWR 192:3
Every good poem is a b. DAY- 86:10
going a b. too far BROW 46:4
to the b.-builders MCAL 205:11
Women, and Champagne, and B. BELL 28:2
briefing b. is what *I* do CALL 51:2
bright future's b. ADVE 3:19
young lady named B. BULL 47:10
brighter women are b. than men LOOS 203:1
brightness leaking the b. away SPEN 304:8
brink trembling on the b. NABO 236:10
walked to the b. DULL 95:8
brinkmanship boasting of his b. STEV 308:11
bristles my skin b. HOUS 160:9
Britain Battle of B. CHUR 66:12
B. a fit country LLOY 201:6
B. did not have MONN 229:6
B. will be honoured HARL 147:10
B. will still be MAJO 213:11
further you got from B. CALL 51:8
I'm backing B. SAYI 289:23
Keep B. tidy OFFI 245:10
speak for B. BOOT 40:9
Without B., Europe ERHA 108:10
Britannia think of Cool B. BENN 29:10
British bones of one B. Grenadier HARR 147:14
B. are coming WELL 333:6
B. journalist WOLF 343:10
B. nation is unique CHUR 67:4
B. pound DYSO 98:5
drunken officer of B. rule WALC 328:14
for b. institutions MAND 215:1
No sex please—we're B. MARR 217:15
rather be B. PAIS 252:8
We are B., thank God MONT 229:14
Britons B. alone use 'Might' WAUG 331:15
broadens travel b. the mind; but CHES 64:14
broccoli b., dear CART 56:5
eat any more b. BUSH 49:8
broke If it ain't b. SAYI 289:19
broken bats have been b. HOWE 160:11
b. heart and a broken home HOOK 160:1
here to B. Hill HUGH 162:12
Morning has b. FARJ 111:7
taken up the b. blade DE G 88:6
brothel b. for the emotions KOES 185:10
playing a piano in a b. MUGG 234:7
brother be the white man's b. KING 181:1
BIG B. IS WATCHING YOU ORWE 250:2
B. can you spare a dime HARB 145:11
brotherhood freedom and our b. LAIN 187:10
table of b. KING 181:6
brother-in-law brother, not b. KING 181:1
brothers live together as b. KING 181:8
two b. and eight cousins HALD 143:12
brown Her b. embrace WALK 329:5
river Is a strong b. god ELIO 102:19
Browning safety-catch of my B. JOHS 172:4
brows pallor of girls' b. OWEN 251:8
Bruce made Adam and B. BRYA 46:11
Brussels drafted in B. BURF 48:3
brutal heart's grown b. YEAT 347:16
brute heart of a b. like you PLAT 259:8
BSE B. holds no terror BAKE 21:1
bubbles frill of b. DUNM 95:11
I'm forever blowing b. KENB 177:3
buck bigger bang for a b. ANON 10:2
b. stops here TRUM 323:12
bucket past is a b. of ashes SAND 286:9
stick inside a swill b. ORWE 250:17
Buckingham Palace guard at B. MILN 225:6
bugger B. Bognor LAST 190:1
bugles Blow out, you b. BROO 44:10
b. calling from sad shires OWEN 251:7
building stuck in this b. LAST 190:8
very old b. OSBO 250:18
built not what they b. FENT 112:7
Who b. Thebes BREC 43:13
bulimia yuppie version of b. EHRE 99:6
bulks come in wee b. LIDD 199:10
bull Dance tiptoe, b. BUNT 47:12
bullet b. through his head ROBI 275:10
Faster than a speeding b. ANON 10:8
bulling b. through wave-wrack MERW 222:13
bull's-eye b. on our chest SHAP 295:1
bully by the bossy for the b. SELD 293:6
such a b. pulpit ROOS 279:3
bum Indicat Motorem B. GODL 136:7

bump b. in the road BUSH 49:10
bumpy going to be a b. night FILM 115:7
bungler Man is a b. SHAW 296:1
bunk History more or less b. FORD 121:11
bunkers gloomy b. were built ESHE 108:13
burden bear any b. KENN 178:3
carry the heavy b. EDWA 99:4
burdened like being b. BAIN 20:11
bureaucracy immobile b. SAMP 286:2
bureaucrats Guidelines for b. BORE 41:2
burglars fear of b. CANE 53:2
burgled We have b. houses GALL 130:13
burgundy naive domestic B. CART 56:4
buried b. at midnight O'BR 244:1
b. in the rain MILL 223:9
b. with me HEWE 154:8
burlesque b. and the newspapers STON 309:6
Burlington B. Bertie HARG 147:8
burn better to b. out YOUN 349:12
B., baby, burn POLI 261:9
b. its children to save MEYE 223:1
B. your bra SAYI 289:4
burned Alexandria's library b. HUGH 162:5
burning b. roof and tower YEAT 347:14
b. the rain forest STIN 308:17
by b. him CEAU 61:4
Is Paris b. HITL 156:15
Keep the Home-fires b. FORD 121:13
lady's not for b. FRY 128:9
burnished Furnish'd and b. BETJ 33:14
burns candle b. at both ends MILL 223:6
burnt b. at the stake as witches SMIT 301:4
if all this was b. cork GREG 140:9
burr aphorism should be like a b. LAYT 193:4
bury anything we want to b. MOOR 230:5
B. my heart at Wounded Knee BENÉ 28:16
b. the blues with me HOOK 160:2
good day to b. bad news MISQ 226:7
physician can b. WRIG 345:14
We will b. you KHRU 180:7
bus Anybody seen in a b. WEST 335:11
Can it be a Motor B. GODL 136:7
missed the b. CHAM 61:12
run over by a b. CARR 54:6
stepping in front of a b. OSBO 250:22
buses men are like bloody b. COPE 77:3
more time on the b. STRU 311:2
bush B. wins it NEWS 240:2
bushes like different b. trimmed QUIN 268:9
bushmen they were not b. HEAD 149:14
business Being good in b. WARH 329:13
b. as usual THAT 317:6
B. carried on as usual CHUR 66:2
B. is like a car SAYI 289:5
b. of the American people COOL 76:9
b. practices improve RODD 276:4
b. to get him in trouble ROBI 276:2
died in b. SAKI 285:7
do b. together THAT 317:7
heart in the b. WATS 331:4
How to succeed in b. MEAD 220:11
I'm in the hurt b. TYSO 325:4
Liberty is unfinished b. ANON 11:10
Murder is a serious b. OPEN 247:9
music b. is not MORR 232:8
no b. like show business BERL 31:6
businessman b. has trampled on NICO 241:9
toward making a b. WATS 331:3
businessmen b. have tried to BLAC 36:10
well-placed b. decide YOUN 349:10
bust dance it b. to bust GREN 140:12
busting June is b. out all over HAMM 144:9
busy b. man has no time MAUR 219:12
B. times ALBR 6:2
Government of the b. SELD 293:6
had a b. day SIGL 298:5
butcher Hog B. for the World SAND 286:5
butler b. did it CATC 58:6
on the b.'s upper slopes WODE 343:6
butter b. for the Royal slice MILN 225:9
guns not with b. GOEB 136:8
no money for b. JOSE 173:4
rather have b. or guns GOER 136:10
Stork from b. ADVE 3:10
butterflies flight of b. SART 287:16
Frogs eat b. STEV 307:14
butterfly breaks a b. on a wheel NEWS 241:2
flap of a b.'s wings LORE 203:4
float like a b. ALI 6:8
buttocks gorgeous b. of the ape HUXL 164:7
butty oul' b. o' mine O'CA 244:7
buy b. a used car POLI 262:7
b. Codham, Cockridden THOM 319:3
b. it like an honest man NORT 243:6
b. me a Mercedes Benz JOPL 173:1
client will beg to b. BURR 48:12
Don't b. a single vote more KENN 177:10
money can't b. me love LENN 196:5
Stop me and b. one ADVE 4:23
by B. and by MCCO 207:5
Byron movement needs a B. POLL 260:2
Byronic think all poets were B. COPE 77:5
bystander never be a b. BAUE 25:2
Byzantium holy city of B. YEAT 348:5

cabinet another to mislead the C. ASQU 15:5
c. minister on a pedestal GRIG 141:5
group of C. Ministers CURZ 83:6
cable little c. cars climb CROS 81:13
of c. television MACK 209:10
Cablinasian I'm a C. WOOD 344:12
cad Cocoa is a c. and coward CHES 64:5

Caesars Sawdust C. NEWS 240:17
worship the C. HUXL 164:1
caff ace c. with a nice museum ADVE 3:2
caftan Iffucan of Azcan in c. STEV 307:11
cage c. upon the wall BISH 36:6
cannot c. the minute MACN 211:17
occupy the same c. WILL 339:10
cake C. or death IZZA 166:9
picked out of a c. RALE 269:7
calamity Oh, c. CATC 59:22
calculating desiccated c. machine BEVA 34:10
Caliban C. casts out Ariel POUN 263:12
California C. is a fine place to live ALLE 6:10
C. to the New York Island GUTH 142:9
Californian C. mall rat PRAT 265:13
Caligula eyes of C. MITT 228:7
call c. it a day COMD 74:1
c. of the wild LOND 202:5
how you c. to me HARD 147:1
May I c. you 338 COWA 79:9
timeless c. SCHL 291:3
calling Germany c. JOYC 174:6
callisthenics c. with words PARK 253:16
calls If anybody c. Say BENT 30:9
calm c. and at peace HUME 163:1
Cambridge C. ladies CUMM 82:12
C. people rarely smile BROO 44:12
either Oxford or C. SNAG 301:10
came I c. through MACA 206:1
camel c. is a horse ISSI 166:3
Take my c., dear OPEN 247:20
Camelot known as C. LERN 196:15
never be another C. ONAS 246:2
camera c. makes everyone SONT 302:15
I am a c. ISHE 166:1
campaign c. in poetry CUOM 82:15
can *c.* nothing but frog-spawn LAWR 192:15
He who c., does SHAW 296:7
know a man who c. ADVE 3:9
Canada all over C. RICH 274:12
C. could have enjoyed COLO 73:13
C. is ten FOTH 123:5
I see C. DAVI 84:10
Canadian C. content THOM 318:3
definition of a C. BERT 32:14
I'm a C. CRON 81:8
sense of doubt—a C. LÉVE 198:1
Canadians C. are Americans with MAHY 213:2
C. are very reluctant CRON 81:6
C. do not like heroes WOOD 344:9
cancelled spring has been c. GILL 134:9
cancer c. close to the Presidency DEAN 86:11
cut out the c. AITK 5:6
up to the word 'c.' KIPL 184:2
white race *is* the c. SONT 302:14
candidate c. of probity HAGU 142:11
candle c. burns at both ends MILL 223:6
c. in that great turnip CHUR 68:1
c. in the wind JOHN 170:11
c. in the wind JOHN 170:14
rather light a c. STEV 308:12
candlelit out for a c. dinner BARN 23:13
candour combines force with c. CHUR 69:3
candy C. is dandy NASH 238:2
canisters steel c. hurtling about CASS 57:4
cannibal c. uses knife and fork LEC 194:10
cannon loose c. like her ANON 12:10
canoe make love in a c. BERT 32:14
can't I c. go on BECK 25:11
capitalism c. is a necessary FRIE 126:4
C. is using its money CAST 57:8
c. of lower classes SPEN 304:10
definition of c. HAMP 145:3
extermination of c. ZINO 350:11
monopoly stage of c. LENI 195:10
unacceptable face of c. HEAT 151:6
capitalist slave of c. society CONN 75:14
Capitol strangers in the C. HEWI 154:10
captain broken by the team c. HOWE 160:11
c. is in his bunk SHAW 295:12
ship's c. complaining POWE 265:6
captains Star c. glow FLEC 120:1
car Business is like a c. SAYI 289:5
buy a used c. POLI 262:7
can't drive the c. TYNA 325:1
c. could go straight upwards HOYL 161:1
c. crash as a sexual event BALL 22:3
c. has become the carapace MCLU 210:9
c. in every garage HOOV 159:3
motor c. was poetry LEWI 199:4
owl of Minerva in a hired c. PAUL 255:8
caravan great c. of humanity SMUT 301:9
carbon c. atom possesses JEAN 169:4
carbuncle monstrous c. CHAR 63:3
carbuncles Monstrous c. SPEN 303:13
carcinoma sing of rectal c. HALD 143:10
card play the race c. SHAP 294:14
stood like a playing c. MAIL 213:5
cardboard C. Iron. Their hardships BOLA 39:11
card-indexes memories are c. CONN 75:10
cards buy a pack of c. COLE 73:7
c. with a man called Doc ALGR 6:6
care better c. of myself BLAK 37:12
c. less and less SAYE 288:10
full of c. DAVI 85:4
she don't c. LENN 196:10
Teach us to c. ELIO 102:3
Took great C. of his Mother MILN 225:7
To say we do not c. WARD 329:11
career c. in tatters MAND 215:9
close my military c. MACA 206:3
Good c. move VIDA 328:9
loyal to his own c. DALT 83:12
our c. and our triumph VANZ 327:2

careful be c. out there CATC 59:19
careless C. talk costs lives OFFI 245:1
have been a little c. CRES 80:7
They were c. people FITZ 119:3
cares Nobody c. MORT 232:15
caricature c. as far as I can SCAR 288:13
caring prosperous or c. society HESE 153:16
carollings little cause for c. HARD 146:9
carpenter I said to the c. CART 55:3
Walrus and C. LEVI 198:4
carpenters special language like c. SEXT 294:11
carrier down from the c.'s cart LEE 195:1
carry c. a big stick ROOS 278:10
cars c. and croissants DYKE 98:2
c. the great Gothic cathedrals BART 24:10
cartoonist life as a c. wonderful PETE 257:6
carving C. is interrelated HEPW 153:4
casbah Come with me to the C. MISQ 226:2
case everything that is the c. WITT 342:8
in our c. we have not got REED 272:3
would have passed in any c. BECK 26:7
casement ghost of Roger C. YEAT 347:10
cash needs good c. TUCK 324:2
Cassidy C.'s hanging hill KAVA 175:12
Cassiopeia C. was over KAVA 175:12
cast C. a cold eye YEAT 348:17
castle C. of lies BOOK 40:8
c. of my skin LAMM 187:15
casualties number of c. GIUL 135:10
cat c. on a hot tin roof WILL 339:9
c. that likes to gallop SMIT 301:1
C. walked by himself KIPL 184:3
Eventually it becomes a c. NASH 237:12
if a c. is black or white DENG 90:1
smile of a cosmic Cheshire c. HUXL 164:9
which way the c. is jumping SULZ 311:10
catalogue c. of human crime CHUR 66:9
catamite in bed with my c. OPEN 247:10
catastrophe education and c. WELL 333:14
unparalleled c. EINS 100:12
Catch-22 anything as good as C. HELL 152:4
C., which specified HELL 152:2
catcher c. in the rye SALI 285:8
category replacement of c.-habits RYLE 284:2
cathedrals cars the great Gothic c. BART 24:10
c. are like DURR 96:12
Catherine child of Karl Marx and C. ATTL 16:4
catholic C. and sensual CHAN 62:10
C. and the Communist ORWE 250:14
C. Church has never come WILL 339:7
if I was not a C. WAUG 332:1
lawful for a C. woman MENC 221:9
Once a C. WILS 340:8
Roman C. Church MACM 211:4
Roman C. women must THOM 319:9
Catholics C. and Communists GREE 139:7
cats C. go on the principle KRUT 186:10
C. look down on us CHUR 69:1
C., no less liquid TESS 315:9
elderly lady who has two c. LEWI 199:6
greater c. with golden eyes SACK 284:6
where c. are cats MARQ 217:7
cattle Actors are c. HITC 156:9
Catullus C. walk that way YEAT 348:6
caught man who shoots him gets c. MAIL 213:8
cause c. may be inconvenient BENN 30:3
Rebel without a c. FILM 118:12
causes aren't any good, brave c. OSBO 250:22
best c. tend to attract FISH 114:10
Tough on the c. of crime BLAI 37:2
caution c. in love RUSS 282:8
cavaliers C. (Wrong but) SELL 293:9
caves c. in which we hide FITZ 119:1
Ceaușescus C.' execution O'DO 244:11
Cecilia Blessed C., appear AUDE 16:12
celebrity c. is a forgery ADAM 2:4
C. is a mask UPDI 325:14
cello of the c. CASA 55:8
cellophane wrapping in c. NICH 241:6
cellos c. of the deep farms STEV 308:14
cells little grey c. CHRI 65:10
Celtic C. Tiger MCAL 205:10
woods of C. antiquity KEYN 179:10
cement Palestine is the c. ARAF 13:6
cemetery Help me down C. Road LARK 189:4
censorship beginning of c. HARE 147:6
extreme form of c. SHAW 296:23
fought without c. WEST 335:12
cent did with every c. FROS 127:9
centaur ant's a c. POUN 264:2
centre c. cannot hold YEAT 348:7
c. is everywhere UPDI 325:10
centuries Through what wild c. DE L 89:1
century c. of the common man WALL 329:8
close the c. MAND 215:4
sad, glittering c. BURC 48:2
So the 20th C. CRAN 80:2
when a new c. begins MANN 216:2
cerebration unconscious c. JAME 167:14
ceremony c. of innocence YEAT 348:7
certain France in a c. way OPEN 248:2
chained probably c. together HUGH 162:11
chains better to be in c. KAFK 175:5
chainsaw imagination and a c. HIRS 156:7
chair speaks of a c. BISH 36:7
chaise-longue hurly-burly of c. CAMP 52:2
chalice c. from the palace FILM 117:7
champagne get no kick from c. PORT 262:12
like c. or high heels BENN 30:3
some c. DEAN 87:1
Women, and C., and Bridge BELL 28:2
chance c. and accident BACO 20:6
C. has appointed her BUNT 47:11

Give peace a c. LENN 196:7
I missed my c. LAWR 192:12
institutions by c. HAIL 143:7
in the last c. saloon MELL 221:4
there is no c. LAST 190:11
too good to leave to c. SIMO 298:15
chandeliers gas c. WHAR 336:2
Chanel C. No. 5 MONR 229:9
change c. at Westminster KING 181:13
'C.' is scientific RUSS 283:7
c. their mind FITZ 119:12
c. the people who teach BYAT 50:4
c. we think we see FROS 127:1
life can c. on a dime LAHR 187:8
Management that wants to c. TUSA 324:7
things will have to c. LAMP 188:3
time for a c. DEWE 91:5
torrent of c. CHES 64:12
try to c. things BOLD 40:3
wind of c. is blowing MACM 211:1
changed changed, c. utterly YEAT 347:5
changed, c. utterly YEAT 347:7
c. upon the blue guitar STEV 307:16
human nature c. WOOL 344:13
If voting c. anything LIVI 200:11
not how he c. MORR 232:6
until I c. myself MAND 215:5
what cannot be c. NIEB 242:4
changing c. countries BREC 43:16
fixed point in a c. age DOYL 94:9
times they are a-c. DYLA 97:17
world is c. ELIZ 106:5
channel Fog in C. CART 56:2
chaos Humour is emotional c. THUR 320:9
means of overcoming c. RICH 274:7
chaps Biography is about C. BENT 30:7
chapter write the next c. JOHN 171:7
character about a fellow's c. REAG 271:11
content of their c. KING 181:7
did not have the c. ROOS 277:11
enormous lack of c. LEVA 197:13
under-appreciated c. trait STIN 309:1
characters Six c. in search PIRA 258:14
charge c. of the clattering train BEAV 25:8
I'm in c. CATC 59:10
charging marching, c. feet JAGG 167:11
charity Keeping books on c. PERÓ 256:10
charlatan c. is always the pioneer DOYL 94:10
charm c. of the bourgeoisie FILM 118:5
C. the great English blight WAUG 331:5
Oozing c. from every pore LERN 197:5
what c. is CAMU 52:6
What is c. LESS 197:9
Charon C. quit poling GINS 135:5
chase have to c. after it KLEE 184:20
chassis worl's in a state o' c. O'CA 244:8
Chattanooga C. Choo-choo GORD 137:16
Chatterley end of the C. ban LARK 188:8
cheap how potent c. music is COWA 79:7
sell it c. SAYI 290:6
to look this c. PART 254:12
Words are c. CHAP 62:14
cheaper c. than a prawn sandwich RATN 270:3
in the c. seats LENN 196:2
cheat cannot c. on DNA WARD 329:11
cheated Old men who never c. BETJ 33:7
cheek dancing c.-to-cheek BERL 31:1
cheeks c. are drawn PARR 254:10
cheer c. when soldier lads march SASS 288:5
which side do they c. for TEBB 314:19
cheerful It's being so c. CATC 59:13
cheeriness Chintzy, Chintzy c. BETJ 33:5
cheerio c. my deario MARQ 217:6
cheers Two c. for Democracy FORS 122:21
cheese like some valley c. AUDE 18:9
of c. FADI 111:2
varieties of c. DE G 88:11
cheeseburger c. will be fine POWE 264:18
chemical made up of c. elements MULL 234:13
two c. substances JUNG 174:13
chemistry c. that works WILL 339:5
chemists c.' war DAVI 85:6
cherished My no longer c. MILL 223:11
Chernobyl cultural C. MNOU 228:11
Three Mile Island and C. O'NE 246:12
cherries just a bowl of c. BROW 46:2
cherry American as c. pie BROW 46:1
Cheshire smile of a cosmic C. cat HUXL 164:9
chest bull's-eye on our chest SHAP 295:1
Chesterton dared attack my C. BELL 27:17
Chevy Drove my C. to the levee MCLE 210:1
chew can't fart and c. gum JOHN 172:1
chewing gum c. for the eyes ANON 12:4
chianti nice c. FILM 115:13
chic *c.* for an atheist RUSS 282:4
Radical C. WOLF 344:4
Chicagowards COCKBURN C. TELE 316:10
chicken c. in every pot HOOV 159:3
c. shit can turn JOHN 171:4
fed the c. every day RUSS 282:15
Some c.! Some neck CHUR 67:7
chickens beside the white c. WILL 340:2
chieftain C. Iffucan of Azcan STEV 307:11
child accused of c. death RICH 274:3
birth of each c. MCWI 212:4
c. becomes an adult SZAS 312:5
c. inherits my body SHAW 297:2
c., punished TREM 321:10
God bless the c. HOLI 158:1
has devoured the infant c. HOUS 160:3
I am to have his c. BURG 48:5
If you strike a c. SHAW 296:9
like a c. in a forest BART 24:9
one c. makes you a parent FROS 126:12

child (*cont.*):
what it is like to be a c. JARR 168:13
childbirth Death and taxes and c. MITC 228:2
childhood C. is Last Chance Gulch STOP 310:4
C. is the kingdom MILL 223:4
dolmens round my c. MONT 229:11
have you seen my c. JACK 167:2
one moment in c. GREE 139:16
children bellies of his c. STEI 306:16
bored by c. TWEE 324:10
burn its c. to save MEYE 223:1
by c. to adults SZAS 312:6
C. and zip fasteners WHIT 337:7
c. are not your children GIBR 134:6
C. aren't happy with NASH 237:16
c. are strangers SCHW 292:5
c. died in the streets AUDE 17:2
C. have never been very good BALD 21:2
C.: one is one SAYI 289:6
c. produce adults DE V 91:1
C.'s talent to endure ANGE 8:14
c. take your hand MCEW 208:13
c. to be a credit RUSS 283:1
c. were lost sight of MOYN 233:10
c. who leave home SLOV 300:1
c. who were rough SPEN 304:4
draw like these c. PICA 258:4
first class, and with c. BENC 28:11
get back from c. NESB 239:5
Goodnight, c. CATC 58:21
idea that all c. ANNE 9:8
interest of the c. SHAW 295:10
made c. laugh EPIT 109:8
music understood by c. STRA 310:8
my c. are frightened of me GEOR 133:6
not much about having c. LODG 201:14
poor get c. KAHN 175:6
reasons for having c. RUSS 283:9
remember the c. you got BROO 45:5
see his c. fed PUDN 267:10
some c., in some schools BLUN 38:8
their unborn c. did DURC 96:7
tiresome for c. SAIN 284:12
violations committed by c. BOWE 41:12
We are c. FORS 122:13
world safer for c. LE G 195:3
Chile Small earthquake in C. COCK 72:9
Chimborazo C., Cotopaxi TURN 324:6
chimpanzee vase in the hands of a c. WAUG 331:16
china Hong Kong's return to C. DENG 90:2
land armies in C. MONT 229:13
wall of C. was finished BREC 43:13
Chinese trust the C. DALA 83:10
went to a C. dinner FLEM 120:11
chintzy Chintzy, C. cheeriness BETJ 33:5
chips c. with everything WESK 334:3
tossed around like poker c. ALBR 6:1
chivalry law of c. SAYE 288:8
chocolates life like a box of c. FILM 117:3
choice from fate to c. SACK 284:4
not your second c. LURI 205:5
choices sum of all the c. DIDI 92:4
choir in the folk mass c. DOYL 94:11
choirs c. of wailing shells OWEN 251:7
choo-choo Chattanooga C. GORD 137:16
choose better to c. the culprits PAGN 252:6
forced to c. YEAT 347:2
I do not c. to run COOL 76:10
wisdom to c. correctly ALLE 6:17
chord just pick a c. VICI 328:1
choreography c. to the audience SZEL 312:12
Christ C. follows Dionysus POUN 263:12
C. perish in torment SHAW 296:22
C. were to return HARE 147:7
Christian C. ideal not been tried CHES 64:15
C. marriage MARG 216:12
most C. of worlds TSVE 324:1
persuades me to be a C. FRY 128:14
Christianity C. most materialistic TEMP 315:3
Disneyfication of C. CUPI 83:1
local thing called C. HARD 147:4
rock 'n' roll or C. LENN 196:3
Christmas call off C. FILM 115:3
child on C. Eve BART 24:9
C. is the Disneyfication CUPI 83:1
C.-morning bells say 'Come!' BETJ 33:3
dreaming of a white C. BERL 31:8
just before a hard C. SMIT 300:3
Let them know it's C. GELD 132:7
not just for C. SAYI 289:13
Out of the C. flame CAUS 60:20
turkeys vote for C. CALL 51:6
very traditional C. WOOD 344:8
Christopher Robin C. has fallen MORT 232:15
C. is saying MILN 225:11
chuck C. it, Smith CHES 63:8
chucked You're c. NYE 243:9
chumps C. make the best husbands WODE 342:11
church C. [of England] should ROYD 280:10
C. of England would ask HARE 147:7
C.'s Restoration BETJ 33:10
Get me to the c. on time LERN 196:16
open the windows of the C. JOHN 170:7
Railways and the C. AWDR 19:10
Churchill voice was that of Mr C. ATTL 16:1
cigar c. called Hamlet ADVE 3:22
really good 5-cent c. MARS 218:2
cigarette c. that bears MARV 218:6
smoked my first c. TOSC 321:3
cigars roller of big c. STEV 307:12
cinema c. is truth 24 times GODA 136:4
circle tightness of the magic c. MACL 210:4

circuit c. learns your job MCLU 210:7
circumcision breast-feeding, c. ORTO 249:1
circus no right in the c. MAXT 219:13
cities c., like teeming sores HOPE 159:6
c. we had learned about JARR 168:10
in the streets of a hundred c. HOOV 159:4
lousy skin scabbed by c. BUNT 47:11
shape of our c. KEAT 176:9
citizens first and second class c. WILL 340:7
citizenship c. Indian TERE 315:8
city c. is not a concrete jungle MORR 231:7
c. of perspiring dreams RAPH 270:1
felled a c. THOM 318:7
modern c. is a place WRIG 345:15
civil c. to everyone SISS 299:4
civilization annihilating all c. SAKH 285:2
C. advances WHIT 337:4
C. and discontents RIVI 275:4
c. has from time ELLI 107:5
C. nothing more than ORTE 248:13
C. the progress RAND 269:9
collapse of c. BELL 28:8
For a botched c. POUN 263:14
history of Western C. TYNA 325:2
last product of c. RUSS 282:9
life-blood of c. TREV 321:11
rottenness of our c. READ 271:1
say c. don't advance ROGE 277:6
soft resort-style c. BAUD 25:1
Speech is c. MANN 216:5
stupid of modern c. KNOX 185:6
thought of modern c. GAND 131:9
civilizes Cricket c. people MUGA 234:1
civil servant c. doesn't make IONE 165:10
Here lies a c. SISS 299:4
civil servants of c. BRID 44:1
Civil Service c. has finished REIT 272:9
C. is deferential CROS 82:2
claim last territorial c. HITL 156:14
claims Extraordinary c. SAGA 284:9
clamour c. of silence TAGO 313:3
clan c. and race MILL 224:6
Clancy C. and Dooley HEWE 154:7
clap c. your hands LENN 196:2
Don't c. too hard OSBO 250:18
If you believe, c. your hands BARR 24:3
Soul c. its hands and sing YEAT 348:4
clapped-out c., post-imperial DRAB 94:13
class c.-ridden society KING 182:3
could have had c. FILM 115:14
first and second c. citizens WILL 340:7
hands of the ruling c. STAL 305:7
merciless c. distinction MORT 232:12
use of *force* by one c. LENI 195:11
While there is a lower c. DEBS 87:13
classes capitalism of lower c. SPEN 304:10
Clashing of C. CONN 75:11
lower c. had such white CURZ 83:8
two c. of travel BENC 28:11
classical c. mind at work PIRS 259:3
classics bellyful of the c. MILL 224:9
classify Germans c. CATH 57:10
classroom in every c. LENO 196:14
clattering charge of the c. train BEAV 25:8
Claus ain't no Sanity C. FILM 116:9
claws pair of ragged c. ELIO 104:6
clay c. grew tall OWEN 251:10
C. is the word KAVA 176:1
had been a lump of c. POPE 260:4
pure c. of time's mud MALA 213:14
clean c. American backyards MAIL 213:3
c. place to die KAVA 176:3
c. the sky ELIO 104:11
lie down in c. postures FOWL 123:7
Not a c. & in-between MCGO 209:4
one more thing to keep c. FRY 128:10
tragedy is c. ANOU 13:2
cleaning militants like c. women TRUF 323:2
cleans guy who c. the river PERO 256:12
sweeps as it c. ADVE 3:29
clear On a c. day LERN 197:1
clercs *trahison des c.* BEND 28:14
clever important to be c. *about* MEDA 221:1
Too c. by half SALI 285:11
cleverest c. member WEBB 332:4
cliché used every c. except CHUR 67:2
clichés new c. GOLD 137:9
click c. with people EISE 102:1
Clunk, c., every trip OFFI 245:2
client c. will crawl through BURR 48:12
cliffs chalk c. of Dover BALD 21:11
white c. of Dover BURT 49:3
climate c. is gentle MCNE 212:2
whole c. of opinion AUDE 17:5
climax works its way up to a c. GOLD 137:11
climb C. ev'ry mountain HAMM 144:8
clipboards people with c. LEAR 193:14
clock After fifty the c. can't LOWE 204:10
c. is always slow SERV 294:2
c. of communism has stopped SOLZ 302:5
c. without the pendulum RUSS 283:8
rock around the c. DE K 88:18
Stands the Church c. BROO 44:13
clocks c. were striking thirteen OPEN 247:8
c. were striking thirteen ORWE 250:1
Stop all the c. AUDE 17:3
clockwork c. orange BURG 48:4
cloned successfully c. a lamb MARC 216:11
Clonmacnoise monks at C. HEAN 150:12
close C. encounters FILM 118:4
c. your eyes before AYCK 19:11
not c. enough CAPA 53:6
peacefully towards its c. DAWS 86:1
closed it was c. FIEL 114:1

closed (*cont.*):
We never c. VAN 326:9
closer Come c., boys LAST 190:2
closest c. friends won't tell you ADVE 3:17
closing c. time in the gardens CONN 75:12
cloth trick of wearing a c. coat BALM 22:7
clothes bought his c. with intelligence AMIE 7:14
C. are our weapons CART 54:9
C. by a man who doesn't CHAN 62:7
C. don't make the man WATS 331:3
C. which make LURI 205:3
poured into his c. WODE 343:7
remarkable suit of c. LOES 202:1
remove her c. in public LAMB 187:14
with your c. on DELL 89:12
clothing sheep in sheep's c. CHUR 69:5
cloud c. in trousers MAYA 220:1
Get off my c. JAGG 167:8
clouds Hullo C. Hullo Sky WILL 339:2
slow movement of c. DAY- 86:7
cloven out pops the c. hoof WODE 342:16
cloverleaf concrete c. MUMF 235:2
clowns Send in the c. SOND 302:11
club don't want to belong to any c. MARX 218:8
most exclusive c. NASH 237:8
that terrible football c. MCGR 209:6
clunk C., click, every trip OFFI 245:2
clurch c. out of the darkness CANE 53:2
clutching c. their gods ELIO 104:1
Clyde poems should be C.-built DUNN 96:2
coaching C. a football team LINE 200:4
coachman France is the c. DE G 88:17
coal island made mainly of c. BEVA 34:3
like miners' c. dust BOOT 40:10
coalition real rainbow c. JACK 167:1
coast c. of Coromandel SITW 299:10
coat long black c. WARR 330:11
Coca-Cola blue jeans and C. GREE 140:4
cocaine C. habit-forming BANK 22:9
cock Our c. won't fight BEAV 25:5
cocktail weasel under c. cabinet PINT 258:13
cock-up adhered to the c. theory INGH 165:7
cocoa c. for Kingsley Amis COPE 77:4
C. is a cad and coward CHES 64:5
coconuts loverly bunch of c. HEAT 151:8
cod photographer is like the c. SHAW 296:24
code trail has its own stern c. SERV 294:1
coffee put poison in your c. CHUR 69:2
with c. spoons ELIO 104:5
coffin in a Y-shaped c. ORTO 249:3
coin bent the c. of my destiny KAVA 176:2
coins for a fistful of c. ZAPA 350:4
coke go better with C. ADVE 4:25
cold Cast a c. eye YEAT 348:17
c. and lonely PAST 255:1
c. coming we had of it ELIO 103:17
c. metal of economic theory SCHU 292:3
c. war BARU 24:12
c. war warrior THAT 315:12
fingers of c. are corpse LAWR 192:18
past the common c. AYRE 20:1
plunging into a c. peace YELT 349:2
spy who came in from the c. LE C 194:12
understand one who's c. SOLZ 302:3
Without the c. war UPDI 325:13
colder c. and dumber than a fish MULD 234:11
colleagues respect fidelity to c. LASK 189:9
colonized culture to be c. by WELS 334:1
colony fuzzy wuzzy c. CAIR 50:10
colour any c. that he wants FORD 121:10
by the c. of their skin KING 181:7
c., culture or ethnic origin MACP 212:3
C. has taken hold of me KLEE 184:20
c. purple WALK 329:6
I know the c. rose ABSE 1:3
It's just my c. MEND 221:13
perceptible through c. MOND 229:2
problem of the c. line DU B 95:5
coloured no 'white' or 'c.' signs KENN 178:12
colourless C. green ideas CHOM 65:6
colours map-makers' c. BISH 36:5
nailing his c. FIEL 113:4
Columbus youth in C., Ohio THUR 320:5
column Fifth c. MOLA 228:12
columns crazy on its smoking c. YEVT 349:6
comb two bald men over a c. BORG 41:5
come believe in the life to c. BECK 25:10
C. to the edge LOGU 202:3
c. up and see me sometime MISQ 227:5
don't want to c. out BERR 32:6
I go—I c. back CATC 59:7
nobody will c. SAND 286:10
shape of things to c. WELL 333:15
they'll c. out for it SKEL 299:12
where do they all c. from LENN 196:6
comeback c. kid CLIN 71:13
comedy All I need to make a c. CHAP 62:13
C. is tragedy that happens CART 54:10
comes Nothing happens, nobody c. BECK 26:5
comfort bourgeois prefers c. HESS 154:4
naught for your c. CHES 63:9
comfortably Are you sitting c. CATC 58:5
comforting always a c. thought MARQ 217:9
cloud of c. convictions RUSS 282:16
comforts recapture the c. BRYS 46:13
comical Beautiful c. things HARV 148:9
coming British are c. WELL 333:6
cold c. we had of it ELIO 103:17
c. for us that night BALD 21:7
Everything's c. up roses SOND 302:9
Yanks are c. COHA 72:16
comma intrusive c. on p. 4 HOUS 160:10
command give a single c. SCHW 292:7

comment C. is free SCOT 292:11
C. is free STOP 309:13
couldn't possibly c. CATC 60:14
commercial you're labelled c. MANN 215:13
commission anyone in the C. ANON 11:5
resigned c. ANON 10:9
committed c. breakfast with it LEWI 198:15
committee C.—a group of men ALLE 6:11
c. a group of unwilling SAYI 289:7
c. divided MCEW 208:10
horse designed by a c. ISSI 166:3
common and still be c. RATT 270:7
century of the c. man WALL 329:8
c. pursuit LEAV 194:1
nor lose the c. touch KIPL 183:7
nothing in c. PYM 267:15
commoner persistent c. BENN 29:2
commons C. has declined in esteem ST J 284:14
member of the House of C. POWE 265:8
common sense C. is nothing more EINS 100:14
communicate birds trying to c. AUDE 19:3
Communism C. is like prohibition ROGE 277:5
communism anti-Christ of C. BUCH 47:6
caused the fall of c. JOHN 171:2
clock of c. has stopped SOLZ 302:5
C. is Soviet power LENI 195:15
C. the illegitimate child ATTL 16:4
trouble with C. LAWR 193:1
Communist member of the C. Party POLI 261:3
communist call me a c. CAMA 51:10
Catholic and the C. ORWE 250:14
Is he a C. STAR 306:1
members of the C. Party MCCA 206:7
Communists came first for the C. NIEM 242:6
communists Catholics and C. GREE 139:7
commuter C.—one who spends WHIT 336:4
commuting not-getting-mugged and c. HORN 159:13
companion gave him a c. VALÉ 326:6
company bought the c. ADVE 3:27
c. he chooses BURT 49:1
soul to the c. store TRAV 321:8
compassion c. of the healer's art ELIO 102:17
c. runs head-on KNAP 185:1
feel c. for fellow men ANNA 9:7
compensates c. for the misery DRAB 95:2
competing register c. attractions KNIG 185:3
competition rigour of c. ANON 10:4
complaint fatal c. of all HILT 156:5
no cause for c. SCOT 293:2
complete become c. yourself FRIE 126:1
complexion schoolgirl c. ADVE 4:6
complicity Our tribe's c. HEAN 150:8
composer c. and *not* homosexual DIAG 91:7
composing C.'s not voluntary BIRT 36:3
compound it's a chemical c. ZAPP 350:5
comprehensible universe is c. EINS 100:10
comprehensive bog-standard c. CAMP 51:14
compris *Je vous ai c.* DE G 88:7
compromise any c. whatever SHAR 295:2
computer c. in every LENO 196:14
if it's got a c. FILM 115:8
modern c. hovers BREN 43:17
requires a c. SAYI 290:11
computers abandoned c. DURR 96:12
C. are anti-Faraday CORN 77:8
C. are composed of AUGA 19:6
so many c. WAŁĘ 329:1
to be left to c. BUCH 47:7
conceit curst c. o' bein' richt MACD 207:10
concentrating not c. on you BARN 23:13
conception present at the c. ORTO 248:15
concepts up the stairs of his c. STEI 306:13
concern indifference to c. HYDE 164:10
concert self-imposed, the c. MILL 224:8
concerto C. to be difficult SCHO 291:8
concession retract your c. GORE 138:1
concrete city is not a c. jungle MORR 231:7
c. and tyres LARK 188:11
c. cloverleaf MUMF 235:2
concubine c. of a warlord OPEN 247:1
concupiscent c. curds STEV 307:12
condemn c. a little more MAJO 213:10
condemned c. to be free SART 287:6
condition c. for freedom FRIE 126:4
first c. of humanity SOYI 303:4
conductors C. must give signals SZEL 312:12
conference ever born in a c. FITZ 119:7
naked into the c. chamber BEVA 34:9
conferences eradication of c. MAYA 220:5
confinement solitary c. WILL 339:13
conflict armed c. EDEN 99:1
field of human c. CHUR 67:1
offered you C. and Art PRIE 266:6
tragic c. of loyalties HOWE 160:12
conflicts C., like living organisms MCEW 208:12
conforms industry applies, man c. ANON 12:2
confront to c. them TRIM 322:5
confused anyone who isn't c. MURR 236:3
confusion in our sea of c. GAMO 131:2
Congo C., creeping through LIND 199:13
conic c. sections were studied WHIT 337:5
conjuring c. trick with bones JENK 169:7
conked c. out on November 15th EPIT 109:15
connect Only c. FORS 122:9
conquered They c. continents DUNN 96:4
conqueror you are a c. ROST 279:13
conscience C.: the inner voice MENC 221:8
c. to bother him LLOY 201:13
cruelty with a good c. RUSS 283:3
taking your c. round BEVI 35:2
will not cut my c. HELL 152:6
consciences binding on the c. JOHN 170:5
consciousness c.-expanding drug CLAR 70:5

consciousness (*cont.*):
C. *isn't* intolerable AMIS 8:9
C. the phenomenon PENR 256:6
tragic c. FUEN 128:17
conscription Not necessarily c. KING 181:16
consent without your c. ROOS 277:12
consenting only between c. adults VIDA 328:3
conservation make a speech on c. STEV 308:13
conservatism c. is based upon CHES 64:12
runs head-on into c. KNAP 185:1
conservative become a c. AREN 14:2
c. been arrested WOLF 343:16
c. is a liberal SAYI 289:8
C. is a man ROOS 278:2
C. Party always MACL 210:5
C. Party at prayer ROYD 280:10
is the C. Party leadable HESE 154:2
make me c. when old FROS 127:14
makes a man more c. KEYN 179:8
conservatives better with the C. POLI 261:24
C. do not believe HAIL 143:3
night for the C. PORT 263:1
conspicuous Vega c. overhead AUDE 18:1
conspiracies c. against the laity SHAW 295:9
conspiracy c. theory of government INGH 165:7
c. to make you happy UPDI 325:11
vast right-wing c. CLIN 71:9
constituencies go back to your c. STEE 306:4
constitution c. does not provide WILL 340:7
establishment of C. CARD 53:11
constructed c. by others ATWO 16:8
consultants c., cars and croissants DYKE 98:2
consume more history than they can c. SAKI 285:5
consumer c. isn't a moron OGIL 244:13
c. is the king SAMU 286:4
c. society ILLI 165:1
consumes c. without producing ORWE 249:4
consuming survive by c. VANE 326:15
contact c. with this Wild Man BLY 38:10
word preserves c. MANN 216:5
contemplation Has left for c. BETJ 33:10
contemptible c. little army ANON 10:7
contender could have been a c. FILM 115:14
content Canadian content THOM 318:3
contest not the victory but the c. COUB 78:3
continent Africa, drifting c. GENE 132:12
C. isolated CART 56:2
ghost c. EISE 101:6
continually think c. of those SPEN 304:2
contraception oral c. ALLE 7:1
contract Social C. nothing more WELL 333:13
verbal c. isn't worth GOLD 137:4
contradict Never c. FISH 114:7
contradiction c. is real LÉVI 198:8
contraire *Au c.* BECK 26:13
contrast enjoyment from a c. FREU 125:6
control Ground c. to Major Tom BOWI 41:16
wrong members in c. ORWE 249:15
controls Who c. the past ORWE 250:3
controversial what is c. EPHR 108:8
convalescence enjoy c. SHAW 295:5
convenience prefers c. to liberty HESS 154:4
convention This c., they BERN 32:2
conventional c. wisdom GALB 130:5
conversation C. is imperative WHIT 336:6
no such thing as c. WEST 335:4
third-rate c. PLOM 259:16
convict c. stain HUGH 161:14
conviction best lack all c. YEAT 348:7
convictions cloud of comforting c. RUSS 282:16
c. are hills FITZ 119:1
convinces man who c. the world DARW 84:8
cook good c., as cooks go SAKI 285:6
cookies baked c. and had teas CLIN 71:8
cool c. as a mountain stream ADVE 3:11
c. web of language GRAV 138:11
rather be dead than c. COBA 72:8
something to be c. LOVE 203:7
think of C. Britannia BENN 29:10
Coolidge admiration for Mr C. ANON 12:8
cooling for c. the blood FLAN 119:15
cooperation partnership and c. ANON 10:4
co-operation belief in c. YAMA 346:6
copperheads c. and the assassin SAND 286:6
cops C. are like a doctor CHAN 62:2
copulating Two skeletons c. BEEC 26:19
copulation Birth, and c. ELIO 104:15
coral like c. insects WARN 330:7
cork c. out of my lunch FIEL 113:11
if all this was burnt c. GREG 140:9
corkscrews crooked as c. AUDE 16:15
cormorant common c. (or shag) ISHE 165:15
corn c. is as high HAMM 144:11
C. King beckoning JARR 168:9
corner At every c., I meet LOWE 204:8
c. of a foreign field OPEN 247:4
just around the c. COWA 79:5
mutters away in a c. CARE 53:12
corny c. as Kansas in August HAMM 144:17
Coromandel coast of C. SITW 299:10
coronation King's C. depends BLUN 38:9
correctness political c. can be JAME 168:7
correlative objective c. ELIO 105:10
corridors c. of power SNOW 301:11
corrupted c. by sentiment GREE 139:9
cosh c. of the English STRA 310:12
cosiness c. and irritation PYM 267:15
cosmetics tired of the c. SEXT 294:7
we make c. REVS 273:3
cost But at what c. BECK 25:9
c. of setting him up NAID 236:13
costs C. merely register KNIG 185:3

Cotopaxi Chimborazo, C. TURN 324:6
cotton c. is high HEYW 155:2
cough all c. in ink YEAT 348:6
coughing keeping people from c. RICH 274:11
one c., and one not SCHN 291:4
coughs C. and sneezes spread OFFI 245:3
council chaos of a Labour c. KINN 182:6
count c. everything CORN 77:8
Don't c. on me RICH 274:2
if you can c. your money GETT 134:2
I won the c. SOMO 302:7
counted c. them all out HANR 145:6
counterpoint Too much c. BEEC 26:18
counting it's the c. STOP 309:9
countries changing c. BREC 43:16
country ask not what your c. KENN 178:7
betraying my c. FORS 122:20
Britain a fit c. LLOY 201:6
Cry, the beloved c. PATO 255:3
died to save their c. CHES 63:14
dying for Queen and c. THOM 320:1
dying for your c. FRAN 124:7
everyday story of c. folk CATC 58:17
fight for its King and C. GRAH 138:9
How can you govern a c. DE G 88:11
In this frozen whited c. HUGH 162:10
King and c. need you SAYI 290:17
love to serve my c. GIBR 134:5
My c. is Kiltartan Cross YEAT 347:12
never let my c. die for me KINN 182:7
no c. for old men YEAT 348:3
Once we had a c. AUDE 18:3
past is a foreign c. OPEN 247:16
peace of each c. JOHN 170:6
put party before c. CREW 80:8
quarrel in a far away c. CHAM 61:9
rather than a c. PILG 258:9
struck our c. POWE 264:19
understand the c. LESS 197:7
vow to thee, my c. SPRI 304:15
what was good for our c. WILS 340:9
While there's a c. lane PARK 254:2
your King and your C. RUBE 280:12
You've never seen this c. PURD 267:11
countryman c. must have praise BLYT 39:1
countryside c. to be laughing FRIE 126:8
county English c. families WAUG 331:6
couples As with most c. LURI 205:4
chasing the naughty c. THOM 318:14
married c. ARCH 13:10
courage C. is the thing BARR 24:6
C. not simply *one* LEWI 198:14
c. to change NIEB 242:4
C. was mine OWEN 251:12
have enough c. MITC 228:1
It takes c. MOWL 233:9
Pathos, piety, c. FORS 122:16
warm c. BUSH 49:13
warm c. ROOS 277:17
court c. jester DYSO 98:3
courting Are yer c. CATC 58:4
courtmartialled c. in my absence BEHA 27:2
cousins two brothers and eight c. HALD 143:12
couture Haute C. should be fun LACR 187:4
covenants Open c. of peace WILS 341:19
cover Duck and c. OFFI 245:7
cow c. is of the bovine ilk NASH 237:6
milk the c. of the world WILB 338:6
Was the c. crossed HERB 153:13
coward sea hates a c. O'NE 246:9
cowardice C., a lack of ability HEMI 152:10
cows contented—for the c. CHAN 62:8
cowslip C. and shad-blow CRAN 79:17
crabs c. in a basket DURR 96:10
crack C. and sometimes break ELIO 102:12
c. in the tea-cup opens AUDE 16:14
cracked You haven't cracked me yet BOGA 39:7
cradle c. rocks above an abyss NABO 236:9
from the c. to the grave CHUR 67:10
rocking the c. ROBI 276:1
crane tall as a c. SITW 299:5
cranks sages and c. QUIN 268:8
crash car c. as a sexual event BALL 22:3
craters passing c., passing fire YEVT 349:6
crazed c. with the spell DE L 89:2
crazy C. like a fox PERE 256:7
c. to fly more missions HELL 152:2
he's football c. MCGR 209:6
Still c. after all SIMO 298:14
two c. people together HART 148:6
create genuinely *c.* Europe MONN 229:4
What I cannot c. FEYN 113:3
created just c. like mistakes EMEC 107:11
creation before you think c.'s FORS 122:19
c. and dissolution AMIS 8:9
I hold C. in my foot HUGH 162:4
world since the C. NIXO 242:9
your niche in c. HALL 144:3
creative Deception is not as c. SAUN 288:7
creator feel at times like the C. BELL 27:9
Of the C. MERW 222:14
creature C. from the Black Lagoon CRON 81:6
credit children to be a c. RUSS 283:1
To c. marvels HEAN 150:11
credulous Man is a c. animal RUSS 283:5
crème c. de la crème SPAR 303:6
Crete people of c. SAKI 285:5
crevasse like a scream from a c. GREE 139:14
crib shadow of the c. BISH 36:6
cricket C.—a game which MANC 214:10
c. as organized loafing TEMP 315:4
C. civilizes people MUGA 234:1
c. test TEBB 314:19

cricket (*cont.*):
c. with their peasants TREV 321:12
everything lost but c. CARD 53:11
play Test c. BRAD 42:10
cried when he c. AUDE 17:2
crime catalogue of human c. CHUR 66:9
C. doesn't pay SAYI 289:9
C. is crime DYSO 98:4
c. rates of the '20s BOAZ 39:3
c. you haven't committed POWE 264:13
Tough on c. BLAI 37:2
UNDULY EMPHASISING C. TELE 316:10
worst c. is WALC 328:16
crimes worst of c. SHAW 295:13
criminal ends I think c. KEYN 179:6
while there is a c. DEBS 87:13
criminals squalid c. REAG 271:13
cringe Australian Cultural C. PHIL 257:13
cultural c. where you have KEAT 176:7
cripples If c., then no matter PAST 255:2
crises age has consisted of c. ATKI 15:11
crisis cannot be a c. next week KISS 184:12
C.? What crisis MISQ 226:3
C.? What Crisis NEWS 240:3
drama out of a c. ADVE 4:30
real c. on your hands THAT 317:2
crisps like eating c. BOY 42:4
critic c. a man who knows TYNA 325:1
c. is a bundle of biases BALL 22:5
function of the c. BELL 27:6
important book, c. assumes WOOL 345:2
in honour of a c. SIBE 298:4
not the c. who counts ROOS 278:13
criticism c.'s motto FORS 122:19
criticized If you are not c. RUMS 281:4
croissants cars and c. DYKE 98:2
Cromwell ruin that C. knocked about BEDF 26:15
cronies money-grabbing c. HAGU 142:10
crook President is a c. NIXO 242:12
crooked c. as corkscrews AUDE 16:15
c. be made straight ELIO 102:7
crooning c. like a bilious pigeon SHAW 296:16
cross first at Cradle and the C. SAYE 288:12
orgasm has replaced the C. MUGG 234:5
There for you to c. PAUL 255:6
crossed Was the cow c. HERB 153:13
crosses Between the c. MCCR 207:7
with c. of fire NERU 239:3
crossroads mankind faces a c. ALLE 6:17
crowd c. will always save COCT 72:13
crowded Across a c. room HAMM 144:14
in a c. theatre MISQ 226:15
crown c. of thorns BEVA 34:7
C., the symbol of permanence JUAN 174:7
neither abdicate the C. JUAN 174:8
never wears the c. HESE 153:14
crucible America is God's C. ZANG 350:3
crucified choose who is to be c. COCT 72:13
crucify God they ought to c. CART 55:3
cruel Such c. glasses HOWE 160:13
cruellest April is the c. month ELIO 104:19
cruelty infliction of c. RUSS 283:3
main sources of c. RUSS 283:6
never really gauged your c. WELC 333:1
crumb c. falls from the tables HUGH 161:9
crumpet thinking man's c. MUIR 234:10
crusade nor is c. KENN 177:4
party is a moral c. WILS 341:3
cry c. all the way to the bank LIBE 199:9
C., the beloved country PATO 255:3
denies you the beer to c. into MARQ 217:12
Don't c. for me Argentina RICE 273:11
Some must c. RHYS 273:5
crystals growing the c. HODG 157:6
Cuban C. Missile Crisis STOC 309:3
cubes sum of two c. RAMA 269:8
Cubism C. has not been understood PICA 258:2
cuckoo c. clock FILM 116:6
rainbow and a c.'s song DAVI 85:2
cuddled c. by a complete stranger ANNE 9:8
culling c. of First Secretaries MORG 231:3
culpable How c. was he HEAN 150:8
culprits better to choose the c. PAGN 252:6
cult c. added to power ANON 12:13
c. of the individual KHRU 180:6
What's a c. ALTM 7:8
cultural Australian C. Cringe PHIL 257:13
c. autonomy GRAY 139:5
c. Chernobyl MNOU 228:11
c. Stalingrad BALL 22:4
in the C. Revolution ANON 12:13
main c. interests HORN 159:13
culture core of a world's c. BOLD 40:1
C. makes life worth ELIO 105:9
c. to be colonised by WELS 334:1
hears the word c. GLEN 136:2
hear the word 'c.' ESHE 108:12
hear the word c. JOHS 172:4
integral part of c. GOUL 138:7
pursue C. in bands WHAR 336:1
What other c. could VIDA 328:2
cultures two c. SNOW 301:12
two great c. LÉVE 198:1
cunning c. plan CATC 59:8
silence, exile, and c. JOYC 173:14
cup prayed my c. might pass KIPL 183:3
curate like a shabby c. AUDE 18:19
curb use the snaffle and the c. CAMP 52:4
cured c. by hanging from a string KING 182:2
c. by more democracy SMIT 300:2
curiosity c. about the future WAUG 331:9
c., freckles, and doubt PARK 253:3
c. of individuals ARTS 14:9

Disinterested c. TREV 321:11
full of 'satiable c. KIPL 184:4
currency debauch the c. KEYN 179:7
curry it's c. JEAN 169:2
curse c. be ended ELIO 102:7
C. the blasted, jelly-boned LAWR 192:15
c. to this country CHUR 67:13
real c. of Eve RHYS 273:6
curtain bloody c. ELIS 105:16
iron c. CHUR 67:14
Iron C. did not reach SOLZ 302:6
curtains keep their c. up DYSO 98:4
cuss don't matter a tinker's c. SHIN 297:13
customer c. is never wrong RITZ 275:3
cut we are going to c. it off POWE 264:15
will not c. my conscience HELL 152:6
cute c. to have the British pound DYSO 98:5
cutting hand is the c. edge BRON 44:6
cyclone South Bend c. RICE 273:10
cyclops view of a paralysed c. HOCK 157:3
cynicism c. about Parliament BOOT 40:11
C. is an unpleasant way HELL 152:5
Cyprus rings black C. FLEC 120:5
Cyril Nice one, C. ADVE 4:15

dabbling d. their fingers MCGR 209:7
dad fuck you up, your mum and d. LARK 189:1
girls in slacks remember D. BETJ 33:3
if the d. is present ORTO 248:15
what I really wanted was a d. JACK 167:3
dada mama of d. FADI 111:3
daddy D., what did you do SAYI 289:10
heart belongs to d. PORT 262:18
think his d. had trouble IVIN 166:7
daffodils d. were for Wordsworth LARK 189:7
daguerrotype stare from d. WARR 330:11
daintily have things d. served BETJ 33:8
dairymaid Queen asked the D. MILN 225:9
damage d. to the earth COUS 78:7
seriously d. your health OFFI 245:13
damaged D. people are dangerous HART 148:2
dame nothin' like a d. HAMM 144:16
damn D. you all to hell FILM 117:15
d. you England OSBO 251:2
don't give a d. FILM 115:9
don't give a d. MITC 228:3
one d. thing over and over MILL 223:12
damnation From sleep and from d. CHES 63:15
damned beautiful and d. FITZ 118:18
brandy of the d. SHAW 295:21
Dan Dangerous D. McGrew SERV 294:4
dance d., dance, little lady COWA 78:8
dancer from the d. YEAT 346:8
d. round in a ring FROS 127:17
d. to the music of time POWE 264:11
Let's face the music and d. BERL 31:3
Lord of the D. CART 55:4
should be able to d. it ZEPH 350:7
too far from the d. POUN 264:3
danced d. with the Prince of Wales FARJ 111:8
dancer d. from the dance YEAT 346:8
dancers d. are all gone ELIO 102:15
dances Slightly bald. Also d. ANON 10:3
truest expression in its d. DE M 89:13
dancing [D.] a perpendicular SHAW 297:3
d. cheek-to-cheek BERL 31:1
D., double-talking CAUS 60:20
d. is to walking WAIN 328:13
like a Mask d. ACHE 1:6
mature women, *d.* FRIE 126:8
Dane-geld paying the D. KIPL 184:1
danger less d. from the wiles NASH 237:9
New Labour, new d. POLI 261:25
dangerous Damaged people are d. HART 148:2
d. to meet it alone WHAR 336:1
more d. than an idea ALAI 5:11
Dante D.'s Inferno BOGA 39:6
dare It wouldn't d. CARR 54:6
Take me if you d. PANK 252:13
dares Who d. wins SAYI 290:16
daring d. starts from within WELT 334:2
dark clean your teeth in the d. JENK 169:6
come out of the d. MANN 216:3
D. as the world of man SITW 299:7
d. for writing LAST 190:11
d. is light enough FRY 128:8
d. night of the soul FITZ 119:6
d. world where gods ROET 276:11
half the world is always d. LE G 195:5
I knew you in the d. OWEN 251:13
In the nightmare of the d. AUDE 17:9
O d. dark dark ELIO 102:16
Out in the d. THOM 319:5
people who live in the d. SHOR 298:1
darker I am the d. brother HUGH 161:7
darkness curse the d. STEV 308:12
d. in ourselves HOPK 159:11
in the d. bind them TOLK 321:2
light in the d. of mere being JUNG 174:11
there is d. everywhere NEHR 238:11
time of d. BREC 43:15
two eternities of d. NABO 236:9
darling call you d. after sex BARN 23:14
d. man, a daarlin' man O'CA 244:7
data some d. was bound to be WATS 331:1
date d. which will live in infamy ROOS 278:6
doubles your chances for a d. ALLE 7:4
last d. slides EWAR 110:6
daughter put your d. on the stage COWA 79:1
to my elder d. THOM 319:3
daughters have three d. RICH 274:9

David D. wrote the Psalms NAYL 238:8
dawn took you away at d. AKHM 5:9
day Action this D. SAYI 289:1
d. the music died MCLE 209:12
d. war broke out CATC 58:9
Doris D. before she was MARX 218:10
Just for one d. BOWI 41:15
long d.'s journey O'NE 246:7
make my d. FILM 115:10
Mars a d. ADVE 4:10
not a second on the d. COOK 76:6
tomorrow is another d. MITC 228:4
write every other d. DOUG 94:3
days Cast your mind on other d. YEAT 348:16
first 1,000 d. KENN 178:6
Ten d. that shook the world REED 272:7
when our d. are done FULL 129:2
dazzled Eyes still d. LIND 200:2
dead been d. 10 or 15 years TRUM 323:8
Better red than d. POLI 261:6
blooming well d. SARO 287:2
cold and pure and very d. LEWI 199:3
d. don't die LAWR 192:17
d. had no speech for ELIO 103:2
d. man's town SPRI 305:2
d. men lost their bones ELIO 105:1
d. writers are remote ELIO 105:12
democracy of the d. CHES 64:11
Either he's d. FILM 115:5
God is d. FROM 126:11
God is not d. ANON 10:11
Harrow the house of the d. AUDE 18:11
he is d., who will not fight GREN 140:13
If the d. talk to you SZAS 312:8
I see d. people FILM 116:7
land of the d. WILD 338:13
left us our Fenian d. PEAR 256:2
more to say when I am d. ROBI 275:9
Not many d. COCK 72:9
only the d. smiled AKHM 5:7
past is the only d. thing THOM 319:2
President Kennedy was d. FORS 123:2
quick, and the d. DEWA 91:4
rather be d. than cool COBA 72:8
remind me of the d. SASS 287:19
saying 'Lord Jones D.' CHES 64:17
simplify me when I'm d. DOUG 93:12
think you are d. or deported HOWE 160:14
thirteen men lay d. HEAN 150:15
walk with the d. FORS 123:1
ways of being d. DAWK 85:9
we are all d. KEYN 179:13
you're ten years d. HAYE 149:12
deaded told you I'd be d. CATC 60:16
deadener Habit is a great d. BECK 26:8
dead-level dread a d. of income TAWN 313:6
deadlock Holy d. HERB 153:11
deadly more d. than the male KIPL 182:15
Dead Sea like a D. fruit MACM 211:3
deal new d. ROOS 277:14
No d. MORG 231:2
square d. afterwards ROOS 278:11
deals D. are my art form TRUM 323:16
dear D. 338171 COWA 79:9
death accused of child d. RICH 274:3
After the first d. THOM 318:11
brooding over d. HILL 155:10
Cake or d. IZZA 166:9
coming up to d. SAUN 288:7
consent to my own d. RODR 276:8
copulation, and d. ELIO 104:15
D. and taxes and childbirth MITC 228:2
d. destroys a man FORS 122:10
D. devours all lovely things MILL 223:10
d. hurtling to and fro HUGH 162:3
D. in Venice MANN 216:1
D. is a master from Germany CELA 61:7
[D. is] nature's way SAYI 289:11
D. is not an event of life WITT 342:10
d. of air ELIO 103:4
D. of a salesman MILL 224:1
d. shall have no dominion THOM 318:4
D. the most convenient time LLOY 201:9
D. the only great emotion FULL 129:6
d.-tick is audible CURZ 83:6
d., who had the soldier DOUG 93:13
D. would summon Everyman HEAN 150:7
died a good d. ACHE 1:7
Even d. is unreliable BECK 26:11
Finality is d. STEP 307:5
go on living even after d. FRAN 124:8
I am become d. OPPE 246:14
If there wasn't d. SMIT 301:8
improved by d. SAKI 285:4
I signed my d. warrant COLL 73:10
isn't sex but d. SONT 302:13
Lead me from d. to life KUMA 186:12
matter of life and d. SHAN 294:13
much possessed by d. ELIO 105:8
No d. in my lifetime HEAN 151:4
no one knew my d. ROET 276:12
nothing but d. UNAM 325:6
reaction to her d. ELIZ 106:4
removes Hazard and d. BOLA 39:12
rendezvous with D. SEEG 293:3
seen birth and d. ELIO 103:18
stars of d. AKHM 5:8
Swarm over, D. BETJ 33:13
Ten years after your d. HUGH 162:9
This is the Black Widow, d. LOWE 204:9
thoughts so crowded with d. GUNN 142:6
up the line to d. SASS 287:17
While there is d. CROS 82:1
Why fear d. LAST 191:8

deaths million d. a statistic STAL 305:10
death sentence d. without a whimper LAWR 192:20
debating D. with him HAGU 142:13
debt deeper in d. TRAV 321:8
National D. SELL 293:10
promise made is a d. unpaid SERV 294:1
debts so we can pay our d. NYER 243:11
decade in the same d. with you ROOS 278:8
Me D. WOLF 344:3
deceiving nearly d. your friends CORN 78:2
December May to D. ANDE 8:10
roses in D. BARR 24:5
decency Have you no sense of d. WELC 333:1
old life of d. LOWE 204:4
deception D. is not as creative SAUN 288:7
decide ministers d. THAT 317:12
decision make a 'realistic d.' MCCA 206:10
monologue is not a d. ATTL 15:14
decisions d. allowed to take PARK 254:7
deck from the bottom of the d. SHAP 294:14
decoded Coward d. for the British LAHR 187:7
deconstructionists D. pulled down WOLF 344:2
decorate painting not made to d. PICA 258:3
decorum Dulce et d. est OWEN 251:9
decrees d. may not change KING 181:2
deduction d. from the smallest EINS 100:15
deed right d. for the wrong ELIO 104:10
deep d. sleep of England ORWE 249:13
defeat d. is an orphan CIAN 69:7
In d.: defiance CHUR 68:12
In d. unbeatable CHUR 68:8
defeated destroyed but not d. HEMI 152:12
even when he is d. KUND 187:3
history to the d. AUDE 18:13
defeats Dewey d. Truman NEWS 240:4
nobility of his later d. TAYL 313:12
defence d. against the atom bomb ANON 9:13
only d. is in offence BALD 21:10
think of the d. of England BALD 21:11
defending d. himself GARC 131:13
means by d. freedom NIEM 242:5
defiance In defeat: d. CHUR 68:12
wilful d. of military SASS 288:6
definite d. maybe GOLD 137:8
definition working d. of hell SHAW 296:14
deformity Art is significant d. FRY 128:13
dehumanizing anecdote d. EPHR 108:7
déjà d. vu all over again BERR 32:7
delay Nothing lost by d. GREE 139:8
delegate When in trouble, d. BORE 41:2
deleted Expletive d. ANON 10:6
delightful it can be d. SHAW 295:6
deliver d. us, good Lord CHES 63:15
demand not a note of d. SCHN 291:5
democracy cured by more d. SMIT 300:2
D. is the theory MENC 221:7
D. is the worst form CHUR 67:15
d. means government ATTL 16:5
D. *not* identical LENI 195:11
d. of the dead CHES 64:11
D. resumed her reign BELL 28:2
D. substitutes election SHAW 296:5
d., tolerance ANNA 9:6
d. unbearable PERE 256:8
d. was renewed DEWA 91:3
five hundred years of d. FILM 116:6
great arsenal of d. ROOS 278:4
justice makes d. possible NIEB 242:2
less d. to save ATKI 15:10
made safe for d. WILS 341:17
no d. can afford BEVE 34:14
no d. in physics ALVA 7:9
not voting that's d. STOP 309:9
pollution of d. WHIT 336:11
Russia an empire or d. BRZE 46:14
Two cheers for D. FORS 122:21
want to understand d. STRU 311:2
democrat Senator, and a D. JOHN 171:5
democratic get on with the d. process BENN 29:9
democratically d. governed HAIL 143:4
Democrats D. and Republicans CLIN 71:11
demolition d. of a man LEVI 198:3
denied Justice d. MILL 223:8
denying they were d. FREE 125:1
dependent d. on other people's ELTO 107:6
depends d. what you mean by CATC 59:12
deported think you are dead or d. HOWE 160:14
deposit greater the d. LAYT 193:5
depression d. when you lose yours TRUM 323:9
deprivation D. is for me LARK 189:7
Derry oak would sprout in D. HEAN 150:15
desert d. is a moving mouth WALC 328:15
d. sighs in the bed AUDE 16:14
my own d. places FROS 127:5
deserve d. to get it MENC 221:7
somehow haven't to d. FROS 127:4
deserves gets what he d. ANON 11:7
desiccated d. calculating machine BEVA 34:10
design masterpiece of d. SMIT 300:4
desirable physically d. MORT 232:12
desire get your heart's d. SHAW 296:3
desired You who d. so much CRAN 80:4
desires d. of the heart AUDE 16:15
desk sleeping under the d. GATE 132:3
subservience to the d. FRAN 124:10
desolation D. in immaculate ROET 276:10
Magnificent d. ALDR 6:4
despair D. is the price GREE 139:10
Do not d. PUDN 267:9

despair (*cont.*):
far side of d. SART 287:12
one path leads to d. ALLE 6:17
sins of d. READ 271:5
Where there is d. THAT 315:13
despise Government I d. KEYN 179:6
destination ultimate d. AWDR 19:10
destined d. to rule BART 24:11
destiny Anatomy is d. FREU 125:7
walking with d. CHUR 68:13
destroy d. the town ANON 11:4
determined to d. himself CUMM 82:10
gods wish to d. CONN 75:6
Whom the mad would d. LEVI 198:6
destroyed d. but not defeated HEMI 152:12
destroyer d. of worlds OPPE 246:14
destruction based on d. BRUC 46:6
mad d. is wrought GAND 131:5
means of total d. SAKH 285:2
to his own d. FRAM 124:3
detached has been slightly d. CAMP 51:13
details God is in the d. ROHE 277:9
mind which reveres d. LEWI 199:5
detective d. novel PRIT 266:11
d. story is about JAME 168:6
detector shock-proof shit d. HEMI 152:15
de Valera Negotiating with d. LLOY 201:12
develop suitable person to d. it DIRA 92:10
developer slipped into d. WILS 340:10
devil *act* like a d. MALC 214:4
believing in the d. KNOX 185:6
blue-eyed d. white man FARD 111:6
D. howling 'Ho' SQUI 305:5
D. knows Latin KNOX 185:7
d.'s walking parody CHES 63:12
Old D. Moon in your eyes HARB 145:13
reference to the d. CHUR 68:15
white man was *created* a d. MALC 214:3
devolution D. Day SALM 285:12
d. takes longer CART 56:7
dialect d. with an army WEIN 332:12
purify the d. ELIO 103:5
diamond d. and safire bracelet LOOS 202:12
d. is forever ADVE 3:12
diamonds d. a girl's best friend ROBI 275:6
to give him d. back GABO 129:10
what beautiful d. WEST 334:16
Diana D., breathless, hunted MOTI 233:7
diaries keep d. to remember O'NE 246:10
diarist To be a good d. NICO 241:8
diary discreet d. CHAN 62:11
keep a d. and some day WEST 334:9
secret d. of Adrian Mole TOWN 321:4
What sort of d. WOOL 345:6
write a d. every day POWE 265:5
write in a d. WARN 330:6
diaspora for the new d. DUNN 96:6
dice God does not play d. EINS 100:4
dictates still d. to us ALLI 7:7
dictation told at d. speed AMIS 8:2
dictator Every d. uses religion BHUT 35:7
dictators D. ride to and fro CHUR 66:6
weed d. may cultivate BEVE 34:14
dictatorship d. impossible PERE 256:8
elective d. HAIL 143:6
establish a d. ORWE 250:7
have a d. TRUM 323:10
inefficiencies of d. GALB 130:10
dictionary ever made the d. WEST 334:17
search for a d. GLEN 136:2
did d. it the hard way EPIT 109:18
I d. it my way ANKA 9:4
die all going to d. BURN 48:9
better to d. on your feet IBAR 164:12
blues will never d. HOOK 160:2
clean place to d. KAVA 176:3
did not wish to d. SHAW 297:6
d. before book is published RUNC 281:7
d. for politicians THOM 320:1
d. for the industrialists FRAN 124:7
d. in my week JOPL 173:2
d. like a true-blue rebel HILL 156:1
Don't d. of ignorance OFFI 245:6
faith is something you d. for BENN 29:5
Hope I d. before TOWN 321:5
I did not d. ANON 10:5
If I should d. ANON 11:1
If I should d. OPEN 247:4
I'll d. young BRUC 46:7
last Jews to d. MEIR 221:2
Let me d. a youngman's death MCGO 209:4
Live and let d. FLEM 120:9
love one another or d. AUDE 18:6
never let my country d. for me KINN 182:7
not afraid to d. ALLE 6:16
Old soldiers never d. FOLE 120:15
only let Him d. STUD 311:5
something he will d. for KING 181:5
taught us how to d. BENN 29:11
these who d. as cattle OWEN 251:6
To d. and know it LOWE 204:9
To d. will be an awfully big BARR 24:2
when to let them d. MCEW 208:12
where myths Go when they d. FENT 112:9
will d. of strangeness MURR 235:16
died D. some, pro patria POUN 263:13
d. to save their country CHES 63:14
He d. that's all MCHA 209:8
If you have d. NERU 239:1
'I never d.,' says he HAYE 149:12
made the books and he d. FAUL 111:12
Mother d. today OPEN 247:2
question why we d. KIPL 182:12
dies kingdom where nobody d. MILL 223:4

man d. in all SOYI 303:3
something in me d. VIDA 328:4
dietary proper d. laws RUSH 281:12
dietetics first law of d. ASIM 15:1
diets feel about d. KERR 179:5
difference d. within the sexes COMP 74:10
has made all the d. FROS 127:16
makes no d. MALL 214:6
What d. does it make GAND 131:5
differences against small d. FREU 125:9
different rich are d. FITZ 118:17
something completely d. CATC 58:2
thought they were d. ELIO 103:18
differently do things d. there OPEN 247:16
one who thinks d. LUXE 205:6
difficult d.; and left untried CHES 64:15
d. takes a little time NANS 237:3
d. we do immediately SAYI 289:12
fascination of what's d. YEAT 347:8
difficulties little local d. MACM 210:15
dig D. for victory OFFI 245:4
expected to d. a trench ADIE 2:6
I could not d. KIPL 182:13
I'll d. with it HEAN 150:10
dignity d. which His Majesty BALD 21:12
individual d. YAMA 346:6
dilly-dally Don't d. on the way COLL 73:9
dime Brother can you spare a d. HARB 145:11
life can change on a d. LAHR 187:8
dinner asking it to d. HALS 144:5
best number for a d. party GULB 142:5
having an old friend for d. FILM 115:15
hungry for d. at eight HART 148:5
went to a Chinese d. FLEM 120:11
dinner-knives with broken d. KIPL 183:4
dinosaurs day of the d. MCAL 205:11
wounded d. BLAC 36:10
diplomacy d. backed up by fairness ANNA 9:5
diplomas d. they can't read GING 134:12
diplomats D. tell lies KRAU 186:4
direct could d. a movie HYTN 164:11
directors way with these d. GOLD 137:6
dirt d. doesn't get any worse CRIS 81:1
master's d. COET 72:14
dirty call d. in our pictures WILD 338:10
d. old town MACC 207:3
give pornography a d. name BARN 23:8
Is sex d. ALLE 6:14
'Jug Jug' to d. ears ELIO 104:22
paid to have d. minds TREV 322:2
You d. rat MISQ 227:6
dirty-mindedness journalistic d. LAWR 192:19
disappointed you have d. us BELL 27:12
disappointing least d. BARU 24:14
disappointment bitter d. HORN 159:12
d. to children POWE 264:10
disaster Triumph and D. KIPL 183:6
disastrous d. and the unpalatable GALB 130:11
discharge d. for loving one MATL 219:2
disciplines by category-d. RYLE 284:2
discontent winter of d. CALL 51:5
Winter of d. NEWS 241:4
discontents Civilization and d. RIVI 275:4
source of all our d. LEAC 193:7
discovered d. the nature of DNA WOLP 344:5
discovery D. consists of seeing SZEN 312:13
invention or d. CARE 54:2
Medicinal d. AYRE 20:1
discreet d. charm FILM 118:5
d. diary CHAN 62:11
discretion D. not the better part STRA 310:6
discriminated men who are d. MEIR 221:3
discussing In d. if it existed GUNN 142:7
discussion government by d. ATTL 16:5
disease biggest d. today TERE 315:7
d. called friendship RENO 272:14
D., Ignorance, Squalor BEVE 35:1
d. in the family TREV 322:3
kind of social d. AMIE 7:12
Life a sexually transmitted d. ANON 11:11
politics is a d. FOTH 123:4
diseases sneezes spread d. OFFI 245:3
disenchantment d. for truth SART 287:8
disestablishment sense of d. KING 181:14
disgruntled if not actually d. WODE 342:14
disguise this identical d. BROO 45:4
dishes who does the d. FREN 125:5
disinterested D. curiosity TREV 321:11
dislike I, too, d. it MOOR 230:7
Disney Mouse over at Disney MAYE 220:7
of Euro D. BALL 22:4
Disneyfication D. of Christianity CUPI 83:1
Disneyland Americans with no D. MAHY 213:2
disorder d. in its geometry DE B 87:5
put back in d. CONN 75:10
there to preserve d. DALE 83:11
dispatch at the D. Box HAGU 142:13
disposable to be d. MILL 224:5
Disraeli D. school of Prime Ministers BLAI 37:7
disregard Atones for later d. FROS 127:15
dissolve d. the people BREC 43:14
distance longest d. between WILL 339:12
distinction make no d. BUSH 49:11
distinguished d. thing JAME 168:4
diver Don't forget the d. CATC 58:11
divided d. by a common language SHAW 297:4
D. by the morning tea MACN 211:13
d. self LAIN 187:9
divine say that D. providence JOHN 171:2
divisions How many d. has *he* got STAL 305:9
divorce grounds for d. DOWD 94:7
DNA cannot cheat on D. WARD 329:11
discovered the nature of D. WOLP 344:5
do as long as they d. what I say THAT 316:13

do (*cont.*):
because we know how to d. them FOX 124:2
Can I d. you now, sir CATC 58:7
d. a girl in ELIO 104:16
d. something about it BURN 48:9
d. those things which KEYN 179:9
d. what had to be done HAVE 148:12
D. what thou wilt CROW 82:3
he'll say d. this TRUM 323:13
Let's d. it LAST 190:13
Let's d. it PORT 262:16
man got to d. STEI 306:14
no-one else will d. FITZ 119:11
way I d. it WEST 335:2
doc cards with a man called D. ALGR 6:6
What's up, D. CATC 60:10
doctors D. in verse THOM 319:10
d. know a hopeless case CUMM 82:9
doctrinal On the d. side QUIN 268:6
doctrine d. something you kill for BENN 29:5
documents d. and friends SPAR 303:5
does D. she or doesn't she ADVE 3:13
dog d. is for life SAYI 289:13
door is what a d. NASH 237:7
drover's d. could lead HAYD 149:11
engine of pollution, the d. SPAR 303:9
hard d. to keep CLIN 71:10
heart to a d. to tear KIPL 183:12
lost d. somewhere ANOU 13:3
man bites a d. BOGA 39:8
nobody knows you're a d. CART 56:8
owning a d. O'RO 248:11
Was there ever d. YEAT 348:13
working like a d. LENN 196:8
your wife and your d. HILL 155:8
doggie How much is that d. MERR 222:8
dogma Any stigma to beat a d. GUED 141:10
dogs D. are Shakespearean SCHW 292:5
d. go on with their doggy life AUDE 17:14
D. look up to us CHUR 69:1
d. of Europe bark AUDE 17:9
go to the d. tonight HERB 153:5
hates d. and babies ROST 279:14
Mad d. and Englishmen COWA 78:14
paparazzi d. of war DENE 89:15
Tom and the other d. EPIT 109:1
doing may not be d. much RUMS 281:4
stop everyone from d. it HERB 153:7
dollar costs only a d. ARDE 13:11
dolls Valley of the d. SUSA 311:12
dolmens d. round my childhood MONT 229:11
dolour d. of pad and paper-weight ROET 276:10
dolphin-torn That d. YEAT 346:11
domes plump with d. THWA 320:10
domestic d. establishment BENN 29:14
domination against white d. MAND 214:11
dominion death shall have no d. THOM 318:4
domino 'falling d.' principle EISE 101:9
don D. John of Austria CHES 64:1
quiet flows the D. SHOL 297:14
Remote and ineffectual D. BELL 27:17
done Been there, d. that SAYI 289:3
decide that nothing can be d. ALLE 6:11
d. very well out of the war BALD 21:8
ever d. for us FILM 117:13
If you want anything d. THAT 315:11
Nothing to be d. BECK 26:1
Something must be d. MISQ 227:2
What is to be d. LENI 195:13
donkeys Lions led by d. SAYI 290:2
don't George—d. do that GREN 140:11
door beating on the d. YEAT 347:10
d. is what a dog NASH 237:7
d. opens and lets the future GREE 139:16
d. we never opened ELIO 102:9
opened the d. DIDD 92:3
through the d. with a gun CHAN 62:6
doormat d. in a world of boots RHYS 273:7
d. or a prostitute WEST 335:7
doors close softly the d. JUST 175:2
no d. or windows MALA 213:16
with both d. open HUGH 161:5
doorstep do this on the d. JUNO 175:1
dorma *Nessun d.* ADAM 1:10
dot pale blue d. SAGA 284:10
double joke with a d. meaning BARK 23:6
Labour's d. whammy POLI 261:23
double-bed peace of the d. CAMP 52:2
doubles d. your chances for a date ALLE 7:4
doublethink D. means the power ORWE 250:6
doubt curiosity, freckles, and d. PARK 253:3
d. and good taste BROD 44:4
Life is d. UNAM 325:6
Dover white cliffs of D. BURT 49:3
down born with D.'s syndrome DE G 88:15
D. and out in Paris ORWE 249:11
d. express in the back WODE 343:2
d. into the darkness MILL 223:5
meet 'em on your way d. MIZN 228:8
downhearted Are we d. KNIG 185:2
Are we d. SAYI 289:2
downhill run by itself except d. SAYI 289:5
drag don't d. wood about SCHW 292:8
dragon d.-green, the luminous FLEC 120:2
d. of the hills SUTT 312:1
O to be a d. MOOR 230:6
drain leave by the first town d. SPOO 304:14
drains comes to unblock your d. GLEN 136:3
drama d. out of a crisis ADVE 4:30
great arena for d. FREE 125:3
draw d. like these children PICA 258:4
drawing room through my d. EDEN 99:2
women in a d. WOOL 345:2
dread Nor d. nor hope attend YEAT 347:4

dreadful d. human beings sitting NORR 243:4
dreadnoughts keep up as two D. LLOY 201:3
dream d. I am dreaming COWA 79:3
d. my dreams away FLAN 119:13
d. that we are dreaming COET 72:15
D. the impossible DARI 84:3
d. things that never were SHAW 295:4
Give birth again To the d. ANGE 8:15
I have a d. KING 181:6
I have a d. KING 181:7
In a d. you are never 80 SEXT 294:10
no longer a d. CLIN 72:1
salesman is got to d. MILL 224:4
till you find your d. HAMM 144:8
dreamed d. I saw Joe Hill HAYE 149:12
d. out in words MURR 235:15
dreamer not a d. FOX 124:1
dreaming d. of a white Christmas BERL 31:8
dreams city of perspiring d. RAPH 270:1
D. are the royal road MISQ 226:4
either d. or swords LOWE 204:2
from uneasy d. OPEN 248:3
interpretation of d. FREU 125:8
scream for help in d. CANE 53:3
dreamt d. I went to Manderley OPEN 247:11
dress automobile changed our d. KEAT 176:9
I like to d. egos VERS 327:7
put on a d. of guilt MCGO 209:2
dressed all d. up BURT 49:2
d. in modern clothing STRA 310:7
dressing remembered for d. well LAMB 187:14
dressmakers Without d. RIDI 274:13
drifted but I d. WEST 334:19
drink d. and drive OFFI 245:5
One more d. PARK 253:20
reason I don't d. ASTO 15:8
your husband I would d. it CHUR 69:2
drinka D. Pinta Milka Day ADVE 3:16
drinks d. as much as you THOM 318:18
dripping electricity was d. THUR 320:6
drive can't d. the car TYNA 325:1
drink and d. OFFI 245:5
D. on, it don't mean nothin' CASH 57:1
driver very good back-seat d. THAT 317:17
driving d. while looking RODD 276:5
droopingly d., but with a hopeful LAWR 191:14
drop d. in the ocean TERE 315:5
one d. of black blood HUGH 161:12
turn on, tune in and d. out LEAR 193:12
drover d.'s dog could lead HAYD 149:11
drowned BETTER D. THAN DUFFERS TELE 316:2
drowning like death by d. FERB 112:11
not waving but d. SMIT 301:3
drug consciousness-expanding d. CLAR 70:5
d. neither moral nor immoral ZAPP 350:5
like a d. MORE 230:10
Words the most powerful d. KIPL 184:8
you can d., with words LOWE 204:2
drugs D. don't cause crime rates BOAZ 39:3
Sex and d. and rock and roll DURY 97:2
so-called soft d. STRA 310:11
drum big bass d. LIND 200:1
still the most effective d. GIRA 135:8
drums beating of war d. KOES 185:13
drunk not d. if you can lie on MART 218:4
not so think as you d. SQUI 305:4
Winston, you're d. CHUR 69:6
drunken d. flame that guides PAZ 255:10
dry d. brain in a dry season ELIO 103:12
into a d. Martini FILM 116:10
old man in a d. month ELIO 103:10
Dubuque for the old lady in D. ROSS 279:9
duchess every D. in London MACD 208:4
married to a d. YOUN 349:11
duck D. and cover OFFI 245:7
just forgot to d. DEMP 89:14
looks like a d. REUT 273:2
ducks d., produce bad parents MORS 232:11
I turn to d. HARV 148:9
duffers BETTER DROWNED THAN D. TELE 316:2
dugs old man with wrinkled d. ELIO 105:6
duke fully-equipped d. LLOY 201:3
dukes drawing room of d. AUDE 18:19
dulce D. et decorum est OWEN 251:9
dull Clean. Christian. D. SHIE 297:11
Heaven would be too d. EPIT 110:5
very d., dreary affair MAUG 219:11
dumb d. son of a bitch TRUM 323:14
So d. he can't JOHN 172:1
takes 40 d. animals SAYI 290:1
dump What a d. FILM 117:12
dung die in their own d. KIPL 183:9
Dunkirk appeals to the D. spirit WILS 341:2
dusk each slow d. OWEN 251:8
dust d. on the nettles THOM 319:6
D. yourself off FIEL 113:10
Excuse My D. EPIT 109:4
fear in a handful of d. ELIO 104:21
dustbin as from a d. GOLD 137:1
d. of history TROT 322:9
duty as much a d. as cooperation GAND 131:8
D. is what FITZ 119:11
Nor law, nor d. YEAT 347:13
sense of d. useful RUSS 282:7
dying achieve it through not d. ALLE 7:5
attend a d. animal YEAT 347:4
dead or d. beast JENK 169:9
D. a very dull, dreary MAUG 219:11
d. breath of Socrates JEAN 169:3
d. breath of Socrates MISQ 226:5
D. is an art PLAT 259:11
d. of the light THOM 318:5
If this is d. LAST 190:7
love to those of the d. LOWR 204:16

dying (*cont.*):
man's d. is more MANN 216:4
nothing new in d. LAST 190:10
Those d. generations YEAT 348:3
dynamite barrel of d. MAYA 220:3

e E = mc^2 EINS 100:2
eagle E. has landed ARMS 14:5
eagles Where e. dare MACL 209:11
ear penetrates the e. with facility BEEC 26:16
earl e. and a knight ATTL 16:3
fourteenth e. HOME 158:10
earlier Here's one I made e. CATC 59:3
early too late or too e. SART 287:13
earned e. on earth THAT 316:11
earrings e. for under £1 RATN 270:3
ears Enemy e. are listening OFFI 245:15
lets the e. lie back IVES 166:5
That man's e. HUGH 161:5
earth call this planet E. CLAR 70:4
damage to the e. COUS 78:7
earned on e. THAT 316:11
e. glow red-hot HAWK 149:8
E., receive an honoured guest AUDE 17:8
E.'s the right place FROS 126:13
feel the e. move HEMI 152:9
he craves the e. SEXT 294:8
pilgrims on this e. RYDE 283:14
Spaceship E. FULL 129:4
surly bonds of e. MAGE 212:8
surly bonds of e. REAG 271:14
earthquake Small e. in Chile COCK 72:9
starts with an e. GOLD 137:11
easier e. job like publishing AYER 19:16
easing e. the Spring REED 272:3
east Britain calls the Far E. MENZ 222:1
face neither E. nor West NKRU 243:2
East End look the E. in the face ELIZ 106:8
Easter E. energy about it HEAN 151:3
E. island statue KEAT 176:5
eastern E. promise ADVE 3:18
easy doesn't make it e. MCEN 208:8
ever said it would be e. MITC 225:14
Life is not meant to be e. FRAS 124:13
Life is not meant to be e. SHAW 295:6
No e. problems EISE 101:11
eat e. at a place called Mom's ALGR 6:6
E. my shorts CATC 58:13
eaten e. by missionaries SPOO 304:13
He has been e. by the bear HOUS 160:3
I have e. the plums WILL 340:3
we've already e. BENN 29:3
eating E. people is wrong FLAN 119:16
Ebenezer Pale E. thought it wrong BELL 28:5
echo e. of a pistol-shot DURR 96:11
waiting for the e. MARQ 217:14
ecology e. and antiwar HUNT 163:5
economic Blithering e. nonsense CLAR 70:9
cold metal of e. theory SCHU 292:3
vital e. interests WEIL 332:11
when I read e. documents HOME 158:9
economical e. with the *actualité* CLAR 69:12
e. with the truth ARMS 14:7
economics E. is the science ROBB 275:5
knew more about e. KEYN 179:14
only the e. MONN 229:5
study of e. SCHU 292:1
economist slaves of defunct e. KEYN 179:12
economists Academic e. JONE 172:8
economy fear of Political E. SELL 293:10
It's the e., stupid POLI 261:19
ecstasy e. of betrayal GENE 132:13
edge at the e. of Being SPEN 304:5
Come to the e. LOGU 202:3
editor e. did it when I was away MURD 235:12
Edna Aunt E. is universal RATT 270:4
educate try to e. people JAGG 167:7
education black kids get an e. POWE 264:16
e. and catastrophe WELL 333:14
e., education, education BLAI 37:4
[E.] has produced TREV 322:1
E. is what survives SKIN 299:14
liberal e. BANK 22:12
poor e. I have received BOTT 41:6
that is e. ROGE 277:1
unplanned e. creates VERW 327:8
effect political e. HAVE 149:1
efficiencies e. of freedom GALB 130:10
efficient have an e. government TRUM 323:10
effort all wasted e. AYER 19:14
redoubling your e. SANT 286:14
effusive don't be too e. ELIZ 106:6
egg e. is a work of art SMIT 300:4
e. on our face BROK 44:5
Go to work on an e. ADVE 3:20
hand that lays the golden e. GOLD 137:6
looks like a poached e. NUFF 243:7
Wall St. lays an e. NEWS 241:1
egghead E. weds hourglass NEWS 240:5
eggs all my e. in one bastard PARK 253:19
Lays e. inside a paper bag ISHE 165:15
ego e. has landed DOBS 93:5
fulfils a man's e. ROOT 279:5
egos I like to dress e. VERS 327:7
eighteen before you reach e. EINS 100:14
eighty dream you are never e. SEXT 294:10
ein *E. Reich, ein Volk* POLI 261:11
Einstein Let E. be SQUI 305:5
elderly e. lady, who mutters away CARE 53:12
elect dissolve the people and e. BREC 43:14
e. the second chamber JAY 169:1
election e. by incompetent many SHAW 296:5

wanted an e. ROOS 277:11
elections e. are won ADAM 1:14
You won the e. SOMO 302:7
elective e. dictatorship HAIL 143:6
Electra Mourning becomes E. O'NE 246:8
electric biggest e. train set WELL 333:7
E. Kool-Aid Acid test WOLF 344:1
tried to mend the E. Light BELL 27:18
electricity e. was dripping THUR 320:6
must use less e. JENK 169:6
electrification power plus e. LENI 195:15
electronic new e. interdependence MCLU 210:6
elegant Most intelligent, very e. BUCK 47:8
so e. So intelligent ELIO 105:2
elementary E., my dear Watson MISQ 226:6
elephant as high as an e.'s eye HAMM 144:11
can say is 'e.' CHAP 62:14
E.'s Child KIPL 184:4
English e. *Never* lies IMLA 165:2
fit the profile of an e. GAMO 131:3
herd of e. pacing DINE 92:8
sleeping with an e. TRUD 323:1
elephants golden e. next SHOR 298:2
shape of identical e. QUIN 268:9
eleven-plus on failing his e. PRES 265:14
elsewhere something that happens e. BENN 30:2
Elvis E. was the greatest LEWI 199:1
embalmer triumph of the e.'s art VIDA 328:6
embarrassment e. and breakfast BARN 23:9
embracing e. knowledge POLA 260:1
emergencies prepared for all e. FORS 122:7
Emily E., hear CRAN 80:4
emotion degree of my aesthetic e. BELL 27:6
escape from e. ELIO 105:13
masses conveying an e. HEPW 153:4
emotional Gluttony an e. escape DE V 90:12
emotions brothel for the e. KOES 185:10
e. were riveted FOOT 121:3
gamut of the e. PARK 253:13
only two e. in a plane WELL 333:9
refusal to admit our e. RATT 270:6
Television strikes at e. DAY 86:2
waste-paper basket of e. WEBB 332:6
world of the e. COLE 73:5
emperor dey makes you E. O'NE 246:5
e. of ice-cream STEV 307:13
E.'s drunken soldiery YEAT 346:10
emperors E. can do nothing BREC 43:7
empire E. strikes back FILM 118:6
e. walking very slowly FITZ 119:4
Greeks in this American e. MACM 210:12
How's the E. LAST 190:5
ideological e. NAIP 237:1
liquidation of British E. CHUR 67:8
lost an e. ACHE 1:8
Russia an e. or democracy BRZE 46:14
way she disposed of an e. HARL 147:10
empires e. of the future CHUR 67:12
empirical *e. scientific system* POPP 260:5
employee In a hierarchy every e. PETE 257:5
employment high e. levels JONE 172:7
emptiness e. The human lack BOLD 40:1
great Australian E. WHIT 336:8
empty Bring on the e. horses CURT 83:5
from an e. chair HESE 154:1
leave a man's hands e. WALC 328:16
enchanted Some e. evening HAMM 144:14
encounters Close e. FILM 118:4
encouraged He e. us EPIT 109:7
end any beginning or any e. POLL 260:3
at the e. of the world DINE 92:8
came to an e. all wars LLOY 201:5
e. cannot justify the means HUXL 163:13
e. is where we start from ELIO 103:7
e. of a thousand years GAIT 130:2
e. of history FUKU 128:18
e. of the beginning CHUR 67:9
e. to beginnings of all wars ROOS 278:9
e. to the old Britain BROW 45:12
evokes the e. of the world BAUD 25:1
have the power to e. it SASS 288:6
In my beginning is my e. ELIO 102:13
In my beginning is my e. OPEN 247:6
not at the e. of the road SULS 311:9
on to the e. of the road LAUD 189:11
Our e. is Life MACN 212:1
there was no e. WHIT 336:7
Waiting for the e. EMPS 108:2
war that will e. war WELL 333:16
where's it all going to e. STOP 310:1
world will e. in fire FROS 127:6
endeavours all my e. are unlucky DOUG 93:11
ended in 1915 the old world e. LAWR 191:13
ending Don't tell the e. TAGL 314:11
way of e. a war ORWE 250:15
endogenous neoclassical e. growth BROW 45:11
ends e. and scarce means ROBB 275:5
It had two e. SOLZ 302:2
similar sounds at their e. LARK 189:8
endure Children's talent to e. ANGE 8:14
props to help him e. FAUL 112:1
endured e. with resignation RUSS 282:7
enemies alone against smiling e. BOWE 41:13
e. of Freedom do not argue INGE 165:3
you are now our e. MUGA 234:2
enemy better class of e. MILL 224:11
e. of good art CONN 75:7
e. to the human race MILL 224:9
I am the e. you killed OWEN 251:13
met the e. CART 56:10
no e. but time YEAT 347:11
quieten your e. by talking CEAU 61:4

enemy (*cont.*):
Sir, no man's e. AUDE 18:10
smitten a sleeping e. YAMA 346:5
sometimes his own worst e. BEVI 35:6
energy important source of e. EINS 100:11
enforceable e. safeguards TRUM 323:5
engine be a Really Useful E. AWDR 19:9
e. of pollution, the dog SPAR 303:9
human e. waits ELIO 105:5
engineers age of the e. HOGB 157:12
e. of human souls STAL 305:8
e. of the soul GORK 138:3
not e. of the soul KENN 178:14
England always be an E. PARK 254:2
bored for E. MUGG 234:6
damn you E. OSBO 251:2
deep sleep of E. ORWE 249:13
E. and America divided SHAW 297:4
E. is a garden KIPL 183:4
E. not the jewelled isle ORWE 249:15
E. one whose centre UPDI 325:10
E.'s native people BURN 48:10
E.'s not a bad country DRAB 94:13
E. will have her neck CHUR 67:7
for ever E. OPEN 247:4
found E. a land of beauty JOAD 170:4
Goodbye, E.'s rose JOHN 170:13
Gott strafe E. FUNK 129:7
History is now and E. ELIO 103:8
lot that make up E. today LAWR 192:15
Speak for E. AMER 7:10
suspended in favour of E. SHAW 295:12
that will be E. gone LARK 188:11
think of the defence of E. BALD 21:11
Wake up, E. GEOR 133:1
we are the people of E. CHES 64:4
world where E. is finished MILL 223:13
You that love E. DAY- 86:7
English baby doesn't understand E. KNOX 185:7
Certain men the E. shot YEAT 347:15
cosh of the E. STRA 310:12
don't hate the E. WELS 334:1
E. book is a blank book PICA 258:2
E. elephant *Never* lies IMLA 165:2
E. know-how COLO 73:13
E. manners more frightening JARR 168:11
E. may not like music BEEC 26:17
E. never smash in a face HALS 144:5
E.-speaking nations THAT 318:2
E. tongue I love WALC 328:14
E. unofficial rose BROO 44:11
E. up with which CHUR 67:16
fragments of the E. scene ORWE 249:16
game which the E. MANC 214:10
great E. blight WAUG 331:5
in the E. language JAME 168:5
make them all learn E. CHUR 68:10
mobilized the E. language MURR 236:2
prefer their E. sloppy SAYE 288:11
raped and speaks E. ANON 9:11
rolling E. road CHES 64:2
You are E. BECK 26:13
Englishman E., even if alone MIKE 223:3
E. to open his mouth SHAW 296:15
No E. is fairly beaten SHAW 296:21
to be an E. NASH 237:8
Englishmen E. never will be slaves SHAW 295:22
Mad dogs and E. COWA 78:14
Englishness all the eternal E. CARD 53:11
Englishwoman E. is so refined SMIT 301:5
Englishwomen E.'s shoes HALS 144:4
enigma mystery inside an e. CHUR 66:7
enjoy e. convalescence SHAW 295:5
enjoyed e. playing tennis IVAN 166:4
e. the last couple of days BECK 26:14
enough e. for everyone's need BUCH 47:5
e. of blood and tears RABI 268:10
e. to go round STEA 306:2
meaning of *e.* AMIS 8:8
Patriotism is not e. CAVE 61:3
two thousand years is e. PIUS 259:5
world's beauty becomes e. MORR 232:5
enterprise leave it to private e. KEYN 179:11
starship E. RODD 276:3
entertain better to e. an idea JARR 168:12
entropy e. of human thought ZAMY 350:1
nor Armageddon, but e. HEWI 154:9
environment humdrum like the e. THAT 317:2
environmental any e. group BRUN 46:8
envy prisoners of e. ILLI 165:1
epigram E.: a wisecrack LEVA 197:14
Impelled to try an e. PARK 253:7
purrs like an e. MARQ 217:13
epitaph e. to be my story FROS 127:10
equal born free and e. ANON 9:10
law has made him e. DARR 84:6
more e. than others ORWE 249:6
talked about e. rights JOHN 171:7
we'll be e. PAST 255:2
Woman is the e. of man LOY 204:17
equality E. for women demands TOYN 321:7
e. in the servants' hall BARR 24:1
neither e. nor freedom FRIE 126:5
not e. or fairness BERL 31:11
equals peace between e. WILS 341:15
Pigs treat us as e. CHUR 69:1
equation e. would halve the sales HAWK 149:4
equations between politics and e. EINS 101:2
fire into the e. HAWK 149:6
have beauty in one's e. DIRA 92:11
eradication e. of conferences MAYA 220:5
erogenous retain our zones e. HARB 145:15

err e. is human SAYI 290:11
error limit to infinite e. BREC 43:5
response to e. GIOV 135:6
errors e. are volitional JOYC 174:2
escape e. from emotion ELIO 105:13
Gluttony an emotional e. DE V 90:12
Eskimo E. forgets his language OKPI 244:16
espionage e. can be recommended WEST 335:5
essential e. ingredient PHIL 257:11
eternity E.'s a terrible thought STOP 310:1
some conception of e. MANC 214:10
who love, time is e. VAN 326:12
etherized patient e. upon a table ELIO 104:2
patient e. upon a table LEWI 198:12
ethical e. dimension COOK 76:7
e. infants BRAD 42:8
ethnological in the e. section EMPS 107:14
Eton during the holidays from E. SITW 299:11
playing-fields of E. ORWE 249:17
étonne *É.-moi* DIAG 91:6
Euclid E. alone has looked MILL 223:7
eunuch Female E. GREE 140:4
prerogative of the e. STOP 309:10
eunuchs seraglio of e. FOOT 121:4
euphemism e. for the fading power BLIS 38:2
euphoric In an e. dream AUDE 18:5
Euphrates bathed in the E. HUGH 161:11
Europe all the nations of E. SALM 285:13
bedrock of E. POWE 264:17
create a nation E. MONN 229:7
dogs of E. bark AUDE 17:9
E. a continent of mongrels FISH 114:5
E. has never existed MONN 229:4
E. in danger of plunging YELT 349:2
E. of nations DE G 88:10
E. the unfinished negative MCCA 206:9
E. will decide DE G 88:8
from mainland E. THAT 318:2
get out of E. BOOK 40:8
going into E. THOM 319:14
going out all over E. GREY 141:1
great stocks of E. YEAT 348:18
keep up with Western E. UPDI 325:9
Leave this E. FANO 111:4
map of E. has been changed CHUR 66:3
take over the whole of E. RIDL 275:1
Without Britain, E. ERHA 108:10
European characteristic of a E. CHAN 62:8
green pastures of the E. VERW 327:8
I'm E. HEWI 154:11
on E. Monetary Union CHIR 65:5
policy of E. integration KOHL 186:2
Europeans second-hand E. HOPE 159:6
Euston in E. waiting-room CORN 77:10
euthanasia that is e. FUEN 128:16
eve E. ate Adam HUGH 162:7
real curse of E. RHYS 273:6
riverrun, past E. and Adam's OPEN 247:17
evening along the road of e. DE L 89:7
E., all CATC 58:15
e.—any evening— LEWI 198:12
five o'clock in an e. BOWE 41:9
Some enchanted e. HAMM 144:14
event not an e. of life WITT 342:10
events E., dear boy MACM 211:5
e. overlapping DURR 96:10
ever have you e. been POLI 261:3
WELL, DID YOU E. PORT 262:19
evermore name liveth for e. EPIT 110:2
every E. day, I am getting better COUÉ 78:4
E. which way but loose FILM 118:7
everybody E. wants to get inta CATC 58:16
everyday crashed against the e. LAST 190:15
e. story of country folk CATC 58:17
everyman Death would summon E. HEAN 150:7
everyone E. burst out singing SASS 288:1
like e. else DE G 88:15
everything against e. KENN 178:17
chips with e. WESK 334:3
E.'s goin' my way HAMM 144:12
e. that is the case WITT 342:8
Life, the Universe and E. ADAM 1:12
robbed a man of *e.* SOLZ 301:14
everywhere children . . . e. CATC 58:21
evidence Extraordinary e. SAGA 284:9
evil banality of e. AREN 14:1
Do e. in return AUDE 18:4
E. visited us yesterday TAYL 314:17
face of 'e.' BURR 48:13
illness identified with e. SONT 302:12
man produces e. GOLD 136:13
means to fight an e. DAWS 85:13
no e. in the atom STEV 308:7
non-cooperation with e. GAND 131:8
What we call e. FORD 121:12
willed no e. STEP 307:8
you agreed to e. RODR 276:7
evils Between two e. WEST 334:15
greatest of e. SHAW 295:13
Two e., monstrous RANS 269:10
evolution e. is more like pushing HEAN 151:3
interested in e. JONE 172:9
exaggeration e. is a truth GIBR 134:8
exam have an e. at II NEIL 238:13
examinations In e., those who do RALE 269:5
examiners Knew more than my e. KEYN 179:14
exception allowing for e. OPEN 247:13
glad to make an e. MARX 218:9
exciting films are too e. BERR 32:13
War the most e. thing DAYA 86:4
exclusion cannot be built on e. ADAM 2:2
e. and prohibition MILL 223:15

excrement in the place of e. YEAT 347:3
excursion made an e. to hell PRIE 266:8
excuse E. My Dust EPIT 109:4
make a good e. SZAS 312:11
excuses e. for our failures FULB 129:1
execute zealous Muslims to e. KHOM 180:4
execution Ceauşescus' e. O'DO 244:11
firing squad at his e. LAST 190:2
public e. FOOT 121:3
executioners respect their e. SART 287:14
shouting at her e. O'DO 244:12
executive e. expression BRIT 44:2
hold the e. to account BOOT 40:11
new powers of the e. DENN 90:5
salary of the chief e. GALB 130:8
exercise E. is the yuppie version EHRE 99:6
exhaust e. the little moment BROO 45:4
exhaustion exhilaration and e. LAHR 187:7
exile silence, e., and cunning JOYC 173:14
exist off-chance that God does e. ELLI 107:3
questioned its right to e. SCHU 292:2
existence e. is but a brief crack NABO 236:9
existential crude e. malpractice FENT 112:8
existing bother of e. HAWK 149:6
exists Everything e. FORS 122:16
exit Such a graceful e. JUNO 175:1
exorcize e. its history MONN 229:6
ex-parrot THIS IS AN E. MONT 230:2
expect E. nothing WALK 329:3
expectations rising e. CLEV 71:6
talents and our e. DE B 87:8
expects Nobody e. MONT 230:3
expediency be sacrificed to e. MAUG 219:4
expedition abandoning the e. DOUG 93:11
expenditure E. rises to meet PARK 254:4
expenses facts are on e. STOP 309:13
expensive how e. it is to be poor BALD 21:3
experience had the e. but missed ELIO 103:1
man of no e. CURZ 83:7
never had much e. MARQ 217:5
refuted by e. POPP 260:5
to be filled in by e. WILS 340:10
we need not e. it FRIS 126:9
experiences e. of our life MANN 216:3
experiment e. needs statistics RUTH 283:11
have them fit e. DIRA 92:11
social and economic e. HOOV 159:1
expert e. in being a minority EWIN 110:11
e. is someone who knows HEIS 151:13
e. knows more and more BUTL 50:1
experts 'e.' make the worst Ministers ATTL 16:6
explain cannot e. to himself CAMP 51:13
e. why it didn't happen CHUR 68:18
Never e. FISH 114:7
Please e. HANS 145:9
explaining forever e. things SAIN 284:12
expletive E. deleted ANON 10:6
explodes line smoulders and e. MAYA 220:3
explorers unlucky e. DOUG 93:11
exploring end of all our e. ELIO 103:6
exposure public e. STON 309:6
express down e. in the back WODE 343:2
expresses music e. itself STRA 310:10
expressing worth e. in music DELI 89:11
exterior this flabby e. LEVA 197:13
exterminate e. a nation SPOC 304:12
Exterminate! E. CATC 58:18
extermination e. of capitalism ZINO 350:11
extinction leads to total e. ALLE 6:17
extraordinary E. claims SAGA 284:9
extreme chooses e. spokesmen SACK 284:5
extremes E. meet MACD 207:10
extremism E. in pursuit JOHN 171:12
e. in the defence GOLD 137:2
exuberance irrational e. GREE 140:1
eye archaeological e. EISE 101:5
Cast a cold e. YEAT 348:17
close one e. DOUG 94:1
e.-catching initiatives BLAI 37:9
e. that can open an oyster WODE 342:17
if you have the e. HOLM 158:6
less in this than meets the e. BANK 22:10
looked into the e. of day YEAT 347:9
My tiny watching e. DE L 89:9
to the e. of God OLIV 245:19
untrusting e. on all they do GELL 132:10
eyeball e. to eyeball RUSK 282:1
eyes bodily hunger in his e. SHAW 295:15
chewing gum for the e. ANON 12:4
close your e. before AYCK 19:11
ever more perfect e. TEIL 315:1
e. as wide as football-pool CAUS 60:21
e. of Caligula MITT 228:7
E. still dazzled LIND 200:2
frightened look in its e. SITW 299:9
good Lord made your e. LEHR 195:6
Looking into his e. PURD 267:12
Smoke gets in your e. HARB 145:10
Stars scribble on our e. CRAN 79:16

Fabians good man fallen among F. LENI 195:14
fabulous It's a f. place MCEN 208:7
face Accustomed to her f. LERN 196:19
f. looks like a weddding-cake AUDE 19:4
f. neither East nor West NKRU 243:2
f. of 'evil' BURR 48:13
has the f. he deserves ORWE 250:16
I am the family f. HARD 146:11
keep your f. CART 55:7
lose its human f. DUBČ 95:4
mask that eats into the f. UPDI 325:14

never forget a f. MARX 218:9
Over the frozen f. CAUS 60:19
stamping on a human f. ORWE 250:8
touched the f. of God MAGE 212:9
unacceptable f. HEAT 151:6
whole life shows in your f. BACA 20:4
faces not having any f. PRIE 266:7
Private f. in public places AUDE 17:17
fact waiting to do away with f. THOM 320:2
factor Falklands F. THAT 317:3
facts accounted for *all* the f. WATS 331:1
f. are lost forever MAIL 213:7
f. are on expenses STOP 309:13
f. are sacred SCOT 292:11
F. do not cease to exist HUXL 164:4
give you all the f. AUDE 18:7
not to deny the f. RYLE 284:1
number of empirical f. EINS 100:15
That's all the f. ELIO 104:15
fade just f. away MACA 206:3
Than to f. away YOUN 349:12
They simply f. away FOLE 120:15
fail F. better BECK 26:9
Others must f. VIDA 328:5
shall not flag or f. CHUR 66:11
failed they f. before POLI 262:9
failure Any f. seems so total QUAN 268:2
different kind of f. ELIO 102:18
effort nor the f. tires EMPS 108:4
f. in life WEST 335:11
f.'s no success at all DYLA 97:12
formula for f. SWOP 312:4
Now we are not a f. VANZ 327:2
political lives end in f. POWE 265:9
success only a delayed f. GREE 139:18
failures f. in love MURD 235:6
fair F. shares for all POLI 261:12
follows that it is F. SWOP 312:3
fairies Do you believe in f. BARR 24:3
f. at the bottom FYLE 129:9
fairness excellence as well as f. ANON 12:12
fairy f. when she's forty HENL 153:1
myth not a f. story RYLE 284:1
faith f. and fire within us HARD 146:13
f. is something you die for BENN 29:5
f. without doubt UNAM 325:6
faithless Human on my f. arm AUDE 17:12
Falklands F. Factor THAT 317:3
F. thing was a fight BORG 41:5
fall Life is a horizontal f. COCT 72:10
Things f. apart YEAT 348:7
fallen Christopher Robin has f. MORT 232:15
good man f. among Fabians LENI 195:14
people who have never f. PAST 254:16
planets had f. on me TRUM 323:3
falling 'f. domino' principle EISE 101:9
f. from stair to stair BAYL 25:3
falls F. the Shadow ELIO 103:15
falsely testifying f. CLIN 72:6
falsifiability *f.* of a system POPP 260:5
fame best f. is a writer's fame LEBO 194:9
defending himself against f. GARC 131:13
F. has a bloody long sell-by date GOSS 138:5
forgery of f. ADAM 2:4
families there are f. THAT 317:9
these old f. HUGH 162:11
family disease in the f. TREV 322:3
f. firm GEOR 133:9
F. history has RUSH 281:12
f.—that dear octopus SMIT 300:5
f. that prays together SAYI 289:15
f., with its narrow privacy LEAC 193:7
f. with the wrong members ORWE 249:15
I am the f. face HARD 146:11
I have a young f. FOWL 123:9
Selling off the f. silver MISQ 226:14
spend more time with f. THAT 317:13
We, your blood f. SPEN 303:12
famine F. sighs like scythe WALC 328:15
famous by that time I was too f. BENC 28:12
f. for fifteen minutes WARH 329:12
F. remarks are very seldom STRU 311:3
When you're first f. LOVE 203:7
world f. RICH 274:12
fan state of the football f. HORN 159:12
fanatic f. a great leader BROU 45:9
fanaticism f. consists in SANT 286:14
fantasies fed the heart on f. YEAT 347:16
fantasy f., like poetry, speaks LE G 195:5
Most modern f. PRAT 265:12
possesses himself of a f. WESK 334:4
fantasyland Web is f. GREE 140:6
far f. side of despair SART 287:12
galaxy f., far away TAGL 314:7
going a bridge too f. BROW 46:4
how f. one can go too far COCT 72:11
much too f. out all my life SMIT 301:3
quarrel in a f. away country CHAM 61:9
Faraday anti-F. machines CORN 77:8
still choose to be F. HUXL 164:8
farce second time as f. BARN 23:12
wine was a f. POWE 264:8
farewell F., my friends LAST 190:3
So f. then CATC 60:4
farm down on the f. LEWI 199:2
farmer F. will never be happy HERB 153:6
farmers inefficient f. LYNN 205:8
farms cellos of the deep f. STEV 308:14
farrow old sow that eats her f. JOYC 173:11
fart can't f. and chew gum JOHN 172:1
farther only much f. away FLEM 120:10
fascinated f. by the darkness HOPK 159:11
fascination f. of what's difficult YEAT 347:8
fascism form of linguistic f. JAME 168:7

fascism (*cont.*):
victims of American F. ROSE 279:8
Fascist Every woman adores a F. PLAT 259:8
fashion F. is more usually OLDF 245:17
in my f. PORT 260:11
never cared for f. BAIL 20:9
fashions fit this year's f. HELL 152:6
fast as f. as the world record COLE 73:3
fasten F. your seat-belts FILM 115:7
faster F. than a speeding bullet ANON 10:8
fat addicted to f. BAKE 21:1
big f. wringer MITC 225:16
Butter merely makes us f. GOER 136:10
F. is a feminist issue ORBA 248:4
f. lady sings SAYI 290:5
f. white woman CORN 77:11
in every f. man CONN 75:9
Life, if you're f. MARG 216:14
outside every f. man AMIS 8:3
thin man inside every f. man ORWE 249:9
fatal most f. complaint of all HILT 156:5
fate Art a revolt against f. MALR 214:9
decide the f. of the world DE G 88:8
from f. to choice SACK 284:4
I feel my f. ROET 276:13
makers of our f. POPP 260:6
father bed fell on my f. THUR 320:5
F. Time and Mother Earth MERR 222:11
f. was a management genius JACK 167:3
f. was self-made ATWO 16:8
I meet my F., my age LOWE 204:8
Lloyd George knew my f. ANON 11:12
my f. and my mother JENN 170:2
than you are as a f. ICE 164:14
fatherland unity of our f. KOHL 186:1
fathers because our f. lied KIPL 182:12
four Our F. DOYL 94:12
fundamental defect of f. RUSS 283:1
My f. can have it THOM 318:17
revolts against its f. MUMF 235:1
Victory has a hundred f. CIAN 69:7
fatigue under the weight of f. CAMU 52:9
fattening illegal, immoral, or f. WOOL 345:12
fault artist is his own f. O'HA 244:15
think it is their f. BROO 45:1
faults f. of his feet BECK 26:2
fava with some f. beans FILM 115:13
favour being in and out of f. FROS 127:1
favourite My second f. organ ALLE 6:15
favourites Sometimes f. don't win FREE 125:3
fawned f. on by rabbits ATWO 16:9
fawns fallow f. invisible THOM 319:5
fear F. and loathing THOM 319:15
F. God. Honour the King KITC 184:16
f. in a handful of dust ELIO 104:21
F. is the main source RUSS 283:6
f. of burglars CANE 53:2
f. of finding something worse BELL 27:11
f. of the Law JOYC 173:7
f. science POLA 260:1
f. those big words JOYC 173:17
f. to negotiate KENN 178:5
f. will turn to love SERO 293:14
first boredom, then f. LARK 188:10
fourth is freedom from f. ROOS 278:5
grief felt so like f. LEWI 198:9
in the direction of our f. BERR 32:11
only thing we have to f. ROOS 277:15
Our deepest f. is not WILL 340:5
without f. the lawless roads MUIR 234:8
feast Paris is a movable f. HEMI 152:11
feather my each f. HUGH 162:4
feather-footed f. through WAUG 331:14
February not Puritanism but F. KRUT 186:9
fed f. the chicken every day RUSS 282:15
fee For a small f. in America SOND 302:8
feed F. the world GELD 132:7
will you still f. me LENN 196:11
feeding Love is mutually f. HEAD 150:1
feel making people f. good CHRÉ 65:8
to *One does f.* KNOX 185:4
feeling Music is f., then STEV 308:1
objectification of f. LANG 188:6
feet better to die on your f. IBAR 164:12
both f. firmly planted ROOS 278:2
careful where he put his f. NICO 241:9
faults of his f. BECK 26:2
fog comes on little cat f. SAND 286:7
hear it through their f. SOUS 303:1
marching, charging f. JAGG 167:11
fell It f. by itself JOHN 171:2
female F. Eunuch GREE 140:4
f. of the species KIPL 182:15
f. principle CLAR 70:1
f. worker is the slave CONN 75:14
no f. Mozart PAGL 252:3
feminine 'f.' principles RODD 276:4
feminism discussions of f. FREN 125:5
feminist call me a f. WEST 335:7
Fat is a f. issue ORBA 248:4
is a f. MUNR 235:4
fen through the plashy f. WAUG 331:14
fence colours to the f. FIEL 113:4
DON'T F. ME IN PORT 262:10
fences Good f. make FROS 127:12
Fenian left us our F. dead PEAR 256:2
Fermanagh dreary steeples of F. CHUR 66:3
fermented drink f. liquids WALT 329:10
ferocious press is f. DIAN 91:13
fertile In such a fix to be so f. NASH 237:4
fertilizer use him as a f. MULL 234:13
few owed by so many to so f. CHUR 67:1
fiction F. is the great virus THOM 320:2
form of continuous f. BEVA 34:12

house of f. JAME 168:1
if she is to write f. WOOL 345:1
Poetry is the supreme f. STEV 307:15
Reality beats f. CONR 76:3
worked into f. WOOL 345:5
fictional My f. project CARE 54:2
fiddle beyond all this f. MOOR 230:7
certainly not a f. MCLE 210:3
fidelity respect f. to colleagues LASK 189:9
stone f. LARK 188:9
field corner of a foreign f. OPEN 247:4
fiend work like a f. THOM 318:16
fifteen always f. years older BARU 24:13
At the age of f. OPEN 247:1
famous for f. minutes WARH 329:12
fifth F. column MOLA 228:12
fifties tranquillized *F.* LOWE 204:7
fifty After f. the clock can't LOWE 204:10
At f., everyone has ORWE 250:16
At f., menopausal STEV 308:15
booze until he's f. FAUL 112:3
until I was nearly f. HEAN 150:11
fight f. and fight again GAIT 130:1
f. for freedom PANK 252:12
f. for its King and Country GRAH 138:9
f. for what I believe CAST 57:5
f. on the beaches CHUR 66:11
f. to the end DIAN 91:12
he is dead, who will not f. GREN 140:13
I f. on THAT 317:15
must f. to the end HAIG 143:2
Never give up the f. MARL 217:2
nor duty bade me f. YEAT 347:13
those who bade me f. EWER 110:8
thought it wrong to f. BELL 28:5
too proud to f. WILS 341:13
when men refuse to f. POLI 262:6
fighter f. not a quitter MAND 215:9
fighting f. for this woman's honour FILM 117:8
In f. to the death DAYA 86:4
not fifty ways of f. MALR 214:7
not f. does matter STEP 307:7
state of affairs worth f. for ORWE 249:12
still f. Blenheim BEVA 34:5
street f. man JAGG 167:12
we keep on f. HEWE 154:7
figure f. a poem makes FROS 128:2
losing her f. or her face CART 55:7
figures f. in words only MURR 235:15
fill O f. me MACN 211:15
trying to f. them CIOR 69:9
films call lusty in foreign f. WILD 338:10
f. the lowest form of art WILD 338:9
seldom go to f. BERR 32:13
filth f. and the fury NEWS 240:6
identical, and so is f. FORS 122:16
final f. solution HEYD 154:12
finality F. is death STEP 307:5
finals This is called F. LODG 201:15
find f. out for yourself FITZ 119:10
Someday I'll f. you COWA 79:3
fine f. romance with no kisses FIEL 113:8
walk a f. line CLIN 72:6
fines paying f. on sorrow MAYA 220:4
finest f. hour CHUR 66:12
finger chills the f. not a bit NASH 238:3
f. lickin' good ADVE 4:1
little f. to become longer SCHO 291:8
Whose f. do you want NEWS 241:3
fingernails paring his f. JOYC 173:13
fingerprints f. across his brain HEND 152:17
fingers cut their own f. EDDI 98:12
dabbling their f. MCGR 209:7
f. do the walking ADVE 4:9
f. of cold are corpse LAWR 192:18
in your yellow f. HEAT 151:9
pulled our f. out PHIL 257:9
finish didn't let me f. BABE 20:3
f. the job CHUR 67:3
Nice guys. F. last DURO 96:9
started so I'll f. CATC 59:15
finished book would have been f. WODE 342:18
f. in the first 100 days KENN 178:6
poem is never f. VALÉ 326:4
where England is f. MILL 223:13
finite knowlege can only be f. POPP 260:10
finned giant f. cars nose forward LOWE 204:5
fire every time She shouted 'F.' BELL 27:14
faith and f. within us HARD 146:13
f. and the rose are one ELIO 103:9
f. into the equations HAWK 149:6
f. in women's bellies CAST 57:6
f. of my loins OPEN 247:12
f. was furry as a bear SITW 299:6
great balls of f. BLAC 37:1
heart is an organ of f. ONDA 246:3
light my f. MORR 232:1
shouting f. MISQ 226:15
tongued with f. ELIO 103:2
world will end in f. FROS 127:6
fires Gorse f. LONG 202:9
Keep the Home-f. burning FORD 121:13
firing faced the f. squad THUR 320:8
firm family f. GEOR 133:9
first culling of F. Secretaries MORG 231:3
done for the f. time CORN 78:1
f. Kinnock in a thousand KINN 182:8
f. line CALV 51:9
f. war of the 21st century BUSH 49:12
is the f. ball BRAD 42:11
men travel f. class GARC 131:12
people who got there f. USTI 325:18
to be called F. Lady ONAS 246:1
fish colder and dumber than a f. MULD 234:11

fish (*cont.*):
f. are having their revenge ELIZ 106:11
F. are jumpin' HEYW 155:2
F. got to swim HAMM 144:7
f. without a bicycle STEI 307:3
no longer f. and chips JEAN 169:2
nose forward like f. LOWE 204:5
No self-respecting f. ROYK 280:11
pretty kettle of f. MARY 218:11
surrounded by f. BEVA 34:3
fishbone monument sticks like f. LOWE 204:6
fishes f. flew and forests walked CHES 63:12
fish-knives Phone for the f. BETJ 33:8
fistful for a f. of coins ZAPA 350:4
fists F. clenched LOGU 202:4
fit isn't f. for humans now BETJ 33:13
only the F. survive SERV 294:3
fitness no test of f. for it SHAW 295:10
five At f. in the afternoon LORC 203:2
bombing begins in f. minutes REAG 271:12
fix don't f. it SAYI 289:19
fixed f. point in a changing age DOYL 94:9
flabby this f. exterior LEVA 197:13
flag f. to which you have pledged BALD 21:6
High as a f. HAMM 144:17
shall not f. or fail CHUR 66:11
flagellation Not f. RATT 270:6
flame Both moth and f. ROET 276:12
F.-capped, and shout SHAW 297:7
tongues of f. are in-folded ELIO 103:9
When a lovely f. dies HARB 145:10
flames amid fierce f. EPIT 109:3
bursting into f. MORR 231:10
F. for a year LAMP 188:4
Flanders In F. fields MCCR 207:7
flappers London wants f. CAMP 52:1
flat Very f., Norfolk COWA 79:6
flattery f. hurts no one STEV 308:4
flavour spearmint lose its f. ROSE 279:6
flaws Psychological f. ANON 12:1
flea literature's performing f. O'CA 244:10
fleas dog that praised his f. YEAT 348:13
educated f. do it PORT 262:16
f. that tease BELL 28:6
fleet whole F.'s lit up WOOD 344:10
flesh F. perishes. I live on HARD 146:11
f. was sacramental ROBI 275:12
world and its shadow, The f. RIDI 274:13
flew and they f. LOGU 202:3
flexible your f. friend ADVE 3:1
float f. like a butterfly ALI 6:8
flooded STREETS F. TELE 316:8
floor lie on the f. without MART 218:4
man has just waxed the f. NASH 238:6
repeat on the Golden F. LAST 191:4
floraisons *mois des f.* ARAG 13:7
flower cracks into furious f. BROO 45:6
drives the f. THOM 318:6
f. of Scotland WILL 340:6
flowers F. are for wrapping NICH 241:6
hundred f. blossom MAO 216:9
Say it with f. ADVE 4:20
Where have all the f. gone SEEG 293:4
flutter F. and bear him up BETJ 33:6
fly show the f. the way out WITT 342:6
try to f. by those nets JOYC 173:10
wouldn't hurt a f. LEAC 193:11
flying like a f. saucer landed DYLA 98:1
foaming f. with much blood POWE 265:3
foe His f. was folly EPIT 109:13
fog f. comes on little cat feet SAND 286:7
F. in Channel CART 56:2
f. that rubs its back ELIO 104:4
fold f., spindle or mutilate SAYI 289:14
Folies-Bergère goes to the F. STOC 309:4
folk all music is f. music ARMS 14:4
in the f. mass choir DOYL 94:11
trouble with a f. song LAMB 187:13
folk-dancing incest and f. ANON 12:15
follies f. a man regrets most ROWL 280:8
folly His foe was f. EPIT 109:13
lovely woman stoops to f. ELIO 105:7
food advertise f. to hungry GALB 130:7
alcohol was a f. WODE 343:4
f. a tragedy POWE 264:8
F. comes first BREC 43:11
give f. to the poor CAMA 51:10
no f. preferences POWE 264:18
problem is f. DONL 93:9
fool As any f. kno WILL 339:1
f. with booze until he's 50 FAUL 112:3
Prove to me that you're no f. RICE 273:12
foolish Beware my f. heart WASH 330:13
more likely to be f. RUSS 282:12
These f. things MARV 218:5
fools flannelled f. at the wicket KIPL 183:8
F.! For I also had my hour CHES 63:13
fools, the fools, the f. PEAR 256:2
perish together as f. KING 181:8
foot foot—f.—sloggin' KIPL 182:11
I hold Creation in my f. HUGH 162:4
silver f. in his mouth RICH 274:5
football Coaching a f. team LINE 200:4
fighting Army f. team RICE 273:10
f. a matter of life SHAN 294:13
F.? the beautiful game PELÉ 256:5
he's f. crazy MCGR 209:6
owe to f. CAMU 52:17
state of the f. fan HORN 159:12
talking about f. BAIL 20:10
footfalls F. echo in the memory ELIO 102:9
footnotes series of f. to Plato WHIT 337:6
forbidden totally f. TYNA 324:13
force combines f. with candour CHUR 69:3

do not respond to f. WHIT 337:7
f. that through the green THOM 318:6
f. with a manoeuvre TROT 322:10
may the f. be with you FILM 116:15
Other nations use 'f.' WAUG 331:15
reduce the use of f. to ORTE 248:13
use of *f.* by one class LENI 195:11
ford F., not a Lincoln FORD 121:7
my friend F. WILL 340:4
Nixon gave us F. ABZU 1:4
foreign call lusty in f. films WILD 338:10
corner of a f. field OPEN 247:4
f. policy COOK 76:7
f. policy: I wage war CLEM 71:1
In this f. land MORR 231:6
into any f. wars ROOS 278:3
journey to a f. land HAGU 142:12
Life is a f. language MORL 231:5
past is a f. country OPEN 247:16
foreigners f. are fiends MITF 228:6
Foreign Secretary attacking the F. BEVA 34:8
F. naked into BEVA 34:9
Foreland Dawn off the F. KIPL 183:10
foreseen What I had not f. SPEN 304:8
forest burning the rain f. STIN 308:17
Cutting through the f. LIND 199:13
In the f. CHES 64:7
To the f. edge DURC 96:7
forests fishes flew and f. walked CHES 63:12
foretell ability to f. CHUR 68:18
foretold who could have f. YEAT 348:10
forever diamond is f. ADVE 3:12
like to live f. LAYT 193:6
you can see f. LERN 197:1
forgery f. of fame ADAM 2:4
forget do not quite f. CHES 64:4
Don't f. the diver CATC 58:11
Don't f. the fruit gums ADVE 3:15
f. there was such a thing WILS 341:18
forgive but do not f. SZAS 312:7
never f. a face MARX 218:9
forgets f. sooner CAMU 52:9
forgetting consist in merely f. MAND 215:3
forgive do not f. those murderers WIES 338:4
F. my little jokes FROS 127:2
f. those who were right MACL 210:5
wise f. but do not forget SZAS 312:7
without hope cannot f. MORR 231:9
woman can f. a man MAUG 219:6
forgiven f. everything SHAW 296:10
forgiveness what f. ELIO 103:11
forgot f. about them AMIE 7:14
just f. to duck DEMP 89:14
forgotten books undeservedly f. AUDE 19:1
F. Army MOUN 233:8
f. man at the bottom ROOS 277:13
learned has been f. SKIN 299:14
things one has f. CANE 53:3
fork pick up mercury with a f. LLOY 201:12
form F. follows function SULL 311:8
formed small, but perfectly f. COOP 77:2
formula 'f.' of the atomic bomb MEDA 220:13
forsaken utterly f. BETT 34:2
forty fairy when she's f. HENL 153:1
Life begins at f. PITK 259:4
Men at f. JUST 175:2
thing about being f. MCCU 207:9
forty-five At f., what next LOWE 204:8
forum on the way to the F. SHEV 297:8
forward nothing to look f. to FROS 127:3
to push things f. MOWL 233:9
fought to have f. well COUB 78:3
foul all f., of course RYDE 283:15
founding f. a bank BREC 43:12
four At the age of f. USTI 326:1
F. legs good ORWE 249:5
f.-year-old child could FILM 117:14
two plus two make f. ORWE 250:4
four-legged f. friend BROO 45:7
fourteenth f. earl HOME 158:10
fox Crazy like a f. PERE 256:7
F. who was my friend READ 271:3
sharp hot stink of f. HUGH 162:8
They've shot our f. BIRC 36:1
foxes second to the f. BERL 31:10
foxholes no atheists in the f. CUMM 82:13
signs on the f. KENN 178:12
fox-hunting prefer f. HAIL 143:3
fracture f. the Labour party KINN 182:9
fragrance Has she f. CAUL 57:11
France F. has lost a battle DE G 88:4
F. in a certain way OPEN 248:2
F. is the coachman DE G 88:17
F. wants you to take part CHIR 65:5
F. will say EINS 100:6
I now speak for F. DE G 88:5
wield the sword of F. DE G 88:6
frankly F., my dear FILM 115:9
fraud not f. or foolishness DAY- 86:8
freaks F. born with their trauma ARBU 13:8
freckles curiosity, f., and doubt PARK 253:3
free as soon write f. verse FROS 128:5
best things in life are f. DE S 90:8
born f. and equal ANON 9:10
but it's f. KRIS 186:8
Comment is f. SCOT 292:11
condemned to be f. SART 287:6
Ev'rything f. in America SOND 302:8
favours f. speech BROU 45:8
f. again SOLZ 301:14
F. at last EPIT 109:5
F. by '93 POLI 261:13
f. man, an American JOHN 171:5
f. society is a society STEV 308:9

free (*cont.*):
F. speech not to be regulated DOUG 94:5
Give a man a f. hand WEST 334:14
I am a f. man MCGO 209:1
I am not f. DEBS 87:13
in chains than to be f. KAFK 175:5
Mother of the F. BENS 30:5
no such thing as a f. lunch SAYI 290:9
not a f. press but a managed RADC 268:12
not only to be f. PANK 252:12
truth makes men f. AGAR 2:10
Universe is a f. lunch GUTH 142:8
Was he f. AUDE 18:15
you are still f. OFFI 245:16
freedom apprenticeship for f. BARA 23:2
conditioned to a f. KENY 179:2
condition for f. FRIE 126:4
efficiencies of f. GALB 130:10
enemies of f. do not argue INGE 165:3
first is f. of speech ROOS 278:5
F. and slavery are mental GAND 131:6
f. for the one who thinks LUXE 205:6
F. is like taking a bath KENN 177:7
F. is not a gift NKRU 243:1
F. is the freedom to say ORWE 250:4
F. of the press SWAF 312:2
F. of the press guaranteed LIEB 199:12
F.'s just another word KRIS 186:8
f. to offend RUSH 281:13
F., what liberties GEOR 133:10
gave my life for f. EWER 110:8
I gave them f. GORB 137:15
means by defending f. NIEM 242:5
neither equality nor f. FRIE 126:5
no easy walk-over to f. NEHR 238:9
peace from f. MALC 214:2
Perfect f. is reserved COLL 73:8
riches and f. WALE 329:1
road toward f. MORR 232:3
there can be no f. LENI 195:12
unless f. is universal HILL 155:7
freedoms four essential human f. ROOS 278:5
freeze f. my humanity MACN 211:15
frei *Arbeit macht f.* ANON 9:12
freight literature goes as f. GARC 131:12
French F. arrange CATH 57:10
F. dinner at nine FLEM 120:11
F. government COLO 73:13
F. went in to protect LYNN 205:8
F. widow in every bedroom HOFF 157:11
F. without tears RATT 270:5
If the F. noblesse TREV 321:12
We are not F. MONT 229:14
Frenchmen Fifty million F. SAYI 289:16
fresh It's tingling f. ADVE 4:4
Freud trouble with F. is that DODD 93:6
Freudian still had her F. papa LOWE 204:4
friend America is our f. MERC 222:7
betraying my f. FORS 122:20
diamonds a girl's best f. ROBI 275:6
four-legged f. BROO 45:7
having an old f. for dinner FILM 115:15
I lose a f. SARG 287:1
lay down his wife for his f. JOYC 174:3
Little F. of all the World KIPL 184:6
Reagan for his best f. WARN 330:5
'Strange f.,' I said OWEN 251:11
than make a f. CURT 83:3
think of him as a f. SMIT 301:6
To find a f. DOUG 94:1
Whenever a f. succeeds VIDA 328:4
wish the author was a f. SALI 285:9
friends best f. are white DURE 96:8
closest f. won't tell you ADVE 3:17
documents and f. SPAR 303:5
f. are necessarily USTI 325:18
f. were not unearthly beautiful RICH 274:4
glory was I had such f. YEAT 347:17
I have lost f. WOOL 345:4
lay down his f. for his life THOR 320:4
little help from my f. LENN 196:12
Money couldn't buy f. MILL 224:11
nearly deceiving your f. CORN 78:2
no absent f. BOWE 41:10
no true f. in politics CLAR 69:11
win f. and influence CARN 54:5
friendship disease called f. RENO 272:14
F. without envy DUNC 95:9
wanted f. MALA 213:15
frighten f. the horses CAMP 52:3
frightened children are f. of me GEOR 133:6
f. look in its eyes SITW 299:9
Why should you be f. WEBB 332:4
frightening never more f. VAN 326:10
fringe form the lunatic f. ROOS 279:4
frog f. remains ROST 279:11
frogs F. eat butterflies STEV 307:14
front for f. runners BUSH 49:10
frontier f. of my Person AUDE 18:2
new f. KENN 178:1
frontiers old f. are gone BALD 21:11
rolled back f. of State THAT 317:10
frost lovely Morning, rich in f. DAVI 85:5
frozen F. anger FREU 125:13
locked and f. AUDE 17:9
fruit like a Dead Sea f. MACM 211:3
trees bear strange f. HOLI 158:2
frustrating imagine how f. it is NOLA 243:3
fuck They f. you up LARK 189:1
word 'f.' is particularly TYNA 324:13
zipless f. JONG 172:11
fudging f. and mudging OWEN 251:3
fugitive f. from th' law CART 56:3
Führer *ein Volk, ein F.* POLI 261:11

fule As any f. kno WILL 339:1
fun Ain't we got f. KAHN 175:6
desire to have all the f. SAYE 288:8
F. is fun but LOOS 202:13
f. to be in the same decade ROOS 278:8
Haute Couture should be f. LACR 187:4
more f. to be with NASH 237:9
most f. you can have DELL 89:12
no reference to f. HERB 153:12
Politics has got to be f. CLAR 69:13
sex was the most f. ALLE 6:12
stop people having f. STRA 310:11
two is f. SAYI 289:6
function Form follows f. SULL 311:8
frightful word [f.] LE C 194:15
fundament frigid on the f. NASH 238:3
funeral heaping up own f. pyre POWE 265:2
funny f. is subversive ORWE 250:13
f. old world FILM 116:8
f. old world THAT 317:16
f. thing happened SHEV 297:8
funny-ha-ha Funny-peculiar or f. HAY 149:10
funny-peculiar F. or funny ha-ha HAY 149:10
fur to make a f. coat SAYI 290:1
furious time cracks into f. flower BROO 45:6
furiously green ideas sleep f. CHOM 65:6
furnish Books do f. a room POWE 264:9
furnished F. and burnish'd BETJ 33:14
furniture don't trip over the f. COWA 79:10
f. on the deck MORT 233:3
rearranges the f. PRAT 265:12
too much of today's f. LAWR 193:1
furry fire was f. as a bear SITW 299:6
further f. away than anywhere RAPH 270:2
f. you got from Britain CALL 51:8
fury filth and the f. NEWS 240:6
fuse line is a f. MAYA 220:3
through the green f. THOM 318:6
future Back to the f. FILM 118:3
bridge to the f. LAWR 192:3
call on past and f. O'NE 246:11
controls the f. ORWE 250:3
curiosity about the f. WAUG 331:9
empires of the f. CHUR 67:12
f. ain't what it used to be BERR 32:5
f. and the past BOLA 39:12
f. can be promised TRUD 322:14
f. not what it was LEVI 198:5
f.'s bright ADVE 3:19
F. shock TOFF 321:1
lets the f. in GREE 139:16
never think of the f. EINS 100:7
once and f. king WHIT 336:9
past, present and f. EINS 101:1
picture of the f. ORWE 250:8
promise of a bright f. AHER 5:3
seen the f. and it works STEF 306:6
walking backward into f. ZHVA 350:8
fuzzy wuzzy f. colony CAIR 50:10
fwowed Tonstant Weader f. up PARK 253:11

gadget g.-filled paradise NIEB 242:3
gadgets worth a thousand g. SCHU 292:4
Gaels great G. of Ireland CHES 63:10
gag tight g. of place HEAN 151:2
Gaia G. a tough bitch MARG 216:15
won't accept G. LOVE 203:11
gaiety only concession to g. THOM 319:8
gaily G. into Ruislip gardens BETJ 33:12
gaining Something may be g. PAIG 252:7
gains no g. without pains STEV 308:6
galaxy g. far, far away TAGL 314:7
Galileo feel like G. LIVI 200:12
G. in two thousand years PIUS 259:5
status of G. merely GOUL 138:6
gallant very g. gentleman EPIT 109:9
gallop G. about doing good SMIT 301:1
Gallup manifesto written by Dr G. BENN 29:4
gamble Life is a g. STOP 310:3
game Anarchism is a g. SHAW 296:12
beautiful g. PELÉ 256:5
best g. I'd ever seen SHAP 294:15
don't like this g. CATC 59:5
g. is about glory BLAN 38:1
how you played the G. RICE 273:8
games G. people play BERN 31:16
gamesmanship practice of g. POTT 263:7
gamut g. of the emotions PARK 253:13
gangsters nations acted like g. KUBR 186:11
gap last g. but one WHIT 336:6
garage to the full g. HOOV 159:3
garbage G. in, garbage out SAYI 289:17
Garbo G. talks TAGL 314:3
garden at the bottom of our g. FYLE 129:9
Back to the g. MITC 227:9
England is a g. KIPL 183:4
g. called Gethsemane KIPL 183:2
gardenias g. in your hair HOLI 158:3
garlands they are g. BENN 29:15
garlic clove of g. round my neck O'BR 244:1
garter knight of the g. ATTL 16:3
gas G. smells awful PARK 253:8
got as far as poison-g. HARD 146:4
when we met the g. KIPL 183:3
gasworks by the g. crofts MACC 207:3
gate Hun is at the g. KIPL 183:1
man at the g. of the year HASK 148:10
gates g. to the glorious FORS 122:4
gauze shoot her through g. BANK 22:13
gay g. man trapped BOY 42:3
reading for g. men STEV 308:15
second best's a g. goodnight YEAT 347:9

gazing g. at each other SAIN 284:13
geese great g. honk northward WARR 330:9
Like g. about the sky AUDE 16:13
gender get My g. right ARNO 14:8
tired of the g. SEXT 294:7
gene selfish g. DAWK 85:11
General Motors good for G. WILS 340:9
generals against the law for g. TRUM 323:14
we're all G. USTI 326:1
generation beat g. KERO 179:3
best minds of my g. GINS 135:2
Every g. revolts MUMF 235:1
g. was stolen FREE 125:1
G. X COUP 78:5
lost g. STEI 306:11
never before has a g. VANE 326:13
generations Those dying g. YEAT 348:3
generosity exercise our g. SART 287:10
genes G. not like blueprints STEW 308:16
true of the g. JONE 172:9
what males do to g. JONE 172:10
genetic g. lottery comes up with PIML 258:10
mechanism for g. material CRIC 80:10
terrible g. defects WATS 331:2
genius g. makes no mistakes JOYC 174:2
g. of Einstein leads PICA 258:7
g. of its scientists EISE 101:7
g. with the IQ VIDA 328:8
talent and g. KENN 178:11
gentle climate is g. MCNE 212:2
Do not go g. THOM 318:5
gentleman g. in Whitehall JAY 168:14
very gallant g. EPIT 109:9
gentlemen G. do not take soup CURZ 83:9
G. go by KIPL 183:13
G. prefer blondes LOOS 202:11
nation of g. MUGA 234:1
gentleness only a willed g. THOM 319:11
genuine place for the g. MOOR 230:7
geography G. is about Maps BENT 30:7
too much g. KING 181:15
geometry disorder in its g. DE B 87:5
George G.—don't do that GREN 140:11
G. the Third Ought never BENT 30:8
Georgia G. on my mind GORR 138:4
red hills of G. KING 181:6
geraniums pot of pink g. MACN 211:11
geriatric years in a g. home AMIS 8:7
German all a G. racket RIDL 275:1
language of poems is G. CELA 61:8
Waiting for the G. verb O'BR 244:5
Germans beastly to the G. COWA 78:9
G. . . . are going to be squeezed GEDD 132:5
G. classify CATH 57:10
G. have historic chance KOHL 186:1
G. went in to cleanse LYNN 205:8
keep the G. down ISMA 166:2
They're G. Don't mention CLEE 70:13
Germany at war with G. CHAM 61:11
Death is a master from G. CELA 61:7
G. calling JOYC 174:6
G. is the horse DE G 88:17
G. will declare EINS 100:6
offering G. too little NEVI 239:8
remaining cities of G. HARR 147:14
germs Kills all known g. ADVE 4:7
Trap the g. OFFI 245:3
gerund Save the g. STOP 309:14
gesture Morality's a g. BOLT 40:4
get G. a life SHAT 295:3
g. what you like SHAW 296:11
g. where I am today without CATC 59:4
What you see is what you g. SAYI 290:14
Gethsemane Garden called G. KIPL 183:2
ghastly G. good taste BETJ 34:1
ghost g. continent EISE 101:6
G. in the Machine RYLE 284:3
g. of Roger Casement YEAT 347:10
I am the g. PLAT 259:9
If the g. cries RAIN 269:4
ghosts g. outnumber us DUNN 96:1
ghoul living on another like a g. HEAD 150:1
giant awaken a sleeping g. FILM 115:16
giants nuclear g. BRAD 42:8
Want one only of five g. BEVE 35:1
gift Freedom is not a g. NKRU 243:1
gifted vividly g. in love DUFF 95:7
young, g. and black HANS 145:7
Young, g. and black IRVI 165:14
gifts buy g. at Jim Gibson's LONG 202:8
gigantic America a g. mistake FREU 125:14
giggles girls got the g. ELIZ 106:12
gin get out the g. REED 272:4
G. was mother's milk SHAW 296:19
Of all the g. joints FILM 117:5
such as g. WALT 329:10
ginless wicked as a g. tonic COPE 77:5
Gipper Win just one for the G. GIPP 135:7
gipsies G. are a litmus test HAVE 149:2
girdle helps you with your g. NASH 237:17
girl can't get no g. reaction JAGG 167:10
danced with a g. FARJ 111:8
diamonds a g.'s best friend ROBI 275:6
do a g. in ELIO 104:16
g. at an impressionable age SPAR 303:7
g. needs good parents TUCK 324:2
g. throwing a ball WOOL 345:3
If you were the only g. GREY 140:15
no g. wants to laugh LOOS 202:13
Poor little rich g. COWA 79:2
pretty g. is like a melody BERL 31:4
girls assumption that g. FRAS 124:12
bombers named for g. JARR 168:10

g. who wear glasses PARK 253:4
It was the g. I liked BAIL 20:9
nude, giant g. SPEN 304:7
process whereby American g. HAMP 145:3
Thank heaven for little g. LERN 197:3
Treaties like g. and roses DE G 88:12
given I would have g. gladly JOHN 171:6
glacier g. knocks in the cupboard AUDE 16:14
glad just g. to see me WEST 334:18
gladly I would have given g. JOHN 171:6
glance O brightening g. YEAT 346:8
glare looked at in merciless g. WILL 339:14
Glasgow G. Empire on a Saturday DODD 93:6
I belong to G. FYFF 129:8
glass baying for broken g. WAUG 331:6
if you break the bloody g. MACN 211:12
liked the Sound of Broken G. BELL 28:1
live in a g. room PEAK 255:13
No g. of ours was raised HEAN 150:13
glasses girls who wear g. PARK 253:4
Such cruel g. HOWE 160:13
glittering g. prizes SMIT 300:6
gloaming Roamin' in the g. LAUD 189:13
global g. thinking LUCE 205:1
image of a g. village MCLU 210:6
globally Think g. SAYI 290:10
globaloney still g. LUCE 205:1
globe-trotting g. Madam YEAT 348:14
glorious Mud! G. mud FLAN 119:15
glory game is about g. BLAN 38:1
g. was I had such friends YEAT 347:17
I go to g. LAST 190:3
Land of Hope and G. BENS 30:5
What price g. ANDE 8:11
gloss gain is g. CUNN 82:14
glove white g. pulpit REAG 271:7
gloves brandy and summer g. JOSE 173:4
through the fields in g. CORN 77:11
glow g. has warmed the world STEV 308:12
gluttony G. an emotional escape DE V 90:12
gnomes g. in Zurich WILS 341:1
go G. ahead, make my day FILM 115:10
g. anywhere I damn well please BEVI 35:3
good cook, as cooks g. SAKI 285:6
G. to jail SAYI 289:18
Here we g. ANON 10:14
I can't g. on BECK 25:11
I g.—I come back CATC 59:7
I have a g. OSBO 250:19
In the name of God, g. AMER 7:11
It's a Rum G. VAUG 327:5
no place to g. BURT 49:2
There you g. again REAG 271:9
to boldly g. RODD 276:3
wherever he wants to g. BRAU 43:1
won't g. quietly DIAN 91:12
you can have another g. QUAN 268:2
goal moving freely, without a g. KLEE 184:19
goals muddied oafs at the g. KIPL 183:8
God as G. loved them GREE 139:11
believe in G. LAST 191:10
bogus g. MACN 211:9
by the hand of G. MARA 216:10
choose a Jewish G. BROW 46:3
don't need any other G. CHAT 63:7
even G. was born too late LOWE 204:13
For G.'s sake, look after LAST 190:4
G. beginning to resemble HUXL 164:9
G. be thanked BROO 44:14
G. bless America BERL 31:2
G. bless the child HOLI 158:1
G. caught his eye MCCO 207:5
g. created life CLIN 72:4
G. does not play dice EINS 100:4
G. does not take sides MITC 225:13
G. gave us memory BARR 24:5
G. has a soft spot TUTU 324:9
G. has been replaced BARA 23:1
G. is a man NICH 241:5
G. is dead FROM 126:11
G. is distant, difficult HILL 155:11
G. is in the details ROHE 277:9
G. is love, but LEE 194:16
G. is not dead ANON 10:11
G. is only another artist PICA 258:6
G. is subtle but not malicious EINS 100:3
G. loves them HUME 163:2
G. must think it exceedingly KNOX 185:5
G. owns heaven SEXT 294:8
G. paints the scenery HART 148:6
G. punish England FUNK 129:7
G. seems to have left KOES 185:12
G. si Love FORS 122:18
G. they ought to crucify CART 55:3
G. this, God that SQUI 305:6
G. to me is a verb FULL 129:3
G. will know the truth EPIT 109:16
G. would give some sign ALLE 7:3
Had G. on his side DYLA 97:18
Honest to G. ROBI 275:11
How odd Of G. EWER 110:9
if G. talks to you SZAS 312:8
industry in the G. business MARC 216:11
In the name of G., go AMER 7:11
into the Hand of G. HASK 148:10
known unto G. EPIT 110:1
like kissing G. BRUC 46:7
might have become a g. RUSS 282:4
next to g. america CUMM 82:5
Not only no G. ALLE 7:2
off-chance that G. does exist ELLI 107:3
only G. can make a tree KILM 180:11
Only G., my dear YEAT 346:9
river Is a strong brown g. ELIO 102:19

God (*cont.*):
saying 'Ta' to G. SPEN 303:14
see G. in the ordinary things EPIT 109:8
Something beautiful for G. MUGG 234:4
something beautiful for g. TERE 315:6
stop believing in G. CHES 64:18
Supreme G. EMPS 107:14
Thanks to G. BUÑU 48:1
to the eye of G. OLIV 245:19
touched the face of G. MAGE 212:9
touch the face of G. REAG 271:14
What G. abandoned HOUS 160:5
women, G. help us SAYE 288:12
would know the mind of G. HAWK 149:7
you are a g. ROST 279:13
godamm Lhude sing G. POUN 263:8
goddess Justice is a blind g. HUGH 161:8
godless decent g. people ELIO 104:14
Godot waiting for G. BECK 26:4
gods clutching their g. ELIO 104:1
dark world where g. ROET 276:11
g. wish to destroy CONN 75:6
Götterdämmerung without the g. MACD 208:2
they first make g. LEVI 198:6
going At the g. down of the sun BINY 35:12
country wears their g. DUNN 96:6
g. gets tough SAYI 290:15
I must be g. SAKI 285:3
puck is g. to be GRET 140:14
to what he was g. HARD 146:14
gold g. filling in a mouthful OSBO 251:1
g. of the day CROS 81:9
judged as g. LESS 197:10
stuffed their mouths with g. BEVA 34:13
Within its net of g. MACN 211:17
golden g. elephants next SHOR 298:2
g. lotus EPIT 109:3
G. Road to Samarkand FLEC 120:4
g. rule is SHAW 296:4
repeat on the G. Floor LAST 191:4
We are g. MITC 227:9
went into a g. land TURN 324:6
your g. hair Margareta CELA 61:5
golf made more Liars than G. ROGE 277:2
thousand lost g. balls ELIO 104:14
gone I'm g. LAST 190:12
gongs Strong g. groaning CHES 64:1
struck regularly like g. COWA 79:8
gong-tormented that g. sea YEAT 346:11
good anything g. to say LONG 202:10
better than the G. Old Days BINC 35:11
For your own g. FRAM 124:3
Gallop about doing g. SMIT 301:1
g. as his parts WIND 342:2
g. becomes indistinguishable DAWS 85:13
g. fences make FROS 127:12
G. girls come in wee bulks LIDD 199:10
'g. old days' a myth ATKI 15:11
g., the bad, and the ugly FILM 118:8
g. time was had by all SMIT 301:7
g. to feel rotten YESE 349:4
g. to listen ADVE 4:2
g. to talk ADVE 4:3
g. unluckily STOP 310:2
g. when it makes sense MCEW 208:11
g. when they do as others do FRAN 124:4
G. women always think BROO 45:1
Great and the G. SAMP 286:1
Greed is g. FILM 115:11
Guinness is g. for you ADVE 3:21
King John was not a g. man MILN 225:8
Lady, be g. GERS 133:12
like a *g.* fiend THOM 318:16
making people fee g. CHRÉ 65:8
Men have never been g. BART 24:8
never had it so g. MACM 210:14
or be thought half as g. WHIT 337:13
policy of the g. neighbour ROOS 277:16
possibility of g. times BRAN 42:12
temptation to be g. BREC 43:3
they were g. men STEP 307:8
very g. day MOOR 230:5
what was g. for our country WILS 340:9
When I'm g. WEST 334:12
would be a g. idea GAND 131:9
goodbye Every time we say g. PORT 262:11
G.!—Good-bye-ee WEST 335:13
g. is really goodbye GANC 131:4
G., moralitee HERB 153:8
G. to all that GRAV 139:2
Without exactly saying it, g. FULL 129:2
goodness G. had nothing to do WEST 334:16
My G., My Guinness ADVE 4:13
goodnight G., children CATC 58:21
John Thomas says g. LAWR 191:14
second best's a gay g. YEAT 347:9
goods when g. are private TAWN 313:7
goodwill In peace: g. CHUR 68:12
goody-goody xsample of a g. WILL 339:2
goose get g. bumps JOHN 170:9
gooseberried g. double bed THOM 318:14
Goose Green on the ground at G. KINN 182:4
Gore Al G. can beat Al Gore NADE 236:12
gore G. is thicker VIDA 328:11
gorse G. fires LONG 202:9
gossip g. and sound bites HURD 163:8
in the g. columns INGH 165:8
got in our case we have not g. REED 272:3
man g. to do STEI 306:14
You've g. approval NESS 239:6
gotcha G. NEWS 240:8
Gothic cars the great G. cathedrals BART 24:10
gotta g. use words when I talk ELIO 104:17

Götterdämmerung G. without the gods MACD 208:2
govern g. in prose CUOM 82:15
g. New South Wales BELL 27:12
government asks you to form a G. ATTL 16:7
at g. expense ARTS 14:9
conspiracy theory of g. INGH 165:7
g. above the law SCAR 290:20
G. and public opinion SHAW 295:22
g. as an adversary BRUN 46:8
g. by discussion ATTL 16:5
G. is big enough FORD 121:9
G. of laws FORD 121:8
G. of the busy SELD 293:6
g. which robs Peter SHAW 295:11
have an efficient g. TRUM 323:10
important thing for G. KEYN 179:9
Labour G. does MORR 231:13
least g. was the best FEIN 112:5
natural party of g. WILS 341:7
no British g. should MACM 211:2
not get all of the g. FRIE 126:7
prepare for g. STEE 306:4
we pretendy g. CONN 75:3
work for a G. I despise KEYN 179:6
working of local g. THAT 317:19
worst form of G. CHUR 67:15
governments G. always want RADC 268:12
g. had better get out EISE 101:10
Never believe g. GELL 132:10
governor *Jimmy Stewart* for g. WARN 330:5
Governor-General save the G. WHIT 337:12
grab all smash and no g. NICO 241:11
grace G. under pressure HEMI 152:14
graces two wonderful g. HUME 163:1
gradual g. day weakening SPEN 304:8
gradualness inevitability of g. WEBB 332:5
grail g. of laughter CRAN 80:1
grain rain is destroying his g. HERB 153:6
grammar destroy every g. school CROS 81:10
don't want to talk g. SHAW 296:17
grand g. to be blooming well dead SARO 287:2
Grand Canyon down the G. MARQ 217:14
grandfathers friends with its g. MUMF 235:1
grandmother We have become a g. THAT 317:11
grant OLD CARY G. FINE TELE 316:6
granted taking things for g. HUXL 164:5
grape G. is my mulatto mother HUGH 162:10
peel me a g. WEST 334:10
grass g. will grow in the streets HOOV 159:4
I am the g. SAND 286:8
grassroots g. revolution BERN 32:1
gratitude give g. FAUL 111:11
g. of women ATWO 16:9
grave from the cradle to the g. CHUR 67:10
into the darkness of the g. MILL 223:5
send you to the g. ORTO 249:3
shovel a g. in the air CELA 61:5
shown Longfellow's g. MOOR 230:9
stand at my g. and cry ANON 10:5
graves g. of little magazines PRES 265:17
look at the g. SAKI 285:7
greasy grey-green, g. Limpopo KIPL 184:5
great All my shows are g. GRAD 138:8
All the world's g. STEI 306:12
G. and the Good SAMP 286:1
g. balls of fire BLAC 37:1
g. life if you don't weaken BUCH 47:2
G. Society JOHN 171:9
g.—the major novelists LEAV 194:3
g. things from the valley CHES 64:8
g. tradition LEAV 194:2
He Was A G. Man ZIEG 350:9
takes a g. owner BRAD 42:5
those who were truly g. SPEN 304:2
Great Britain G. has lost an empire ACHE 1:8
greatest Elvis was the g. LEWI 199:1
I'm not the g. CLAR 69:14
I'm the g. ALI 6:7
greatness g. within them CAMU 52:11
greed G. is all right BOES 39:4
G. is good FILM 115:11
not enough for everyone's g. BUCH 47:5
Greek G. as a treat CHUR 68:10
G. the language they gave me ELYT 107:9
half G., half Latin SCOT 292:12
Greeks G. had a word AKIN 5:10
G. in this American empire MACM 210:12
green Colourless g. ideas CHOM 65:6
drives my g. age THOM 318:6
G. how I love you LORC 203:3
g. shoots of recovery MISQ 226:8
Her g. lap WALK 329:5
How g. was my valley LLEW 201:1
Make it a *g.* peace DARN 84:4
My passport's g. HEAN 150:13
Praise the g. earth BUNT 47:11
Wherever g. is worn YEAT 347:7
greenery In a mountain g. HART 148:6
greenhouse g. gases MARG 216:15
Greenpeace G. had a ring to it HUNT 163:5
greens healing g. ABSE 1:3
grey but black and g. GREE 139:15
little g. cells CHRI 65:10
grey-green g., greasy Limpopo KIPL 184:5
grief g. felt so like fear LEWI 198:9
G. has no wings QUIL 268:5
g. is like a minefield WARN 330:8
Of g. I died ROET 276:12
grievance Scotsman with a g. WODE 342:12
gringo g. in Mexico FUEN 128:16
groans g. of love LOWR 204:16
grope Group G. THOM 319:14

Groucho G. tendency ANON 11:8
ground G. control to Major Tom BOWI 41:16
when I hit the g. SPRI 305:2
grow never g. out of it USTI 326:1
Please help me g. God BLUM 38:3
They shall g. not old BINY 35:12
growing g. the crystals HODG 157:6
problem of g. old MORR 232:6
grown-ups facts about g. JARR 168:13
growth neoclassical endogenous g. BROW 45:11
grumbling rhythmical g. ELIO 105:15
gruntled far from being g. WODE 342:14
guardians good grey g. of art WILB 338:8
guards Brigade of G. MACM 211:4
guerrilla g. wins if he does not KISS 184:11
guest receive an honoured g. AUDE 17:8
guests G. can be delightful ELIZ 106:13
guided g. missiles and misguided KING 181:11
guile squat, and packed with g. BROO 44:12
guillotine blade of the g. PAZ 255:10
guilt assumption of g. CROS 81:12
beggar would recognise g. PARS 254:11
g. of Stalin GORB 137:13
put on a dress of g. MCGO 209:2
guinea g. pigs in laboratory WILL 339:8
Guinness G. is good for you ADVE 3:21
My Goodness, My G. ADVE 4:13
guitar blue g. STEV 307:16
gulag G. archipelago SOLZ 302:1
word 'g.' did not appear WU 346:3
gum can't fart and chew g. JOHN 172:1
gums Don't forget the fruit g. ADVE 3:15
gun g. in your pocket WEST 334:18
Happiness is a warm g. LENN 196:1
no g., but I can spit AUDE 18:2
out of the barrel of a g. MAO 216:7
through the door with a g. CHAN 62:6
gun-boat answer is to send a g. BEVA 34:5
gunfire towards the sound of g. GRIM 141:6
guns G. aren't lawful PARK 253:8
g. not with butter GOEB 136:8
hundred men with g. PUZO 267:14
monstrous anger of the g. OWEN 251:6
not the g. that kill HEST 154:5
rather have butter or g. GOER 136:10
gunslinger Hip young g. ANON 10:15
Gutenberg G. made everybody MCLU 210:11
guts Mrs Thatcher 'showed g.' KINN 182:4
Spill your g. at Wimbledon CONN 75:15
gutter in the g. with that guy EISE 101:8
Journalists belong in g. PRIE 266:3
guys Nice g. Finish last DURO 96:9

habit Growing old a bad h. MAUR 219:12
H. is a great deadener BECK 26:8
h. is hell for those HOLI 158:4
habit-forming Cocaine h. BANK 22:9
haddock hold on sausage and h. WOOL 345:9
Haig ask for H. ADVE 3:14
hail one H. Mary DOYL 94:12
hair And not your yellow h. YEAT 346:9
anything with long h. MASO 219:1
h. blown about PRES 265:16
smoothes her h. ELIO 105:7
half finished in h. the time WODE 342:18
H. dead and half alive BETJ 33:5
Too clever by h. SALI 285:11
half-a-crown help to h. HARD 146:12
Hallelujah H. . . . Never again ALBR 6:1
halo What is a h. FRY 128:10
halt tan with henna hackles, h. STEV 307:11
Hamlet cigar called H. ADVE 3:22
had not written *H.* WOLP 344:5
H. so much paper and ink PRIE 266:6
not Prince H. ELIO 104:7
hamster Freddie Starr ate my h. NEWS 240:7
hand by the h. of God MARA 216:10
children take your h. MCEW 208:13
Give a man a free h. WEST 334:14
h. into the Hand of God HASK 148:10
h. is the cutting edge BRON 44:6
h. not yet contented MERW 222:14
h. that lays the golden egg GOLD 137:6
h. that signed the paper THOM 318:7
Have still the upper h. COWA 79:4
invisible h. in politics FRIE 126:3
kiss the h. that wrote JOYC 174:5
Left h. down a bit CATC 59:18
Put out my h. and touched MAGE 212:9
Took me by the h. TURN 324:6
handbag hitting it with her h. CRIT 81:4
wield a h. HESE 154:1
handclasp h.'s a little stronger CHAP 62:15
Handel tunes of H. SITW 299:10
handful fear in a h. of dust ELIO 104:21
handicap h. her in competition LURI 205:3
handkerchief scent on a pocket h. LLOY 201:8
hands blood on their h. SPEN 303:10
Holding h. at midnight GERS 133:15
handstand H. IN SHOWER TELE 316:9
hang let him h. there EHRL 99:8
will not h. myself today CHES 63:11
hanged if they'd been h. DENN 90:6
hanging cured by h. from a string KING 182:2
postcards of the h. DYLA 97:5
hangman fit for the h. LASK 189:9
happen poetry makes nothing h. AUDE 17:7
what may h. STEI 307:1
happened after they have h. IONE 165:13
funny thing h. SHEV 297:8
happening believe what isn't h. COLE 73:2

happens h. anywhere LARK 188:12
Nothing h., nobody comes BECK 26:5
happiness fatal to true h. RUSS 282:8
H. a cigar ADVE 3:22
h. alone is salutary PROU 267:6
H. is an imaginary SZAS 312:6
H. is a warm gun LENN 196:1
H. is a warm puppy SCHU 291:11
h. makes up in height FROS 127:8
h. was a warm puppy EPHR 108:6
Last Chance Gulch for h. STOP 310:4
lifetime of h. SHAW 295:19
or justice or human h. BERL 31:11
politics of h. HUMP 163:4
right to h. RAYN 270:10
happy ask if they were h. CHAN 62:8
aware that you are h. KRIS 186:7
conspiracy to make you h. UPDI 325:11
H. the hare at morning AUDE 16:16
prevent from being h. ANOU 13:3
remembers the h. things LOVE 203:9
someone may be h. MENC 221:6
This is the h. warrior READ 271:4
Was he h. AUDE 18:15
harbour h., the bridge ANON 10:10
those who h. them BUSH 49:11
hard did it the h. way EPIT 109:18
h. day's night LENN 196:8
h. dog to keep CLIN 71:10
h. man is good to find WEST 335:1
h. rain's a gonna fall DYLA 97:8
To ask the h. question AUDE 18:14
hard-faced h. men who look as if BALD 21:8
hard-sell h. or soft-sell TV push NASH 237:15
hardships h. parcelled within them BOLA 39:11
hardworking quite so h. FIEL 113:6
hare Happy the h. at morning AUDE 16:16
h. sitting up LAWR 192:6
harlot Prerogative of the h. KIPL 184:9
Harlow *t* is silent, as in *H.* ASQU 15:7
harpsichord describing the h. BEEC 26:19
harrow H. the house of the dead AUDE 18:11
Harvard glass flowers at H. MOOR 230:9
hat get ahead, get a h. ADVE 3:26
puttin' on my top h. BERL 31:7
think without his h. BECK 26:6
way you wear your h. GERS 134:1
hate h. a song that has sold BERL 31:9
h. myself in the morning LARD 188:7
how much men h. them GREE 140:3
I h. war ROOS 277:18
letter of h. OSBO 251:2
man you love to h. TAGL 314:9
of love is not h. WIES 338:2
People must learn to h. MAND 215:2
players who h. your guts STEN 307:4
seen much to h. here MILL 223:13
you h. something in him HESS 154:3
hated Make hatred h. FRAN 124:6
never h. a man enough GABO 129:10
hates h. dogs and babies ROST 279:14
hating h., my boy, is an art NASH 238:1
hatless lands h. from the air BETJ 33:7
hatred good rancorous h. WARN 330:7
Great h., little room YEAT 348:2
intellectual h. YEAT 348:1
Make h. hated FRAN 124:6
Regulated h. HARD 146:2
set against the h. MCEW 208:14
What we need is h. GENE 132:11
Haughey H. buried at midnight O'BR 244:1
have with what you h. HANS 145:8
having h. an old friend for dinner FILM 115:15
hawking h. his conscience round BEVI 35:2
Hays Will H. is my shepherd FOWL 123:7
haze Purple h. is in my brain HEND 152:16
he H. would, wouldn't he RICE 273:13
Who h. ROSS 279:10
head dark hole of the h. HUGH 162:8
if S-E-X rears its h. AYCK 19:11
If you can keep your h. KIPL 183:5
Inside your h. HUGH 162:3
Johnny-h.-in-air PUDN 267:9
keep your h. PUDN 267:10
purpose of the h. RIDI 274:13
world in my h. HEWE 154:8
healer compassion of the h.'s art ELIO 102:17
Time not a great h. COMP 74:4
health come with a h. warning HENM 153:2
h. of the whole human race TOYN 321:6
H. Service is safe THAT 317:4
seriously damage your h. OFFI 245:13
toasts to my h. PHIL 257:12
When you have both, it's h. DONL 93:9
hear can't h. what they say SMIT 300:11
Can you h. me, mother CATC 58:8
h. it through their feet SOUS 303:1
H. ye! Hear ye ANON 10:13
prefer not to h. AGAR 2:10
want to h. from your sweater LEBO 194:6
heard h. it's in the stars PORT 262:19
You ain't h. nuttin' yet JOLS 172:5
heart Beware my foolish h. WASH 330:13
bicycle-pump the human h. AMIS 8:4
Bury my h. at Wounded Knee BENÉ 28:16
committed adultery in my h. CART 55:2
ease a h. like a satin gown PARK 253:9
examine my own h. DE V 90:9
fed the h. on fantasies YEAT 347:16
Fourteen h. attacks JOPL 173:2
get your h.'s desire SHAW 296:3
h. and its values BUSH 49:14
h. belongs to Daddy PORT 262:18
h. grows old YEAT 348:10

heart (*cont.*):
h. in the business WATS 331:4
h. is a lonely hunter MCCU 207:8
h. is an organ of fire ONDA 246:3
h. likes a little disorder DE B 87:5
h. *prefers* to move UPDI 325:8
h.'s stalled motor MAYA 220:6
h. to a dog to tear KIPL 183:12
h. was warm and gay HAMM 144:10
h. was with the Oxford men LETT 197:12
left my h. in San Francisco CROS 81:13
make a stone of the h. YEAT 347:6
may not change the h. KING 181:2
memory of the h. CAMU 52:9
rag and bone shop of the h. YEAT 346:12
waters of the h. THOM 318:8
heart-beat just a h. away STEV 308:10
hearthstone squats on the h. QUIL 268:5
heartless h., witless nature HOUS 160:6
restrain the h. KING 181:2
hearts H. wound up with love SPEN 304:6
queen in people's h. DIAN 91:10
heat furnace that gives no h. RAYM 270:9
If you can't stand the h. TRUM 323:15
white h. of technology MISQ 227:4
heather bonnie bloomin' h. LAUD 189:12
cries 'Nothing but h.' MACD 208:1
heaven any better in H. WILL 340:4
God owns h. SEXT 294:8
H. knows I'm miserable MORR 232:9
H. would be too dull EPIT 110:5
Pennies don't fall from h. THAT 316:11
pennies from h. BURK 48:7
people we find in h. TUTU 324:9
thirtieth year to h. THOM 318:9
heaventree h. of stars JOYC 174:4
heavy h. bear who goes with me SCHW 292:6
Sob, h. world AUDE 16:11
Hebrew H. and Arabic mingling RUME 281:1
Hebrides seas colder than the H. FLEC 120:1
Hector H. took off his plume CORN 77:10
hedgehogs belongs to the h. BERL 31:10
throwing h. under me KHRU 180:9
heels like champagne or high h. BENN 30:3
heigh-ho H., heigh-ho MORE 230:11
height Happiness makes up in h. FROS 127:8
someone that h. look regal AMIE 7:13
Heinz Beanz meanz H. ADVE 3:7
Helen H.'s face in hell PARK 253:6
hell Damn you all to h. FILM 117:15
do science in h. VAUG 327:3
h. for those you love HOLI 158:4
H. full of musical amateurs SHAW 295:21
H. is oneself ELIO 102:5
H. is other people SART 287:7
If Hitler invaded h. CHUR 68:15
I say the h. with it CART 56:5
made an excursion to h. PRIE 266:8
my idea of h. BAIL 20:10
not be H. if you are there EPIT 110:5
probably redesigned H. PRIC 266:2
they think it is h. TRUM 323:7
walked eye-deep in h. POUN 263:13
War is h., and all that HAY 149:9
why they invented H. RUSS 283:3
working definition of h. SHAW 296:14
would be h. on earth SHAW 295:19
hellhound h. always a hellhound WODE 342:15
hello H., good evening CATC 59:1
help any h. in help MURR 235:14
do something to h. me LAUR 189:15
h. and support of the woman EDWA 99:4
little h. from my friends LENN 196:12
look on and h. LAWR 192:17
present h. in trouble ANON 9:9
scream for h. in dreams CANE 53:3
you can't h. it SMIT 300:7
helper mother's little h. JAGG 167:9
helpless as h. as everybody else MAND 215:10
hen better take a wet h. KHRU 180:8
henna tan with h. hackles STEV 307:11
herald h. angels sing ANON 10:12
herbs intolerance to h. WALT 329:10
here H.'s looking at you FILM 115:12
H. we go ANON 10:14
If we can't stay h. alive MONT 229:12
I'm still h. HOPE 159:9
Kilroy was h. ANON 11:9
only h. for the beer ADVE 3:28
heretic oppressor or a h. CAMU 52:15
heretics H. are the only remedy ZAMY 350:1
hero Show me a h. FITZ 119:8
Herod for an hour of H. HOPE 159:7
H. is his name CAUS 60:20
heroes Canadians do not like h. WOOD 344:9
fit country for h. LLOY 201:6
land that needs h. BREC 43:4
speed glum h. SASS 287:17
We can be h. BOWI 41:15
heroing H. is one of the shortest ROGE 277:4
herring shoals of h. MACC 207:4
hick Sticks nix h. pix NEWS 240:18
hidden h. persuaders PACK 251:15
hide he can't h. LOUI 203:6
nothing to h. CHUR 69:4
wise man h. a pebble CHES 64:7
hiding they got a bloody good h. GRAN 138:10
high corn is as h. HAMM 144:11
get h. with a little help LENN 196:12
Pile it h. SAYI 290:6
taking the h. ground MAND 215:8
highest to the h. office MCCA 206:6
high-tech thing with h. HOCK 157:5
high-water h. mark of my youth THUR 320:5

highway each and ev'ry h. ANKA 9:4
hilarity h. like a scream GREE 139:14
hill all gone under the h. ELIO 102:15
light on the h. CHIF 65:2
over the top of the h. SHAP 295:1
hills convictions are h. FITZ 119:1
h. are alive HAMM 144:15
red h. of Georgia KING 181:6
hindsight H. is always twenty-twenty WILD 338:11
hinterland She has no h. HEAL 150:5
hip have a h. replacement CLEE 70:12
H. is the sophistication MAIL 213:6
H. young gunslinger ANON 10:15
hippies h. wanted peace COOP 77:1
hips armchairs tight about the h. WODE 343:5
Or Mae West's h. EWAR 110:7
when your h. stick NASH 237:17
hipsters angelheaded h. burning GINS 135:2
hired They h. the money COOL 76:13
Hiroshima After H. BOLD 40:3
bomb on H. TRUM 323:4
Einstein leads to H. PICA 258:7
historians h. left blanks POUN 263:11
history cancer of human h. SONT 302:14
Does h. repeat itself BARN 23:12
dustbin of h. TROT 322:9
end of h. FUKU 128:18
exorcize its h. MONN 229:6
Family h. has RUSH 281:12
from the lessons of h. HUXL 163:11
h. came to a . SELL 293:12
H. gets thicker TAYL 313:9
H. is a nightmare JOYC 174:1
H. is not what you thought SELL 293:8
h. is now and England ELIO 103:8
h. is on our side KHRU 180:7
H. littered with the wars POWE 265:1
h.-making creature AUDE 18:18
H. more or less bunk FORD 121:11
H. teaches us that men EBAN 98:6
h. to the defeated AUDE 18:13
h. will record MORS 232:10
hope and h. rhyme HEAN 150:9
Human h. becomes more WELL 333:14
more h. than they can consume SAKI 285:5
more of their own h. HUGH 162:1
name is h. THWA 320:10
No h. much DURR 96:11
no h. of mankind POPP 260:8
not learning from h. BLAI 37:3
rattling good h. HARD 147:3
reverberates through h. KOES 185:13
teaching of h. MOLT 228:13
thousand years of h. GAIT 130:2
too much h. KING 181:15
writing h. with lightning WILS 341:11
hit H. the road, Jack MAYF 220:8
Hitler H.'s level of accuracy TAYL 313:11
H. was mad LIVI 200:13
If H. invaded hell CHUR 68:15
If I can't love H. MUST 236:5
kidding, Mister H. PERR 257:1
like kissing H. CURT 83:4
thank heaven for Adolf H. BUCH 47:6
hitting h. it with her handbag CRIT 81:4
hoarder h. of two things SPAR 303:5
hobbit there lived a h. OPEN 247:5
hock weak h. and seltzer BETJ 33:2
hog Not the whole h. MILL 224:10
hogs Men eat h. STEV 307:14
hold love them, and h. on DUNN 96:3
hole dark h. of the head HUGH 162:8
first h. made through MOOR 230:4
if you knows of a better h. CART 56:12
In a h. in the ground OPEN 247:5
making a h. in a sock EINS 101:4
mint with the h. ADVE 4:12
holiday perpetual h. SHAW 296:14
to take a h. RUSS 282:5
holidays during the h. from Eton SITW 299:11
hollow We are the h. men ELIO 103:13
Hollywood H. money isn't money PARK 253:18
not have been invited to H. CHAN 62:4
play H. lookalikes SMIT 300:9
holocaust Somme is like the H. BARK 23:5
holy H. deadlock HERB 153:11
h.-water death MCGO 209:4
home all the comforts of h. BRYS 46:13
can't go h. again WOLF 343:14
children who leave h. SLOV 300:1
E.T. phone h. FILM 115:6
get all that at h. BENN 29:12
H. is the place where FROS 127:4
H. is where you come to THAT 317:18
H. James HILL 156:4
house is not a h. ADLE 2:8
I tank I go h. GARB 131:11
Keep the H.-fires burning FORD 121:13
look as much like h. FRY 128:12
no place like h. LANC 188:5
White House or h. DOLE 93:7
years in a geriatric h. AMIS 8:7
Homer had the voice of H. HALD 143:10
house on H.'s shores ELYT 107:9
homes In h., a haunted apparatus RAIN 269:4
Stately H. of England COWA 79:4
homing flock of h. pigeons HUGH 162:14
homosexual composer and *not* h. DIAG 91:7
homosexuality If h. were normal BRYA 46:11
honest buy it like an h. man NORT 243:6
h. and intelligent ORWE 250:14
H. to God ROBI 275:11
Keep the bastards h. POLI 261:20

honey bee produces h. GOLD 136:13
h. still for tea BROO 44:13
h. to smear his face SCHW 292:6
Hong Kong H.'s return to China DENG 90:2
honour Fear God. H. the King KITC 184:16
for this woman's h. FILM 117:8
great peaks of h. LLOY 201:4
h. almost greater than YOUN 349:11
H. is like a match PAGN 252:5
peace with h. CHAM 61:10
signed with their h. SPEN 304:3
we h. it SHIE 297:12
years and h. to the grave KIPL 183:9
honours good card to play for H. BENN 30:4
hoover onto the board of H. GREE 140:5
hope culture without h. MORR 231:9
h. and history rhyme HEAN 150:9
H. is definitely not HAVE 148:11
in the store we sell h. REVS 273:3
Land of H. and Glory BENS 30:5
may we bring h. THAT 315:13
Nor dread nor h. attend YEAT 347:4
Some blessed H. HARD 146:9
there is h. CROS 82:1
two thousand years of h. WEIZ 332:14
hopeful with a h. heart LAWR 191:14
hopefulness Lord of all h. STRU 311:4
hopeless doctors know a h. case CUMM 82:9
hopes h. of its children EISE 101:7
horizon just beyond the h. KISS 184:15
horizontal h. desire SHAW 297:3
Life is a h. fall COCT 72:10
horn won't come out of your h. PARK 253:1
horns memories are hunting h. APOL 13:4
horribilis annus h. ELIZ 106:3
horror h. of sunsets PROU 267:2
h.! The horror CONR 76:1
horse feeds the h. enough oats GALB 130:9
h. designed by a committee ISSI 166:3
never heard no h. sing ARMS 14:4
sick h. nosing around KAVA 176:3
sounds like a saddle h. ONAS 246:1
torturer's h. scratches AUDE 17:14
where's the bloody h. CAMP 52:4
Horseguards be in the H. RATT 270:7
horseman H., pass by YEAT 348:17
horsemen Four H. rode again RICE 273:10
horses Bring on the empty h. CURT 83:5
don't spare the h. HILL 156:4
frighten the h. CAMP 52:3
if you cannot ride two h. MAXT 219:13
I saw the h. HUGH 162:6
They shoot h. don't they MCCO 207:6
horseshoe h. over his door BOHR 39:9
horticulture lead a h. PARK 254:1
hose out of the turret with a h. JARR 168:8
hospitality shrink from acts of h. SHIE 297:10
host I'd have been under the h. PARK 253:20
hostile universe is not h. HOLM 158:5
hot long h. summer FILM 118:9
On a h., hot day LAWR 192:11
only in h. water REAG 271:6
hounds by your own quick h. MOTI 233:7
hour finest h. CHUR 66:12
for an h. of Herod HOPE 159:7
I also had my h. CHES 63:13
its h. come round at last YEAT 348:8
matched us with His h. BROO 44:14
hourglass Egghead weds h. NEWS 240:5
hours better wages and shorter h. ORWE 250:10
see the h. pass CIOR 69:9
house Harrow the h. of the dead AUDE 18:11
h. a machine for living in LE C 194:14
H. Beautiful is play lousy PARK 253:12
h. is not a home ADLE 2:8
in 'The H. at Pooh Corner' PARK 253:11
man in the h. is worth WEST 334:8
This H. today is a theatre BALD 21:12
threshold of a new h. ATWO 16:10
With usura hath no man a h. POUN 263:9
houseful three is a h. SAYI 289:6
householder think she's a h. WILD 338:14
housekeeper make a h. think WILD 338:14
housekeeping good h. to the winds KEYN 180:2
houses h. are all gone ELIO 102:15
spaces between the h. FENT 112:7
housework H. expands to fill CONR 76:5
h., with its repetition DE B 87:4
no need to do any h. CRIS 81:1
Houston H., we've had a problem LOVE 203:10
how H. do they know PARK 253:17
howitzer h. squatting GRIG 141:5
howls going to be h. of anguish HEAL 150:2
Howth H. Castle and Environs OPEN 247:17
huff leave in a h. FILM 116:1
hullo H. Clouds Hullo Sky WILL 339:2
human all h. life is there ADVE 3:3
dreadful h. beings sitting NORR 243:4
emptiness. The h. lack BOLD 40:1
health of the whole h. race TOYN 321:6
h. beings are more alike ANGE 9:3
H. kind Cannot bear ELIO 102:10
h. nature changed WOOL 344:13
H. nature not black and white GREE 139:15
h. rose to haunt us RICH 274:4
h., they suffered WARR 330:11
h. zoo MORR 231:7
lose its h. face DUBČ 95:4
love h. beings GREE 139:11
not made on a h. scale MALR 214:8
people are only h. COMP 74:5
robot may not injure a h. ASIM 14:10
To err is h. SAYI 290:11

ultimate h. mystery MILL 224:6
wish I loved the H. Race RALE 269:6
humanity belief in h. YAMA 346:6
first condition of h. SOYI 303:4
freeze my h. MACN 211:15
H. a work in progress WILL 339:8
Oh, the h. MORR 231:10
humankind answers h. invented PAZ 255:11
human rights tolerance and h. ANNA 9:6
humans isn't fit for h. now BETJ 33:13
Humean H. predicament QUIN 268:6
humiliating without h. them FITZ 119:12
humiliation Art is born of h. AUDE 19:2
called shame and h. O'RO 248:8
humming hear the virus h. DOTY 93:10
hummy at that word 'h.' PARK 253:11
humour h. for humour NEIL 238:13
H. is emotional chaos THUR 320:9
my h. is based BRUC 46:6
They have no sense of h. LEAR 193:14
Hun H. is at the gate KIPL 183:1
hundred h. flowers blossom MAO 216:9
hundredth your h. birthday TELE 316:7
hunger bodily h. in his eyes SHAW 295:15
H. allows no choice AUDE 18:6
h. is not only in STEI 306:16
h. to be beautiful RHYS 273:6
hungry advertise food to h. GALB 130:7
got to be kept h. DIMA 92:6
hunter heart is a lonely h. MCCU 207:8
H.'s waking thoughts AUDE 16:16
Hunter Dunn Miss J. H. BETJ 33:14
hunters see the first h. PURD 267:12
hurdles don't really see the h. MOSE 233:4
hurricane h. on the way FISH 114:3
hurry H. up please it's time ELIO 105:3
hurt I'm in the h. business TYSO 325:4
never h. a hair STUD 311:5
never h. anybody ELTO 107:7
no one was to be h. BROO 45:2
wish to h. BRON 44:8
Yes it h. POLI 262:8
hurting If the policy isn't h. MAJO 213:9
once it has stopped h. BOWE 41:11
people h. people MAIL 213:4
hurtling death h. to and fro HUGH 162:3
husband Bigamy is one h. too many ANON 10:1
h. what is left of a lover ROWL 280:7
left her h. because MURD 235:5
My h. and I ELIZ 106:2
husbands Chumps make the best h. WODE 342:11
how many h. she had had GABO 129:12
hush H.! Hush! Whisper who dares MILN 225:11
hyacinths h. and biscuits SAND 286:11
hydrogen telescope or h. bomb LOVE 203:8
hyphenated h. Americanism ROOS 279:1
hypochondria h. has always seemed DIAM 91:8
hypocrisy world safe for h. WOLF 343:13
hypothermia dying of h. BENN 29:10
hypotheses smallest number of h. EINS 100:15
hypothesis discard a pet h. LORE 203:5

I I am a camera ISHE 166:1
I plus my surroundings ORTE 248:12
My husband and I ELIZ 106:2
IBM for buying I. ADVE 4:16
ice after the last i. age PURD 267:12
I. formed on the butler WODE 343:6
It's fresh as i. ADVE 4:4
piece of i. on a hot stove FROS 128:3
Some say in i. FROS 127:6
Vulgarity often cuts i. BEER 26:21
iceberg grew the I. too HARD 146:7
i., you know DEAN 87:1
ill-concealed i. LAWS 193:3
icebox plums that were in the i. WILL 340:3
ice-cream emperor of i. STEV 307:13
i. out of the container BRYS 46:12
iceman i. cometh O'NE 246:6
id PUT THE I. BACK IN YID ROTH 280:1
idea better to entertain an i. JARR 168:12
does get an i. MARQ 217:10
good i. but it won't work ROGE 277:5
good i.—son CATC 58:19
i. And the reality ELIO 103:15
i. of death saves him FORS 122:10
i. whose time has come SAYI 290:8
more dangerous than an i. ALAI 5:11
no grand i. was ever born FITZ 119:7
originator of a new i. DIRA 92:10
responsibility for that i. BIRT 36:3
to whom the i. first occurs DARW 84:8
would be a good i. GAND 131:9
ideal i. for which I am prepared MAND 214:11
i. reader suffering from JOYC 173:6
idealism morphine or i. JUNG 174:12
ideals i. of a nation DOUG 94:2
shoes with broken high i. MCGO 209:2
ideas Colourless green i. CHOM 65:6
From it our i. are born GENE 132:11
genuine i., Bright Ideas BENT 30:10
hold two opposed i. FITZ 119:5
identical they exist, but are i. FORS 122:16
identify I can i. with her MADO 212:7
idle he would be i. CRAN 79:15
if I. you can keep your head KIPL 183:5
ignorance Disease, I., Squalor BEVE 35:1
Don't die of i. OFFI 245:6

ignorance (*cont.*):
evil is simply i. FORD 121:12
I. is an evil weed BEVE 34:14
i. is never better FERM 112:13
i. necessarily infinite POPP 260:10
i. so abysmal MEDA 220:13
sincere i. KING 181:10
ignorant Asking the i. ZOBE 351:1
become an i. man again STEV 307:17
many i. men are sure DARR 84:5
ignore nothing to i. NASH 237:16
ignored because they are i. HUXL 164:4
ignores poetry i. most people MITC 225:12
Ike I like I. POLI 261:15
Poor I. TRUM 323:13
I'll I. be back FILM 116:3
ill i.-trained spaniel CRAN 79:13
warn you not to fall i. KINN 182:5
illegal i., immoral, or fattening WOOL 345:12
means that it is not i. NIXO 242:14
Nothing is i. if YOUN 349:10
illegitimate no i. children GLAD 135:12
ill-housed nation i., ill-clad ROOS 278:1
illness i. identified with evil SONT 302:12
i. the night-side of life SONT 302:16
makes i. worthwhile SHAW 295:5
man's illness BACA 20:5
ill-nourished ill-clad, i. ROOS 278:1
ills i. of democracy SMIT 300:2
illuminated i. trouser-clip MORT 233:1
illusion only an i. EINS 101:1
image just an i. GODA 136:5
live without any i. MURD 235:7
imagery for their i. MCEW 208:9
images Fresh i. beget YEAT 346:11
i. change as they repeat WARH 330:2
i. of life BERG 30:12
I. split the truth LEVE 197:16
unpurged i. of day YEAT 346:10
imagination i. sleeps CAMU 52:16
literalists of the i. MOOR 230:8
suspend the i. HEMI 152:10
takes a lot of i. BAIL 20:8
Television contracts i. WOGA 343:8
those that have no i. SHAW 296:22
imitate i. each other HOFF 157:9
Immature poets i. ELIO 105:11
never failed to i. them BALD 21:2
imitation I. lies at the root FRAN 124:4
immanent I. Will that stirs HARD 146:6
immaturity expression of human i. BRIT 44:2
immoral illegal, i., or fattening WOOL 345:12
immorality i. what they dislike WHIT 337:2
immortal that couldn't be i. SZYM 313:1
immortality i. can be assured GALB 130:12
i. through my work ALLE 7:5
Milk's leap toward i. FADI 111:2
Millions long for i. ERTZ 108:11
organize her own i. LASK 189:10
impartiality i. is bias REIT 272:10
impatient growing i. to see him SMIT 301:6
impeachment articles of i. ANON 10:13
not grounds for i. DOWD 94:7
imperialism I.'s face AUDE 18:5
I. the monopoly stage LENI 195:10
imperialisms prey of rival i. KENY 179:2
imperialist Through its i. system MAND 215:1
impertinent ask an i. question BRON 44:7
importance taking decisions of i. PARK 254:7
important i. book, critic assumes WOOL 345:2
i. to be clever *about* MEDA 221:1
same as i. PRAT 265:11
impossible art of the i. HAVE 148:13
Dream the i. DARI 84:3
i. takes little longer NANS 237:3
i. takes longer SAYI 289:12
i. to carry the burden EDWA 99:4
says that it is i. CLAR 70:3
two words, 'i.' GOLD 137:5
impostors treat those two i. KIPL 183:6
impressionable at an i. age SPAR 303:7
improbability high degree of i. FISH 114:11
statistical i. DAWK 85:10
improved i. by death SAKI 285:4
improvisation I. is too good SIMO 298:15
impure all things are i. LAWR 191:12
in KNEW YOU HAD IT I. YOU TELE 316:3
inadequate how i. intelligence is EINS 100:9
not that we are i. WILL 340:5
inadvertence by chance or i. HAIL 143:7
incest i. and folk-dancing ANON 12:15
i. flourished LEE 195:2
include i. me out GOLD 137:3
inclusion Life being all i. JAME 168:2
income dread a dead-level of i. TAWN 313:6
he has i. NASH 237:11
rises to meet i. PARK 254:4
income tax I. made more liars ROGE 277:2
incompatibility i. is the spice NASH 237:11
incompetence rise to level of i. PETE 257:5
sheer i. JONE 172:7
incomplete i. until he has married GABO 129:11
incomprehensible most i. fact EINS 100:10
use the i. ZOBE 351:1
inconceivable i. idea of the sun STEV 307:17
i. that I should be the age MERW 222:12
inconvenient cause may be i. BENN 30:3
lie even when i. VIDA 328:10
increased i. by one penny CART 56:9
incredible i. as if you fired RUTH 283:12
indecent for i. behaviour WAUG 331:7
independence i. as dearly ANON 12:12
i. of judges DENN 90:4

war for i. MCAL 205:12
India final message of I. FORS 122:18
I. will awake to life NEHR 238:10
Nothing in I. FORS 122:15
Indians I. are you BALD 21:6
indifference from total i. HYDE 164:10
it's i. WIES 338:2
indifferent It is simply i. HOLM 158:5
indignation Savage i. there YEAT 348:12
individual cult of the i. KHRU 180:6
i. men and women THAT 317:9
individualism system of rugged i. HOOV 159:2
individuality had its own i. RYDE 283:15
individually I. you agreed to evil RODR 276:7
individuals things i. are doing KEYN 179:9
indomitable i. Irishry YEAT 348:16
industrial i. worker would sooner BLYT 39:1
industrialists die for the i. FRAN 124:7
industry permit a cottage i. MARC 216:11
Science finds, i. applies ANON 12:2
ineffectual Remote and i. Don BELL 27:17
inefficiencies i. of dictatorship GALB 130:10
inevitability i. of gradualness WEBB 332:5
inevitable foresee the i. ASIM 14:11
inexactitude terminological i. CHUR 66:1
infamy date which will live in i. ROOS 278:6
I., infamy FILM 116:5
infection i. of things gone LOWE 204:14
inferior make you feel i. ROOS 277:12
inferno Dante's I. BOGA 39:6
i. of his passions JUNG 174:10
infinite door to i. wisdom BREC 43:5
ignorance necessarily i. POPP 260:10
Space is almost i. QUAY 268:3
infinitive care what a split i. FOWL 123:8
when I split an i. CHAN 62:5
inflation I. one form of taxation FRIE 126:6
pay to get i. down LAMO 188:1
inflections beauty of i. STEV 308:3
influence i. on human life MULL 234:14
i. people CARN 54:5
i. to your son ICE 164:14
information jester of the i. industry DYSO 98:3
lost in i. ELIO 104:13
informed badly-i. labrador NYE 243:10
inhale didn't i. CLIN 71:12
if he doesn't i. STEV 308:4
initiatives eye-catching i. BLAI 37:9
injustice I. anywhere a threat KING 181:3
i. makes democracy NIEB 242:2
ink all cough in i. YEAT 348:6
inn remember an I., Miranda BELL 28:6
inner have no I. Resources BERR 32:12
innocence assumption of i. easy CROS 81:12
ceremony of i. YEAT 348:7
i. is like a dumb leper GREE 139:17
I. no earthly weapon HILL 155:11
not in i. ARDR 13:12
innocent i. and the beautiful YEAT 347:11
We are i. ROSE 279:7
innuendoes beauty of i. STEV 308:3
inoperative statements i. ZIEG 350:10
inquisition before the I. LIVI 200:12
Spanish I. MONT 230:3
inscription like a rough i. YEVT 349:5
insect gigantic i. OPEN 248:3
insecurity international i. NIEB 242:3
inside i. the tent pissing out JOHN 171:13
I've lived i. myself DAVI 84:11
insignificance of the utmost i. CURZ 83:7
insomnia suffering from ideal i. JOYC 173:6
instincts i. already catered for BENN 29:14
true to your i. LAWR 192:5
institution always an i. DAY 86:3
change an i. TUSA 324:7
transformed into i. SART 287:15
institutional i. racism MACP 212:3
institutions acquiring their i. HAIL 143:7
instrument State is an i. STAL 305:7
insulted never *hope* to get i. DAVI 85:7
insults our visible i. CART 54:9
insurance form of moral i. BROD 44:3
National compulsory i. CHUR 67:10
intact is there, i. TRIM 322:6
integration policy of European i. KOHL 186:2
intellect i. of man is forced YEAT 347:2
intellectual i. hatred YEAT 348:1
i. is someone whose CAMU 52:12
'I.' suggests AUDE 17:15
i. who underrates KUND 186:13
practical i. STRO 311:1
wanted to be an i. SCHW 292:8
intellectuals treachery of the i. BEND 28:14
intelligence arresting human i. LEAC 193:10
bewitchment of i. WITT 342:5
bought his clothes with i. AMIE 7:14
first-rate i. FITZ 119:5
how inadequate i. is EINS 100:9
I. is quickness WHIT 337:1
underestimating i. MENC 221:10
intelligent honest and i. ORWE 250:14
i. minority CLAR 70:6
Most i., very elegant BUCK 47:8
rule of i. tinkering EHRL 99:7
so i. ELIO 105:2
intensity full of passionate i. YEAT 348:7
intentions only had good i. THAT 316:12
interact do not i. at all UPDI 325:15
intercourse positions in i. KEAT 176:9
interest compete for her i. LEWI 199:6
gives them an i. BAIN 20:11
interested i. in the arts AYCK 19:12
only i. in art SHAW 297:1
interesting proposition be i. WHIT 336:13

interesting (*cont.*):
Very i. . . . but CATC 60:7
interlude present is an i. O'NE 246:11
international i. finance system LIVI 200:13
I. life DEBR 87:11
i. wrong AUDE 18:5
Internet I. is an élite CHOM 65:7
On the I., nobody CART 56:8
posted on the I. LENO 196:14
thanks to the I. WILE 338:16
interpose i. my body STRA 310:5
intersecting i. monologues WEST 335:4
intervene i.—before breakfast HESE 153:17
interviewer i. allows you to say BENN 29:8
intolerable behaviour was i. MAJO 213:13
intolerance I. of groups FREU 125:9
intolerant not to tolerate the i. POPP 260:7
intrusive i. comma on p. 4 HOUS 160:10
invent i. the universe SAGA 284:8
invented i. the brake NEME 238:14
only lies are i. BRAQ 42:14
invention i. of a mouse DISN 93:3
i. or discovery CARE 54:2
Marriage a wonderful i. CONN 75:2
see past our i. STOP 309:8
invisible i. hand in politics FRIE 126:3
i., refined out of JOYC 173:13
no i. means of support BUCH 47:3
priest of the i. STEV 307:10
Iraq creating I. BELL 27:9
Ireland coming to I. today GEOR 133:2
great Gaels of I. CHES 63:10
I. holds these graves PEAR 256:2
I. hurt you into poetry AUDE 17:6
I. is the old sow JOYC 173:11
I. we dreamed of DE V 90:11
jurisdiction in I. ADAM 2:1
Out of I. have we come YEAT 348:2
Romantic I.'s dead YEAT 348:9
what I have got for I. COLL 73:10
Irish answer to the I. Question SELL 293:11
I. poets, learn your trade YEAT 348:15
Let the I. vessel lie AUDE 17:8
symbol of I. art JOYC 173:16
what the I. people wanted DE V 90:9
Irishman secondarily, I'm an I. HEWI 154:11
Irishmen appeal to all I. GEOR 133:2
Irishry indomitable I. YEAT 348:16
iron he's got i. teeth GROM 141:8
i. curtain CHUR 67:14
I. Curtain did not reach SOLZ 302:6
i. lady ANON 11:3
I. Lady THAT 315:12
irrational i. exuberance GREE 140:1
i. is rational STEV 307:18
irrigation numerical i. system AUGA 19:6
irritation cosiness and i. PYM 267:15
is what the meaning of 'i.' is CLIN 72:3
Islam I. has established them KHOM 180:3
island at this i. now AUDE 17:11
everyone on this i. AHER 5:4
i. made mainly of coal BEVA 34:3
soggy little i. UPDI 325:9
isolated Continent i. CART 56:2
isolationist you'll find an i. RUSK 282:2
it It's just I. KIPL 184:7
Italy I. under the Borgias FILM 116:6
itsy I. bitsy teenie weenie VANC 326:8
ivy it was agony, I. CATC 58:14

jack news of my boy J. KIPL 183:11
jack-knife j. has Macheath BREC 43:10
jail dey gits you in j. O'NE 246:5
Go to j. SAYI 289:18
j. of infinite space HUGH 162:1
jam j. we thought was for BENN 29:3
jamais j. triste archy MARQ 217:8
James Bond. J. Bond FILM 115:2
Home J. HILL 156:4
J. I, James II GUED 142:2
J. James Morrison Morrison MILN 225:7
Jane J., Jane, tall as a crane SITW 299:5
Me Tarzan, you J. MISQ 226:11
Japan to J.'s advantage HIRO 156:6
Japanese reconcile J. action CHUR 67:6
jaw-jaw To j. is always better CHUR 68:3
jazz If you're in j. MANN 215:13
J. is the only music COLE 73:4
J. music is to be played MORT 233:2
J. will endure SOUS 303:1
Picasso, sunbathing and j. WAUG 331:11
jealousy J. is feeling alone BOWE 41:13
To j. nothing is more SAGA 284:11
jeans blue j. and Coca-Cola GREE 140:4
jeepers J. Creepers MERC 222:4
Jeeves J. shimmered out WODE 342:13
Jefferson when J. ate alone KENN 178:11
Jellicoe J. was the only man CHUR 68:17
jelly blasted, j.-boned swines LAWR 192:15
shivers like the j. PIRO 259:1
jellybeans way of eating j. REAG 271:11
jest laughing at some j. KIPL 182:14
jester j. of the information industry DYSO 98:3
Jesus J. loves you more SIMO 298:12
j. told him; he wouldn't CUMM 82:7
J. wants me for a sunbeam TALB 313:4
more popular than J. now LENN 196:3
thinks he is J. Christ CLEM 71:2
to the heart of J. TERE 315:8
When J. came to Birmingham STUD 311:5
jet blood j. is poetry PLAT 259:10
Jew declare that I am a J. EINS 100:6

J. and the language CELA 61:8
Just J.-*ish* MILL 224:10
saved one J. from Auschwitz AUDE 19:5
jewellery just rattle your j. LENN 196:2
Jewish J. man with parents alive ROTH 279:15
murderers of J. children WIES 338:4
national home for the J. people BALF 22:1
solution of J. question GOER 136:11
Jews all poets are J. TSVE 324:1
But spurn the J. BROW 46:3
came for the J. NIEM 242:6
condition of the J. SART 287:16
last J. to die MEIR 221:2
To choose The J. EWER 110:9
jigsaw piece in a j. puzzle FILM 117:2
Jim worried about J. CATC 59:11
job circuit learns your j. MCLU 210:7
do his j. when he doesn't feel AGAT 2:11
doing a pretty good j. NADE 236:12
easier j. like publishing AYER 19:16
finish the j. CHUR 67:3
he's doing a grand j. CATC 60:2
j. working-class parents ABBO 1:1
looking for a j. MORR 232:9
neighbour loses his j. TRUM 323:9
jobs create j. TSVA 323:17
jogging alternative to j. FITT 118:16
John King J. was not a good man MILN 225:8
Johnny J.-head-in-air PUDN 267:9
joints Of all the gin j. FILM 117:5
joke every j. a custard pie ORWE 250:13
j. with a double meaning BARK 23:6
not seen the j. VIDA 328:2
jokes doesn't make j. IONE 165:10
Forgive my little j. FROS 127:2
jolt j. in the perspective WOOL 345:5
journal page of your j. HUGH 162:9
journalism J. largely consists CHES 64:17
journalist British j. WOLF 343:10
never was a j. DAY 86:3
journalistic j. dirty-mindedness LAWR 192:19
journalists J. belong in gutter PRIE 266:3
j. dabbling MCGR 209:7
tell lies to j. KRAU 186:4
journey j. *really* necessary OFFI 245:8
j. to a foreign land HAGU 142:12
long day's j. O'NE 246:7
now begin the j. REAG 272:1
journeying sat the j. boy HARD 146:14
joy oh! weakness of j. BETJ 33:15
shock of your j. HUGH 162:9
Strength through j. POLI 261:21
tables of j. HUGH 161:9
Judas J. was paid POWE 265:4
Whether J. Iscariot DYLA 97:18
judge Before you j. me JACK 167:2
best j. of a run WHAR 335:14
Here come de j. CATC 59:2
not j. this movement kindly READ 271:1
judged nation is j. LÉVE 198:2
judgement j. of your parents UPDI 325:12
nation fit to sit in j. WILS 341:12
wait for the last j. CAMU 52:8
judges independence of j. DENN 90:4
j. can tap MARS 218:3
J. must follow their oaths ZOBE 351:2
jug 'J. Jug' to dirty ears ELIO 104:22
juggle how to j. work, love, home FRIE 126:2
July on the Fourth of J. HAMM 144:17
jumped We have j. TRIM 322:7
jumpers Angels in j. LEWI 199:8
June J. is bustin' out all over HAMM 144:9
jungle city is not a concrete j. MORR 231:7
monkeys in the j. CASH 57:1
wise primitive in giant j. MAIL 213:6
juniper j. talks to the oak PAUL 255:7
under a j.-tree ELIO 102:4
junk flung up old j. CANN 53:4
J. is the ideal product BURR 48:12
jurisdiction j. in Ireland ADAM 2:1
just be British than j. PAIS 252:8
j. an image GODA 136:5
J. like that CATC 59:16
j. one of those things PORT 262:15
J. say no OFFI 245:9
may not be a j. peace IZET 166:8
talk of a j. war SORL 302:17
justice I don't want j. HUGH 162:13
If this is j. HISL 156:8
j. and the American way ANON 10:8
J. denied MILL 223:8
J. is a blind goddess HUGH 161:8
J. is the first condition SOYI 303:4
j. makes democracy possible NIEB 242:2
J. should not only be done HEWA 154:6
ounce of j. TANS 313:5
pursuit of j. GOLD 137:2
victors' j. SHAW 297:5
justifiable not a j. act of war BELL 27:8

Kaiser put the kibosh on the K. ELLE 106:14
Kane of *Citizen K.* THOM 320:2
Kansas corny as K. in August HAMM 144:17
keep If you can k. your head KIPL 183:5
K. the bastards honest POLI 261:20
some day it'll k. you WEST 334:9
keeps gave it us for k. AYRE 20:1
Kennedy President K. was dead FORS 123:2
you're no Jack K. BENT 30:11
Kensal Green by way of K. CHES 64:3
go to K. SAKI 285:7
Kentucky Long ago in K. WARR 330:9

kept I k. my word DE L 89:6
kettle k.'s breath HILL 155:10
pretty k. of fish MARY 218:11
Khrushchev not have married Mrs K. VIDA 328:7
kibosh put the k. on the Kaiser ELLE 106:14
kick first k. I took SPRI 305:2
great k. at misery LAWR 192:16
Nixon to k. around NIXO 242:8
kid comeback k. CLIN 71:13
have one k. O'RO 248:11
Here's looking at you, k. FILM 115:12
kiddies k. have crumpled BETJ 33:8
kidding k., Mister Hitler PERR 257:1
kids don't have any k. yourself LARK 189:2
how many k. did you kill POLI 261:14
just a couple of k. OPEN 247:14
kill bombers to k. the babies LE G 195:3
get out and k. something LEAC 193:11
how many kids did you k. POLI 261:14
k. a mockingbird LEE 194:17
k. animals and stick in NICO 241:10
K. millions of men ROST 279:13
k. you in a new way ROGE 277:6
licensed to k. FILM 116:2
Licensed to k. FLEM 120:6
Otherwise k. me MACN 211:16
prepared to k. one another SHAW 295:18
something you k. for BENN 29:5
they k. people TAGL 314:13
we are going to k. it POWE 264:15
killed don't mind your being k. KITC 184:17
Go to Spain and get k. POLL 260:2
I am the enemy you k. OWEN 251:13
k. in the war POWE 265:7
k. lots of men MOYN 233:11
not get k. FILM 116:2
(who k. him) thought BELL 28:5
killer lover and k. are mingled DOUG 93:13
killing medal for k. two men MATL 219:2
kills grip that k. it TAGO 313:2
it k. me KANE 175:7
K. all known germs ADVE 4:7
k. more people LIVI 200:13
suicide k. two people MILL 223:14
that which k. DE B 87:2
Kilroy K. was here ANON 11:9
Kiltartan My country is K. Cross YEAT 347:12
kin one's own k. and kith NASH 237:9
kind People will always be k. SASS 287:18
kindness k. and reconciliation MUNR 235:3
k. of strangers WILL 339:16
milk of human k. GUED 142:1
king fight for its K. and Country GRAH 138:9
God save the K. MOYN 233:11
If the K. asks you ATTL 16:7
K. and country need you SAYI 290:17
K. asked the Queen MILN 225:9
k. of banks and stones KAVA 176:4
K.'s life moving peacefully DAWS 86:1
K.'s Moll Reno'd NEWS 240:13
leave without the k. ELIZ 106:9
once and future k. WHIT 336:9
unless you're a k. HULL 162:15
your K. and your Country RUBE 280:12
kingfish call me the K. LONG 202:6
kings five k. left FARO 111:9
k. haul up the lumps BREC 43:13
walk with K. KIPL 183:7
Kinnock If K. wins NEWS 240:9
Kipling K. and his views AUDE 17:10
kiss k. is still a kiss HUPF 163:6
Kiss K. Bang Bang KAEL 175:3
k. my ass in Macy's window JOHN 171:14
k. on the hand ROBI 275:6
k. the hand that wrote JOYC 174:5
wanting to k. me MACD 208:4
kissed k. his sad Andromache CORN 77:10
k. my first woman TOSC 321:3
never k. an ugly girl EPIT 109:10
kisses fine romance with no k. FIEL 113:8
kissing I wasn't k. her MARX 218:7
k. your hand LOOS 202:12
like k. God BRUC 46:7
like k. Hitler CURT 83:4
kitchen get out of the k. TRUM 323:15
send me to eat in the k. HUGH 161:7
whip in k. cups STEV 307:12
Kitchener K. is a great poster ASQU 15:6
Kit-Kat have a K. ADVE 3:23
kitten trouble with a k. NASH 237:12
kleine eine k. Pause LAST 191:2
knees I don't really like k. SAIN 285:1
live on your k. IBAR 164:12
knew If you looked away, you k. SERE 293:13
K. YOU HAD IT IN YOU TELE 316:3
told what he k. AMIS 8:2
knife cannibal uses k. and fork LEC 194:10
He who wields the k. HESE 153:14
knighthoods looking for your k. KEAT 176:7
knights lances of ancient k. ROOT 279:5
knitter beautiful little k. SITW 299:8
knives night of the long k. HITL 156:12
knob holding the k. DIDD 92:3
knocked ruin that Cromwell k. about BEDF 26:15
we k. the bastard off HILL 156:3
what they k. down FENT 112:7
knocking K. on the moonlit door DE L 89:5
K. on the moonlit door OPEN 247:7
k. the American system CAPO 53:8
know all I k. is what I read ROGE 277:3
because we k. how to do them FOX 124:2
do not pretend to k. DARR 84:5

don't k. what I'm doing BRAU 43:2
don't k. who he is FOTH 123:6
How do they k. PARK 253:17
I do not believe . . . I k. JUNG 174:16
I k. what I like BEER 26:20
k. a man who can ADVE 3:9
k. better what is good JAY 168:14
k. the place for the first time ELIO 103:6
K. what I mean, Harry BRUN 46:10
k. what I think WALL 329:9
k. what we are talking about RUSS 282:13
k. when I am having a good time ASTO 15:8
Not many people k. that CAIN 50:9
say 'I don't k.' RUMS 281:3
things they didn't k. POUN 263:11
those who do not wish to k. RALE 269:5
wanted to k. about sex REUB 273:1
wouldn't k. how to work it FILM 115:8
You k. more than you think SPOC 304:11
you k. who ADVE 4:21
you'll never k. MISQ 226:10
knowing Bewrapt past k. HARD 146:14
knowingly Never k. undersold ADVE 4:14
knowledge After such k. ELIO 103:11
k. can only be finite POPP 260:10
k. they cannot lose OPPE 246:15
k. we have lost ELIO 104:13
make k. available BLAC 36:13
never better than k. FERM 112:13
search for k. RUSS 282:3
show of k. DOUG 94:4
known k. and the unknown PINT 258:12
k. unto God EPIT 110:1
knows if you k. of a better 'ole CART 56:12
K. Things MILN 225:5
sits in the middle and k. FROS 127:17
Knox John K. in Paradise PARK 253:6
koompartoo make a *K.* BURN 48:10
Korea doing in K. TRUM 323:6
Kray talking about the K. brothers TAYL 314:16
Kremlin howl by the K. AKHM 5:9

la in L. La land HOPK 159:10
laboratory guinea pigs in l. WILL 339:8
used to be a l. RICH 274:8
labour believes that new L. DAVI 84:9
chaos of a L. council KINN 182:6
Don't let L. ruin it POLI 261:24
fracture the L. party KINN 182:9
is L.'s call POLI 261:12
L. Government does MORR 231:13
L. isn't working POLI 261:22
L. Party learns to love BLAI 37:8
L. Party owes more PHIL 258:1
L.'s double whammy POLI 261:23
L. spin doctors CAMP 51:11
[L.] the natural party WILS 341:7
leader for the L. Party BEVA 34:10
never visualised l. WEBB 332:3
New L., new danger POLI 261:25
not enter the L. Party BENN 29:4
Of the L. Party JENK 169:9
to live without l. TAWN 313:8
labrador badly-informed l. NYE 243:10
lace Nottingham l. BETJ 33:2
lacy l. sleeve with vitriol WOOL 345:11
ladder l. of important things STIP 309:2
ladders where all the l. start YEAT 346:12
ladies l., God bless them SAYE 288:12
L., just a little more TREE 321:9
l. who lunch SOND 302:10
worth any number of old l. FAUL 112:2
lads We are l. GALL 130:13
lady elderly l., who mutters away CARE 53:12
for the old l. in Dubuque ROSS 279:9
iron l. ANON 11:3
L., be good GERS 133:12
l. loves Milk Tray ADVE 3:5
l.'s not for burning FRY 128:9
l.'s not for turning THAT 316:15
l. that's known as Lou SERV 294:4
little l. comes by GAY 132:4
talk like a l. SHAW 296:17
to be called First L. ONAS 246:1
why the l. is a tramp HART 148:5
Lafayette *L., nous voilà* STAN 305:11
laid l. end to end PARK 253:15
laity conspiracies against the l. SHAW 295:9
lake meal on a l. MEND 221:12
lambs new-born l. GILL 134:9
lame without religion is l. EINS 100:1
lamp post leaning on a l. GAY 132:4
lamps l. are going out GREY 141:1
land L. of Hope and Glory BENS 30:5
l. of my fathers THOM 318:17
L. that I love BERL 31:2
l. that needs heroes BREC 43:4
l. was ours before FROS 127:7
more precious than l. SADA 284:7
One Law, one L., one Throne KIPL 183:15
seen the promised l. KING 181:9
This l. is your land GUTH 142:9
landed ego has l. DOBS 93:5
landing fight on the l. grounds CHUR 66:11
landmarks fewer l. in space CAMU 52:9
landscape Who owns this l. MCCA 206:5
landslide pay for a l. KENN 177:10
language by means of l. WITT 342:5
cool web of l. GRAV 138:11
divided by a common l. SHAW 297:4
growing up in the same l. QUIN 268:9
In such lovely l. LAWR 192:14

language (*cont.*):
l. charged with meaning POUN 264:6
L. is a form of human reason LÉVI 198:7
l. of Shakespeare SHAW 296:16
l. of the unheard KING 181:12
L. tethers us LIVE 200:9
laogai in every l. WU 346:3
laughter in a l. GOLD 136:12
learning the l. CLIN 72:4
Life is a foreign l. MORL 231:5
limits of my l. WITT 342:9
mobilized the English l. MURR 236:2
mystery of l. KELL 177:2
Political l. is designed ORWE 250:11
rich and delicate l. WAUG 331:16
Slang is a l. SAND 286:12
suicides have a special l. SEXT 294:11
languages between and across l. CRAW 80:5
'primitive' l. CHAT 63:6
speaks eighteen l. PARK 253:14
laogai want to see *l.* ended WU 346:3
lascivious l. gloating STOP 309:7
lash sodomy, prayers, and the l. CHUR 68:2
lassie I love a l. LAUD 189:12
last Free at l. EPIT 109:5
l. breath of Julius Caesar JEAN 169:3
l. day of an era past YELT 349:3
L. night I dreamt OPEN 247:11
l. person who has sat on him HAIG 143:1
l. time I saw Paris HAMM 144:10
l. while they last DE G 88:12
Look thy l. DE L 89:4
Nice guys. Finish l. DURO 96:9
wait for the l. judgement CAMU 52:8
We were the l. romantics YEAT 347:1
won the l. war ROOS 277:10
Las Vegas loathing in L. THOM 319:15
late offering even that too l. NEVI 239:8
rather l. for me LARK 188:8
This is a l. parrot MONT 230:2
too l. or too early SART 287:13
later l. than you think SERV 294:2
lateral l. thinking DE B 87:7
Latin Devil knows L. KNOX 185:7
half Greek, half L. SCOT 292:12
learn L. as an honour CHUR 68:10
latrine mouth used as a l. AMIS 8:1
laugh no girl wants to l. LOOS 202:13
Others may be able to l. RHYS 273:5
why people l. FIEL 113:15
laughing fun I ever had without l. ALLE 6:12
killed while l. KIPL 182:14
l. at us FRIE 126:8
laughter L. . . . civilized music USTI 325:17
l. in a language GOLD 136:12
L. would be bereaved USTI 326:2
more frightful than l. SAGA 284:11
laurels want l. for ourselves LOWE 204:3
lava in its l. I still find WOOL 345:8
law against the l. for generals TRUM 323:14
dead-level of l. and order TAWN 313:6
fear of the L. JOYC 173:7
government above the l. SCAR 290:20
had people not defied the l. SCAR 290:18
have a l. DYSO 98:4
judgement of the l. JACK 167:4
keystone of the rule of l. DENN 90:4
l. has made him equal DARR 84:6
l. not supported by people HUMP 163:3
l. of the Yukon SERV 294:3
Nor l., nor duty YEAT 347:13
One L., one Land, one Throne KIPL 183:15
whole of the L. CROW 82:3
lawn Get your tanks off my l. WILS 341:9
on the l. I lie in bed AUDE 18:1
scooters off my l. CLAR 70:7
laws Government of l. FORD 121:8
If l. are needed KHOM 180:3
l. of God will be suspended SHAW 295:12
neither l. made JOHN 170:5
scientist's l. QUIN 268:7
lawyer freely as a l. interprets GIRA 135:9
l. with his briefcase PUZO 267:14
to a corporate l. COMM 74:2
lay L. your sleeping head AUDE 17:12
layout Perfection of planned l. PARK 254:6
Lazarus L. mystified HILL 155:9
LBJ All the way with L. POLI 261:2
Hey, L., how many kids POLI 261:14
lead can't see who's in the l. SNAG 301:10
couldn't l. a flock HUGH 162:14
l. a horticulture PARK 254:1
leadable is the Conservative Party l. HESE 154:2
leader fanatic a great l. BROU 45:9
Take me to your l. CATC 60:5
test of a l. LIPP 200:6
Wanna be the l. MCGO 209:3
leaders idle l. CRAN 79:15
leadership L. is not about being KEAT 176:8
L. means making CHRÉ 65:8
leading submarines than l. ladies MILL 224:14
leaf wise man hide a l. CHES 64:7
leaguer become a big l. DIMA 92:6
leaking L. is what you do CALL 51:2
leap giant l. for mankind ARMS 14:6
learn clever ones l. Latin CHUR 68:10
l. how to be aged BLYT 39:2
People must l. to hate MAND 215:2
learned l. has been forgotten SKIN 299:14
learning not l. from history BLAI 37:3
least l. government was the best FEIN 112:5
leave forever taking l. RILK 275:2
If you can't l. in a taxi FILM 116:1

if you l. things alone CHES 64:12
l. the country NEWS 240:9
l. without the King ELIZ 106:9
You better l. DYLA 97:6
leaves l. will fall on my breast NERU 239:1
lecture first to l. you ELTO 107:6
tried to l. *me* PAGL 252:4
lectures hissed my mystery l. SPOO 304:14
left L. hand down a bit CATC 59:18
position was on the l. MOSL 233:5
leftovers nothing but l. ULLM 325:5
left-wing social contract is l. DEBR 87:11
leg does not resemble a l. APOL 13:5
legacies l. of empire SAMP 286:2
legend managing one's l. DEBR 87:10
Your l. ever did JOHN 170:11
Your l. ever will JOHN 170:14
legends Men must have l. MURR 235:16
legs born with your l. apart ORTO 249:3
Four l. good ORWE 249:5
leisure absence of l. to reflect HAVE 148:12
fill l. intelligently RUSS 282:9
length for what it lacks in l. FROS 127:8
Lenin L. was right KEYN 179:7
leopard l. does not change COMP 74:8
leopards three white l. sat ELIO 102:4
leper innocence is like a dumb l. GREE 139:17
Lesbia L. with her sparrow MILL 223:10
less about l. and less MAYO 220:9
l. in this than meets the eye BANK 22:10
L. is a bore VENT 327:6
L. is more ROHE 277:8
less than $10,000 EVAN 108:14
more about l. and less BUTL 50:1
more and more in l. and less YATE 346:7
One square foot l. BENC 28:13
lessons from the l. of history HUXL 163:11
l. to be drawn ELIZ 106:4
let L.'s go to work FILM 116:11
Lethe waters of L. GINS 135:5
letter don't think this is a l. RENO 272:14
l. by strange letter HEAN 150:6
Someone wants a l. ADVE 4:22
letters can't write l. BISH 36:8
l. get in wrong places MILN 225:4
l. to a non-existent LEWI 198:13
levee Drove my Chevy to the l. MCLE 210:1
levers shan't be pulling the l. THAT 317:17
Levis sold a million pairs of L. BURR 48:11
lexicons We are walking l. LIVE 200:10
liar answered 'Little L.' BELL 27:14
proved l. HAIL 143:5
liars Income Tax made more L. ROGE 277:2
liberal first L. leader STEE 306:4
l. education BANK 22:12
l. is a conservative who WOLF 343:16
L. is a man who uses ROOS 278:2
l. who has been mugged SAYI 289:8
liberals l. can understand BRUC 46:5
liberation Women's L. is just MEIR 221:3
liberationists furious about the l. LOOS 203:1
liberties Freedom, what l. GEOR 133:10
liberty defence of l. GOLD 137:2
holy name of l. GAND 131:5
L. is liberty, not BERL 31:11
L. is precious LENI 195:17
L. is unfinished business ANON 11:10
L. means responsibility SHAW 296:6
safeguards of l. FRAN 124:9
survival and success of l. KENN 178:3
library Alexandria's l. burned HUGH 162:5
less time in the l. STRU 311:2
l. is thought in SAMU 286:3
you have a public l. BENN 29:7
licence l. to act like an asshole ZAPP 350:5
l. to print money THOM 320:3
licenced based upon l. premises O'BR 244:3
licensed l. to kill FILM 116:2
L. to kill FLEM 120:6
licking finger l. good ADVE 4:1
lie Bodies never l. DE M 89:13
definition of a l. ANON 9:9
Every word she writes is a l. MCCA 206:11
fall victim to a big l. HITL 156:16
home to a l. POUN 263:13
l. even when inconvenient VIDA 328:10
l. that makes us realize truth PICA 258:8
l. to them remorselessly FORS 122:11
old L.: Dulce et decorum OWEN 251:9
possible to l. for the truth ADLE 2:7
lied because our fathers l. KIPL 182:12
I l. to please the mob KIPL 182:13
lies Africa was swaddled in l. NAIP 236:14
Castle of lies BOOK 40:8
Here l. Groucho Marx EPIT 109:10
l. about the Democrats STEV 308:5
L. are the mortar WELL 333:13
l. of tongue and pen CHES 63:15
make l. sound truthful ORWE 250:11
Matilda told such Dreadful L. BELL 27:13
only l. are invented BRAQ 42:14
Without l. humanity would FRAN 124:5
life actor's l. for me WASH 330:12
afternoon of human l. JUNG 174:14
all human l. is there ADVE 3:3
believe in l. DU B 95:6
believe in the l. to come BECK 25:10
can be a daring l. WELT 334:2
contempt for l. VANE 326:13
content to manufacture l. BERN 31:14
destroying practically all l. KING 180:13
dog is for l. SAYI 289:13
essence of l. DAWK 85:10
Further sacrifice of l. DE V 90:10

life (*cont.*):
gave my l. for freedom EWER 110:8
Get a l. SHAT 295:3
God created l. CLIN 72:4
goes through l. holding on ELLI 107:2
great l. if you don't weaken BUCH 47:2
images of l. BERG 30:12
isn't l. a terrible thing THOM 318:15
I've had a wonderful l. LAST 191:3
lay down his friends for his l. THOR 320:4
lay down my l. for HALD 143:12
Lead me from death to l. KUMA 186:12
l. a glorious cycle of song PARK 253:2
l. and loves of a she-devil WELD 333:3
l. a series of images WARH 330:2
L. a sexually transmitted disease ANON 11:11
L. begins at forty PITK 259:4
L. being all inclusion JAME 168:2
l. exists in the universe JEAN 169:4
L., friends, is boring BERR 32:12
l. had been ruined BROO 45:3
l. in the village LEE 195:1
l. is 6 to 5 against RUNY 281:10
L. is a foreign language MORL 231:5
L. is a gamble STOP 310:3
L. is a great surprise NABO 236:8
L. is a horizontal fall COCT 72:10
L. is an offensive WHIT 336:12
L. is a rainbow which YEVT 349:7
L. is Colour and Warmth GREN 140:13
L. is doubt UNAM 325:6
L. is first boredom LARK 188:10
l. is generally something BENN 30:2
L. is just one damned HUBB 161:4
L. is not having been told NASH 238:6
L. is nothing much to lose HOUS 160:7
L. is not meant to be easy FRAS 124:13
L. is not meant to be easy SHAW 295:6
l. is one damn thing MILL 223:12
L. is the other way round LODG 201:14
l. is the thing SMIT 300:13
L. is too short to stuff CONR 76:4
l. is washed in the speechless BARZ 24:16
L. just a bowl of cherries BROW 46:2
l. like a box of chocolates FILM 117:3
l. of any important person PRIE 266:4
L. says: she did this BARN 23:11
L.'s better with POLI 261:24
l. sentence goes on CONL 74:11
l.'s rich pageant MARS 218:1
L., the Universe and Everything ADAM 1:12
live out my l. talking VANZ 327:2
looked at l. from both sides MITC 227:8
makes l. worth living ELIO 105:9
matter of l. and death SHAN 294:13
matters in your l. RUSH 281:11
measured out my l. ELIO 104:5
men confused with l. FRID 125:16
more a way of l. ANON 11:16
no l. that couldn't be SZYM 313:1
not an event of l. WITT 342:10
not in giving l. DE B 87:2
not the men in my l. that counts WEST 334:13
one's own l. lacks BARK 23:4
On l., on death YEAT 348:17
only living l. O'NE 246:11
Our end is L. MACN 212:1
outer l. of telegrams FORS 122:8
parallels your l. COPP 77:7
Perfection of the l. YEAT 347:2
priceless gift of l. ROSE 279:7
reflection of l. FREE 125:3
remaining years of l. MAND 214:12
Reverence for L. SCHW 292:9
shilling l. will give you AUDE 18:7
sketchy understanding of l. CRIC 80:9
some problems with my *l.* SIMO 298:10
sons and daughters of L. GIBR 134:6
taking l. by the throat FROS 128:4
There is l., but not for you MORT 232:14
university of l. BOTT 41:6
Water is l.'s *mater* SZEN 312:14
What is this l. DAVI 85:4
whole l. shows in your face BACA 20:4
Who owns my life RODR 276:8
Without work, l. goes rotten CAMU 52:18
you lived your l. JOHN 170:11
lifeless virtue is l. PAST 254:16
life sentence escape the l. LAWR 192:20
lifetime l. of happiness SHAW 295:19
light brief crack of l. NABO 236:9
dark is l. enough FRY 128:8
dying of the l. THOM 318:5
Give me a l. HASK 148:10
gives a lovely l. MILL 223:6
l. at the end of the tunnel DICK 92:1
l. at the end of the tunnel LOWE 204:12
L. breaks where no sun THOM 318:8
l. has gone out NEHR 238:11
l. in the darkness JUNG 174:11
l. my fire MORR 232:1
l. on the hill CHIF 65:2
speed far faster than l. BULL 47:10
tried to mend the Electric L. BELL 27:18
waited for the l. ROBI 275:10
while the l. fails ELIO 103:8
lightest poor tread the l. HARR 148:1
lighthouse great l. which stands JENK 169:11
lightness unbearable l. of being KUND 187:1
lightning known the l.'s hour DAY- 86:6
writing history with l. WILS 341:11
lights all-the-l.-on man REED 272:5
glare of l. CHRÉ 65:9
turn out the l. NEWS 240:9

watching the tail l. CRAN 80:2
like but you'll l. it CATC 60:15
don't know whether I l. it VAUG 327:4
don't l. this game CATC 59:5
I know what I l. BEER 26:20
I L. Ike POLI 261:15
l. everyone else DE G 88:15
l. everyone else SHIE 297:9
l. is not necessarily good BELL 27:7
l. what you get SHAW 296:11
man you don't l. THOM 318:18
liked l. it so much ADVE 3:27
wish to be l. RUSS 282:7
would have l. to be Perón PERÓ 256:11
likely Not bloody l. SHAW 296:20
likes does know what she l. RATT 270:4
does what he l. to do GILL 134:10
lilac l. and the roses ARAG 13:7
lilacs breeding L. ELIO 104:19
Lilibet this special day. L. TELE 316:7
limbs deck your lower l. in pants NASH 238:5
limelight backing into the l. BERN 31:17
limited so whizzed the L. CRAN 80:2
limits l. of my language WITT 342:9
limousine One perfect l. PARK 253:5
limpet miserable l. CRAN 79:14
Limpopo grey-green, greasy L. KIPL 184:5
Lincoln Ford, not a L. FORD 121:7
L. County Road DYLA 97:15
L. was shovelled SAND 286:6
L. went to New Orleans HUGH 161:11
line active l. on a walk KLEE 184:19
first l. CALV 51:9
l. is a fuse MAYA 220:3
playing on the l. FORS 122:13
problem of the colour l. DU B 95:5
through colour and l. MOND 229:2
lines awful banal l. GUIN 142:4
I plant l. WALC 328:17
Just say the l. COWA 79:10
sentiment in short l. LARK 189:8
linguistic form of l. fascism JAME 168:7
l. philosophy RUSS 283:8
link You are the weakest l. CATC 60:12
linoleum shoot me through l. BANK 22:13
lion nation that had l.'s heart CHUR 68:6
lions L. led by donkeys SAYI 290:2
lips already born before my l. MAND 215:12
Is it Lombard's l. EWAR 110:7
My l. are sealed MISQ 226:12
Read my l. BUSH 49:7
Watch my l. BLUN 38:6
Watch my l. BLUN 38:7
lipstick bears a l.'s traces MARV 218:6
too much l. NASH 237:17
liquid Cats, no less l. TESS 315:9
liquidation l. of British Empire CHUR 67:8
liquor l. is quicker NASH 238:2
listen don't want to l. to *you* LEBO 194:6
good to l. ADVE 4:2
Stop-look-and-l. OFFI 245:14
listening ain't l. GLAS 136:1
hearing without l. SIMO 298:13
l., lying in wait THOM 319:4
lit whole Fleet's l. up WOOD 344:10
literalists l. of the imagination MOOR 230:8
literary l. equivalent WHAR 336:2
Of all the l. scenes PRES 265:17
literature as for l. POUN 264:1
Great l. is POUN 264:6
life ruined by l. BROO 45:3
like their l. clear LEWI 199:3
l. can and should do BYAT 50:4
l. goes as freight GARC 131:12
l. is more dependable BROD 44:3
L. is mostly about LODG 201:14
L. is news POUN 264:5
L.'s always a good card BENN 30:4
l.'s performing flea O'CA 244:10
L. the orchestration WILD 338:15
real l. can exist only MACD 207:13
Remarks are not l. STEI 306:7
rest is l. VALÉ 326:5
Russian l. saved RATU 270:8
litmus Gypsies are a l. test HAVE 149:2
little having too l. COMP 74:6
L. boxes on the hillside REYN 273:4
l. boys who wanted STEI 306:12
l. grey cells CHRI 65:10
L. man, you've had a busy SIGL 298:5
L. one! Oh, little one STEP 307:6
l. people pay taxes HELM 152:7
l. ships of England GUED 141:11
offering Germany too l. NEVI 239:8
live enable its citizens to l. WEIL 332:11
find a way to l. CRON 81:7
he isn't fit to l. KING 181:5
If you don't l. it PARK 253:1
like to l. forever LAYT 193:6
L. and let die FLEM 120:9
l. at all is miracle PEAK 255:12
l. in an unlivable situation LAIN 187:11
l. on your knees IBAR 164:12
l. our lives RILK 275:2
l. this long BLAK 37:12
l. through someone else FRIE 126:1
l. to be over ninety ABBO 1:2
l. together as brothers KING 181:8
Man is born to l. PAST 254:14
might as well l. PARK 253:8
Sacco's name will l. VANZ 327:1
taught us how to l. BENN 29:11
lived I've l. inside myself DAVI 84:11
Never to have l. is best YEAT 347:9

liver ate his l. FILM 115:13
lives Careless talk costs l. OFFI 245:1
woman who l. for others LEWI 198:10
liveth name l. for evermore EPIT 110:2
living go on l. even after death FRAN 124:8
I *love* l. SIMO 298:10
I shall go on l. NERU 239:1
land of the l. WILD 338:13
L. and partly living ELIO 104:9
l. in a time BREC 43:15
l. in Philadelphia EPIT 109:11
L. is abnormal IONE 165:12
Look to the l. DUNN 96:3
machine for l. in LE C 194:14
no l. of its own JENN 170:1
not learning from but l. BLAI 37:3
not l. with you WILL 339:10
way of l. with the Negro BALD 21:4
well and l. in ANON 11:6
world does not owe us a l. PHIL 257:9
Livingstone I wouldn't vote for Ken L. SCAR 290:19
Lloyd George L. knew my father ANON 11:12
loafing cricket as organized l. TEMP 315:4
loathing Fear and l. THOM 319:15
local little l. difficulties MACM 210:15
l. thing called Christianity HARD 147:4
working of l. government THAT 317:19
locally act l. SAYI 290:10
loft windy, untidy l. CANN 53:4
log big rotting l. WHIT 336:5
logic l. of our times DAY- 86:9
nothing more than l. gates AUGA 19:6
logical l. positivists AYER 19:15
loins shudder in the l. engenders YEAT 347:14
Lolita L., light of my life OPEN 247:12
London 1938 in L. MIDL 223:2
L. Pride handed down to us COWA 78:12
L. spread out in the sun LARK 189:5
L. Transport diesel-engined FLAN 119:17
Londoner because I'm a L. GREG 140:7
loneliness l. of long-distance SILL 298:7
well of l. HALL 144:2
lonely All the l. people LENN 196:6
heart is a l. hunter MCCU 207:8
Only the l. ORBI 248:5
long anything with l. hair MASO 219:1
In the l. run KEYN 179:13
live this l. BLAK 37:12
L. ago in Kentucky WARR 330:9
l. and the short HUGH 161:6
l. hot summer FILM 118:9
l. time ago TAGL 314:7
l. way to Tipperary JUDG 174:9
l. week-end FORS 122:3
night of the l. knives HITL 156:12
week is a l. time in politics WILS 341:6
long-distance l. runner SILL 298:7
longer devolution takes l. CART 56:7
impossible takes l. SAYI 289:12
longitude l. with no platitude FRY 128:11
look and l. another HEDR 151:11
l. after our people LAST 190:4
l. at the record IVIN 166:6
L. back in anger OSBO 250:20
l. on and help LAWR 192:17
L., stranger AUDE 17:11
l. the East End in the face ELIZ 106:8
L. thy last DE L 89:4
Stop-l.-and-listen OFFI 245:14
lookalikes play Hollywood l. SMIT 300:9
looked better to be l. over WEST 334:7
If you l. away, you knew SERE 293:13
l. at in merciless glare WILL 339:14
more he l. inside MILN 225:1
looking Here's l. at you FILM 115:12
keep l. over his shoulder BARU 24:15
l. in the same direction SAIN 284:13
someone may be l. MENC 221:8
stop other people from l. BLAC 36:13
looking glass cracked l. JOYC 173:16
looks l. like a duck REUT 273:2
needs good l. TUCK 324:2
looney L. Tunes REAG 271:13
loophole l. through which pervert BRON 44:8
loose Every which way but l. FILM 118:7
l. cannon like her ANON 12:10
Lorca L. was killed, singing READ 271:3
lord in the L.'s bosom HOLU 158:7
L. of all hopefulness STRU 311:4
L. of the Dance CART 55:4
L. survives the rainbow LOWE 204:11
Praise the L. FORG 121:14
saying 'L. Jones Dead' CHES 64:17
thank the L. I'm Welsh MATT 219:3
we battle for the L. ROOS 278:14
Lord Copper Up to a point, L. WAUG 331:13
lords L. a matter of controversy ST J 284:14
one of the l. of life LAWR 192:12
lordships good enough for their l. ANON 12:7
lose hurts to l. DOLE 93:8
l. the war in an afternoon CHUR 68:17
nothing much to l. HOUS 160:7
quickest way is to l. ORWE 250:15
waste it is to l. one's mind QUAY 268:4
we don't want to l. you RUBE 280:12
wins if he does not l. KISS 184:11
losing l. your brain FOX 123:10
l. your sight SASS 287:18
loss text was l. CUNN 82:14
lost Balls will be l. always BERR 32:10
France has not l. the war DE G 88:4
l. an empire ACHE 1:8
l. dog somewhere ANOU 13:3

l. generation STEI 306:11
not that you won or l. RICE 273:8
paradises we have l. PROU 267:5
Though lovers be l. THOM 318:4
Vietnam was l. in MCLU 210:10
what is l. in translation FROS 128:6
wherever we're l. in FRY 128:12
lot not a l. . . . but you'll like CATC 60:15
Lothian West L. DALY 83:13
West-L. DALY 84:1
lottery genetic l. comes up with PIML 258:10
l. forms a principal part BORG 41:3
L., with weekly pay-out ORWE 250:5
lotus l. can be planted EPIT 109:3
Lou lady that's known as L. SERV 294:4
lousy *House Beautiful* is play l. PARK 253:12
L. but loyal SAYI 290:3
lout l.'s game WEST 335:5
love All you need is l. LENN 196:4
Any kiddie in school can l. NASH 238:1
bridge is l. WILD 338:13
capable of l. AYER 19:15
caution in l. RUSS 282:8
doesn't l. a wall FROS 127:11
failures in l. MURD 235:6
fell in l. with himself POWE 264:7
for us, it's love BOUS 41:8
From Russia with l. FLEM 120:8
God is l., but LEE 194:16
God si L. FORS 122:18
greater l. hath no man THOR 320:4
Greater l. than this JOYC 174:3
groans of l. LOWR 204:16
Hearts wound up with l. SPEN 304:6
If I can't l. Hitler MUST 236:5
I'll l. you AUDE 16:13
I l. you BURN 48:9
I l. you LAST 190:8
It's not l. FOND 121:2
It's so simple, l. PRÉV 266:1
Land that I l. BERL 31:2
learns to l. Peter BLAI 37:8
Let's fall in l. PORT 262:16
longing for l. RUSS 282:3
l. affair with America MAIL 213:3
l. and work FREU 125:12
l. boat has crashed LAST 190:15
L., curiosity, freckles PARK 253:3
l. does not consist in SAIN 284:13
L. doesn't just sit there LE G 195:4
L. Flames for a year LAMP 188:4
L. has pitched his mansion YEAT 347:3
l. human beings GREE 139:11
l. in another's soul LAYT 193:5
l. is a thing that can never PARK 253:2
L. is a universal migraine GRAV 139:1
L. is discovery of reality MURD 235:10
L. is given HUGH 161:9
l. is given over-well PARK 253:6
l. is here to stay GERS 133:14
L. is just a system BARN 23:14
L. is mutually feeding HEAD 150:1
L. is one of the answers PAZ 255:11
L. is the delusion MENC 221:5
L. makes the world go round MACK 209:9
L. means not ever having TAGL 314:8
L.? most natural painkiller LAST 191:1
l. one another or die AUDE 18:6
l. one's country ANNA 9:7
L. set you going PLAT 259:13
l. that asks no question SPRI 304:15
L. the Beloved Republic FORS 122:21
l. them, and hold on DUNN 96:3
L.-thirty, love-forty BETJ 33:15
l. . . . whatever that may CHAR 63:2
l. will steer the stars RADO 269:1
l. without the rhetoric STOP 309:15
l. you for yourself alone YEAT 346:9
make l. in a canoe BERT 32:14
Make l. not war SAYI 290:4
man in l. is incomplete GABO 129:11
Man's l. is of man's life AMIS 8:4
man you l. to hate TAGL 314:9
money can't buy me l. LENN 196:5
Most people l. love PAST 254:15
Need we say it was not l. MILL 223:11
never l. anybody STOP 309:8
never l. a stranger BENS 30:6
no l. for such THOM 319:11
Onstage I make l. JOPL 173:3
opposite of l. WIES 338:2
programmed to l. completely BAIN 20:12
revolution where l. not allowed ANGE 9:2
right place for l. FROS 126:13
search for l. WAŁĘ 329:1
support of the woman I l. EDWA 99:4
There is only l. MCEW 208:14
they're in l. TAGL 314:13
thought that l. would last AUDE 17:4
tired of L. BELL 27:16
vividly gifted in l. DUFF 95:7
When l. congeals HART 148:4
Where l. rules JUNG 174:15
who l., time is eternity VAN 326:12
wilder shores of l. BLAN 37:13
will survive of us is l. LARK 188:9
Work is l. made visible GIBR 134:7
You can only l. one war GELL 132:9
loved l. you, so I drew these tides LAWR 192:21
thirst to be l. RHYS 273:6
wish I l. the Human Race RALE 269:6
lovely l. woman stoops to folly ELIO 105:7
on all things l. DE L 89:4
Wouldn't it be l. LERN 197:4

lover l. and killer are mingled DOUG 93:13
l.'s quarrel with the world FROS 127:10
what is left of a l. ROWL 280:7
lovers l. and tribes ONDA 246:4
Though l. be lost THOM 318:4
wonder if it's l. MULD 234:12
loves God l. them HUME 163:2
lady l. Milk Tray ADVE 3:5
life and l. of a she-devil WELD 333:3
Who l. ya, baby CATC 60:11
woman whom nobody l. CORN 77:11
loving Can't help l. dat man HAMM 144:7
discharge for l. one MATL 219:2
savage l. has made me BECK 26:12
low l. road to the highest MCCA 206:6
lowbrow first militant l. BERL 31:13
lower capitalism of l. classes SPEN 304:10
l. classes had such white CURZ 83:8
l. than vermin BEVA 34:4
While there is a l. class DEBS 87:13
loyal Lousy but l. SAYI 290:3
l. to his own career DALT 83:12
loyalties l. which centre upon CHUR 68:14
tragic conflict of l. HOWE 160:12
loyalty I want *l.* JOHN 171:14
L. is the Tory's secret KILM 180:12
l. we feel to unhappiness GREE 139:12
LSD L.? Nothing much happened AUDE 19:3
L. reminds me of minks GRAV 139:4
PC is the L. of the '90s LEAR 193:13
luck believes in l. STEA 306:3
but it is l. FORS 122:13
watching his l. SERV 294:4
lucky l. if he gets out of it FILM 116:8
lugubrious l. man in a suit ELIZ 106:12
lullaby Once in a l. HARB 145:14
lump had been a l. of clay POPE 260:4
lumps l. in it STEP 307:5
lunatic all in l. asylums CHES 64:10
form the l. fringe ROOS 279:4
lunatics lunatic asylum run by l. LLOY 201:10
l. have taken charge ROWL 280:9
lunch cork out of my l. FIEL 113:11
ladies who l. SOND 302:10
L. is for wimps FILM 116:12
no such thing as a free l. SAYI 290:9
no trench, no l. ADIE 2:6
unable to l. today PORT 262:17
Universe is a free l. GUTH 142:8
luncheon do not take soup at l. CURZ 83:9
lungs from froth-corrupted l. OWEN 251:9
lures l. the truth WESK 334:4
lust despair rather than l. READ 271:5
horrible that l. and rage YEAT 348:11
l. and calls it advertising LAHR 187:6
l. and rape and incest BENN 29:12
to l. after it LEWI 198:15
lusty call l. in foreign films WILD 338:10
luxury Every l. lavished on you ORTO 249:1
To trust people is a l. FORS 122:6
lying branch of the art of l. CORN 78:2
listening, l. in wait THOM 319:4
One of you is l. PARK 253:10
Lyonnesse When I set out for L. HARD 147:2
lyric now it's l. verse WAUG 331:10

M dreaded four M.'s STRE 310:13
Macavity M. WASN'T THERE ELIO 104:12
Macbeth I appeared as M. HARG 147:9
Little Nell and Lady M. WOOL 345:11
Macheath jack-knife has M. BREC 43:10
machine desiccated calculating m. BEVA 34:10
Ghost in the M. RYLE 284:3
m. for living in LE C 194:14
m. for turning red wine DINE 92:9
sausage m. CHRI 65:11
machines M. are the new proletariat ATTA 15:12
M. are worshipped RUSS 283:2
M. have less problems WARH 330:3
whether m. think SKIN 299:13
macht *Arbeit m. frei* ANON 9:12
mad Everybody's a m. scientist CRON 81:7
M. about the boy COWA 78:13
M. dogs and Englishmen COWA 78:14
men that God made m. CHES 63:10
they call you m. EMIN 107:13
Whom the m. would destroy LEVI 198:6
madam globe-trotting M. YEAT 348:14
made Here's one I m. earlier CATC 59:3
I m. it FILM 115:1
m., like bread LE G 195:4
Madeira M., m'dear FLAN 119:14
madeleine little piece of m. PROU 267:4
Madelon *Ce n'est que M.* BOUS 41:8
mademoiselle M. from Armenteers ANON 11:13
madhouse don't want m. EMPS 108:3
madmen M. in authority KEYN 179:12
madness destroyed through m. GINS 135:2
m. is terrific WOOL 345:8
M.! Madness FILM 116:13
M. need not be breakdown LAIN 187:12
m. of TV PAGL 252:2
moment of m. DAVI 85:1
Madonnas M. or Mary Magdalenes WILL 339:7
Mafia not as M.-like CAST 57:9
magazines graves of little m. PRES 265:17
magic indistinguishable from m. CLAR 70:2
mistake medicine for m. SZAS 312:9
old black m. MERC 222:6
tell you what I want. M. WILL 339:15

manners (*cont.*):
English m. more frightening JARR 168:11
m. out of men DICK 92:2
manoeuvre force with a m. TROT 322:10
mansion Love has pitched his m. YEAT 347:3
manufacture content to m. life BERN 31:14
manunkind busy monster, m. CUMM 82:8
manure liquid m. from the West SOLZ 302:6
many so much owed by so m. CHUR 67:1
map make a m. JONE 172:9
m.-makers' colours BISH 36:5
maps Geography is about M. BENT 30:7
marathon fought near M. GRAV 138:12
march do not m. on Moscow MONT 229:13
don't m. as alternative FITT 118:16
m. my troops towards GRIM 141:6
m. towards it CALL 51:4
Men who m. away HARD 146:13
marching m., charging feet JAGG 167:11
Margaret It's me, M. BLUM 38:3
Marie I am M. of Roumania PARK 253:2
marijuana experimented with m. CLIN 71:12
market enterprise of the m. ANON 10:4
m. has no morality HESE 153:15
on m. research RODD 276:5
Market Harborough AM IN M. TELE 316:1
market-place gathered in the m. CAVA 61:1
Marlowe quoting from this M. STAR 306:1
marriage Christian m. MARG 216:12
get anywhere in a m. MURD 235:9
M. 2001-style FELT 112:6
M. a wonderful invention CONN 75:2
M. is a bribe WILD 338:14
M. isn't a word FILM 116:16
M. is popular because SHAW 296:8
M. is waste-paper basket WEBB 332:6
m. on the rocks MERR 222:11
So that is m. WOOL 345:3
three of us in this m. DIAN 91:11
value of m. is not DE V 91:1
marriages All the unhappy m. WODE 342:11
no 'mixed' m. MORR 232:7
married can't get m. at all FILM 117:11
Each thirteenth year he m. MERR 222:10
getting m. in the morning LERN 196:16
Getting you m. is not easy SETH 294:5
incomplete until he has m. GABO 129:11
m. beneath me ASTO 15:9
m.—to be the more together MACN 211:13
Onassis would not have m. VIDA 328:7
trendy Smug M. FIEL 113:5
when they got m. OPEN 247:14
marry men we wanted to m. STEI 307:2
Martha had enough of M. MACM 211:6
Martians understand than M. SOLZ 301:13
martinetissimo I am a m. STOK 309:5
Martini into a dry M. FILM 116:10
martyr regarded as a m. KHOM 180:4
martyrdom m. must run its course AUDE 17:14
marvel m. my birthday away THOM 318:10
marvels to credit m. HEAN 150:11
Marx illegitimate child of Karl M. ATTL 16:4
in M.'s pages SCHU 292:3
M is for M. CONN 75:11
Marxism more to Methodism than M. PHIL 258:1
Marxist M.—Groucho tendency ANON 11:8
Mary one Hail M. DOYL 94:12
time for some M. MACM 211:6
Mary Jane matter with M. MILN 225:10
Mary Magdalenes Madonnas or M. WILL 339:7
mask like a M. dancing ACHE 1:6
m. that eats into the face UPDI 325:14
masochistic m. form OLIV 245:20
masons Where did the m. go BREC 43:13
mass two thousand years of m. HARD 146:4
Massachusetts denied in M. MILL 223:8
masses calling 'em the m. PRIE 266:7
If it is for the m. SCHO 291:7
m. conveying an emotion HEPW 153:4
Movement of M. CONN 75:11
master Death is a m. from Germany CELA 61:7
m.'s dirt COET 72:14
masterpiece knows, at sight, a m. POUN 264:1
masters never wrong, the Old M. AUDE 17:13
We are not the m. BLAI 37:5
We are the m. now MISQ 227:3
mastery I had m. OWEN 251:12
mastodons like m. bellowing WODE 343:3
masturbation Don't knock m. ALLE 6:13
M. is the thinking HAMP 145:2
m. of war RAE 269:2
match Honour is like a m. PAGN 252:5
never win a m. again IVAN 166:4
matched m. us with His hour BROO 44:14
matches have a box of m. HOME 158:9
my m. should HENM 153:2
with that stick of m. MAND 215:6
materialistic m. of religions TEMP 315:3
mateship as dearly as m. ANON 12:12
mathematician appear as a pure m. JEAN 169:5
mathematics avoid pregnancy by m. MENC 221:9
In m. you don't NEUM 239:7
M. may be defined RUSS 282:13
M., rightly viewed RUSS 282:14
no place for ugly m. HARD 146:3
Matilda M. told such Dreadful Lies BELL 27:13
matter Does it m. SASS 287:18
not fighting does m. STEP 307:7
position of m. RUSS 282:11

What is the m. MILN 225:10
mattering can go on m. BOWE 41:11
matters m. in your life RUSH 281:11
Nobody that m. MILL 223:4
What can I do that m. SPEN 304:9
mattress crack it open on a m. MILL 224:2
maturing mind is m. late NASH 237:14
mausoleum used as its m. AMIS 8:1
may M. to December ANDE 8:10
maybe definite m. GOLD 137:8
M., just maybe ADVE 4:11
mayor running for M. of Toytown SCAR 290:19
watch the m. LETT 197:11
MBEs looking for your M. KEAT 176:7
McCarthyism M. [cartoon text] CART 56:13
M. is Americanism MCCA 206:8
McDonald M.'s wrapper FELT 112:6
McNamara M.'s War MCNA 211:7
me M. Decade WOLF 344:3
meal building a m. MEND 221:12
gives a m. man-appeal ADVE 4:17
m. was never found ULLM 325:5
mean depends what you m. by CATC 59:12
Down these m. streets CHAN 62:3
even if you don't m. it TRUM 323:11
Know what I m., Harry BRUN 46:10
M., Moody and Magnificent TAGL 314:10
poem should not m. but be MACL 210:2
whatever that may m. CHAR 63:2
meaning emptied of m. CAMU 52:16
Is there a m. to music COPL 77:6
joke with a double m. BARK 23:6
language charged with m. POUN 264:6
m. doubtless objectionable ANON 12:6
missed the m. ELIO 103:1
real m. lies underneath CARE 54:1
meanings With words and m. ELIO 102:14
means decide all m. are permitted DAWS 85:13
end cannot justify the m. HUXL 163:13
ends and scarce m. ROBB 275:5
Whatever 'in love' m. DUFF 95:7
meant it's what I m. VAUG 327:4
'w-a-t-e-r' m. the wonderful KELL 177:2
measles m. of the human race EINS 101:3
measured m. out my life ELIO 104:5
measurements easier to make m. SULL 311:7
meat teeth are in the real m. GRIM 141:7
mechanized m. slaughterhouses VANE 326:14
medal m. for killing two men MATL 219:2
media exposed to the m. BOWI 42:1
m. It sounds like STOP 309:11
medical in advance of m. thought WODE 343:4
medicinal M. discovery AYRE 20:1
medicine mistake m. for magic SZAS 312:9
rotational m. MORG 231:1
mediocre middle-aged and m. STRE 310:13
Some men are born m. HELL 152:3
mediocrity m. of the apparatus TROT 322:11
m. thrust upon them HELL 152:3
meditation light with m. DUNN 96:5
medium call it a m. because ACE 1:5
m. is the message MCLU 210:8
mother and m. SZEN 312:14
meet m. 'em on your way down MIZN 228:8
We'll m. again PARK 254:3
meeting great ordeal of m. me CHUR 68:5
megalith M.-still HUGH 162:6
melody m. lingers on BERL 31:5
pretty girl is like a m. BERL 31:4
melting-pot M. where all races ZANG 350:3
member accept me as a m. MARX 218:8
memoir point of any m. FORS 123:1
memoirs write m. is to speak ill PÉTA 257:4
memorandum m. is written ACHE 1:9
memorials there are no m. YEVT 349:5
memories m. are card-indexes CONN 75:10
m. are hunting horns APOL 13:4
M. are not shackles BENN 29:15
m. insist on cherishing O'NE 246:10
memory Footfalls echo in the m. ELIO 102:9
God gave us m. BARR 24:5
m. remembers the happy things LOVE 203:9
m. revealed itself PROU 267:4
M. says: Want RICH 274:2
no force can abolish m. ROOS 278:7
No m. of having starred FROS 127:15
Poor people's m. CAMU 52:9
quits the m. with difficulty BEEC 26:16
sense them like a m. MOSE 233:4
stay in a man's m. KIPL 184:7
Thanks for the m. ROBI 275:7
men all m. are rapists FREN 125:4
how much m. hate them GREE 140:3
I eat m. like air PLAT 259:12
If m. could get pregnant KENN 177:5
If m. had to have babies DIAN 91:9
manners out of m. DICK 92:2
m. are like bloody buses COPE 77:3
M. are so honest LERN 196:17
M. at forty JUST 175:2
m. confused with life FRID 125:16
M. eat hogs STEV 307:14
m. hurrying back MULD 234:12
M. seldom make passes PARK 253:4
M.! the only animal to fear LAWR 192:9
m. we wanted to marry STEI 307:2
m. who are discriminated MEIR 221:3
M. who march away HARD 146:13
m. with the muck-rakes ROOS 278:12
not the m. in my life that counts WEST 334:13
twenty-five-year-old m. MCCU 207:9
war between m. and women THUR 320:7
We are the hollow m. ELIO 103:13
menace m. to be defeated SCAR 290:20

mend Make do and m. OFFI 245:11
mental dissolution of m. forms AMIS 8:9
Freedom and slavery are m. GAND 131:6
m. processes HALD 143:9
mentor m. and my tormentor BROW 45:13
Mercedes buy me a M. Benz JOPL 173:1
merciless looked at in m. glare WILL 339:14
mercury pick up m. with a fork LLOY 201:12
mercy I want m. HUGH 162:13
mermaids heard the m. singing ELIO 104:8
merrygoround It's no go the m. MACN 211:10
mess Another fine m. LAUR 189:14
m. we have made of things ELIO 102:6
message if there is a m. PAXM 255:9
medium is the m. MCLU 210:8
m. of your play BEHA 27:3
putting a m. in a bottle HODG 157:7
messages m. should be delivered GOLD 137:10
messenger m.-boy Presidency SCHL 291:1
met m. the enemy CART 56:10
We m. at nine LERN 196:18
metaphor it's a lovely m. LOVE 203:11
metaphysical m. brothel KOES 185:10
Methodism more to M. than Marxism PHIL 258:1
Mexico gringo in m. FUEN 128:16
mice as long as it catches m. DENG 90:1
slept with m. COWA 79:12
Michelangelo M. left a proof YEAT 348:14
Talking of M. ELIO 104:3
Mickey Mouse live in M. land HOPK 159:10
M. could direct HYTN 164:11
microphone paid for this m. REAG 271:8
middle in the m. of the road BEVA 34:6
Secret sits in the m. FROS 127:17
middle age dead centre of m. ADAM 1:13
pleasures of m. POUN 264:4
reckless m. YEAT 347:19
middle-aged Grown m. WINT 342:4
Middle Ages go and live in the M. SMIT 301:4
M. ended in the 1950s HOBS 157:1
middle class m. morality SHAW 296:18
midnight Holding hands at m. GERS 133:15
M. Without Pity JOHN 171:3
stroke of the m. hour NEHR 238:10
might Britons alone use 'M.' WAUG 331:15
migraine Love is a universal m. GRAV 139:1
miles m. to go before I sleep FROS 128:1
milestone We're at a m. SULS 311:9
militant first m. lowbrow BERL 31:13
m. pacifist EINS 100:8
militants m. like cleaning women TRUF 323:2
military close my m. career MACA 206:3
entrust to m. men CLEM 71:5
m. man approaches SHAW 296:2
milk end is moo, the other, m. NASH 237:6
Gin was mother's m. SHAW 296:19
lady loves M. Tray ADVE 3:5
m. and the yoghurt TRIL 322:4
m. of human kindness GUED 142:1
M.'s leap toward immortality FADI 111:2
m. the cow of the world WILB 338:6
putting m. into babies CHUR 67:11
milka Drinka Pinta M. Day ADVE 3:16
millennium end of a m. promises HEWI 154:9
nonsense of the m. BONO 40:7
Third M. CLAR 70:6
million Fifty m. Frenchmen SAYI 289:16
make a m. ANON 11:2
m. deaths a statistic STAL 305:10
m. million spermatozoa HUXL 164:6
millionaire I am a M. SHAW 295:14
m. who bought it MCCA 206:5
old-fashioned m. FISH 114:9
Who wants to be a m. PORT 262:20
millions I will be m. EPIT 109:14
M. long for immortality ERTZ 108:11
that of m. of others LOEW 202:2
minarets Fretted with m. THWA 320:10
mind all in the m. WOLF 343:12
beat at your m. HECH 151:10
Cast your m. on other days YEAT 348:16
change their m. FITZ 119:12
could not make up his m. OLIV 245:18
cutting edge of the m. BRON 44:6
don't m. if I do CATC 59:6
empires of the m. CHUR 67:12
forces of the m. PROU 267:6
Georgia on my m. GORR 138:4
losing your m. FOX 123:10
m. begins to roam SOLZ 301:13
M. in its purest play WILB 338:7
m. is just like a spin-dryer NOLA 243:3
m. is maturing late NASH 237:14
M. my bike CATC 59:20
m. of Lord Beaverbrook ATTL 16:1
m. of the oppressed BIKO 35:9
m. that can write AHER 5:5
m. the least of possessions WHIT 336:8
m. watches itself CAMU 52:12
m. which reveres details LEWI 199:5
not to have a m. QUAY 268:4
no way out of the m. PLAT 259:7
out of my m. OPEN 247:3
sex in the m. LAWR 192:8
they're wrong. M. it FORS 122:12
travel broadens the m. CHES 64:14
Until reeled the m. GIBB 134:4
violence in the m. ALDI 6:3
Why m. being wrong AYER 19:17
would know the m. of God HAWK 149:7
mindful M. of the Church's teaching MARG 216:12
minds M. like beds always made up WILL 340:1

m. of ordinary men BRON 44:8
paid to have dirty m. TREV 322:2
mine lovin' dat man of m. HAMM 144:7
she is m. for life SPAR 303:7
minefield grief is like a m. WARN 330:8
if you're fat, is a m. MARG 216:14
miners like m.' coal dust BOOT 40:10
Minerva owl of M. PAUL 255:8
mines m. reported in the fairway KIPL 183:10
Mineworkers National Union of M. MACM 211:4
minister last m. is strangled NAIR 237:2
M. whose stubbornness JENK 169:10
Yes, M.! No, Minister CROS 82:2
ministers 'experts' make the worst M. ATTL 16:6
group of Cabinet M. CURZ 83:6
how much my M. talk THAT 316:13
m. decide THAT 317:12
mink trick of wearing m. BALM 22:7
minks LSD reminds me of m. GRAV 139:4
minor change from major to m. PORT 262:11
minorities treats its m. LÉVE 198:2
We are all m. EWIN 110:11
minority not enough to make a m. ALTM 7:8
mint m. with the hole ADVE 4:12
minute cannot cage the m. MACN 211:17
fill the unforgiving m. KIPL 183:7
minutes famous for fifteen m. WARH 329:12
have the seven m. COLL 73:11
miracle is m. enough PEAK 255:12
miracles believe in m. FOX 124:1
Miranda remember an Inn, M. BELL 28:6
mirror in the rear m. RODD 276:5
miserable Heaven knows I'm m. MORR 232:9
m. limpet CRAN 79:14
misery great kick at m. LAWR 192:16
Man hands on m. to man LARK 189:2
misfits m., Looney Tunes REAG 271:13
misguided missiles and m. men KING 181:11
mislead one to m. the public ASQU 15:5
misleading bound to be m. WATS 331:1
misquotation M. is the privilege PEAR 256:3
misrule Thirteen years of Tory m. POLI 262:4
missed m. the bus CHAM 61:12
Woman much m. HARD 147:1
misses m. family and friends EPIT 109:15
missiles guided m. and misguided KING 181:11
missionaries eaten by m. SPOO 304:13
Mississippi singing of the M. HUGH 161:11
mistake America a gigantic m. FREU 125:14
author made a m. DIRA 93:1
have made a great m. MORS 232:10
make a m., it's a beaut LA G 187:5
m. shall not be repeated EPIT 109:17
Shome m., shurely CATC 60:3
mistakes genius makes no m. JOYC 174:2
If he makes m. CHUR 68:14
just created like m. EMEC 107:11
M. are a fact GIOV 135:6
some of the worst m. HEIS 151:13
misunderstood don't want to be m. FRUM 128:7
through being m. COCT 72:12
mites with m. of stars MAYA 220:2
Mitty Walter M., the undefeated THUR 320:8
mixed no 'm. ' marriages MORR 232:7
moanday m., tearsday, wailsday JOYC 173:7
mob I lied to please the m. KIPL 182:13
mockingbird kill a m. LEE 194:17
model m. of modern Prime Minister HENN 153:3
provide logical m. LÉVI 198:8
moderate white m. devoted to KING 181:4
moderation m. in the pursuit GOLD 137:2
M. the highest virtue JOHN 171:12
modern All art was m. once SERO 293:14
m. Prime Minister HENN 153:3
modernity M. is the transition SACK 284:4
modest good deal to be m. about CHUR 68:4
M.? My word, no REED 272:5
mois *m. des floraisons* ARAG 13:7
molecule inhales one m. of it JEAN 169:3
molecules without understanding m. CRIC 80:9
moll King's M. Reno'd NEWS 240:13
Moloch M., national sovereignty MEYE 223:1
mom place called M.'s ALGR 6:6
moment Exhaust the little m. BROO 45:4
if only for a m. SZYM 313:1
m. of awakening COET 72:15
m. of madness DAVI 85:1
one brief shining m. LERN 196:15
momentary Beauty m. in the mind STEV 308:2
momentum M. part of exhilaration LAHR 187:7
monarch m. of the road FLAN 119:17
relations with the M. BLAI 37:7
monarchy m. become only popular ST J 284:14
US presidency a Tudor m. BURG 48:6
money ain't got a barrel of m. WOOD 344:11
bank will lend you m. if HOPE 159:8
Capitalism is using its m. CAST 57:8
corrupted by m. GREE 139:9
costs a lot of m. PART 254:12
divided up their m. STEA 306:2
haven't got the m. RUTH 283:13
He had m. as well THAT 316:12
Hollywood m. isn't money PARK 253:18
if you can count your m. GETT 134:2
If you have m. you spend it KENN 178:18
licence to print m. THOM 320:3
listen to m. singing LARK 189:6
long enough to get m. from LEAC 193:10

money (*cont.*):
lost m. by underestimating MENC 221:10
M. are like money AMIS 8:8
m. can't buy me love LENN 196:5
M. couldn't buy friends MILL 224:11
M. doesn't talk, it swears DYLA 97:9
M. gives me pleasure BELL 27:16
m.-grabbing cronies HAGU 142:10
m. gushes into politics WHIT 336:11
M. is like a sixth sense MAUG 219:7
m. I spend on advertising LEVE 197:15
M. was exactly like sex BALD 21:5
m. was not time MERR 222:10
must put the m. in BULL 47:9
Never ask of m. spent FROS 127:9
nobody ever lost m. DEED 88:2
not having any m. WHIT 337:9
not spending m. alone EISE 101:7
only interested in m. SHAW 297:1
poet can earn more m. AUDE 18:17
poetry in m. GRAV 139:3
rub up against m. RUNY 281:8
Take the m. and run FILM 118:15
they have more m. FITZ 118:17
They hired the m. COOL 76:13
use the m. for the poor PERÓ 256:10
voice is full of m. FITZ 119:2
voter who uses his m. SAMU 286:4
When you have m., it's sex DONL 93:9
mongrels energetic m. FISH 114:5
monkey attack the m. BEVA 34:8
make a m. of a man BENC 28:10
monkeys m. banging on typewriters WILE 338:16
m. in the jungle CASH 57:1
m. strumming on typewriters EDDI 98:8
you get m. SAYI 289:21
monks m. at Clonmacnoise HEAN 150:12
monogamy M. is the same ANON 10:1
monologue m. is not a decision ATTL 15:14
monologues Intersecting m. WEST 335:4
monopoly best of all m. profits HICK 155:4
m. stage of capitalism LENI 195:10
Monroe mouth of Marilyn M. MITT 228:7
monster busy m., manunkind CUMM 82:8
monstrous m. carbuncle CHAR 63:3
M. carbuncles SPEN 303:13
month April is the cruellest m. ELIO 104:19
m. of metamorphoses ARAG 13:7
m. of tension LESS 197:8
monument m. sticks like fishbone LOWE 204:6
moo One end is m. NASH 237:6
moocow m. coming down along the road OPEN 247:15
moody Mean, M. and Magnificent TAGL 314:10
moon Don't let's ask for the m. FILM 115:4
landing a man on the M. KENN 178:8
land on the m. KOES 185:14
looking at the full m. GINS 135:3
m. belongs to everyone DE S 90:8
m. in lonely alleys CRAN 80:1
m. is in the seventh house RADO 269:1
m. shone bright ELIO 105:4
m. the stars TRUM 323:3
m. walks the night DE L 89:8
Old Devil M. in your eyes HARB 145:13
only a paper m. HARB 145:12
Only you beneath the m. PORT 262:14
wanted the m. STEI 306:12
moonlight m. and music BERL 31:3
M. behind you COWA 79:3
moonlit Knocking on the m. door DE L 89:5
on the m. door OPEN 247:7
moral don't have a m. plan CRON 81:8
form of m. insurance BROD 44:3
It *is* a m. issue NEWS 240:10
Mankind's m. test KUND 187:2
m. as soon as unhappy PROU 267:7
No m. system can rest AYER 19:13
party is a m. crusade WILS 341:3
purely m. act HAVE 149:1
moralists delight to m. RUSS 283:3
morality Goodbye, m. HERB 153:8
know about m. CAMU 52:17
market has no m. HESE 153:15
middle-class m. SHAW 296:18
M.'s a gesture BOLT 40:4
two kinds of m. RUSS 282:17
What is m. WHIT 337:2
morals Food first, then m. BREC 43:11
more believing m. and more YATE 346:7
knows m. and more MAYO 220:9
Less is m. ROHE 277:8
m. and more about less BUTL 50:1
m. equal than others ORWE 249:6
m. Piglet wasn't there MILN 225:1
m. than somewhat RUNY 281:9
M. will mean worse AMIS 8:5
morning arrested one fine m. OPEN 247:18
autumn arrives in the m. BOWE 41:9
Come, lovely M. DAVI 85:5
getting married in the m. LERN 196:16
Good m., sir CATC 58:20
hate myself in the m. LARD 188:7
m. again in America POLI 261:17
M. has broken FARJ 111:7
take you in the m. BALD 21:7
what a beautiful m. HAMM 144:12
Mornington M. Crescent HARG 147:9
Morocco we're M. bound BURK 48:8
moron consumer isn't a m. OGIL 244:13
IQ of a m. VIDA 328:8
Morris M. Minor prototype NUFF 243:7
mortar Lies are the m. WELL 333:13

Moscow do not march on M. MONT 229:13
mosquito just another m. OKPI 244:16
moth Both m. and flam ROET 276:12
mother artist man and m. woman SHAW 295:20
Can you hear me, m. CATC 58:8
Did this happen to your m. WALK 329:2
have a beautiful m. WALK 329:5
I have been a m. to you O'DO 244:12
m. and medium SZEN 312:14
M. died today OPEN 247:2
m. of all battles HUSS 163:9
m. of all treachery PAIS 252:9
M. of the Free BENS 30:5
m.'s little helper JAGG 167:9
m. will be there HERB 153:5
my father and my m. JENN 170:2
my m. I see in myself FRID 125:15
rob his m. FAUL 112:2
Took great care of his M. MILN 225:7
mothers Come m. and fathers DYLA 97:17
m. go on getting blamed WHIT 337:8
m. no longer sing MENU 221:14
mothers-in-law m. and Wigan Pier BRID 44:1
motion poetry in m. KAUF 175:10
motor heart's stalled m. MAYA 220:6
motorcycle art of m. maintenance PIRS 259:2
mould frozen in an out-of-date m. JENK 169:8
mountain Climb ev'ry m. HAMM 144:8
go up to the m. KING 181:9
In a m. greenery HART 148:6
last blue m. FLEC 120:3
mourn no cause to m. OWEN 251:11
mourners let the m. come AUDE 17:3
mourning Don't waste time in m. HILL 156:1
M. becomes Electra O'NE 246:8
mouse invention of a m. DISN 93:3
that damned M. MAYE 220:7
mouth Englishman to open his m. SHAW 296:15
Keep your m. shut OFFI 245:15
m. of Marilyn Monroe MITT 228:7
m. used as a latrine AMIS 8:1
My m. went across NERU 239:3
poet's m. be silent YEAT 347:18
silver foot in his m. RICH 274:5
z is keeping your m. shut EINS 100:13
mouthful filling in a m. of decay OSBO 251:1
mouths examining his wives' m. RUSS 282:10
stuffed their m. with gold BEVA 34:13
movable Paris is a m. feast HEMI 152:11
move feel the earth m. HEMI 152:9
moved We shall not be m. SAYI 290:12
moves If it m., salute it SAYI 289:20
movie could direct a m. HYTN 164:11
m. was shot in 3B FILM 117:10
movies M. should have a beginning GODA 136:6
pay to see bad m. GOLD 137:7
thing that can kill the m. ROGE 277:1
Mozart no female M. PAGL 252:3
MP Being an M. ABBO 1:1
Being an M. PARR 254:9
MPs healthy cynicism of M. CREW 80:8
much not m. for them to be COMP 74:5
so m. owed by so many CHUR 67:1
muckrakes men with the m. ROOS 278:12
mud M.! Glorious mud FLAN 119:15
pure clay of time's m. MALA 213:14
muddle This was a m. MCLE 210:3
mudging fudging and m. OWEN 251:3
mugged liberal who has been m. SAYI 289:8
not-getting-m. HORN 159:13
mulatto Grape is my m. mother HUGH 162:10
Mulligan plump Buck M. OPEN 247:19
mum fuck you up, your m. and dad LARK 189:1
oafish louts remember M. BETJ 33:3
mumble When in doubt, m. BORE 41:2
mumbo-jumbo enough of the m. GUIN 142:4
murder about a m. ORWE 249:10
brought m. into the home HITC 156:10
commit a m. VAN 326:11
decided to m. his wife OPEN 247:9
m. by the throat LLOY 201:7
m. men everywhere FANO 111:4
m. respectable ORWE 250:11
m. the thinker WESK 334:5
not m. but the restoration JAME 168:6
stick to m. and leave art EPST 108:9
to m., for the truth ADLE 2:7
We hear war called m. MACD 208:3
murderer m. for fancy prose style NABO 236:7
shoot your m. ACHE 1:7
murderers m. of Jewish children WIES 338:4
Murdoch wrapped in a M. newspaper ROYK 280:11
muscles M. better and nerves more CUMM 82:11
muse tenth American m. BRON 44:9
Why does my M. only speak SMIT 301:2
museum ace caff with a nice m. ADVE 3:2
m. inside our heads LIVE 200:10
mush m. and slush OWEN 251:3
mushroom supramundane m. LAUR 191:11
too short to stuff a m. CONR 76:4
music all m. is folk music ARMS 14:4
Beauty in m. IVES 166:5
body swayed to m. YEAT 346:8
dance to the m. of time POWE 264:11
day the m. died MCLE 209:12
don't like my m. LOEW 202:2
English may not like m. BEEC 26:17
Good m. is that which BEEC 26:16

music (*cont.*):
how potent cheap m. is COWA 79:7
I got m. GERS 133:11
Is there a meaning to m. COPL 77:6
Jazz is the only m. COLE 73:4
Let's face the m. and dance BERL 31:3
most civilized m. USTI 325:17
M. begins to atrophy POUN 264:3
m. business is not MORR 232:8
m. expresses itself STRA 310:10
M. is feeling, then STEV 308:1
M. is your own experience PARK 253:1
m. that excels FISH 114:8
m. the brandy of the damned SHAW 295:21
My m. is best understood STRA 310:8
real m. was sex DOYL 94:11
sound of m. HAMM 144:15
twang, and you've got m. VICI 328:1
What do you think about m. VAUG 327:5
What m. is more enchanting SMIT 300:11
What the m. says BOWI 41:17
worth expressing in m. DELI 89:11
musician m., if he's a messenger HEND 152:17
Muslims zealous M. to execute KHOM 180:4
must you m. go on BECK 25:11
mutilate fold, spindle or m. SAYI 289:14
myriad There died a m. POUN 263:14
myself my mother I see in m. FRID 125:15
mystery grasped m. of the atom BRAD 42:7
I had m. OWEN 251:12
riddle wrapped in a m. CHUR 66:7
myth m. not a fairy story RYLE 284:1
purpose of m. LÉVI 198:8
thing itself and not the m. RICH 274:1
myths Science must begin with m. POPP 260:9
where m. Go when they die FENT 112:9

nabobs nattering n. AGNE 5:2
nagging N. is the repetition SUMM 311:11
nail I n. my pictures together SCHW 292:10
nailing n. his colours FIEL 113:4
naive n. domestic Burgundy CART 56:4
n. forgive and forget SZAS 312:7
naked n. ape MORR 231:8
n. into the conference chamber BEVA 34:9
name In the n. of God, go AMER 7:11
know, yet can't quite n. LARK 188:13
n. at the top of the page CHUR 68:9
n. is history THWA 320:10
n. is Mandy PARR 254:10
n. liveth for evermore EPIT 110:2
prefer a self-made n. HAND 145:5
problem that has no n. FRIE 125:17
problem that has no n. FRIE 126:2
state with the prettiest n. BISH 36:4
writing our n. there HEAN 150:6
named N. Shamed NEWS 240:14
names confused things with n. SART 287:9
in love with American n. BENÉ 28:15
n. of all these particles FERM 112:12
naming n. of parts REED 272:2
napalm smell of n. in the morning FILM 116:4
Napoleon thinks he is N. CLEM 71:2
Napoleons Caesars and N. HUXL 164:1
narrative descriptive n. EPHR 108:7
nastier how much n. I would be WAUG 332:1
nasty n. in the woodshed GIBB 134:3
nation AMERICA thus top n. SELL 293:12
broad mass of a n. HITL 156:16
create a n. Europe MONN 229:7
exterminate a n. SPOC 304:12
n. engaged in heaping up POWE 265:2
n. fit to sit in judgement WILS 341:12
n. is judged LÉVE 198:2
N. shall speak peace REND 272:12
n. talking to itself MILL 224:7
n. that had lion's heart CHUR 68:6
no rainbow n. MAND 215:7
one-third of a n. ROOS 278:1
pillars of the n. state PROD 266:12
take a n.'s pulse WHIT 336:3
terrorize a whole n. MURR 236:1
what our N. stands for BETJ 33:11
national N. Debt SELL 293:10
n. dish no longer JEAN 169:2
n. home for the Jewish people BALF 22:1
nationalism N. is an infantile EINS 101:3
nations Europe of n. DE G 88:10
Let n. rage BISH 36:6
n. acted like gangsters KUBR 186:11
n. which have put mankind INGE 165:5
Other n. use 'force' WAUG 331:15
three small n. STRA 310:12
native England's n. people BURN 48:10
'N.' always means STEI 306:8
our ideas about the n. LESS 197:7
NATO N. exists for three reasons ISMA 166:2
Nato N. is the bedrock of Europe POWE 264:17
nattering n. nabobs AGNE 5:2
natural n. party of government WILS 341:7
N. selection a mechanism FISH 114:11
nature Defying n., it surpasses PAGL 252:1
heartless, witless n. HOUS 160:6
interpreted n. as freely GIRA 135:9
left-wing, like n. DEBR 87:11
n. cannot be fooled FEYN 113:2
n. makes it so hard MCNE 212:2
N., Mr Allnutt, is what FILM 117:4
n. replaces it with WILL 339:11
n.'s way of telling you SAYI 289:11
whatever N. has in store FERM 112:13
naught n. for your comfort CHES 63:9

naughty N. but nice FILM 118:10
Navajo Don't speak N. NEZ 239:11
naval N. tradition CHUR 68:2
navy army and a n. WEIN 332:12
Neanderthal N. skeleton HAWK 149:3
of N. man STRA 310:7
necessarily ain't n. so HEYW 155:1
Not n. conscription KING 181:16
necessary journey *really* n. OFFI 245:8
neck at last wrings its n. RUSS 282:15
Some chicken! Some n. CHUR 67:7
necklace with our n. MAND 215:6
need All you n. is love LENN 196:4
enough for everyone's n. BUCH 47:5
face of total n. BURR 48:13
People who n. people MERR 222:9
things that people don't n. WARH 330:1
Will you still n. me LENN 196:11
negative Europe the unfinished n. MCCA 206:9
n. waiting to be slipped WILS 340:10
prefers a n. peace KING 181:4
negotiate n. out of fear KENN 178:5
not here to n. TRIM 322:5
negotiating N. with de Valera LLOY 201:12
when I was n. MAND 215:5
Negro American N. problem BALD 21:4
life of the N. race DARR 84:6
N.'s great stumbling block KING 181:4
one drop of N. blood HUGH 161:12
places where the average N. DAVI 85:7
Negroes culture of the N. PADE 251:16
neighbour policy of the good n. ROOS 277:16
neighbours make good n. FROS 127:12
Nell Little N. and Lady Macbeth WOOL 345:11
neoclassical n. endogenous growth BROW 45:11
neo-conservative n. ideas AMIE 7:12
nerve do not lose my n. NEHR 238:12
n. has been extracted ROWL 280:7
nervous n. breakdown RUSS 282:5
nessun *N. dorma* ADAM 1:10
nest not a n.-egg person JOHN 170:10
net surfing the N. ELIZ 106:7
nets try to fly by those n. JOYC 173:10
nettles dust on the n. THOM 319:6
neurosis n. is a secret TYNA 325:3
N. is a way of avoiding TILL 320:12
neurotics come to us from n. PROU 267:3
neutral apart, studiously n. WILS 341:14
neutrality Armed n. WILS 341:16
Just for a word 'n.' BETH 33:1
N. helps the oppressor WIES 338:3
neutrinos N., they are very small UPDI 325:15
never N. explain FISH 114:7
n. had it so good MACM 210:14
N. in the field CHUR 67:1
N. knowingly undersold ADVE 4:14
N. mind the quality POWE 265:10
N. on Sunday FILM 118:11
N. to have lived is best YEAT 347:9
We n. closed VAN 326:9
new beginning of a n. month MANN 216:2
believes that n. Labour DAVI 84:9
Few n. truths have ever won BERL 31:12
kill you in a n. way ROGE 277:6
n. clichés GOLD 137:9
n. deal ROOS 277:14
N. Frontier was not SCHL 291:3
N. Hampshire has long BUSH 49:10
New Labour, n. danger POLI 261:25
n. world order BUSH 49:9
nothing n. in dying LAST 190:10
pulse of this n. day ANGE 8:15
shock of the n. DUNL 95:10
so quite n. a thing CUMM 82:11
threshold of a n. house ATWO 16:10
wrote MAKE IT N. POUN 263:10
Youth is something very n. CHAN 62:9
New England charge against N. KRUT 186:9
news good n. yet to hear CHES 64:3
HERE IS THE N. HEAN 151:1
how much n. there is DOUG 94:3
man bites a dog, that is n. BOGA 39:8
news that STAYS n. POUN 264:5
New South Wales govern N. BELL 27:12
newspaper make a great n. BRAD 42:5
Murdoch n. ROYK 280:11
n. is a nation talking MILL 224:7
n. is to be Accurate SWOP 312:3
n. touches a story MAIL 213:7
newspapers burlesque and the n. STON 309:6
n. I can't stand STOP 309:12
n. paid too much MURD 235:13
read the n. avidly BEVA 34:12
writing for the n. LEWI 199:6
New York kind of N. USTI 326:3
N. makes one think BELL 28:8
present in N. CHAP 63:1
three o'clock in N. MIDL 223:2
New Yorker *N.* will be ROSS 279:9
New Yorkers begin again as N. CLIN 71:11
next n. to god america CUMM 82:5
used to be the n. president GORE 138:2
nice all the n. people OPEN 247:13
involving not very n. people FRAN 124:9
Naughty but n. FILM 118:10
N. guys. Finish last DURO 96:9
N. one, Cyril ADVE 4:15
n. to people on your way up MIZN 228:8
N. to see you CATC 59:21
N. work if you can get it GERS 133:15
not about being n. KEAT 176:8
thoroughly n. people PYM 267:15
nicely That'll do n. ADVE 3:4

nicens n. little boy OPEN 247:15
niche your n. in creation HALL 144:3
Nigeria daughter of N. EMEC 107:10
nigger n. of the world ONO 246:13
night blue of the n. CROS 81:9
dark n. of the soul FITZ 119:6
fit n. out for man or beast FIEL 113:13
gentle into that good n. THOM 318:5
hard day's n. LENN 196:8
Illness the n.-side of life SONT 302:16
journey into n. O'NE 246:7
language of the n. LE G 195:5
moon walks the n. DE L 89:8
N. and day PORT 262:14
N. Mail crossing the Border AUDE 17:16
n. of the long knives HITL 156:12
N., snow, and sand NERU 239:2
n. starvation ADVE 3:25
something of the n. WIDD 338:1
terrible n. PORT 263:1
nightgowns tweed n. GING 134:11
nightingale n. sang in Berkeley MASC 218:13
nightingales n. are singing near ELIO 104:18
nightmare History is a n. JOYC 174:1
In the n. of the dark AUDE 17:9
national n. is over FORD 121:8
nightmares Don't have n. CATC 58:12
n. about two things STOC 309:3
nineteen since n.-eighteen AHER 5:4
ninety live to be over n. ABBO 1:2
n.-minute patriots SILL 298:6
nix Sticks n. hick pix NEWS 240:18
Nixon N. impeached himself ABZU 1:4
no can't say N. in any of them PARK 253:14
It's n. go the merrygoround MACN 211:10
Just say n. OFFI 245:9
land of the omnipotent N. BOLD 40:2
man who says n. CAMU 52:13
N.! No! No THAT 317:14
n. you always meant RUME 281:2
she said 'n.' ALLE 7:1
We say N. WRIG 345:16
Noah N. he often said to his wife CHES 64:6
one poor N. HUXL 164:6
Nobel dinner for N. Prizewinners KENN 178:11
nobility n. without pride DUNC 95:9
noble days of the N. Savage BIKO 35:8
nobody N. came GINS 135:1
n. knows you're a dog CART 56:8
n.'s going to stop 'em BERR 32:6
n.'s perfect FILM 117:11
n. tells me anything GALS 130:16
n. will come SAND 286:10
Nothing happens, n. comes BECK 26:5
there is n. there KEYN 180:1
nod Old N., the shepherd DE L 89:7
one great n. after the other NOLA 243:3
noise Go placidly amid the n. EHRM 99:9
loud n. at one end KNOX 185:8
love the n. it makes BEEC 26:17
n.! And the people ANON 11:14
n. is an effective means GOEB 136:9
prisoners of n. MORE 230:10
noisy into the n. crowd TAGO 313:3
non-being avoiding n. TILL 320:12
non-cooperation n. with evil GAND 131:8
nonexistent obsolescent and n. BREN 43:17
nonsense Blithering economic n. CLAR 70:9
n. of the millennium BONO 40:7
non-violence N. the first article GAND 131:7
norfan N., both sides WELL 333:11
Norfolk bear him up the N. sky BETJ 33:6
Very flat, N. COWA 79:6
normal N. is the good smile SHAF 294:12
north answer from the N. KIPL 183:15
heart of the N. is dead LAWR 192:18
He was my N., my South AUDE 17:4
to us the near n. MENZ 222:1
North America Mr and Mrs N. WINC 342:1
northern N. reticence HEAN 151:2
nose run up your n. dead against BALD 21:13
thirty inches from my n. AUDE 18:2
very shiny n. MARK 217:1
noses turn up our n. SHIE 297:12
where the n. would go HEMI 152:8
nostalgia N. isn't what it used ANON 11:15
not find out what you are *n.* LOY 204:17
n. I, but the wind LAWR 192:13
N. so much a programme ANON 11:16
N. while I'm alive BEVI 35:6
say 'Why n.' SHAW 295:4
note longest suicide n. KAUF 175:9
same n. can be played COLE 73:4
notebook in a little n. LASK 189:10
notes n. I handle no better SCHN 291:6
nothing don't believe in n. CHES 64:18
Emperors can do n. BREC 43:7
individually can do n. ALLE 6:11
N. ain't worth nothin' KRIS 186:8
N. happens, nobody comes BECK 26:5
N. is ever done SHAW 295:18
N. is more dangerous ALAI 5:11
N., like something LARK 188:12
N. to be done BECK 26:1
n. to look backward to FROS 127:3
n. to say CAGE 50:7
resent having n. COMP 74:6
say n. HEAN 151:2
You ain't heard n. yet JOLS 172:5
nothingness N. haunts being SART 287:5
notice not escaped our n. CRIC 80:10
taken no n. of HARE 147:5
noun verb not a n. FULL 129:3
novel n. is the one bright book LAWR 192:2

n. tells a story FORS 122:1
novelists great—the major n. LEAV 194:3
novels you lose two n. MCWI 212:4
now not right n. JAY 168:15
We are the masters n. MISQ 227:3
nowness n. of everything POTT 263:2
nuclear n. giants BRAD 42:8
safety record of n. O'NE 246:12
nudge nudge n., snap snap MONT 230:1
nuisance exchange of one n. ELLI 107:4
n. in time of war CHUR 67:13
nuisances small n. of peace-time HAY 149:9
NUM against the Pope or the N. BALD 21:13
number best n. for a dinner party GULB 142:5
called the wrong n. CART 56:11
I am not a n. MCGO 209:1
n. of the question CHUR 68:9
very interesting n. RAMA 269:8
numbers Noting the n. of trains MAXW 219:14
n. that rocket the mind WILB 338:5
numerical n. irrigation system AUGA 19:6
Nuremberg of the N. trials SHAW 297:5
prosecution at N. JACK 167:4
nurse always keep a-hold of N. BELL 27:11
N. UNUPBLOWN TELE 316:5
nuts N. MCAU 206:4

oafs muddied o. at the goals KIPL 183:8
oak juniper talks to the o. PAUL 255:7
O., and Ash, and Thorn KIPL 183:14
o. would sprout in Derry HEAN 150:15
oaths Judges must follow their o. ZOBE 351:2
oats feeds the horse enough o. GALB 130:9
obedience life of o. EICH 99:10
obey people would immediately o. SCHW 292:7
obituary except your own o. BEHA 27:4
o. in serial form CRIS 81:2
objectification o. of feeling LANG 188:6
objectionable meaning doubtless o. ANON 12:6
objective have a great o. CHIF 65:2
o. correlative ELIO 105:10
obligation o. goes unrecognized WEIL 332:7
obliteration policy is o. BELL 27:8
oblivion love, and then o. MCEW 208:14
obscenity 'o.' is not a term RUSS 283:4
obsolescence planned o. STEV 307:9
obsolescent o. and nonexistent BREN 43:17
obsolete war is o. or men are FULL 129:5
obvious in obvious o. BALF 22:2
occurred Ought never to have o. BENT 30:8
ocean blanket of o. CAUS 60:19
drop in the o. TERE 315:5
Earth when it is clearly O. CLAR 70:4
October O., that ambiguous month LESS 197:8
octopus dear o. SMIT 300:5
odd But not so o. BROW 46:3
How o. Of God EWER 110:9
must think it exceedingly o. KNOX 185:5
odds mass of o. and ends WOOL 345:6
off I want to be o. it PAXM 255:9
offence I was like to give o. FROS 127:13
only defence is in o. BALD 21:10
offend freedom to o. RUSH 281:13
offensive extremely o. SMIT 300:7
Life is an o. WHIT 336:12
what is merely o. EPHR 108:8
offer o. he can't refuse PUZO 267:13
office in o. but not in power LAMO 188:2
o. party is not WHIT 337:10
ousted from o. LIEB 199:11
official No sane local o. SMIT 300:3
This high o., all allow HERB 153:9
officialism Where there is o. FORS 122:17
Ohioan black O. swan WRIG 346:2
oil foreign o. controlling DYLA 97:16
Scotland's o. POLI 261:18
sound of o. wells FISH 114:8
oiled O. his way around the floor LERN 197:5
Okie O. means you're scum STEI 306:15
old attendance on my o. age YEAT 348:11
die before I get o. TOWN 321:5
first sign of o. age HICK 155:5
getting too o. DISN 93:2
Growing o. a bad habit MAUR 219:12
Growing o. is like POWE 264:13
heart grows o. YEAT 348:10
HOW O. CARY GRANT TELE 316:6
I grow o. . . . I grow old ELIO 104:8
know they're o. JENN 170:2
make me conservative when o. FROS 127:14
no country for o. men YEAT 348:3
not bored is never o. CASA 55:9
now am not too o. BLUN 38:5
o. age always fifteen years BARU 24:13
O. age is the most unexpected TROT 322:12
O. age should burn THOM 318:5
o. age, the last gap but one WHIT 336:6
o. heads on young shoulders SPAR 303:6
o. is having lighted rooms LARK 188:13
o. man in a dry month ELIO 103:10
O. man river HAMM 144:13
O. soldiers never die FOLE 120:15
outrageous o. fellow HOYL 161:2
planned by o. men RICE 273:9
problem of growing o. MORR 232:6
that horror—the o. woman COLE 73:7
They shall grow not o. BINY 35:12
too o. to rush up to the net ADAM 1:13
until they're o. BINC 35:10
warn you not to grow o. KINN 182:5
When I am an o. woman JOSE 173:4

older ask somebody o. than me BLAK 37:11
for us o. ones ELIZ 106:5
grow o. and older SAYE 288:10
O. men declare war HOOV 159:5
so much o. then DYLA 97:14
old-fashioned o. millionaire FISH 114:9
omelette o. all over our suits BROK 44:5
omelettes make o. properly BELL 28:7
omens grievous o. SUTT 312:1
omnibus horse power o. FLAN 119:17
omnipotent land of the o. No BOLD 40:2
Onassis O. would not have married VIDA 328:7
once o. and future king WHIT 336:9
O. we had a country AUDE 18:3
one But the O. was Me HUXL 164:6
centre upon number o. CHUR 68:14
How to be o. up POTT 263:5
o. for my baby MERC 222:5
square root of minus o. BECK 26:11
oneself Hell is o. ELIO 102:5
only If you were the o. girl GREY 140:15
It's the o. thing SAND 286:13
O. connect FORS 122:9
O. the lonely ORBI 248:5
onstage O. I make love JOPL 173:3
onwards o. and upwards YORK 349:9
oozing O. charm from every pore LERN 197:5
open in the great o. spaces MARQ 217:7
O. covenants of peace WILS 341:19
opened o. the door DIDD 92:3
opera o. ain't over SAYI 290:5
O. is when a guy gets GARD 132:1
operatic so romantic, so o. PROU 267:2
operations o. we can perform WHIT 337:4
opinion form a clear o. BONH 40:6
Government and public o. SHAW 295:22
o. has been widely held RUSS 282:12
what is my o. LOEW 202:2
whole climate of o. AUDE 17:5
opponents o. eventually die PLAN 259:6
opportunity maximum of o. SHAW 296:8
o. for achievement KEIL 176:11
when he had the o. ROWL 280:8
opposite o. of people STOP 309:16
opposition effective means of o. GOEB 136:9
oppressed mind of the o. BIKO 35:9
oppression violence and o. SOLZ 302:4
war against o. MCAL 205:12
oppressor ends as an o. CAMU 52:15
Neutrality helps the o. WIES 338:3
weapon in hands of o. BIKO 35:9
opprobrium term of o. MOYN 233:10
optimism not the same as o. HAVE 148:11
optimist o. is a guy MARQ 217:5
o. proclaims CABE 50:5
opulence private o. GALB 130:6
oral o. contraception ALLE 7:1
orange clockwork o. BURG 48:4
future's O. ADVE 3:19
happen to be an o. ALLE 6:10
orchestra signals to the o. SZEL 312:12
orchestration o. of platitudes WILD 338:15
order new world o. BUSH 49:9
not necessarily in that o. GODA 136:6
restoration of o. JAME 168:6
war creates o. BREC 43:6
wretched rage for o. MAHO 212:11
orders led by o. EICH 99:10
ordinary learn to see the o. BAIL 20:8
O. made beautiful SHAF 294:12
see God in the o. things EPIT 109:8
warn you not to be o. KINN 182:5
organ heart is an o. of fire ONDA 246:3
o. grinder is present BEVA 34:8
organisms Conflicts, like living o. MCEW 208:12
organization about the o. man WHYT 337:14
o. is and must be MILL 223:15
o. of forms CART 55:6
organize o. her own immortality LASK 189:10
waste time mourning—o. HILL 156:1
organized it's got to be o. HOCK 157:4
organizing Only an o. genius BEVA 34:3
organs o. have been transplanted HARB 145:15
orgasm o. has replaced the Cross MUGG 234:5
original o. is unfaithful BORG 41:4
saves o. thinking SAYE 288:9
originality O. is deliberate HOFF 157:9
originator o. of a new idea DIRA 92:10
orphan defeat is an o. CIAN 69:7
O., both sides WELL 333:11
Oscar assume that O. said it PARK 253:7
other happens to *o.* people CART 54:10
O. is ourselves THOM 319:13
O. voices, other rooms CAPO 53:9
Prudence is the o. woman ANON 11:18
wonderful for o. people KERR 179:5
others woman who lives for o. LEWI 198:10
Otis Miss O. regrets PORT 262:17
ought didn't o. never to have BEVI 35:4
something o. to be done WELL 333:17
ourselves Other is o. THOM 319:13
out best way o. is always through FROS 127:19
counted them all o. HANR 145:6
get o. while we're young SPRI 305:3
include me o. GOLD 137:3
truth is o. there CATC 60:6
outcast o. on the world HEWI 154:10
outer o. life of telegrams FORS 122:8
outlaw attacks from o. states REAG 271:13
outlaws o. Russia forever REAG 271:12
outrageous o. old fellow HOYL 161:2
outside just going o. LAST 190:6
just going o. MAHO 212:10

parents (*cont.*):
p. obey their children EDWA 99:5
p. were created for NASH 237:16
produce bad p. MORS 232:11
punished by selfish p. TREM 321:10
sue its p. WATS 331:2
Paris after they've seen P. LEWI 199:2
Down and out in P. ORWE 249:11
Is P. burning HITL 156:15
last time I saw P. HAMM 144:10
P. is a movable feast HEMI 152:11
park come out to the ball p. BERR 32:6
p., a policeman CHAP 62:13
Poisoning pigeons in the p. LEHR 195:7
parking put up a p. lot MITC 227:7
parley-voo Hinky, dinky, p. ANON 11:13
parliament desire to get here [P.] BOOT 40:10
enables P. to do SHAW 295:17
function of P. BOOT 40:11
modern P. CONN 74:12
[p.] a lot of hard-faced men BALD 21:8
p. of whores O'RO 248:9
P. would not exist SCAR 290:18
Scottish P. EWIN 110:10
Scottish p. SALM 285:14
shall be a Scottish p. ANON 12:5
shall be a Scottish p. DEWA 91:2
parliamentarian pleasure for a p. CRIT 81:3
parody devil's walking p. CHES 63:12
parrot has become a p. PAIS 252:10
This is a late p. MONT 230:2
parsley P. is gharsley NASH 237:10
part What isn't p. of ourselves HESS 154:3
particles names of all these p. FERM 112:12
parting p. has to come MUNR 235:3
partly Living and p. living ELIO 104:9
parts good as his p. WIND 342:2
naming of p. REED 272:2
refreshes the p. ADVE 3:24
save all the p. EHRL 99:7
so many moving p. SHAP 294:15
party great p. is not to be HAIL 143:5
in the p. manifestoes ROTH 280:2
natural p. of government WILS 341:7
office p. is not WHIT 337:10
p.'s over COMD 74:1
p.'s over CROS 81:11
put p. before country CREW 80:8
save the P. we love GAIT 130:1
pasarán *No p.* IBAR 164:13
pass Do not p. go SAYI 289:18
p. the ammunition FORG 121:14
prayed my cup might p. KIPL 183:3
They shall not p. IBAR 164:13
They shall not p. SAYI 289:22
passed That p. the time BECK 26:7
Timothy has p. EPIT 110:3
passengers p. off in small boats LAST 191:5
passeront *Ils ne p. pas* SAYI 289:22
passes beauty p. DE L 89:3
Men seldom make p. PARK 253:4
passing-bells p. for these OWEN 251:6
passion p. to which he has always POWE 264:7
prose and the p. FORS 122:9
vows his p. is infinite PARK 253:10
passionate full of p. intensity YEAT 348:7
passions inferno of his p. JUNG 174:10
passport My p.'s green HEAN 150:13
past always praising the p. SMIT 301:4
call on p. and future O'NE 246:11
cannot remember the p. SANT 286:15
last day of an era p. YELT 349:3
neither repeat his p. AUDE 18:18
nothing but the p. KEYN 179:8
p., brittle with relics THOM 319:12
p. exudes legend MALA 213:14
p. is a bucket of ashes SAND 286:9
p. is a foreign country OPEN 247:16
p. is lost CHAP 63:1
p. is the only dead thing THOM 319:2
p. not getting any better LEVI 198:5
p., present and future EINS 101:1
Remembrance of things p. PROU 267:1
Time present and time p. ELIO 102:8
under the bloody p. AHER 5:3
Utopia is a blessed p. KISS 184:15
Who controls the p. ORWE 250:3
pathless Truth is a p. land KRIS 186:6
pathos P., piety, courage FORS 122:16
patience had taught her p. COLE 73:6
other people's p. UPDI 325:7
patient p. etherized upon a table ELIO 104:2
p. etherized upon a table LEWI 198:12
patients poets are their own p. THOM 319:10
patria Died some, pro p. POUN 263:13
patries *Europe des p.* DE G 88:10
patriotism knock the p. out SHAW 296:13
P. is not enough CAVE 61:3
patriots ninety-minute p. SILL 298:6
patrol P. the halls WILB 338:8
pattable she is p. NASH 237:11
pattern Art is p. informed by READ 271:2
Art is the imposing of p. WHIT 337:3
Pauli P. [exclusion] principle GAMO 131:2
pause eine kleine P. LAST 191:2
pauses p. between the notes SCHN 291:6
paved If you p. the way HUGH 162:12
p. paradise MITC 227:7
paw ear on its p. MAYA 220:2
pay Can't p., won't pay POLI 261:10
Crime doesn't p. SAYI 289:9
Not a penny off the p. COOK 76:6
p. any price KENN 178:3
p. to see my Aunt Minnie WILD 338:12

p. us, pass us CHES 64:4
sum of things for p. HOUS 160:5
we are made to p. for FRIE 126:7
We won't p. FO 120:12
paycock till night like a p. O'CA 244:6
paying p. the Dane-geld KIPL 184:1
price well worth p. LAMO 188:1
PC P. is the LSD of the '90s LEAR 193:13
peace curse in time of p. CHUR 67:13
Give p. a chance LENN 196:7
hard and bitter p. KENN 178:2
have you known p. WEST 335:3
In p.: goodwill CHUR 68:12
In the arts of p. SHAW 296:1
Let p. fill our heart KUMA 186:12
Make it a *green* p. DARN 84:4
make your p. with authority MORR 232:4
may not be a just p. IZET 166:8
no p. is truly safe ANNA 9:6
not a p. treaty FOCH 120:14
no way to p. MUST 236:6
Open covenants of p. WILS 341:19
p. between equals WILS 341:15
P. cannot be built ADAM 2:2
p. for our time CHAM 61:10
p. from freedom MALC 214:2
P. is indivisible LITV 200:8
P. is much more precious SADA 284:7
P. is no longer a dream CLIN 72:1
P. is poor reading HARD 147:3
p. like retarded pygmies PEAR 256:4
P. nothing but slovenliness BREC 43:6
p. of the double-bed CAMP 52:2
P., political p. MITC 225:15
p. there may be in silence EHRM 99:9
p. will guide the planets RADO 269:1
p. with honour CHAM 61:10
people want p. so much EISE 101:10
plunging into a cold p. YELT 349:2
potent advocates of p. GEOR 133:3
prefers a negative p. KING 181:4
speak p. unto nation REND 272:12
tell me p. has broken out BREC 43:8
than to make p. CLEM 71:3
war and p. in 21st century KOHL 186:2
peaceful p. revolution impossible KENN 178:10
quietly pacifist p. WALK 329:4
peacefully p. towards its close DAWS 86:1
peach dare to eat a p. ELIO 104:8
peaches p. and what penumbras GINS 135:4
peacock till night like a p. O'CA 244:6
peak small things from the p. CHES 64:8
peanuts hate it as much as p. WELL 333:8
If you pay p. SAYI 289:21
pear go round the prickly p. ELIO 103:14
pearl splendid p. SEXT 294:9
Pearl Harbor since P. NATT 238:7
peas ability to sort p. HOLU 158:8
peasant cross woman's p. origins O'DO 244:12
I am a West Indian p. MCDO 208:5
p. by the shoulders WEST 335:3
peasants cricket with their p. TREV 321:12
pebble wise man hide a p. CHES 64:7
pederasty not p. RATT 270:6
pedestrians two classes of p. DEWA 91:4
peel orange p. picked out RALE 269:7
p. me a grape WEST 334:10
peepers where you get them p. MERC 222:4
peepshow ticket for the p. MACN 211:10
peer Not a reluctant p. BENN 29:2
peerage When I want a p. NORT 243:6
pellet p. with the poison FILM 117:7
pen spark-gap mightier than p. HOGB 157:12
squat p. rests HEAN 150:10
pencils feel for their blue p. ESHE 108:12
sadness of p. ROET 276:10
penicillin trials of p. HODG 157:6
pennies P. don't fall from heaven THAT 316:11
p. from heaven BURK 48:7
penny Not a p. off the pay COOK 76:6
pension hang your hat on a p. MACN 211:11
spend my p. on brandy JOSE 173:4
pentagon P., immense monument FRAN 124:10
people American p. have spoken CLIN 72:5
as if p. mattered SCHU 292:1
law not supported by p. HUMP 163:3
look after our p. LAST 190:4
Most p. ignore most poetry MITC 225:12
noise! And the p. ANON 11:14
no petty p. YEAT 348:18
Not many p. know that CAIN 50:9
p. are only human COMP 74:5
p. are the masters BLAI 37:5
p. hurting people MAIL 213:4
People p., but books never ROOS 278:7
P.'s Princess BLAI 37:6
p. were a kind of solution CAVA 61:2
People who need p. MERR 222:9
Power to the p. POLI 262:1
same as if they was p. DURE 96:8
we are the p. of England CHES 64:4
What kind of a p. CHUR 67:6
Peoria It'll play in P. POLI 261:16
pepper Sergeant P. TYNA 325:2
percentage reasonable p. BECK 26:3
perdition led to *p.* by a man WEST 335:10
perestroika [p.] combines GORB 137:14
started the process of p. GORB 137:15
perfect ever more p. eyes TEIL 315:1
It's not p. BINC 35:11
nobody's p. FILM 117:11
Nothing is p. STEP 307:5
One p. rose PARK 253:5

perfection P. of planned layout PARK 254:6
P. of the life YEAT 347:2
perfectly small, but p. formed COOP 77:2
perform p. without thinking WHIT 337:4
period p. of silence on your part ATTL 16:2
periphrastic p. study ELIO 102:14
perish p. together as fools KING 181:8
perished Now that love is p. MILL 223:11
perishes p. every day GOSS 138:5
Perón not been born P. PERÓ 256:11
perpendicular p. expression SHAW 297:3
perpetrator thou shalt not be a p. BAUE 25:2
persecuted because he is p. GOUL 138:6
Persians Truth-loving P. GRAV 138:12
persistence take the place of p. COOL 76:14
person no more than a p. AUDE 17:5
P. from Porlock SMIT 301:6
third p. was in the room POPE 260:4
personal P. isn't the same PRAT 265:11
p. is political POLI 261:26
P. relations FORS 122:8
warm p. gesture GALB 130:8
personalities meeting of two p. JUNG 174:13
p. of the two sexes MEAD 220:10
ten independent p. FOTH 123:5
personality good p. TUCK 324:2
product of his own p. FROM 126:10
personally should be p. associated BLAI 37:9
perspective jolt in the p. WOOL 345:5
perspiring city of p. dreams RAPH 270:1
persuaders hidden p. PACK 251:15
persuasive p. argument FRAM 124:3
pertinent way to a p. answer BRON 44:7
perversion War the universal p. RAE 269:2
perversity p. is the soul's UPDI 325:8
pervert loophole through which p. BRON 44:8
pessimist p. fears this is true CABE 50:5
p. waiting for rain COHE 73:1
petal dropping a rose p. MARQ 217:14
Peter government which robs P. SHAW 295:11
petrol price of p. has been increased CART 56:9
pets hate a word like 'p.' JENN 170:1
pettiness to expiate: a p. LAWR 192:12
petty no p. people YEAT 348:18
phagocytes stimulate the p. SHAW 295:8
phallic P. and ambrosial POUN 263:12
phallus future is the p. LAWR 192:3
Philadelphia living in P. EPIT 109:11
went to P., but FIEL 114:1
philistinism our yawning P. PRIT 266:11
philosophers separation of p. QUIN 268:8
philosophical p. tradition WHIT 337:6
philosophy linguistic p. RUSS 283:8
P. is a battle WITT 342:5
P. is the replacement RYLE 284:2
phoenix expect a p. hour DAY- 86:5
phone answer the p. CART 56:11
call him up on the p. SALI 285:9
E.T. p. home FILM 115:6
never even made a p. call CHOM 65:7
P. for the fish-knives BETJ 33:8
p. has not rung MITC 228:5
p. is for you LEBO 194:8
photograph p. is a secret ARBU 13:9
photographer p. is like the cod SHAW 296:24
to be a good p. BAIL 20:8
photography p. is all right if HOCK 157:3
P. is truth GODA 136:4
p. of an event CART 55:6
physical lightly called p. COLE 73:5
physician p. can bury mistakes WRIG 345:14
physicists p. have known sin OPPE 246:15
p.' war DAVI 85:6
physics no democracy in p. ALVA 7:9
p. or stamp collecting RUTH 283:10
pianists no better than many p. SCHN 291:6
piano help with moving the p. WEST 335:9
playing a p. in a brothel MUGG 234:7
Picardy Roses are flowering in P. WEAT 332:2
Picasso abhorred plastics, P. WAUG 331:11
pick p. it up SAYI 289:20
P. yourself up FIEL 113:10
pickle weaned on a p. ANON 12:8
picnic Teddy Bears have their P. KENN 177:8
picture no go the p. palace MACN 211:11
One p. is worth BARN 23:7
pictures I nail my p. together SCHW 292:10
P. are for entertainment GOLD 137:10
p. aren't good enough CAPA 53:6
p. didn't have beginning POLL 260:3
p. that got small FILM 118:2
pie make an apple p. SAGA 284:8
Miss American P. MCLE 210:1
p. in the sky when you die HILL 155:12
pig from p. to man ORWE 249:7
p. got up and walked away BURT 49:1
pigeon crooning like a bilious p. SHAW 296:16
pigeon-holed branded, p. PRES 265:14
pigeons flock of homing p. HUGH 162:14
Poisoning p. LEHR 195:7
pigs P. treat us as equals CHUR 69:1
pike p. in the thatch DE C 88:1
Pilate water like P. GREE 139:7
pile P. it high SAYI 290:6
P. the bodies high SAND 286:8
pilgrims land of the p. CUMM 82:5
We are all p. RYDE 283:14
We are the P. FLEC 120:3
pill little yellow p. JAGG 167:9
sleeping p. is white SEXT 294:9
something of a p. WODE 343:1
women may take the p. THOM 319:9
pillars p. of the nation state PROD 266:12
pillow like the feather p. HAIG 143:1

pilot what do I tell the p. LAST 191:6
pimples scratching of p. WOOL 345:7
pink bright p. dress SHUL 298:3
p. right down to NIXO 242:7
pinko-grey really p. FORS 122:14
pinstripe come in a p. suit FEIN 112:4
pint p. of plain O'BR 244:4
p.—that's very nearly GALT 131:1
pinta Drinka P. Milka Day ADVE 3:16
pioneer always the p. DOYL 94:10
pips until the p. squeak GEDD 132:5
piranha p. strikes SZYM 312:15
piss worth a pitcher of warm p. GARN 132:2
pissed p. in our soup BENN 29:13
pissing inside the tent p. out JOHN 171:13
pistol echo of a p.-shot DURR 96:11
I reach for my p. JOHS 172:4
p. in your pocket WEST 334:18
pistons black statement of p. SPEN 304:1
pitchfork use my wit as a p. LARK 189:3
pity Midnight Without P. JOHN 171:3
P. the feeling which arrests JOYC 173:12
p. this busy monster CUMM 82:8
Poetry is in the p. OWEN 251:4
unbearable p. RUSS 282:3
pix Sticks nix hick p. NEWS 240:18
place at the wrong p. BRAD 42:9
In p. of strife CAST 57:7
in the wrong p. DYLA 97:6
know your p. in the set-up KING 182:3
places all p. were alike to him KIPL 184:3
been things and seen p. WEST 334:11
distance between two p. WILL 339:12
placidly Go p. amid the noise EHRM 99:9
plagiarism one author, it's p. MIZN 228:9
plagiarist No p. can excuse HAND 145:4
plagiarize P.! Let's no one LEHR 195:6
plain no p. women on television FORD 121:6
pint of p. O'BR 244:4
plan by his p. of attack SASS 288:3
coherent p. to the universe HOYL 161:3
cunning p. CATC 59:8
don't have a moral p. CRON 81:8
plane It's a p. ANON 10:8
only two emotions in a p. WELL 333:9
planet hanging from a round p. EDDI 98:10
planets stars and all the p. TRUM 323:3
plank landing on a p. travelling EDDI 98:10
planned p. obsolescence STEV 307:9
planning p. is indispensable EISE 101:12
plans p. are useless EISE 101:12
plant I p. lines WALC 328:17
plantation still working on a p. HOLI 158:3
planter Ulsterman, of p. stock HEWI 154:11
plants talk to the p. CHAR 63:4
plasterer agog at the p. HEAN 150:6
plastic cannot pass through p. JOHN 170:8
plastics abhorred p., Picasso WAUG 331:11
platitude longitude with no p. FRY 128:11
p. is simply a truth BALD 21:9
stroke a p. until MARQ 217:13
platitudes orchestration of p. WILD 338:15
Plato p. told him: he couldn't CUMM 82:7
series of footnotes to P. WHIT 337:6
play Did that p. of mine send out YEAT 347:15
every time I p. it JOHN 170:9
Games people p. BERN 31:16
It'll p. in Peoria POLI 261:16
P. it again, Sam FILM 115:17
P. it again, Sam MISQ 226:13
p. it over again LAMB 187:13
P. it tough BRAD 42:10
p. things as they are STEV 307:16
work, rest and p. ADVE 4:10
y is p. EINS 100:13
players p. who hate your guts STEN 307:4
playing p. on the line FORS 122:13
stood like a p. card MAIL 213:5
work terribly hard at p. MORT 232:13
plays enjoyed going to p. UPDI 325:16
please P. explain HANS 145:9
try to p. everyone SWOP 312:4
pleased 'p.' is pronounced MURR 235:14
so p. with themselves ROBI 275:8
pleasure give that sort of p. GLEN 136:3
greater than the p. YOUN 349:11
No p. worth giving up AMIS 8:7
P.'s for those who are bad YESE 349:4
pleasures p. of the senses ESHE 108:13
pleats witty little p. BAIL 20:9
plebiscite justice by p. ZOBE 351:2
ploughs p., ladies, bears CANN 53:4
plumber choose to be a p. EINS 100:16
getting a p. on weekends ALLE 7:2
I can't get a p. SCHW 292:7
p. comes to unblock GLEN 136:3
plume in blast-beruffled p. HARD 146:8
plums I have eaten the p. WILL 340:3
p. and orange peel RALE 269:7
pluralism p. in social attitudes BOWI 42:2
poacher p. staggering MCCA 206:5
pocket gun in your p. WEST 334:18
pound in your p. WILS 341:8
poem Every good p. is a bridge DAY- 86:10
figure a p. makes FROS 128:2
p. is never finished VALÉ 326:4
p. lovely as a tree KILM 180:10
p. must ride on its own melting FROS 128:3
p. should not mean but be MACL 210:2
write a p. after Auschwitz ADOR 2:9
poems P. are made by fools KILM 180:11
p. should be Clyde-built DUNN 96:2
poet All a p. can do is warn OWEN 251:5
ask a p. to sing BOLD 40:3

poet (*cont.*):
hate what every p. hates KAVA 176:4
No p. ever interpreted GIRA 135:9
p. can earn more money AUDE 18:17
p. is always indebted MAYA 220:4
p. is the priest STEV 307:10
p.'s hope: to be AUDE 18:9
p.'s inward pride DAY- 86:6
p.'s mouth be silent YEAT 347:18
p.'s voice need not merely FAUL 112:1
p. will give up writing CELA 61:8
there is a p. indulging MAHO 212:11
worst tragedy for a p. COCT 72:12
poetry blood jet is p. PLAT 259:10
campaign in p. CUOM 82:15
deeper intimacy with p. NERU 239:4
Ireland hurt you into p. AUDE 17:6
no more define p. HOUS 160:8
p. begins to atrophy POUN 264:3
p. ignores most people MITC 225:12
p. in money GRAV 139:3
p. in motion KAUF 175:10
P. is a way to taking life FROS 128:4
[P.] is capable of saving RICH 274:7
P. is in the pity OWEN 251:4
P. is not most important THOM 318:19
P. is the achievement SAND 286:11
P. is the supreme fiction STEV 307:15
P. is to prose WAIN 328:13
P. is what is lost FROS 128:6
p. makes nothing happen AUDE 17:7
P. not a turning loose ELIO 105:13
p. should be alive ZEPH 350:7
p. strays into my memory HOUS 160:9
P. unearths from among HILL 155:9
saying it and that is p. CAGE 50:7
Writing a book of p. MARQ 217:14
poets all p. are Jews TSVE 324:1
impossible to hold the p. GIRA 135:8
Irish p., learn your trade YEAT 348:15
mature p. steal ELIO 105:11
No death has hurt p. more HEAN 151:4
Nor till the p. among us MOOR 230:8
p. are their own patients THOM 319:10
Should p. bicycle-pump AMIS 8:4
think all p. were Byronic COPE 77:5
point rather make a p. CURT 83:3
Up to a p., Lord Copper WAUG 331:13
poison got as far as p.-gas HARD 146:4
put p. in your coffee CHUR 69:2
Slowly the p. EMPS 108:4
poisoning P. pigeons LEHR 195:7
poker tossed around like p. chips ALBR 6:1
polecat semi-house-trained p. FOOT 121:5
polemic don't watch BBC for p. SIMP 299:1
police among p. officers ORTO 249:2
p. are those who arrest HARR 147:13
p. can beat you SHAW 296:12
p. were to blame GRAN 138:10
policeman p. and a pretty girl CHAP 62:13
p. is there to preserve DALE 83:11
terrorist and the p. CONR 76:2
policemen aren't enough p. LEC 194:11
how young the p. look HICK 155:5
sadists become p. CONN 75:5
policy foreign p. COOK 76:7
home p.: I wage war CLEM 71:1
If the p. isn't hurting MAJO 213:9
instrument of national p. BRIA 43:18
My [foreign] p. BEVI 35:3
p. of the good neighbour ROOS 277:16
polite no allies to be p. to GEOR 133:7
politeness suave p. KNOX 185:4
political fear of P. Economy SELL 293:10
half your p. life THAT 317:2
personal is p. POLI 261:26
p. autonomy GRAY 139:5
p. correctness can be JAME 168:7
P. language is designed ORWE 250:11
p. lives end in failure POWE 265:9
p. significance HAVE 149:1
p. will LYNN 205:9
politician judge a p. IVIN 166:6
my life as a p. POWE 265:8
p. does get an idea MARQ 217:10
p. is an arse upon CUMM 82:6
p. to complain about POWE 265:6
p. urges them to rebel PERU 257:3
p. was a person LLOY 201:11
statesman is a p. TRUM 323:8
politicians die for p. THOM 320:1
p. hear the word 'culture' ESHE 108:12
to be left to the p. DE G 88:9
words of the p. MORR 231:6
politics between p. and equations EINS 101:2
do not go in for p. CAMU 52:11
In p., if you want anything THAT 315:11
invisible hand in p. FRIE 126:3
no true friends in p. CLAR 69:11
p. and little else CAMP 52:5
P., executive expression BRIT 44:2
P. has got to be fun CLAR 69:13
p. is a disease FOTH 123:4
P. is not the art GALB 130:11
P. is the Art BUTL 50:3
P. is war without bloodshed MAO 216:6
p. making us unhappy FILI 114:2
p. of happiness HUMP 163:4
p. of Versailles MONN 229:5
P. supposed to be REAG 271:10
p. the art of impossible HAVE 148:13
P. the art of preventing VALÉ 326:7
P. too serious a matter DE G 88:9
week is a long time in p. WILS 341:6

prayer Conservative Party at p. ROYD 280:10
p. factories DURR 96:12
wing and a p. ADAM 2:5
wish for p. is a prayer BERN 31:15
prayers saying his p. MILN 225:11
prays family that p. together SAYI 289:15
preach p. but do not practise RUSS 282:17
precedent dangerous p. CORN 78:1
precious p. it must be rationed LENI 195:17
predecessors as his p. were CAST 57:9
predicament human p. QUIN 268:6
It is a p. BENN 30:1
predict only p. things after IONE 165:13
preference special p. for beetles HALD 143:11
preferences no food p. POWE 264:18
pregnancy avoid p. by mathematics MENC 221:9
pregnant If men could get p. KENN 177:5
prejudices deposit of p. laid EINS 100:14
proprietor's p. SWAF 312:2
premature p. anti-Fascist ANON 12:16
premises based upon licenced p. O'BR 244:3
prepare not to p. for life PAST 254:14
prepared BE P. BADE 20:7
p. for all emergencies FORS 122:7
prerogative p. of the eunuch STOP 309:10
P. of the harlot KIPL 184:9
prescription p. of a quick dip WESL 334:6
presence posted p. of the watcher JAME 168:1
present know nothing but the p. KEYN 179:8
no p. in Wales THOM 319:12
past, p. and future EINS 101:1
perpetuates the p. DE B 87:4
p. in New York CHAP 63:1
p. is an interlude O'NE 246:11
p., yes, we are in it LOWE 204:14
Time p. and time past ELIO 102:8
who controls the p. ORWE 250:3
preserve do not p. myself ORTE 248:12
there to p. disorder DALE 83:11
Whom God P. MORT 233:1
presidency cancer close to the P. DEAN 86:11
heart-beat from the P. STEV 308:10
I will seek the p. DOLE 93:7
messenger-boy P. SCHL 291:1
pursuit of the P. JOHN 171:12
Teflon-coated P. SCHR 291:9
US p. a Tudor monarchy BURG 48:6
vice-p. isn't worth GARN 132:2
want the p. MCCA 206:6
president All the P.'s men BERN 32:3
anybody could become p. DARR 84:7
any boy may become P. STEV 308:8
choose to run for P. COOL 76:10
first p. to be ousted LIEB 199:11
going to be your next p. CART 55:1
P. is a crook NIXO 242:12
p. is the most visible BUSH 49:14
P., not a Pope STRE 310:14
P.'s spouse BUSH 49:4
security around the p. MAIL 213:8
to hide from the P. CHUR 69:4
used to be the next p. GORE 138:2
vote for the best P. PETE 257:6
We are the P.'s men KISS 184:14
When the P. does it NIXO 242:14
press complain about the p. POWE 265:6
Freedom of the p. SWAF 312:2
Freedom of the p. guaranteed LIEB 199:12
Let's go to p. WINC 342:1
lose your temper with the P. PANK 252:11
not a free p. but a managed RADC 268:12
popular p. is drinking MELL 221:4
power of the p. NORT 243:5
p. is ferocious DIAN 91:13
p. still hounded you JOHN 170:12
p. would kill her SPEN 303:10
with you on the free p. STOP 309:12
pressed p. out of shape FROS 127:18
pressure Grace under p. HEMI 152:14
presumption amused by its p. CART 56:4
pretender Old P. GUED 142:2
pretendy wee p. government CONN 75:3
pretext not looking for a p. RAHM 269:3
pretty lived in a p. how town CUMM 82:4
policeman and a p. girl CHAP 62:13
p. girl is like a melody BERL 31:4
We're so p. ROTT 280:4
prevent not knowing how to p. RUSS 283:9
preventing Politics the art of p. VALÉ 326:7
price love that pays the p. SPRI 304:15
pay any p. KENN 178:3
p. of petrol has been increased CART 56:9
p. well worth paying LAMO 188:1
What p. glory ANDE 8:11
Wot p. Selvytion nah SHAW 295:16
prices reduce the rise in p. HEAT 151:5
prick paint with my p. MISQ 226:9
prickly go round the p. pear ELIO 103:14
pride here have P. and Truth YEAT 347:19
lacks a proper p. MACD 207:11
London P. handed down to us COWA 78:12
look backward to with p. FROS 127:3
save its p. MEYE 223:1
priest p. of the invisible STEV 307:10
p. persuades humble people PERU 257:3
priggish p. schoolgirl GRIG 141:3
prime One's p. is elusive SPAR 303:8
Prime Minister best P. we have BUTL 50:2
HOW DARE YOU BECOME P. TELE 316:4
last British P. ADAM 2:1
modern P. HENN 153:3
next P. but three BELL 27:12
No woman will be P. THAT 315:10

P. has nothing to hide CHUR 69:4
P. shuffling along HEAL 150:4
Unknown P. ASQU 15:4
Prime Ministers Disraeli school of P. BLAI 37:7
P. dissatisfied JENK 169:12
primitive call it a 'p. society' GREG 140:8
'p.' languages CHAT 63:6
wise p. in giant jungle MAIL 213:6
prince Advise the p. ELIO 104:7
danced with the P. of Wales FARJ 111:8
P. of Wales not a position BENN 30:1
princess People's P. BLAI 37:6
P. of Wales was DOWD 94:6
principle little of the p. left REIT 272:9
standing up for a p. O'RO 248:7
useful thing about a p. MAUG 219:4
print licence to p. money THOM 320:3
priorities p. have gone all wrong BEVA 34:11
prison at home in p. WAUG 331:8
born in p. MALC 214:1
forever p.-pent WOLF 343:11
while there is a soul in p. DEBS 87:13
prisoner your being taken p. KITC 184:17
prisoners p. of addiction ILLI 165:1
p. of noise MORE 230:10
weapons of all p. COLE 73:6
privacy society of p. RAND 269:9
private P. faces in public places AUDE 17:17
p. opulence GALB 130:6
p. . . . secret . . . intimate STOP 309:16
p. territory BACA 20:5
privilege only extended p. HILL 155:7
privileges p. you were born with BROW 45:12
prize Pulitzer P. ready to be won CHIL 65:4
prized local, but p. elsewhere AUDE 18:9
prizes glittering p. SMIT 300:6
winners of the big p. ORWE 250:5
probity p. and integrity HAGU 142:11
problem can't see the p. CHES 64:13
Houston, we've had a p. LOVE 203:10
p.-solving minds KAUN 175:11
p. that has no name FRIE 125:17
p. that has no name FRIE 126:2
p. to be overcome KEIL 176:11
you're part of the p. CLEA 70:11
problems all our p. THAT 318:2
Machines have less p. WARH 330:3
No easy p. EISE 101:11
proceed reason to p. RAHM 269:3
procrastination p. is the art MARQ 217:4
producing consumes without p. ORWE 249:4
production means of p. ANON 12:9
products p. people really want NASH 237:15
profession important p. SHAW 295:10
second oldest p. REAG 271:10
second p. in reserve NICO 242:1
professional p. is a man who can AGAT 2:11
professions p. are conspiracies SHAW 295:9
shortest-lived p. ROGE 277:4
professor p. of rotational medicine MORG 231:1
profits best of all monopoly p. HICK 155:4
programme Not so much a p. ANON 11:16
programmed p. to love completely BAIN 20:12
progress Humanity a work in p. WILL 339:8
illusion of p. ANON 12:11
p. if a cannibal uses LEC 194:10
P. is a comfortable disease CUMM 82:8
'p.' is ethical RUSS 283:7
'p.' is the exchange ELLI 107:4
social p., order JOHN 170:6
prohibition Communism is like p. ROGE 277:5
enacting P. HOOV 159:1
exclusion and p. MILL 223:15
P. makes you want MARQ 217:12
project less ambitious p. ANON 10:11
p. will be complete BLAI 37:8
proletariat new p. ATTA 15:12
prolonged deliberately p. SASS 288:6
promise Eastern p. ADVE 3:18
p. made is a debt unpaid SERV 294:1
p. of their early years POWE 264:10
promised reach the p. land CALL 51:4
seen the p. land KING 181:9
promises have p. to keep FROS 128:1
man who p. least BARU 24:14
p. and panaceas ROTH 280:2
promising first call p. CONN 75:6
prone position for women is p. CARM 54:3
pronounced 'please' is p. MURR 235:14
pronunciation p. reigned HEAN 151:1
proof America is the p. MCCA 206:9
propaganda on p. CORN 78:2
P. can be defined DEBR 87:10
purely for p. BEAV 25:7
property Private p. is necessary TAWN 313:7
Thieves respect p. CHES 64:9
through p. that we shall PANK 252:13
prophet not as a p. MAND 214:12
prophets ceased to pose as its p. POPP 260:6
proposition meaning of a p. SCHL 291:2
proprietor p.'s prejudices SWAF 312:2
props p. to help him endure FAUL 112:1
prose Good p. like a window-pane ORWE 249:8
govern in p. CUOM 82:15
Poetry is to p. WAIN 328:13
p. and the passion FORS 122:9
prose-song Gertrude Stein's p. LEWI 199:7
prosperous p. or caring society HESE 153:16
prostitute doormat or a p. WEST 335:7
made into a p. BOWI 41:17
prostitutes small nations like p. KUBR 186:11
prostitution banking and p. WRIG 345:15
protection calls mutely for p. GREE 139:17

Protestant P. counterpoint BEEC 26:18
P. with a horse BEHA 27:1
White-Anglo Saxon-P. BALT 22:8
proud too p. to fight WILS 341:13
prove I could p. everything PINT 258:11
to p. it I'm here CATC 59:14
Provence found it in P. WILL 340:4
proverbs Solomon wrote the P. NAYL 238:8
providence way that P. dictates HITL 156:13
provinces Brought up in the p. BENN 30:2
prudence P. is the other woman ANON 11:18
prurient p. curiosity STOP 309:7
psalms David wrote the P. NAYL 238:8
psychiatrist p. is a man who goes STOC 309:4
psychological P. flaws ANON 12:1
psychopath p. is the furnace RAYM 270:9
public admired in p. life ROOS 277:11
give the p. something SKEL 299:12
I and the p. know AUDE 18:4
immaculate p. places ROET 276:10
one to mislead the p. ASQU 15:5
Private faces in p. places AUDE 17:17
p. rallies around an idea ASIM 14:12
p. squalor GALB 130:6
respect p. opinion RUSS 282:6
tell the p. which way SULZ 311:10
publications previous p. HILB 155:6
publicity no such thing as bad p. BEHA 27:4
now called p. O'RO 248:8
oxygen of p. THAT 317:8
public relations precedence over p. FEYN 113:2
public school to an English p. WAUG 331:8
publish p. and be sued INGR 165:9
published before this book is p. RUNC 281:7
publisher makes everybody a p. MCLU 210:11
publishers become p. CONN 75:5
publishing easier job like p. AYER 19:16
p. faster PAUL 255:5
puck p. is going to be GRET 140:14
Pulitzer P. Prize ready to be won CHIL 65:4
pulpit such a bully p. ROOS 279:3
white glove p. REAG 271:7
pulse p. of this new day ANGE 8:15
take a nation's p. WHIT 336:3
two people with the one p. MACN 211:14
punch p. above its weight HURD 163:7
punctual Aunt Minnie always p. WILD 338:12
punished child, p. TREM 321:10
punk p. was a good idea COLL 73:12
punt better fun to p. SAYE 288:8
puppets not party p. CANA 53:1
puppy Happiness is a warm p. SCHU 291:11
happiness was a warm p. EPHR 108:6
pure p. as the driven slush BANK 22:11
purify p. the dialect ELIO 103:5
Puritan to the P. all things are LAWR 191:12
Puritanism not P. but February KRUT 186:9
P. The haunting fear MENC 221:6
purple colour p. WALK 329:6
deep p. falls PARI 252:15
I shall wear p. JOSE 173:4
P. haze is in my brain HEND 152:16
purpose happy sense of p. O'RO 248:7
purrs p. like an epigram MARQ 217:13
pursuit common p. LEAV 194:1
pushed and he p. LOGU 202:3
put up with which I will not p. CHUR 67:16
pygmies peace like retarded p. PEAR 256:4
pyjamas in p. for the heat LAWR 192:11
pylons P., those pillars bare SPEN 304:7
pyramid economic p. ROOS 277:13
pyre heaping up own funeral p. POWE 265:2

quack q. of yesterday DOYL 94:10
quad No one about in the Q. KNOX 185:5
quality Never mind the q. POWE 265:10
quarks Three q. for Muster Mark JOYC 173:8
quarrel lover's q. with the world FROS 127:10
no q. with the Viet Cong ALI 6:9
q. in a far away country CHAM 61:9
takes one to make a q. INGE 165:4
Quebec Long Live Free Q. DE G 88:13
Québecois I am a Q. LÉVE 198:1
queen dying for Q. and country THOM 320:1
have the Q. as their aunt MARG 216:13
Q. has the quality PHIL 257:11
q. in people's hearts DIAN 91:10
To toast *The Q.* HEAN 150:13
queerer q. than we suppose HALD 143:8
questing passes the q. vole WAUG 331:14
question Answer to the Great Q. ADAM 1:12
ask an impertinent q. BRON 44:7
asked any clear q. CAMU 52:6
mere asking of a q. FORS 122:15
q. is absurd AUDE 18:15
q. why we died KIPL 182:12
secretly changed the Q. SELL 293:11
To ask the hard q. AUDE 18:14
very simple q. LARD 188:7
what is the q. LAST 191:7
questions *all* q. were stupid WEIS 332:13
ask q. of those RALE 269:5
queue orderly q. of one MIKE 223:3
quick q., and the dead DEWA 91:4
quiet is a q. life HICK 155:4
never have a q. world SHAW 296:13
q. flows the Don SHOL 297:14
q. on the western front REMA 272:11
should be kept very q. LOOS 203:1
quieten q. your enemy by talking CEAU 61:4

quietly q. pacifist peaceful WALK 329:4
won't go q. DIAN 91:12
quit try again. Then q. FIEL 113:16
quitter fighter not a q. MAND 215:9
quotation always have a q. SAYE 288:9
get a happy q. anywhere HOLM 158:6
q. is a national vice WAUG 331:10
q. what a speaker wants BENN 29:8
quotations heaps of q. DOUG 94:4
read books of q. CHUR 68:11
quote man is to q. him BENC 28:10
quoted very seldom q. correctly STRU 311:3
quotes q. give us acquaintance WILL 339:4

rabbit r. in a snare STEP 307:6
rabbits fawned on by r. ATWO 16:9
race clan and r. MILL 224:6
play the r. card SHAP 294:14
r. between education WELL 333:14
white r. *is* the cancer SONT 302:14
races People don't mix r. MORR 232:7
so-called white r. FORS 122:14
racism institutional r. MACP 212:3
racist do not fear the r. MORR 231:6
racket all a German r. RIDL 275:1
Once in the r. CAPO 53:7
radar writer's r. HEMI 152:15
radical dared be r. when young FROS 127:14
R. Chic WOLF 344:4
R. is a man ROOS 278:2
radio had the r. on MONR 229:8
R. and television SARR 287:3
r. expands it WOGA 343:8
rag foul r. and bone shop YEAT 346:12
Shakespeherian R. ELIO 105:2
rage horrible that lust and r. YEAT 348:11
r. to live VANE 326:13
wretched r. for order MAHO 212:11
ragged pair of r. claws ELIO 104:6
railway big r. station NABO 236:10
by r. timetables TAYL 313:10
lying across a r. line JENK 169:9
R. termini FORS 122:4
railways R. and the Church AWDR 19:10
rain buried in the r. MILL 223:9
glazed with r. water WILL 340:2
hard r.'s a gonna fall DYLA 97:8
r. in Spain LERN 197:2
r. is destroying his grain HERB 153:6
real sad r. CASH 57:2
Singin' in the r. FREE 124:14
Still falls the r. SITW 299:7
waiting for it to r. COHE 73:1
waiting for r. ELIO 103:10
wedding-cake in the r. AUDE 19:4
rainbow Follow ev'ry r. HAMM 144:8
Lord survives the r. LOWE 204:11
no r. nation MAND 215:7
r. and a cuckoo's song DAVI 85:2
R. gave thee birth DAVI 85:3
r. which includes black YEVT 349:7
real r. coalition JACK 167:1
Somewhere over the r. HARB 145:14
rains r. pennies from heaven BURK 48:7
Ramsbottom Mr and Mrs R. EDGA 99:3
rancour without r. BLAC 36:12
rape procrastinated r. PRIT 266:10
r. isn't the worst thing WELD 333:5
r., ultra-violence and Beethoven TAGL 314:2
you r. it DEGA 88:3
raped r. and speaks English ANON 9:11
when they were r. PAGL 252:4
Raphael draw like R. PICA 258:4
rapist r. bothers to buy a bottle DWOR 97:3
rapists all men are r. FREN 125:4
rapper to your son as a r. ICE 164:14
rappers first r. of Europe BJÖR 36:9
rat anthropomorphic view of r. KOES 185:11
Anyone can r. CHUR 66:4
giant r. of Sumatra DOYL 94:8
terrier can define a r. HOUS 160:8
You dirty r. MISQ 227:6
rational irrational is r. STEV 307:18
make life more r. AYER 19:14
only r. position DIAM 91:8
rationed precious it must be r. LENI 195:17
rats r.' alley ELIO 105:1
rattle Shake, r. and roll CALH 51:1
ray r. of sunshine WODE 342:12
razor arse full of r. blades KEAT 176:5
mirror and a r. OPEN 247:19
r. rusting PLAT 259:9
reach I r. for my pistol JOHS 172:4
other beers cannot r. ADVE 3:24
r. the promised land CALL 51:4
reaches further r. ARCH 13:10
reaction can't get no girl r. JAGG 167:10
if there is any r. JUNG 174:13
reactionaries r. are paper tigers MAO 216:8
reactionary R. is a somnambulist ROOS 278:2
read his books were r. BELL 28:4
not r. Eliot, Auden RICH 274:10
people who can't r. ZAPP 350:6
r. any good books lately CATC 58:22
r., much of the night ELIO 104:20
R. my lips BUSH 49:7
r. the life of any important PRIE 266:4
r. too widely PEAR 256:3
superfluous to r. HILB 155:6
what I r. in the papers ROGE 277:3
who don't r. the books BYAT 50:4
Why r. FITZ 119:10

reader ideal r. suffering from JOYC 173:6
not to inform the r. ACHE 1:9
reading careful of his r. LEWI 198:11
lie in a hot bath r. THOM 318:19
Like R., only farther FLEM 120:10
Peace is poor r. HARD 147:3
prefer r. SMIT 300:13
R. isn't an occupation ORTO 249:2
R. it slower WOOD 344:7
what is worth r. TREV 322:1
readmission r. to the human race LYNN 205:8
real Be r. CONN 75:4
event is r. SHIE 297:12
home to a r. world TURK 324:5
r. slow walk CASH 57:2
washed in the speechless r. BARZ 24:16
realest one of the r. things SHAP 294:15
realism I don't want r. WILL 339:15
realistic make a 'r. decision' MCCA 206:10
reality Cannot bear very much r. ELIO 102:10
employs r. as little MOND 229:3
It is a r. CLIN 72:1
Love is discovery of r. MURD 235:10
other people's r. SONT 302:15
principal part of r. BORG 41:3
R. beats fiction CONR 76:3
r. take precedence FEYN 113:2
they are a r. DEWA 91:2
really be a R. Useful Engine AWDR 19:9
what I r. really want ROWB 280:6
reaping No, r. BOTT 41:7
reason form of human r. LÉVI 198:7
for the wrong r. ELIO 104:10
r. to proceed RAHM 269:3
reasonable They were r. people BROO 45:2
reasons r. for the rule change STRA 310:9
We want better r. RUSS 283:9
rebel die like a true-blue r. HILL 156:1
R. without a cause FILM 118:12
What is a r. CAMU 52:13
rebellion r. and revivalism THOM 319:7
rebels One final tip to r. NICO 242:1
receipt Applause is a r. SCHN 291:5
receiver left the r. off the hook KOES 185:12
recession r. that Australia had to have KEAT 176:6
r. when your neighbour TRUM 323:9
spend way out of a r. CALL 51:3
recherche *A la r. du temps perdu* PROU 267:1
recipes like r. in a cookbook STEW 308:16
r. always successful VALÉ 326:5
recirculation commodious vicus of r. OPEN 247:17
recognize only a trial if I r. it KAFK 175:4
reconciliation bridge of r. RUNC 281:5
kindness and r. MUNR 235:3
stability and r. MITC 225:15
True r. does not MAND 215:3
reconvened hereby r. EWIN 110:10
record as fast as the world r. COLE 73:3
look at the r. IVIN 166:6
not merely be the r. FAUL 112:1
red Better r. than dead POLI 261:6
not even r. brick OSBO 250:21
r. wheel barrow WILL 340:2
rise with my r. hair PLAT 259:12
reds honour the indomitable R. DUNN 96:2
redundancy handing out r. notices KINN 182:6
redwood From the r. forest GUTH 142:9
reeled Until r. the mind GIBB 134:4
referee having two you are a r. FROS 126:12
refined Englishwoman is so r. SMIT 301:5
refinement r. scrapes at vainly BEER 26:21
refreshes r. the parts ADVE 3:24
refuse offer he can't r. PUZO 267:13
regal someone that height look r. AMIE 7:13
reggae what r. is TAYL 314:16
regret perfunctory r. SAKI 285:3
r., but without rancour BLAC 36:12
regrets I have no r. CRES 80:6
Miss Otis r. PORT 262:17
regrette *Je ne r. rien* CRES 80:6
regulated R. hatred HARD 146:2
speech is not to be r. DOUG 94:5
reheat cannot r. a soufflé MCCA 207:2
Reich *Ein R., ein Volk* POLI 261:11
reindeer Red-nosed R. MARK 217:1
rejoice r. at that news THAT 317:1
r., rejoice HEAT 151:7
relations in personal r. RUSS 282:7
not have sexual r. CLIN 71:14
Personal r. FORS 122:8
relationship human r. suffers FORS 122:17
r. that was not CLIN 72:2
Their r. consisted GUNN 142:7
relationships R., relationships FISH 114:4
relative Success is r. ELIO 102:6
relaxed feel terribly r. DAYA 86:4
religion Art and R. are two roads BELL 27:5
can't talk r. to SHAW 295:15
Every dictator uses r. BHUT 35:7
in Quebec a r. FOTH 123:4
r. has always been to me POTT 263:3
R. is the frozen thought KRIS 186:5
r. weak SZAS 312:9
r. without science EINS 100:1
start your own r. ANON 11:2
That is my r. SHAW 295:14
tourism is their r. RUNC 281:6
trust the old r. LOWE 204:13
wisest r. HAIL 143:3
religions materialistic of r. TEMP 315:3
they who found r. PROU 267:3
religiose r. And mystic DUNN 96:5

religious great r. art CLAR 70:1
reluctant Not a r. peer BENN 29:2
remarkable anything r. about it PAST 254:15
remarks Famous r. are very seldom STRU 311:3
R. are not literature STEI 306:7
remember cannot r. the past SANT 286:15
I r. it well LERN 196:18
keep diaries to r. O'NE 246:10
r. for ever WARN 330:6
R. me when I am dead DOUG 93:12
r. the children you got BROO 45:5
r. this, a kiss is HUPF 163:6
We will r. them BINY 35:12
what you can r. SELL 293:8
Yes; I r. Adlestrop THOM 319:1
yet never can, r. THOM 319:4
remembered like to be r. POWE 265:7
r. around the world DISN 93:3
remembrance R. of things past PROU 267:1
remind foolish things r. me MARV 218:5
remorse doesn't understand r. SZYM 312:15
remove not malignant and r. it WAUG 331:18
r. her clothes in public LAMB 187:14
rendezvous r. with Death SEEG 293:3
Reno'd Kings Moll R. NEWS 240:13
renounce I r. war FOSD 123:3
rent r. we pay for our room CLAY 70:10
reorganized we would be r. ANON 12:11
repeat condemned to r. it SANT 286:15
images change as they r. WARH 330:2
neither r. his past AUDE 18:18
repeated mistake shall not be r. EPIT 109:17
simply a truth r. BALD 21:9
repetition Nagging is the r. SUMM 311:11
repetitious r. mechanism WHIT 336:12
republic Australian r. MURR 235:17
democratically governed r. HAIL 143:4
destroyed the R. DE V 90:10
Love the Beloved R. FORS 122:21
sweet equal r. PAUL 255:7
repulsive Right but R. SELL 293:9
reputation don't need a r. MITC 228:1
re-rat takes ingenuity to r. CHUR 66:4
rescuers firing on the r. WOOL 345:10
research Basic r. is what BRAU 43:2
r. the art of the soluble MEDA 220:14
steal from many, it's r. MIZN 228:9
resigned I am not r. MILL 223:5
r. commission ANON 10:9
resistance break the r. STAL 305:7
lot of r. DICK 92:2
resistentialism R. is concerned JENN 170:3
resistible r. rise of Arturo Ui BREC 43:9
resort-style soft r. civilization BAUD 25:1
resources Have no Inner R. BERR 32:12
respect r. for women NYE 243:9
r. of the people MARS 218:3
would increase the r. MAND 215:1
respectability r. and air conditioning BARA 23:1
save a shred of r. READ 271:1
respiration artificial r. BURG 48:5
response r. to error GIOV 135:6
responsibility Liberty means r. SHAW 296:6
no sense of r. KNOX 185:8
Power without r. KIPL 184:9
r. without power STOP 309:10
slightest sense of r. ANON 11:5
rest r. the tongues HOLU 158:7
Swift has sailed into his r. YEAT 348:12
work, r. and play ADVE 4:10
restaurant table at a good r. LEBO 194:9
resting-place give us a r. WEIZ 332:14
restoration Church's R. BETJ 33:10
restraint praise the firm r. CAMP 52:4
restructuring r. combines GORB 137:14
results quick and effective r. BULL 47:9
reticence Northern r. HEAN 151:2
retire don't r. in this business MITC 228:5
retiring r. at high speed toward HALS 144:6
retreating my right is r. FOCH 120:13
seen yourself r. NASH 238:5
return I shall r. MACA 206:1
I will r. EPIT 109:14
r. of democratic control STEE 306:5
revelation first hole is a r. MOOR 230:4
revelations offers stupendous r. HOFF 157:11
revenge fish are having their r. ELIZ 106:11
gave us Ford as his r. ABZU 1:4
r. by the culture PADE 251:16
tribal, intimate r. HEAN 150:14
reverence R. for Life SCHW 292:9
revisited r. ideas OLDF 245:17
revivalism rebellion and r. THOM 319:7
revolt r., disorder MORR 232:3
revolution after the r. AREN 14:2
grassroots r. BERN 32:1
peaceful r. impossible KENN 178:10
r. is the kicking down HEAN 151:3
r. where love not allowed ANGE 9:2
r. will raise its head LUXE 205:7
safeguard a r. ORWE 250:7
volcano of r. ELLI 107:5
revolutionary Every r. ends CAMU 52:15
forge his r. spirit GUEV 142:3
his r. triumph TAYL 313:12
r. in a bathroom LINK 200:5
revolutions modern r. have ended CAMU 52:14
revolver reaches for a r. GLEN 136:2
resembles a r. FANO 111:5
reward r. is when we die RYDE 283:14
rhetoric love without the r. STOP 309:15
Rhine think of the R. BALD 21:11

Rhodesia majority rule in R. SMIT 300:10
rhyme hope and history r. HEAN 150:9
r. is a barrel MAYA 220:3
R. is still most effective GIRA 135:8
still more tired of R. BELL 27:16
rhythm I got r. GERS 133:11
sweet, soft, plenty r. MORT 233:2
rhythmical r. grumbling ELIO 105:15
Ribstone Pippin Right as a R. BELL 27:15
rice *r. pudding for dinner* MILN 225:10
rich all the r. people STEA 306:2
by chance grow r. THOM 319:3
can't spend ourselves r. BLAC 36:11
never be too r. or too thin WIND 342:3
no boy from a r. family DIMA 92:6
not really a r. man GETT 134:2
parish of r. women AUDE 17:6
people r. enough to pay HEAL 150:2
Poor little r. girl COWA 79:2
r. are different FITZ 118:17
r. get rich KAHN 175:6
r. is better TUCK 324:3
r. wage war SART 287:4
save the few who are r. KENN 178:4
sincerely want to be r. CORN 77:9
to tax r. people LLOY 201:9
richness r. of lovers and tribes ONDA 246:4
riddle r. of the sands CHIL 65:3
r. wrapped in a mystery CHUR 66:7
ride if you cannot r. two horses MAXT 219:13
She's got a ticket to r. LENN 196:10
ridiculous heart of the r. MAHO 212:10
right convinced that they are r. VAN 326:10
curst conceit o' bein' r. MACD 207:10
exclusively in the r. HUXL 164:3
forgive those who were r. MACL 210:5
have to do what's right BARE 23:3
just not r. PARK 254:8
man of the r. MOSL 233:5
no r. in the circus MAXT 219:13
not only to be r. SZAS 312:5
not r. now JAY 168:15
one WAS r. POUN 264:4
questioned its r. to exist SCHU 292:2
R. as a Ribstone Pippin BELL 27:15
R. but Repulsive SELL 293:9
r. deed for the wrong ELIO 104:10
r. goes unrecognized WEIL 332:7
R. Now is a lot better BINC 35:11
r. to happiness RAYN 270:10
scientists are probably r. ASIM 14:12
Self-government is our r. CASE 55:10
Two wrongs don't make a r. SZAS 312:11
vast r.-wing conspiracy CLIN 71:9
Want to do r. RICH 274:2
righteous seen the r. forsaken BLUN 38:5
rights Bill of R. seems COMM 74:2
equal in dignity and r. ANON 9:10
sick had no r. FORS 122:11
Stand up for your r. MARL 217:2
talked about equal r. JOHN 171:7
your r. become only CASE 55:11
right-wing life is r. DEBR 87:11
rime r. was on the spray HARD 147:2
ring One R. to rule them all TOLK 321:2
rings postman always r. twice CAIN 50:8
riot r. is the language of KING 181:12
ripper no female Jack the R. PAGL 252:3
rise into this world to r. above FILM 117:4
resistible r. of Arturo Ui BREC 43:9
r. at ten thirty HARG 147:8
still, like air, I'll r. ANGE 9:1
risen r. without trace MUGG 234:3
rises sun also r. HEMI 152:13
rising r. expectations CLEV 71:6
risks just one of the r. he takes STEV 308:8
We took r. SCOT 293:2
ritual body building is r. PAGL 252:1
river guy who cleans the r. PERO 256:12
Ol' man r. HAMM 144:13
r. Is a strong brown god ELIO 102:19
Sleepless as the r. CRAN 80:3
riverrun r., past Eve and Adam's OPEN 247:17
rivers I've known r. HUGH 161:10
road ads and not the r. NASH 237:13
Follow the yellow brick r. HARB 146:1
Golden R. to Samarkand FLEC 120:4
Goodbye yellow brick r. JOHN 171:1
Hit the r., Jack MAYF 220:8
in the middle of the r. BEVA 34:6
one more for the r. MERC 222:5
on to the end of the r. LAUD 189:11
r. through the woods KIPL 183:16
r. toward freedom MORR 232:3
rolling English r. CHES 64:2
roads How many r. DYLA 97:4
Two r. diverged FROS 127:16
where r. were bad LEE 195:2
without fear the lawless r. MUIR 234:8
roam mind begins to r. SOLZ 301:13
roaming R. in the gloamin' LAUD 189:13
roar called upon to give the r. CHUR 68:6
r. of London's traffic ANON 11:17
roareth that r. thus GODL 136:7
roast R. beef and Yorkshire ORWE 249:10
rob r. his mother FAUL 112:2
robbed We was r. JACO 167:5
robbing r. a bank BREC 43:12
Robinson here's to you, Mrs R. SIMO 298:12
robot r. may not injure a human ASIM 14:10
robotics Rules of R. ASIM 14:10
robs government which r. Peter SHAW 295:11
rock being in a r. band STIP 309:2
like the R. of Gibraltar GAMO 131:2

r. around the clock DE K 88:18
R. is like a battery CLAP 69:10
R. journalism is people ZAPP 350:6
Sex and drugs and r. and roll DURY 97:2
simple r. and roll reasons GELD 132:6
rocked r. the system ROBI 276:1
rocket not r. science LINE 200:4
numbers that r. the mind WILB 338:5
Rockies R. may crumble GERS 133:14
rocks marriage on the r. MERR 222:11
r. remain HERB 153:10
role not yet found a r. ACHE 1:8
roll R. over, Beethoven BERR 32:9
Shake, rattle and r. CALH 51:1
rolled bottoms of my trousers r. ELIO 104:8
rolling jus' keeps r. along HAMM 144:13
Like a r. stone DYLA 97:11
r. English road CHES 64:2
Roman Before the R. came to Rye CHES 64:2
romance fine r. with no kisses FIEL 113:8
music and love and r. BERL 31:3
Romans R. ever done FILM 117:13
romantic R. Ireland's dead YEAT 348:9
ticket to r. places MARV 218:6
Wrong but R. SELL 293:9
romantics We were the last r. YEAT 347:1
Rome Treaty [of R.] is like DENN 90:3
romping r. of sturdy children DE V 90:11
roof cat on a hot tin r. WILL 339:9
room about to enter a r. EDDI 98:10
All I want is a r. LERN 197:4
Books do furnish a r. POWE 264:9
boys in the back r. LOES 201:16
Great hatred, little r. YEAT 348:2
money and a r. of her own WOOL 345:1
smoke-filled r. SIMP 299:2
rooms boys in the back r. BEAV 25:6
lighted r. inside your head LARK 188:13
Other voices, other r. CAPO 53:9
rope fourfold r. of nerves HEAT 151:9
see a piece of r. DALA 83:10
rose English unofficial r. BROO 44:11
fire and the r. are one ELIO 103:9
Goodbye, England's r. JOHN 170:13
I know the colour r. ABSE 1:3
Into the r.-garden ELIO 102:9
One perfect r. PARK 253:5
R. is a rose STEI 306:10
Roves back the r. DE L 89:1
white r. of Scotland MACD 207:12
rosebud R. is just a piece FILM 117:2
roses ash the burnt r. leave ELIO 103:3
Everything's coming up r. SOND 302:9
R. are flowering in Picardy WEAT 332:2
r. in December BARR 24:5
Treaties like girls and r. DE G 88:12
rot it must be all r. NICH 241:5
rotational r. medicine MORG 231:1
rotted simply r. early NASH 237:14
rotten good to feel r. YESE 349:4
You r. swines CATC 60:16
rottenness r. of our civilization READ 271:1
rotting big r. log WHIT 336:5
rough children who were r. SPEN 304:4
round R. and round the circle ELIO 102:7
R. up the usual suspects FILM 116:14
Roundheads R. (Right but) SELL 293:9
Rousseau R. was the first BERL 31:13
royal If you have a R. Family PIML 258:10
My children are not r. MARG 216:13
needed no r. title SPEN 303:11
royalty R. the gold filling OSBO 251:1
rub r. up against money RUNY 281:8
rubble crushed by the r. SOLZ 302:5
rubs fog that r. its back ELIO 104:4
rudest r. voice wins SACK 284:5
Rudolph R., the Red-nosed MARK 217:1
rugby R. Union which is THOM 319:7
rugged system of r. individualism HOOV 159:2
rugs like a million bloody r. FITZ 119:4
ruin r. himself in twelve months GEOR 133:4
r. that Cromwell knocked about BEDF 26:15
ruined They r. us DUNN 96:4
Ruislip Gaily into R. gardens BETJ 33:12
rule golden r. is SHAW 296:4
One Ring to r. them all TOLK 321:2
reasons for the r. change STRA 310:9
R. I, on page I MONT 229:13
r. by amateurs ATTL 16:6
r. the world BART 24:11
You work, we r. DUNN 96:4
rules keep making up these sex r. SALI 285:10
R. of Robotics ASIM 14:10
rum It's a R. Go VAUG 327:5
r., sodomy, prayers CHUR 68:2
what a R. Go everything is WELL 333:12
run best judge of a r. WHAR 335:14
born to r. SPRI 305:3
He can r. LOUI 203:6
In the long r. KEYN 179:13
Now Teddy must r. KENN 179:1
Take the money and r. FILM 118:15
They get r. down BEVA 34:6
What makes Sammy r. SCHU 291:10
runaway r. Presidency SCHL 291:1
rung phone has not r. MITC 228:5
runner long-distance r. SILL 298:7
running R.'s like breathing FREE 125:2
Russia forecast the action of R. CHUR 66:7
From R. with love FLEM 120:8
innocent R. squirmed AKHM 5:8
outlaws R. forever REAG 271:12
R. an empire or democracy BRZE 46:14
Russian embrace the R. bear CHAN 62:12

Russian (*cont.*):
R. literature saved RATU 270:8
Russians keep the R. out ISMA 166:2
Rutherford R. was a disaster BULL 47:9
rye Before the Roman came to R. CHES 64:2
catcher in the r. SALI 285:8

Sacco S.'s name will live VANZ 327:1
sack S. the lot FISH 114:6
sacrament abortion would be a s. KENN 177:5
sacramental flesh was s. ROBI 275:12
sacrifice final s. SPRI 304:15
Further s. of life DE V 90:10
great pinnacle of S. LLOY 201:4
Too long a s. YEAT 347:6
you refused a lesser s. MARY 218:12
sacrificed be s. to expediency MAUG 219:4
sacrifices forgive him for the s. MAUG 219:6
sad It's very s. CURT 83:3
real s. rain CASH 57:2
sadists repressed s. CONN 75:5
safe Health Service is s. THAT 317:4
made s. for democracy WILS 341:17
S. is spelled D-U-L-L CLAR 69:13
s. to be unpopular STEV 308:9
s. to go back in the water TAGL 314:6
world s. for hypocrisy WOLF 343:13
safeguards enforceable s. TRUM 323:5
safer world s. for children LE G 195:3
safety strike against public s. COOL 76:8
sagas frosty s. CRAN 79:16
peoples who memorized s. BJÖR 36:9
said if you want anything s. THAT 315:11
sailed I have s. the seas YEAT 348:5
saint call me a s. CAMA 51:10
s. or incarnation of Satan MADO 212:7
Sloane turned secular s. BURC 48:2
sake Art for art's s. DIET 92:5
salad turn to chicken s. JOHN 171:4
salary s. of the chief executive GALB 130:8
sales equation would halve the s. HAWK 149:4
salesman Death of a s. MILL 224:1
s. is got to dream MILL 224:4
salmon primordial as a s. WHIT 336:10
smoked s. and tinned WILS 341:4
saloon in the last chance s. MELL 221:4
salt s. rubbed into their wounds WEST 335:6
salute If it moves, s. it SAYI 289:20
salvation Wot prawce s. nah SHAW 295:16
Sam Play it again, S. FILM 115:17
Play it again, S. MISQ 226:13
Samaritan remember the Good S. THAT 316:12
Samarkand Golden Road to S. FLEC 120:4
Samarra tonight in S. MAUG 219:8
Sammy What makes S. run SCHU 291:10
sand Night, snow, and s. NERU 239:2
sands riddle of the s. CHIL 65:3
sandwich cheaper than a prawn s. RATN 270:3
raw-onion s. BARN 23:12
sane if he was s. he had to fly HELL 152:2
San Francisco left my heart in S. CROS 81:13
sanity ain't no S. Claus FILM 116:9
sank s. my boat KENN 178:15
Sighted sub, s. same MASO 218:14
Santa shoot S. Claus SMIT 300:3
sap dried the s. out of my veins YEAT 347:8
new s. running HEWE 154:7
sardines s. will be thrown CANT 53:5
sat everyone has s. except a man CUMM 82:6
Satan casting out S. by Satan SORL 302:17
saint or incarnation of S. MADO 212:7
Satanic Verses author of *The S.* KHOM 180:4
satellite With s. TV O'DO 244:11
satiable full of s. curtiosity KIPL 184:4
satin ease a heart like a s. gown PARK 253:9
satire S. is what closes Saturday KAUF 175:8
satisfaction can't get no s. JAGG 167:10
satisfied can't be s. HUGH 161:13
Saturday closes S. night KAUF 175:8
Glasgow Empire on a S. DODD 93:6
saucer like a flying s. landed DYLA 98:1
sausage hold on s. and haddock WOOL 345:9
s. machine CHRI 65:11
savage days of the Noble S. BIKO 35:8
s. loving has made me BECK 26:12
savaged s. by a dead sheep HEAL 150:3
save destroy the town to s. it ANON 11:4
God s. the King MOYN 233:11
helped s. the world KEYN 180:2
s. the Governor-General WHIT 337:12
S. the pound POLI 262:2
through life trying to s. ROGE 277:7
To s. your world AUDE 17:1
saved could have s. sixpence BECK 25:9
only s. the world CHES 63:14
saving capable of s. us RICH 274:7
saw *I s. you do it* STOP 309:16
sawdust S. Caesars NEWS 240:17
say anything good to s. LONG 202:10
more to s. when I am dead ROBI 275:9
nothing to s. CAGE 50:7
S. it with flowers ADVE 4:20
s. nothing HEAN 151:2
see what I s. FORS 122:2
see what I s. WALL 329:9
way I s. it WEST 335:2
wink wink, s. no more MONT 230:1
scale not made on a human s. MALR 214:8
scandal because of a s. HAIL 143:5
scar wears their going like a s. DUNN 96:6
scare can't s. him STEI 306:16
s. myself with my own FROS 127:5

scarlet His sins were s. BELL 28:4
scarves underneath its s. CARE 54:1
scenery among savage s. HOFF 157:11
God paints the s. HART 148:6
scent s. on a pocket handkerchief LLOY 201:8
scepticism s. kept her SART 287:11
schedule my s. is already full KISS 184:12
schizophrenic s. is a special LAIN 187:11
you are a s. SZAS 312:8
school At s. I never minded MORT 232:13
destroy every grammar s. CROS 81:10
schoolchildren What all s. learn AUDE 18:4
schoolgirl priggish s. GRIG 141:3
s. complexion ADVE 4:6
schoolmaster becoming a s. WAUG 331:7
schoolmasters bunch of s. JAGG 167:7
schools some children, in some s. BLUN 38:8
science aim of s. BREC 43:5
All s. is either physics RUTH 283:10
do s. in hell VAUG 327:3
essence of s. BRON 44:7
fear s. POLA 260:1
grand aim of all s. EINS 100:15
In s. the credit goes DARW 84:8
Modern s. largely conceived LEBO 194:5
no less true than s. DAY- 86:10
plundered this new s. MCEW 208:9
redefined the task of s. HAWK 149:5
S. aggregate of recipes VALÉ 326:5
S. finds, industry applies ANON 12:2
S. is an edged tool EDDI 98:12
S. is part of culture GOUL 138:7
s. is satisfying the curiosity ARTS 14:9
s. is strong SZAS 312:9
S. may have found a cure KELL 177:1
S. must begin with myths POPP 260:9
s. reassures BRAQ 42:13
S. without religion EINS 100:1
separation of state and s. FEYE 113:1
triumph of modern s. WAUG 331:18
science fiction S. writers foresee ASIM 14:11
scientific *empirical s. system* POPP 260:5
importance of s. work HILB 155:6
new s. truth PLAN 259:6
scientist distinguished s. says CLAR 70:3
Everybody's a mad s. CRON 81:7
exercise for research s. LORE 203:5
not try to become a s. EINS 100:16
s.'s laws QUIN 268:7
s. thinks of a method PERU 257:3
We believe a s. RICH 274:6
scientists in the company of s. AUDE 18:19
s. are probably right ASIM 14:12
than most young s. MEDA 221:1
scissors end up using s. HOCK 157:5
scooters s. off my lawn CLAR 70:7
score time required to s. 500 COMP 74:3
scorer One Great S. RICE 273:8
Scotch as a S. banker DAVI 84:10
Mary, ma S. Bluebell LAUD 189:12
Scotland flower of S. WILL 340:6
In S. we live between CRAW 80:5
new voice of S. CONN 75:1
our infinite S. MACD 208:1
popular in S. DAVI 84:9
renewed in S. DEWA 91:3
same s. as Scotland JONE 172:6
S., land of omnipotent No BOLD 40:2
S.'s oil POLI 261:18
S.'s rightful heritage CONN 74:12
S. will be reborn NAIR 237:2
sing Flower of S. SILL 298:6
white rose of S. MACD 207:12
Scotsman S. on the make BARR 24:4
S. with a grievance WODE 342:12
Scottish S. Parliament EWIN 110:10
S. parliament SALM 285:14
shall be a S. parliament ANON 12:5
shall be a S. parliament DEWA 91:2
Scotty Beam me up, S. MISQ 226:1
scouts s.' motto BADE 20:7
scrabble s. with all the vowels ELLI 107:1
scrap s. of paper BETH 33:1
scrape s. your strings darker CELA 61:6
scratching s. of pimples WOOL 345:7
scream like a s. from a crevasse GREE 139:14
no one can hear you s. TAGL 314:5
s. till I'm sick CROM 81:5
screw seek the right s. HOLU 158:8
scum Okie means you're s. STEI 306:15
They are s. MAUG 219:9
scuttling S. across the floors ELIO 104:6
scythe sighs like s. WALC 328:15
sea black s.-brute bulling MERW 222:13
complaining about the s. POWE 265:6
In a solitude of the s. HARD 146:5
in our s. of confusion GAMO 131:2
like bathing in the s. LEIG 195:8
Put out to s. MACN 212:1
s.-change in politics CALL 51:7
s. curling Star-climbed MERW 222:14
s. hates a coward O'NE 246:9
s. is the universal COUS 78:6
serpent-haunted s. FLEC 120:2
snotgreen s. JOYC 173:15
seagulls When s. follow a trawler CANT 53:5
seal heard a s. bark CART 56:1
sealed My lips are s. MISQ 226:12
seals aroma of performing s. HART 148:4
seams Amusing little s. BAIL 20:9
search in s. of an author PIRA 258:14
seas floors of silent s. ELIO 104:6
s. colder than the Hebrides FLEC 120:1
s. of pity lie AUDE 17:9

seas (*cont.*):
s. roll over HERB 153:10
season dry brain in a dry s. ELIO 103:12
man has every s. FOND 121:1
seat-belts Fasten your s. FILM 115:7
second elect the s. chamber JAY 169:1
grow a s. tongue MONT 229:10
not a s. on the day COOK 76:6
not your s. choice LURI 205:5
s. best's a gay goodnight YEAT 347:9
s. oldest profession REAG 271:10
s. profession in reserve NICO 242:1
second-best s. is anything but LESS 197:6
second-hand s. Europeans HOPE 159:6
secret girls that have no s. SPEN 304:7
neurosis is a s. TYNA 325:3
photograph is a s. ARBU 13:9
s. diary of Adrian Mole TOWN 321:4
s. in the Oxford sense FRAN 124:11
S. sits in the middle FROS 127:17
secretary being S. of State STIP 309:2
secretive make sex less s. SZAS 312:10
secrets privacy and tawdry s. LEAC 193:7
throw their guilty s. PRIE 266:3
security otherwise styled s. MADA 212:5
s. around the president MAIL 213:8
seduction In s., the rapist DWOR 97:3
see come up and s. me sometime MISQ 227:5
I'll s. you again COWA 78:11
I s. dead people FILM 116:7
I shall never s. KILM 180:10
Nice to s. you CATC 59:21
s. and hear nothing THOM 319:4
s. the hours pass CIOR 69:9
s. things and say 'Why' SHAW 295:4
s. what I say WALL 329:9
wait and s. ASQU 15:2
What you s. is what you get SAYI 290:14
seeing s. what everybody has seen SZEN 312:13
seem Let be be finale of s. STEV 307:13
seen being s. for what one is DRAB 95:2
I have s. war ROOS 277:18
s. one city slum AGNE 5:1
should be s. to be done HEWA 154:6
when you've s. one Western WHIT 337:11
You've never s. this country PURD 267:11
segregation S. now WALL 329:7
selection discrimination and s. JAME 168:2
Natural s. a mechanism FISH 114:11
no more s. BLUN 38:7
no s. by examination BLUN 38:6
self divided s. LAIN 187:9
self-assertion s. abroad WAUG 331:12
self-contempt S., well-grounded LEAV 194:4
self-defence it was in s. MARL 217:3
self-determination act of s. AHER 5:4
self-government S. is our right CASE 55:10
selfish accept the s. gene LOVE 203:11
s. gene DAWK 85:11
small and s. is sorrow ELIZ 106:10
self-made father was s. ATWO 16:8
s. man is one who STEA 306:3
s. man may prefer HAND 145:5
self-respect starves your s. PARR 254:9
self-revelation s., whether it be LANC 188:5
self-sufficiency S. at home WAUG 331:12
sell I'll s. him LEAC 193:9
s. it cheap SAYI 290:6
s. Jack like soapflakes KENN 178:16
to s. time TAWN 313:8
selling S. off the family silver MISQ 226:14
s. postcards DYLA 97:5
seltzer weak hock and s. BETJ 33:2
semen no frozen s. ever read a story WILL 339:6
semi-house-trained s. polecat FOOT 121:5
senator S., and a Democrat JOHN 171:5
sensations easy prey to s. TREV 322:1
sense good when it makes s. MCEW 208:11
Have you no s. of decency WELC 333:1
Money is like a sixth s. MAUG 219:7
s. out of the nonsense BONO 40:7
something makes s. HAVE 148:11
talk s. to American people STEV 308:6
senseless kind of s. wit WILB 338:7
senses pleasures of the s. ESHE 108:13
thrusting of my s. PEAK 255:13
sensibility dissociation of s. ELIO 105:14
informed by s. READ 271:2
sensitively lie to them s. NYE 243:9
sensual Catholic and s. CHAN 62:10
sensuality s., rebellion THOM 319:7
sentence it's a s. FILM 116:16
life s. goes on CONL 74:11
what a s. NEWS 240:15
sentenced s. to death in my absence BEHA 27:2
sentences Backward ran s. GIBB 134:4
sentiment corrupted by s. GREE 139:9
separate can't s. peace MALC 214:2
do not want to be s. SALM 285:13
separating s. us FILI 114:2
separation real s. of powers DENN 90:4
s. of state and science FEYE 113:1
September When you reach S. ANDE 8:10
seraglio s. of eunuchs FOOT 121:4
serenity called the s. of age BLIS 38:2
sergeant S. Pepper TYNA 325:2
serial obituary in s. form CRIS 81:2
serious Murder is a s. business OPEN 247:9
War is too s. a matter CLEM 71:5
You cannot be s. MCEN 208:6
seriously S., though CATC 60:2
sermon rejected S. on the Mount BRAD 42:7

serpent s. ate Eve HUGH 162:7
s.-haunted sea FLEC 120:2
servant answer to the s. problem LEBO 194:5
as a humble s. MAND 214:12
lookingglass of a s. JOYC 173:16
s. to the devil SISS 299:4
s. worth a thousand gadgets SCHU 292:4
servanthood essence of s. COET 72:14
servants choice of s. WAUG 331:17
equality in the s.' hall BARR 24:1
wish your wife or s. GRIF 141:2
serve love to s. my country GIBR 134:5
service devoted to your s. ELIZ 106:1
Pressed into s. FROS 127:18
s. of my love SPRI 304:15
s.? The rent we pay CLAY 70:10
sesquippledan S. verboojuice WELL 333:10
settled s. will STEE 306:5
seven have the s. minutes COLL 73:11
s.-stone weakling ADVE 4:5
S. types of ambiguity EMPS 108:5
seventh moon is in the s. house RADO 269:1
seventies s. started 21st century BOWI 42:2
seventy another s. years LAYT 193:6
Oh, to be s. again CLEM 71:4
sewer s. in a glass-bottomed boat MIZN 228:10
universal s. COUS 78:6
sex attempt to insult s. LAWR 192:1
Battles and s. MCAR 205:13
call you darling after s. BARN 23:14
if s. rears its ugly head AYCK 19:11
isn't s. but death SONT 302:13
Is s. dirty ALLE 6:14
make s. less secretive SZAS 312:10
men think. S., work FISH 114:4
Money was exactly like s. BALD 21:5
mostly about having s. LODG 201:14
No s. please—we're British MARR 217:15
only unnatural s. act KINS 182:10
portray this [s.] relation ROBI 275:12
practically conceal its s. NASH 237:4
real music was s. DOYL 94:11
S. and drugs and rock and roll DURY 97:2
S. and taxes JONE 172:10
s. business isn't worth LAWR 193:2
s. in the mind LAWR 192:8
S. is something I really SALI 285:10
S. never an obsession BOY 42:4
s. on the basketball court SEIK 293:5
s. that brings forth DE B 87:2
s. was the most fun ALLE 6:12
s. with someone I love ALLE 6:13
wanted to know about s. REUB 273:1
what age the s. drive goes BLAK 37:11
When you have money, it's s. DONL 93:9
sexes difference within the s. COMP 74:10
personalities of the two s. MEAD 220:10
sexophones s. wailed HUXL 163:10
sexual car crash as a s. event BALL 22:3
draws so oddly with the s. GUNN 142:6
not have s. relations CLIN 71:14
S. intercourse began LARK 188:8
shock of s. astonishment WESL 334:6
sexuality relinquish their s. WOLF 343:9
sexually Life a s. transmitted disease ANON 11:11
shabby tamed and s. tigers HODG 157:8
shackles Memories are not s. BENN 29:15
shade whiter s. of pale REID 272:8
shadow Falls the S. ELIO 103:15
live under the s. of a war SPEN 304:9
s. stands over us ALLI 7:7
shadows cold white s. WRIG 346:2
less liquid than their s. TESS 315:9
long s. on county grounds MAJO 213:11
shafts Its s. remain ROET 276:9
shake S., rattle and roll CALH 51:1
shaken S. and not stirred FLEM 120:7
Shakespeare Even if I could be S. HUXL 164:8
I can do S. HOPK 159:10
If S. had not written WOLP 344:5
reproduce works of S. WILE 338:16
S., another Newton HUXL 164:6
S. is like bathing LEIG 195:8
S. is so tiring HULL 162:15
S.—the nearest thing OLIV 245:19
When I read S. LAWR 192:14
Shakespearean Dogs are S. SCHW 292:5
Shakespearian That S. rag BUCK 47:8
Shakespeherian S. Rag ELIO 105:2
shaking s. an apple tree COLL 73:12
shall picked the was of s. CUMM 82:10
shame called s. and humiliation O'RO 248:8
feels no s. SZYM 312:15
mourn with her in s. EMEC 107:10
secret s. destroyed RICH 274:10
terrible s. for me YOKO 349:8
shamed Named S. NEWS 240:14
shape pressed out of s. FROS 127:18
s. and definition BARK 23:4
s. of things to come WELL 333:15
shares Fair s. for all POLI 261:12
shark s. has pretty teeth BREC 43:10
sharks s. circling, and waiting CLAR 69:11
shed disused s. in Co. Wexford MAHO 213:1
she-devil life and loves of a s. WELD 333:3
sheep savaged by a dead s. HEAL 150:3
s. in sheep's clothing CHUR 69:5
s. to pass resolutions INGE 165:4
sheepdog if it was a s. MASO 219:1
sheet brought in the white s. LORC 203:2
sheets polyester s. FARR 111:10
shelf s. life of the modern TRIL 322:4
shell aggressive s. MCLU 210:9

shell (*cont.*):
fired a 15-inch s. RUTH 283:12
shells choirs of wailing s. OWEN 251:7
sheltered s. life can be WELT 334:2
shepherd Old Nod, the s. DE L 89:7
sheriff I shot the s. MARL 217:3
sherry first-rate s. flowing PLOM 259:16
shift s. in what the public wants CALL 51:7
shilling s. life will give you AUDE 18:7
shimmered Jeeves s. out WODE 342:13
shimmy s. like my sister Kate PIRO 259:1
ship as the smart s. grew HARD 146:7
like a sinking s. WOOL 345:10
s. appeared in the air HEAN 150:12
ships all the s. at sea WINC 342:1
little s. of England GUED 141:11
s. have been salvaged HALS 144:6
s. sail like swans asleep FLEC 120:5
wrong with our bloody s. BEAT 25:4
shires bugles calling from sad s. OWEN 251:7
shit chicken s. can turn JOHN 171:4
ocean of s. TANS 313:5
shock-proof s. detector HEMI 152:15
shivering s. human soul PAST 255:1
shivers s. like the jelly PIRO 259:1
shoals s. of herring MACC 207:4
shock Future s. TOFF 321:1
s. of the new DUNL 95:10
s. of your joy HUGH 162:9
sudden s. of joy BLIS 38:2
shocked not s. by this subject BOHR 39:10
shocking something s. PORT 260:12
shocks s. the magistrate RUSS 283:4
shoe other s. to drop MURR 235:17
shoes changing s. BREC 43:16
Englishwomen's s. HALS 144:4
never tied my s. PU 267:8
s. with broken high ideals MCGO 209:2
shoeshine smile and a s. MILL 224:4
shook Ten days that s. the world REED 272:7
shoot s. me in my absence BEHA 27:2
s. me through linoleum BANK 22:13
s. Santa Claus SMIT 300:3
s. your murderer ACHE 1:7
They s. horses don't they MCCO 207:6
they shout and they s. INGE 165:3
You'd s. a fellow down HARD 146:12
shooting war minus the s. ORWE 250:12
shoots green s. of recovery MISQ 226:8
man who s. him gets caught MAIL 213:8
shop foul rag and bone s. YEAT 346:12
shopping main thing today—s. MILL 224:5
Whole families s. GINS 135:4
shore To the other s. PAUL 255:6
shores wilder s. of love BLAN 37:13
short long and the s. HUGH 161:6
shorts Eat my s. CATC 58:13
shot Certain men the English s. YEAT 347:15
I s. the sheriff MARL 217:3
They've s. our fox BIRC 36:1
shoulder keep looking over his s. BARU 24:15
standing s. to shoulder HAWK 149:8
stand s. to shoulder BLAI 37:10
shoulders City of the Big S. SAND 286:5
old heads on young s. SPAR 303:6
s. held the sky HOUS 160:5
shout they s. and they shoot INGE 165:3
show got the s. business right BERN 32:2
wrong if someone can s. you AYER 19:17
show business no business like s. BERL 31:6
s. with blood BRUN 46:9
shower HANDSTAND IN S. TELE 316:9
sweetness of a s. THOM 319:6
showman great s. whose technique TAYL 313:14
shows All my s. are great GRAD 138:8
shrimp s. learns to whistle KHRU 180:5
shrink discussed it with his s. FARR 111:10
s. from acts of hospitality SHIE 297:10
shroud stiff dishonoured s. ELIO 104:18
striped s. THOM 319:8
shudder s. in the loins engenders YEAT 347:14
shuffle All s. there YEAT 348:6
shutter click the s. EISE 102:1
shy life has made me s. BERG 30:12
sick kingdom of the s. SONT 302:16
Pass the s. bag, Alice CATC 60:1
scream till I'm s. CROM 81:5
s. had no rights FORS 122:11
think we're s. WOLF 343:12
Sid Tell S. ADVE 4:24
Sidcup get down to S. PINT 258:11
side S. by side WOOD 344:11
which s. do they cheer for TEBB 314:19
sides everyone changes s. CONN 75:13
God does not take s. MITC 225:13
holding on to the s. ELLI 107:2
looked at life from both s. MITC 227:8
Norfan, both s. WELL 333:11
sidestreets down the s. GINS 135:3
siege She kept the s. HILL 155:10
Siegfried washing on the S. Line KENN 177:9
siesta Englishmen detest a s. COWA 78:14
sigh s. is just a sigh HUPF 163:6
sights few more impressive s. BARR 24:4
sign God would give some s. ALLE 7:3
signed hand that s. the paper THOM 318:7
I s. my death warrant COLL 73:10
significance s. of an event CART 55:6
s. of its own JUNG 174:14
signs no 'white' or 'coloured' s. KENN 178:12
s. of his awareness BLUN 38:9
silence clamour of s. TAGO 313:3
Deep is the s. DRIN 95:3

slaves (*cont.*):
sons of former s. KING 181:6
sledge great s. drops in vain ROET 276:9
sleep deep s. of England ORWE 249:13
Do s. well CATC 58:12
from my mother's s. JARR 168:8
green ideas s. furiously CHOM 65:6
have to go to s. LAST 190:9
Let us s. now OWEN 251:14
miles to go before I s. FROS 128:1
None shall s. ADAM 1:10
put the world to s. MUIR 234:9
S. is when all GOLD 137:1
wake to s. ROET 276:13
when you s. you remind me SASS 287:19
sleeping Lay your s. head AUDE 17:12
s. pill is white SEXT 294:9
s. under the desk GATE 132:3
s. with an elephant TRUD 323:1
smitten a s. enemy YAMA 346:5
waken a s. giant FILM 115:16
sleepless S. as the river CRAN 80:3
sleeps while the world s. NEHR 238:10
sleepwalker assurance of a s. HITL 156:13
sleepy I'm not s. DYLA 97:13
sleeve Ash on an old man's s. ELIO 103:3
lacy s. with vitriol WOOL 345:11
sleeves Americanism with its s. MCCA 206:8
rolls up its s. SAND 286:12
slept s. with mice COWA 79:12
slice S. him where you like WODE 342:15
slightly has been s. detached CAMP 51:13
slip S., slop, slap OFFI 245:12
slitty-eyed you'll all be s. PHIL 257:10
Sloane S. turned secular saint BURC 48:2
slogans instead of principles, s. BENT 30:10
refuse to repeat s. CLAR 70:8
slogged s. up to Arras SASS 288:3
slop Slip, s., slap OFFI 245:12
slopes on the butler's upper s. WODE 343:6
slot stuck in the s. KAVA 176:2
slouches S. towards Bethlehem YEAT 348:8
Slough friendly bombs, fall on S. BETJ 33:13
slovenliness Peace nothing but s. BREC 43:6
slow telling you to s. down SAYI 289:11
Time is too s. VAN 326:12
slower had to be s. FRAS 124:12
Reading it s. WOOD 344:7
slowly Architecture acts most s. DIMN 92:7
twist s. in the wind EHRL 99:8
slum free diversions in s. life MCAR 205:13
In almost any s. HARR 147:13
seen one city s. AGNE 5:1
slums gay intimacy of the s. WAUG 331:8
slurp s. into the barrels FISH 114:8
slush mush and s. OWEN 251:3
pure as the driven s. BANK 22:11
smack give them such a s. MERC 222:7
Just a s. at Auden EMPS 108:1
small pictures that got s. FILM 118:2
s., but perfectly formed COOP 77:2
S. is beautiful SCHU 292:1
s. states—Israel, Athens INGE 165:5
s.-talking. world FRY 128:11
they are very s. UPDI 325:15
smash all s. and no grab NICO 241:11
English never s. in a face HALS 144:5
smell s. and hideous hum GODL 136:7
s. of napalm in the morning FILM 116:4
Sweet s. of success FILM 118:14
smile Asians could still s. HEAD 149:14
Cambridge people rarely s. BROO 44:12
faint fleeting s. THUR 320:8
good s. in a child's eyes SHAF 294:12
has a nice s. GROM 141:8
Is it Colman's s. EWAR 110:7
It's OK to s. OFFI 245:16
s. and a shoeshine MILL 224:4
S. at us, pay us CHES 64:4
s. dwells a little longer CHAP 62:15
s. of a cosmic Cheshire cat HUXL 164:9
smiled only the dead s. AKHM 5:7
smith Chuck it, S. CHES 63:8
smitten s. a sleeping enemy YAMA 346:5
smoke rise then as s. to the sky CELA 61:6
S. gets in your eyes HARB 145:10
smoked s. my first cigarette TOSC 321:3
smoke-filled s. room SIMP 299:2
smoking S. can seriously damage OFFI 245:13
smug s.-faced crowds SASS 288:5
trendy S. Married FIEL 113:5
snails pace of s. KING 181:13
snake bitten by a s. DALA 83:10
s. came to my water-trough LAWR 192:11
snakes S. eat frogs STEV 307:14
snare rabbit in a s. STEP 307:6
sneaky snouty, s. mind NICO 241:8
sneezes Coughs and s. spread OFFI 245:3
snipe could shoot s. off him POWE 264:12
snippy no need to get s. GORE 138:1
snobbery bereaved if s. died USTI 326:2
S. with Violence BENN 29:16
snotgreen s. sea JOYC 173:15
snouty s., sneaky mind NICO 241:8
snow congealed s. PARK 253:18
dark over the s. THOM 319:5
first fall of s. PRIE 266:5
like the s. geese OKPI 244:16
Night, s., and sand NERU 239:2
s. falling faintly JOYC 173:5
woods fill up with s. FROS 127:20
wrong kind of s. WORR 345:13
snowed s. for six days THOM 318:12
Snow White used to be S. WEST 334:19

soaked s. to the skin COHE 73:1
soap mouths out with s. NEZ 239:11
soapflakes sell Jack like s. KENN 178:16
sob S., heavy world AUDE 16:11
sober tomorrow I shall be s. CHUR 69:6
social kind of s. disease AMIE 7:12
s. and economic experiment HOOV 159:1
S. Contract nothing more WELL 333:13
s. progress, order JOHN 170:6
socialism lots of ways to get s. KINN 182:9
S. can only arrive VIER 328:12
S. does not mean ORWE 250:10
S. is what MORR 231:13
S. nothing but capitalism SPEN 304:10
s. would not lose DUBČ 95:4
socialists s. throw it away CAST 57:8
socially often s. impressive WILL 339:4
society affluent s. GALB 130:4
call it a 'primitive s.' GREG 140:8
class-ridden s. KING 182:3
good s. is one MCEW 208:11
Great S. JOHN 171:9
litmus test of civil s. HAVE 149:2
nature of our s. POWE 264:19
No s. can survive GING 134:12
no such thing as S. THAT 317:9
prosperous or caring s. HESE 153:16
so-called affluent s. BEVA 34:11
S. is built on MAIL 213:4
S. needs to condemn MAJO 213:10
s. of privacy RAND 269:9
s. where it is safe STEV 308:9
sock making a hole in a s. EINS 101:4
socks have to wash your s. DE B 87:6
Socrates dying breath of S. MISQ 226:5
soda wash their feet in s. water ELIO 105:4
Sodom S. and Gomorrah BELL 28:8
sodomy rum, s., prayers CHUR 68:2
sofa s. upholstered in panther PLOM 259:17
soft s. under-belly of Europe MISQ 227:1
softly S. along the road DE L 89:7
soggy s. little island UPDI 325:9
soldier British s. stand up to SHAW 295:7
s. of the Great War EPIT 110:1
s.'s life is terrible hard MILN 225:6
s. trying to violate STRA 310:5
who had the s. singled DOUG 93:13
soldiers Old s. never die FOLE 120:15
old s. never die MACA 206:3
young Argentinian s. RUNC 281:5
soldiery Emperor's drunken s. YEAT 346:10
solidity appearance of s. ORWE 250:11
s. was knocked out LEAC 193:8
solitary s. confinement WILL 339:13
solitude feel his s. more keenly VALÉ 326:6
Solomon S. wrote the Proverbs NAYL 238:8
soluble art of the s. MEDA 220:14
solution can't see the s. CHES 64:13
either part of the s. CLEA 70:11
final s. HEYD 154:12
people were a kind of s. CAVA 61:2
total s. GOER 136:11
solutions all the s. THAT 318:2
s. are not ASIM 14:11
some S. mishtake, shurely CATC 60:3
somebody life of s. else DAVI 84:11
someday S. I'll find you COWA 79:3
someone s. may be happy MENC 221:6
S. wants a letter ADVE 4:22
something s. completely different CATC 58:2
S. may be gaining PAIG 252:7
S. must be done MISQ 227:2
s. of the night WIDD 338:1
Time for a little s. MILN 225:3
was there s. CATC 58:20
sometime come up and see me s. MISQ 227:5
woman is a s. thing HEYW 155:3
somewhat more than s. RUNY 281:9
somewhere S. over the rainbow HARB 145:14
Somme S. is like the Holocaust BARK 23:5
son good idea—s. CATC 58:19
s. was killed while laughing KIPL 182:14
song carcase of an old s. THOM 319:12
hate a s. that has sold BERL 31:9
only s. where I get JOHN 170:9
s. is ended (but the melody) BERL 31:5
s. was wordless SASS 288:2
trouble with a folk s. LAMB 187:13
sons s. and daughters of Life GIBR 134:6
sophistication Hip is the s. MAIL 213:6
Sorbonne one day at the S. STEV 307:18
sordid this s. saga LIEB 199:11
soreness leave a little s. LAYT 193:4
sorrow paying fines on s. MAYA 220:4
small and selfish is s. ELIZ 106:10
S. in all lands SUTT 312:1
sorry having to say you're s. TAGL 314:8
S. for itself LAWR 192:10
sort ability to s. peas HOLU 158:8
soteriological In s. terms FENT 112:8
soufflé cannot reheat a s. MCCA 207:2
sought least s. for CRAN 80:4
soul dark night of the s. FITZ 119:6
engineers of the s. GORK 138:3
give his own s. BOLT 40:5
literature saved my s. RATU 270:8
Lord take my s. LAST 190:14
love in another's s. LAYT 193:5
not engineers of the s. KENN 178:14
owe my s. to the company store TRAV 321:8
shivering human s. PAST 255:1
S. clap its hands and sing YEAT 348:4
s. swooned slowly JOYC 173:5
soulless when work is s. CAMU 52:18

souls engineers of human s. STAL 305:8
furnished s. CUMM 82:12
only in men's s. STEV 308:7
stuff of other people's s. MCGR 209:7
sound feeling, then, not s. STEV 308:1
s. of music HAMM 144:15
s. of surprise BALL 22:6
soundbite s. all an interviewer BENN 29:8
trade the s. DOBS 93:4
soundbites can't speak in s. CLAR 70:8
gossip and s. HURD 163:8
sounds similar s. at their ends LARK 189:8
soup do not take s. at luncheon CURZ 83:9
pissed in our s. BENN 29:13
south go s. in the winter ELIO 104:20
I want to go s. LAWR 192:18
Yes, but not in the S. POTT 263:6
South Africa S., renowned CAMP 52:5
southern S. trees bear strange HOLI 158:2
souvenirs *s. sont cors de chasse* APOL 13:4
sovereign advise my s. WAUG 331:17
change for a s. NESB 239:5
sovereignties addition of s. MONN 229:4
Soviet S. power plus electrification LENI 195:15
Soviets All power to the S. POLI 261:1
Soviet Union S. has indeed FULB 129:1
sow old s. that eats her farrow JOYC 173:11
space art of how to waste s. JOHN 172:3
cantos of unvanquished s. CRAN 79:16
In s., no one can hear you TAGL 314:5
more s. where nobody is STEI 306:9
S. is almost infinite QUAY 268:3
S. is blue HEIS 152:1
S. isn't remote HOYL 161:1
untrespassed sanctity of s. MAGE 212:9
spaces s. between the houses FENT 112:7
spaceship S. Earth FULL 129:4
spade pick up a s. FITZ 119:10
Spain Go to S. and get killed POLL 260:2
nor leave S. JUAN 174:8
permanence and unity of S. JUAN 174:7
spain rain in S. LERN 197:2
spam they offered s. MALA 213:15
Spaniards not the power of the S. SCHU 291:12
spaniel ill-trained s. CRAN 79:13
spanner their throats with a s. BETJ 33:9
spare Brother can you s. a dime HARB 145:11
do in his s. time GILL 134:10
spark-gap s. mightier than pen HOGB 157:12
sparrow Lesbia with her s. MILL 223:10
sparrows pass through for the s. GALB 130:9
speak I didn't s. up NIEM 242:6
I now s. for France DE G 88:5
s. before you think FORS 122:19
s. for Britain BOOT 40:9
S. for England AMER 7:10
s. ill of everybody except PÉTA 257:4
S. softly ROOS 278:10
whereof one cannot s. WITT 342:7
speaking talking without s. SIMO 298:13
speaks s. of a chair BISH 36:7
spearmint s. lose its flavour ROSE 279:6
special all s. cases CAMU 52:7
specialist definition of a s. MAYO 220:9
spectacle global s. DEBO 87:9
spectacular assured by a s. error GALB 130:12
spectators anything more than s. ASQU 15:3
speech dead had no s. for ELIO 103:2
gift of articulate s. SHAW 296:16
make a s. on conservation STEV 308:13
our concern was s. ELIO 103:5
quick of s. WINT 342:4
s. from Ernest Bevin FOOT 121:3
S. is civilization MANN 216:5
speechless from among the s. dead HILL 155:9
washed in the s. real BARZ 24:16
speed s. far faster than light BULL 47:10
s. glum heroes SASS 287:17
Unsafe at any s. NADE 236:11
spelling s. is Wobbly MILN 225:4
spend can't s. ourselves rich BLAC 36:11
If you have money you s. it KENN 178:18
s., and spend, and spend NICH 241:7
s. more time with my family FOWL 123:9
s. your way out CALL 51:3
spender big s. FIEL 113:7
spending better of s. RODD 276:6
spent Never ask of money s. FROS 127:9
spermatozoa million million s. HUXL 164:6
spider s. trying to hide NERU 239:3
spill let them not s. me MACN 211:16
S. your guts at Wimbledon CONN 75:15
spin Labour s. doctors CAMP 51:11
Sob, as you s. AUDE 16:11
spinach I say it's s. CART 56:5
spindle fold, s. or mutilate SAYI 289:14
spin-doctors s. in spin clinics BENN 29:9
spin-dryer mind is just like a s. NOLA 243:3
spinner S. of the Years HARD 146:7
spires grey s. of Oxford LETT 197:12
spirit appeals to the Dunkirk s. WILS 341:2
forge his revolutionary s. GUEV 142:3
sacramental of the s. ROBI 275:12
spirits S. of well-shot woodcock BETJ 33:6
spiritual approach the s. in art MOND 229:3
Music is s. MORR 232:8
not being a s. people MANC 214:10
spiritualist you are a s. SZAS 312:8
spiritualists convention of s. STOP 309:11
spit no gun, but I can s. AUDE 18:2
spite In S. of Everything ZIEG 350:9
splintered pass through the s. walls PEAK 255:13
splinters teeth like s. CAUS 60:21

split care what a s. infinitive FOWL 123:8
Images s. the truth LEVE 197:16
when I s. an infinitive CHAN 62:5
spoken American people have s. CLIN 72:5
spongy on s. shoes WILB 338:8
spoons world locks up its s. SHAW 296:2
sport owe to s. CAMU 52:17
Serious s. ORWE 250:12
thing about s. GREA 139:6
sportsman s. is a man who LEAC 193:11
spots s. rather a credit COMP 74:8
spotted s., silent, unfancied MORT 232:12
spouse President's s. BUSH 49:4
spray rime was on the s. HARD 147:2
spring beckoning to his S. Queen JARR 168:9
easing the S. REED 272:3
first hour of s. BOWE 41:9
only the right to s. FOND 121:1
s. breaks through again COWA 78:11
s. has been cancelled GILL 134:9
s. has kept in its folds ARAG 13:7
s. is wound up tight ANOU 13:1
s. now comes unheralded CARS 54:8
s. summer autumn winter CUMM 82:4
spur s. me into song YEAT 348:11
spy s. who came in from the cold LE C 194:12
squalor public s. GALB 130:6
square S. deal afterwards ROOS 278:11
squat s., and packed with guile BROO 44:12
squats s. on the hearthstone QUIL 268:5
squawking seven stars go s. AUDE 16:13
squeak until the pips s. GEDD 132:5
stab saw him s. READ 271:4
stability political s. MITC 225:15
stage put your daughter on the s. COWA 79:1
stain bright s. on the vision GRAV 139:1
convict s. HUGH 161:14
s. upon the silence BECK 26:10
stained hole in a s. glass window CHAN 62:1
stair falling from s. to stair BAYL 25:3
stake s. driven through his heart O'BR 244:1
Stalin guilt of S. GORB 137:13
S. himself rose TROT 322:11
Stalingrad cultural S. BALL 22:4
stall Baby in an ox's s. BETJ 33:4
stalled heart's s. motor MAYA 220:6
stallions bared teeth of s. CRAN 79:17
stamp physics or s. collecting RUTH 283:10
stamps stick in s. NICO 241:10
stand Get up, s. up MARL 217:2
no time to s. and stare DAVI 85:4
S. by your man WYNE 346:4
s. up to anything except SHAW 295:7
supposed to s. on that? CART 56:13
standard defending s. of living NIEM 242:5
standing s. armies of power RADC 268:11
s. by my man CLIN 71:7
still s. GREE 140:2
star Being a s. made it possible DAVI 85:7
By a high s. our course MACN 212:1
got to come back a s. FILM 118:1
guiding s. CARS 54:7
S. captains glow FLEC 120:1
stardust We are s. MITC 227:9
stare dead s. in a million adults SHAF 294:12
never to s. at people BALF 22:2
no time to stand and s. DAVI 85:4
starless s. and bible-black OPEN 248:1
starred No memory of having s. FROS 127:15
stars heard it's in the s. PORT 262:19
heaventree of s. JOYC 174:4
knowledge of the s. leads EDDI 98:11
reaches for the s. KOES 185:14
seven s. go squawking AUDE 16:13
s. of death AKHM 5:8
S. scribble on our eyes CRAN 79:16
We have the s. FILM 115:4
We've got more s. MAYE 220:7
with mites of s. MAYA 220:2
starship s. Enterprise RODD 276:3
start end is where we s. from ELIO 103:7
S. all over again FIEL 113:10
s. in the streets KENN 177:6
wholly new s. ELIO 102:18
started arrive where we s. ELIO 103:6
s. so I'll finish CATC 59:15
starter few thought he was a s. ATTL 16:3
Your s. for ten CATC 60:17
starvation night s. ADVE 3:25
starve let our people s. NYER 243:11
state no such thing as the S. AUDE 18:6
reinforcement of the S. CAMU 52:14
rolled back frontiers of S. THAT 317:10
separation of s. and science FEYE 113:1
s. has no place TRUD 322:13
S. is an instrument STAL 305:7
s. with the prettiest name BISH 36:4
While the S. exists LENI 195:12
stately S. Homes of England COWA 79:4
S., plump Buck Mulligan OPEN 247:19
statement black s. of pistons SPEN 304:1
statements s. inoperative ZIEG 350:10
statesman he was a s. LLOY 201:11
set a s. right YEAT 347:18
s. is a politician TRUM 323:8
statistic million deaths a s. STAL 305:10
statistical s. improbability DAWK 85:10
s. possibilities DIAM 91:8
statistics experiment needs s. RUTH 283:11
statue s. has never been set up SIBE 298:4
status quo restored the s. SQUI 305:5
stay If we can't s. here alive MONT 229:12
love is here to s. GERS 133:14
s. up all night BRYS 46:12

stay (*cont.*):
things to s. as they are LAMP 188:3
stays prays together s. together SAYI 289:15
steak not the meat of the s. PRIE 266:9
wanted s. MALA 213:15
steal s. from many, it's research MIZN 228:9
s. more than a hundred men PUZO 267:14
stealing For de little s. O'NE 246:5
steamers little holiday s. PRIE 266:8
steaming wealth of s. phrases SCHU 292:3
steel s. canisters hurtling about CASS 57:4
surgeon plies the s. ELIO 102:17
steeples dreary s. of Fermanagh CHUR 66:3
step One more s. along CART 55:5
one small s. for a man ARMS 14:6
take this s. with regret BLAC 36:12
step-parents especially s. POWE 264:10
sterilized thoroughly s. SAKI 285:3
stick carry a big s. ROOS 278:10
rattling of a s. inside ORWE 250:17
should s. together HUGH 162:11
Work was like a s. SOLZ 302:2
sticks S. nix hick pix NEWS 240:18
stigma Any s. to beat a dogma GUED 141:10
still I'm s. here HOPE 159:9
S. crazy after all SIMO 298:14
S. falls the rain SITW 299:7
s., like air, I'll rise ANGE 9:1
s. point ELIO 102:11
s. standing GREE 140:2
stillness present s. WARR 330:10
stimulate s. the phagocytes SHAW 295:8
sting s. like a bee ALI 6:8
stirred Shaken and not s. FLEM 120:7
stocking glimpse of s. PORT 260:12
stole son of a bitch s. my watch FILM 117:9
stolen generation was s. FREE 125:1
s. his wits away DE L 89:2
stone bomb them back into S. Age LEMA 195:9
caught the first s. POWE 264:14
Let them not make me a s. MACN 211:16
Like a rolling s. DYLA 97:11
make a s. of the heart YEAT 347:6
through a piece of s. MOOR 230:4
stood should of s. in bed JACO 167:6
stop nobody's going to s. 'em BERR 32:6
S. all the clocks AUDE 17:3
s. everyone from doing it HERB 153:7
S.-look-and-listen OFFI 245:14
S. me and buy one ADVE 4:23
S. the world NEWL 239:9
stops buck s. here TRUM 323:12
s. at 1945 MOLT 228:13
storage thought in cold s. SAMU 286:3
store in the s. we sell hope REVS 273:3
stork S. from butter ADVE 3:10
Stormont Ulster Parliament at S. GEOR 133:2
stormy S. weather KOEH 185:9
story dreaming s. JARR 168:9
novel tells a s. FORS 122:1
s. is ephemeral and doomed FAUL 111:13
St Paul's Say I am designing S. BENT 30:9
straight nothing ever ran quite s. GALS 130:14
strain train take the s. ADVE 4:8
Words s. ELIO 102:12
strand never alone with a S. ADVE 4:32
walk down the S. HARG 147:8
strange 'S. friend,' I said OWEN 251:11
strangeness will die of s. MURR 235:16
stranger by a complete s. ANNE 9:8
I, a s. and afraid HOUS 160:4
Look, s. AUDE 17:11
never love a s. BENS 30:6
s. and alone WOLF 343:11
wiles of the s. NASH 237:9
You may see a s. HAMM 144:14
strangers kindness of s. WILL 339:16
s. in the Capitol HEWI 154:10
strangled last minister is s. NAIR 237:2
strappy s. sandals SHUL 298:3
straw Headpiece filled with s. ELIO 103:13
strawberry S. fields forever LENN 196:9
stream cool as a mountain s. ADVE 3:11
street don't do it in the s. CAMP 52:3
inability to cross the s. WOOL 345:4
s. fighting man JAGG 167:12
sunny side of the s. FIEL 113:9
talking at s. corners VANZ 327:2
worth two in the s. WEST 334:8
streets children died in the s. AUDE 17:2
Down these mean s. CHAN 62:3
grass will grow in the s. HOOV 159:4
start in the s. KENN 177:6
S. FLOODED TELE 316:8
Streltsy like wives of the S. AKHM 5:9
strength S. through joy POLI 261:21
stretch s. the human frame SCAR 288:13
strife In place of s. CAST 57:7
step towards an end of s. GEOR 133:2
strike s. against public safety COOL 76:8
s. it in anger SHAW 296:9
strings scrape your s. darker CELA 61:6
striped s. shroud THOM 319:8
stroke at a s., reduce the rise HEAT 151:5
strong nature of s. people BONH 40:6
only the S. shall thrive SERV 294:3
realize how s. she is REAG 271:6
river Is a s. brown god ELIO 102:19
struck s. regularly like gongs COWA 79:8
structuralists S. constructed WOLF 344:2
struggle s. between artist man SHAW 295:20
s. continues LAST 190:14
s. towards the heights CAMU 52:10
to-day the s. AUDE 18:12

struggled s. against tyranny TUTU 324:8
stubbornness self-righteous s. JENK 169:10
stuck s. in the slot KAVA 176:2
s. in this building LAST 190:8
studiously apart, s. neutral WILS 341:14
study proper s. of mankind HUXL 163:12
stuff too short to s. a mushroom CONR 76:4
stumbles how the strong man s. ROOS 278:13
stump mount the s. STEV 308:13
stupid *all* questions were s. WEIS 332:13
interesting . . . but s. CATC 60:7
It's the economy, s. POLI 261:19
not as s. as he seems CAST 57:9
on the part of the s. WARN 330:7
pretend to be more s. STAR 305:12
s. neither forgive nor SZAS 312:7
style cut, the s., the line LOES 202:1
has no real s. PICA 258:6
Mandarin s. CONN 75:8
murderer for fancy prose s. NABO 236:7
sub Sighted s., sank same MASO 218:14
subject not shocked by this s. BOHR 39:10
sublime most s. noise FORS 122:5
ridiculous, the s. MAHO 212:10
submarines worked with more s. MILL 224:14
substitute no s. for talent HUXL 164:2
no s. for victory MACA 206:2
substitutes Ours is the age of s. BENT 30:10
subtle s. but not malicious EINS 100:3
suburbia come from s. RAPH 270:2
subversive funny is s. ORWE 250:13
subway in a New York s. STRA 310:7
succeed How to s. in business MEAD 220:11
If at first you don't s. FIEL 113:16
not enough to s. VIDA 328:5
not going to s. MORT 232:14
possible to s. RENO 272:13
s. in America IZZA 166:10
succeeds Whenever a friend s. VIDA 328:4
success If *A* is a s. in life EINS 100:13
made me a s. ANDR 8:13
no s. like failure DYLA 97:12
s. is like fresh fruit GOSS 138:5
S. is relative ELIO 102:6
s. only a delayed failure GREE 139:18
Sweet smell of s. FILM 118:14
successful recipes always s. VALÉ 326:5
successors dissatisfield with s. JENK 169:12
gold by our s. LESS 197:10
none of my s. MAJO 213:13
sucker give a s. an even break FIEL 113:12
sue s. its parents WATS 331:2
sued publish and be s. INGR 165:9
suet-pudding cold, black s. LEWI 199:7
Suez S.—a smash and grab raid NICO 241:11
S. Canal flowing through EDEN 99:2
suffering About s. they were AUDE 17:13
not true that s. ennobles MAUG 219:5
sufferings constant in human s. JOYC 173:12
sufficient S. conscience LLOY 201:13
sugar no s. cane for miles HOLI 158:3
suicide infamous s. PLAT 259:9
it is s. MACD 208:3
longest s. note KAUF 175:9
possibility of s. CIOR 69:8
s. kills two people MILL 223:14
suicides s. have a special language SEXT 294:11
sui generis say I am *s.* LONG 202:7
suit lugubrious man in a s. ELIZ 106:12
suitable s. case for treatment MERC 222:2
suites get to the s. KENN 177:6
suits omelette all over our suits BROK 44:5
sum s. of all the choices DIDI 92:4
Sumatra giant rat of S. DOYL 94:8
summer long hot s. FILM 118:9
on a hot s. afternoon ANON 12:7
s. afternoon JAME 168:5
S. time and the livin' HEYW 155:2
sun At the going down of the s. BINY 35:12
Born of the s. SPEN 304:3
inconceivable idea of the s. STEV 307:17
staring at the s. BELL 27:10
s. also rises HEMI 152:13
S. backs Blair NEWS 240:19
s. doesn't revolve LIVI 200:12
s. set on your wrath MILL 224:15
S. Wot Won It NEWS 240:12
watched the s. going down VAN 326:11
where no s. shines THOM 318:8
sunbathing Picasso, s. and jazz WAUG 331:11
sunbeam Jesus wants me for a s. TALB 313:4
Sunday Never on S. FILM 118:11
rainy S. afternoon ERTZ 108:11
S., bloody Sunday FILM 118:13
S. go-to-meeting clothes SHIE 297:11
working week and S. best AUDE 17:4
sundial s., and I make a botch BELL 28:3
sunlight s. on the garden MACN 211:17
sunlit broad, s. uplands CHUR 66:12
sunny some s. day PARK 254:3
s. side of the street FIEL 113:9
sunset s. of my life REAG 272:1
sunsets Autumn s. exquisitely HUXL 164:7
horror of s. PROU 267:2
sunshine ray of s. WODE 342:12
superior S. people never make MOOR 230:9
superman godlike s. WODE 343:1
It's S. ANON 10:8
superstition main source of s. RUSS 283:6
supplies just bought fresh s. BREC 43:8
support depend on the s. of Paul SHAW 295:11
no invisible means of s. BUCH 47:3
s. of the woman I love EDWA 99:4

tambourine Mr T. Man DYLA 97:13
tango Takes two to t. HOFF 157:10
tank tiger in your t. ADVE 4:19
tanks Get your t. off my lawn WILS 341:9
tanstaafl acronym T. SAYI 290:9
tarnished neither t. nor afraid CHAN 62:3
Tarot readers of T. cards JONE 172:8
tarted should be t. up BOWI 41:17
tarts action of two t. MACM 211:2
Tarzan Me T., you Jane MISQ 226:11
tasks dear unfinished t. ANON 11:1
taste bouquet better than the t. POTT 263:4
doubt and good t. BROD 44:4
ghastly good t. BETJ 34:1
underrating public t. DEED 88:2
tasted t. your worm SPOO 304:14
tastes if it t. good, it's bad ASIM 15:1
tattered t. coat upon a stick YEAT 348:4
wars have t. his ears HUGH 162:2
taught t. us how to live BENN 29:11
t. what is BRUC 46:6
tax power to t. BLAC 36:11
to t. rich people LLOY 201:9
taxation Inflation one form of t. FRIE 126:6
taxes Death and t. and childbirth MITC 228:2
little people pay t. HELM 152:7
no new t. BUSH 49:7
Sex and t. JONE 172:10
taxi If you can't leave in a t. FILM 116:1
t. throbbing waiting ELIO 105:5
taxi-cab look like a t. HUGH 161:5
taxis hiring t. to scuttle round KINN 182:6
tea honey still for t. BROO 44:13
T., although an Oriental CHES 64:5
T. and sympathy ANDE 8:12
t. for two CAES 50:6
t.'s out of the way REED 272:4
teabag woman is like a t. REAG 271:6
teach change the people who t. BYAT 50:4
T. us to care ELIO 102:3
teaches He who cannot, t. SHAW 296:7
teaching t. of history MOLT 228:13
tea-cup crack in the t. opens AUDE 16:14
tea-girl t.'s chance to kiss WHIT 337:10
tear Wipe the t., baby dear WEST 335:13
tears blood, toil, t. and sweat CHUR 66:8
bursting into t. WOOD 344:8
enough of blood and t. RABI 268:10
French without t. RATT 270:5
t. I cannot hide HARB 145:10
tearsday moanday, t., wailsday JOYC 173:7
tease fleas that t. BELL 28:6
technical few t. details NYE 243:10
technically t. sweet OPPE 246:16
Technik *Vorsprung durch T.* ADVE 4:27
technique t. improved as the real TAYL 313:14
technology advanced t. CLAR 70:2
in relation to our t. BERR 32:8
T. . . . the knack FRIS 126:9
white heat of t. MISQ 227:4
teddy Now T. must run KENN 179:1
T. Bears have their Picnic KENN 177:8
teenager as a t. LEBO 194:8
teenie Itsy bitsy t. weenie VANC 326:8
teeth clean their t. in the dark JENK 169:6
he's got iron t. GROM 141:8
old bitch gone in the t. POUN 263:14
shark has pretty t. BREC 43:10
t. are in the real meat GRIM 141:7
women have fewer t. RUSS 282:10
Teflon T.-coated Presidency SCHR 291:9
telegram visual t. CASS 57:3
telegrams life of t. and anger FORS 122:8
telephones Tudor monarchy with t. BURG 48:6
telescope t. or hydrogen bomb LOVE 203:8
television first law of t. ADAM 2:3
I hate t. WELL 333:8
It's t., you see HOWE 160:14
no plain women on t. FORD 121:6
of t. WILD 338:9
on t. as an agent EYRE 111:1
On t. I feel like MUGG 234:7
Radio and t. SARR 287:3
see bad t. for nothing GOLD 137:7
Some t. programmes ANON 12:4
T. brought brutality MCLU 210:10
T. closer to reality PAGL 252:2
T. contracts imagination WOGA 343:8
T. has brought murder HITC 156:10
T. has made dictatorship PERE 256:8
T. is for appearing on COWA 79:11
T. is simultaneously JAME 167:13
T. thrives on unreason DAY 86:2
T.? word is half Greek SCOT 292:12
thinking man's t. HAMP 145:2
when t. presents SACK 284:5
tell closest friends won't t. you ADVE 3:17
Don't ask, don't t. NUNN 243:8
Don't t. the ending TAGL 314:11
T. Sid ADVE 4:24
T. them I came DE L 89:6
t. them of us and say EPIT 110:4
What do I t. the pilot LAST 191:6
telling t. you something DUNM 95:11
tells nobody t. me anything GALS 130:16
t. the truth MUNR 235:4
temper including my t. NEHR 238:12
Never lose your t. with PANK 252:11
never to lose me t. O'CA 244:9
truth that has lost its t. GIBR 134:8
temperature acquire a t. SCHU 292:3
temps *A la recherche du t. perdu* PROU 267:1
temptation maximum of t. SHAW 296:8

timing real bad sense of t. MCGO 209:5
Timothy T. has passed EPIT 110:3
T. Winters comes CAUS 60:21
tin cat on a hot t. roof WILL 339:9
on a corrugated t. roof BEEC 26:19
Tina acronym T. THAT 316:14
like T. Brown FIEL 113:6
tingling It's t. fresh ADVE 4:4
tinker don't matter a t.'s cuss SHIN 297:13
tinkering rule of intelligent t. EHRL 99:7
tinned smoked salmon and t. WILS 341:4
tiny My t. watching eye DE L 89:9
Tipperary long way to T. JUDG 174:9
tipster racing t. who only TAYL 313:11
tiptoe Dance t., bull BUNT 47:12
tired I'm t. LAST 190:9
I was t. of it PARK 254:8
sin to be t. MOSS 233:6
t. of being a woman SEXT 294:7
t. of Love BELL 27:16
Tiresias T., old man ELIO 105:6
tiring Shakespeare is so t. HULL 162:15
tit get her t. caught MITC 225:16
titanic deck of the T. MORT 233:3
title needed no royal t. SPEN 303:11
toad Give me your arm, old t. LARK 189:4
let the t. work LARK 189:3
toads gardens with real t. MOOR 230:8
toast accumulation of t. PHIL 257:12
today get where I am t. without CATC 59:4
standing here t. JOHN 171:6
T. is the last day YELT 349:3
t. the struggle AUDE 18:12
T. we have naming of parts REED 272:2
we gave our t. EPIT 110:4
will not hang myself t. CHES 63:11
toe big t. ends up making a hole EINS 101:4
toil blood, t., tears and sweat CHUR 66:8
told I t. you so EPIT 109:6
like to be t. the worst CHUR 67:4
plato t. him: he couldn't CUMM 82:7
tolerance such a thing as t. WILS 341:18
T. the essential PHIL 257:11
tolerant being t. for nothing GREG 140:9
tolerate not to t. the intolerant POPP 260:7
tolerated women not merely t. AUNG 19:8
Tom gone to join T. EPIT 109:1
Ground control to Major T. BOWI 41:16
tomato You like t. GERS 133:13
tomb t. of a mediocre talent SMIT 300:12
tombs in the cool t. SAND 286:6
tomcat t. lies stretched flat HUGH 162:2
tomorrow For your t. we gave EPIT 110:4
Leave t. behind COWA 78:8
T. for the young AUDE 18:12
t. is another day MITC 228:4
we thought was for t. BENN 29:3
what to see t. STEI 307:1
tongue grow a second t. MONT 229:10
lies of t. and pen CHES 63:15
tip of the t. OPEN 247:12
tongues nor spoke with t. of gold RICH 274:4
t. of beggards HOLU 158:7
tons Sixteen t. TRAV 321:8
Tony straight from T. PARR 254:10
tool Science is an edged t. EDDI 98:12
tools Give us the t. CHUR 67:3
toothache Venerable Mother T. HEAT 151:9
toothaches underrates t. KUND 186:13
toothpaste t. is out of the tube HALD 144:1
top made it to the t. MALL 214:6
T. of the world FILM 115:1
T. people ADVE 4:26
topography T. displays BISH 36:5
torch t. passed to new generation KENN 178:2
tormentor mentor and my t. BROW 45:13
tornado set off a t. in Texas LORE 203:4
Toronto T. is a kind USTI 326:3
torso remain only a t. ERHA 108:10
torture mind that will t. you AHER 5:5
self-imposed t. MILL 224:8
So does t. AUDE 18:16
torturer t.'s horse scratches AUDE 17:14
Tory hatred for the T. Party BEVA 34:4
Thirteen years of T. misrule POLI 262:4
to like T. MPs CAMP 51:11
T.'s secret weapon KILM 180:12
total t. solution GOER 136:11
totalitarian lead to the t. state DENN 90:5
totalitarianism name of t. GAND 131:5
totem t.-symbol in his hand KOES 185:14
totter t. towards the tomb SAYE 288:10
tough in t. joints RUNY 281:9
t. get going SAYI 290:15
T. on crime BLAI 37:2
toughness T. doesn't have to come FEIN 112:4
tourism t. is their religion RUNC 281:6
What an odd thing t. is BRYS 46:13
tourist makes everyone a t. SONT 302:15
t. of wars GELL 132:8
town destroy the t. ANON 11:4
Dirty old t. MACC 207:3
go down to the end of the t. MILN 225:7
lived in a pretty how t. CUMM 82:4
Toytown running for Mayor of T. SCAR 290:19
trace risen without t. MUGG 234:3
tracing fitful t. of a portal STEV 308:2
tracks hungry on the t. CRAN 80:2
trade Irish poets, learn you t. YEAT 348:15
There isn't any T. HERB 153:9
tradition great t. LEAV 194:2
T. means giving votes CHES 64:11
traduced t. Joseph K. OPEN 247:18
traffic reckless motor t. DEWA 91:4

truth Art is not t. PICA 258:8
Believing T. is staring BELL 27:10
economical with the t. ARMS 14:7
forsake this t. ROSE 279:7
here have Pride and T. YEAT 347:19
how many people know the t. WEST 335:8
Images split the t. LEVE 197:16
just tell the t. TRUM 323:7
keep t. safe in its hand TAGO 313:2
know the t. at last EPIT 109:16
lawyer interprets the t. GIRA 135:9
lures the t. WESK 334:4
mistook disenchantment for t. SART 287:8
new scientific t. PLAN 259:6
possesses not only t. RUSS 282:14
seek to suppress t. SOYI 303:2
simply a t. repeated BALD 21:9
stop telling the t. STEV 308:5
sword of t. AITK 5:6
to lie for the t. ADLE 2:7
t. 24 times per second GODA 136:4
t. about herself MUNR 235:4
t., beauty, and goodness WEIL 332:9
t. cannot be told SOLZ 301:13
T. exists, only lies BRAQ 42:14
T. is a pathless land KRIS 186:6
T. is never undone ROET 276:9
t. is out there CATC 60:6
t., justice and the American way ANON 10:8
T.-loving Persians GRAV 138:12
t. makes men free AGAR 2:10
t. that has lost its temper GIBR 134:8
unpleasant way of saying t. HELL 152:5
write the t. KANE 175:7
truths all t. are half-truths WHIT 336:14
Few new t. have ever won BERL 31:12
old universal t. FAUL 111:13
repetition of unpalatable t. SUMM 311:11
t. being in and out FROS 127:1
try Nice t. MORG 231:2
t., try again FIEL 113:16
We t. harder ADVE 4:29
trying I am t. to be SMIT 300:7
just goes on t. PICA 258:6
without really t. MEAD 220:11
tsar no t., but the slaves ZAMY 350:2
T-shirt got the T. SAYI 289:3
tube toothpaste is out of the t. HALD 144:1
Tudor US presidency a T. monarchy BURG 48:6
tumour aspirin for a brain t. CHAN 62:2
ripens in a t. ABSE 1:3
tune guy who could carry a t. EPIT 109:12
turn on, t. in and drop out LEAR 193:12
tunes t. of Handel SITW 299:10
tunnel back down the time t. KEAT 176:7
light at the end of the t. DICK 92:1
light at the end of the t. LOWE 204:12
turkeys t. vote for Christmas CALL 51:6
turn and quickly t. away YEAT 347:9
Because I do not hope to t. ELIO 102:2
t. on, tune in and drop out LEAR 193:12
T. that off WILL 339:14
turning lady's not for t. THAT 316:15
point of the t. world ELIO 102:11
turnip candle in that great t. CHUR 68:1
turret washed me out of the t. JARR 168:8
turtle t. lives 'twixt plated NASH 237:4
TV blight has hit the T. industry STRE 310:13
by T. stupor SOLZ 302:4
T.—a clever contraction ACE 1:5
twang t., and you've got music VICI 328:1
tweed t. nightgowns GING 134:11
twelve snowed for t. days THOM 318:12
twentieth close of the t. century HEWI 154:9
half of the t. century QUAN 268:1
language of the t. century BEVA 34:5
t. century belongs TRUD 322:14
t. century will be TOYN 321:6
twenty at T. I tried to vex AUDE 18:8
twenty-first first war of the t. century BUSH 49:12
started t. century BOWI 42:2
t. century CLAR 70:6
twenty-five t.-year-old men MCCU 207:9
twenty-twenty Hindsight is always t. WILD 338:11
twice Don't think t. DYLA 97:7
must do t. as well as men WHIT 337:13
postman always rings t. CAIN 50:8
twist t. slowly in the wind EHRL 99:8
twisted You silly t. boy CATC 60:18
two Takes t. to tango HOFF 157:10
tea for t. CAES 50:6
t. by two in the ark LEVE 197:17
t. cultures SNOW 301:12
t. glasses and two chairs MACN 211:14
t. is fun SAYI 289:6
t. plus two make four ORWE 250:4
We're number t. ADVE 4:29
worth t. in the street WEST 334:8
types Seven t. of ambiguity EMPS 108:5
typewriter t. separated me from NERU 239:4
typewriters banging on million t. WILE 338:16
monkeys strumming on t. EDDI 98:8
tyranny against a monstrous t. CHUR 66:9
conditions of t. AREN 14:3
silent in the face of t. SOYI 303:3
struggled against t. TUTU 324:8
unnecessary t. RUSS 282:6
tyres concrete and t. LARK 188:11

ugly Bessie, you're u. CHUR 69:6

ugly *(cont.)*:
good, the bad, and the u. FILM 118:8
no place for u. mathematics HARD 146:3
UK within the U. STRA 310:12
Ulster betrayal of U. CAIR 50:10
Ulsterman U., of planter stock HEWI 154:11
ultimate u. blandness ROTT 280:5
unable u. to find work COOL 76:15
unacceptable u. face HEAT 151:6
unaware And I was u. HARD 146:9
unbearable in victory u. CHUR 68:8
u. lightness of being KUND 187:1
unbeatable In defeat u. CHUR 68:8
unbeautiful are u. and have CUMM 82:12
unborn possible to talk to the u. BARZ 24:16
unbroken part of u. stream HAWK 149:3
uncertainty u. principle HAWK 149:5
Uncle Sam U. came along NEZ 239:11
unconscious royal road to the u. MISQ 226:4
u. cerebration JAME 167:14
uncool U. people ELTO 107:7
undecided five who are u. STEN 307:4
under got you u. my skin PORT 262:13
I'd have been u. the host PARK 253:20
under-appreciated highly u. STIN 309:1
under-belly soft u. of Europe MISQ 227:1
underestimating u. intelligence MENC 221:10
underneath U. the Arches FLAN 119:13
underrates u. toothaches KUND 186:13
underrating u. public taste DEED 88:2
undersold Never knowingly u. ADVE 4:14
understand child could u. FILM 117:14
don't u. things NEUM 239:7
don't u. too hot SALI 285:10
failed to u. it BOHR 39:10
Grown-ups never u. SAIN 284:12
I do not u. FEYN 113:3
liberals can u. BRUC 46:5
much that I did not u. ORWE 249:12
u. a little less MAJO 213:10
u. nothing CORN 77:8
u. the situation MURR 236:3
What you can't u. DYLA 97:17
understanding sketchy u. of life CRIC 80:9
understatement that was an u. MITC 225:14
understood don't care if I'm u. FRUM 128:7
I have u. you DE G 88:7
music u. by children STRA 310:8
undertaking no such u. CHAM 61:11
underwear right down to her u. NIXO 242:7
undeservedly books u. forgotten AUDE 19:1
undeserving u. poor SHAW 296:18
uneconomic shown it to be 'u.' SCHU 292:2
uneducated u. man to read books CHUR 68:11
unemployment leave it to u. KEYN 179:11
rising u. LAMO 188:1
u. results COOL 76:15
unexpected most u. of all things TROT 322:12
unexplained you're u. as yet HALL 144:3
unfaithful original is u. BORG 41:4
unfinished Liberty is u. business ANON 11:10
unfit chosen from the u. SAYI 289:7
unforgiveness alp of u. PLOM 259:15
unforgiving fill the u. minute KIPL 183:7
unfree Ireland u. shall never be at peace PEAR 256:2
unhappily bad end u. STOP 310:2
unhappiness loyalty we feel to u. GREE 139:12
putting-off of u. GREE 139:8
u. develops the forces of the mind PROU 267:6
U. is best defined DE B 87:8
vocation of u. SIME 298:9
unhappy making us u. FILI 114:2
moral as soon as u. PROU 267:7
only speak when she is u. SMIT 301:2
U. the land that needs BREC 43:4
unheard language of the u. KING 181:12
unhurt U. people not much good STAR 305:13
uninspiring may be u. GEOR 133:5
union Act of U. is there TRIM 322:6
u. has been guiding star CARS 54:7
United Kingdom in this our U. DEWA 91:3
unity national u. BUSH 49:13
national u. ROOS 277:17
u. of our fatherland KOHL 186:1
universal u. sewer COUS 78:6
universe Architect of the U. JEAN 169:5
coherent plan to the u. HOYL 161:3
fact about the u. EINS 100:10
good u. next door CUMM 82:9
Life, the U. and Everything ADAM 1:12
mechanism of the U. WHIT 336:12
Somewhere in the u. TAGL 314:12
u. go to all the bother HAWK 149:6
U. is a free lunch GUTH 142:8
u. is not hostile HOLM 158:5
u. is not only queerer HALD 143:8
u.'s existence made known PENR 256:6
u. sleeps MAYA 220:2
universities men who go to the u. MAUG 219:9
university able to get to a u. KINN 182:8
u. of life BOTT 41:6
u. of the air WILS 341:5
u. training AMIS 8:5
unjoined *u.* system ANON 10:16
unknowable decide on the u. ZOBE 351:1
unknown glorious and the u. FORS 122:4
known and the u. PINT 258:12
tread safely into the u. HASK 148:10
U. Prime Minister ASQU 15:4
unluckily good u. STOP 310:2
unlucky It was his u. night MCHA 209:8
so u. that he runs into MARQ 217:11
unmaking things are in the u. KING 181:14

unnatural only u. sex act KINS 182:10
unnecessary to do the u. SAYI 289:7
unofficial English u. rose BROO 44:11
unpalatable disastrous and the u. GALB 130:11
unplayable another u. work SCHO 291:8
unpopular safe to be u. STEV 308:9
unprincipled sold by the u. CAPP 53:10
unproductive wholly u. HAGU 142:13
unreality u. of painted people UPDI 325:16
unreason Television thrives on u. DAY 86:2
unreliable Even death is u. BECK 26:11
unsafe U. at any speed NADE 236:11
unsayable say the u. RUSH 281:14
unscathed u. tourist of wars GELL 132:8
unselfishly U. so we might have MCHA 209:8
unsolicited u. advice COOL 76:11
unsorted all the u. stuff GOLD 137:1
unspeakable speak the u. RUSH 281:14
unspun I am u. DOBS 93:4
untalented product of the u. CAPP 53:10
unthought never be u. DÜRR 97:1
untouchable dying from being u. HEGG 151:12
untried difficult; and left u. CHES 64:15
untrue man who's u. to his wife AUDE 17:15
unupblown NURSE U. TELE 316:5
unwanted feeling of being u. TERE 315:7
unwell Jeffery Bernard is u. WATE 330:14
unwilling group of the u. SAYI 289:7
u. or unable WILL 340:1
up nice to people on your way u. MIZN 228:8
U. to a point, Lord Copper WAUG 331:13
uplands broad, sunlit u. CHUR 66:12
upper Like many of the U. Class BELL 28:1
prove the u. classes COWA 79:4
uppity feeling a bit u. CLOU 72:7
upstanding clean u. chap like you KING 182:1
upwards car could go straight u. HOYL 161:1
onwards and u. YORK 349:9
uranium element u. may be turned EINS 100:11
urine red wine of Shiraz into u. DINE 92:9
us he is u. CART 56:10
USA Born in the U. SPRI 305:1
use u. words as they are used COMP 74:9
used ain't what they u. to be PERS 257:2
buy a u. car POLI 262:7
get u. to them NEUM 239:7
useful be a Really U. Engine AWDR 19:9
what is apparently u. WHIT 337:5
useless plans are u. EISE 101:12
usual Business carried on as u. CHUR 66:2
usura With u. hath no man a house POUN 263:9
usury u. is contrary to Scripture TAWN 313:8
uterus what your u. looks like EPHR 108:6
Utopia U. is a blessed past KISS 184:15
utterance such a door of u. MACD 207:13
U-turn media catch-phrase, the U. THAT 316:15
vacant v. interstellar spaces ELIO 102:16
We're v. ROTT 280:4
vacuum behind the v. cleaner GREE 140:5
v. a hell of a lot better WILL 339:11
vague don't be v. ADVE 3:14
valley great things from the v. CHES 64:8
How green was my v. LLEW 201:1
V. of the dolls SUSA 311:12
value Nothing has v. FORS 122:16
values authentic and pure v. WEIL 332:9
Victorian v. THAT 317:5
van Follow the v. COLL 73:9
vanished this v. being HAWK 149:3
vanities bonfire of the v. WOLF 343:15
vanity feeds your v. PARR 254:9
vase Sèvres v. in the hands WAUG 331:16
vast v. right-wing conspiracy CLIN 71:9
vaulting V. the sea CRAN 80:3
Vega V. conspicuous overhead AUDE 18:1
vengeance stay the hands of v. JACK 167:4
Venice Death in V. MANN 216:1
verb God to me is a v. FULL 129:3
Waiting for the German v. O'BR 244:5
verbal v. contract isn't worth GOLD 137:4
verboojuice Sesquippledan v. WELL 333:10
verdict opportunity to pass their v. AHER 5:4
verifiability not the *v.* POPP 260:5
verification method of its v. SCHL 291:2
vermin lower than v. BEVA 34:4
Versailles politics of V. MONN 229:5
verse as soon write free v. FROS 128:5
died to make v. free PRES 265:17
Doctors in v. THOM 319:10
give up v., my boy POUN 264:1
No subject for immortal v. DAY- 86:9
write it out in a v. YEAT 347:7
very Be v. afraid TAGL 314:1
V. interesting . . . but CATC 60:7
vessel v. with the pestle FILM 117:7
vice Art is v. DEGA 88:3
defence of liberty is no v. GOLD 137:2
English v. RATT 270:6
quotation is a nation v. WAUG 331:10
vices V. are general MURD 235:8
vicious didn't know what v. was AUNG 19:7
Sid V. of the Sex Pistols DURC 96:7
victim Any v. demands allegiance GREE 139:13
oppressor, never the v. WIES 338:3
thou shalt not be a v. BAUE 25:2
victims blame to its 'v.' SONT 302:12
v. of American Fascism ROSE 279:8
v. who respect SART 287:14
Victoria take a ticket at V. BEVI 35:3
Victorian stuffy V. family ORWE 249:15
V. values THAT 317:5
victors v.' justice SHAW 297:5
victory Dig for v. OFFI 245:4

In v.: magnanimity CHUR 68:12
in v. unbearable CHUR 68:8
no substitute for v. MACA 206:2
not the v. but the contest COUB 78:3
peace without v. WILS 341:15
produce v. parades HOBS 157:2
smells like v. FILM 116:4
v. by a woman WEST 335:10
V. has a hundred fathers CIAN 69:7
v. in spite of all terror CHUR 66:10
v. in war KEEG 176:10
wallow in our v. PRES 265:15
we never had a v. CHUR 68:16
Viet Cong no quarrel with the V. ALI 6:9
Vietnam since the V. war WHIT 336:5
To win in V. SPOC 304:12
V. as a war PILG 258:9
V. was lost in MCLU 210:10
V. was the first WEST 335:12
views Kipling and his v. AUDE 17:10
village image of a global v. MCLU 210:6
life in the v. LEE 195:1
villages V. ruled by conformism DEBO 87:9
vinegar have it tinned. With v. WILS 341:4
vines advise client to plant v. WRIG 345:14
violations no end to the v. BOWE 41:12
violence rape, ultra-v. and Beethoven TAGL 314:2
Snobbery with V. BENN 29:16
v. in the mind ALDI 6:3
v. is necessary BROW 46:1
violent v. revolution inevitable KENN 178:10
violet At the v. hour ELIO 105:5
violin v. so much wood and catgut PRIE 266:6
vipers plays with his v. CELA 61:5
virgin before she was a v. MARX 218:10
V. is the possibility BRAN 42:12
virginity little more v. TREE 321:9
virtuality voyager in v. TURK 324:5
virtue v. at the testing point LEWI 198:14
virtues v. are particular MURD 235:8
virus dying not from the v. HEGG 151:12
Fiction is the great v. THOM 320:2
hear the v. humming DOTY 93:10
v. from unprotected sex SEIK 293:5
visible not reproduce the v. KLEE 184:18
Work is love made v. GIBR 134:7
vision single central v. BERL 31:10
trouble with 'the v. thing' IVIN 166:7
v. thing BUSH 49:5
visions Cecilia, appear in v. AUDE 16:12
visits never make long v. MOOR 230:9
visual v. telegram CASS 57:3
vitriol sleeve with bottle of v. WOOL 345:11
vivacious v. and a bit wild EMIN 107:13
vivid v. rather than happy LOVE 203:9
vocabulary mastery of v. SAYE 288:11
vocation v. of unhappiness SIME 298:9
voice I've lost my v. MORR 231:11
new v. of Scotland CONN 75:1
v. is full of money FITZ 119:2
v. was that of Mr Churchill ATTL 16:1
v. we know so well WRIG 345:16
voices Other v., other rooms CAPO 53:9
v. of young people SMIT 300:11
voids attempts to fill v. WEIL 332:8
volcano crust over a v. ELLI 107:5
vole passes the questing v. WAUG 331:14
Volk *Ein Reich, ein V.* POLI 261:11
Volkswagen V. parked in the gap MULD 234:12
Voltaire V. in the Bastille DE G 88:16
volume unequipped with v. knobs SETH 294:6
voluntary Composing's not v. BIRT 36:3
vomit returning to one's own v. POWE 265:5
Vorsprung *V. durch Technik* ADVE 4:27
vote always v. *against* FIEL 113:14
Don't buy a single v. more KENN 177:10
turkeys v. for Christmas CALL 51:6
v. against somebody ADAM 1:14
v. for the best President PETE 257:6
V. for the man who promises BARU 24:14
voted Today we v. CLIN 71:11
voters v. don't know FOTH 123:6
votes some v. down there BUCH 47:4
V. for women POLI 262:5
v. to get the things done SAMU 286:4
voting If v. changed anything LIVI 200:11
not v. that's democracy STOP 309:9
vow v. to thee, my country SPRI 304:15
vowels with all the v. missing ELLI 107:1
voyages v. of the starship RODD 276:3
vulgar v., vulgar, vulgar CHAR 63:5
vulgarity V. often cuts ice BEER 26:21
v. of the human heart BROD 44:4

wage home policy: I w. war CLEM 71:1
wages better w. and shorter hours ORWE 250:10
wagon w. of his 'Plan' PAST 255:2
wait too slow for those who w. VAN 326:12
w. and see ASQU 15:2
waited w. nearly 300 years CONN 75:1
waiter dam' good head w. GULB 142:5
waiting opposite of talking is w. LEBO 194:7
w. for Godot BECK 26:4
W. for the end EMPS 108:2
W. for the German verb O'BR 244:5
w. seven hundred years COLL 73:11
What are we w. for CAVA 61:1
wake W. up, England GEOR 133:1
when I w. up MATT 219:3
waken w. a sleeping giant FILM 115:16

waking take my w. slow ROET 276:13
Wales no present in W. THOM 319:12
Princess of W. was DOWD 94:6
still parts of W. THOM 319:8
W.'s own annual blood sport MORG 231:3
W. to gain the same JONE 172:6
whole world . . . But for W. BOLT 40:5
walk machine that would w. APOL 13:5
never learned to w. forward ROOS 278:2
no easy w.-over to freedom NEHR 238:9
W. across my swimming pool RICE 273:12
w. hard enough CHAT 63:7
w. on the wild side ALGR 6:5
w. with the dead FORS 123:1
You'll never w. alone HAMM 145:1
walked Cat w. by himself KIPL 184:3
W. day and night LOGU 202:4
walking boots are made for w. HAZL 149:13
dancing is to w. WAIN 328:13
empire w. very slowly FITZ 119:4
fingers do the w. ADVE 4:9
w. with destiny CHUR 68:13
walks Ministry of Silly W. CLEE 70:12
w. through a wall MALA 213:16
wall against a w. of stone WILB 338:7
doesn't love a w. FROS 127:11
walks through a w. MALA 213:16
w. to a layman COMM 74:2
Watch the w., my darling KIPL 183:13
walling What I was w. in FROS 127:13
wallow w. in our victory PRES 265:15
Wall St. W. lays an egg NEWS 241:1
walrus W. and Carpenter LEVI 198:4
waltz dance a second w. SHIE 297:11
goes out of a beautiful w. GREN 140:12
wandering I'm just w. MURD 235:11
wanna W. be the leader MCGO 209:3
want get what you w. LURI 205:5
people know what they w. MENC 221:7
something they w. to see SKEL 299:12
third is freedom from w. ROOS 278:5
W. one only of five giants BEVE 35:1
we w. it now MORR 232:2
What does a woman w. FREU 125:11
what I really really w. ROWB 280:6
what we all w. SHIE 297:9
war After each w. ATKI 15:10
ain't gonna be no w. MACM 210:13
anyone who wasn't against w. LOW 204:1
at w. with Germany CHAM 61:11
beating of w. drums KOES 185:13
bungled, unwise w. PLOM 259:15
cold w. BARU 24:12
cold w. warrior THAT 315:12
condemn recourse to w. BRIA 43:18
day w. broke out CATC 58:9
done very well out of the w. BALD 21:8
Don't mention the w. CLEE 70:13
easier to make w. CLEM 71:3
enable it to make w. WEIL 332:11
first w. fought without WEST 335:12
first w. of the 21st century BUSH 49:12
First World W. had begun TAYL 313:10
for w. like precocious giants PEAR 256:4
France has not lost the w. DE G 88:4
going to the w. CHES 64:1
home policy: I wage w. CLEM 71:1
if someone gave a w. GINS 135:1
I hate w. ROOS 277:18
I have seen w. ROOS 277:18
involve us in the wrong w. BRAD 42:9
In w.: resolution CHUR 68:12
I renounce w. FOSD 123:3
killed in the w. POWE 265:7
live under the shadow of a w. SPEN 304:9
lose the w. in an afternoon CHUR 68:17
Make love not w. SAYI 290:4
Mankind must put an end to w. KENN 178:9
McNamara's W. MCNA 211:7
no declaration of w. EDEN 99:1
not a justifiable act of w. BELL 27:8
nuisance in time of w. CHUR 67:13
Older men declare w. HOOV 159:5
Once lead this people into w. WILS 341:18
page 1 of the book of w. MONT 229:13
paparazzi dogs of w. DENE 89:15
quaint and curious w. is HARD 146:12
rich wage w. SART 287:4
seek no wider w. JOHN 171:10
seven days w. MUIR 234:9
soon as w. is declared GIRA 135:8
subject is W. OWEN 251:4
talk of a just w. SORL 302:17
tempered by w. KENN 178:2
they'll give a w. SAND 286:10
third world w. TRUM 323:6
understood this liking for w. BENN 29:14
Vietnam as a w. PILG 258:9
wage w. against CHUR 66:9
w. and peace in 21st century KOHL 186:2
W. being deliberately prolonged SASS 288:6
w. between men and women THUR 320:7
w. creates order BREC 43:6
w. for independence MCAL 205:12
w. has used up words JAME 168:3
w. in which everyone CONN 75:13
W. is hell, and all that HAY 149:9
W. is not the word KENN 177:4
w. is obsolete or men are FULL 129:5
w. is politics with bloodshed MAO 216:6
W. is too serious a matter CLEM 71:5
W. makes good history HARD 147:3
w. minus the shooting ORWE 250:12
w. of words CAMP 51:12

w. on poverty JOHN 171:8
w. run to show the Third World BERR 32:8
w. situation has developed HIRO 156:6
w. that will end war WELL 333:16
W. the most exciting thing DAYA 86:4
W. the universal perversion RAE 269:2
W. too serious a business BUCH 47:7
w. which existed to produce HOBS 157:2
W. will cease when POLI 262:6
waste of God, w. STUD 311:6
way of ending a w. ORWE 250:15
We hear w. called murder MACD 208:3
what a lovely w. LITT 200:7
what did you do in the W. SAYI 289:10
win an atomic w. BRAD 42:6
without having won the w. YOKO 349:8
won the last w. ROOS 277:10
You can only love one w. GELL 132:9
wardrobe open your w. WELD 333:4
warfare Armed w. must be preceded ZINO 350:11
warlord concubine of a w. OPEN 247:1
warm man who's w. to understand SOLZ 302:3
w. courage BUSH 49:13
w. courage ROOS 277:17
warn All a poet can do is w. OWEN 251:5
w. you not to be ordinary KINN 182:5
warning come with a health w. HENM 153:2
War Office except the British W. SHAW 295:7
warrior cold war w. THAT 315:12
This is the happy w. READ 271:4
wars brought us to these w. DAY- 86:8
came to an end all w. LLOY 201:5
end to beginnings of all w. ROOS 278:9
History littered with the w. POWE 265:1
how do w. start KRAU 186:4
into any foreign w. ROOS 278:3
not armaments that cause w. MADA 212:5
tourist of w. GELL 132:8
w. planned by old men RICE 273:9
wartime this w. atmosphere CONR 76:3
war-war better than to w. CHUR 68:3
was picked the w. of shall CUMM 82:10
wash have to w. your socks DE B 87:6
w. the wind ELIO 104:11
washed never w. my own feet PU 267:8
w. in the blood LIND 200:1
washes Persil w. whiter ADVE 4:18
washing w. on the Siegfried Line KENN 177:9
wasp everything about the w. THOM 318:13
White-Anglo Saxon-Protestant (w.) BALT 22:8
waste art of how to w. space JOHN 172:3
Don't w. time in mourning HILL 156:1
w. it is to lose one's mind QUAY 268:4
W. of Blood STUD 311:6
w. remains and kills EMPS 108:4
wasted all w. effort AYER 19:14
spend on advertising is w. LEVE 197:15
waste-paper file your w. basket BENN 29:7
w. basket of emotions WEBB 332:6
watch done much better by a w. BELL 28:3
like a fat gold w. PLAT 259:13
or my w. has stopped FILM 115:5
sit out front and w. me BARR 24:7
son of a bitch stole my w. FILM 117:9
W. my lips BLUN 38:6
W. my lips BLUN 38:7
w. the mayor LETT 197:11
W. the wall, my darling KIPL 183:13
watcher posted presence of the w. JAME 168:1
watching BIG BROTHER IS W. YOU ORWE 250:2
My tiny w. eye DE L 89:9
watchmaker *blind* w. DAWK 85:8
water bridge over troubled w. SIMO 298:11
go back in the w. TAGL 314:6
That stretch of w. PAUL 255:6
W. is life's *mater* SZEN 312:14
w. like Pilate GREE 139:7
'w.' meant the wonderful KELL 177:2
w.'s the same shape COPP 77:7
where the w. goes CHES 64:6
Waterloo battle of W. won ORWE 249:17
watermelons down by the w. GINS 135:4
Watson Elementary, my dear W. MISQ 226:6
Good old W. DOYL 94:9
wave age is rocking the w. MAND 215:11
bulling through w.-wrack MERW 222:13
waving not w. but drowning SMIT 301:3
waxed man has just w. the floor NASH 238:6
way All the w. with LBJ POLI 261:2
did it the hard w. EPIT 109:18
Every which w. but loose FILM 118:7
have it your own w. CART 56:1
I did it my w. ANKA 9:4
If w. to the Better there be HARD 146:10
more a w. of life ANON 11:16
no w. out of the mind PLAT 259:7
on the w. to the Forum SHEV 297:8
see no other w. DAY- 86:8
w. I do it WEST 335:2
ways w. of making you talk CATC 60:9
weak w. always have to decide BONH 40:6
w. from your loveliness BETJ 33:15
W. shall perish SERV 294:3
weaken great life if you don't w. BUCH 47:2
weakening w. the will SPEN 304:8
weakest You are the w. link CATC 60:12
weakling seven-stone w. ADVE 4:5
weakness oh! w. of joy BETJ 33:15
weaned w. on a pickle ANON 12:8
weapon art is not a w. KENN 178:14
his w. wit EPIT 109:13
Innocence no earthly w. HILL 155:11
offensive and dangerous w. PICA 258:3

weapon (*cont.*):
Tory's secret w. KILM 180:12
w. in hands of oppressor BIKO 35:9
w. with worker at each end POLI 261:5
weapons all word of the w. WILB 338:5
books are w. ROOS 278:7
Clothes are our w. CART 54:9
W. are like money AMIS 8:8
wear what you are going to w. WELD 333:4
weary got the W. Blues HUGH 161:13
weasel w. under cocktail cabinet PINT 258:13
w. word ROOS 279:2
weather Stormy w. KOEH 185:9
w. turned around THOM 318:10
you won't hold up the w. MACN 211:12
web cool w. of language GRAV 138:11
W. is a tremendous BERN 32:1
World Wide W. GREE 140:6
Webster Like W.'s Dictionary BURK 48:8
W. was much possessed ELIO 105:8
wedding-cake face looks like a w. AUDE 19:4
weds Egghead w. hourglass NEWS 240:5
wee come in w. bulks LIDD 199:10
w. pretendy government CONN 75:3
weed Ignorance is an evil w. BEVE 34:14
weeds Give me w. NICH 241:6
grubbing w. from gravel KIPL 183:4
week die in my w. JOPL 173:2
greatest w. in the history NIXO 242:9
That was the w. that was BIRD 36:2
w. is a long time in politics WILS 341:6
weekend long w. FORS 122:3
w. starts here CATC 60:8
weekends getting a plumber on w. ALLE 7:2
weight one and half times own w. UPDI 325:7
punch above its w. HURD 163:7
w. of the backside ADAM 2:3
weirdo thought patterns of a w. GREE 140:6
welcome good evening, and w. CATC 59:1
welfare lead to the w. state DENN 90:5
W. became a term MOYN 233:10
w.-state TEMP 315:2
well alive and w. ANON 11:6
all shall be w. ELIO 103:9
Didn't she do w. CATC 58:10
Do sleep w. CATC 58:12
w. of loneliness HALL 144:2
Welsh thank the Lord I'm W. MATT 219:3
west construction of the W. NAIP 237:1
face neither East nor W. NKRU 243:2
in the gardens of the W. CONN 75:12
liquid manure from the W. SOLZ 302:6
W. Lothian DALY 83:13
W.-Lothian DALY 84:1
where the W. begins CHAP 62:15
western delivered by W. Union GOLD 137:10
quiet on the w. front REMA 272:11
When you've seen one W. WHIT 337:11
Westerners W. have aggressive KAUN 175:11
West Indian I am a W. peasant MCDO 208:5
Westminster change at W. KING 181:13
puppets sent to W. CANA 53:1
wet out of these w. clothes FILM 116:10
so w. you could shoot snipe POWE 264:12
Wexford disused shed in Co. W. MAHO 213:1
whale Save the w. SAYI 290:7
screw the w. STOP 309:14
whales W. play WILL 339:3
whammy Labour's double w. POLI 261:23
what know what's w. WEST 334:17
W. is to be done LENI 195:13
W.'s up, Doc CATC 60:10
w., when and why WARN 330:4
wheat packed like squares of w. LARK 189:5
wheel breaks a butterfly on a w. NEWS 241:2
created the w. APOL 13:5
invented the w. NEME 238:14
red w. barrow WILL 340:2
wheels w. of black Marias AKHM 5:8
when forgotten to say 'W.!' WODE 343:7
what, w. and why WARN 330:4
where w. do they all come from LENN 196:6
W. OUGHT I TO BE TELE 316:1
W. were you? TAGL 314:15
whereof w. one cannot speak WITT 342:7
whimper Not with a bang but a w. ELIO 103:16
whimsical say something w. LOVE 203:7
whin three w. bushes rode across KAVA 175:12
whining w. Californian mall rat PRAT 265:13
whisky good old boys drinkin' w. MCLE 210:1
W. makes it go round MACK 209:9
whisper my w. was already born MAND 215:12
W. who dares MILN 225:11
whispering just w. in her mouth MARX 218:7
whistle shrimp learns to w. KHRU 180:5
W. while you work MORE 230:12
You know how to w. FILM 117:1
white American w. man to find BALD 21:4
best friends are w. DURE 96:8
be the w. man's brother KING 181:1
blue-eyed devil w. man FARD 111:6
dreaming of a w. Christmas BERL 31:8
fat w. woman CORN 77:11
no 'w.' or 'coloured' signs KENN 178:12
say this for the w. race GREG 140:8
shake a bat at a w. man GREG 140:10
so-called w. races FORS 122:14
W.-Anglo Saxon-Protestant BALT 22:8
w. heat of technology MISQ 227:4
w. man's cruelties MALC 214:4
w. man was *created* a devil MALC 214:3
w. race does not really STEI 306:8
w. race *is* the cancer SONT 302:14

white-collar not the w. people WHYT 337:14
Whitehall gentleman in W. JAY 168:14
White House imported the W. ANON 10:16
W. or home DOLE 93:7
whitewash at the W. NIXO 242:11
whiter Persil washes w. ADVE 4:18
w. shade of pale REID 272:8
whites need the knowledge of w. TSVA 323:17
whitewash w. at the White House NIXO 242:11
Whitman tonight, Walt W. GINS 135:3
Walt W.— CRAN 79:17
who W. am I going to be today WELD 333:4
W. he ROSS 279:10
w. the hell are you CATC 59:9
W.? Whom LENI 195:16
whom Who? W. LENI 195:16
whores parliament of w. O'RO 248:9
second-rate w. PLOM 259:16
Who's Who been in *W.* WEST 334:17
why about the wasp, except w. THOM 318:13
see things and say 'W.' SHAW 295:4
W. not? Why not? Yeah LAST 191:9
w. people laugh FIEL 113:15
Would this man ask w. AUDE 17:1
WI war of words with the W. CAMP 51:12
wicked August is a w. month O'BR 244:2
wicket flannelled fools at the w. KIPL 183:8
wider seek no w. war JOHN 171:10
w. still and wider BENS 30:5
widow French w. in every bedroom HOFF 157:11
W. The word consumes itself PLAT 259:14
width feel the w. POWE 265:10
wields He who w. the knife HESE 153:14
wife decided to murder his w. OPEN 247:9
If I were your w. CHUR 69:2
lay down his w. for his friend JOYC 174:3
man who's untrue to his w. AUDE 17:15
riding to and from his w. WHIT 336:4
she is your w. OGIL 244:13
talks frankly only with his w. BABE 20:2
w. does not like PRES 265:16
wish your w. or servants GRIF 141:2
your w. and your dog HILL 155:8
Wigan mothers-in-law and W. Pier BRID 44:1
road to W. Pier ORWE 250:9
wild call of the w. LOND 202:5
never saw a w. thing LAWR 192:10
walk on the w. side ALGR 6:5
wilder w. shores of love BLAN 37:13
wilderness Women have no w. BOGA 39:5
will Immanent W. that stirs HARD 146:6
political w. LYNN 205:9
settled w. STEE 306:5
w. to carry on LIPP 200:6
wrote my w. across the sky LAWR 192:21
willed only a w. gentleness THOM 319:11
wilt Do what thou w. CROW 82:3
Wimbledon Spill your guts at W. CONN 75:15
wimps Lunch is for w. FILM 116:12
win From w. and lose MITC 227:8
spend it, and w. KENN 178:18
that's to w. MALR 214:7
To w. in Vietnam SPOC 304:12
w. an atomic war BRAD 42:6
W. just one for the Gipper GIPP 135:7
wind answer is blowin' in the w. DYLA 97:4
candle in the w. JOHN 170:11
how the w. doth ramm POUN 263:8
not I, but the w. LAWR 192:13
Not with this w. blowing KIPL 183:11
solidity to pure w. ORWE 250:11
twist slowly in the w. EHRL 99:8
wash the w. ELIO 104:11
w. of change is blowing MACM 211:1
windbags W. can be right FENT 112:10
windbeaten w. verbs ELYT 107:9
window argument of the broken w. PANK 252:14
back upon the w.-panes ELIO 104:4
doggie in the w. MERR 222:8
Good prose like a w.-pane ORWE 249:8
has not one w. JAME 168:1
hole in a stained glass w. CHAN 62:1
kiss my ass in Macy's w. JOHN 171:14
windows open the w. of the Church JOHN 170:7
windscreen through the w. DUNM 95:11
wine doesn't get into the w. CHES 64:6
red sweet w. of youth BROO 44:10
red w. of Shiraz into urine DINE 92:9
w. was a farce POWE 264:8
wing w. and a pray'r ADAM 2:5
wings Grief has no w. QUIL 268:5
on laughter-silvered w. MAGE 212:8
wink wink w., say no more MONT 230:1
winning more fun w. DOLE 93:8
W. is everything HILL 155:8
w. isn't everything SAND 286:13
wins Who dares w. SAYI 290:16
w. if he does not lose KISS 184:11
Winston W. is back ANON 12:14
winter furious w. blowing RANS 269:10
go south in the w. ELIO 104:20
rich and lovely W.'s Eve DAVI 85:5
W. is icummen in POUN 263:8
w. of discontent CALL 51:5
W. of discontent NEWS 241:4
wisdom conventional w. GALB 130:5
door to infinite w. BREC 43:5
W. was mine OWEN 251:12
w. we have lost ELIO 104:13
wise Astrologers or three w. men LONG 202:8

wise (*cont.*):
w. forgive but do not forget SZAS 312:7
wisecrack w. that played Carnegie Hall LEVA 197:14
wisecracking w. and wit PARK 253:16
wisely nations behave w. once EBAN 98:6
wish If otherwise w. I SHAW 297:6
w. for prayer is a prayer BERN 31:15
w. I loved the Human Race RALE 269:6
wit his weapon w. EPIT 109:13
W. has truth in it PARK 253:16
witch-doctors Accountants are w. HARM 147:11
witches burnt at the stake as w. SMIT 301:4
without get where I am today w. CATC 59:4
witnessed worst thing I've ever w. MORR 231:11
witnesses w. to the desolation GEOR 133:3
wits stolen his w. away DE L 89:2
witty Thou swell! Thou w. HART 148:7
wives left the w. and joined WELD 333:2
several chilled w. MERR 222:10
wobbly spelling is W. MILN 225:4
wolf afraid of the big bad w. CHUR 65:12
w. of a different opinion INGE 165:4
Wolsey W.'s Home Town NEWS 240:13
woman artist man and mother w. SHAW 295:20
comfort about being a w. STAR 305:12
done, ask a w. THAT 315:11
Every w. adores a Fascist PLAT 259:8
fat white w. CORN 77:11
just like a w. DYLA 97:10
like a beautiful w. CASA 55:8
No w. will be Prime Minister THAT 315:10
One is not born a w. DE B 87:3
one w. differs from another MENC 221:5
prime truth of w. CHES 64:16
Prudence is the other w. ANON 11:18
that horror—the old w. COLE 73:7
tired of being a w. SEXT 294:7
trapped in a w.'s body BOY 42:3
victory by a w. WEST 335:10
What does a w. want FREU 125:11
Why can't a w. be LERN 196:17
w. can be proud and stiff YEAT 347:3
w. can forgive a man MAUG 219:6
w. is a sometime thing HEYW 155:3
w. is like a teabag REAG 271:6
W. is the equal of man LOY 204:17
W. much missed HARD 147:1
w. must have money WOOL 345:1
w. only the right to spring FOND 121:1
W. the nigger of the world ONO 246:13
w. who lives for others LEWI 198:10
w. without a man STEI 307:3
womankind packs off its w. SHAW 296:2
wombs think with our w. LUCE 205:2
women all these surplus w. RICH 274:9
blame the w.'s movement TWEE 324:11
Certain w. should be struck COWA 79:8
claim our right as w. PANK 252:12
Equality for w. demands TOYN 321:7
feelings of w. in drawing room WOOL 345:2
fight to get w. out GREE 140:5
fire in w.'s bellies CAST 57:6
Good w. always think BROO 45:1
how w. felt PAGL 252:4
joined a w.'s group STEV 308:15
joined the w. WELD 333:2
man who doesn't know w. CHAN 62:7
no plain w. on television FORD 121:6
position for w. is prone CARM 54:3
Some w.'ll stay KIPL 184:7
turn into American w. HAMP 145:3
Votes for w. POLI 262:5
war between men and w. THUR 320:7
Whatever w. do WHIT 337:13
W., and Champagne, and Bridge BELL 28:2
w. are brighter than men LOOS 203:1
W. are programmed to love BAIN 20:12
w. become unnaturally thin WOLF 343:9
w. come and go ELIO 104:3
w., God help us SAYE 288:12
w. have fewer teeth RUSS 282:10
W. have no wilderness BOGA 39:5
W. have very little idea GREE 140:3
W. never have young minds DELA 89:10
w. not merely tolerated AUNG 19:8
W.'s Liberation is just MEIR 221:3
w. were first at the Cradle SAYE 288:12
won I w. the count SOMO 302:7
No one w. ROOS 277:10
not that you w. or lost RICE 273:8
not to have w. COUB 78:3
Sun Wot W. It NEWS 240:12
wonder boneless w. CHUR 66:5
moon-washed apples of w. DRIN 95:3
wonderful I've had a w. life LAST 191:3
Yes, w. things CART 54:11
won't administrative w. LYNN 205:9
woodcock Spirits of well-shot w. BETJ 33:6
woods go down in the w. today KENN 177:8
road through the w. KIPL 183:16
Whose w. are whose O'RO 248:10
Whose w. these are FROS 127:20
w. against the world BLUN 38:4
w. are lovely, dark FROS 128:1
woodshed nasty in the w. GIBB 134:3
Woodstock W. rises from his pages BURR 48:11
Woolf afraid of Virginia W. ALBE 5:12
word Every w. she writes is a lie MCCA 206:11
for whom the w. 'fuck' TYNA 324:13

Greeks had a w. AKIN 5:10
I kept my w. DE L 89:6
most contradictory w. MANN 216:5
up to the w. 'cancer' KIPL 184:2
War is not the w. KENN 177:4
weasel w. ROOS 279:2
words answer you in two w. GOLD 137:5
dreamed out in w. MURR 235:15
fear those big w. JOYC 173:17
few w. of my own EDWA 99:4
gotta use w. when I talk ELIO 104:17
long w. Bother me MILN 225:2
may w. matter to you SMIT 300:8
not even with w. BROO 45:2
shoot me with your w. ANGE 9:1
subtle terrorism of w. GAIT 130:3
threw w. like stones SPEN 304:4
Trying to learn to use w. ELIO 102:18
use words as they are w. COMP 74:9
war has used up w. JAME 168:3
war of w. CAMP 51:12
W. are cheap CHAP 62:14
w. are emptied CAMU 52:16
w. cascade down into my lap NOLA 243:3
w. for moral ideas CHAT 63:6
W. strain ELIO 102:12
W. the most powerful drug KIPL 184:8
worth ten thousand w. BARN 23:7
wrestle With w. ELIO 102:14
you can drug, with w. LOWE 204:2
Wordsworth daffodils were for W. LARK 189:7
work good idea but it won't w. ROGE 277:5
got my w. cut out SQUI 305:6
Go to w. on an egg ADVE 3:20
immortality through my w. ALLE 7:5
in w. does what he wants COLL 73:8
Let's go to w. FILM 116:11
let the toad w. LARK 189:3
looked for w. TEBB 314:18
love and w. FREU 125:12
Man grows beyond his w. STEI 306:13
men think. Sex, w. FISH 114:4
men w. more and dispute less TAWN 313:7
never have to w. again TWIG 324:12
Nice w. if you can get it GERS 133:15
off to w. we go MORE 230:11
of the life, or of the w. YEAT 347:2
slaughterhouses of w. VANE 326:14
unable to find w. COOL 76:15
watch them at work BARN 23:13
Whistle while you w. MORE 230:12
Without w., life goes rotten CAMU 52:18
W. and pray HILL 155:12
W. expands PARK 254:5
W. is love made visible GIBR 134:7
W. is of two kinds RUSS 282:11
w. is terribly important RUSS 282:5
W. is the call MORR 231:12
W. is *x* EINS 100:13
W. liberates ANON 9:12
w. like a fiend THOM 318:16
w. parallels your life COPP 77:7
w., rest and play ADVE 4:10
w. terribly hard at playing MORT 232:13
W. to survive VANE 326:15
W. was like a stick SOLZ 302:2
wouldn't know how to w. it FILM 115:8
You w., we rule DUNN 96:4
worked So on we w. ROBI 275:10
yes it w. POLI 262:8
worker weapon with w. at each end POLI 261:5
w. is the slave CONN 75:14
workers not the w. WHYT 337:14
organized w. of the country SHIN 297:13
secure for the w. ANON 12:9
working in his w. time GILL 134:10
it isn't w. MAJO 213:9
killin' meself w. O'CA 244:6
kind of like w. BISH 36:8
Labour isn't w. POLI 261:22
w. like a dog LENN 196:8
working-class job w. parents want ABBO 1:1
working classes worst fault of w. MORT 232:14
works seen the future and it w. STEF 306:6
w. and is not bored CASA 55:9
w. even if you don't BOHR 39:9
world adventure in the w. of Aids PERK 256:9
all the towns in all the w. FILM 117:5
along the W. I go CART 55:5
blamed for worsening the w. JAME 167:13
decide the fate of the w. DE G 88:8
Feed the w. GELD 132:7
funny old w. THAT 317:16
Hog Butcher for the W. SAND 286:5
in 1915 the old w. ended LAWR 191:13
In a w. I never made HOUS 160:4
limits of my w. WITT 342:9
Little Friend of all the W. KIPL 184:6
loosed upon the w. YEAT 348:7
Love makes the w. go round MACK 209:9
new w. order BUSH 49:9
only girl in the w. GREY 140:15
only saved the w. CHES 63:14
point of the turning w. ELIO 102:11
put the w. to sleep MUIR 234:9
rule the w. BART 24:11
Sob, heavy w. AUDE 16:11
Stop the w. NEWL 239:9
sword the axis of the w. DE G 88:14
Ten days that shook the w. REED 272:7
third w. war TRUM 323:6
Top of the w. FILM 115:1

world (*cont.*):
war run to show the w. BERR 32:8
way the w. ends ELIO 103:16
We want the w. MORR 232:2
woods against the w. BLUN 38:4
w. beauty becomes enough MORR 232:5
w. empty of people LAWR 192:6
w. famous RICH 274:12
w. in my head HEWE 154:8
w. is an oyster MILL 224:2
w. is becoming like asylum LLOY 201:10
w. is changing ELIZ 106:5
w. is everything that is WITT 342:8
w. like a Mask dancing ACHE 1:6
w. must be made safe WILS 341:17
w. of silence EPIT 109:2
w. safe for hypocrisy WOLF 343:13
w.'s in a state o' chassis O'CA 244:8
w. stood like a playing card MAIL 213:5
w.'s worst wound SASS 288:4
W. War III DAVI 85:6
w. will end in fire FROS 127:6
worlds best of all possible w. CABE 50:5
destroyer of w. OPPE 246:14
worm tasted your w. SPOO 304:14
worms diet of w. FENT 112:8
worried may not be w. into being FROS 128:3
w. about Jim CATC 59:11
worse bad against the w. DAY- 86:9
fear of finding something w. BELL 27:11
If my books had been any w. CHAN 62:4
More will mean w. AMIS 8:5
w. off for having known STEP 307:8
worsening blamed for w. the world JAME 167:13
worship second is freedom to w. ROOS 278:5
worst full look at the w. HARD 146:10
intellectual hatred the w. YEAT 348:1
like to be told the w. CHUR 67:4
rape isn't the w. thing WELD 333:5
While the w. are full YEAT 348:7
world's w. wound SASS 288:4
w. form of Government CHUR 67:15
w. is yet to come JOHN 172:2
w. thing I've ever witnessed MORR 231:11
w. time of the year ELIO 103:17
You do your w. CHUR 67:5
worth confident of their own w. AUNG 19:8
makes life w. living ELIO 105:9
w. doing badly CHES 64:16
Worthington on the stage, Mrs W. COWA 79:1
wotthehell w. archy MARQ 217:8
would He w., wouldn't he RICE 273:13
wound Hearts w. up with love SPEN 304:6
world's worst w. SASS 288:4
w., not the bandage POTT 263:3
Wounded Knee Bury my heart at W. BENÉ 28:16
wounds salt rubbed into their w. WEST 335:6
wow make people say 'W.!' SMIT 300:9
wrapper McDonald's w. FELT 112:6
wreck w. and not the story RICH 274:1
wreckers not the w. MCAL 205:11
wrestled w. for perhaps too long HOWE 160:12
wringer big fat w. MITC 225:16
wrings at last w. its neck RUSS 282:15
wrinklies not because ageing w. STRA 310:11
write love to w. them BISH 36:8
mind that can w. AHER 5:5
people who can't w. ZAPP 350:6
w. all the books EDDI 98:8
w. every other day DOUG 94:3
w. the truth KANE 175:7
writer best fame is a w.'s fame LEBO 194:9
For a w., success is GREE 139:18
I'm a w. WALC 328:17
modern hardback w. TRIL 322:4
No w. can give that GLEN 136:3
protect the w. ACHE 1:9
things a w. is for RUSH 281:14
w. must refuse SART 287:15
w.'s only responsibility FAUL 112:2
w.'s radar HEMI 152:15
writers dead w. are remote ELIO 105:12
writing continue w. GARC 131:13
get it in w. LEE 194:16
little point in w. AMIS 8:6
live and despise w. SMIT 301:2
no talent for w. BENC 28:12
thought *nothing* of her w. SITW 299:8
W. is not a profession SIME 298:9
written being w. about BELL 28:9
wrong but also to be w. SZAS 312:5
called the w. number CART 56:11
customer is never w. RITZ 275:3
different kinds of w. COMP 74:7
Eating people is w. FLAN 119:16
excuse the w. by showing HAND 145:4
Fifty million Frenchmen can't be w. SAYI 289:16
Had anything been w. AUDE 18:15
in the w. place DYLA 97:6
involve us in the w. war BRAD 42:9
majority are w. DEBS 87:12
never w., the Old Masters AUDE 17:13
only an accumulated w. CASE 55:11
ran w. through all the land MUIR 234:8
right deed for the w. ELIO 104:10
something has gone w. POTT 263:5
thought it w. to fight BELL 28:5
very probably w. CLAR 70:3
We were w. MCNA 211:8
Why mind being w. AYER 19:17

W. but Wromantic SELL 293:9
w. kind of snow WORR 345:13
w. members in control ORWE 249:15
w. with our bloody ships BEAT 25:4
wrongs Two w. don't make a right SZAS 312:11
wysiwyg shortened to *w.* SAYI 290:14

X Generation X. COUP 78:5
xerox X. makes everybody MCLU 210:11
XXXX wouldn't give a X. ADVE 3:6

Yale libel on a Y. prom PARK 253:15
Yanks Y. are coming COHA 72:16
year man at the gate of the y. HASK 148:10
thirtieth y. to heaven THOM 318:9
years after all these y. SIMO 298:14
take away 30 y. RODD 276:6
two thousand y. of hope WEIZ 332:14
yellow And not your y. hair YEAT 346:9
Follow the y. brick road HARB 146:1
Goodbye y. brick road JOHN 171:1
y. polkadot bikini VANC 326:8
yes getting the answer y. CAMU 52:6
never hear the word 'Y.' WEST 335:3
We say Y. WRIG 345:16
Y., but not in the South POTT 263:6
Y., I believe LAST 191:10
Y.; I remember Adlestrop THOM 319:1
Y. it hurt POLI 262:8
Y., Minister! No, Minister CROS 82:2
Y.! we have no bananas SILV 298:8
y. you don't mean RUME 281:2
yesterday Evil visited us y. TAYL 314:17
I believe in y. LENN 196:13
keeping up with y. MARQ 217:4
perhaps it was y. OPEN 247:2
Y.'s men POLI 262:9
yid PUT THE ID BACK IN Y. ROTH 280:1
yoghurt bin bag full of y. FRY 128:15
York Duchess of Y. is a vulgarian CHAR 63:5
you Y.'ve got approval NESS 239:6
young angry and defrauded y. KIPL 182:13
Being y. is not minding WHIT 337:9
Being y. is overestimated QUAN 268:2
get out while we're y. SPRI 305:3
Hip y. gunslinger ANON 10:15
how y. the policemen look HICK 155:5
I have been y. BLUN 38:5
I'll die y. BRUC 46:7
resolute, the y. KIPL 183:9
They're y. TAGL 314:13
too y. to fall asleep SASS 287:19
too y. to take up golf ADAM 1:13
voices of y. people SMIT 300:11
Women never have y. minds DELA 89:10
y. are quick of speech WINT 342:4
y., gifted and black HANS 145:7
Y., gifted and black IRVI 165:14
y. men think it is HOUS 160:7
y. regard me as outrageous HOYL 161:2
y. whom I hope to bother AUDE 18:8
younger y. than that now DYLA 97:14
y. with time CASA 55:8
youngster going out a y. FILM 118:1
youth belongs to Y. QUAN 268:1
it is y. who must fight HOOV 159:5
red sweet wine of y. BROO 44:10
shake their wicked sides at y. YEAT 347:19
y. and laughter go SASS 288:5
Y. is something very new CHAN 62:9
Y. is vivid LOVE 203:9
Y., which is forgiven SHAW 296:10
Yugoslavia Y. is running KOST 186:3
yuppie y. version of bulimia EHRE 99:6

Zaire Z. is the trigger FANO 111:5
zeal tempering bigot z. KNOX 185:4
Zen Z. and the art PIRS 259:2
zip Children and z. fasteners WHIT 337:7
zipless z. fuck JONG 172:11
zones retain our z. erogenous HARB 145:15
zoo human z. MORR 231:7
running a z. O'RO 248:11
Zurich gnomes in Z. WILS 341:1

Selective Thematic Index

Computing

Drinks

Education

Environment

Europe

Family

Fashion

Film

Fitness

Food

Future

Health

Law

Literature

Love

Marriage

Men and Women

Music

Past

only dead thing that smells sweet THOM 319:2
past is a bucket of ashes SAND 286:9
Stands the Church clock at ten to three BROO 44:13
suddenly in the 1950s HOBS 157:1

Photography

camera makes everyone a tourist SONT 302:15
cod which produces a million eggs SHAW 296:24
in a fraction of a second CART 55:6
learn to see the ordinary BAIL 20:8
more important to click with people EISE 102:1
point of view of a paralysed cyclops HOCK 157:3
secret about a secret ARBU 13:9
you aren't close enough CAPA 53:6

Politics

argument of the broken window pane PANK 252:14
Art of the Possible BUTL 50:3
can take a nation's pulse WHIT 336:3
election by the incompetent many SHAW 296:5
expression of human immaturity BRIT 44:2
feeds your vanity PARR 254:9
got the show business right BERN 32:2
government by discussion ATTL 16:5
Instead of rocking the cradle ROBI 276:1
man who promises least BARU 24:14
must have an ethical dimension COOK 76:7
ninety-minute patriots SILL 298:6
not the voting that's democracy STOP 309:9
only safe pleasure CRIT 81:3
Organize yourselves CAST 57:6
Safe is spelled D-U-L-L CLAR 69:13
second oldest profession REAG 271:10
start in the streets KENN 177:6
too serious to be left to politicians DE G 88:9
war without bloodshed MAO 216:6
week is a long time in politics WILS 341:6
Women, and Champagne BELL 28:2

Popular Culture

anything with long hair MASO 219:1
decisive moment TYNA 325:2
famous for fifteen minutes WARH 329:12
first rappers of Europe BJÖR 36:9
I think of it as a cultural Stalingrad BALL 22:4
It's like kissing God BRUC 46:7
more popular than Jesus LENN 196:3
more than ten people like you MANN 215:13
no hard-sell or soft-sell TV push NASH 237:15
pay to see bad movies GOLD 137:7
shaking an apple tree COLL 73:12
turn on, tune in, drop out LEAR 193:12
want to hear from your sweater LEBO 194:6
Whole families shopping at night GINS 135:4

Present

controls the past ORWE 250:3
Exhaust the little moment BROO 45:4
gadget-filled paradise NIEB 242:3
Ours is the age of substitutes BENT 30:10
past is lost CHAP 63:1
strange interlude O'NE 246:11
We are now in the Me Decade WOLF 344:3

Press

cut out the cancer AITK 5:6
drinking in last chance saloon MELL 221:4
editor did it when I was away MURD 235:12
elderly lady in Hastings LEWI 199:6
facts are lost forever MAIL 213:7
facts are on expenses STOP 309:13
facts are sacred SCOT 292:11
Go to where the silence is GOOD 137:12
if a man bites a dog, that is news BOGA 39:8
It forgives nothing DIAN 91:13
It takes a great owner BRAD 42:5
men with the muck-rakes ROOS 278:12
more than you can get out of baked beans O'RE 248:6
my one form of continuous fiction BEVA 34:12
nation talking to itself MILL 224:7
not a free press but a managed one RADC 268:12
omelette all over our suits BROK 44:5
paparazzi nothing but dogs of war DENE 89:15
saying 'Lord Jones Dead' CHES 64:17
such of the proprietor's prejudices SWAF 312:2
When seagulls follow a trawler CANT 53:5

Quotations

achieve unexpected felicities HOLM 158:6
for an uneducated man to read CHUR 68:11
make a monkey out of a man BENC 28:10
make quite a fair show of knowledge DOUG 94:4
plums and orange peel picked out RALE 269:7
privilege of the learned PEAR 256:3
what a speaker wants to say BENN 29:8
Windbags can be right FENT 112:10

Religion

Royalty

Science

Sex

Society

Sport

Technology

always end up using scissors HOCK 157:5
indistinguishable from magic CLAR 70:2
invented the brake NEME 238:14
Machines are the new proletariat ATTA 15:12
make a machine that would walk APOL 13:5
need not experience the world FRIS 126:9
practical intellectual STRO 311:1
reality must take precedence FEYN 113:2
spark-gap is mightier than the pen HOGB 157:12
white heat of technology MISQ 227:4

Television

contracts the imagination WOGA 343:8
licence to print money THOM 320:3
male, middle class, middle-aged STRE 310:13
manufacture of banality SARR 287:3
No good can come of it SCOT 292:12
playing a piano in a brothel MUGG 234:7
rudest voice wins SACK 284:5
sanction of switching off EYRE 111:1
so much chewing gum for the eyes ANON 12:4
taken no notice of HARE 147:5
Television is for appearing on COWA 79:11
Television thrives on unreason DAY 86:2
We are surfing food MACK 209:10

Transport

any colour so long as it is black FORD 121:10
automobile changed our dress, manners KEAT 176:9
dreadful human beings alongside NORR 243:4
great Gothic cathedrals BART 24:10
lances of ancient knights ROOT 279:5
looks like a poached egg NUFF 243:7
Night Mail crossing the Border AUDE 17:16
one who spends his life WHIT 336:4
only two emotions in a plane WELL 333:9
seen in a bus over the age of 30 WEST 335:11
steel canisters hurtling about CASS 57:4
Take my camel, dear OPEN 247:20
the car his perilous excursion ashore LEWI 199:4

Travel

Abroad is bloody GEOR 133:8
'abroad' to be Catholic and sensual CHAN 62:10
Been there, done that SAYI 289:3
broadens the mind; but CHES 64:14
first class, and with children BENC 28:11
redesigned Hell from airport layouts PRIC 266:2
this is an awful place SCOT 293:1
tourism is their religion RUNC 281:6

War

air power has prevailed KEEG 176:10
blood, toil, tears and sweat CHUR 66:8
bomber will always get through BALD 21:10
bomb them back into the Stone Age LEMA 195:9
counted them all back HANR 145:6
fight for its King and Country GRAH 138:9
first war of the 21st century BUSH 49:12
give a war and nobody will come SAND 286:10
guerrilla wins if he does not lose KISS 184:11
In Flanders fields, the poppies blow MCCR 207:7
no allies to be polite to GEOR 133:7
no one will win the next ROOS 277:10
no substitute for victory MACA 206:2
Patriotism is not enough CAVE 61:3
Peace is indivisible LITV 200:8
rather have butter or guns GOER 136:10
real slow walk CASH 57:2
Rule 1, on page 1 MONT 229:13
Somme is like the Holocaust BARK 23:5
so much owed by so many to so few CHUR 67:1
survival is all there is FULL 129:6
this may not be a just peace IZET 166:8
war has used up words JAME 168:3
way to win an atomic war BRAD 42:6
when men refuse to fight POLI 262:6
without the gods MACD 208:2

Youth

Any failure seems so total QUAN 268:2
At eighteen our convictions are hills FITZ 119:1
door opens and lets the future in GREE 139:16
forgotten what it is like JARR 168:13
Grown-ups never understand SAIN 284:12
have you seen my childhood JACK 167:2
more of an influence to your son ICE 164:14
no one mentioned it CHAN 62:9
not minding not having any money WHIT 337:9
phone is for you LEBO 194:8
times they are a-changin' DYLA 97:17
vivid rather than happy LOVE 203:9

AskOxford.com
Oxford Dictionaries *Passionate about language*

For more information about the background to Oxford Quotations Dictionaries, and much more about Oxford's commitment to language exploration, why not visit the world's largest language learning site, ***AskOxford.com?***

Passionate about English?

What were the original 'brass monkeys'? ***AskOxford.com***

How do new words enter the dictionary? ***AskOxford.com***

How is 'whom' used? ***AskOxford.com***

Who said, 'For also knowledge itself is power?' ***AskOxford.com***

How can I improve my writing? ***AskOxford.com***

If you have a query about the English language, want to look up a word, need some help with your writing skills, are curious about how dictionaries are made, or simply have some time to learn about the language, bypass the rest and ask the experts at ***AskOxford.com***.

Passionate about language?

If you want to find out about writing in French, German, Spanish, or Italian, improve your listening and speaking skills, learn about other cultures, access resources for language students, or gain insider travel tips from those in the know, ask the experts at ***AskOxford.com***.